Northern Territory

David Andrew
Hugh Finlay

D1540277

LONELY PLANET PUBLICATIONS
Melbourne • Oakland • London • Paris

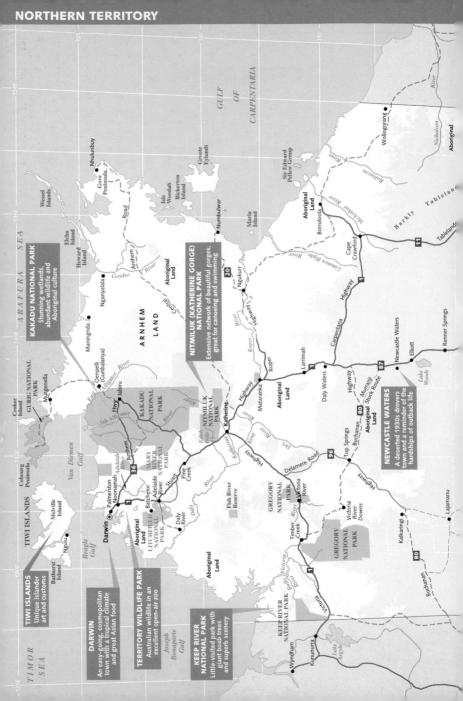

NORTHERN TERRITORY

KAKADU NATIONAL PARK
Stunning wetlands, abundant wildlife and Aboriginal culture

NITMILUK (KATHERINE GORGE) NATIONAL PARK
Extensive network of beautiful gorges, great for canoeing and swimming

NEWCASTLE WATERS
A deserted 1930s drovers town and a reminder of the hardships of outback life

TIWI ISLANDS
Unique islander art and customs

DARWIN
An easy-going, cosmopolitan town with a tropical climate and great Asian food

TERRITORY WILDLIFE PARK
Australian wildlife in an excellent open-air zoo

KEEP RIVER NATIONAL PARK
Little-visited park with giant boab trees and superb scenery

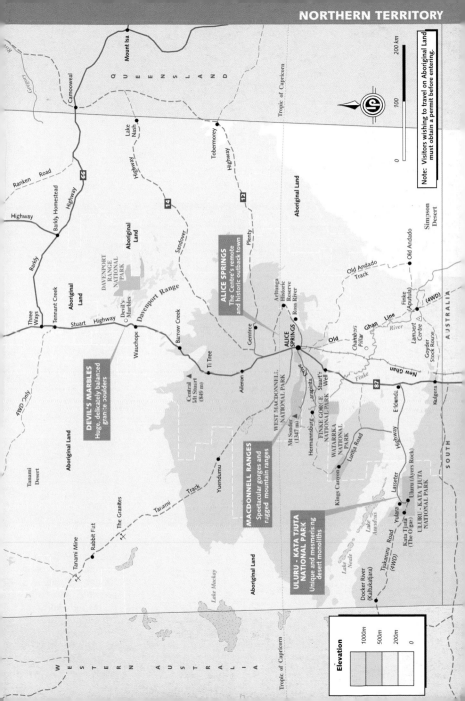

Northern Territory
2nd edition – August 1999
First published – September 1996

Published by
Lonely Planet Publications Pty Ltd A.C.N. 005 607 983
192 Burwood Rd, Hawthorn, Victoria 3122, Australia

Lonely Planet Offices
Australia PO Box 617, Hawthorn, Victoria 3122
USA 150 Linden St, Oakland, CA 94607
UK 10a Spring Place, London NW5 3BH
France 1 rue du Dahomey, 75011 Paris

Photographs
Many of the images in this guide are available for licensing from
Lonely Planet Images.
email: lpi@lonelyplanet.com.au

Front cover photograph
Storm over Uluru (Gareth McCormack)

ISBN 0 86442 791 3

Contents – Text

Contents – Maps

MAP INDEX

LP

The Authors

David Andrew

In various incarnations David Andrew has worked as a public servant, restaurant manager, research assistant at Kakadu National Park and book editor for Lonely Planet. But all things considered, he believes there are few things in the world more fun than birdwatching and travel. Consequently he has visited many parts of the world to stand in swamps, crawl through vines and freeze in snowfields in the hope of glimpsing birds and other wildlife. Before updating this edition of *Northern Territory* he updated the East Malaysia chapters of the *Malaysia, Singapore & Brunei* book, and has written wildlife and birdwatching sections for many other Lonely Planet guides.

Hugh Finlay

Deciding there must be more to life than civil engineering, Hugh took off around Australia in the mid-70s, working at everything from spray painting to diamond prospecting before hitting the overland trail. He joined Lonely Planet in 1985 and has written *Jordan & Syria* and co-authored *Kenya, Morocco, Algeria & Tunisia* and updated *Nepal, Queensland* and *Australia*. He lives in central Victoria.

FROM THE AUTHOR

David Andrew My profuse thanks to all those who helped in updating this book, in particular John van Commenee and Debbie Turner in Darwin; Greg Miles and Ian Irvine in Kakadu National Park; and Brendan Bainbridge, Paul Simpson and Max Davidson for making Arnhem Land and Gurig National Park possible at short notice. Thanks also to Britz: Australia for assistance, and the many helpful staff at the various Regional Tourist Associations and hostels throughout the Territory. And as always heartfelt thanks to my wife Robyn for her help and company on the long drive, and for clicking away with her camera.

And many thanks are also owed to the editors and designers at Lonely Planet – the unsung heroes of book production.

This Book

The 1st edition of *Northern Territory* was researched and written by Hugh Finlay. This 2nd edition was updated by David Andrew.

From the Publisher
This edition of *Northern Territory* was produced in Lonely Planet's Melbourne office. Editing was co-ordinated by Arabella Bamber, who thanks Errol Hunt for all his help with editing and proofing. Barbara Benson co-ordinated the cartography and design, with Kusnandar's mapping assistance. Thanks also go to Robert Allen for his erudite contribution to the Aboriginal Art special section, Guillaume Roux for his cover design, Kate Nolan for her delicate illustrations and to Tim Uden for his invaluable expertise in matters Quarkish. Finally, thank you to Mark Griffiths, David Bamber, Wendy Vismans and Digby Horwood.

Thanks
Many thanks to the travellers who used the last edition and wrote to us with their useful comments and suggestions:

Tania, Helen & Paul, Karen Anthony, Elizabeth Arango, Mark Atkinson, Ruth Baggs, Philip Baker, Dave Ballen, Adam J Beale, Peter Beyerle, Jen Campbell, Betty Chen, Trish Clark, Paul Cook, Jenni Dean, Linley Denson, Deidre Doyle, Jason Dyer, Anne Evins, Miriam Fetzer, Nicki Folland, Joanne Harris, Alistair Hart, Bill Heath, Nell Heath, James & Lea Hobbs, Debbie Isherwood, Richard Johnson, Ian Loftus, Doreen A McGregor, Wendy Monger, Beth Morris, Beryl Mulder, Peter Myska, Nicola Neesham, David Odling-Smee, Belinda Park, Louise Pearce, Jeff Phillips, GS Roberts, Carol Robertson, Ute Saunders, Eric Scott, Sue Smith, Warren Smith, Jason Sowerby, Mark Taylor, Hiran Thabrew, David Thomson, Corinne Toune, Jenny Ward, Roger Wyett.

Foreword

ABOUT LONELY PLANET GUIDEBOOKS

The story begins with a classic travel adventure: Tony and Maureen Wheeler's 1972 journey across Europe and Asia to Australia. Useful information about the overland trail did not exist at that time, so Tony and Maureen published the first Lonely Planet guidebook to meet a growing need.

From a kitchen table, then from a tiny office in Melbourne (Australia), Lonely Planet has become the largest independent travel publisher in the world, an international company with offices in Melbourne, Oakland (USA), London (UK) and Paris (France).

Today Lonely Planet guidebooks cover the globe. There is an ever-growing list of books and there's information in a variety of forms and media. Some things haven't changed. The main aim is still to help make it possible for adventurous travellers to get out there – to explore and better understand the world.

At Lonely Planet we believe travellers can make a positive contribution to the countries they visit – if they respect their host communities and spend their money wisely. Since 1986 a percentage of the income from each book has been donated to aid projects and human rights campaigns.

Updates Lonely Planet thoroughly updates each guidebook as often as possible. This usually means there are around two years between editions, although for more unusual or more stable destinations the gap can be longer. Check the imprint page (following the colour map at the beginning of the book) for publication dates.

Between editions up-to-date information is available in two free newsletters – the paper *Planet Talk* and email *Comet* (to subscribe, contact any Lonely Planet office) – and on our Web site at www.lonelyplanet.com. The *Upgrades* section of the Web site covers a number of important and volatile destinations and is regularly updated by Lonely Planet authors. *Scoop* covers news and current affairs relevant to travellers. And, lastly, the *Thorn Tree* bulletin board and *Postcards* section of the site carry unverified, but fascinating, reports from travellers.

Correspondence The process of creating new editions begins with the letters, postcards and emails received from travellers. This correspondence often includes suggestions, criticisms and comments about the current editions. Interesting excerpts are immediately passed on via newsletters and the Web site, and everything goes to our authors to be verified when they're researching on the road. We're keen to get more feedback from organisations or individuals who represent communities visited by travellers.

> Lonely Planet gathers information for everyone who's curious about the planet – and especially for those who explore it first-hand. Through guidebooks, phrasebooks, activity guides, maps, literature, newsletters, image library, TV series and Web site we act as an information exchange for a worldwide community of travellers.

Research Authors aim to gather sufficient practical information to enable travellers to make informed choices and to make the mechanics of a journey run smoothly. They also research historical and cultural background to help enrich the travel experience and allow travellers to understand and respond appropriately to cultural and environmental issues.

Authors don't stay in every hotel because that would mean spending a couple of months in each medium-sized city and, no, they don't eat at every restaurant because that would mean stretching belts beyond capacity. They do visit hotels and restaurants to check standards and prices, but feedback based on readers' direct experiences can be very helpful.

Many of our authors work undercover, others aren't so secretive. None of them accept freebies in exchange for positive write-ups. And none of our guidebooks contain any advertising.

Production Authors submit their raw manuscripts and maps to offices in Australia, USA, UK or France. Editors and cartographers – all experienced travellers themselves – then begin the process of assembling the pieces. When the book finally hits the shops, some things are already out of date, we start getting feedback from readers and the process begins again ...

WARNING & REQUEST

Things change – prices go up, schedules change, good places go bad and bad places go bankrupt – nothing stays the same. So, if you find things better or worse, recently opened or long since closed, please tell us and help make the next edition even more accurate and useful. We genuinely value all the feedback we receive. Julie Young coordinates a well travelled team that reads and acknowledges every letter, postcard and email and ensures that every morsel of information finds its way to the appropriate authors, editors and cartographers for verification.

Everyone who writes to us will find their name in the next edition of the appropriate guidebook. They will also receive the latest issue of *Planet Talk*, our quarterly printed newsletter, or *Comet*, our monthly email newsletter. Subscriptions to both newsletters are free. The very best contributions will be rewarded with a free guidebook.

Excerpts from your correspondence may appear in new editions of Lonely Planet guidebooks, the Lonely Planet Web site, *Planet Talk* or *Comet*, so please let us know if you *don't* want your letter published or your name acknowledged.

Send all correspondence to the Lonely Planet office closest to you:

Australia: PO Box 617, Hawthorn, Victoria 3122
USA: 150 Linden St, Oakland, CA 94607
UK: 10A Spring Place, London NW5 3BH
France: 1 rue du Dahomey, 75011 Paris

Or email us at: talk2us@lonelyplanet.com.au

For news, views and updates see our Web site: www.lonelyplanet.com

HOW TO USE A LONELY PLANET GUIDEBOOK

The best way to use a Lonely Planet guidebook is any way you choose. At Lonely Planet we believe the most memorable travel experiences are often those that are unexpected, and the finest discoveries are those you make yourself. Guidebooks are not intended to be used as if they provide a detailed set of infallible instructions!

Contents All Lonely Planet guidebooks follow roughly the same format. The Facts about the Destination chapters or sections give background information ranging from history to weather. Facts for the Visitor gives practical information on issues like visas and health. Getting There & Away gives a brief starting point for researching travel to and from the destination. Getting Around gives an overview of the transport options when you arrive.

The peculiar demands of each destination determine how subsequent chapters are broken up, but some things remain constant. We always start with background, then proceed to sights, places to stay, places to eat, entertainment, getting there and away, and getting around information – in that order.

Heading Hierarchy Lonely Planet headings are used in a strict hierarchical structure that can be visualised as a set of Russian dolls. Each heading (and its following text) is encompassed by any preceding heading that is higher on the hierarchical ladder.

Entry Points We do not assume guidebooks will be read from beginning to end, but that people will dip into them. The traditional entry points are the list of contents and the index. In addition, however, some books have a complete list of maps and an index map illustrating map coverage.

There may also be a colour map that shows highlights. These highlights are dealt with in greater detail in the Facts for the Visitor chapter, along with planning questions and suggested itineraries. Each chapter covering a geographical region usually begins with a locator map and another list of highlights. Once you find something of interest in a list of highlights, turn to the index.

Maps Maps play a crucial role in Lonely Planet guidebooks and include a huge amount of information. A legend is printed on the back page. We seek to have complete consistency between maps and text, and to have every important place in the text captured on a map. Map key numbers usually start in the top left corner.

Although inclusion in a guidebook usually implies a recommendation we cannot list every good place. Exclusion does not necessarily imply criticism. In fact there are a number of reasons why we might exclude a place – sometimes it is simply inappropriate to encourage an influx of travellers.

Introduction

The Northern Territory is untamed and sometimes surreal Australia. Even to most Australians it is still 'never never land', the real outback; life on a Territory cattle station is as remote from the cappuccino-swilling city dwellers down south as it is from the *palazzos* of Europe. The Territory's mystique draws people from around the world.

The bones of the earth's crust have been laid bare in spectacular fashion from instantly recognisable landmarks such as Uluru (Ayers Rock) in the aptly-named Red Centre to lost valleys of palms; beautiful gorges and glowing red mesas dot the vast plains of the outback.

The land and climate have created unique environments, and a greater contrast between the arid deserts and the lush tropics couldn't be imagined. Populating it all is a fantastic selection of beautiful and spectacular wildlife, from the famous kangaroos of the plains to awesome crocodiles, spring blooms covering desert dunes to lily-carpeted tropical lagoons.

Aboriginal culture and lore is inextricably linked with the landscape and wildlife, and excellent interpretive material in national parks will leave you with an inkling of what this country means to Aboriginal people. Several excellent tours can provide greater insight into their lifestyle.

Perhaps none felt the harshness of this demanding country more than the early explorers and settlers. Deluded they may have

NORTHERN TERRITORY LOCATOR

been, but they were also resourceful and determined. Examples of their exploits – and frequent failures – stand as poignant reminders all over the Territory.

Each element of the Territory can be experienced separately or enjoyed as a part of a greater whole. Most sights are easy to get to, yet somehow they maintain an aura of remote timelessness. And when you hanker for the trappings of modern life you can retreat to the outback town of Alice Springs or tropical Darwin with all its distractions.

It's a bit rough around the edges at times, but there's a sense of raw fun to be enjoyed at noisy festivals (where else is there an annual boat regatta on a dry river bed?) and rodeos. And there's the still genuine hospitality shown by people who – literally and regularly – fight against overwhelming disasters such as floods, drought and cyclones.

Few people visit the Northern Territory and come away untouched by the experience – it's that sort of place.

Facts about the Northern Territory

HISTORY

The Australian continent was the last great landmass to be discovered by Europeans. Long before the British claimed it, European explorers and traders had been dreaming of the riches to be found in the unknown – some said mythical – southern land (*terra australis*) that was supposed to counterbalance the landmass north of the equator. The continent they eventually found had already been inhabited for tens of thousands of years.

Aboriginal Settlement

Australian Aboriginal (which literally means 'indigenous') society has the longest continuous cultural history in the world, with origins dating back to the last Ice Age. Although mystery shrouds many aspects of Australian prehistory, it seems almost certain that the first humans came here across the sea from South-East Asia. Heavy-boned people whom archaeologists call Robust arrived around 70,000 years ago, and more slender Gracile people around 50,000 years ago. Gracile people are the ancestors of Australian Aboriginal people.

They arrived during a period when the sea level was more than 50m lower than it is today. This created more land between Asia and Australia than there is now, but watercraft were still needed to cross some stretches of open sea. Although much of Australia is today arid, the first migrants found a much wetter continent, with large forests and numerous inland lakes teeming with fish.

Because of the favourable conditions, archaeologists suggest that within a few thousand years Aboriginal people had moved through and populated much of the continent, although central Australia was not occupied until about 24,000 years ago.

The last Ice Age came to an end 15,000 to 10,000 years ago. The sea level rose dramatically with the rise in temperature, and an area of Australia the size of Western Australia was flooded during a process that would have seen strips of land 100km wide inundated in just a few decades. Many of the inland lakes dried up and vast deserts formed. Thus, although the Aboriginal population was spread fairly evenly throughout the continent 20,000 years ago, the coastal areas became more densely occupied.

Early Contact

The first European to sight Australia's north coast was probably a Portuguese, sometime in the 16th century. Before that it is believed that units of an Asian fleet commanded by Chinese eunuch admiral Cheng Ho (Zheng He) may have visited the northern Australian coast in the 15th century. In 1879 a small, carved figure of the Chinese god, Shao Lao, was found lodged in the roots of a banyan tree at Doctor's Gully in Darwin – it dated from the Ming Dynasty (1368-1644). As the fleet definitely reached Timor it is quite plausible that they also made it to Australia.

In the early 17th century the Dutch were keen to control the lucrative spice trade. By then the existence of the Great South Land was generally accepted, and the Dutch set out to find it. But it was not until 1623, after Dirk Hartog had discovered the west coast and several ships had been wrecked on its uncharted coast, that the Dutch decided to explore in more detail. The *Arnhem*, skippered by Willem van Colster, in company with the *Pena*, skippered by Jan Carstensz, sailed north-west from the foot of the Gulf of Carpentaria, making landfall at Groote Eylandt and Cape Arnhem. Both vessels

EUROPEAN EXPLORATION

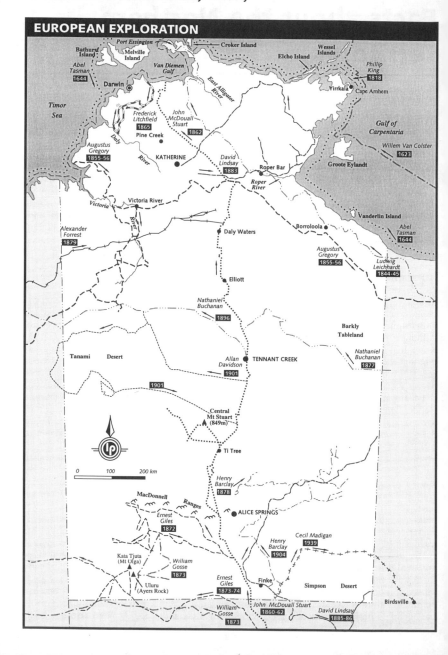

EUROPEAN EXPLORATION

— · — · —	Willem van Colster (*Duyfken*, 1623)
· · · · · · · · ·	Abel Tasman (Limmen, Zeemeeuw & Bracq, 1644)
— — — —	Phillip King (*Mermaid*, 1818)
— · · — · · · —	Ludwig Leichhardt (1844-1845)
— — — — —	Augustus Gregory (1855-56)
· · · · · · · · · · · ·	John McDouall Stuart (1860-62)
═══════	Frederick Litchfield (1865)
— — — — —	Ernest Giles (1872, 1873-74)
— · — · —	William Gosse (1873)
— · · · — · · · —	Nathaniel Buchanan (1877, 1896)
— · — · —	Henry Barclay (1878, 1904)
⊢———⊣	Alexander Forrest (1879)
─────────	David Lindsay (1883, 1885-86)
· · · · · · · · · · · · ·	Allan Davidson (1901)
⊢ + + + ⊣	Cecil Madigan (1939)

came into contact with Aboriginal people, whom they dismissed as 'indigent and miserable men'.

Further exploratory voyages, fuelled by the hope that the Aboriginal people would have something worth trading, led to the mapping of the northern Arnhem Land coast. The great Dutch navigator, Abel Tasman, sailed the entire north coast from Cape York to beyond the Kimberley in Western Australia. This great feat of navigation was deemed a failure because no commercial gain resulted from it, and Tasman's achievements were largely unrecognised.

Other visitors to the northern shores of Australia, from perhaps as early as the mid-17th century, were Macassan traders from the island of Celebes (now Sulawesi). Sailing in their wooden-hulled *praus*, the Macassans came in search of the sea cucumber known as *trepang*. These slimy and rather repulsive looking creatures were highly prized by the Chinese, and were found in profusion in Australian waters.

Unlike the Europeans, the Macassans had largely peaceful contact with Aboriginal people. They would set up camps for three months at a time, gathering and curing trepang and trading with the Aboriginal people, who found use for dugout canoes, metal items, food, tobacco and glass objects. A number of Macassans fathered children by Aboriginal women, some Aboriginal people made the journey to Macassar, and a few even lived there. The Macassans generally

had little impact on the local Aboriginal culture as they were pretty much self-sufficient, and were harvesting a resource not used by the Aboriginal people.

British Expeditions

With naval might at its peak, and the colony at Botany Bay now established, the British were keen to fully explore the coast of Australia. In 1801 Matthew Flinders set out on an ambitious mission to chart the entire coastline of Australia. By the time he reached the Gulf, his rotten vessel, the *Investigator*, was in danger of falling apart, so he gave the northern coast little more than a cursory glance, although many place names along the coast are a reminder of his trip. A couple of years later a French ship, *Le Géographe*, charted some of the western Territory coast, and names such as Joseph Bonaparte Gulf and Perron Islands date from this voyage.

The first person to really chart the waters of the Northern Territory was a remarkable young hydrographer, Phillip King. In four voyages between 1817 and 1821, King charted the coast in great detail and was the first to discover that Bathurst and Melville islands were in fact islands. The Cobourg Peninsula and the East, South and West Alligator rivers were all named by King. Such was his accuracy that King's charts form the basis for modern navigational charts of these waters.

Although King had noted the existence of Darwin harbour, he did not actually enter it, and this was undertaken by John Wickham, commander of the *Beagle*, and one of his senior officers, John Lort Stokes. Aboard one of the ship's whaling boats, Stokes explored the bay, then named it Port Darwin, after the soon-to-be-famous naturalist who had sailed on the *Beagle* to South America. It was on this voyage that Stokes and Wickham discovered and named the Victoria and Fitzroy rivers to the west.

British Attempts at Settlement

The British government was persuaded by a merchant, William Barns, and the mercantile body known as the East India Trade Committee that a settlement in northern Australia would be able to cash in on the trepang and spice trades, and deter rivals such as the French, Dutch and Americans.

In 1824 a military settlement was established on Melville Island. Despite early optimism, Fort Dundas, as named by its founder Captain Gordon Bremer, lasted barely 18 months.

Undeterred by their initial failure, a second garrison settlement, Fort Wellington, was set up at Raffles Bay on the mainland near Croker Island by Captain James Stirling. This small settlement also soon foundered, despite some hopeful reports from the last commandant, Captain Barker, and by 1829 it too had been abandoned.

Back in England the Colonial Office was still keen to settle northern Australia, and in 1838 a third party was equipped and despatched with orders to try again at Port Essington on the Cobourg Peninsula. A settlement called Victoria was established, where 36 marines and a few family members constructed a number of buildings, including a hospital, governor's residence, church and a number of military buildings.

Early hope once again faded, to be replaced by gloom and despair brought on by isolation, disease, death, white ants and a cruel climate. The hoped-for commercial boom failed to materialise. For a further four years the settlers battled on, all the while their spirits draining, until finally the decision was taken to abandon what had taken 11 years to establish. Race relations were for the most part pretty good – Aboriginal people helped in the construction of many buildings and, having had contact with Macassan trepangers, were familiar with working on boats. Today the ruins of Victoria lie within the Cobourg National Park.

Inland Exploration

In the early 1840s there was great demand by squatters in New South Wales for cheap Asian labour, and pressure was put on the government to find an overland route to the Port Essington settlement. It was hoped this

Prussian explorer Ludwig Leichhardt

would not only provide an easy route in for labourers, but also a route out for exports of horses and cattle.

In 1844 the government refused to fund an expedition, but a Prussian scientist by the name of Ludwig Leichhardt raised the necessary funds by private subscription and set off from the Darling Downs in Queensland. The party reached the Gulf of Carpentaria after nine months, and then headed north-west along the coast, on the way discovering and naming a number of major rivers including the McArthur, Roper, Limmen and Wickham.

The party suffered great privations: a number of the horses were drowned in the Roper River and so most of the zoological and botanical specimens had to be abandoned, members were killed in Aboriginal attacks at the Gulf, and food was pretty much limited to bush tucker. They eventually crossed the Arnhem Land escarpment and struggled into Victoria on 17 December 1845, 14 months after setting out. Although Leichhardt became something of a hero, the trip itself was largely a failure as the route was far too difficult for regular use and no new promising grazing areas were discovered.

Another major figure in the exploration of the Top End is Augustus Charles Gregory. In 1854 the Colonial Office in London, in consultation with the Royal Geographical Society, financed the North Australian Expedition whose main brief was to explore east from the Victoria River to the Gulf in the hope of finding new grazing lands for future pastoral development. Gregory was invited to lead the expedition, and another member of the party was the botanist Ferdinand von Mueller (who later designed the botanic gardens in Darwin, Castlemaine and Melbourne).

The party of 18 journeyed up the Victoria River aboard the *Tom Tough* and set up camp near present-day Timber Creek. Gregory spent six months exploring the Victoria River district, even probing down into the Great Sandy Desert. They then headed east, crossing the Daly and Roper rivers.

The eastward route from the Roper River to the Gulf was largely the reverse of Leichhardt's earlier expedition and both explorers missed finding the vast Mitchell grass plains of the Barkly Tableland. Gregory eventually arrived in Brisbane after 15 months. The success of the expedition lay in Gregory's sound judgment. His favourable reports of the Victoria River district led to the eventual opening up of that area.

During the 1850s two South Australian speculators, James Chambers and William Finke, employed a young Scottish surveyor, John McDouall Stuart, to head north and find new grazing lands. It was the beginning of a quest which would eventually lead Stuart to the north coast of Australia, and a place in the history books as arguably the greatest explorer of the Australian interior.

In March 1858 Stuart's small party of just three men and 13 horses set off, and by mid-April had reached the Finke River and the MacDonnell Ranges, which he named after the South Australian governor. They continued north, reaching Central Mount Sturt (named by Stuart for his former boss, explorer Charles Sturt), and tried, unsuccessfully, to cross the inhospitable country north-west to the Victoria River. Already weakened by disease and short on supplies, the party eventually turned back after a hostile encounter with a group of Warumungu Aboriginal men at a place that Stuart named Attack Creek.

Stuart returned to Adelaide to a hero's welcome and within a matter of weeks was back on the trail north in a government-funded attempt to cross the continent from south to north. With a party of 11 men and 45 horses he returned to Attack Creek and managed to continue for a further 250km before being forced once again to return south.

Within a month of returning, the dogged Scotsman was heading north again and this time he reached the mangrove-lined shores of the north coast at Point Stuart on 24 July 1862. During the four month return trip to Adelaide, Stuart's health failed rapidly. After a loud but brief welcome back in Adelaide, Stuart soon fell from the public eye, and with his ambition now achieved and his health in tatters he was seemingly a broken man. He returned to Britain where he died just four years after his famous expedition.

Colonial Expansion

Partly as a result of favourable reports by Gregory and Stuart, there was a push by South Australian governors to annex the Northern Territory. The Colonial Office was reluctant to spend any more British money on developing the north of Australia, and so in 1863 it agreed to South Australia's claims.

Having gained the Northern Territory, South Australia's hope was that they would be able to develop it successfully at little cost to the public. It was a hope that remained largely unfulfilled, as by Federation in 1901 the Territory had a huge debt and pastoralism, although well established, was hardly booming. The main success was the establishment of a permanent settlement on the north coast.

In an effort to encourage pioneering pastoralists, half a million acres of cheap land was put on the market in 1864. Ominously, most was taken up by wealthy speculators in London and Adelaide who hoped to turn a fast profit. Selling the land was the easy bit – the South Australian government then had to find and survey the 160-acre plots for the new land holders, and establish a new northern coastal settlement and port.

In 1864 the task was given to Boyle Finniss, a surveyor, who had orders to investigate the Adam Bay area at the mouth of the Adelaide River and establish a settlement. The area proved unsuitable as a port as the waters were difficult to navigate and the hinterland was waterlogged in the Wet, but Finniss went ahead and established a settlement at Escape Cliffs. It wasn't long before Finniss faced censure from his fellow officers and eventually the South Australian government.

Finally, South Australian Surveyor-General George Goyder was sent north in 1869 to settle and survey the area, and he headed straight for Port Darwin, having read the journals of John Lort Stokes who sailed into the harbour in 1839. The settlement was officially named Palmerston.

Settlement of the north was slow as the prospective landholders down south proved reluctant to move north. Most forfeited their holding and demanded refunds.

A saviour was urgently needed – and came in the form of the submarine telegraph cable which was to connect Australia with Britain.

The Overland Telegraph Line

In 1870 the South Australian government won the right to build a telegraph cable overland between Port Augusta and Darwin, where it would connect with a submarine cable connecting Java with India and England. The scheme would for the first time put Australia in direct communication with England. Previously all communication had had to travel by sea, so a governor in NSW might wait six months or more for a reply from the Colonial Office in London.

South Australia won the right only after somewhat rashly committing itself to finishing the cable in just two years – around 3000km of cable were to be laid across harsh and largely unpopulated land.

Private contracts were awarded for the construction of the 800km southern and northern sections, leaving a 1100km middle section which would be constructed by the South Australian government, under the supervision of Postmaster-General and Superintendent of Telegraphs, (later Sir) Charles Todd.

The southern section, from Port Augusta to near Charlotte Waters, was completed ahead of schedule by Ned Bagot. The central section was split into five parts, each under an experienced surveyor, and the names of these men today appear regularly in street names throughout the Territory – McMinn, Mills, Woods, Knuckey and Harvey. John Ross was given the job of scouting and blazing the route. Basically the line roughly followed the route pioneered by Stuart some years earlier, although Ross found a shorter route through the MacDonnell Ranges. Despite massive logistical problems, the southern and central sections were completed on time.

It was on the northern section that the project really ran into problems. The private contractors seriously underestimated the effect the wet season was going to have on their ability to complete the task. By June 1872 the line was complete except for the 350km section between Daly Waters and Tennant Creek, which was bridged by a pony relay until the lines were physically joined some months later.

Upon its completion in 1872, it was possible to send a message from Adelaide to London in a mere seven hours!

While the completion of the line and the opening of the OTL gave a good deal of prestige to South Australia, the state gained little direct benefit. By 1889 the line was largely superseded by another line which came ashore at Broome in Western Australia. However, the line opened up the country for further exploration and development. In the 1870s Ernest Giles and South Australian surveyor William Gosse both made expeditions west of Alice Springs, while Peter Warburton toughed it out by camel from Alice Springs across the Great Sandy Desert to the De Grey River near Port Hedland, surviving for much of the way on dried camel meat.

Gold!

The next major event in the opening up of the Territory was the discovery of gold in an OTL post hole at Yam Creek, about 160km south of Darwin. The find spurred on prospectors and it wasn't long before other finds had been made at nearby Pine Creek.

The finds sparked a minor rush and it was hoped that this would finally be the economic hurry-up that the South Australian government still so desperately needed. Men arrived by ship in Port Darwin – which was where their problems started. Equipment was expensive and there was no road south to the goldfields. Those that did make it found that most of the hopeful prospects had been claimed by speculative companies from Adelaide. Gold production from the Pine Creek fields was never high, peaking at £100,000 in 1880 and again in 1890, before dropping away sharply.

While the finds in the Territory were minuscule compared with those in Victoria and Western Australia, they generated activity in an area that was economically very unattractive. In an effort to encourage more people to the area, the South Australian government decided in 1883 to build a railway line from Palmerston (Darwin) to Pine Creek. The line was built by Chinese labourers, who had started coming to the Territory in the 1870s at the instigation of the South Australian premier, the prevailing view at the time being that it would be impossible to really develop the Territory without Asian labour.

By 1888 the European population was outnumbered four to one by Chinese immigrants, who dominated the goldfields. As had happened elsewhere in Australia, the Chinese faced serious obstacles – mainly in the form of racism – and many returned home after the gold had petered out. Many, however, stayed on in the Top End. Darwin had a thriving Chinatown until WWII, after which it was not rebuilt.

Cattle Industry

The increased confidence of the 1870s and 80s in the eastern colonies led to a pastoral boom in the Territory and the foundation of the cattle industry, which for many years was the mainstay of the Territory economy. Cattle were brought in overland from Queensland, initially along the route pioneered by Leichhardt, to stock the new runs of the north, while those in the Centre were stocked from South Australia along the Telegraph route. Stock routes pioneered by drovers such as Nat Buchanan, Thomas Pearce, Thomas Kilfoyle, Darcy Uhr and the Duracks of the Kimberley soon crisscrossed the Top End.

Such was the optimism of the era that many of the new stations were established on marginal or unviable land. Many stations simply didn't survive the economic crash of the 1890s, while others changed hands numerous times, usually at a loss. Gradually the individual runs were consolidated and became bigger, with large companies such as Goldsborough Mort and the British Vestey Brothers taking up large holdings. Even they had to struggle against poor land, distant markets and inadequate road access.

Federation & the Early 20th Century

The strident push for a Commonwealth of Australia by the eastern colonies was never strong in the Territory, although in a referendum of 1898 Territorians still voted overwhelmingly for it. Soon after Federation the South Australian government offered its Northern Territory to the Federal government. The great optimism of just a generation ago had turned to a resignation that the Territory was just too tough. Despite efforts to develop it, most projects (and many such as sugar, tobacco and coffee were tried) had failed completely or provided only minimal

Sidney Kidman, The Cattle King

More than any other enterprise, pastoralism – and in particular the cattle industry – led to white settlement in much of inland Australia. Rearing cattle was an arduous and risky business: grazing country was often marginal, the climate harsh, and there were vast distances to be travelled to civilisation, with the thought of marauding Aborigines never far away. Yet there was no shortage of starters prepared to give it a go and some went on to make major contributions.

Sir Sidney Kidman was the undisputed cattle king of Australia. Born in Adelaide in 1857, he ran away from home at the age of 13 and headed north for the 'corner country' of north-western New South Wales. Here he worked on outback stations, and over the years became an expert bushman and stockman.

It was in the latter part of the 19th century that vast expanses of outback Australia were settled. The infrastructure was virtually nil and getting cattle to markets in good condition was a major problem. Kidman came up with a bold yet simple solution: 'chains' of stations along strategic routes which would allow the gradual movement of stock from inland to the coastal markets. This in effect split the entire outback into a number of paddocks.

Starting with £400 which he inherited at the age of 21, Kidman traded in cattle and horses, and later in mines at Broken Hill, and gradually built up a portfolio of land-holdings which gave him the envisaged 'chains'. Eventually he owned or controlled about 170,000 sq km of land (an area 2½ times the size of Tasmania, or about the size of Washington state in the USA) in chains. One chain ran from the Gulf of Carpentaria south through western Queensland and New South Wales to Broken Hill and into South Australia, and another stretched from the Kimberley into the Northern Territory and then down through the Red Centre and into South Australia.

Such was Kidman's stature as a pastoralist that at one time the north-western area of New South Wales was known as 'Kidman's Corner'. His life was portrayed, somewhat romantically, in Ion Idriess' book *The Cattle King*. Kidman was knighted in 1921 and died in 1935.

Sir Sidney Kidman

returns, speculators and investors had lost faith and the Territory remained an economic backwater.

Opposition to the transfer to the Commonwealth came from Adelaide-based investors who held leases in the Territory and from conservative politicians. All were pinning their hopes on the completion of the transcontinental railway line which would link Adelaide with Darwin, and provide easy and rapid access to Asian markets. The transfer finally came in 1911, and it was conditional on the Federal government reimbursing the South Australians the £6 million spent on the Port Augusta-Oodnadatta railway, and completing the north-south transcontinental rail link. Unfortunately no time limit was placed on the latter condition, and it was only in 1999 that the final section from Alice to Darwin was given approval.

The Federal government set about trying to find an economic saviour for its new possession. Apparently having learnt little from the South Australians' experience, money was poured into experimental farms in the Top End but virtually everything failed.

In the 1920s, the Federal government concluded that the Territory was in fact two different places, and divided it into the separate administrative entities of North Australia and Central Australia, the dividing line being the 20° south parallel of latitude. Based largely on the fear that the populous Asian nations to the north were jealous of this vast and empty land, the three-man commission administrating North Australia was given almost a free hand to develop the infrastructure necessary to expand the pastoral industry. A change of government in 1929 forced a rethink and all development plans were shelved.

The 1930s saw yet more forays into commercial ventures, none of them wildly successful. Peanuts became the latest agricultural experiment, but it was only import restrictions protecting the local industry that allowed any of the farmers to make any money at all. Competition from Queensland nuts, combined with marketing problems and the poor Territory soils, meant that only the very biggest producers could make a decent profit. A fledgling pearl industry developed from Darwin, but it relied on cheap Asian labour and was severely hampered by competition from Japanese vessels. Other industries, such as the hunting of crocodiles and snakes for their skins, took off but failed to survive the severe depression of the early 1930s.

While the Territory struggled to pay its way, advances in technology and communications meant that it wasn't entirely isolated.

The fledgling aviation industry put Darwin on the map as passenger flights, operated by Qantas, had to make an overnight refuelling stop there, and pioneer aviators such as Amy Johnson also landed in Darwin. Other towns, too, started to develop – Tennant Creek became a minor boom town thanks to mining, and Alice Springs now had a rail connection to Adelaide.

20th-Century Exploration

Around the turn of the century, Baldwin Spencer, a biologist, and Francis Gillen, an anthropologist, teamed up to study the Aboriginal people of central Australia and Arnhem Land. The results of their study are a detailed record of a vanished way of life.

Donald Thomson led his first expedition to Arnhem Land in 1935 and his work in northern Australia is still highly regarded by anthropologists and naturalists.

Allan Davidson was the first European to explore the Tanami Desert in any detail. In 1900 he set out looking for gold and found a number of good prospects which led to a minor rush some years later.

In the 1930s, aerial mapping of the Centre began in earnest. Surveys were carried out over the Simpson Desert, the only large stretch of the country still to be explored on foot. In 1939, CT Madigan led an expedition that crossed this forbidding landscape from Old Andado to Birdsville; today the untracked route attracts a number of experienced adventurers.

In 1948 the largest scientific expedition ever undertaken in Australia was led by Charles Mountford into Arnhem Land. Financed by the National Geographic Society and the Australian government, it collected over 13,000 fish, 13,500 plant specimens, 850 birds and over 450 animal skins, along with thousands of Aboriginal implements and weapons.

WWII

When Britain declared war on Germany at the outbreak of WWII, Australia did likewise. Australian troops and ships were dispatched to Europe; the only troops stationed in Darwin were there to defend Indonesian islands against a Japanese attack. With the bombing of Pearl Harbor in late 1941 these troops were deployed to Ambon and Singapore, leaving Darwin with a pitifully small defence force. By early 1942, however, there were some 14,000 Australian and American troops stationed in the Top End, although they had nothing in the way of air or naval support.

Darwin's isolation also proved a nightmare for military planners. Spurred on by the demands of the war effort, the road from the southern railhead at Alice Springs to Larrimah was pushed through, and the first military convoy passed along it in early 1941; by October 1943 it was sealed all the way.

With the fall of Singapore to the Japanese in February 1941, the threat to Darwin became real, although it was underestimated by those in charge in Darwin. Nonetheless, women and children of the city were evacuated late that year.

At 9.57 am on 19 February 1942 the first bombs fell on Darwin. Nearly 200 Japanese aircraft bombed the harbour and the RAAF base at Larrakeyah, not far from the city centre. At noon a second fleet of 54 Betty bombers attacked the city. The loss of life in the raids was heavy, and there was severe damage to the city's buildings. In all, Darwin was attacked 64 times during the war and 243 people lost their lives; it was the only place in Australia to suffer prolonged attacks.

In March 1942 the entire Territory north of Alice Springs was placed under military control; convoys of men were trucked north and by December there were 32,000 men stationed in the Top End. The infrastructure needed to support these convoys was hastily put in place, and many reminders of this era can still be seen along or just off the Stuart Hwy between Alice Springs and Darwin.

While the war certainly devastated Darwin, the war effort had produced a number of lasting benefits for the Territory – among them sealed roads from Darwin to Alice Springs and Queensland, and much improved telephone, power and water facilities.

Post-War to the Present

A post-war immigration boom led to high growth in the urban areas of Darwin and Alice Springs, but a shortage of Federal funds for the Territory meant there was little development and the rebuilding of Darwin proceeded at a snail's pace.

One of the main beneficiaries of the war was the pastoral industry, which had the novel experience of having a ready market and high demand for its product – beef. This demand saw the construction of thousands of kilometres of Commonwealth funded 'beef roads' in the Territory into the late 1960s. This meant that most cattle were now trucked to markets or railheads by road trains, which virtually spelt the doom of the drovers who had played such a vital part in opening up the Territory.

Mining is one of only two industries (the other is tourism) that has really gone ahead since WWII. Copper and gold from Tennant Creek, oil and gas from the Amadeus basin in the Centre, gold from the Tanami, bauxite from Gove, manganese from Groote Eylandt and uranium from Batchelor – and more recently Kakadu – have all played an important role in the economic development of the Territory.

The big success story of the last 20 years, however, is tourism. At the end of WWII the population of Alice Springs was around 1000; today it has risen to over 20,000, purely on the strength of the tourist industry. For most Australians the outback is where the 'real' Australia lies, and as Uluru (Ayers Rock) lies in the Territory, the Territory has become the major outback destination. The rise in environmental awareness and ecotourism has also led to the huge popularity of Kakadu National Park, and Uluru and Kakadu each receive close to half a million visitors each year.

The 1970s was a time of great optimism in the Territory, an optimism that was severely tested (although, it seems, undiminished) by the occurrence of the worst natural disaster in Australia's history. On Christmas Eve in 1974 Cyclone Tracy ripped through Darwin, killing 66 people and destroying 95% of the city's dwellings. Within four years the city had been largely rebuilt and has never looked back since.

Despite its increasing sophistication, the Northern Territory is still frontier country to most Australians, the 'never never', where, it has been said, men are men and women aren't ladies. It's also a place full of surprises – in 1995 the Northern Territory government was the first in the world to legislate on voluntary euthanasia, yet it also steadfastly refused to introduce a methadone program for heroin users, preferring instead to give them a one-way bus ticket south.

Aboriginal Land Rights Britain settled Australia on the legal principle of *terra nullius*, a land belonging to no-one, which meant that the country was legally unoccupied. The settlers could take land from Aboriginal people without signing treaties or providing compensation. The concept of land ownership was completely foreign to Aboriginal people and their view of the world in which land did not belong to individuals: people belonged to the land, were formed by it and were a part of it like everything else.

After WWII Aboriginal people became more organised and better educated, and a political movement for land rights developed. In 1962 a bark petition was presented to the Federal government by the Yolngu people of Yirrkala, in north-east Arnhem Land, demanding that the government recognise Aboriginal peoples' occupation and ownership of Australia since time immemorial. The petition was ignored, and the Yolngu people took the matter to court and lost. In the famous Yirrkala Land Case in 1971, Australian courts accepted the government's claim that Aboriginal people had no meaningful economic, legal or political relationship to land. The case upheld the principle of *terra nullius*, and the common-law position that Australia was unoccupied in 1788.

The Yirrkala Land Case was based on an inaccurate (if not outright racist) assessment of Aboriginal society, and the Federal government came under increasing pressure to legislate for Aboriginal land rights. In 1976 it eventually passed the Aboriginal Land Rights (Northern Territory) Act, which is often referred to as the Land Rights Act.

Aboriginal Land Rights (NT) Act This remains Australia's most powerful and comprehensive land rights legislation. Promises were made to legislate for national land rights, but these were abandoned after opposition from mining companies and state governments. The 1976 act established three Aboriginal Land Councils, who are empowered to claim land on behalf of traditional Aboriginal owners.

However, under the act the only land claimable is unalienated land outside town boundaries – land that no-one else owns or leases, usually semi-desert or desert. Thus, when the traditional Anangu owners of Uluru claimed traditional ownership of Uluru and Kata Tjuta (the Olgas), their claim was disallowed because the land was within a national park. It was only by amending two acts of parliament that Uluru-Kata Tjuta National Park was handed back to traditional Anangu owners on the condition that it was immediately leased back to the Australian Nature Conservation Agency (now Parks Australia).

At present almost half of the Northern Territory has either been claimed, or is being claimed, by its traditional Aboriginal owners. The claim process is extremely tedious and can take many years to complete, largely because almost all claims have been opposed by the Territory government. Many elderly claimants die before the matter is resolved. Claimants are required to prove that under Aboriginal law they are responsible for the sacred sites on the land being claimed.

Once a claim is successful, Aboriginal people have the right to negotiate with mining companies and ultimately accept or reject exploration and mining proposals. This right is strongly opposed by the mining lobby, despite the fact that traditional Aboriginal owners in the Northern Territory only reject about a third of these proposals outright.

Mabo & the Native Title Act It was only recently that the non-Aboriginal community, including the Federal government, came to grips with the fact that a meaningful conciliation between white Australia and its indigenous population was vital to the psychological well-being of all Australians.

In May 1982, five Torres Strait Islanders led by Eddie Mabo began an action for a declaration of native title over the Queensland Murray Islands. They argued that the legal principle of *terra nullius* had wrongfully usurped their title to land, as for thousands of years Murray Islanders had enjoyed a relationship with the land that included a notion of ownership. In June 1992 the High Court of Australia rejected *terra nullius* and the myth that Australia had been unoccupied. In doing this, it recognised that a principle of native title existed before the arrival of the British.

The High Court's judgment became known as the Mabo decision, one of the most controversial decisions ever handed down by an Australian court. It was ambiguous, as it didn't outline the extent to which native title existed in mainland Australia. It received a hostile reaction from the mining and other industry groups, but was hailed by Aboriginal people and Labor Prime Minister Paul Keating as an opportunity to create a basis of reconciliation between Aboriginal and non-Aboriginal Australians.

To define the principle of native title, the Federal parliament passed the Native Title Act in December 1993. Contrary to the cries of protest from the mining industry, the act gives Australian Aboriginal people very few new rights. It limits the application of native title to land which no-one else owns or leases, and to land with which Aboriginal people have continued to have a physical association. The act states that existing ownership or leases extinguish native title, although native title may be revived after mining leases have expired. If land is successfully claimed by Aboriginal people under the act, they will have no veto over developments including mining. Despite (or because of) its complexity, it will no doubt take a number of years and court cases before the implications of the Native Title Act are fully understood.

The Wik Decision Several months prior to the Native Title Act becoming law, the Wik and Thayorre peoples had made a claim for native title in the Federal Court to land on Cape York Peninsula. The area claimed included two pastoral leases. Neither had ever been permanently occupied for that purpose, but the Wik and Thayorre peoples had been in continuous occupation of them. They argued that native title co-existed with the pastoral leases.

In January 1996 the Federal Court decided that the claim could not succeed as the granting of pastoral leases under Queensland law extinguished any native title rights. The Wik people appealed that decision in the High Court, which subsequently overturned it.

The High Court determined that, under the law that created pastoral leases in Queensland, native title to the leases in question had not been extinguished. Further, it said that native title rights could continue at the same time that land was under lease, and that pastoralists did not have exclusive right of possession to their leases. Importantly, it also ruled that where the two were in conflict, the rights of the pastoralists would prevail.

Despite the fact that lease tenure was not threatened, the Wik decision brought a hue and cry from pastoral lessees across Australia, who demanded that the Federal government step in to protect them by legislating to limit native title rights, as was intended in the original act. Aboriginal leaders were equally adamant that native title must be preserved.

In late 1997 the government responded with its 10 Point Plan, a raft of proposed legislative amendments to the Native Title Act which only further entrenches the pastoralists' position and effectively extinguishes native title, something the Wik judgement does not do. Whatever the outcome of the Federal government's response to Wik, it's obvious that failure to resolve the native title issue will put new and extravagant meaning into the phrase 'lawyers' picnic', and will make reconciliation less rather than more likely.

GEOGRAPHY

The Northern Territory covers an area of around 1.35 million sq km, about 17% of the Australian landmass, roughly equal to the combined areas of Spain, France and Italy in Europe, or the state of Florida in the USA. Although roughly 80% of the Territory is in the tropics – the Tropic of Capricorn cuts across just north of Alice Springs – only the northern 25%, known as the Top End, has anything resembling the popular idea of a tropical climate.

The 5440km coastline is generally flat and backed by swamps, mangroves and mudflats, rising to a plateau no higher than 450m. The ruggedly beautiful ochre-red ridges of the MacDonnell Ranges, which reach heights of more than 600m, cut an east-west swathe through the Centre either side of Alice Springs. The famous monolith, Uluru, 348m high, is in the south-western part of the Territory.

The Top End is a distinct region of savanna woodlands and pockets of rainforest. In the north-east, the Arnhem Land plateau rises abruptly from the plain and continues to the coast of the Gulf of Carpentaria. Much of the southern three-quarters of the Territory consists of desert or semi-arid plain.

The main rivers in the north-west are the Victoria and the Daly, which flow into the Timor Sea; east of Darwin the Adelaide, Mary, South Alligator and East Alligator rivers flow into the Arafura Sea; and further south there are the Roper and McArthur rivers, flowing into the Gulf of Carpentaria. Inland rivers, such as the Finke, Todd and Hugh, are dry most of the year. When they do flow, however, their waters often cover a great area before being lost in the wilds of the Simpson Desert.

CLIMATE

The two geographical zones – the Top End and the Centre – also correspond to the two climatic zones. The climate of the Top End is influenced by the tropical monsoons and so has two distinct seasons – the Wet (November to April) and the Dry (May to October). During the Wet the Top End receives virtually all of its annual rainfall (around 1600mm), usually in heavy late-afternoon thunderstorms. During the Dry rainfall is minimal and humidity is low, making it an ideal time for a visit. Temperatures throughout the year remain constant, with minimum/maximum temperatures of around 25/32°C in the Wet and 19/30°C in the Dry.

The Centre has a much drier climate and greater extremes of temperature. In winter daytime temperatures of around 15-20°C are comfortable, although there are often cold winds. Night-time temperatures are surprisingly low, making camping out a difficult prospect unless you have good gear – at Yulara the mercury often plunges below 0°C at night during winter, catching out many an unwary camper. In summer daytime temperatures are generally far too hot for comfort – an average of around 33°C

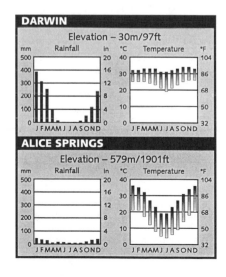

but often much higher – making spring and autumn the ideal times for a visit. Rainfall in the Centre is low all year round.

Alice Springs

There are maximums of 30°C and above from October to March – 30°C is a cool day in summer! – minimums are 10°C and below from May to September. From December to February there's an average of 40mm of rain per month.

Darwin

Temperatures are even year round, with maximums from 30-34°C and minimums from 19-26°C; rainfall is minimal from May to September, but from December to March there's 250-380mm a month.

NATIONAL PARKS & RESERVES

The Northern Territory has more than 100 national parks and reserves – nonurban protected wilderness areas of environmental or natural importance. As a rule, the parks and reserves are administered by the Parks & Wildlife Commission of the Northern Territory. The exceptions are Kakadu and Uluru-Kata Tjuta national parks, which come under the domain of the Federal national parks body, Parks Australia (formerly the Australian Nature Conservation Agency – ANCA).

Public access is encouraged if safety and conservation regulations are observed. In all parks you're asked to do nothing to damage or alter the natural environment. Approach roads, camping grounds (often with toilets and showers), walking tracks and information centres are often provided for visitors. Pets and firearms are not allowed in national parks and nature reserves.

Some national parks are so isolated, rugged or uninviting that you wouldn't want to do much except look unless you were an experienced, well-prepared bushwalker or climber. Other parks, however, are among Australia's major attractions and two in the Territory – Kakadu and Uluru-Kata Tjuta – have been included on the World Heritage List (a United Nations list

of natural or cultural places of world significance that would be an irreplaceable loss to the planet if they were altered).

Other popular parks in the Northern Territory include Litchfield National Park, which is only a few hours from Darwin and has some superb swimming holes and waterfalls; Nitmiluk (Katherine Gorge) National Park, with its series of rugged gorges which are great fun to canoe along; Watarrka National Park, which has as its centrepiece the outrageously picturesque Kings Canyon; and the West MacDonnell National Park, which encompasses some of the most spectacular gorge country in central Australia and offers excellent bushwalking opportunities.

For Parks & Wildlife offices see Useful Organisations in the Facts for the Visitor chapter.

GOVERNMENT & POLITICS
Federal Government

Australia is a monarchy, but although Britain's ruler is also Australia's, Australia is fully autonomous. The British sovereign is represented by the governor-general and the state governors, whose nominations for their posts by the respective governments are ratified by the reigning monarch.

Federal parliament is based in Canberra, the capital of the nation. Like Washington DC in the USA, Canberra is in its own separate area of land, the Australian Capital Territory (ACT), and is not under state rule.

The Federal government is elected for a maximum of three years but elections can be (and often are) called earlier. Voting in Australian elections is by secret ballot and is compulsory for persons 18 years of age and over. Voting can be somewhat complicated as a preferential system is used whereby each candidate has to be listed in order of preference. This can result, for example, in Senate elections with 50 or more candidates to be ranked!

In Federal parliament the two main political groups are the Australian Labor Party (ALP) and the coalition between the Liberal (conservative) Party and the National Party. These parties also dominate state politics but sometimes the Liberal and National parties are not in coalition. On 3 October 1998 the Liberals, led by John Howard, and the National Party were returned for a second term in office.

The Cabinet, presided over by the prime minister, is the government's major policy-making body, and is comprised of about half the full ministry. It meets in private (usually in Canberra) and its decisions are ratified by the Executive Council, a formal body presided over by the governor-general.

Northern Territory Government
Politically the Northern Territory is something of an anomaly in Australia. In 1947 the Chifley government in Canberra created the Northern Territory Legislative Council, a 13 member body (six elected, seven appointed by Canberra) which had the power to do pretty well anything as long as it did not offend Canberra, which retained the right of veto. One NT parliamentarian commented that it gave Territorians no more rights than 'the inhabitants of Siberian Russia or the inmates of a gaol'.

The elected council members agitated for self-government, but Canberra remained unmoved. In 1958 the size of the council was increased and the MP for the Northern Territory in the House of Representatives in Canberra was finally allowed to vote in the House – but only on matters pertaining to the Territory. It was not until 1974 that the Territory got a fully elected Legislative Assembly, and representation in the Senate in Canberra. Self-government (akin to statehood) came in 1978, although Canberra still has a greater say than it does in the states.

The motion that the Northern Territory should be granted statehood was narrowly defeated at a referendum in October 1998.

The leader of the Territory's 25 seat parliament is the Chief Minister. The Territorian Country Liberal Party has been in power since 1974 and holds all but the eight seats held by the ALP. There is no Upper House, although if statehood were granted one would be established.

ECONOMY
The Northern Territory economy is dominated by two major industries – tourism and mining – with other primary industry coming a distant third.

Mining & Energy
Mining in the Northern Territory contributes about 20% of gross state product.

The major minerals mined in the Territory are: bauxite, with the third-largest bauxite mine in Australia at Gove; gold, with mines in the Pine Creek area, the Tanami Desert and the Tennant Creek area; manganese on Groote Eylandt, one of the world's four major producers of high grade ore; zinc, lead and silver, including one of the world's largest known ore bodies at McArthur River near Borroloola; and uranium, with 10% of the world's reserves lying in or close to Kakadu National Park.

Oil production is dominated by the offshore fields of Jabiru, Challis/Cassini and Skeea. Gas production is from the Mereenie gas fields west of the MacDonnell Ranges in central Australia.

Tourism
Tourism is one of the fastest-growing industries. Almost a million people travel to or within the Territory each year, compared with about half that number a decade ago.

Primary Industry
There are more than 200 pastoral holdings in the Northern Territory producing cattle for Australian and South-East Asian markets. These vary from small stations of around 200 sq km to huge properties such as Brunette Downs on the Barkly Tableland, which is a shade over 12,000 sq km. Live cattle exports from the Territory are worth around $30 million annually.

Prawn fishing is another important industry, with an annual catch of around 5500 tonnes valued at around $60 million.

POPULATION & PEOPLE
Although the Northern Territory accounts for nearly 20% of the Australian landmass,

it has just 1% of the country's population. Around 38,000 of the Territory's 189,991 people are of Aboriginal descent. The non-Aboriginal population is cosmopolitan. Darwin also has a significant population of Chinese Australians, descendants of the first non-European migrants into the Territory last century.

At June 1998, the population of Darwin was 86,576, while other major centres of population are Alice Springs (25,522), Nhulunbuy (3719), Katherine (9856) and Tennant Creek (3862).

Aboriginal People

When whites first settled in Australia, it is believed there were about 300,000 Aboriginal people and around 250 different languages were spoken, many as distinct from each other as English is from Chinese.

In such a society, based on family groups with an egalitarian political structure, a co-ordinated response to the colonisers was not possible. Despite the presence of the Aboriginal people, the newly arrived Europeans considered the new continent to be *terra nullius* – a land belonging to no-one. They saw no recognisable system of government, no commerce or permanent settlements and no evidence of land ownership.

Many Aboriginal people were driven from their land by force, and many more succumbed to exotic diseases such as small-pox, measles, venereal disease, influenza, whooping cough, pneumonia and tuberculosis. Others voluntarily left their lands to travel to the fringes of settled areas to obtain new commodities such as steel and cloth, and experience hitherto unknown drugs such as tea, tobacco and alcohol.

The delicate balance between Aboriginal people and nature was broken, as the invaders cut down forests and introduced domestic animals. Cattle destroyed waterholes and ruined the habitats that had for tens of thousands of years sustained mammals, reptiles and vegetable foods. Several species of plants and animals disappeared altogether.

There was considerable conflict between Aborigines and pastoralists. Aboriginal people occasionally speared cattle or attacked isolated stations, then suffered fierce reprisal raids which left many of them dead. An attack on the Barrow Creek telegraph station in which two whites were killed led to punitive raids in which up to 50 Aborigines were killed. A similar attack on a lonely Daly River copper mine in 1884 led to the deaths of three miners and a government reprisal raid during which it is believed many Aboriginal people were killed. Very few were prosecuted for killing Aboriginal people, although the practice was widespread.

By the early 1900s, legislation designed to segregate and 'protect' Aboriginal people was passed in all states. The legislation imposed restrictions on Aboriginal people's rights to own property and seek employment, and the Aboriginals Ordinance of 1918 even allowed the state to remove children from Aboriginal mothers if it was suspected that the father was non-Aboriginal. In these cases the parents were considered to have no rights over the children, who were placed in foster homes or child-care institutions.

Many Aboriginal people are still bitter about having been separated from their families and forced to grow up apart from their people. On the other hand, the Ordinance gave a degree of protection for 'full-blood' Aborigines living on reserves, as non-Aboriginal people could enter only with a permit, and mineral exploration was forbidden. Arnhem Land was declared an Aboriginal reserve in 1931.

In these early years of the 20th century, most Territory Aboriginal people were confined to government-allotted reserves or Christian missions. Others lived on cattle stations where they were employed as skilful but poorly paid stockmen or domestic servants, or lived a half life on the edges of towns. Only a few – some of those on reserves and cattle stations, and those in the remote outback – maintained much of their traditional way of life.

Continued on page 39

ABORIGINAL
ART

V isual imagery is a fundamental part of Aboriginal life, a connection between past and present, supernatural and earthly, people and the land. The initial forms of artistic expression by Aborigines were rock carvings (petroglyphs), body painting and ground designs, and the earliest engraved designs known to exist date back at least 30,000 years.

While it has always been an integral part of Aboriginal culture, Aboriginal art, with some noteable exceptions, was largely ignored by non-Aboriginals, or simply seen as an anthropological curiosity. Then in 1971 an event took place which changed non-Aboriginal perceptions of Aboriginal art. At Papunya, 240 km north-west of Alice Springs, Long Jack Phillipus Tjakamarra and Billy Stockman Tjapaltjarri, both elders of the community employed as groundsmen at the school, were encouraged to paint a mural on one of the school's external walls. Shortly after work commenced, other members of the community became enthused by the project and joined in creating the mural named *Honey Ant Dreaming*. Government regulations later saw the mural destroyed, but its effect on the community was profound. Images of spiritual significance had taken on a very public form, and the desire to paint spread through the community. Initially the paintings were executed on smallish boards, though within a short time canvases were used.

From this quiet beginning in a remote Aboriginal community one of the most important art movements of the late 20th century grew and spread. That it developed in Papunya is not without irony. Papunya was established in 1960 under the auspices of the Australian government's cultural assimilation policy; a policy designed in combination with others, such as the forced removal of Aboriginal children from their families, to undermine Aboriginal culture. *Honey Ant Dreaming* and the creative and cultural energy it unleashed, helped to strengthen Aboriginal culture and led to the abandonment of these policies.

While the dot paintings of the central deserts are among the more readily identifiable and probably most popular form of contemporary Aboriginal art, there's a huge range of material being produced – bark paintings from Arnhem Land, wood carving and silk-screen printing from the Tiwi Islands north of Darwin, batik printing and wood carving from central Australia, didgeridoos and more.

ROCK ART
Arnhem Land

Arnhem Land, in Australia's tropical Top End, is possibly the area with the richest artistic heritage. Recent finds suggest that rock paintings were being made as early as 60,000 years ago, and some of the rock art galleries in the huge sandstone Arnhem Land plateau are at least 18,000 years old.

The art of Arnhem Land is vastly different from that of the central deserts. Here, Dreaming stories are depicted far more literally, with easily

Title page: Aboriginal art on display at Kakadu National Park (photo by Richard I'Anson).

recognisable (though often stylised) images of ancestors, animals, and even Macassans – Indonesian mariners from Sulawesi who regularly visited the north coast until banned by government regulations in 1906.

The paintings contained in the Arnhem Land rock art sites range from hand prints to paintings of animals, people, mythological beings and European ships, constituting one of the world's most important and fascinating rock art collections. They provide a record of changing environments and lifestyles over the millennia.

In some places they are concentrated in large 'galleries', with paintings from more recent eras sometimes superimposed over older paintings. Some sites are kept secret – not only to protect them from damage, but also because they are private or sacred to the Aboriginal owners. Some are believed to be inhabited by dangerous beings, who must not be approached by the ignorant. However, two of the finest sites have been opened up to visitors, with access roads, walkways and explanatory signs. These are Ubirr and Nourlangie in Kakadu National Park.

The rock paintings show how the main styles succeeded each other over time. The earliest hand or grass prints were followed by a 'naturalistic' style, with large outlines of people or animals filled in with colour. Some of the animals depicted, such as the thylacine (Tasmanian tiger), have long been extinct on mainland Australia.

After the naturalistic style came the 'dynamic', in which motion was often depicted (a dotted line, for example, to show a spear's path through the air). In this era the first mythological beings appeared, with human bodies and animal heads.

The next style mainly showed simple human silhouettes, and was followed by the curious 'yam figures', in which people and animals were drawn in the shape of yams (or yams in the shape of people and animals!). Fish were depicted in the art of this period, and the style known as 'x-ray', which showed creatures' bones and internal organs, appeared.

By about 1000 years ago many of the salt marshes had turned into freshwater swamps and billabongs. The birds and plants which provided new food sources in this landscape appeared in the art of this time.

From around 400 years ago, Aboriginal artists also depicted the human newcomers to the region – Macassan traders and, more recently, Europeans – and the things they brought, or their modes of transport such as ships or horses.

PAINTING
Western Desert Painting

Following the developments at Papunya (see introduction) and with the growing importance of art, both as an economic and a cultural activity, an association was formed to help the artists sell their work. The Papunya Tula company in Alice Springs is still one of the relatively few galleries in central Australia to be owned and run by Aboriginal people.

Painting in central Australia has flourished to such a degree that it is now an important educational activity for children, through which they can learn different aspects of religious and ceremonial knowledge. This is especially true now that women are so much a part of the painting movement.

Dot painting partly evolved from 'ground paintings', which formed the centrepiece of dances and songs. These were made from pulped plant material, and the designs were made on the ground using dots of this mush. Dots were also used to outline objects in rock paintings, and to highlight geographical features or vegetation.

While dot paintings may look random and abstract, they usually depict a Dreaming journey, and so can be seen almost as aerial landscape maps. Many paintings feature the tracks of birds, animals and humans, often identifying the ancestor. Subjects are often depicted by the imprint they leave in the sand – a simple arc depicts a person (as that is the print left by someone sitting), a *coolamon* (wooden carrying dish) is shown by an oval shape, a digging stick by a single line, a camp fire by a circle. Males or females are identified by the objects associated with them – digging sticks and coolamons for women, spears and boomerangs for men. Concentric circles usually depict Dreaming sites, or places where ancestors paused in their journeys. These symbols are widely used, but their meaning within each individual painting is known only by the artist and the people closely associated with him or her – either by group or by the Dreaming – and different groups apply different interpretations to each painting. So sacred stories can be publicly portrayed, as the deeper meaning is not evident to most viewers.

The colours used in central Australian dot paintings include reds, blues and purples which may seem overly vivid but can be seen in the outback landscape.

Art & the Dreaming

All early Aboriginal art was based on the various peoples' ancestral Dreaming – the 'Creation', when the earth's physical features were formed by the struggles between powerful supernatural ancestors such as the Rainbow Serpent, the Lightning Men and the Wandjina. Codes of behaviour were also laid down in the Dreaming, and although these laws have been diluted and adapted in the last 200 years, they still provide the basis of Aboriginal law today. Ceremonies, rituals and sacred paintings are all based on the Dreaming.

A Dreaming can relate to a person, an animal or a physical feature, while others are more general, relating to a region, a group of people, or natural forces such as floods and wind. Australia is covered by a vast network of Dreamings, and any one person may have connections to several.

Top: Ancient Ewaninga rock engravings (petroglyphs) south of Alice Springs; courtesy of the NT Tourist Commission

Bottom: *Bush Tucker and Flowers*, silk scarf by Rosemary Petyarre; courtesy of Utopia Awely Batik, Utopia Women's Centre

Top: *Pelican story* by Amy Jirwulurr Johnson; acrylic on canvas; 185 x 175cm; 1994; Ngukurr, NT; represented by Alcaston House Gallery, Melbourne

Bottom: Lightning Brothers rock art site at Katherine River; courtesy of the NT Tourist Commission

Kumoken (Freshwater crocodile) with Mimi Spirits by Djawida, b.c. 1935, Yulkman clan; Kunwinjku language, Kurrudjmuh, western Arnhem Land; earth pigments on bark; 151 x 71cm; 1990; purchased 1990 by National Gallery of Victoria

Top: Decorative central Australian scorched carvings made from river red gum root; Maraku Arts & Crafts, Uluru; courtesy of DESART

Bottom: *Possum, Snake, Potato Dreaming* by Paddy Japaljarri Sims and Bessie Nakamarra Sims; acrylic on linen; 91 x 153cm, 1992; War-lukurlangu Artists Association, Yuendumu, NT; courtesy of DESART

Bark Painting

While bark painting is a more recent art form, it is still an important part of the cultural heritage of Arnhem Land Aboriginal people. It's difficult to establish when bark was first used, partly because it is perishable and old pieces simply don't exist. European visitors in the early 19th century noted the practice of painting the inside walls of bark shelters.

The bark used is from the stringybark tree (*Eucalyptus tetradonta*), and it is taken off the tree in the wet season when it is moist and supple. The rough outer layers are removed and the bark is dried by placing it over a fire and then under weights on the ground to keep it flat. In a couple of weeks the bark is dry and ready for use. A typical bark painting made today has sticks across the top and bottom of the sheet to keep it flat.

The pigments used in bark paintings are mainly red and yellow (ochres), white (kaolin) and black (charcoal). The colours were gathered from special sites by the traditional owners, and they were then traded. These natural pigments are still used today, giving the paintings their superb soft and earthy finish. Binding agents such as egg yolks, wax and plant resins were added to the pigments. Recently these have been replaced by synthetic agents such as wood glue. Similarly, the brushes used in the past were obtained from the bush materials at hand – twigs, leaf fibres, feathers, human hair and the like – but these too have largely been replaced by modern brushes.

One of the main features of Arnhem Land bark paintings is the use of cross-hatching designs. These designs identify the particular clans, and are based on body paintings of the past. The paintings can also be broadly categorised by their regional styles. In the west the tendency is towards naturalistic images and plain backgrounds, while to the east the use of geometric designs is more common.

The art reflects Dreaming themes that vary by region. In eastern Arnhem Land the prominent ancestor beings are the Djangkawu, who travelled the land with elaborate *dilly* bags (carry bags) and digging sticks (for making waterholes), and the Wagilag Sisters, who are associated with snakes and waterholes. In western Arnhem Land the Rainbow Serpent, Yingarna, is the significant being (according to some clans), but one of her offspring, Ngalyod, and Nawura are also important. The *mimi* spirits are another feature of western Arnhem Land art, both on bark and rock. These mischievous spirits are attributed with having taught the Aborigines of the region many things, including hunting, food gathering and painting skills.

Contemporary Painting

Since the late 1980s the artists of Ngukurr ('nook-or'), near Roper Bar in south-eastern Arnhem Land, have been producing works using acrylic paints on canvas. Although ancestral beings still feature prominently, the works are generally much more modern, with free-flowing forms and often have little in common with traditional formal structure.

ARTEFACTS & CRAFTS

Objects traditionally made for practical or ceremonial use – musical instruments and weapons such as clubs *(nula nulas)*, spears and spearthrowers *(woomeras)* – often featured intricate and symbolic decoration. In recent years many communities have also developed non-traditional craft forms that have created employment and income, and the growing tourist trade has seen demand and production increase steadily.

Didgeridoos

The most widespread craft items seen for sale these days are didgeridoos. There has been a phenomenal boom in popularity and they can be found in shops around the country.

Originally they were used as ceremonial musical instruments by Aboriginal people in Arnhem Land (where they are known as *yidaki*). The traditional instrument was made from particular eucalypt branches which had been hollowed out by termites. The tubes were often fitted with a wax mouthpiece made from sugarbag (native honey bee wax) and decorated with traditional designs.

Although they may look pretty, most didgeridoos made these days bear little relation to traditional ones: they may be made from the wrong or inferior wood, have been hollowed out using mechanical or other means, have poor sound quality, and most have never had an Aboriginal person anywhere near them! (See Buying Aboriginal Art & Artefacts.)

Boomerangs

Boomerangs are curved wooden throwing sticks used for hunting and also as ceremonial clapping sticks. Contrary to popular belief, not all boomerangs are designed to return when thrown – the idea is to hit the animal being hunted! Returning boomerangs were mostly used in south-eastern and western Australia. Although they all follow the same

---

Hollow-Log Coffins

Hollowed-out logs were often used for reburial ceremonies in Arnhem Land, and were also a major form of artistic expression. They were highly decorated, often with many of the Dreaming themes, and were known as *dupun* in eastern Arnhem Land and *lorrkon* in western Arnhem Land.

In 1988 a group of Arnhem Land artists made a memorial as their contribution to the movement highlighting injustices against Aborigines – this was, of course, the year when non-Aboriginal Australians were celebrating 200 years of European settlement. The artists painted 200 log coffins – one for each year of settlement – with traditional clan and Dreaming designs, and these now form a permanent display in the National Gallery in Canberra.

fundamental design, boomerangs come in a huge range of shapes, sizes and decorative styles, and are made from a number of different wood types.

Wooden Sculptures

Traditionally most wooden sculptures were made to be used for particular ceremonies and then discarded. Arnhem Land artists still produce soft-wood carvings of birds, fish, other animals and ancestral beings, which were originally used for ceremonial purposes. The lightweight figures are engraved and painted with intricate symbolic designs.

Early in this century, missionaries encouraged some communities and groups to produce wooden sculptures for sale.

Scorched Carvings

Also very popular are the wooden carvings which have designs scorched into them with hot fencing wire. These range from small figures, such as possums, up to quite large snakes and lizards, although none of them have any Dreaming significance. In central Australia one of the main outlets for these is the Maruku Arts & Crafts shop at the Uluru-Kata Tjuta National Park Cultural Centre, where it's possible to see the crafts being made. Although much of the artwork is usually done by women, men are also involved at the Maruku shop. The Mt Ebenezer Roadhouse, on the Lasseter Highway (the main route to Uluru), is another Aboriginal-owned enterprise and one of the cheapest places for buying sculpted figures.

Tiwi Island Art

Due to their isolation, the Aborigines of the Tiwi Islands (Bathurst and Melville islands, off the coast of Darwin) have developed art forms – mainly sculpture – not found anywhere else, although there are some similarities with the art of Arnhem Land.

The *pukumani* burial rites are one of the main rituals of Tiwi religious life, and it is for these ceremonies that many of the art works are created – *yimwalini* (bark baskets), spears and *tutini* (burial poles). These carved and painted ironwood poles, up to 2.5m long, are placed around the grave, and represent features of the deceased person's life.

In the last 50 or so years the Tiwi islanders have been producing sculptured animals and birds, many of these being Creation ancestors (the Darwin Museum of Arts & Sciences has an excellent display). More recently, bark painting and silk-screen printing have become popular, and there are workshops on both islands where these items are produced.

Fibre Craft

Articles made from fibres are a major art form among women. String or twine was traditionally made from bark, grass, leaves, roots and other materials, hand-spun and dyed with natural pigments, then woven to make dilly bags, baskets, garments, fishing nets and other items. Strands or fibres from the leaves of the pandanus palm (and other palms or grasses) were also woven to make dilly bags and mats. While all these objects have utilitarian purposes, many also have ritual uses.

Textiles

The women of Utopia, 260km north-east of Alice Springs, are known for their production of batik material. In the mid-1970s the Anmatyerre and Alyawarre people started to reoccupy their traditional lands around Utopia, and this was given a formal basis in 1979 when they were granted title to the station. A number of scattered outstations, rather than a central settlement, were set up, and around this time the women were introduced to batik as part of a self-help program. The art form flourished and Utopia Women's Batik Group was formed in 1978 (the group was later incorporated and is now called Utopia Awely Batik Aboriginal Corporation, trading as Utopia Silks). The brightly coloured silk batiks were based on traditional women's body-painting designs called *awely*, and on images of flora and fauna.

In the late 1980s techniques using acrylic paints on canvas were introduced at Utopia, and Utopian art is now receiving international acclaim.

Pottery

The Arrernte people from Hermannsburg have recently begun to work with pottery, a craft which is not traditionally Aboriginal. They have incorporated moulded figures and surface treatments adapted from Dreaming stories.

BUYING ABORIGINAL ART & ARTEFACTS

One of the best and most evocative reminders of your trip is an Aboriginal work of art or artefact. By buying *authentic* items you are supporting Aboriginal culture and helping to ensure that traditional skills and designs endure. Unfortunately much of the so-called Aboriginal art sold as souvenirs is either ripped off from Aboriginal people or is just plain fake. Admittedly it is often difficult to tell whether an item is genuine, or whether a design is being used legitimately, but it is worth trying to find out.

The best place to buy artefacts is either directly from the communities which have craft outlets or from galleries and shops which are owned and operated by Aboriginal communities (see the following list for some suggestions). This way you can be sure that the items are genuine and that the money you spend goes to the right people. There are many Aboriginal artists who get paid very small sums for their work, only to find it being sold for thousands in big city galleries.

Didgeridoos are the hot item these days, and you need to decide whether you want a decorative piece or an authentic and functional musical instrument. Many of the didgeridoos sold are not made by Aboriginal people, and there are even stories of backpackers in Darwin earning good money by making or decorating didgeridoos. From a community outlet such as Injalak (Oenpelli) or Manyallaluk (Katherine) you could expect to pay $100 to $200 for a functional didgeridoo which has been painted with ochre paints, and you may even get to meet the maker. On the other hand, from a souvenir shop in Darwin you could pay anything from $200 to $400 or more for something which looks pretty but is really little more than a painted bit of wood.

Dot paintings are also very popular, although they tend to be expensive. As with any art, works by lesser known artists are cheaper than big-name works. A dot painting measuring 1 sq m could be as little as $200, but you can be sure it's no masterpiece. Bargains are hard to find and basically it comes down to whether you think you are getting value for money.

Major Aboriginal Craft Outlets

The following are some Aboriginal owned and operated places where you can buy artefacts and crafts:

Alice Springs
Aboriginal Arts & Culture Centre
(☎ 8952 3408, aborart@ozemail.com.au, 86 Todd St)
Gallery and craft outlet with a good variety of dot paintings and other desert crafts.
Papunya Tula Artists
(☎ 8952 4731, fax 8953 2509, 78 Todd St)
Specialising in western desert dot paintings; high prices but good quality.
DESART
(☎ 8953 4736, fax 8953 4517, 1 Heenan Bldg, Gregory Terrace)
A resource and advocacy organisation representing 22 owner-operated Aboriginal art centres in central Australia.
Warumpi Arts
(☎ 8952 9066, Gregory Terrace)
Wholesale and retail of fine Aboriginal art from Papunya Community.

Darwin
Raintree Aboriginal Fine Arts
(☎ 8941 9933, 20 Knuckey St)
One of the major commercial outlets in Darwin, with medium to high prices but top quality paintings and artefacts.

Kakadu National Park

Injalak Arts & Crafts
(☎ 8979 0190, fax 8979 0119, Oenpelli)
Just over the East Alligator River from Ubirr in Kakadu National Park, Injalak has probably the best selection of Top End arts and crafts anywhere; prices are very reasonable and the staff can pack and ship orders (permits are required to visit, but are easily available on the spot).

Warradjan Aboriginal Cultural Centre
(☎ 8979 0051, Cooinda, Kakadu National Park)
High exposure and consequently high prices, but good fabrics, T-shirts and didgeridoos.

Katherine Region

Manyallaluk Community
(☎ 8975 4727, fax 8975 4724, PMB 134, Katherine)
This small community of Top End Aboriginal people, 100km from Katherine, has a small but impressive array of artefacts including didgeridoos and bark paintings, and some of the best prices you'll come across anywhere.

Uluru-Kata Tjuta National Park

Maruku Arts & Crafts
(☎ 8956 2153, fax 8956 2410, Uluru-Kata Tjuta Cultural Centre)
Good for artefacts, especially scorched wood carvings – craftspeople usually work on the site.

Continued from page 28

White tolerance was still generally low, and punitive raids which saw the deaths of many still occurred – such as at Coniston Station north-west of Alice springs in 1928. On this occasion, however, there was enough public outrage, mostly from the urban centres in the eastern states, to prompt a public inquiry. The police were exonerated in this case and another in Arnhem Land in 1934, but the time had finally come when people could no longer kill Aboriginal people and expect to get away with it.

The process of social change for Aboriginal people was accelerated by WWII. After the war 'assimilation' of Aborigines became the stated aim of the government. To this end, Aboriginal rights were subjugated even further: the government had control over everything, from where Aborigines could live to whom they could marry. Many people were forcibly moved to townships, the idea being that they would adapt to European culture which would in turn aid their economic development. The boys were trained to be stockmen, the women domestic servants, and while many excelled in their field, the policy itself was a dismal failure.

In the 1960s the assimilation policy came under a great deal of scrutiny, and white Australians became increasingly aware of the inequity of the treatment of Aborigines. In 1967 non-Aboriginal Australians voted to give Aboriginal people and Torres Strait Islanders the status of citizens, and gave the national government power to legislate for them in all states. The states had to provide them with the same services as were available to other citizens, and the national government set up the Department of Aboriginal Affairs to identify the special needs of Aboriginal people and legislate for them.

The assimilation policy was finally dumped in 1972, to be replaced by the government's policy of self-determination, which for the first time enabled Aborigines to participate in decision-making processes by granting them rights to their land.

Although the latest developments give rise to cautious optimism, many Aboriginal people still live in appalling conditions, and alcohol and drug abuse remain a widespread problem, particularly among young and middle-aged men. Aboriginal communities have taken up the challenge to eradicate these problems – many communities are now 'dry', and there are a number of rehabilitation programs for alcoholics and other drug users. The problem of petrol sniffing is slowly being addressed. Thanks for much of this work goes to Aboriginal women, many of whom have found themselves on the receiving end of domestic violence.

All in all it's been a tough 200 years for Australia's indigenous people. Their resilience has enabled them to withstand the pressures on their culture, traditions and dignity, and, after so many years of domination, to keep so much of that culture intact.

EDUCATION

Schooling is compulsory in the Territory between the ages of six and 15. There are about 37,000 pupils enrolled in around 170 primary, secondary, area and Aboriginal community schools. In some areas, Aboriginal pupils are taught in both English and their tribal language. The larger towns also have residential colleges for Aboriginal students.

The Northern Territory University in Darwin is the largest provider of tertiary education in the Territory. The University's Institute of Technical & Further Education provides a wide range of trade and technical courses.

ARTS
White Australian Art

In the 1880s a group of young artists developed the first distinctively Australian style of painting. Working from a permanent bush camp near Melbourne they captured the unique qualities of Australian life and light. The work of this group is generally referred to as the Heidelberg School. In Sydney a contemporary movement worked near Sydney Harbour. Both groups were influenced by the French plein-air painters, whose practice of working outdoors to capture the effects of natural light led directly to impressionism. The main artists were Tom Roberts, Arthur Streeton, Frederick McCubbin and Charles Conder.

In the 1940s a new generation of young artists redefined the direction of Australian art, for the first time blending cultural motifs and historical figures into a modern style. Among them are some of Australia's most famous modern artists, including the late Sir Sidney Nolan and Arthur Boyd.

But the formal demands of landscape painting don't often happily meet the challenges of outback landscape, and few painters even attempted to approach the subject matter. Russell Drysdale was one, and more recently painters such as Fred Williams and John Olsen have lent their own unique interpretations to this difficult subject. Sydney artist Brett Whiteley also drew inspiration from Australian landscape and wildlife.

The Museum & Art Gallery of the Northern Territory (see the Darwin chapter) has a good collection of modern painters who have worked in the Northern Territory, although it's not always on display.

Literature
Aboriginal Song & Narrative Aboriginal oral traditions are loosely and misleadingly described as 'myths and legends'. Their single uniting factor is the Dreamtime, when the totemic ancestors formed the landscape, fashioned the laws and created the people who would inherit the land. Translated and printed in English, these renderings of the Dreamtime often lose much of their intended impact. Gone are the sounds of sticks, didgeridoo and the rhythm of the dancers which accompany each poetic line; the words fail to fuse past and present, and the spirits and forces to which the lines refer lose much of their animation.

At the turn of the 19th century, Catherine Langloh Parker was collecting Aboriginal legends and using her outback experience to interpret them sincerely but synthetically. She compiled *Australian Legendary Tales: Folklore of the Noongah-burrahs* (1902).

Professor Ted Strehlow was one of the first methodical translators, and his *Aranda Traditions* (1947) and *Songs of Central Australia* (1971) are important works. Equally important is the combined effort of Catherine and Ronald Berndt. There are 188 songs in the collection *Djanggawul* (1952), 129 sacred and 47 secular songs in the collection *Kunapipi* (1951), and *The Land of the Rainbow Snake* (1979) focuses on children's stories from western Arnhem Land.

More recently, many Dreamtime stories have appeared in translation, illustrated and published by Aboriginal artists. Some representative collections are *Joe Nangan's Dreaming: Aboriginal Legends of the North-West* (Joe Nangan & Hugh Edwards, 1976); *Milbi: Aboriginal Tales from Queensland's Endeavour River* (Tulo Gordon & J B Haviland, 1980); *Visions of Mowanjum: Aboriginal Writings from the Kimberley* (Kormilda Community College, Darwin; 1980); and *Gularabulu* (Paddy Roe & Stephen Muecke, 1983).

Modern Aboriginal Literature Aboriginal writers have fused the English language with aspects of their traditional culture. The result often carefully to exposes the injustices they have been subjected to, especially as urban dwellers. The first Aboriginal writer to be published was David Unaipon (*Native Legends*) in 1929.

Aboriginal literature now includes drama, fiction and poetry. The poet Oodgeroo Noonuccal (Kath Walker), one of the best-known of modern Aboriginal writers, was the first Aboriginal woman to have work published (*We Are Going*, 1964). *Paperbark: A collection of Black Australian writings* (1990) presents a great cross-section of modern Aboriginal writers, including dramatist Jack Davis and novelist Mudrooroo Narogin (Colin Johnson). This book has an excellent bibliography of Aboriginal Australian writing.

There are a number of modern accounts of Aboriginal life in remote parts of Australia. *Raparapa Kularr Martuwarra: Stories from the Fitzroy River Drovers* (1988) is a Magabala Books production. This company, based in Broome, energetically promotes Aboriginal literature, as does IAD Press in Alice Springs.

Autobiography and biography have become an important branch of Aboriginal literature – look for *Moon and Rainbow* (Dick Roughsey, 1971), *My Country of the Pelican Dreaming* (Grant Ngabidj, 1981), *Yami* (Yami Lester, 1993) and *Snake Dreaming* (Roberta Sykes, 1997).

The Aboriginal in White Literature

Aboriginal people have often been used as characters in white outback literature. Usually the treatment was patronising and somewhat short-sighted. There were exceptions, especially in the subject of interracial sexuality between white men and Aboriginal women.

Rosa Praed, in her short piece *My Australian Girlhood* (1902), drew heavily on her outback experience and her affectionate childhood relationship with Aboriginal people. Jeannie Gunn's *Little Black Princess* was published in 1904, but it was *We of the Never Never* (1908) that brought her renown. Her story of the life and trials on Elsey Station includes an unflattering, patronising depiction of the Aboriginal people on and around the station.

Catherine Martin, in 1923, wrote *The Incredible Journey*. It follows the trail of two black women, Iliapo and Polde, in search of a little boy who had been kidnapped by a white man. The book describes in careful detail the harsh desert environment they traverse.

Katharine Susannah Prichard contributed a great deal to outback literature in the 1920s. A journey to Turee Station in the cattle country of the Ashburton and Fortescue rivers, in 1926, inspired her lyric tribute to the Aboriginal, *Coonardoo* (1929), which delved into the then almost taboo love between an Aboriginal woman and a white station boss. Later, Mary Durack's *Keep Him My Country* (1955) explored the theme

of a white station manager's love for an Aboriginal girl, Dalgerie.

Outback Novelists Nevil Shute's *A Town Like Alice* (1950) would have been the first outback-based novel that many people read. Other Shute titles with outback themes were *In the Wet* (1953) and *Beyond the Black Stump* (1956).

Perhaps the best local depicter of the outback was the aforementioned Katharine Susannah Prichard. She produced a string of novels with outback themes into which she wove her political thoughts. *Black Opal* (1921) was the study of the fictional opal mining community of Fallen Star Ridge; *Working Bullocks* (1926) examined the political side of work in the karri forests of Western Australia; and *Moon of Desire* (1941) follows its characters in search of a fabulous pearl from Broome to Singapore. Her controversial trilogy of the Western Australian goldfields was published separately as *The Roaring Nineties* (1946), *Golden Miles* (1948) and *Winged Seeds* (1950).

Xavier Herbert's *Capricornia* (1938) stands as one of the great epics of outback Australia, with its sweeping descriptions of the northern country. His second epic, *Poor Fellow My Country* (1975), is a documentary of the fortunes of a northern station owner. Herbert uses the characters to voice his bitter regret at the failure of reconciliation between the white despoilers of the land and its indigenous people.

One of the great non-fiction pieces is Mary Durack's family chronicle, *Kings in Grass Castles* (1959), which relates the white settlement of the Kimberley ranges. Her sequel was *Sons in the Saddle* (1983).

Australia's Nobel prize winner, Patrick White, used the outback as the backdrop for a number of his monumental works. The most prominent character in *Voss* (1957) is an explorer, perhaps loosely based on Ludwig Leichhardt; *The Tree of Man* (1955) has all the outback happenings of flood, fire and drought; and the journey of *The Aunt's Story* (1948) begins on an Australian sheep station.

Kenneth Cook's nightmarish novel set in outback New South Wales, *Wake in Fright* (1961), has been made into a film.

Contemporary Novelists Miles Franklin was one of Australia's early feminists and made a decision early in her life to become a writer rather than the traditional wife and mother. Her best-known book is *My Brilliant Career*. On her death she endowed an annual award for an Australian novel; today the Miles Franklin Award is the most prestigious in the country.

The works of Patrick White are arguably some of the best to come out of Australia in the second half of the 20th century. He won the Miles Franklin Award twice, for *Voss* (1957) and *The Riders in the Chariot* (1961), and the Nobel Prize for *The Eye of the Storm* (1973).

Thomas Keneally has won two Miles Franklin Awards and one Booker Prize, and is well known for his novels, such as *The Chant of Jimmy Blacksmith* (1972), which deal with the suffering of oppressed peoples, in this case Aboriginal people.

Thea Astley is far from a household name, yet she is one of the finest writers in the country, and three-times winner of the Miles Franklin Award. Her best books include *The Slow Natives* (1965), *The Acolyte* (1972) and *It's Raining in Mango* (1987), the last of which is probably Astley's finest work and expresses her outrage at the treatment of Aboriginal people.

Cinema

The Australian film industry began as early as 1896, a year after the Lumiere brothers opened the world's first cinema in Paris. Maurice Sestier, one of the Lumieres' photographers, came to Australia and made the first films in the streets of Sydney and at Flemington Race Course during the Melbourne Cup.

In the 1930s, film companies like Cinesound made 17 feature films, many based on Australian history or literature. Early Australian actors who became famous both at home and overseas include Errol Flynn and Chips Rafferty (born John Goffage). One successful Chips Rafferty film with an outback theme is *The Overlanders*.

Before the introduction of government subsidies during 1969 and 1970, the Australian film industry found it difficult to compete with US and British interests. But the 1970s saw something of a renaissance of Australian cinema, and films like *Picnic at Hanging Rock* drew acclaim and appealed to large local and international audiences.

The Northern Territory has a landscape that appeals to international and local directors, and several notable films have been filmed there. Nicholas Roeg's *Walkabout* is an outback classic and worth catching. A few film versions of outback novels, such as *We of the Never Never* and *A Town Like Alice*, have a languid appeal, and although they are hardly incisive they're probably worth a look also. Others, such as *Jedda*, a bleak story of Aboriginal life, are quite compelling. Part of Jedda was filmed at Katherine Gorge.

Of course the most famous Territory movie was *Crocodile Dundee*, a phenomenally successful film that did much to boost tourism in the Top End. It concerns the unlikely adventures of Mick 'Crocodile' Dundee, a bush Everyman who visits the big smoke for the first time. The film's success spawned a sequel and a host of look-alike tour guides in the Top End.

Meryl Streep made a good fist of an Australian accent in *Evil Angels*, the infamous story of Lindy Chamberlain who was wrongfully imprisoned for killing her child after it was snatched by a dingo at Uluru.

The great Werner Herzog tried to capture something of the Aboriginal land rights issue in his disjointed but well-meaning *Where the Green Ants Dream* – even though it was filmed near Coober Pedy in South Australia. This bizarre landscape has featured in many Australian movies, including *Ground Zero*, *Mad Max III* and more recently *Priscilla – Queen of the Desert*.

Music

Popular Music Like its movies, Australia's popular music since the 1950s has been a frustrating mix of good, indifferent, lousy and excellent. Little of the popular music created here has had anything noticeably different from that coming from overseas.

However, the success of Aboriginal music, and its merging with rock, is something different and refreshing. The band Yothu Yindi is perhaps the most famous example. Their song about the dishonoured white-man's agreement, *Treaty*, perhaps did more than anything else to popularise Aboriginal land-rights claims. Lead singer, Mandawuy Yunupingu, was named Australian of the Year in 1993.

Other Aboriginal names include Coloured Stone, Kev Carmody, Archie Roach, Scrap Metal, the Sunrise Band, Ruby Hunter, Christine Anu (from the Torres Strait Islands), and the bands that started it all but no longer exist, No Fixed Address and Warumpi Band.

White country music owes much to Irish heritage and American country influences, often with a liberal sprinkling of dry outback humour. Names to watch out for include Slim Dusty, Ted Egan, John Williamson, Chad Morgan, Lee Kernaghan, Neil Murray, Gondwanaland and Smokey Dawson.

The live music circuit of Australia really is something to crow about, although the Territory is definitely a backwater when it comes to touring bands.

Folk Music Australian folk music is derived from a mixture of English, Irish and Scottish roots. Bush bands, playing fast-paced and high-spirited folk music for dancing, can be anything from performers trotting out standards such as *Click Go The Shears* to serious musicians who happen to like a rollicking time.

Fiddles, banjos and tin whistles feature prominently, plus there's the indigenous 'lagerphone', a percussion instrument made from a great many beer-bottle caps nailed to a stick, which is then shaken or banged on the ground. If you have a chance to go to a bush dance or folk festival, don't pass it up.

Architecture

Australia's first white settlers arrived in the country with memories of Georgian grandeur, but the lack of materials and tools meant that most of the early houses were almost caricatures of the real thing. One of the first concessions to the climate, and one which was to become a feature of Australian houses, was the addition of a wide verandah which kept the inner rooms of the house dark and cool.

By the turn of the century, at a time when the separate colonies were combining to form a new nation, a simpler, more 'Australian' architectural style had evolved, and this came to be known as Federation style. Built between about 1890 and 1920, Federation houses typically feature red-brick walls, and an orange-tiled roof decorated with terracotta ridging and chimney pots. Also a feature was the rising sun motif on the gable ends, symbolic of the dawn of a new age for Australia.

The variety of climates led to some interesting regional variations. In the 1930s houses were designed specifically for the tropical climate by the Northern Territory Principal Architect, Beni Carr Glynn Burnett. The elevated buildings featured louvres and casement windows, so the ventilation could be adjusted according to the weather conditions at the time. Internal walls were only three quarter height and also featured lower louvres to allow for cross-ventilation. The eaves were also left open to aid ventilation. This style has developed into the modern 'troppo' (tropical) style of architecture, which is not only practical, but also takes into account that cyclones are a major feature of the climate.

The immigration boom that followed WWII led to today's urban sprawl – cities and towns expanded rapidly, and the 'brick veneer' became the dominant housing medium, and remains so today. On the fringe of any Australian city you'll find acres of new, low cost, brick-veneer suburbs – as far as the eye can see it's a bleak expanse of terracotta roofs and bricks in various shades. Alice Springs has some fine examples of this urban blight.

Modern Australian architecture struggles to maintain a distinctive style, with overseas trends dominating large projects. There are some notable exceptions, of course, and in the Territory these are found in Kakadu and Uluru-Kata Tjuta national parks where the Federal government has spent large amounts on excellent visitor/cultural centres. Also of interest is the Strehlow Research Centre in Alice Springs, which features a huge rammed-earth wall.

SOCIETY & CONDUCT
Aboriginal Society

Australia's Aboriginal people were tribal, living in extended family groups or clans, with clan members descended from a common ancestral being. Tradition, rituals and laws linked the people of each clan to the land they occupied and each clan had various sites of spiritual significance, places to which their spirits would return when they died. Clan members came together to perform rituals to honour their ancestral spirits and the creators of the Dreaming.

It was the responsibility of the clan, or particular members of it, to correctly maintain and protect the sites so that the ancestral beings were not offended and continued to protect the clan. Traditional punishments for those who neglected these responsibilities were severe, as their actions could easily affect the well-being of the whole clan – food and water shortages, natural disasters or mysterious illnesses could all be attributed to disgruntled or offended ancestral beings.

Many Aboriginal communities were semi-nomadic, others sedentary, one of the deciding factors being the availability of food. Where food and water were readily available, the people tended to remain in a limited area. When they did wander, however, it was to visit sacred places to carry out rituals, or to take advantage of seasonal foods available elsewhere. They did not, as is still often believed, roam aimlessly and desperately in the search for food and water.

The traditional role of the men was that of hunter, tool-maker and custodian of male law; the women reared the children, and gathered and prepared food. There was also female law and ritual for which the women would be responsible. Ultimately, the shared effort of men and women ensured the continuation of their social system.

Wisdom and skills obtained over millennia enabled Aboriginal people to use their environment to the maximum. An intimate knowledge of the behaviour of animals and the correct time to harvest the many plants they utilised ensured that food shortages were rare. Like other hunter-gatherer peoples of the world, Aboriginal people were true ecologists.

Although Aborigines in northern Australia had been in regular contact with the fishing and farming peoples of Indonesia for at least 1000 years, the cultivation of crops and the domestication of livestock held no appeal. The only major modification of the landscape practised by Aboriginal people was the selective burning of undergrowth in forests and dead grass on the plains. This encouraged new growth, which in turn attracted game animals to the area. It also prevented the build-up of combustible material in the forests, making hunting easier and reducing the possibility of major bush fires. Dingoes were domesticated to assist in the hunt and to guard the camp from intruders.

Similar technology – for example the boomerang and spear – was used throughout the continent, but techniques were adapted to the environment and the species being hunted. In the wetlands of northern Australia, fish traps hundreds of metres long made of bamboo and cord were built to catch fish at the end of the wet season.

Contrary to the common image, some tribes did build permanent dwellings, varying widely depending on climate, the materials available and likely length of use; in the deserts semicircular shelters were made with arched branches covered with native grasses or leaves. Such dwellings were used mainly for sleeping. At Keep River National Park (see the Katherine & Victoria River District chapter) there's an example of a stone shelter used to trap birds.

The early Australian Aboriginal people were also traders. Trade routes crisscrossed the country, dispersing goods and a variety of produced items along their way. Many of the items traded, such as certain types of stone or shell, were rare and had great ritual significance. Boomerangs and ochre were other important trade items. Along the trading networks which developed, large numbers of people would often meet for 'exchange ceremonies', where not only goods but also songs and dances were passed on.

Aboriginal Beliefs & Ceremonies

Early European settlers and explorers usually dismissed the entire Aboriginal population as 'savages' and 'barbarians', and it was some time before the Aboriginal peoples' deep, spiritual bond with the land, and their relationship to it, was understood by white Australians.

The perceived simplicity of the Aboriginal peoples' technology contrasts with the sophistication of their cultural life. Religion, history, law and art are integrated in complex ceremonies which depict the activities of their ancestral beings, and prescribe codes of behaviour and responsibilities for looking after the land and all living things. The link between the Aboriginal people and the ancestral beings are totems, each person having their own totem, or Dreaming. These totems take many forms, such as caterpillars, snakes, fish and magpies. Songs explain how the landscape contains these powerful creator ancestors who can exert either a benign or a malevolent influence. They tell of the best places and times to hunt, and where to find water in drought years. They can also specify kinship relations and correct marriage partners.

Ceremonies are still performed in many parts of Australia; many of the sacred sites are believed to be dangerous and entry is prohibited under traditional Aboriginal law. These restrictions may seem merely the result of superstition, but in many cases they have a pragmatic origin. For instance, fishing from a certain reef was traditionally prohibited. This restriction was scoffed at by local whites until it was discovered that fish from this area had a high incidence of ciguatera which renders fish poisonous if eaten by humans.

Many Aborigines living an urban life also maintain their Aboriginality – some still speak their indigenous language (or a mix) every day, and they mix largely with other Aboriginal people. Much of their knowledge of the environment, bush medicine and food ('bush tucker') has been retained, and many traditional rites and ceremonies are being revived.

See the later Religion section for more on Aboriginal beliefs, ceremonies and sacred sites.

Outback Life

Life on remote station properties has been much improved by modern developments such as the Royal Flying Doctor Service, the School of the Air and the expanding national telephone network, but many outback communities are still affected by the tyranny of distance. Not many city people can imagine living perhaps 500km from the nearest doctor and supermarket, or having their children sitting down in front of a high-frequency (HF) radio transceiver to go to school.

School of the Air Until recent times, outback children living away from towns either attended boarding school or obtained their education through written correspondence lessons. In 1944, Adelaide Meithke recognised that HF radio transceivers could be used to improve the children's education as well as their social life by giving them direct contact both with trained teachers and their fellow students. Her idea for a classroom of the airwaves, using the RFDS radio facilities, became a reality when Australia's first School of the Air opened in Alice Springs in 1951.

Today there are 14 Schools of the Air (three in the Territory) and most use the RFDS network as their classroom. The major

Royal Flying Doctor Service

Established by the Reverend John Flynn with a single aircraft in 1928, the original Flying Doctor has grown into a national organisation, the Royal Flying Doctor Service (RFDS), which provides a comprehensive medical service to outback residents. Sick and injured people in even the most isolated communities are now assured of receiving expert medical assistance within hours instead of weeks.

Almost as important is the social function of the RFDS's HF radio network, which allows anyone without a telephone to send and receive telegrams and to take part in special broadcasts known as galah sessions. Like party lines, these open periods of radio time allow distant neighbours to keep in touch with each other and with events around them in a way the telephone can never rival.

education method is still correspondence lessons – materials and equipment are sent to students, who return set written and audio work by mail – which are supplemented by radio classes lasting 20 to 30 minutes. Students speak to their teachers daily and each has a 10-minute personal session with their teacher once a week. Although face-to-face contact is limited, students and teachers do meet at least once a year on special get-togethers, and teachers visit each of their students on patrols by 4WD vehicle and light aircraft.

With 14 teachers and eight support staff, the Alice Springs School of the Air teaches about 140 children in nine grades, from pre-school to year seven, over a broadcast area of 1.3 million sq km, the furthest student living 1000km away. In 1992 the school broke new ground once again when it beamed 'live' lessons by satellite to its students.

Shopping Most stations are far from even the most basic facilities such as post offices, libraries and shops, and often neighbours can be 50km or more apart. Most isolated communities receive mail and newspapers either weekly or fortnightly when the mail plane or mail truck does its rounds. Perishable groceries and minor freight can be sent out with the mail, but a major shopping expedition can mean a round trip of 1000km or more to the nearest decent shops.

It's not all Bad The outback presents its share of difficulties. Most of these can be attributed to isolation, but as the famous Australian poet AB (Banjo) Paterson wrote in *Clancy of the Overflow*, bush people do 'have pleasures that the townsfolk never know'. One of these is the ready accessibility of wide-open spaces untainted by air pollution, traffic noise and crowds. Another is the sense of self-reliance and independence that's still strong in the outback.

Being forced to make their own entertainment encourages people living hundreds of kilometres apart to get together (usually on the RFDS radio network, although increasingly by telephone) to organise social functions such as horse-race meetings, campdrafts (rodeos) and gymkhanas. This strong sense of community spirit, even when the 'community' may be spread over a vast area, means that even neighbours who don't get on will more than likely assist each other in a crisis. It's these aspects of outback life that help to make the hardships worthwhile.

Dos & Don'ts

Water Most pastoralists are happy for travellers to make use of their water supplies, but they do ask that they be treated with respect. This means washing clothes, dishes and sweaty bodies in a bucket or basin, not in the water supply itself. Always remember that animals and people may have to drink it when you've finished.

Camping right beside watering points is also to be avoided. In the outback the stock is often half wild and will hang back if you're parked or have your tent pitched right where they normally drink. They'll eventually overcome their fear through necessity, which means you'll be covered in dust and develop grey hair as the thirst-crazed mob mills around your camp at midnight. If you must camp in the vicinity, keep at least 200m away and stay well off the paths that animals have worn as they come in to drink.

Much the same applies if you drive up to a bore or dam and find the stock having a drink. Stay well back until they've finished, then you can move in for your share. The thing to remember at all times is that this isolated pool or trough might be the only water in a radius of 30km or more.

Gates The golden rule with any gate is to *leave it as you find it*. You must do this even if a sign by an open gate says to keep it closed – it may have been left open for any number of reasons, such as to let stock through to water. It's fairly common for animals to perish because tourists have closed gates that a pastoralist left open.

Floods Sometimes the outback receives a large part of its annual rainfall in a matter of days. When this happens, unsealed roads and tracks become extremely slippery and boggy. The correct thing to do in this event is either to get out before the rain soaks in or to stay put on high ground until the surface dries out. Otherwise your vehicle may gouge great ruts in the road surface, which of course won't endear you to the locals who must live with the mess you've made. Quite apart from that, you'll probably get well and truly stuck in some dreadful place far from anywhere. This is one of the reasons to carry plenty of extra stores on an outback trip. If a road is officially closed because of heavy rain, you can be fined for travelling on it – the norm is $1000 per wheel!

Bushfires There are bushfires every year in Australia. Don't be the mug who starts one. In hot, dry, windy weather, be extremely careful with any naked flame – no cigarette butts out of car windows, please. On a total fire ban day (listen to the radio or watch the billboards on country roads), it is forbidden

even to use a camping stove in the open. The locals will not be amused if they catch you breaking this particular law; they'll happily dob you in, and the penalties are severe.

If you're unfortunate enough to find yourself driving through a bushfire, stay inside your car and try to park it off the road in an open space, away from trees, until the danger's past. Lie on the floor under the dashboard, covering yourself with a wool blanket if possible. The front of the fire should pass quickly, and you will be much safer than if you were out in the open. It is very important to cover up with a wool blanket or wear protective clothing, as it has been proved that heat radiation is the big killer in bushfire situations.

Bushwalkers should take local advice before setting out. On a day of total fire ban, don't go – delay your trip until the weather has changed. Chances are that it will be so unpleasantly hot and windy, you'll be better off anyway in an air-conditioned pub sipping a cool beer.

If you're out in the bush and you see smoke, even at a great distance, take it seriously. Go to the nearest open space, downhill if possible. A forested ridge is the most dangerous place to be. Bushfires move very quickly and change direction with the wind.

Dogs The tourist's best friend is a contentious issue in the outback at the best of times. There's no doubt that the best way to avoid dog-related hassles is not to bring the hound in the first place. If you do have to bring it you will find that many of the best spots in the Territory – such as the national parks – will be closed to you.

Courtesy These days most outback pastoralists are on the telephone and it's a common courtesy to contact them before you invade their property. Straight-through travel on established roads is not a problem, but if you're thinking of going camping or fishing in some remote spot, the landholder will expect you to ask permission. You'll usually rise in the estimation of the more isolated people if you drop off some very recent newspapers or ask if there's anything they'd like brought out from town. Always remember to take-your-own-everything, as station folk seldom organise their shopping around the needs of ill-prepared visitors.

Cross-Cultural Etiquette Many of the outback's original inhabitants lead lives that are powerfully influenced by ancient traditions, and the average tourist is almost entirely ignorant of Aboriginal social customs. You won't go far wrong if you treat outback Aboriginal people as potential friends. Also, remember that Aboriginal people generally have great senses of humour and love a good laugh.

Most larger communities have a store staffed by white people, and this is the place to go first for information. The store is usually easy to find. If you're not sure, ask someone rather than head off on an unauthorised sightseeing tour that raises dust and could make you unpopular. One sure way to wear out a welcome is to drive around taking photographs without permission.

When speaking with outback Aboriginal people, it's important to remember that English is very much the second language on most remote communities and may not be spoken at all well. Speak distinctly and reasonably slowly, using straightforward English and a normal tone of voice.

Alcohol Unfortunately many non-Aboriginal Australians have the idea that Aboriginal people in general drink to excess. This assertion is hypocritical and inaccurate. In actual fact, a smaller percentage of Aboriginal people drink than do non-Aboriginals.

However, Aboriginal people who consume alcohol are more likely than their non-Aboriginal counterparts to drink in public. One reason for this is the fact that Aboriginal councils have banned the possession and consumption of alcohol in many of their communities. In addition, the Liquor Act prohibits the possession, consumption and bringing of alcohol into restricted areas on Aboriginal lands. As a result, many outback Aboriginal people have irregular access to alcohol, and only drink when they go to town. Unfortunately, this is the only time many non-Aboriginal people (and tourists) see them.

Throughout the Territory (and Australia), Aborigines are actively involved in the fight against alcoholism. With the assistance of lawyers, they have persuaded some outback hotels and takeaway outlets not to sell alcohol to local Aboriginal people, and signs at such outlets explain that Aboriginal elders ask tourists not to buy alcohol for Aboriginal people. Also, some outlets may refuse to sell you alcohol if you're heading towards an Aboriginal community. Please respect such efforts to combat alcoholism.

RELIGION

A shrinking majority of people in Australia (around 70%) are at least nominally Christian. Three Protestant churches have merged to become the Uniting Church; others still operating independently include Lutherans (there are a number of Lutheran missions in the Territory) and Reformed. The Anglican Church of Australia (formerly called Church of England) has remained separate. The Catholic Church is popular (about a third of Christians are Catholics), with the original Irish adherents now joined by the large numbers of Mediterranean immigrants.

Non-Christian minorities abound, the main ones being Buddhist, Jewish and Muslim.

Aboriginal Religion

Traditional Aboriginal cultures either have very little religious component or are nothing but religion, depending on how you look at it. Is a belief system which views every event, no matter how trifling, in a non-material context a religion? The early Christian missionaries certainly didn't think so. For them a belief in a deity was an essential part of a religion, and anything else was mere superstition.

Sacred Sites Aboriginal sacred sites are a perennial topic of discussion. Their presence can lead to headline-grabbing controversy when they stand in the way of developments such as roads, mines and dams. This is because most other Australians still have great difficulty understanding the Aboriginal peoples' deep spiritual bond with the land.

Aboriginal religious beliefs centre on the continuing existence of spirit beings that lived on Earth during the Dreamtime, which occurred before the arrival of humans. These beings created all the features of the natural world and were the ancestors of all living things. They took different forms but behaved as people do, and as they travelled about they left signs to show where they passed.

Despite being supernatural, the ancestors were subject to ageing and eventually they returned to the sleep from which they'd awoken at the dawn of time. Here their spirits remain as eternal forces that breathe life into the newborn and influence natural events. Each ancestor's spiritual energy flows along the path it travelled during the Dreamtime and is strongest at the points where it left physical evidence of its activities, such as a tree, riverbed, hill or claypan. These features are sacred sites.

Every person, animal and plant is believed to have two souls – one mortal and one immortal. The latter is part of a particular ancestral spirit and returns to the sacred sites of that ancestor after death, while the mortal soul simply fades into oblivion. Each person is spiritually bound to the sacred sites that mark the land associated with his or her ancestor. It is the individual's obligation to help care for these sites by performing the necessary rituals and singing the songs that tell of the ancestor's deeds. By doing this, the order created by that ancestor is maintained.

Some of the sacred sites are believed to be dangerous and entry is prohibited under traditional Aboriginal law. These restrictions often have a pragmatic origin. One site in northern Australia was believed to cause sores to break out all over the body of anyone visiting the area. Subsequently, the area was found to have a dangerously high level of radiation from naturally occurring radon gas.

Aboriginal sacred sites are not like Christian churches, which can be deconsecrated before the bulldozers move in. Neither can they be bought, sold or transferred. Other Australians find this difficult to accept because they regard land as belonging to the individual, whereas in Aboriginal society the reverse applies. Aboriginal people believe that to destroy or damage a sacred site threatens not only the living but also the spirit inhabitants of the land. It is a distressing and dangerous act, and one that no responsible person would condone.

Throughout much of Australia, when pastoralists were breaking the Aboriginal peoples' link to the land many Aboriginal people sought refuge on missions and became Christians. However, becoming Christians has not, for most Aboriginal people, meant renouncing their traditional religion. Many senior Aboriginal law men are also devout Christians.

LANGUAGE

Any visitor from abroad who thinks English is all they'll hear when they arrive is wrong. For many Northern Territorians Italian, Greek, or Vietnamese is their first language. And you will hear more Aboriginal languages here than anywhere else in Australia.

Australian English

Australian English is remarkable perhaps for two reasons: firstly because the vocabulary and accent hardly change from one end of the continent to the other, and secondly because similar slang is used – frequently and volubly – from the lowliest road worker to the most deluded politician.

Australian is simply a variant of English/American, owing much of its old slang to British and Irish roots. Like all other versions of English, it also includes the worst of newspeak from American TV. However, there are a few surprises, including the incorporation of some Aboriginal terms, which do set Australian English apart.

The accent, despite its distinctiveness, is difficult to master. Rest assured, however, that no matter how much you distort your vowels you will probably be understood. Affecting the Aussie 'twang' takes much practice, but you can achieve an approximation by pinching your nose as you speak. There is a slight regional variation in the Australian accent, while the difference between city and country speech is mainly a matter of speed. Some of the most famed Aussie words are hardly heard at all – 'mates' are more common than 'cobbers'.

Lonely Planet publishes the *Australian* phrasebook – an introduction to both Australian English and Aboriginal languages. The Glossary at the end of this book may also help.

Aboriginal Languages

At the time of European contact there were around 250 separate Australian languages, comprising about 700 dialects. Often three or four adjacent tribes would speak what amounted to dialects of the same language, but another adjacent tribe might speak a completely different language.

It is believed that all the languages evolved from a single language family as the Aboriginal people gradually moved out over the entire continent and split into new groups. There are a number of words that occur right across the continent, such as *jina* (foot) and *mala* (hand), and similarities also exist in the often complex grammatical structures.

Following European contact the number of Aboriginal languages was drastically reduced. At least eight separate languages were spoken in Tasmania alone, but none of these were recorded before the native speakers either died or were killed. Of the original 250 or so languages, only around 30 are today spoken on a regular basis and are taught to children.

Aboriginal Kriol is a new language which has developed since European arrival in Australia. It is spoken across northern Australia and has become the 'native' language of many young Aboriginal people. Although many words are English they often have different meanings and the spelling is phonetic. Pronunciation and grammatical construction are along Aboriginal lines. For example, the English sentence 'He was amazed' becomes 'I bin luk kwesjinmak' in Kriol.

There are a number of generic terms which Aboriginal people use to describe themselves, and these vary according to the region. The most common of these is Koori, used for the people of south-east Australia. Nunga is used to refer to the people of coastal South Australia, Murri for those from the north-east, and Nyoongah is used in the country's south-west.

Lonely Planet's *Australian* phrasebook gives detailed information about Aboriginal languages.

FAUNA & FLORA

Wildlife is abundant in the Territory, especially in national parks and other reserves, and is definitely one of the highlights of a visit (see the various chapters for information on national parks). Plants and animals vary according to habitat, and influence each other in a complex balance of predator and prey. Broadly speaking, there are two distinct habitat zones in the Territory shaped by climate – the arid zone, and the wet-dry tropics to the north, which include the entire Top End.

The arid zone is characterised by low rainfall and hardy, stunted vegetation. When rain falls in this country, life moves into top gear: flowers and woody plants burst into bloom; the sandhills, plains and rocky ridges come alive with nectar-eating birds and insects; and predators enjoy the bumper harvest. For nature lovers this is the best time to visit the inland.

Title page: Big, bouncy boxing kangaroos (photo by Richard I'Anson).

Sulphur-crested cockatoo eating pandanas fruit

Wildlife is also attuned to the dramatic annual cycle of wet and dry seasons in the Top End. The warm, clear days of the Dry cause waterholes to shrink and large concentrations of wildlife gather near billabongs. The late Dry is an excellent time to see wildlife in northern Australia. By the early Wet most animals are gearing up to breed, migratory birds arrive from South-East Asia and many different species of insects hatch out. With the wet season rains breeding is in full swing, drawing to a close as the rains peter out and the cycle begins again.

FAUNA

Many Australian animals need no introduction and some, such as the kangaroo, are world famous. The Territory is a great place to see many native mammals, a host of birds and some impressive reptiles.

Mammals

The major group of Australian mammals, and the one which contains the most famous examples, is the marsupials. These mammals raise their tiny young inside a pouch, or marsupium, and show numerous other adaptations to the unique Australian environment.

Kangaroos are probably the most instantly recognisable Australian mammal and hardly need a description. The name really applies to only a few large species; there are dozens of smaller, similar animals called wallabies. All kangaroos and wallabies feed on plants and raise a single young.

The distinctive **red kangaroo** is the largest of the group – a fully grown male can stand 2m high. Only males usually have the attractive reddish coat; females are often a blue-grey colour. Red kangaroos range over most of inland Australia.

The Top End's most common representative is the **agile wallaby**, which is about 1.7m long when fully grown. It has become quite used to people in national parks such as Nitmiluk and Kakadu.

The various rock wallabies are generally small (around 1m long) and are superbly adapted to foraging on cliffs and rock slopes. The **black footed rock wallaby** is an attractively marked species which can usually be seen at Heavitree Gap (Alice Springs), Ormiston Gorge and Standley Chasm. The **short**

Rock wallaby

Wildlife Top 10

The Territory boasts some impressive wildlife, including the world's largest crocodiles, huge numbers of birds and some very annoying insects. The following list (in no particular order) will give you a taste of some of the memorable creatures and plants you might encounter.

Crocodiles No-compromise killing machines that command a grim fascination – if not outright terror. Watch out for them just about anywhere near water in the Top End, and be prepared for a photo opportunity at Yellow Water (Kakadu) or Adelaide River crossing.

Roos & Wallabies These famous and abundant marsupials come in many shapes and sizes, from the great red kangaroos of the inland plains to dainty rock wallabies leaping up precipices at Standley Chasm and tame agile wallabies in the camp ground at Nitmiluk.

A Pigeon for Every Occasion There seems to be a different type of pigeon wherever you go, and the Territory has no less than 15 species. There are fat little spinifex pigeons at Ormiston Gorge, dazzling white imperial pigeons in the Wet and rock pigeons at Nourlangie Rock (Kakadu).

Wildflowers The desert comes alive after rains: dunes are carpeted in showy flowers, such as desert peas and poached egg daisies, and the usually featureless scrub is suddenly adorned with desert roses, grevilleas and wattle.

Sturt's desert rose – floral emblem of the Northern Territory

eared rock wallaby is a smaller, rather plain species which can sometimes be seen at Ubirr in Kakadu. Rock wallabies are prodigious jumpers and can scale seemingly pathless cliffs. The **euro**, a species of wallaroo, can also be seen on rocky outcrops in the foothills of the MacDonnell Ranges.

Apart from the dingo, there are no large flesh-eating mammals on the Australian mainland. Rather,

Wildlife Top 10

Frilled Lizards Everybody's favourite lizard, commonly seen in the early Wet pretending to be a tree stump by the road or trundling through the bush on its hind legs. The frill only opens when it's in a bad mood – but it's almost worth provoking one.

Cockatoos Colourful, common and eccentric. The choices include foolish galahs in tasteful pink and grey, swirling flocks of little corellas and huge red-tailed black cockatoos calling like a rusty gate.

Wild Horses Domestic stock gone wild – known as 'brumbies' – once attained pest proportions. Numbers have declined to the point where the sight of one now has some appeal in a countryside usually devoid of large animals.

Waterbirds Top End waterholes in the Dry are full of great flocks of waterfowl – honking magpie geese and whistling ducks – plus armies of stately herons, egrets and storks. Overhead look for marauding kites and fish-catching sea eagles.

Termites These tiny, blind insects would probably go unnoticed but for their magnificent feats of engineering – the solid mounds of earth that stretch to the horizons all over the tropics. Ideal subjects for wildlife photos because they don't move.

Banteng A Territory anomaly – Indonesia's wild ox was introduced during settlement at Gurig, and the descendants are now the only wild herd left in the world.

the predatory marsupials are a mixed bag of small but voracious animals which prey on insects, reptiles and birds. The **northern quoll** is the largest hunting marsupial in the Territory, although it is only as big as a domestic cat. Its ginger fur is attractively marked with white spots, but being nocturnal it is not often seen by visitors. Smaller predators include a number of mouse-like marsupials called **antechinus** and **dunnarts**.

Bandicoots are rather plain, inoffensive mammals that eat mainly insects but also some plant material. They are largely nocturnal, but can occasionally be seen scampering around camp grounds.

The rare **bilby** is an attractive little animal found in remote deserts, such as the Tanami, but has been all but wiped out by competition from rabbits. It is subtly marked in greys and white, with rabbit-like ears. Major efforts have been made to ensure its survival, but your only real chance of seeing one is at the Alice Springs Desert Park.

Bilby or rabbit-bandicoot

Possums and gliders are a wide-ranging group that generally live in forests and woodlands, although the **northern brushtail** has become habituated to life in the city and may be seen scrounging around garbage bins in parts of Darwin. The **rock possum** is a smaller species which lives on sandstone escarpments in the Top End. Gliders live almost exclusively in trees and with a fold of loose skin between front and rear legs, can glide up to 100m from the top of one tree to the trunk of another. The **sugar glider**, found in tropical woodland, generally feeds on nectar from flowering trees and shrubs.

An even more unusual group of mammals found in Australia, the monotremes, lays eggs. The **echidna**, or spiny anteater, is the only example found in the Northern Territory. It is a football-sized, slow moving animal covered in stout spines with a tube-like snout through which it gathers ants and termites, its sole prey.

The **dingo** is Australia's native dog, although it was brought into the country from South-East Asia some 6000 years ago and domesticated by Aboriginal people. It is now widespread and common in many parts of the outback, where its howls may be heard at night. Dingoes can successfully interbreed with domestic dogs and pure strains are becoming rare in some areas. Dingoes prey mainly on rabbits, rats and mice, although when other food is scarce they sometimes attack livestock and are therefore considered vermin by many station owners.

Birds

The Territory's birdlife is as beautiful as it is varied, and several species are unique to the Top End.

The largest is the primitive **emu**, a flightless bird that lives on inland plains and is related to the ostrich of Africa. After the female lays her six to 12 large, dark green eggs the male hatches them and raises the young.

The **bustard** is also a large bird of the plains, sometimes mistaken for the emu, although it is much smaller and can fly well. Bustards are sometimes seen feeding next to highways in the early morning.

It would be virtually impossible to travel in the Territory without seeing at least one member of the cockatoo family. The pink and grey **galah** is probably the most common, and often scratches for seeds on roadsides. The pure white **sulphur-crested cockatoo** is a

Magpie geese

noisy bird that often ends up as a caged pet. Another white cockatoo is the **little corella**, whose feathers are sometimes stained with earth where it has been rooting for bulbs. The most striking of the cockatoos is the large **red-tailed black cockatoo**; it is usually heard before it's seen – listen for its 'creaking gate' call.

Also conspicuous all over the Territory are the many species of parrots. Perhaps the most famous is the **budgerigar**, a small bright green bird of arid regions that is the wild ancestor of the world's most popular cage bird. Wild budgies often fly in flocks of thousands. The aptly-named **rainbow lorikeet** is extravagantly colourful, with a blue head, orange breast and green body. It is common in noisy, fast flying flocks across the Top End. Another common parrot is the **red-winged parrot**, in electric green and scarlet. The **hooded parrot** is unique to the Top End, where it nests in the large termite mounds of the tropical woodlands.

Several species of birds of prey are conspicuous in open country. The **wedge-tailed eagle** is the largest, with a wingspan of up to 2m, and is easily identified in flight by its wedge-shaped tail. 'Wedgies' are often seen in outback Australia, either soaring to great heights or feeding on road-kills. The **black kite** can be seen virtually anywhere and also scavenges road kills; it is an untidy-looking bird with a distinctive forked tail. The **white-bellied sea eagle** is almost as big as a wedgie and handsomely marked in grey and white. It is common around large waterways, where it feeds by swooping to pluck fish from just below the surface.

The Top End's many wetlands are host to a great variety of birdlife and this habitat is a great place to get acquainted with several species in a short space of time. The many different types employ different feeding strategies, from ducks puddling about on the surface, to cormorants diving beneath and herons standing motionless in the shallows waiting to spear a frog or fish.

One of the most distinctive is the **jabiru**, a handsome black and white stork standing more than 1m tall. Its plumage is iridescent and shines green or blue, depending on the light. It is popularly thought that 'jabiru' is its Aboriginal name, but the name in fact comes from a South American stork.

The **magpie goose** is a large, black and white goose commonly seen in tropical wetlands. Flocks

Jabiru

numbering thousands congregate towards the end of the Dry, when their honking is a familiar sound. A variety of ducks often feed with magpie geese, including two species of **whistling ducks**, which call with a soft whistling; the diminutive, bottle-green **pygmy goose**; and the striking **Radjah shelduck**, also known as the Burdekin duck. The graceful **black swan** is the world's only all-black swan.

The **brolga** is a member of the crane family which inhabits wetlands as well as drier habitats. Standing more than 1m high, the brolga is grey in colour with a distinctive red head. Its courtship displays are loud and spectacular, and have been incorporated into Aboriginal lore and dances.

Parks and gardens in the Top End provide well-watered oases for birds in the Dry. The **great bowerbird** is a crow-sized bird common around gardens and roadhouses in the tropics. It is rather drably coloured, but has an extraordinary courtship behaviour: the male builds a bower which he decorates with various coloured objects to attract females. A female inspects the bowers and, when she like the look of one, mates with its owner. The male then leaves the nesting up to her and pursues other females.

The black and white **magpie** is found virtually throughout the country. Its melodious carolling is one of the most distinctive sounds of the Australian bush; the closely related **pied butcherbird** is also common in the Territory and it, too, has a beautiful song.

The little **willy wagtail** is a small black and white bird that gets quite cheeky when used to people, and will fearlessly harass large eagles and other predators. The willy wagtail appears as a sign of bad luck in Aboriginal stories.

Reptiles

Crocodiles

There are two types of crocodile in Australia: the inoffensive **freshwater crocodile**, or 'freshie' as it's known, and the extremely dangerous **saltwater crocodile** or 'saltie' (see the boxed text in the Kakadu & Arnhem Land chapter for more on salties).

Freshies are smaller than salties – anything over 4m should be regarded as a saltie. Freshies tend to be shy, and can be recognised by their finer build and much narrower snout. Freshies feed almost exclu-

Freshwater crocodile

Saltwater or estuarine crocodile

sively on fish, and can sometimes be seen in quiet reaches of the Roper River and in Kakadu.

Turtles & Tortoises

In Australia, 'turtle' is the name generally given to the large marine reptiles that come ashore only to lay their eggs; several species nest on remote beaches in the Top End. Australian 'tortoises' all inhabit fresh water and cross dry land only to look for breeding sites or a new feeding ground. Freshwater tortoises are commonly seen sunning themselves on logs or mud banks near billabongs.

Snakes

The Territory's snakes are generally shy and come in contact with humans only by chance. There are various species of **python**, some of which are beautifully marked, which kill their prey by constriction ie squeezing them to death. Olive and water pythons hunt at night for rats and can grow quite large.

Most other snake species are poisonous, although only a few are dangerous. **Whip snakes** are slender, fast moving species common in the Top End. **Blind snakes** are tiny, inoffensive snakes like large earthworms that live underground and feed on termites. Several large, venomous species should be avoided at all times; arguably the most dangerous is the **death adder**, which lies hidden in the undergrowth and will bite if stepped on.

Whip snake

Lizards

The **frilled lizard** is Australia's most famous lizard and is commonly seen in the Top End during the Wet. It gets its name from a loose flap of skin which normally hangs flat around the neck – when alarmed or threatened, the frill is raised and the mouth opened to give a more ferocious appearance. The frilled lizard is quite large – up to 1m long – and runs on its hind legs when threatened.

The richest communities of lizards are found in the sandy deserts, where up to 50 species shelter among spinifex or burrow into the sand. Lizards have very low moisture requirements and thus proliferate in this arid environment. Many are small but some, particularly the various species of **geckos**, are beautifully patterned.

The dozen or so species of **goannas** (the name is a corruption of 'iguana') range in size from the

Frilled lizard

pygmy monitors of the tropics, which reach only 30cm in length, to the large **perentie** of the sandy deserts, which can grow to more than 2m long. Goannas are most common in the Top End and often scrounge for scraps around picnic areas. With their forked tongue and loud hiss they appear quite formidable but they're harmless unless provoked.

FLORA

Australia's vegetation is as unique and distinct as its animal life, and adapted to cycles of drought, flood and fire. The most famous – and largest – plants are the eucalypts, or gum trees, which grow in nearly every habitat. Gum trees vary greatly in form and height, from tall, straicght hardwoods to stunted, twisted, shrub-like 'mallees'.

Acacias are probably best known as the woody trees that dot the plains of Africa, but more than 600 species grow naturally in Australia, about 100 of which are found in the Territory. Many are commonly known as wattle; they tend to be fast growing and short lived, and grow in many forms, from tall, weeping trees to prickly shrubs. Despite their many differences, all wattles have furry yellow flowers shaped either like a spike or a ball.

Also known as she-oaks, casuarinas are hardy trees that are almost as much a part of the Australian landscape as eucalypts. They are characterised by feather like 'leaves', which are actually branchlets, the true leaves are small scales at the joints of the branchlets.

Many varieties of acacias, or wattles, are found in the Northern Territory.

Arid Zone

Much of the Territory is arid land where all life forms must be adapted to low rainfall. In the great deserts of the southern region, such as the Tanami and Simpson, endless fields of rolling red sand dunes support little but spinifex, a hardy grass that grows in dense, dome-shaped clumps. In dry times its long, needle-like leaves roll into tight cylinders to reduce the number of pores exposed to the sun and wind. This keeps water loss through evaporation to a minimum. Spinifex stands are very difficult to walk through – the explorer Ernest Giles called spinifex 'that abominable vegetable production'. Spinifex leaves have a high resin content, and this resin was used by Aboriginal people to fasten heads to spears and as a general adhesive.

In sheltered pockets between high dunes or rocky ridges stands of **desert oak** may grow. These magnificent trees are a type of casuarina and are common around Uluru and Kings Canyon, near Alice Springs. Young desert oaks resemble tall hairy broomsticks; adult trees have a broad shady crown and dark weeping foliage. The sighing music of the wind in its 'leaves' makes the desert oak an inspiring feature of its sand-plain habitat.

Desert oaks

After good spring rains the inland explodes in a multicoloured carpet of vibrant wildflowers. The most common of these ephemerals, or short-lived plants, are the numerous species of daisy. The **poached-egg daisy** is aptly named, with white petals surrounding a pale yellow middle. **Sturt's desert pea** is a showy desert flower whose distinctive red petals have a black centre. Common flowering shrubs of the inland include the **desert bottlebrush**, **honey grevillea**, which has beautiful golden flower spikes, and the **holly grevillea**, with holly-like leaves and red flowers.

Mulga is probably the most widespread of the arid zone wattles, sometimes forming dense thickets (the explorer John McDouall Stuart complained how the scrub near Alice Springs tore his clothes and pack saddles to bits) but usually growing as open woodland. Mulga leaves are very resistant to water loss and the tree's shape directs any rain down to the base of the trunk where the roots are most dense. The hard wood is excellent for fence posts and was preferred by Aboriginal people for making spears and other implements. They also ground the mulga seeds for flour.

Gidgee is another wide-ranging acacia. It has distinctive silvery grey-green foliage and is also known as stinking wattle because of the pungent smell given off by the leaves when crushed.

The **ghost gum** is one of the most attractive eucalypts, thanks to its bright green leaves and smooth white bark. Ghost gums are found throughout central and northern Australia, and were a popular subject for artists such as Albert Namatjira.

Two unusual plants more often associated with areas of high rainfall grow in sheltered parts of the rugged MacDonnell Ranges. The **MacDonnell Range cycad** belongs to an ancient family of very slow growing plants like primitive palms. The reproductive cones that grow at the tip of the short trunk are poisonous, but were eaten by Aboriginal people after the toxins had been leached out. The **cabbage palm** of Palm Valley, in Finke Gorge National Park, grows to 30m high, and is unique to this area. The growing tip of the tree consists of tender green leaves which were a source of bush tucker to Aboriginal people. The nearest relatives of both grow hundreds of kilometres away, and both are all that remains of extensive stands that grew when the climate in the Centre was wetter.

Rivers & Billabongs

Many waterways and lakes in the arid zone are dry for years on end, only flooding after exceptional rains. Consequently, the vegetation they support must be able to tap deep into the soil for underground water. **River red gums** are stately eucalypts that generally line watercourses and can grow to 40m high. Red gums have smooth, often beautifully marked grey, tan and cream bark. They also have a habit of dropping large limbs, so while they may be good shade trees it's certainly not wise to camp under one.

Waterways and billabongs in the Top End are usually lined with **paperbarks**, or *Melaleucas* – recognisable by loose, papery bark which hangs in thin sheets around the trunk. This is actually dead bark which insulates the tree from extreme temperatures and moisture loss. The bark was used by Aboriginal people to fashion water carriers, rafts, shelters and food coverings.

Pandanus palms are distinctive palms that often grow in association with paperbarks. They can easily be recognised by their long, drooping, pointed leaves and slender stalks.

Waterlilies of several species form floating mats of large, roundish leaves on freshwater lagoons and swamps right across the tropical north. The roots are prized as food by Aboriginal people, who dig them out of the mud and eat them either raw or cooked. Yellow Water in Kakadu is a fine place to see waterlilies.

Tropical Woodland

The dominant vegetation in the tropics is open woodland with an understorey of grasses and shrubs.

Cabbage palm

This habitat covers vast areas and virtually the whole of the Top End, broken only by rocky outcrops, rivers or flood plains. A feature of this landscape is thousands of termite mounds formed from hard, packed earth. Built by tiny insects, these mounds come in many shapes and colours, and can be up to 6m high (see the boxed text in the Around Darwin chapter for more on termites).

The **Darwin woollybutt** is one of the most common woodland trees of the Top End. This medium-sized tree has rough, dark bark on the main trunk, but smooth white bark on the upper limbs. This is the tree's in-built fire protection as this thick bark insulates the trunk from grass fires that sweep through during the Dry. The activity of termites hollowing out its limbs provides the essential part for that famous instrument, the didgeridoo. The distinctive **salmon gum**, with its smooth, straight pink trunk and dark green canopy is another beautiful tree found throughout the Top End.

Australia's grotesque **boab** tree is found only from Victoria River west to the Kimberley in Western Australia. It grows on flood plains and rocky areas. Its huge, grey, swollen trunk topped by a mass of contorted branches make it a fascinating sight, particularly during the dry season when it loses its leaves and becomes 'the tree that God planted upside-down'. Although boabs rarely grow higher than 20m, their moisture-storing trunks can measure over 23m around.

Much tropical woodland has an understorey of grass, which can grow to 2m in height after the wet season and whose seeds are eaten by many species of insects and birds.

Boab tree

Mangroves

Much of the northern coast is fringed by dense forests of unusual trees called mangroves. These remarkable plants have adapted to life in salt water and some species have pneumatophores – exposed roots that can take in air when exposed at low tide. Once dismissed as useless 'swamps', mangrove communities are now recognised as an important nursery for young fish and crustaceans. Fruit bats and many waterbirds use mangroves for shelter and nesting.

There are also **freshwater mangroves** that grow on the fringes of flood plains.

Carpet of calandrinia flowers in the central desert near Uluru

CHRIS MELLOR

Red lily, Iligadjarr Wetlands, Kakadu

RICHARD I'ANSON

Ancient cycads, Finke Gorge National Park

HUGH FINLAY

Sturt desert pea, a striking sight in the wild

ROBYN COVENTRY

RICHARD I'ANSON

Boabs and eucalypts, Keep River National Park

RICHARD I'ANSON

Pandanus palms, Keep River National Park

PAUL SINCLAIR

Ghost gum, West MacDonnell National Park

CHRIS MELLOR

Saltwater, or estuarine, crocodile keeping cool on the banks of a billabong

CHRIS MELLOR

Australia's native dog, the dingo

DAVID CURL

Northern quoll, a nocturnal marsupial

Mobs of kangaroos are often seen at dusk

RICHARD I'ANSON

Flocks of galahs are seen all over the Territory

Great Egret, common in Kakadu wetlands

The rare Leichhardt's grasshopper, Kakadu

A sprightly and iridescent Rainbow bee-eater

Sea-eagle, Yellow Water, Kakadu

Facts for the Visitor

THE BEST

The Territory is outdoor-adventure country. With such a variety of landscapes and climate, the main appeal lies in the wealth of natural attractions which rival anything else in Australia. The obvious attraction is Uluru (Ayers Rock), probably Australia's most readily identifiable symbol after Sydney's Opera House. There's also the UN World Heritage listed Kakadu National Park, with its abundant flora and fauna and superb wetlands; Litchfield National Park, with cool plunge pools and waterfalls; Nitmiluk National Park with the superb Katherine Gorge; and the spectacular Kings Canyon in Watarrka National Park. Other less visited parks, such as Gregory National Park in the Victoria River District and Rainbow Valley south of Alice Springs, are also well worth exploring, although you'll need a 4WD vehicle to fully appreciate them.

The Territory is also where Australia's Aboriginal cultural heritage is at its most accessible – the rock-art sites of Kakadu, and Aboriginal-owned and run tours of Arnhem Land, Manyallaluk (near Katherine), King's Canyon and Uluru are just a few of the possibilities.

The European history of the Territory is one of hardship and struggle in a hostile and unfamiliar environment. Relics of those days leave a strong impression – the Alice Springs Telegraph Station, the ghost town of Newcastle Waters, the Elsey Cemetery near Katherine and the ruins of Victoria Settlement on the Cobourg Peninsula are all vivid and poignant reminders that life in the Territory has never been easy.

And it's got some of the most accessible – common and less common – wildlife in Australia. Among it are the famous outback marsupials such as kangaroos, wallabies and euros, hundreds of bird species – including many colourful parrots, cockatoos and finches, and some unusual and rather large lizards.

THE WORST

The downside of the great outdoors and the otherwise superb wildlife is the incredible number of annoying insects that bite, get up your nose or otherwise make themselves unwelcome. The worst are the bushflies in the Centre – and if you leave your visit until too late in the year they really will spoil it.

And there's the great frustration of not being able to swim nearly everywhere in the Top End because of crocodiles and/or sea stingers, despite the searing heat. The stingers are only around for half the year, but the crocs, well those guys just never take a break.

The incredible distances between stops make driving tedious and seem neverending. That can't be helped, of course, but it's made worse at times by having only the execrable food at roadhouses to look forward to along the way.

The Territory is generally an expensive place and transportation costs doubtless keep the price of commodities high. But to pay through the nose for ordinary and dilapidated 'budget' accommodation – as you do at big attractions such as Uluru and Cooinda – smacks of exploitation.

Last but not least, we shouldn't forget the NT Government's fabulous 5% 'bed tax' – as if the cost of a motel room isn't high enough already!

PLANNING
When to Go

The Dry season (winter) is generally considered to be the best time to visit the Territory, although this should certainly not deter you from visiting at another time.

Summer in the centre of the country is just too damned hot to do anything much, while in the far north summer is the wet season and even though it is usually not as hot as down south, the heat and humidity can make life pretty uncomfortable. To make matters worse, swimming in the sea in the north is not possible because of the 'stingers' (box jellyfish) which frequent the waters at this time. On the other hand, if you want to see the Top End green and free of dust, be treated to some spectacular electrical storms and have the best of the barramundi fishing while all the other tourists are down south, this is the time to do it.

In winter the Top End is dry and warm, but also dusty and brown. In the Centre the fierce summer heat has been replaced by cool sunny days and surprisingly cold nights – overnight temperatures as low as -5°C are not uncommon at Uluru in winter, which is no fun if you're camping! Spring and autumn are good times to be in the Centre, although spring can be marred by plagues of bushflies if there has been any amount of rain. Spring is also the time for wildflowers in the outback and these can be stunning after rains.

The other major consideration when travelling in Australia is school holidays. Australian families take to the road (and air) en masse at these times and many places are booked out, prices rise and things generally get a bit crazy. See Public Holidays & Special Events later in this chapter for details.

Maps

There's no shortage of maps available, although many of them are of pretty average quality. Among the best are those published by Hema, whose maps are updated regularly. It produces a 1:800,000 *Northern Territory* map which is useful for road travel throughout the Territory, and the 1:2,000,000 *Top End and Western Gulf* which covers this end of the land in more detail. There's also a good 1:25,000 Darwin city map and various others cover regions such as Kakadu. The best map for the Alice Springs and Centre seems to be *Alice Springs and Central Australia* published by Alderri, although none seems to be perfect.

Good road maps published by the various oil companies – Shell, BP, Mobil – are readily available from service stations and roadhouses.

Maps NT (a branch of the Department of Lands, Planning & Environment) stocks a good range of maps, and has offices in Darwin and Alice Springs.

For bushwalking, off-road 4WD driving and other activities that require large-scale maps, the topographic sheets put out by the Australian Surveying & Land Information Group (AUSLIG) are the ones to get. The more popular sheets are often available over the counter at shops which sell specialist bushwalking gear and outdoor equipment. AUSLIG also has special interest maps showing various types of land use, for example, population densities or tribal and linguistic groupings on Aboriginal land. For more information, or a catalogue, contact AUSLIG, Department of Administrative Services, Scrivener Building, Dunlop Court, Bruce, ACT 2617 (☎ toll-free 1800 800 173).

TOURIST OFFICES

There are a number of information sources for visitors to the Northern Territory and you could easily smother yourself in brochures and booklets, maps and leaflets.

The Northern Territory Tourism Commission (NTTC) is very active in promoting the Territory both domestically and overseas. It doesn't maintain tourist offices as such, but does publish very useful *Holiday Guides* to the Centre and the Top End. These guides list accommodation and tour options throughout the Territory, and include prices and booking information. The NTTC also has a NT Holiday Centre HELPLINE (☎ toll-free 1800 621 336), or you can visit them on the World Wide Web at: www.nttc.com.au.

Offices in other Australian States are as follows:

Adelaide
 (☎ 08-8272 3744, fax 8272 3755)
 Level 1, 2 Greenhill Rd, SA 5000
Brisbane
 (☎ 07-3368 2021, fax 3367 1015)
 Suite 17, Savoir Faire, 16 Park Rd, Milton, Qld 4064

Melbourne
(☎ 03-9686 1255, fax 9686 1191)
Suite 5, 51 City Rd, Southbank, Vic 3006
Perth
(☎ 09-387 3517, fax 284 9994)
236 Jersey St, Wembley, WA 6014
Sydney
(☎ 02-9360 5333; fax 9360 2770)
Suite 207, 80 Williams St, Woolloomooloo,
NSW 2011

Local Tourist Offices

Tourist offices are maintained by the local tourism authorities, in Alice Springs, Darwin, Katherine and Tennant Creek. They stock mountains of leaflets and brochures on tours and accommodation, and are generally very helpful.

Alice Springs
(☎ 8952 5199, fax 8953 0295)
Central Australian Tourism Industry Association (CATIA), Gregory Terrace
Darwin
(☎ 8981 4300, fax 8981 0653)
Darwin Region Tourism Association Information Centre, corner of Mitchell & Knuckey Sts
Katherine
(☎ 8972 2650)
Katherine Region Tourist Association, Stuart Highway
Tennant Creek
(☎ 8962 3388)
Tennant Creek Visitor Centre, Battery Hill, Peko Rd

Tourist Offices Abroad

The Northern Territory Tourism Commission (NTTC) has several office overseas which also distribute some tourist literature in the local language. Offices are as follows:

Germany
(☎ 720 714, fax 723 651, nttc_frankfurt_m@t-online.de)
2nd floor, Bockenheimer Landstrasse 45, 60325 Frankfurt am Main
Japan
(☎ 03-5214 0781, fax 5214 0784, nttcty@gol.com)
New Otani Garden Court Bldg 28F, 4-1 Kioicho, Chiyoda-ku, Tokyo 102

New Zealand
(☎ 09-303 2207, fax 303 2136, delamer@ihug.co.nz)
c/o De La Mer Communications Ltd, 13/88 Cook St, Auckland
Singapore
(☎ 324 1849; fax 324 1848, nttcsin@singnet.com.sg) 100 Amoy St, Singapore 0105
UK
(☎ 020-8944 2992, fax 8944 2993, carolyn@outbackaustralia.demon.co.uk)
1st floor, Beaumont House, Lambton Rd, London SW20 0LW
USA
(☎ 310 643 2636, fax 643 2637, realoutback@earthlink.net)
3601 Aviation Blvd, Suite 2100, Manhattan Beach CA 90266

The Australian Tourist Commission (ATC) is the government body that promotes and provides information about Australia to potential foreign visitors. The ATC is strictly an external operator; it does minimal promotion within the country and has little contact with visitors to Australia.

The ATC also maintains a number of Helplines that independent travellers can ring or fax to get specific information about Australia.

VISAS & DOCUMENTS

All visitors to Australia need a visa. Only New Zealand nationals are exempt, and even they receive a 'special category' visa on arrival.

Visa application forms are available from either Australian diplomatic missions overseas or travel agents, and you can apply by mail or in person. The type of visa depends on the reason for your visit.

Visas

Tourist Visas These are issued by Australian consular offices abroad; they are the most common type and entitle you to a stay of either three or six months. For either visa there is a $50 fee.

The visa is valid for use within 12 months of the date of issue and can be used to enter and leave Australia several times within that 12 months.

When you apply for a visa, you must present your passport and a passport photo and sign an undertaking that you have an onward or return ticket and 'sufficient funds' – the latter is obviously open to interpretation.

You can also apply for a long-stay visa, which is a multiple-entry, four-year visa that allows for stays of up to six months on each visit.

Working Holiday Visas Young, single visitors from the UK, Canada, Korea, Holland and Japan may be eligible for a 'working holiday' visa. 'Young' is fairly loosely interpreted as around 18 to 25, although exceptions are made and people up to 30, and young married couples without children, may be given a working holiday visa, but it's far from guaranteed.

A working holiday visa allows for a stay of up to 12 months, but the emphasis is supposed to be on casual employment rather than a full-time job, so you are supposed to work for only three months. This visa can only be applied for from outside Australia (preferably, but not necessarily, in your country of citizenship), and you can't change from a tourist visa to a working holiday visa.

Conditions attached to a working holiday visa include having sufficient funds for a ticket out, and taking out private medical insurance; a fee of about $145 is payable when you apply for the visa.

See the Work section later in this chapter for details of what sort of work might be available and where.

Visa Extensions The maximum stay visitors are allowed in Australia is one year, including extensions.

Visa extensions are made through the Department of Immigration & Multicultural Affairs office (☎ 8946 3100, 40 Cavenagh St, Darwin) and, as the process takes some time, it's best to apply about a month before your visa expires. There is an application fee of $145, and even if they turn down your application they can still keep your money! To qualify for an extension you are required to take out private medical insurance to cover the period of the extension, and have a ticket out of the country. Some offices are more strict in enforcing these conditions than others.

If you're trying to stay for longer in Australia the books *Temporary to Permanent Resident in Australia* and *Practical Guide to Obtaining Permanent Residence in Australia*, both published by Longman Cheshire, might be useful.

Driving Licence

You can use your own foreign driver's licence in Australia, as long as it is in English (if it's not, a translation must be carried). As an International Licence cannot be used on its own and must be supported by your home licence, there's not much point in getting one.

Medicare Card

Under reciprocal arrangements, visitors from the UK, New Zealand, Finland, Malta, Italy and the Netherlands are entitled to free or heavily subsidised medical treatment under Medicare, Australia's compulsory national health scheme. To enrol you must show your passport and health-care card or certificate from your own country, and you will be given a Medicare card.

With your card you can get necessary treatment at public hospitals and can claim for visits to a private doctor, although in this case you may have to pay for the consultation first then claim from Medicare. You should also find out how much the doctor's consultation fee is because Medicare only covers a certain amount and you must pay the balance. Look for clinics which 'bulk bill' because the bill for the treatment gets sent direct to Medicare.

For more information phone Medicare on ☎ 13 2011.

EMBASSIES & CONSULATES
Australian Embassies & Consulates

Australian consular offices overseas include the following:

Canada
    (☎ 613-236 0841, fax 236 4376)
    Suite 710, 50 O'Connor St, Ottawa
    also in Toronto and Vancouver
France
    (☎ 01 40 59 33 00, fax 4059 3310)
    4 Rue Jean Rey, 75724 Paris Cedex 15 Paris
Germany
    (☎ 0228-81 030, fax 376 268)
    Godesberger Allee 107, 53175 Bonn
    also in Frankfurt and Berlin
Indonesia
    Jakarta:
    (☎ 021-522 7111, fax 522 7101)
    Jalan H R Rasuna Said Kav C 15-16, Jakarta
    Selatan 12940
    Denpasar:
    (☎ 0361-23 5092, fax 23 1990)
    Jalan Prof Moh Yamin 51, Renon, Denpasar,
    Bali
Ireland
    (☎ 01-676 1517, fax 678 5185)
    Fitzwilton House, Wilton Terrace, Dublin 2
Japan
    Tokyo:
    (☎ 03-5232 4111, fax 5232 4149)
    2-1-14 Mita, Minato-ku, Tokyo 108
    Osaka:
    (☎ 06-941 9271, fax 920 4543)
    Twin 21 MID Tower, 29th Floor, 2-1-61 Shi-
    romi, Chuo-ku, Osaka 540
    Fukuoka:
    (☎ 092-734 5055, fax 724 2304)
    7th Floor, Tsuruta Keyaki Bldg, 1-1-5 Akasaka
    Chuo-ku, Fukuoka City 810, Kyushu
    Nagoya:
    (☎ 052-211 0630, fax 211 0632)
    8th Floor, Ikko Fushimi Bldg, 1-20-10 Nishiki,
    Naka-ku, Nagoya 460
    also in Sapporo and Sendai
Malaysia
    (☎ 03-242 3122, fax 241 5773)
    6 Jalan Yap Kwan Seng, Kuala Lumpur 50450
    also in Kuching and Penang
New Zealand
    Wellington:
    (☎ 04-473 6411, fax 498 7118)
    72-78 Hobson St, Thorndon, Wellington
    Auckland:
    (☎ 09-303 2429, fax 377 0798)
    Union House, 32-38 Quay St, Auckland 1
Thailand
    (☎ 02-287 2680, fax 287 2029)
    37 South Sathorn Rd, Bangkok 10120
UK
    (☎ 020-7379 4334, fax 7465 8210)
    Australia House, The Strand, London WC2B
    4LA
    also in Edinburgh and Manchester

USA
    (☎ 202-797 3000, fax 797 3168)
    1601 Massachusetts Ave NW, Washington DC
    20036
    also in Atlanta, Boston, Chicago, Denver, Hon-
    olulu, Houston, Los Angeles, New York and
    San Francisco

Embassies & Consulates in Australia

The following countries have consulates (or honorary consuls) in Darwin. Call first to find out when they are open:

France
    (☎ 8981 3411) 47 Knuckey St, Darwin
Germany
    (☎ 8984 3770) Berrimah Rd, Berrimah
Indonesia
    (☎ 8941 0048) 20 Harry Chan Ave, Darwin
Japan
    (☎ 8981 8722) 19 Lindsay St, Darwin
Portugal
    (☎ 8927 1956) 15 Colsters Crescent, Wagaman
Sweden
    (☎ 8981 2971) 22 Mitchell St, Darwin

CUSTOMS

When entering Australia you can bring most articles in free of duty provided that Customs is satisfied they are for personal use and that you'll be taking them with you when you leave. There's also the usual duty-free per person quota of 1125ml of alcohol, 250 cigarettes and dutiable goods up to the value of A$400.

With regard to prohibited goods, there are two areas to which you must pay particular attention. Number one is, of course, drugs – Australian Customs have a mania about the stuff and can be extremely efficient when it comes to finding them. Unless you want to make first-hand investigations of conditions in Australian jails, don't bring any with you. This particularly applies if you are arriving from South-East Asia or the Indian Subcontinent.

Problem two is animal and plant quarantine. You will be asked to declare all goods of animal or vegetable origin – wooden spoons, straw hats, the lot – and show them to an official. The authorities are naturally keen to prevent weeds, pests or diseases getting into the country. Fresh food, particularly meat, cheese, fruit, and vegetables, and flowers, are also unpopular. There are also restrictions on taking fruit and vegetables between states (see the boxed text 'Interstate Quarantine' in the Getting There & Away chapter).

Weapons and firearms are either prohibited or require a permit and safety testing. Other restricted goods include products made from protected wildlife species (such as ivory), non-approved telecommunications devices and live animals.

When it is time to leave there are duty-free stores at the international airports and their associated cities. Treat them with healthy suspicion. 'Duty-free' is one of the world's most overworked catch phrases, and it is often just an excuse to sell things at prices you can easily beat by shopping around a little.

MONEY
Currency
Australia's currency is the Australian dollar, which comprises 100 cents. There are coins for 5c, 10c, 20c, 50c, $1 and $2, and notes for $5, $10, $20, $50 and $100. Although the smallest coin in circulation is 5c, some prices are still marked in single cents then rounded to the nearest 5c when you pay.

The only major restriction on importing or exporting currency or travellers cheques is that you may not take out more than $5000 in cash without prior approval.

Exchange Rates
The Australian dollar fluctuates quite markedly against the US dollar, but it seems to stay pretty much in the 60c range – a disaster for Australians travelling overseas but a real bonus for inbound visitors.

country	unit		dollar
Canada	C$1	=	A$1.05
euro	€1	=	A$1.65
France	FF10	=	A$2.51
Germany	DM1	=	A$0.84
Hong Kong	HK$10	=	A$1.99
Japan	¥100	=	A$1.31
New Zealand	NZ$1	=	A$0.84
United Kingdom	UK£1	=	A$2.49
United States	US$1	=	A$1.55

Exchanging Money
Changing foreign currency or travellers cheques is no problem at almost any bank or licensed moneychanger such as Thomas Cook or American Express. The foreign exchange booth at Darwin airport opens for all incoming international flights.

Travellers Cheques There is a variety of ways to carry your money around with you. If your stay is limited then travellers cheques are the most straightforward and they generally enjoy a better exchange rate than foreign cash in Australia.

American Express, Thomas Cook and other well-known international brands of travellers cheques are all widely used. A passport will usually be adequate for identification; it would be sensible to carry a driving licence, credit cards or other form of identification in case of problems.

Fees for changing foreign-currency travellers cheques seem to vary from bank to bank and year to year. Currently, of the 'big four' banks (ANZ, Commonwealth, National and Westpac), Commonwealth and National charge a flat $5; ANZ charges $6.50 for foreign currency and up to $3000 in A$; and Westpac charges $7 for foreign currency and up to $500 in A$.

Buying Australian dollar travellers cheques is an option worth looking at. These can be exchanged immediately at the bank cashier's window without being converted from a foreign currency.

ATMs Most travellers these days opt for an account which includes a cash card, which you can use to access cash from ATMs (Automatic Telling Machines) found in just about every town. You simply put your card in the machine, key in your personal identification number (PIN) and withdraw funds from your account. In all but the most remote places there'll be at least one place where you can withdraw money from these 'hole in the wall' machines. Major international banks and credit agencies often have reciprocal arrangements with Australian banks, enabling you to use their ATMs – check with your bank.

ATMs can be used day or night, and it is possible to use the machines of some other banks: Westpac ATMs accept Commonwealth Bank cards and vice versa; National Bank ATMs accept ANZ cards and vice versa. There is usually a daily limit to how much you can withdraw from your account – check with your bank.

Many businesses, such as service stations, supermarkets and convenience stores, are linked into the EFTPOS system (Electronic Funds Transfer at Point Of Sale), and at places with this facility you can use your bank cash card to pay for services or purchases direct, and sometimes withdraw cash as well. Bank cash cards and credit cards can also be used to make local, STD and international phone calls in certain public telephones, although in the Territory you'll find these only in big towns.

Credit Cards A good alternative to carrying large numbers of travellers cheques is the credit card. Visa, MasterCard, Diners Club and American Express are all widely accepted.

Cash advances from credit cards are available over the counter and from many ATMs, depending on the card.

A credit card makes life much simpler if you're planning to rent a vehicle while travelling around the Territory. In fact, many rent-a-car agencies simply won't rent you a vehicle if you don't have a card.

Local Bank Accounts If you're planning to stay longer than a month or so, it's worth considering other ways of handling money that give you more flexibility and are more economical.

Opening an account at an Australian bank is not all that easy, especially for overseas visitors. An identification points system operates and you need to score a minimum of 100 points before you can have the privilege of letting the bank take your money. Passports, driving licences, birth certificates and other 'major' IDs earn you 40 points; minor ones such as credit cards get you 20 points (just like a TV game show!). However, if visitors apply to open an account during the first six weeks of their visit, then just showing their passport will suffice.

If you don't have an Australian Tax File Number (see the Work section later in this chapter), interest earned from your funds will be taxed at the rate of 48% and this money goes straight to our old mate, the Deputy Commissioner of Taxation.

Costs

If you've just arrived from South-East Asia, the cost of living in Australia will probably give you the conniptions! And compared with other states, and southern Australia generally, the Northern Territory is still an expensive place to travel. The worst culprits are accommodation (except at the budget end) and food (cheap takeaway food is available, but it's usually poor quality); fuel in some areas is very expensive and long distances mean you'll have to buy plenty of it.

But it's not all bad news. Compared with Canada, the USA and much of Europe, Australia is cheaper in some ways and more expensive in others and the exchange rate means it can be reasonably priced for some visitors.

All major towns have a backpackers hostel, where a dorm bed usually goes for $15 or so; they can also be found at major attractions, such as Uluru-Kata Tjuta (Ayers Rock), where you'll find some of the country's most expensive dorms.

The biggest cost in any trip is going to be transport, simply because it's such a vast country. If there's a group of you, buying a second-hand car is probably the most economical way to go.

On average you can expect to spend about $40-50 per day if you budget fiercely and *always* take the cheapest option; $75 gives you much greater flexibility. Obviously if you stay for longer periods in each place and can take advantage of discounts given on long-term accommodation, or even move into a share-house with other people, this helps to keep your costs to a minimum.

Tipping

Tipping is optional and virtually unheard of in a taxi (of course, the driver won't hurl a tip back at you). If you feel the service warrants it, it's only customary to tip in more expensive restaurants; 10% of the bill is sufficient.

POST & COMMUNICATIONS

Post offices are open from 9 am to 5 pm Monday to Friday (and the main post office in Darwin opens on Saturday morning). Some newsagents double as local post offices and sell postage stamps.

Postal Rates

Letters Australia's postal services are relatively efficient. It costs 45c to send a standard letter or postcard within Australia.

Air-mail letters/postcards cost 75/70c to New Zealand, 85/80c to Singapore and Malaysia, 95/90c to Hong Kong and India, $1.05/95c to the USA and Canada, and $1.20/1.00 to Europe and the UK.

Parcels By sea mail a 1 to 2kg parcel costs $13.50 to $21 to India and $16 to $25 to the USA, Europe or the UK. Each 500g over 2kg costs $2 to India and $3 to the USA, Europe or the UK, with a maximum of 20kg for all destinations. Air-mail rates are considerably more expensive.

Receiving Mail

All post offices will hold mail and the main post offices in Darwin and Alice Springs have efficient poste restante counters.

Telephone

Local Calls There is no time limit on local calls. From public/private phones they cost 40c/30c; you can make local calls from gold or blue phones – often found in shops, hotels, bars, etc – and from payphones.

Phonecards There's a wide range of local and international phonecards. Lonely Planet's eKno Communication Card (see the insert at the back of this book) is aimed specifically at travellers and provides cheap international calls, a range of messaging services and free email – for local calls, you're usually better off with a local card. To join the eKno service from the Northern Territory dial ☎1800 674100 and to access it dial ☎ 1800 114478. For further information, visit the eKno Web site at www.ekno.lonelyplanet.com.

Many public phones accept Telstra Phonecards, which are very convenient. The cards come in $5, $10, $20 and $50 denominations, and are available from retail outlets such as newsagents and pharmacies.

Some public phones take only bank cards or credit cards, and these too are convenient, although the cost can quickly mount up. The minimum charge for a call on one of these phones is $1.20.

STD Calls Subscriber Trunk Dialling – long-distance – calls can be made from virtually any public phone. Without a card you'll need plenty of coins handy and be prepared to feed them through at a fair rate. STD calls are cheaper in off-peak hours – see the front of a local telephone book for the different rates.

The STD area code for the Northern Territory, Western Australia and South Australia is 08.

International Calls From most STD phones you can also make ISD (International Subscriber Dialling) calls. Connections to overseas numbers are almost as quick as to local numbers and if your call is brief it needn't cost very much. Just dial 0011 for overseas, the country code (44 for Britain, 1 for the USA or Canada, 64 for New Zealand), the city code (020 for London, 212 for New York etc), and then the phone number. All phone directories have a listing of international access codes.

You can also make ISD calls with Optus rather than Telstra. The fee structure varies slightly between the two companies, and if you are phoning one country constantly it may be worth comparing the two. This option is only available from private phones in certain areas. Phone Optus (☎ toll-free 1800 500 005) for details of their services.

International calls from Australia are among the cheapest you'll find anywhere. A Telstra call to the USA or Britain costs 84c a minute Monday to Friday (45c on weekends); New Zealand is 69c a minute Monday to Friday (42c on weekends); a 15c connection fee applies to all these calls. See the back of White Pages phone books, or call ☎ 1225 for assistance or ☎ 1222 for costs. Weekends are usually the cheapest time to ring.

Country Direct is a service which gives travellers in Australia direct access to operators in nearly 50 countries, to make collect or credit card calls. For a full list of the countries in this system, check any local White Pages phone book. They include: Canada (☎ 1800 881 150), Germany (☎ 0011 800 0049 049), Japan (☎ 1800 551 181), New Zealand (☎ 1800 551 164), UK (☎ 1800 551 104) and USA (☎ 1800 551 155).

Toll-Free Calls Many businesses, including tour operators, some places to stay and some government departments operate a toll-free service, so no matter where you are ringing from around the country, it's a free call. These numbers have the prefix 1800 and we've listed them wherever possible throughout the book.

Many companies, such as the airlines, have six-digit numbers beginning with 13, and these are charged at the rate of a local call. Often they'll be Australia-wide numbers, but sometimes are applicable only to a specific STD district. Unfortunately there's no way of telling without actually ringing the number.

Mobile Phones Phone numbers with the prefixes 014, 015, 016, 018 or 041 are mobile or car phones. The three mobile operators are Telstra, Optus and Vodaphone. Calls to mobile numbers are charged at special STD rates and can be expensive.

The call range of mobile phones is quite limited in the Territory and services are usually available only near major centres.

Information Calls Other odd numbers you may come across are numbers starting with 0055 and 1900. The 0055 numbers, usually recorded information services and the like, are provided by private companies, and your call is charged in multiples of 25c (40c from public phones) at a rate selected by the provider (40-75c per minute).

Numbers beginning with 1900 are also information services, but they are charged on a fixed fee basis, which can vary from as little as 35c to as much as $30!

Email & Internet Access

If you want to surf the Net, even if it's only to access your email, there are a couple of service providers in the Territory. With some, such as Pegasus Networks, you can dial from anywhere in the country for the cost of a local call. Typical casual rates are about $5 per half hour.

If you want to open your own on-line account, costs vary, but a typical price structure is a $20 registration fee (which may include a few hours of on-line time), plus $20 per month for 10 hour on-line time. A few of the current big operators include:

Taunct
   (☎ 8941 0699, www.taunet.net.au)
TOPEND.COM.AU
   (☎ toll-free 1800 686 455,
   www.topend.com.au)
Pegasus Networks
   (☎ toll-free 1800 812 812, www.peg.apc.org)
Telstra Big Pond
   (☎ toll-free 1800 804 282, www.bigpond.au)

CompuServe users who want to access the service locally should phone CompuServe (☎ toll-free 1800 025 240) to get the local log-in numbers.

INTERNET RESOURCES

The World Wide Web is rapidly expanding to become a major source of information on anything you care to name.

The Lonely Planet site (www.lonelyplanet.com.au) is not specific to the Northern Territory (or even Australia) but is still definitely worth a look (well, we would say that, wouldn't we?).

Although things on the Net change rapidly, some sites which currently contain a range of information on the Northern Territory include:

Guide to Australia
www.csu.edu.au/education/australia.html
(This site, maintained by the Charles Sturt University in NSW, is a mine of information, with links to federal and Northern Territory government departments, weather information, books, maps etc.)
The Aussie Index
www.aussie.com.au/aussie.htm
(A fairly comprehensive list of Australian companies, educational institutions and government departments which maintain Web sites.)
Australian Government
http://gov.info.au
(The federal government has a site, which is predictably unexciting, but it is wide-ranging and a good source for things like visa information.)
Taunet
www.taunet.net.au
(The only service provider in the Territory, with a few links to local sites, and snippets of local info which may be useful.)
Northern Territory Tourism Commission
www.nttc.com.au/pfm/
(A comprehensive guide to tourist destinations in the Territory.)

BOOKS

In almost any bookshop in the country you will find a section devoted to Australiana with books on every Australian subject you care to mention. Although Darwin has far and away the best range, there are bookshops – including second-hand bookshops – in Darwin, Katherine and Alice Springs. The best ones are mentioned in the appropriate sections.

Lonely Planet

If you are pushing beyond the borders to see more of the country, Lonely Planet's *Australia* is the book to take. In addition, each state is covered in its own guide – check out the *Western Australia*, *Queensland* or *South Australia* books for the next stage in your trip. There's also a book covering *Islands of Australia's Great Barrier Reef* if you're heading that way.

If you're going on outback trips under your on steam take the LP *Outback Australia* guide. Lonely Planet's *Bushwalking in Australia* describes over 35 walks of different lengths and difficulty in various parts of the country, including some in the Territory.

To get a handle on some of the slang you'll hear on your travels, there's Lonely Planet's *Australian* phrasebook.

And if you're travelling by road for any distance in the NT, you'll empathise with *Sean & David's Long Drive*, one of the titles in Lonely Planet's 'Journeys' travel literature series, a hilarious, offbeat road book by Sean Condon.

Guidebooks

Burnum Burnum's Aboriginal Australia is subtitled 'a traveller's guide'. If you want to explore Australia from the Aboriginal point of view, this large and lavish hardback is the book for you.

The late Brian Sheedy's *Outback on a Budget* includes lots of practical advice. There are a number of other books about vehicle preparation and driving in the outback, including *Explore Australia by Four-Wheel Drive* by Peter & Kim Wherrett.

Cassettes For that long haul up the Stuart Hwy, *Take a Tour Guide* is an informative commentary on two cassettes that gives general background information and explains a bit about each town or site between Port Augusta (SA) and Darwin. It's available from 38 Beaumaris Parade, Highett, Vic 3190 (☎ 03-9555 8419) and each tape costs $5 (plus $2 postage).

Travel

Accounts of travels in Australia include the marvellous *Tracks*, by Robyn Davidson. It's the amazing story of a young woman who set out alone to walk from Alice Springs to the Western Australia coast with her camels. It almost single-handedly inspired the current Australian interest in camel safaris!

Quite another sort of travel is Tony Horwitz's *One for the Road*, an often hilarious account of a high-speed hitchhiking trip around Australia (Oz through a windscreen). In contrast, *The Ribbon and the Ragged Square*, by Linda Christmas, is an intelligent, sober account of an investigatory trip round Oz by an English journalist. There's lots of background and history as well as first-hand reporting and interviews.

The late Bruce Chatwin's book *The Songlines* tells of his experiences among central Australian Aboriginal people and makes more sense of the Dreamtime, sacred sites, sacred songs and the traditional Aboriginal way of life than 10 learned tomes put together. It's one of the great modern books on the outback.

The journals of the early European explorers can be fairly hard going but make fascinating reading. The hardships that many of these men (and they were virtually all men) endured is nothing short of amazing. The original accounts are usually available in main libraries. Men such as Sturt, Eyre, Leichhardt, Davidson, King (on the Burke and Wills expedition), Stuart and many others all kept detailed journals.

History & Politics

For a good introduction to Australian history, read *A Short History of Australia*, a most accessible and informative general history by Manning Clark, the much-loved Aussie historian, or *The Fatal Shore*, Robert Hughes' best-selling account of the convict era.

Geoffrey Blainey's *The Tyranny of Distance* is an engrossing study of the problems of transport in this harsh continent and how they shaped the pattern of white settlement: transporting produce hundreds of miles by bullock cart from an inland farm to a port cost more than shipping it from the port around the globe to Europe – a handicap that only wool and later gold were profitable enough to overcome.

Finding Australia, by Russel Ward, traces the story of the early days from the first Aboriginal arrivals up to 1821. It's strong on Aboriginal people, women and

the full story of foreign exploration, not just Captain Cook's role.

The Exploration of Australia, by Michael Cannon, is a coffee table book in size, presentation and price, but it's a fascinating reference book about the gradual European uncovering of the continent.

The Fatal Impact, by Alan Moorehead, begins with the voyages of James Cook, regarded as one of the greatest and most humane explorers, and tells the tragic story of the European impact on Australia, Tahiti and Antarctica in the years that followed Cook's great voyages of discovery. It details how good intentions and the economic imperatives of the time led to disaster, corruption and annihilation.

John Pilger's *A Secret Country* is a vividly written book that deals with Australia's historical roots, its shabby treatment of Aboriginal people and the current political complexion.

Far Country, by Alan Powell, is a very readable history of the Northern Territory. Ernestine Hill's *The Territory* is another worthwhile volume on the history of the Territory.

The Front Door, by Douglas Lockwood, is a history of Darwin from 1869 to 1969. For some good pictures of Darwin during WWII, try *Darwin's Air War*, published by the Historical Society of the Northern Territory.

Stores & Stories by Jean Bagshaw delves into the life of a woman running general stores on Aboriginal communities in the 1970s and '80s.

For a taste of Alice Springs early this century, get hold of *Alice on the Line* by Doris Blackwell & Douglas Lockwood. The early days of the Daly River area are recorded in *Spirit of the Daly* by Peter Forrest.

Other books which give an insight into the pioneering days in the outback include *Packhorse & Waterhole* by Gordon Buchanan, son of legendary drover Nat Buchanan who was responsible for opening up large areas of the Northern Territory; *The Big Run*, by Jock Makin, a history of the huge Victoria River Downs cattle station in the Victoria River district; and *The Cattle King* by Ion Idriess, which details the life of the remarkable Sir Sidney Kidman, the man who set up a chain of stations in the outback early this century.

Aboriginal People

The Australian Aborigines by Kenneth Maddock is a good cultural summary. The award-winning *Triumph of the Nomads*, by Geoffrey Blainey, chronicles the life of Australia's original inhabitants, and convincingly demolishes the myth that Aboriginal people were 'primitive' people trapped on a hostile continent. It's an excellent read.

For a sympathetic historical account of what's happened to the original Australians since Europeans arrived read *Aboriginal Australians* by Richard Broome. *A Change of Ownership*, by Mildred Kirk, covers similar ground to Broome's book, but does so more concisely, focusing on the land rights movement and its historical background.

The Other Side of the Frontier, by Henry Reynolds, uses historical records to give a vivid account of an Aboriginal view of the arrival and takeover of Australia by Europeans. His book *With the White People* identifies the essential Aboriginal contributions to the survival of the early white settlers. *My Place*, Sally Morgan's prize-winning autobiography, traces her discovery of her Aboriginal heritage. *The Fringe Dwellers* by Nene Gare describes just what it's like to be Aboriginal growing up in a white-dominated society.

Don't Take Your Love to Town by Ruby Langford and *My People* by Oodgeroo Noonuccal (Kath Walker) are also recommended reading for people interested in the experiences of Aboriginal people.

Songman, by Allan Baillie, is a fictional account of the life of an adolescent Aboriginal boy growing up in Arnhem Land in the days before white settlement.

NEWSPAPERS & MAGAZINES

The Territory's only daily is the tabloid *NT News*, which is pretty lightweight and usually features a rogue croc story at least once a week. In Alice Springs the twice-weekly *Centralian Advocate* provides a bit of local news.

The *Australian* is Australia's only national daily and widely available in the Territory.

Weekly magazines include an Australian edition of *Time* and a combined edition of the Australian news magazine the *Bulletin* and *Newsweek*. The *Guardian Weekly* is widely available and good for international news. Asian weekly mags such as *Asiaweek* and *Far Eastern Economic Review* are available in Darwin.

Business Review Weekly is an Australian weekly magazine that explores business matters.

Good outdoor and adventure magazines include *Wild*, *Rock* and *Outdoor Australia*. There are plenty of magazines devoted to fishing and 4WD driving as well.

Magazines from the UK and USA are also available, but usually with a delay of a month or so.

RADIO & TV

At least one radio and TV station can be picked up all over the Territory, but in some remote areas there may be nothing at all.

The national advertising-free (so far) TV and radio network is the Australian Broadcasting Corporation (ABC). You should be able to pick up Radio National (sometimes on AM and sometimes by FM relays) and ABC TV nearly everywhere.

Triple J is an ABC youth FM radio station which plays excellent music from outside the pop mainstream and plugs into Australia's youth culture. Unfortunately, you can pick it up only in Darwin and Alice Springs.

Far and away the best TV network in Australia is SBS, which broadcasts great films and documentaries, and has the best news service by a country mile. Unfortunately, you're only likely to pick it up in Darwin and Alice Springs.

In most places in the Territory you can pick up an ABC radio station and ABC TV, and/or a couple of AM or FM commercial stations.

Imparja is an Aboriginal owned and run commercial TV station that operates out of Alice Springs and has a 'footprint' which covers one third of the country (mainly the Northern Territory, South Australia and western NSW). It broadcasts a variety of programs, ranging from soaps to pieces made by and for Aboriginal people.

On the pay TV front Australia is really dragging its feet. It's only available to a fraction of the population, and at relatively high cost. The major players in the industry are still jockeying for position, and until the dust settles pay TV is a bit of a non-starter.

VIDEO SYSTEMS

Australia uses the PAL system and pre-recorded videos purchased in Australia may be incompatible with overseas systems. Check this before you buy.

PHOTOGRAPHY & VIDEO

Australian film prices are not too far out of line with those of the rest of the western world. Including developing, 36-exposure Kodachrome 64 or Fujichrome 100 slide film costs around $25, but with a little shopping around you can find it for around $20 – even less if you buy it in quantity.

There are a number of camera shops in Darwin and Alice Springs and standards of camera service are high. Print film in major brands is readily available, but a good range of slide film is available only in Darwin and Alice – you should stock up before you go if you have any preference for brand or stock.

Developing standards are also high; many places offer one-hour developing of print film, and in Darwin and Alice you can get E6 (slide) processing done overnight if not within a few hours.

Photography is no problem, but in the outback you have to allow for the exceptional intensity of the light. Best results in the outback regions are obtained early in the morning and late in the afternoon. As the sun gets higher, colours appear washed out. Especially in the summer, allow for temperature extremes and do your best to keep film as cool as possible, particularly after exposure. Other film and camera hazards are dust in the outback and humidity in the Top End.

As in any country, politeness goes a long way when taking photographs; ask before taking pictures of people. Note that many Aboriginal people do not like to have their photographs taken, even from a distance.

TIME

The Northern Territory is on Central Standard Time, which is plus 9½ hours from GMT/UTC. This is half an hour behind the eastern states, 1½ hours ahead of Western Australia, and the same as South Australia.

Things get screwed up in summer as daylight savings does not apply in the Northern Territory, so from November to March (approximately), the eastern states are 1½ hours ahead of Northern Territory time, and South Australia is one hour ahead.

ELECTRICITY

Voltage is 220-240V 50Hz and the plugs are three-pin, but not the same as British three-pin plugs. Users of electric shavers or hairdryers should note that, apart from in top-end hotels, it's difficult to find converters to take either US flat two-pin plugs or the European round two-pin plugs. Adaptors for British plugs can be found in good hardware shops, chemists and travel agents.

WEIGHTS & MEASURES

Australia uses the metric system. Petrol and milk are sold by the litre, apples and potatoes by the kilogram, distance is measured by the metre or kilometre, and speed limits are displayed in kilometres per hour (km/h).

For those who need help with metric units there's a conversion table at the back of this book.

HEALTH

Australia is a remarkably healthy country to travel in, considering that such a large portion of it lies in the tropics. So long as you have not visited an infected country in the past 14 days (aircraft refuelling stops do not count) no vaccinations are required for entry. There are, however, a few routine vaccinations that are recommended worldwide whether you are travelling or not, and it's always worth checking whether your tetanus booster is up to date.

Medical care in Australia is first class and only moderately expensive. A typical visit to the doctor costs around $35. If you have an immediate health problem, phone or visit the casualty section at the nearest public hospital.

Health Insurance

Ambulance services in Australia are self-funding (ie they're not free) and can be frightfully expensive, so you'd be wise to take out travel insurance for that reason alone. Make sure the policy specifically includes ambulance, helicopter rescue and a flight home for you and anyone you're travelling with, should your condition warrant it. Also check the fine print: some policies exclude 'dangerous activities' such as scuba diving, motorcycling and even trekking. If such activities are on your agenda, you don't want that policy.

Basic Rules

Heat In northern and outback areas you can expect the weather to be hot between October and April, and travellers from cool climates may feel uncomfortable, even in winter. 'Hot' is a relative term, depending on what you are used to. The sensible thing to do on a hot day is to avoid the sun between mid-morning and mid-afternoon. Infants and elderly people are most at risk from heat exhaustion and heatstroke.

Water People who first arrive in a hot climate may not feel thirsty when they should; the body's 'thirst mechanism' often needs a few days to adjust. The rule of thumb is that an active adult should drink at least 4 litres of water per day in warm weather, more when physically very active, such as when cycling or walking. Use the colour of your urine as a guide: if it's clear you're probably drinking enough, but if it's dark you need to drink more. Remember that body moisture will evaporate in the dry air with no indication that you're sweating.

Everyday Health

Normal body temperature is 37°C or 98.6°F; more than 2°C (4°F) higher indicates a high fever. The normal adult pulse rate is 60 to 100 per minute (children 80 to 100, babies 100 to 140). As a general rule the pulse increases about 20 beats per minute for each °C (2°F) rise in fever.

Respiration (breathing) rate is also an indicator of illness. Count the number of breaths per minute: between 12 and 20 is normal for adults and older children (up to 30 for younger children, 40 for babies). People with a high fever or serious respiratory illness breathe more quickly than normal. More than 40 shallow breaths a minute may indicate pneumonia.

Tap water is safe to drink in towns and cities throughout the Territory. In outback areas, bore water may not be fit for human consumption, so seek local advice before drinking it.

Always beware of water from rivers, creeks and lakes, as it may have been infected by stock or wildlife. The surest way to disinfect water is to thoroughly boil it for 10 minutes.

Environmental Hazards

Fungal Infections These occur more commonly in hot weather and are usually found on the scalp, between the toes (athlete's foot) or fingers, in the groin and on the body (ringworm). Ringworm, which is a fungal infection, not a worm, can be caught from infected animals or other people. Moisture encourages these infections.

To prevent fungal infections wear loose, comfortable clothes, avoid artificial fibres, wash frequently and dry yourself carefully. If you do get an infection, wash the infected area at least daily with a disinfectant or medicated soap and water, and rinse and dry well. Apply an antifungal cream or powder like tolnaftate (Tinaderm). Try to expose the infected area to air or sunlight as much as possible. Wash all towels and underwear in hot water, change them often and let them dry in the sun.

Heat Exhaustion Dehydration and salt deficiency can cause heat exhaustion. Take time to acclimatise to high temperatures, drink sufficient liquids and do not do anything that is physically too demanding. Heat exhaustion is a strong possibility in the Territory during summer – make sure you carry sufficient water at all times.

Salt deficiency is characterised by fatigue, lethargy, headaches, giddiness and muscle cramps; extra salt in your food may help, but an electrolyte replacement drink (such as Gatorade or Staminade) is better.

Heatstroke This serious, occasionally fatal, condition can occur if the body's heat-regulating mechanism breaks down and the body temperature rises to dangerous levels. Long, continuous periods of exposure to high temperatures and insufficient fluids can leave you vulnerable to heatstroke.

The symptoms are feeling unwell, not sweating very much (or at all) and a high body temperature (39 to 41°C or 102 to 106°F). Where sweating has ceased, the skin becomes flushed and red. Severe, throbbing headaches and lack of coordination will also occur, and the sufferer may be confused or aggressive. Eventually the victim will become delirious or convulse. Hospitalisation is essential, but in the interim get victims out of the sun, remove their clothing, cover them with a wet sheet or towel and then fan continually. Give fluids if they are conscious.

Prickly Heat This itchy rash is caused by excessive perspiration trapped under the skin. It usually strikes people who have just arrived in a hot climate. Keeping cool, bathing often, drying the skin and using a mild talcum or prickly heat powder, and/or resorting to air-conditioning may help.

Sunburn In the tropics, the desert or at high altitude you can get sunburnt surprisingly

Medical Kit Check List

Following is a list of items you should consider including in your medical kit – consult your phamacist for brands available in your country.

☐ **Aspirin** or **paracetamol** (acetaminophen in the US) – for pain or fever.
☐ **Antihistamine** – for allergies, eg hay fever; to ease the itch from insect bites or stings; and to prevent motion sickness.
☐ **Antibiotics** – consider including these if you're travelling well off the beaten track; see your doctor, as they must be prescribed, and carry the prescription with you.
☐ **Loperamide** or **diphenoxylate** – 'blockers' for diarrhoea; **prochlorperazine** or **metaclopramide** for nausea and vomiting.
☐ **Rehydration mixture** – to prevent dehydration, eg due to severe diarrhoea; particularly important when travelling with children.
☐ **Insect repellent, sunscreen, lip balm** and **eye drops.**
☐ **Calamine lotion, sting relief spray** or **aloe vera** – to ease irritation from sunburn and insect bites or stings.
☐ **Antifungal cream** or **powder** – for fungal skin infections and thrush.
☐ **Antiseptic** (such as povidone-iodine) – for cuts and grazes.
☐ **Bandages, Band-Aids (plasters)** and other wound dressings.
☐ **Water purification tablets** or **iodine.**
☐ **Scissors, tweezers** and a **thermometer** (note that mercury thermometers are prohibited by airlines).
☐ **Syringes** and **needles** – in case you need injections in a country with medical hygiene problems. Ask your doctor for a note explaining why you have them.
☐ **Cold** and **flu tablets, throat lozenges** and **nasal decongestant.**
☐ **Multivitamins** – consider for long trips, when dietary vitamin intake may be inadequate.

quickly, even through cloud. Use a sunscreen, a hat, and a barrier cream for your nose and lips. Calamine lotion or Stingose are good for mild sunburn. Protect your eyes with good quality sunglasses, particularly if you will be near water or sand.

Infectious Diseases

Diarrhoea Simple things like a change of water, food or climate can all cause a mild bout of diarrhoea, and a few rushed toilet trips with no other symptoms do not indicate a major problem.

Dehydration is the main danger with any diarrhoea, and can occur quite quickly in children or the elderly. Under all circumstances *fluid replacement* (at least equal to the volume being lost) is the most important thing to remember. Weak black tea with a little sugar, soda water, or soft drinks allowed to go flat and diluted 50% with clean water are all good. With severe diarrhoea a rehydrating solution, to replace lost minerals and salts, is preferable. Commercially available oral rehydration salts (ORS) are very useful; add them to boiled or bottled water.

Gut-paralysing drugs such as Lomotil or Imodium can be used to bring relief from the symptoms, although they do not actually cure the problem. Only use these drugs if you do not have access to toilets, eg if you *must* travel. For children under 12 years Lomotil and Imodium are not recommended. Do not use these drugs if the person has a high fever or is severely dehydrated.

Hepatitis Hepatitis B is spread through contact with infected blood, blood products or body fluids, for example through sexual contact, unsterilised needles, blood transfusions, or contact with blood via small breaks in the skin. Other risk situations include having a shave, and tattoo or body piercing with contaminated equipment. Hepatitis B can lead to long term problems such as chronic liver damage, liver cancer or a long term carrier state.

HIV & AIDS Infection with the human immunodeficiency virus (HIV) may lead to acquired immune deficiency syndrome (AIDS), which is a fatal disease. Any exposure to blood, blood products or body fluids may put the individual at risk. The disease is often transmitted through sexual contact or dirty needles – vaccinations, acupuncture, tattooing and body piercing are potentially as dangerous as intravenous drug use.

Sexually Transmitted Diseases Gonorrhoea, herpes and syphilis are among these diseases; sores, blisters or rashes around the genitals and discharges or pain when urinating are common symptoms. In some STDs, such as wart virus or chlamydia, symptoms may be less marked or not observed at all, especially in women. Syphilis symptoms eventually disappear completely but the disease continues and can cause severe problems in later years. While abstinence from sexual contact is the only 100% effective prevention, using condoms is also effective. The treatment of gonorrhoea and syphilis is with antibiotics. The different sexually transmitted diseases each require specific antibiotics. There is no cure for herpes or AIDS.

Cuts, Bites & Stings

There are plenty of unpleasant creatures waiting to cut, bite and sting in the Territory. The most serious bites are inflicted by sharks and crocodiles (see Dangers & Annoyances), but apart from disease-carrying mosquitoes none should be a serious concern if common sense is used.

Bites & Stings Take care when collecting firewood – ants, spiders and scorpions all may live under fallen wood. Ant, bee and wasp stings are usually painful rather than dangerous. However, in people who are allergic to them severe breathing difficulties may occur and require urgent medical care. Calamine lotion or Stingose spray will give relief and ice packs will reduce the pain and swelling.

Some spiders have nasty bites – the only potentially deadly species in the Territory is the redback (similar to the American black widow), but the antivenin is usually available. Keep away from all large spiders and don't walk around barefoot at night. Scorpions are common in rocky parts of the Centre; their stings are painful but not dangerous. They may shelter in shoes or clothing, so if you are camping shake these things out before putting them on in the morning.

Certain cone shells found in Australian coastal waters can inflict a dangerous – even fatal – sting. Various fish and other sea creatures may have a dangerous sting or bite, or are dangerous to eat – seek local advice. Don't handle unfamiliar live shells and don't walk barefoot on coral reefs.

Jellyfish Avoid contact with these sea creatures, which have stinging tentacles – seek local advice and don't swim in inshore waters between October and May, when the extremely poisonous box jellyfish is present. Stings from most jellyfish are simply rather painful. Dousing in vinegar will deactivate any stingers which have not 'fired'. Calamine lotion, antihistamines and analgesics may reduce the reaction and relieve the pain.

Leeches & Ticks Leeches may be present in damp forest; they attach themselves to your skin to suck your blood. Salt or a lighted cigarette end will make them fall off. Do not pull them off, as the bite is then more likely to become infected. Clean and apply pressure if the point of attachment is bleeding. An insect repellent may keep them away.

You should always check all over your body if you have been walking through a potentially tick-infested area as ticks can cause skin infections and other more serious diseases. If a tick is found attached, press down around its head with tweezers, grab the head and gently pull upwards. Avoid pulling the rear of the body as this may squeeze the tick's gut contents through the attached mouth parts into the skin, increasing the risk of infection and disease. Smearing chemicals on the tick will not make it let go and is not recommended.

Snakes There are plenty of these in the Territory, although most are harmless and nearly all are shy. The important things to remember are to leave any snake alone (never try to catch or kill it), and don't walk around barefoot at night. There are several large, deadly species, but the most dangerous is probably the death adder, which sits motionless in the undergrowth and can be stepped on if you are unlucky. To minimise your chances of being bitten always wear boots, socks and long trousers when walking through undergrowth where snakes may be present. Don't put your hands into holes and crevices, and be careful when collecting firewood.

Snakebites do not cause instant death and antivenins are available for all dangerous species. Immediately wrap the entire bitten limb tightly, as you would for a sprained ankle, and then attach a splint to immobilise it. Calm the victim, keep them still and seek medical help. Do not attempt to catch the snake, it's not vital to identify the snake and you risk being bitten again. Don't use a tourniquet, don't clean poison from the skin near the wound and don't try to suck out the poison. Certainly don't cut the skin near the wound, you're trying to keep the victim calm remember?

Women's Health
Gynaecological Problems Antibiotic use, synthetic underwear, sweating and contraceptive pills can lead to fungal vaginal infections, especially when travelling in hot climates. Fungal infections are characterised by a rash, itch and discharge and can be treated with a vinegar or lemon-juice douche, or with yoghurt. Nystatin, miconazole or clotrimazole pessaries or vaginal cream are the usual treatment. Maintaining good personal hygiene and wearing loose-fitting clothes and cotton underwear may help prevent these infections.

Sexually transmitted diseases are a major cause of vaginal problems. Symptoms include a smelly discharge, pain during intercourse and sometimes a burning sensation when urinating. Medical attention should be sought and male sexual partners must also be treated. Remember that in addition to these diseases, HIV or hepatitis B may be acquired during exposure. Besides abstinence, the best thing is to practise safe sex using condoms.

Pregnancy Most miscarriages occur during the first three months of pregnancy, so this is the most risky time to travel as far as your own health is concerned. Miscarriage is not uncommon, and can occasionally lead to severe bleeding. The last three months should also be spent within reasonable distance of good medical care. A baby born as early as 24 weeks stands a chance of survival, but only in a good modern hospital. Pregnant women should avoid all unnecessary medication, but vaccinations and malarial prophylactics should still be taken where possible. Additional care should be taken to prevent illness and particular attention should be paid to diet and nutrition. Alcohol and nicotine, for example, should be avoided.

WOMEN TRAVELLERS

The Northern Territory is generally a safe place for women travellers, although it's probably best to avoid walking alone late at night. Sexual harassment is unfortunately still second nature to some Aussie males. In the Territory the macho male image is still big and it's generally true to say your average Territory male is fairly unenlightened about women's issues.

Hitching is certainly not recommended for solo women, and even pairs should exercise care at all times (see the section on hitching in the Getting Around chapter).

GAY & LESBIAN TRAVELLERS

While Australia in general is rapidly becoming a popular destination among gay and lesbian travellers, attitudes in the Northern Territory are a good few years behind those you find on the east coast and elsewhere – the predominant attitude you're likely to come across outside the main towns is still pretty homophobic. Having said that, there is an active lesbian scene in Alice Springs.

Graylink (☎ 8948 0089, fax 8948 1777, PO Box 3826, Darwin, NT 0801) is a gay-friendly, Darwin-based company which co-ordinates independent travel and group tours through the Top End of Australia. It also operates a local tour booking agency and information centre by the international arrivals gate at Darwin Airport.

GN News is a newsletter put out by the fledgling gay community of the Top End; phone ☎ 8948 0216 for further information.

USEFUL ORGANISATIONS
Automobile Associations

The Automobile Association of the Northern Territory (AANT) provides an emergency breakdown service, and literature on accommodation and camp grounds.

The AANT also has reciprocal arrangements with the various other state motoring organisations in Australia and with similar organisations overseas. So, if you're a member of the National Roads & Motorists Association (NRMA) in New South Wales, you can use AANT services facilities in the Territory. The same applies if you're a member of the AAA in the USA or the RAC or AA in the UK.

The AANT has two offices in the Territory, located at 79-81 Smith St, Darwin (☎ 8981 3837, fax 8941 2965), and at 58 Sargent St, Alice Springs (☎ 8952 1087).

Emergency Road Service The numbers to ring for breakdown service throughout the Territory are:

Adelaide River	☎ 8976 7046
Alice Springs	☎ 8952 1087
Batchelor	☎ 8976 0196
Darwin	☎ 8941 0611
Elliott	☎ 8969 2025
Katherine	☎ 8972 3177
Tennant Creek	☎ 8962 2468
Yulara (Uluru)	☎ 8956 2188

Parks & Wildlife Commission

The Northern Territory's many parks and reserves are administered by the Parks & Wildlife Commission. The exceptions are Kakadu and Uluru-Kata Tjuta national parks, which come under the jurisdiction of the Federal national parks body – Parks Australia.

The facilities provided in the various parks by Parks & Wildlife are among the best in the country. Most parks have at the very least picnic areas and interpretive signs, while those that get heavier use have marked walking trails, camp grounds with facilities (sometimes including free gas barbecues) and ranger-guided activities during the tourist season (generally in winter).

Parks & Wildlife also produces informative leaflets on just about every park or reserve under its administration, and these are available from their regional offices, or often from the rangers or park visitor centres on site.

Parks & Wildlife Offices The most useful Parks & Wildlife offices for visitors to Darwin and Alice Springs are at the main tourist information centres. All major centres also have a regional office.

Alice Springs
  (☎ 8952 5199) CATIA office, Gregory Terrace
Darwin
  (☎ 8981 4300) Darwin Regional Tourism Association Information Centre
  (☎ 8999 5511) Main office: PO Box 496, Palmerston
Katherine
  (☎ 8973 8888) Giles Street
Tennant Creek
  (☎ 8962 4599) corner of Irvine and Schmidt Sts

Parks Australia Formerly the Australian Nature Conservation Agency (ANCA), this is the Federal body which administers Kakadu and Uluru-Kata Tjuta national parks. You probably won't have anything to do with them normally, but any inquiries should be directed to the excellent visitor centres at these parks (see the Kakadu & Arnhem Land and Uluru-Kata Tjuta National Park chapters for details).

Australian Trust for Conservation Volunteers

This nonpolitical, nonprofit group organises practical conservation projects (such as tree planting, track construction and flora and fauna surveys) for volunteers to take part in.

Travellers are welcome and it's an excellent way to get involved with the conservation movement and, at the same time, visit some of the more interesting areas of the country, such as Tasmania, Kakadu and Fraser Island.

Most projects are either for a weekend or a week and all food, transport and accommodation is supplied in return for a small contribution to help cover costs. Most travellers who take part in ATCV join a Conservation Experience Package that lasts six weeks and includes six different projects. The cost is $840, and further weeks can be added for $140.

Contact the head office (☎ toll-free 1800 032 501, info@atcv.com.au, www.atcv.com.au) at PO Box 423, Ballarat, Vic 3350, or the local office (☎ 8981 3206) at PO Box 2358, Darwin, NT 0801.

WWOOF

WWOOF (Willing Workers on Organic Farms) is a relatively new organisation in Australia, although it is well established in other countries. The idea is that you do a few hours work each day on a farm in return for bed and board. Some places have a minimum stay of a couple of days but many will take you for just a night. Some will let you stay for months if they like the look of you, and you can get involved with some interesting large-scale projects.

Becoming a WWOOFer is a great way to meet interesting people and to travel cheaply. There are about 1100 WWOOF associates in Australia, with about eight near Darwin and one in the Alice Springs area.

As the name says, the farms are supposed to be organic but that isn't always so. Some places aren't even farms – you might help out at a pottery or do the books at a seed wholesaler. There are even a few commercial farms which exploit WWOOFers as cheap harvest labour, although these are quite rare. Whether they have a farm or just a vegie patch, most participants in the

Northern Territory for the Disabled Traveller

The general level of disability awareness in Australia is encouraging, but information about accessible accommodation and tourist attractions is fragmented and available on a regional basis only. The practical level of awareness is generally high and new accommodation must meet standards set down by law.

Information

The Australian Tourist Commission publishes an information fact sheet *Travel in Australia for People with Disabilities* containing addresses of organisations that provide assistance to the disabled.

NICAN (National Information Communications Awareness Network), PO Box 407, Curtin, ACT 2605 (☎ toll-free 1800 806 769, fax 285 3714) is an Australia-wide directory providing information on accessible accommodation, sporting and recreational activities.

ACROD (Australian Council for the Rehabilitation of the Disabled), PO Box 60, Curtin, ACT 2605 (☎ 02-6282 4333, fax 281 3488), can provide information about help organisations, accommodation and tour operators providing specialised tours.

Other sources to contact are the Northern Territory Visual Impairment Resource Unit (☎ 8981 5488) and the Deafness Association of the Northern Territory (☎ 8945 2016, fax 8945 1880). Publications to look for include:

Access in Alice published by the Disability Services of Central Australia (☎ 8952 3351)
Darwin – City Without Steps and *Free in Darwin – Places to Go*, available from the local council, Darwin Civic Centre, Harry Chan Ave (☎ 8982 2511) and from the Darwin Region Tourism Association, corner of Mitchell and Knuckey Sts (☎ 8981 4300) which also has a list of Darwin's wheelchair-accessible accommodation. Information is also available from the Community Care Centre for Disability Workers in Darwin (☎ 8989 2876)
Easy Access Australia – A Travel Guide to Australia ($24.80), a book researched and written by wheelchair users (order from PO Box 218, Kew, Victoria 3101)
Smooth Ride Guides – Australia & New Zealand, published in the UK but available in Australia
A Wheelie's Handbook of Australia, another book written by a wheelchair user (order from Colin James, PO Box 89, Coleraine, Victoria 3315).

Organised Tours

Few tour operators are equipped for wheelchairs but in Darwin, Land-a-Barra Tours (☎ 8932 2543) operates a boat on which a wheelchair can be anchored securely, providing a safe fishing session. Also in Darwin, Sahara Tours (☎ 8953 0881) runs tours in a wheelchair-hoist-equipped bus.

Boat cruises on Yellow Water (☎ 8979 0111) can cope with wheelchairs with advance warning.

---

scheme are concerned to some extent with alternative lifestyles.

To join WWOOF send $35 ($40 for couples) or, from overseas A$40 ($45) to WWOOF, RSD, Buchan, Vic 3885 (☎ 03-5155 0218), and they will send you a membership number and a booklet which lists WWOOF places all over Australia.

National Trust

The National Trust is dedicated to preserving historic buildings. The Trust actually owns several buildings throughout the Territory which are open to the public. Many other buildings, not open to the public, are 'classified' by the National Trust to ensure their preservation.

Northern Territory for the Disabled Traveller

Places to Stay
Accommodation in the Territory is generally good, the difficulty is finding out about it. Always ask at tourist offices for lists of wheelchair-accessible accommodation and tourist attractions.

Darwin and Alice Springs both have large hotels and a number of motels which provide accessible rooms. Motel chains such as Flag and Best Western are also well represented.

There are other accommodation providers that have accessible rooms and most proprietors will do what they can to assist you. The guides published by the state motoring organisations are very comprehensive and give wheelchair-access information. However, it is best to confirm that the facilities would suit your needs.

For campers there are wheelchair-accessible showers and toilets at Cooinda, Merl, Muirella Park and Gunlom (Kakadu), Yulara (Uluru-Kata Tjuta), Edith Falls and Katherine Gorge (Nitmiluk) and at Florence Falls and Wangi (Litchfield) camp grounds.

Getting Around
Air Travel by air is easy; Qantas and Ansett welcome disabled passengers. Qantas staff undergo disability training and Ansett has instituted ANSACARE, a system of recording your details once only eliminating repetition at booking and obviating the need for further medical certificates. Neither airline requires a medical certificate for long-term, stable disabilities. Darwin, Alice Springs and Yulara airports all have facilities for the disabled traveller, including parking spaces, wheelchair access to terminals and accessible toilets. However, there are no air bridges at Alice or Yulara so the airlines use a forklift to raise an enclosed platform to transfer wheelchair passengers. Some Qantas jets have an accessible toilet on board.

Bus Long-distance bus travel is not yet a viable option for the wheelchair user.

Train The *Ghan,* which runs weekly between Alice Springs, Adelaide and Melbourne, has one compartment fitted out for wheelchair users.

Taxi Taxis in Darwin (☎ toll-free 131008 or 8981 8777) include three station wagons and one van converted to carry a wheelchair. In Alice (☎ 131008) a modified stretch vehicle is available.

Car Rental Avis and Hertz offer hire cars with hand controls at no extra charge for pick up at the major airports, but advance notice is required.

Parking The international wheelchair symbol for parking in allocated bays is widely recognised.

Bruce Cameron

The National Trust also produces some excellent literature, including a fine series of small booklets on places such as Newcastle Waters, Katherine and also Myilly Point (Darwin). These guides are available from the National Trust offices and cost $2 each.

In Darwin the National Trust office is in the historic old buildings of Myilly Point, between the city centre and the casino (☎ 8981 2848, 4 Burnett Place, Myilly Point, Darwin, NT 0820).

DANGERS & ANNOYANCES
Animal Hazards
Among Australia's unique and lovable wildlife there are a few less-than-pleasant – even

downright dangerous – inhabitants of the bush, although it's unlikely that you'll come across many of them. Here's a rundown just in case.

Crocodiles Saltwater crocodiles can be a real danger and have killed a number of people (travellers and locals). They are found in river estuaries and large rivers, sometimes a long way inland, so before diving into that inviting, cool water find out from the locals whether it's croc-free.

Snakes Although the Territory has many species, few are dangerous and their reputation and abundance are exaggerated by locals and visitors like. However, the dangerous ones are *very* dangerous, and you'd be well advised to leave any snake alone if you don't know what you're playing with. Few are aggressive, and unless you have the bad fortune to stand on one it's unlikely that you'll be bitten. See the Flora & Fauna section in the Facts about the Northern Territory chapter and the Health section earlier in this chapter for more information.

Box Jellyfish The box jellyfish, also known as the sea wasp or 'stinger', is present in Territory waters during summer and the sting from its tentacles can be fatal. The stinging tentacles spread several metres away from its body and by the time you see it you're likely to have been stung. If someone is stung, they are likely to run out of the sea screaming and collapse on the beach, with weals on their body as though they've been whipped. See the Health section for information about treating a sting.

Stay out of the sea when the sea wasps are around – the locals are ignoring that lovely water for an excellent reason.

Flies & Mosquitoes

For four to six months of the year you'll have to cope with those two banes of the Australian outdoors – the fly and the mosquito.

The bushfly is a disgusting, persistent little fly that seeks out moisture on your skin, in your eyes and up your nose – one reason people in country areas talk without opening their mouth is to keep the damned flies out! In the towns the flies are not too bad; it's in the country that it starts getting out of hand, and the further 'out' you get the worse the flies seem to be.

In central Australia the flies start to come out with the warmer spring weather (late August), particularly if there has been any amount of spring rain, and last through until winter. They are such a nuisance that virtually every shop sells the Genuine Aussie Fly Net (made in Korea), which fits on a hat and is rather like a string onion bag but is very effective. It's either that or the 'Great Australian Wave' to keep them away. Repellents such as Aerogard and Rid go some way to deterring the little bastards.

The only biting fly is the March fly – and its activities are not restricted to March – a large, usually striped fly with red eyes. Fortunately they fly slowly and can usually be killed easily.

Mosquitoes (mossies) too can be a problem, especially in the Top End – in Kakadu there are droves of them year round. It's a good idea to avoid being bitten as far as possible; mosquito-borne diseases such as dengue and Ross River fever are not unknown in the Territory.

On the Road

Animals Kangaroos, wandering cattle and two Territory specialities – camels and wild horses – can be a real hazard to the driver. A collision with one will badly damage your vehicle and probably kill the animal.

Other Drivers Australians ain't the world's greatest drivers and in fact the national rate of death on the roads is staggering (as a percentage of population it's among the highest in the world). Alcohol (ie drunk-driving) has something to do with the toll, but just as frightening is the fact that some 80% of accidents *don't* involve alcohol. Fatigue is a killer and after driving over hundreds of kilometres on straight roads you'll understand why. Visitors from countries where they don't drive on the left also come to grief occasionally, and inexperienced drivers on outback roads often crash.

The dangers posed by stray animals and drunks are particularly enhanced at night, so it's best to avoid travelling after dark. See the Getting Around chapter for more on driving hazards.

EMERGENCY

In the case of a life-threatening situation, dial ☎ 000. This call is free from any phone and the operator will connect you with either the police, ambulance or fire brigade. To dial any of these services direct, check the inside front cover of the White Pages section of the telephone book.

For other telephone crisis and personal counselling services (such as sexual assault, poisons information or alcohol and drug problems), check the Community Information pages of the telephone book.

BUSINESS HOURS

Most shops close at 5 or 5.30 pm weekdays, and either noon or 5 pm on Saturday. There's not much in the way of late-night trading, although a couple of major supermarkets in Alice Springs and Darwin are open 24 hours.

Banks are open from 9.30 am to 4 pm Monday to Thursday, and until 5 pm on Friday.

Of course there are some exceptions to these somewhat restricting opening hours and all sorts of places stay open late and all weekend – particularly milk bars, convenience stores and roadhouses and facilities in tourist areas.

PUBLIC HOLIDAYS & SPECIAL EVENTS

The Christmas holiday season is part of the long summer school vacation and the time you are most likely to find accommodation booked out and long queues in most of Australia. However, the winter months are the busiest in the Territory, with cooler temperatures in the Centre and the Dry in the Top End. There are three other shorter school-holiday periods during the year, falling from early to mid-April, late June to mid-July, and late September to early October.

The following is a list of the main national and local public holidays observed in the Northern Territory.

National & Territory Holidays

New Year's Day	1 January
Australia Day	26 January
Easter	March/April – Good Friday and Easter Saturday, Sunday and Monday
Anzac Day	25 April
May Day	1st Monday in May
Queen's Birthday	2nd Monday in June
Picnic Day	1st Monday in August
Christmas Day	25 December
Boxing Day	26 December

Local Holidays

Alice Springs Show Day	1st Friday in July
Tennant Creek Show Day	2nd Friday in July
Katherine Show Day	3rd Friday in July
Darwin Show Day	4th Friday in July

Special Events

Some of the most enjoyable Australian festivals are, naturally, the ones that are most typically Australian – like the outback horse-race meetings, which draw together isolated townsfolk, the tiny communities from the huge stations and more than a few eccentric bush characters. There are happenings and holidays in the Territory all year round, but particularly during the winter.

January
Australia Day
This national holiday, commemorating the arrival of the First Fleet in Sydney in 1788, is observed on 26 January.

April
Anzac Day
A national public holiday, on 25 April, commemorating the landing of Anzac troops at Gallipoli in 1915. Memorial marches by the returned soldiers of both world wars and the veterans of Korea and Vietnam are held all over the country.
NT Country Music Talent Quest
Held in Adelaide River, it's a lively three days with acts from all over Australia participating.

May

Alice Springs Cup Horse Racing Carnival
Three weeks of horse racing, culminating in the Alice Springs Cup.

Bangtail Muster
Alice Springs' parade and festival honouring outback cattlemen.

June

Barunga Wugularr Sports & Cultural Festival
For the four days over the Queen's Birthday long weekend in June, Barunga, 80 km southeast of Katherine, becomes a gathering place for Aboriginal people from all over the Territory. There are traditional arts and crafts, as well as dancing and athletics competitions.

Merrepen Arts Festival
Held in June or July, Nauiya Nambiyu on the banks of the Daly River is the venue for this festival. Several Aboriginal communities from around the district, such as Wadeye, Nauiya and Peppimenarti, display their arts and crafts.

July

NT Royal Shows
These agricultural shows are held in Darwin, Katherine, Tennant Creek and Alice Springs.

Alice Springs Camel Cup
Held in Blatherskite Park, this annual event is Australia's biggest camel racing day.

Darwin Cup Carnival
An eight day racing festival, the highlight of which is the running of the Darwin Cup.

Darwin to Ambon Yacht Race
This prestigious yacht race starts in Darwin and boasts an international field.

August

Darwin Rodeo
This rodeo includes international team events between Australia, the USA, Canada and New Zealand.

Darwin Beer Can Regatta
These boat races are for boats constructed entirely out of beer cans, of which there are plenty in this heavy drinking city.

Yuendumu Festival
Aboriginal people from the central and western desert region meet in Yuendumu, northwest of Alice Springs, over the long weekend in early August. There's a mix of traditional and modern sporting and cultural events.

Oenpelli Open Day
Oenpelli is in Arnhem Land, not far from Jabiru in Kakadu National Park. On the first Saturday in August an open day is held where there's a chance to buy local artefacts and watch the sports and dancing events.

Festival of Darwin
This mainly outdoor arts and culture festival highlights Darwin's unique position in Australia with its large Asian and Aboriginal populations.

Australian Safari Race
A 6000km Adelaide to Darwin cross-country road rally which attracts an international field of contestants.

October

Henley-on-Todd Regatta
A series of races for leg-powered bottomless boats on the (usually) dry Todd River.

World Solar Car Challenge
An event which sees weird and wonderful solar-powered vehicles sailing down the Stuart Highway from Darwin to Adelaide. It generates a huge amount of interest in the Territory, and attracts contestants from around the world.

ACTIVITIES

There are plenty of activities that you can take part in while travelling through the Territory. Here is just an idea of what's available:

Bushwalking

One of the best ways of really getting away from it all in the Territory is to go bushwalking. There are many fantastic walks in the various national parks, particularly Kakadu, Litchfield and Watarrka (Kings Canyon). See the various chapters for information on marked walking trails in national parks.

Willis' Walkabouts (☎ 8985 2134) is one company which offers extended bushwalks year round in both the Top End and the Centre.

Scuba Diving

There's great scuba diving in Darwin harbour on old WWII and Cyclone Tracy wrecks. See the Darwin section for details of companies offering dives and courses.

Cycling

You often see people cycling in the Northern Territory, but the stops between drinks can be uncomfortably long and you need to be well prepared. For the not-so-masochistic there are plenty of great day trips around Darwin and in the MacDonnell Ranges out of Alice Springs.

Camel Riding

For the more adventurous, camel riding has really taken off in the country around Alice Springs. If you've done it in India or Egypt or you just fancy yourself as the explorer/outdoors type, then here's your chance. You can take anything from a five minute stroll to a 14 day expedition.

Hot-Air Ballooning

Hot-air ballooning is another popular adventure option in Alice Springs, with at least two companies offering early morning flights over the outback.

Fossicking

Fossicking is a popular pastime in the Northern Territory, although it is really only an option if you have a 4WD. About 30% of Australia's land area consists of basins which have been filled with sediments poor in gemstones other than precious opal. Some exceptions are the Harts Range in central Australia (see the North of Alice chapter) and the Top End goldfields.

In order to fossick you must first obtain a fossicking permit. Permission to fossick on freehold land and mineral leases must usually be obtained from the owner or leaseholder. Sadly, the actions of the thoughtless minority in trespassing and abuse of property have brought the hobby into disrepute in many areas and fossickers are no longer always welcome.

Contact the Department of Mines & Energy in Darwin, Tennant Creek or Alice Springs for information on mining law, permits and the availability of geological maps, reports and fossicking guides.

Barramundi Fishing

For many visitors to the northern regions of Australia, one of the primary motivations for their visit is to land a 'barra' – Australia's premier native sport fish.

The barra is a highly prized fish mainly because of its great fighting qualities: once it takes a lure or fly, it fights like hell to be free. As you try to reel one in, chances are it will play the game for a bit, then make some powerful runs, often leaping clear of the water and shaking its head in an attempt to throw the hook. Even the smaller fish (3-4kg) can put up a decent fight, but when they are about 6kg or more you have a battle on your hands which can last several minutes.

Landing the barra is a challenge, but it's only half the fun; the other half is eating it. In the Territory, at least, the barramundi is a prized table fish, although the taste of the flesh does depend to some extent on where the fish is caught. Those caught in saltwater or tidal rivers are generally found to have the sweetest flavour; those in landlocked waterways can have a muddy flavour and soft flesh if the water is a bit murky.

The fish is found throughout coastal and riverine waters of the Top End. The best time to catch them is the post-Wet, ie around late March to the end of May. At this time the floods are receding from the rivers and the fish tend to gather in the freshwater creeks which are full of young fish. The best method is to fish from an anchored boat and cast a lure into a likely spot, such as a small creek mouth or floodway.

Bag & Size Limits It's in everyone's interest to follow the legal restrictions when fishing for barra. In the Northern Territory, the minimum size limit is 55cm, and the bag limit is five fish in one day. They may not be retained on a tether line at any time. Certain areas of the Northern Territory are closed to fishing between 1 October and 31 January.

Information The following addresses may be useful:

Amateur Fishermen's Association of the Northern Territory
(☎ 8989 2499) PO Box 1231, Darwin, NT 0810
Darwin Game Fishing Club
(☎ 8984 4327) GPO Box 3629, Darwin, NT 0801
Northern Territory Game Fishing Association
(☎ 8946 9846) GPO Box 128, Darwin, NT 0801
Recreational Fisheries Division, Department of Primary Industries & Fisheries
(☎ 8999 4395)

Organised Fishing Trips & Charters
There are a host of commercial operators offering fishing trips for barra and other sporting fish. Some of them include:

Barra Bash
(☎ toll-free 1800 632 225) GPO Box 2253, Darwin, NT 0801. It does day trips out of Darwin.
Big Barra Fishing Safaris
(☎ 8932 1473) 11 Bailey Circuit, Driver, NT 0830. It offers one-day trips to the Mary River system east of Darwin, or extended tours in north-western Arnhem Land (one of only two operators to have permission to fish in Arnhem Land).
Land-a-Barra Tours
(☎ 8932 2543) 10 Fagan Court, Gray, NT 0830.

WORK

If you come to Australia on a 12 month 'working holiday' visa you can officially work for only three out of those 12 months, but working on a regular tourist visa is not on. Many travellers on tourist visas do find casual work, especially in the Territory, where there is a demand for seasonal labour in tourist resorts, backpackers hostels and on cattle stations.

With the current boom in tourism, casual work is often not hard to find at the major tourist centres. Alice Springs and Darwin are both good prospects, but opportunities are usually limited to the peak holiday seasons.

Other good prospects for casual work include factories, bar work, waiting on tables or washing dishes, other domestic chores at outback roadhouses, nanny work, fruit picking (mangoes are big from Katherine northwards) and collecting for charities.

Although many travellers do find work, if you are coming to Australia with the intention of working, make sure you have enough funds to cover you for your stay, or have a contingency plan if the work is not forthcoming.

The government employment service has been privatised and there's now a plethora of smaller 'job placement agencies' throughout the Territory. The staff usually have a good idea of what's available where.

The various backpackers magazines, newspapers and hostels are good information sources – some local employers even advertise on their notice boards.

Tax File Number

It's important to apply for a Tax File Number (TFN) if you plan to work (or open a bank account – see the Money section earlier in this chapter) in Australia, not because it's a condition of employment, but without a TFN tax will be deducted from any wages you earn at the maximum rate, which is currently 48.5%! To get a TFN, contact the local branch of the Australian Taxation Office for a form. It's a straightforward procedure, and you will have to supply adequate identification, such as a passport and driving licence. The issue of a TFN takes about four weeks.

Paying Tax

Yes, it's one of the certainties in life! If you have supplied your employer with a Tax File Number, tax will be deducted from your wages at the rate of 29% if your annual income is below $20,700. As your income increases, so does the tax rate, with the maximum being 48.5% for that part of an income over $50,000. For nonresident visitors, tax is payable from the first dollar you earn, unlike residents who have something like a $6000 tax-free threshold. For this reason, if you have had tax deducted at the correct rate as you earn, it is unlikely you'll be entitled to a tax refund when you leave.

If you have had tax deducted at 48.5% because you have not submitted a Tax File Number, you will be entitled to a partial refund. Once you lodge a tax return (which must include a copy of the Group Certificate all employers issue to salaried workers at the end of the financial year or within seven days of leaving a job), you will be refunded the extra tax you have paid. Before you can lodge a tax return, however, you must have a Tax File Number.

ACCOMMODATION

The Northern Territory government levies a 5% 'bed tax' to stay in all hotel and motel rooms. Thankfully, it doesn't apply to budget accommodation such as backpackers hostels or camping and caravan sites. Sometimes it's included in a quoted price, but often it's not – ask before settling on a room for the night.

Darwin and the three main towns in the Northern Territory are well supplied with youth hostels, backpackers hostels and caravan parks with camp grounds – the cheapest shelter you can find. In addition to this there are plenty of motels.

A typical town will have a basic motel at around $50 for a double, an old town centre pub with rooms (shared bathrooms) at say $30, and a caravan park probably with camp sites for around $10 and on-site vans or cabins for $35 for two. If there's a group of you, the rates for three or four people in a room are always worth checking. Often there are larger 'family' rooms or units with two bedrooms.

There are a couple of free backpackers newspapers and booklets available at hostels around the country, and these have fairly up-to-date listings of hostels, although they give neither prices nor details of each hostel.

There's a wide variation in seasonal prices for accommodation. At busy times, school holidays in particular, prices are at their peak, whereas at other times useful discounts can be found. This particularly applies to the Top End, where the wet season (summer) is the low season and prices can drop by as much as 30%. In this book high season prices are quoted unless indicated otherwise.

Bush Camping

Camping in the bush, either freelance or at designated spots in national parks and reserves, is for many people one of the highlights of a visit to Australia. This is especially so in the Northern Territory where the national parks are a major attraction. Nights spent around a campfire under the stars are unforgettable.

In the Centre you don't even need a tent – swags are definitely the way to go. These ready made zipped canvas bedrolls, complete with mattress, are widely available as both singles and doubles, and are extremely convenient – it takes literally a few seconds to pack or unpack.

In the Top End it's still possible to use swags in the Dry, the only addition you'll need is a mosquito net. In the Wet sleeping out is a risky business and you basically need a tent.

There are a few basic rules to camping in the wild:

- Most of the land in Australia belongs to someone, even if you haven't seen a house for 100 km or so, and you need permission to camp on it. In national parks and on Aboriginal land you will need permits. On public land observe all the rules and regulations.
- Select your camping spot carefully. Start looking well before nightfall and choose a spot that makes you invisible from the road. You'll notice any number of vehicle tracks leading off the main road into the bush: explore a few and see what you find.
- Some trees (for instance, river red gums and ironwood) are notorious for dropping limbs. Know your trees, or don't camp under large branches.
- Ants live everywhere, and it's embarrassingly easy to set up camp on underground nests. Also beware of the wide variety of mean spiny seeds on the ground which can ruin your expensive tent groundsheet with pinprick holes – carry a tarpaulin or sheet of thick plastic to use as an underlay.
- Carry out all the rubbish you take in, don't bury it. Wild animals dig it up and spread it everywhere.
- Observe fire restrictions – where and when you can light a fire – and make sure it is safe. Use a trench and keep the area around the fire clean of flammable material.
- Don't chop down trees or pull branches off living trees to light your fire. Don't use dead wood that's become a white-ant habitat (it won't burn well either). If the area is short of wood, go back down the track a little and collect some there. If that is not possible, use a gas stove for cooking.
- Respect the wildlife. This also means observing crocodile warnings and keeping away from suspect river banks.
- Don't camp right beside a water point. Stock and wildlife won't come in while you are there, and if it is the only water around they may die of thirst.

Early morning in the Finke River – swags are perfect for camping in the Centre

- Don't camp close enough to a river or stream to pollute it. In most parks the minimum distance is 20m.
- Don't use soap or detergent in any stream, river, dam or any other water point.
- Use toilets where they are provided. If there isn't one, find a handy bush, dig a hole, do the job and then fill in the hole. Bury all human waste well away from any stream.

Camping & Caravan Parks

In cities and towns, camping at caravan parks is the cheapest way of all, with nightly costs for two of around $10 to $15. There are a great number of caravan parks and you'll almost always find space available, especially if you only want an unpowered site.

Australian caravan parks are well kept, conveniently located and excellent value. One of the drawbacks is that camp sites are often intended more for caravanners (house trailers for any North Americans out there) than for campers and the tent campers get little thought in these places.

On-Site Vans & Cabins Many – but not all – caravan parks have on-site vans that you can rent for the night. These give you the comfort of a caravan without the inconvenience of actually towing one of the damned things. On-site cabins are also widely available, and these are more like a small self-contained unit. They usually have their own bathroom and toilet and are much less cramped than a caravan. The price difference is not always that great – say $25 to $30 for an on-site van, $30 to $50 for a cabin.

Hostels

YHA There are YHA or affiliate hostels in Alice Springs, Yulara, Darwin, Kakadu, Katherine, Mataranka and Tennant Creek.

YHA hostels provide basic accommodation, usually in small dormitories or bunk rooms although most provide twin rooms for couples (about $30 to $35). The nightly charges are very reasonable, usually between $14 and $20 a night and $3 more for non-members. To become a full YHA member in Australia costs $27 a year (there's also a $17 joining fee, although if you're an overseas resident joining in Australia you don't have to pay this). You can join at the YHA Travel Centre in Darwin (in the Transit Centre in Mitchell St) or at any of the YHA hostels.

The YHA has the Aussie Starter Pack, whereby Australian residents joining the YHA receive two vouchers worth $8 each to use at a hostel in their state. International visitors joining the YHA at a hostel receive their first night at that hostel for free. The scheme has standardised the additional nightly fee charged to non-YHA members at $3 per night. When staying at a hostel nonmembers receive an Aussie Starter Card, to be stamped each night by the YHA. Once the card has been stamped nine times, you are given a year's free membership.

You must have a regulation sheet sleeping bag or bed linen – for hygiene reasons a regular sleeping bag will not do. If you haven't got sheets they can be rented at many hostels (usually for $3), but it's cheaper, after a few nights' stay, to have your own. YHA offices and some larger hostels sell the official YHA sheet bag.

All hostels have cooking facilities and 24-hour access, and there's usually some communal area where you can sit and talk. There are usually laundry facilities and often excellent notice boards. Many hostels have a maximum-stay period because it would hardly be fair for people to stay too long when others are being turned away.

YHA members are also entitled to a number of handy discounts around the country on things such as car hire, camping shops, activities, tours and accommodation, and these are detailed in the *Discounts* booklet, published each year.

Inquiries about membership in the NT can be made by phoning ☎ 8981 6344.

Backpacker Hostels There are backpacker hostels in Darwin, Katherine, Tennant Creek and Alice Springs. Most are purpose-built as backpackers hostels and have a good range of facilities.

Prices at backpackers hostels are generally in line with YHA hostels, typically $12 to $20, although discounts may be available.

There's at least one organisation (VIP) which you can join where, for a modest fee (typically $15), you'll receive a discount card (valid for 12 months) and a list of participating hostels. This is hardly a great inducement to join but you do also receive useful discounts on other services, such as bus passes, so they may be worth considering.

Nomads backpackers (☎ 8941 9722) is another organisation which runs pubs and hostels right around the country.

Some roadhouses along major highways also have backpackers beds.

Motels, Serviced Apartments & Holiday Flats

If you've got transport and want a modern place with your own bathroom and other facilities, then you're moving into the motel bracket. Motels line the highways of Australia, just like in the USA, but they're usually located away from the city centres. Prices vary and singles are often not much cheaper than doubles. Most places start at $60.

Holiday flats and serviced apartments are much the same thing. A holiday flat is much like a motel room but usually has cooking facilities, and you don't get your bed made every morning nor the cups washed up. Most motels provide at least tea and coffee-making facilities and a small fridge, but a holiday flat will also have cooking utensils, cutlery, crockery and so on.

Holiday flats are often rented on a weekly basis but even in these cases it's worth asking if daily rates are available. Paying for a week, even if you stay only for a few days, can still be cheaper than having those days at a higher daily rate. If there are more than just two of you, another advantage of holiday flats is that you can often find them with two or more bedrooms. A two bedroom holiday flat is typically priced at about 1½ times the cost of a comparable single bedroom unit.

FOOD

Meat, meat and more meat is the message in the Territory, where old habits die hard and cholesterol is something which only affects wimps down south. If you are into dinner-plate sized, inch-thick steaks, you've come to the right place. Novelty meats such as kangaroo, camel, crocodile and buffalo also feature prominently, especially in places where tourists are the main patrons. You might try them for their novelty value, but they're usually well overpriced.

Fish, in particular the ubiquitous – and overrated – barramundi (universally known as 'barra'), is another favourite in the Top End.

At the bottom end of the food scale is the Australian meat pie. The standard pie is an awful concoction of anonymous meat and dark gravy in a soggy pastry case. You'll have to try one though; the number consumed in Australia each year is phenomenal, and they're a real part of Australian culture. In country towns where pies are made by the local baker they can actually be pretty good.

Vegetarian Food

Vegetarians are not well catered for. In Darwin and Alice Springs a number of cafes offer a few vegetarian dishes on the menu. Elsewhere you will have to resort to the fairly ordinary salad bars at pub bistros, or cook for yourself.

Shopping for Food

While a wide range of produce is sold in supermarkets, most of it has been trucked in from elsewhere and so is not always as fresh as it might be. The exception is beef, which is produced locally and is cheap. Despite the distances most food has travelled before hitting the local shelves, prices are not too out of line with what you pay elsewhere around the country.

Where to Eat

Takeaway Food In Darwin and Alice Springs you'll find all the well-known international fast-food chains – Hungry Jack's, KFC, Pizza Hut etc – all typically conspicuous.

Milk bars sell an assortment of pies, pasties, sandwiches and milkshakes and there are a few fish and chip shops (which nearly all sell nothing but barra in one of its less appetising incarnations) or hamburger joints. The fare is usually filling, rather than wholesome. All towns of any size have at least one pizza joint.

Roadhouses The death rate on Australia's roads is something of a byword, but some wag once commented about the hidden toll from eating the food from service stations. And the worst offenders in this category are the roadhouses that line the highways across the Territory. Greasy, overpriced food is kept lukewarm for hours and dished out by grumpy staff almost everywhere you go. Vile coffee is also available.

Give these places a miss unless you have absolutely no choice.

Restaurants & Cafés Dining out has finally caught on in some parts of the Territory, and Darwin and Alice Springs, at least, have a selection of good eateries with à la carte menus. However, they are rarely cheap and your money goes a lot further in southern capitals. Best value are the modern and casual cafés, where for $15 to $20 you can get a good feed. Most are licensed to sell alcohol.

While eating out is a pleasure in Darwin and Alice, in smaller towns it can be something of an ordeal. The food will be predictable and unexciting, and is usually of the 'meat and three veg' variety.

Pubs Most pubs serve two types of meals: bistro meals, which are usually in the $10 to $15 range and are served in the dining room or lounge bar, where there's usually a self-serve salad bar; and bar (or counter) meals which are filling, simple, no-frills meals eaten in the public bar, and these usually cost less than $10, sometimes as little as $5.

The quality of pub food varies enormously, and while it's usually fairly basic and unimaginative, it's generally pretty good value. The usual meal times are from noon to 2 pm and from 6 to 8 pm.

Food Markets Where the climate allows there are often outdoor food stalls and markets, and these can be an excellent place to sample a variety of cuisines, with Asian being the most popular. Darwin's Thursday and Sunday evening Mindil Beach Market is probably the largest of its type in the country, and the range of cuisines is very impressive.

DRINKS

Plain water in bottles is now served at some restaurants in Darwin and perhaps in Alice, but you may have to ask for it and there may be a charge.

Beer

Beer drinking is as much part of the culture in the Territory as latte is down south, although it's a part of the Territory image that local tourist authorities are trying, with difficulty, to shake off.

Australian beer will be fairly familiar to North Americans; it's similar to what's known as lager in the UK. It may taste like lemonade to the European real-ale addict, but it packs quite a punch. It is chilled before drinking.

The only beer indigenous to the Territory is NT Draught, but it's not terribly popular.

Among the best-known in the Territory are the beers made by Victoria's CUB – Fosters, Victoria Bitter (or VB) and Carlton Draught, which are known locally by the can colour – blue, green and white, respectively. Other popular beers are XXXX (pronounced four-ex), and Tooheys Red. Recent additions to the stable of old favourites include Carlton Cold, Diamond Draught and lower alcohol beers like Tooheys Blue and Lite Ice, and styles other than your average Aussie lager, such as Blue Bock and Old Black Ale, both made by Tooheys.

The smaller breweries generally seem to produce better beer – Cascade (Tasmania) and Coopers (South Australia) being two examples. Coopers also produce a stout, which is popular among connoisseurs, and their Black Crow is a delicious malty, dark beer. These brands are not so easy to get in the Territory, and can be costly.

Standard beer generally contains around 4.9% alcohol, although the trend in recent years has been towards low-alcohol beers, with an alcohol content of between 2% and 3.5%. Tooheys Blue is a particularly popular light beer.

Excessive use of alcohol is a problem in many Aboriginal communities and for this reason many are now 'dry', and it is an offence to carry alcohol into these places. The problem has also led to restricted trading hours and even 'dry days' in some places – in Alice Springs, for instance, takeaway liquor outlets don't open until noon.

Wine

If you don't fancy a beer, then turn to wine like many Australians are doing. Parts of Australia have a climate conducive to wine production, and good-quality wines are relatively cheap and readily available all over the country. Most wine is sold in 750mL bottles or in 2 and 4L 'casks' (a great Australian innovation, sometimes known as Chateau Cardboard).

Wine drinking is not really the norm in the Territory – it's not unusual to see men drinking beer from bottles at the dinner table! Waiting staff outside Darwin and Alice will probably think you're pretty posh if you ask for a glass of wine – but don't be surprised if they offer you Chateau Cardboard.

It takes a little while to become familiar with Australian wines and their styles, especially since the manufacturers are being forced to delete generic names from their labels as exports increase; the biggest victim is 'champagne', which is now called 'sparkling wine'.

White wines are almost always drunk chilled and in summer or the outback many people chill their reds too.

Australia also produces excellent ports (perfect at a campfire) and superb muscats, but only mediocre sherries.

ENTERTAINMENT
Discos & Nightclubs

These are pretty much limited to Darwin, where there's a reasonable choice. Admission charges range from around $6 to $12.

Some places have certain dress standards, but it is generally left to the discretion of the people at the door – if they don't like the look of you, bad luck.

Live Music

A few pubs in Darwin and Alice Springs have live music, which are often great places for catching bands. The best way to find out about the local scene is to get to know some locals, or travellers who have spent some time in the place. Otherwise there are often listings in newspapers, particularly on Friday.

Cinemas
In Darwin, Alice Springs and Katherine there are a couple of commercial cinemas showing new-release mainstream movies. Elsewhere it's video only.

SPECTATOR SPORTS
Unfortunately the Territory doesn't offer a great deal to the armchair – or wooden bench – sports fan. Aussie Rules is the main game, although it is only played on local club level. Unlike down south when the football season is winter, in the Territory it is during the Wet.

During the non-football half of the year there's cricket, although again it is only played on a local level. Occasionally an interstate side will play a couple of games for some out-of-season match practice.

Australia loves to gamble, and hardly any town of even minor import is without a horse-racing track or a Totalisator Agency Board (TAB) betting office. Most towns host at least one annual country race meeting, and these can be great fun. Darwin and the Alice both have racing carnivals. In addition to these are rodeos held in major towns throughout the Territory in winter.

SHOPPING
There are lots of things definitely not to buy – plastic boomerangs, fake Aboriginal ashtrays and T-shirts, and all the other terrible souvenirs which fill the tacky souvenir shops in the big cities. Most of them come

from Taiwan or Korea anyway. Before buying an Australian souvenir, make sure it was actually made here!

Aboriginal Art
Aboriginal artwork has been 'discovered' by the international community, and prices are correspondingly high.

For most people the only thing remotely affordable are small carvings and some very beautiful screen-printed T-shirts produced by Aboriginal craft cooperatives. Didgeridoos and boomerangs are also popular purchases, but just be aware that unless you pay top dollar, what you are getting is something made purely for the tourist trade – these are certainly not the real thing.

Australiana
The term 'Australiana' is a euphemism for souvenirs. These are the things you buy as gifts for all the friends, aunts and uncles, nieces and nephews. They are supposedly representative of Australia and its culture, although many are extremely dubious.

The seeds of many of Australia's native plants are on sale all over the place. Try growing kangaroo paws back home (if your own country will allow them in).

Also gaining popularity are 'bush tucker' items such as tinned witchetty grubs, or honey ants. Bon appetit.

Opals
The opal is Australia's national gemstone and opals and jewellery made with it are popular souvenirs. It's a beautiful stone, but buy wisely and shop around – quality and prices can vary widely from place to place. There are a couple of shops in Alice Springs that specialise in opal jewellery.

Getting There & Away

AIR (INTERNATIONAL)

Basically getting to Australia means flying, although it is sometimes possible to hitch a ride on a yacht from Indonesia or the southwest Pacific.

The main problem with getting to Australia is that it's a long way from anywhere. Coming from Asia, Europe or North America there are lots of competing airlines and a wide variety of air fares, but there's no way you can avoid those great distances. Australia's current international popularity adds another problem – flights are often heavily booked. If you want to fly to Australia at a particularly popular time of year (the middle of summer, ie Christmas time, is notoriously difficult) or on a particularly popular route (like Hong Kong or Singapore to Sydney or Melbourne) then you need to plan well ahead.

In the Northern Territory the only international entry point is Darwin, and there are only limited options from here. The majority of visitors to the Northern Territory arrive here either by road or air from elsewhere in Australia.

Discount Tickets

Buying airline tickets these days is like shopping for a car, a stereo or a camera – five different travel agencies will quote you five different prices. Rule number one if you're looking for a cheap ticket is to go to an agent, not directly to the airline. The airline can usually only quote you the absolutely by-the-rule-book regular fare. An agent, on the other hand, can offer all sorts of special deals, particularly on competitive routes.

Ideally an airline would like to fly all its flights with every seat in use and every passenger paying the highest fare possible. Fortunately life usually isn't like that and airlines would rather have a half-price passenger than an empty seat. When faced with the problem of too many seats, they will either let agents sell them at cut prices, or oc-casionally make one-off special offers on particular routes – watch the travel ads in the press.

Of course what's available and what it costs depends on what time of year it is, what route you're flying and who you're flying with. If you're flying on a popular route (like from Hong Kong) or one where the choice of flights is very limited (like from South America or, to a lesser extent, from Africa) then the fare is likely to be higher or there may be nothing available but the official fare.

Similarly the dirt cheap fares are likely to be less conveniently scheduled, go by a less convenient route or be with a less popular airline. Flying London-Sydney, for example, is most convenient with airlines like Qantas, British Airways, Thai International or Singapore Airlines. They have flights every day, they operate the same flight straight through to Australia and they're good, reliable, comfortable, safe airlines. At the other extreme you could fly from London to an Eastern European or Middle Eastern city on one flight, switch to another flight from there to Asia, and change to another airline from there to Australia. It takes longer, there are delays and changes of aircraft along the way, the airlines may not be so good and, furthermore, the connection only works once a week and that means leaving London at 1.30 on a Wednesday morning. The flip side is it's cheaper.

Round-the-World Tickets

Round-the-World (RTW) tickets are very popular these days and many of these will take you through Australia. The airline RTW tickets are often real bargains and since Australia is pretty much at the other side of the world from Europe or North America it can work out no more expensive, or even cheaper, to keep going in the same direction right round the world rather than U-turn to return.

Air Travel Glossary

Baggage Allowance This will be written on your ticket and usually includes one 20kg item to go in the hold, plus one item of hand luggage.

Bucket Shops These are unbonded travel agencies specialising in discounted airline tickets.

Bumped Just because you have a confirmed seat doesn't mean you're going to get on the plane (see Overbooking).

Cancellation Penalties If you have to cancel or change a discounted ticket, there are often heavy penalties involved; insurance can sometimes be taken out against these penalties. Some airlines impose penalties on regular tickets as well, particularly against 'no-show' passengers.

Check-In Airlines ask you to check in a certain time ahead of the flight departure (usually one to two hours on international flights). If you fail to check in on time and the flight is overbooked, the airline can cancel your booking and give your seat to somebody else.

Confirmation Having a ticket written out with the flight and date you want doesn't mean you have a seat until the agent has checked with the airline that your status is 'OK' or confirmed. Meanwhile you could just be 'on request'.

Courier Fares Businesses often need to send urgent documents or freight securely and quickly. Courier companies hire people to accompany the package through customs and, in return, offer a discount ticket which is sometimes a phenomenal bargain. In effect, what the companies do is ship their freight as your luggage on regular commercial flights. This is a legitimate operation, but there are two shortcomings – the short turnaround time of the ticket (usually not longer than a month) and the limitation on your luggage allowance. You may have to surrender all your allowance and take only carry-on luggage.

Full Fares Airlines traditionally offer 1st class (coded F), business class (coded J) and economy class (coded Y) tickets. These days there are so many promotional and discounted fares available that few passengers pay full economy fare.

ITX An ITX, or 'independent inclusive tour excursion', is often available on tickets to popular holiday destinations. Officially it's a package deal combined with hotel accommodation, but many agents will sell you one of these for the flight only and give you phoney hotel vouchers in the unlikely event that you're challenged at the airport.

Lost Tickets If you lose your airline ticket an airline will usually treat it like a travellers cheque and, after inquiries, issue you with another one. Legally, however, an airline is entitled to treat it like cash and if you lose it then it's gone forever. Take good care of your tickets.

MCO An MCO, or 'miscellaneous charge order', is a voucher that looks like an airline ticket but carries no destination or date. It can be exchanged through any International Association of Travel Agents (IATA) airline for a ticket on a specific flight. It's a useful alternative to an onward ticket in those countries that demand one, and is more flexible than an ordinary ticket if you're unsure of your route.

No-Shows No-shows are passengers who fail to show up for their flight. Full-fare passengers who fail to turn up are sometimes entitled to travel on a later flight. The rest are penalised (see Cancellation Penalties).

On Request This is an unconfirmed booking for a flight.

Air Travel Glossary

Onward Tickets An entry requirement for many countries is that you have a ticket out of the country. If you're unsure of your next move, the easiest solution is to buy the cheapest onward ticket to a neighbouring country or a ticket from a reliable airline which can later be refunded if you do not use it.

Open Jaw Tickets These are return tickets where you fly out to one place but return from another. If available, this can save you backtracking to your arrival point.

Overbooking Airlines hate to fly empty seats and since every flight has some passengers who fail to show up, airlines often book more passengers than they have seats. Usually excess passengers make up for the no-shows, but occasionally somebody gets bumped. Guess who it is most likely to be? The passengers who check in late.

Point-to-Point Tickets These are discount tickets that can be bought on some routes in return for passengers waiving their rights to a stopover.

Promotional Fares These are officially discounted fares, available from travel agencies or direct from the airline.

Reconfirmation At least 72 hours prior to departure time of an onward or return flight, you must contact the airline and 'reconfirm' that you intend to be on the flight. If you don't do this the airline can delete your name from the passenger list and you could lose your seat.

Restrictions Discounted tickets often have various restrictions on them – such as needing to be paid for in advance and incurring a penalty to be altered. Others are restrictions on the minimum and maximum period you must be away, such as a minimum of 14 days or a maximum of one year.

Round-the-World Tickets RTW tickets give you a limited period (usually a year) in which to circumnavigate the globe. You can go anywhere the carrying airlines go, as long as you don't backtrack. The number of stopovers or total number of separate flights is decided before you set off and they usually cost a bit more than a basic return flight.

Stand-by This is a discounted ticket where you only fly if there is a seat free at the last moment. Stand-by fares are usually available only on domestic routes.

Travel Agencies Travel agencies vary widely and you should choose one that suits your needs. Some simply handle tours, while full-services agencies handle everything from tours and tickets to car rental and hotel bookings. If all you want is a ticket at the lowest possible price, then go to an agency specialising in discounted tickets.

Transferred Tickets Airline tickets cannot be transferred from one person to another. Travellers sometimes try to sell the return half of their ticket, but officials can ask you to prove that you are the person named on the ticket. This is less likely to happen on domestic flights, but on an international flight tickets are compared with passports.

Travel Periods Ticket prices vary with the time of year. There is a low (off-peak) season and a high (peak) season, and often a low-shoulder season and a high-shoulder season as well. Usually the fare depends on your outward flight – if you depart in the high season and return in the low season, you pay the high-season fare.

The official airline RTW tickets are usually put together by a combination of two airlines, and permit you to fly anywhere you want on their route systems so long as you do not backtrack. Other restrictions are that you (usually) must book the first sector in advance and cancellation penalties then apply. There may be restrictions on how many stops you are permitted and usually the tickets are valid from 90 days up to a year. A typical price for a South Pacific RTW ticket is around US$2000.

An alternative type of RTW ticket is one put together by a travel agent using a combination of discounted tickets from a number of airlines. A UK agent like Trailfinders can put together interesting London-to-London RTW combinations including Australia for between £895 and £1100.

Departure Tax

There is a $30 departure tax when leaving Australia, but this is often incorporated into the price of your air ticket and so is not always paid as a separate tax.

The UK

The cheapest tickets in London are from the numerous 'bucket shops' (discount-ticket agencies) which advertise in magazines and papers like *Time Out*, *Southern Cross* and *TNT*. Pick up one or two of these publications and ring round a few bucket shops to find the best deal. The magazine *Business Traveller* also has a great deal of good advice on air-fare bargains. Most bucket shops are trustworthy and reliable but the occasional sharp operator appears – *Time Out* and *Business Traveller* give some useful advice on precautions to take.

Trailfinders (☎ 020-7938 3366) at 194 Kensington High St, London W8 7RC, and STA Travel (☎ 020-7581 4132) at 74 Old Brompton Rd, London SW7 3LQ, and 117 Euston Rd, London NW1 2SX (☎ 020-7465 0484) are good, reliable agents for cheap tickets.

The cheapest London to Sydney or Melbourne bucket-shop (not direct) tickets are about £339/550 one way/return. Cheap fares to Perth are around £309/549 one way/return. Such prices are usually only available if you leave London in the low season – March to June. In September and mid-December fares go up by about 30%, while the rest of the year they're somewhere in between. Average direct high-season fares to Sydney and Melbourne are £554/700 one way/return and for Perth £459/699 one way/return.

From Australia you can expect to pay around A$895/1075 one way/return to London and other European capitals, with stops in Asia on the way, in the low season, and A$1399/1870 in the high season.

North America

There is a variety of connections across the Pacific from Los Angeles, San Francisco and Vancouver to Australia, including direct flights, flights via New Zealand, island-hopping routes and more circuitous Pacific rim routes via nations in Asia. Qantas, Air New Zealand and United all fly USA-Australia; Qantas, Air New Zealand and Canadian Airlines International fly Canada-Australia. An interesting option from the east coast is Northwest's flight via Japan.

To find good fares to Australia check the travel ads in the Sunday travel sections of papers such as the *Los Angeles Times*, *San Francisco Chronicle-Examiner*, *New York Times* or *Toronto Globe & Mail*. You can typically get a one-way/return ticket from the west coast for US$998/1498 in the low season, US$1058/1558 in the high season (Australian summer/Christmas period) or from the east coast for US$1179/1378 one way/return in the low season and US$1609/1878 in the high season. In the USA good agents for discounted tickets are the two student travel operators, Council Travel and STA Travel, both of which have lots of offices around the country. Canadian west-coast fares out of Vancouver will be similar to those from the US west coast. From Toronto fares go from around C$1790/2200 one way/return during the low season and C$2055/2550 in the high season; from Vancouver they cost C$1370/

1610 during the low season and C$1790/2110 during the high season.

If Pacific island-hopping is your aim, check out the airlines of Pacific island nations, some of which have good deals on indirect routings. Qantas can give you Fiji or Tahiti along the way, while Air New Zealand can offer both and the Cook Islands as well.

One-way/return fares available from Australia include: San Francisco A$1030/1530 in the low season (high season A$1030/1830), New York A$1200/1780 (A$1200/2080) and Vancouver A$1030/1530 (A$1030/1830).

New Zealand

Air New Zealand and Qantas operate a network of trans-Tasman flights linking Auckland, Wellington and Christchurch in New Zealand with most major Australian gateway cities. You can fly directly between a lot of places in New Zealand and a lot of places in Australia.

Fares vary depending on which cities you fly between and when you do it, but from New Zealand to Sydney you're looking at around NZ$345/459 one way/return in the low season, NZ$425/650 high season, and to Melbourne NZ$470/529 in the low season, NZ$495/730 high season. There is a lot of competition on this route, with United and British Airways both flying it as well as Qantas and Air New Zealand, so there is bound to be some good discounting going on.

Cheap fares to New Zealand from Europe will usually be for flights via the USA. A straightforward London-Auckland return bucket-shop ticket costs around £599 in the low season, £800 high season. Coming via Australia you can continue right around on a RTW ticket which will cost from around £895 for a ticket with a comprehensive choice of stopovers.

Asia

Ticket discounting is widespread in Asia, particularly in Singapore, Hong Kong, Bangkok and Penang. There are a lot of fly-by-night operators in the Asian ticketing scene so a little care is required. Also the Asian routes have been particularly caught up in the capacity shortages on flights to Australia. Flights between Hong Kong and Australia are notoriously heavily booked while flights to or from Bangkok and Singapore are often part of the longer Europe-Australia route so they are also sometimes very full. Plan ahead. For much more information on South-East Asian travel and on to Australia see Lonely Planet's *South-East Asia on a shoestring*.

Typical one-way fares to Australia from Singapore are S$638 to Darwin (or Perth), S$895 to Sydney or Melbourne.

The cheapest way out of Australia is to take the Merpati flight between Darwin and Kupang, on the island of Timor. One-way/return fares are A$244/396 (low season) and A$319/489 (high season). Because of political changes you must be able to show an onward ticket on arrival in Kupang, and Merpati will not issue a ticket without an onward (or return) booking.

Africa

The flight possibilities between Africa and Australia have increased markedly in the last few years, and there are a number of direct flights each week between Perth and Harare (Zimbabwe) or Johannesburg (South Africa). Both routes cost around A$1060/1590 one way/return in the low season (high season A$1200/1890).

Other airlines that connect southern Africa and Australia include Malaysia Airlines (via Kuala Lumpur), Singapore Airlines (via Singapore) and Air Mauritius (via Mauritius).

From East Africa the options are to fly via Mauritius or Zimbabwe, or via the Indian subcontinent, and on to South-East Asia, then connect from there to Australia.

AIR (DOMESTIC)

Australia is so vast (and in many parts so empty) that unless your time is unlimited you will probably have to take to the air sooner or later.

There are only two main domestic carriers within Australia, Qantas (☎ 13 1313) and Ansett (☎ 13 1300). For 40-odd years Australia had a 'two-airline policy' but, despite the fact that the airline industry is deregulated, they have a duopoly on domestic flights.

With this cosy cohabitation the airlines charge virtually what they like and operate virtually identical schedules. Domestic airline travel within Australia is expensive and the choices of flights limited, particularly on the low-volume routes, although discounting is now a regular feature of the domestic flights scene.

Unfortunately there is only limited discounting on flights into and out of the Northern Territory, so advance-purchase deals are about the best you can hope for.

Note that all domestic flights in Australia are nonsmoking. Because Qantas flies both international and domestic routes, flights leave from both the international and domestic terminals at Australian airports. Flights with flight numbers from QF001 to QF399 operate from international terminals; flight numbers QF400 and above operate from domestic terminals.

Cheap Fares
Random Discounting A major feature of the deregulated air-travel industry is random discounting. As the airlines try harder to fill planes, they often offer substantial discounts on selected routes – mainly the heavy volume routes but that's not always the case.

To make the most of the discounted fares, you need to keep in touch with what's currently on offer, mainly because there are usually conditions attached to cheap fares – such as booking 14 or so days in advance, flying only on weekends or between certain dates and so on. Also the number of seats available is usually fairly limited. The further ahead you can plan the better.

It is fair to say that on virtually any route in the country covered by Qantas or Ansett the full economy fare will not be the cheapest way to go. Because the situation is so fluid, the special fares will more than likely have changed by the time you read this. For that reason we list the full one-way economy fares. Discounts are generally greater for return rather than one-way travel.

Some Possibilities If you're planning a return trip and you have 14 days up your sleeve then you can save 45% by travelling Apex. You have to book for your tickets 14 days in advance, pay at least three days before flying and you must stay away at least one Saturday night. You must allow 14 days if you wish to change flight details, but the tickets are nonrefundable. If you book seven days in advance the saving is 35% off the full fare.

For one-way travel, if you can book three days in advance a saving of around 10% is offered; for five days a savings of 15%, seven-day advance booking the discount is around 20% and if you have the time a 21-day advance booking has a discount of around 60%.

University or other higher education students under the age of 26 can get a 25% discount off the regular economy fare. An airline tertiary concession card (available from the airlines) is required for Australian students. Overseas students can use their International Student Identity Card.

All nonresident international travellers can get up to a 40% discount on internal Qantas flights and 30% on Ansett flights simply by presenting their international ticket when booking. It seems there is no limit to the number of domestic flights you can take, it doesn't matter which airline you fly into Australia with, and it doesn't have to be on a return ticket. Note that the discount applies only to the full economy fare, and so in many cases it will be cheaper to take advantage of other discounts offered. The best advice is to ring around and explore the options before you buy.

Air Passes
With discounting being the norm these days, air passes do not represent the value they did in pre-deregulation days. However, there are a few worth checking out if you plan to fly quite a bit in Australia. If the Territory is your only destination, a pass would be of no use at all.

Qantas Two passes are offered by Qantas. The Boomerang Pass can only be purchased overseas and involves purchasing coupons for either short-haul flights at $220 one way, or for long-haul sectors (such as from just about anywhere to Yulara, the service village for Uluru-Kata Tjuta National Park) for $275. You must purchase a minimum of two coupons before you arrive in Australia, and at the time of buying your international ticket. When you are in Australia you can buy up to eight more, but only if you can show proof of your international ticket and the first two coupons.

There is also the Qantas Backpackers Pass, which can only be bought in Australia on production of identification such as a YHA membership, a VIP Backpackers or Independent Backpackers Card or ISIC. You must initially purchase a minimum of three one-way coupons (such as Sydney-Yulara, Yulara-Darwin and Darwin-Cairns), and stay away a minimum of seven nights. Additional coupons can be purchased two at a time (six is the maximum); you must stay away at least two nights at each stop. The coupons are valid for 12 months. Fares are nonrefundable but you can rebook or reroute subject to payment of extra fare if applicable. The discount is quite substantial; a sample fare using this pass is Sydney to Yulara for $292 one way, as against the full economy fare of $558.

Ansett Two similar passes are also offered by Ansett. The G'day Airpass works the same as the Qantas Boomerang Pass – the fares are identical and it must also be purchased overseas.

The Ansett Backpackers Pass works much the same way as the Qantas Backpackers Pass except there is no restriction on the maximum amount of coupons you can buy.

Airport Transport
There are private or public bus services at Darwin, Alice Springs and Yulara airports. In smaller places you'll probably be able to cadge a lift with airline staff, who often make a special trip to the airport/airstrip to meet the flight.

Warning
This section is particularly vulnerable to change – prices for international travel are volatile, routes are introduced and cancelled, schedules change, rules are amended, special deals come and go. Airlines and governments seem to take a perverse pleasure in making price structures and regulations as complicated as possible and you should check directly with the airline or travel agent to make sure you understand how a fare (and ticket you may buy) works.

In addition, the travel industry is highly competitive and there are many lurks and perks. The upshot of this is that you should get quotes and advice from as many airlines and travel agents as possible before you part with your hard-earned cash. The details given in this chapter should be regarded only as pointers and cannot be any substitute for your own careful, up-to-date research.

AIR-BUS PASSES
A company called OZ Experience (☎ 1300 301 359) offers the Air-Bus Pass – various combinations that allow you to do part of your trip by air (say, the boring parts) and part by road at competitive prices. There are some 20 available combinations throughout Australia, a number of which include the Northern Territory. All flights are with Qantas and the bus sections are with various tour operators. You can get off and on at any of the stops along the bus routes. These passes are only available to international travellers with proof that their travel originated from a country other than Australia. Restrictions include that a ticket becomes void after the passing of a confirmed departure date, although you can change your date of travel, that you must confirm your seat 48 hours prior to departure and there is a 100% cancellation fee.

For example, the 'Devils Bollocks Pass' is valid for 12 months and allows you to fly

Sydney-Darwin, bus Darwin-Alice Springs, fly Alice Springs-Cairns, bus Cairns-Sydney for A$1085; and with the 'Wombat Pass', also valid for 12 months, you can fly Sydney-Alice Springs then Alice Springs-Cairns, and take a bus Cairns-Sydney for A$815. Some of the bus routes go off the beaten-track and include side trips and guides.

LAND

Basically to get to the Territory overland you must travel a bloody long way. The nearest state capital to Darwin is Brisbane, a distance of about 3500km!

Bus

A great many travellers see Australia by bus because it's one of the best ways to come to grips with the country's size and changing landscape. The bus companies have comprehensive networks (far more comprehensive, in fact, than the railway system) on which you can have the freedom to get off and on wherever you choose. The buses all look pretty similar, and are equipped with air-conditioning, toilets and videos.

There are two major bus companies in Australia – Greyhound Pioneer (☎ toll-free 13 2030), which has routes all over the mainland; and McCafferty's (☎ toll-free 13 1499), which operates out of Brisbane and services all mainland states except WA.

Greyhound Pioneer operates services into and out of the Territory on three routes – the Western Australian route from Broome, Derby and Kununurra; the Queensland route through Mt Isa to Three Ways; or straight up the Stuart Hwy from Adelaide.

McCafferty's operates the Queensland route and up from Adelaide.

Fares can vary a bit between the companies, but if one discounts a fare the other tends to follow quite quickly. Greyhound Pioneer has advance-purchase fares which can be as much as 50% off the normal fare if you book ahead (usually at least 15 days).

Greyhound Pioneer and McCafferty's have a variety of passes available, and if you are travelling extensively in Australia

they can be excellent value. The set-route passes are the most popular as they give you a set amount of time (usually three, six or 12 months) to cover a route; many of these include the highlights of the Territory – Uluru and Kakadu – as well Darwin, Alice Springs and all the towns along the Stuart Hwy.

The Kilometre Passes are also good value, allowing you to travel any route, get off and on as you choose and even backtrack until all your purchased kilometres have run out.

Discounts apply to YHA, VIP, Nomads, Student and Independent Backpacker card holders. The fares quoted here are all full one-way fares.

Queensland Sample fares and times from Queensland to Darwin include Mt Isa ($176; 21 hours), Cairns ($289; 40 hours) and Brisbane ($310; 47 hours). A one-way trip from Cairns to Alice Springs costs $266 and takes 34 hours.

Most services from Queensland have a change of buses at Tennant Creek.

Western Australia Greyhound Pioneer leaves Perth daily for Darwin, travelling through Kununurra, Broome and Port Hedland en route. All buses stop at Katherine.

Some sample fares and times to Darwin from points in WA are Perth ($436; 58 hours), Broome ($202; 27 hours) and Kununurra ($102; 12 hours).

An alternative is to go from Perth to Port Augusta (in South Australia) and up the centre to Alice Springs ($324; 55 hours).

South Australia From Adelaide it is possible to go direct to Alice Springs via Coober Pedy, or you can get off at Erldunda and connect with services to Yulara (Uluru-Kata Tjuta National Park), 244km to the west along the Lasseter Hwy.

Greyhound Pioneer and McCafferty's have daily services from Adelaide to Alice Springs ($135; 19 hours). From Coober Pedy the fare is $75 and the journey takes about eight hours.

Interstate Quarantine

When travelling between states in Australia, whether by land or air, you may come across signs (mainly at airports, interstate railway stations and state borders) warning of the possible dangers of carrying fruit, plants and vegetables which may be infected with a disease or pest from one area to another.

The reason is that certain pests and diseases – fruit fly, cucurbit thrips, grape phylloxera and potato cyst nematodes, to name a few – are prevalent in some areas but not in others and authorities are trying to limit the spread of such problems. Most quarantine control relies on honesty and some quarantine posts at the state/territory borders are not always staffed.

One exception is the border with Western Australia which is manned 24 hours and sometimes employs dogs to sniff out offending matter. This may seem excessive (after all, insects don't respect state borders), but it's taken very seriously. It's prohibited to carry fresh fruit and vegetables, plants, flowers, and even nuts and honey across the Northern Territory/Western Australia border in either direction. The controls with South Australia and Queensland are less strict – there's usually an honesty bin for disposal even if the post isn't manned. Check at the borders.

In the Top End there are also checkpoints on the Arnhem Hwy en route to Kakadu National Park and south down the Stuart Hwy near the Batchelor turn-off. If you buy any fruit or vegetables before heading out this way, make sure you get a quarantine certificate from the place you bought them – it's a formality only – and keep the offending items in their bags until you pass the checkpoint.

If you want to go direct to Yulara, the journey from Adelaide takes 20 hours and costs $135 ($100; eight hours from Coober Pedy).

Other Bus Options There are a few companies that offer flexible transport options in various parts of the country, and are a good alternative to the big bus companies. The trips are generally aimed at budget travellers and so are good fun, and are a combination of straightforward bus travel and an organised tour. The buses are generally smaller and so not necessarily as comfortable as those of the big bus companies, but it's a much more interesting way to travel – see the Organised Tours section later in this chapter.

Train

The famous *Ghan* train (see the boxed text) connects the Centre with Adelaide and Melbourne. It is a popular route into the Territory, mainly because it means you don't have to drive all the way or sit on a bus.

Modes of travel are economy seat (no sleeper and no meals), economy berth (a sleeper with shared facilities and no meals) and 1st class sleeper (a self-contained sleeper and meals).

The cost one way from Melbourne to Alice Springs is $250/525/840 for an economy seat/economy berth/1st class sleeper. The *Ghan* departs Melbourne once a week – on Wednesday – at 10.35 pm.

The train departs Adelaide on Monday and Thursday at 3 pm, arriving in Alice Springs the next day at 10 am. From Alice Springs the departure is on Tuesday and Friday at 1 pm, arriving in Adelaide the next day at 7.40 am. Between Adelaide and Alice Springs the *Ghan* costs $170/351/539.

You can also join the *Ghan* at Port Augusta, the connection point on the Sydney to Perth railway route. Fares between Alice Springs and Port Augusta are $136/295/500.

It's a popular route and bookings are recommended. Discounted fares are sometimes offered, especially in the low season (February through June excluding Christmas). For bookings phone ☎ 13 2232.

It is also possible to put your car on the *Ghan*, which gives you transport when you arrive and again saves the long drive from

The Ghan

One of the best ways to get to the Territory is on the famous *Ghan* train. Although it's not the adventure it once was, it is still one of the great Australian railway journeys.

The *Ghan* saga started in 1877, when it was decided to build a railway line from Adelaide to Darwin. The line took more than 50 years to reach Alice Springs and as we head into the 21st century they're still thinking about laying the final 1500km to Darwin. But things didn't get off to an auspicious beginning – the line was built in the wrong place to start with.

Because all the creek beds north of Marree were bone dry and nobody had ever seen rain out there, it was concluded that rain wouldn't fall in the future. In fact the initial stretch of line was laid right across a flood plain and when the rain came, even though it soon dried up, the line was simply washed away. In the century or so that the original *Ghan* line survived the tracks were washed away regularly.

The wrong route was only part of the *Ghan's* problems. At first it was built as a wide gauge track to Marree, then extended as narrow gauge to Oodnadatta in 1884. But the foundations were flimsy, the sleepers too light, the grading too steep and the whole thing meandered hopelessly. It was hardly surprising that right up to the end the top speed of the old *Ghan* was a flat-out 30km/h!

Early rail travellers went from Adelaide to Marree on the broad-gauge line, changed there for Oodnadatta, then had to make the final journey to Alice Springs by camel train. The Afghani-led camel trains had pioneered transport through the outback and it was from these Afghanis that the *Ghan* took its name.

Finally in 1929 the line was extended from Oodnadatta to Alice Springs. Though the *Ghan* was a great adventure, it was slow and uncomfortable as it bounced and bucked its way down the badly laid line. It was unreliable and expensive to run, and worst of all, a heavy rainfall could strand it at either end or even in the middle. Parachute drops of supplies to stranded train travellers became part of outback lore and on one occasion the *Ghan* rolled in 10 days late!

By the early 1970s the South Australian state railway system was taken over by the Federal government and a new line to Alice Springs was planned. At a cost of A$145 million, a standard gauge was to be laid from Tarcoola, north-west of Port Augusta on the transcontinental line, to Alice Springs – and it would be laid where rain would not wash it out. In 1980 the line was completed in circumstances that would be unusual for any major project today, let alone an Australian one – it was ahead of time and on budget.

In the late '80s the old *Ghan* made its last run and the old line was subsequently torn up. One of its last appearances was in the film *Mad Max III*.

Whereas the old train took 140 passengers and, under ideal conditions, made the trip in 50 hours, the new train is a rather more modern and comfortable affair that takes twice as many passengers and does it in 24 hours. The *Ghan* may not be the adventure it once was, but it's still a great trip.

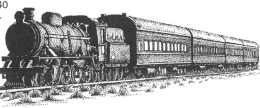

The old Ghan

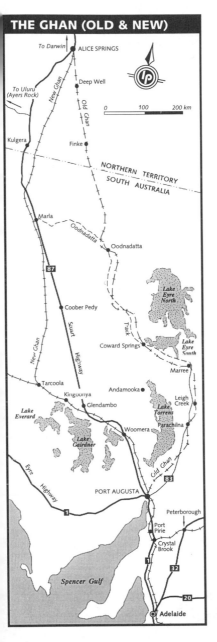

THE GHAN (OLD & NEW)

To Darwin — ALICE SPRINGS
Deep Well
To Uluru (Ayers Rock)
Kulgera
Finke
NORTHERN TERRITORY
SOUTH AUSTRALIA
Marla
Oodnadatta
Oodnadatta
87
Lake Eyre North
Coober Pedy
Lake Eyre South
Coward Springs
Marree
Tarcoola
Andamooka
Kingoonya
Leigh Creek
Glendambo
Lake Torrens
Lake Everard
Woomera
Parachilna
Lake Gairdner
Old Ghan
83
Eyre Highway
PORT AUGUSTA
Peterborough
Port Pirie
Crystal Brook
1
32
Spencer Gulf
20
Adelaide

the south. The cost from Alice Springs to Adelaide is $220 (but it's $300 from Adelaide to Alice Springs) and $380 between Melbourne and Alice Springs. Check the time by which you need to have your car at the terminal for loading: it's normally several hours before departure so the train can be 'made up'.

Car & Motorcycle
See the Getting Around chapter for details of road rules, driving conditions and information on buying and renting vehicles.

The main roads into the Territory are the Barkly Hwy from Mt Isa and north Queensland; the Victoria Hwy from the Kimberley in Western Australia; and the Stuart Hwy from South Australia. All are bitumen roads in excellent condition, the main problem being the sheer distances involved.

Hitching
Hitching is never entirely safe in any country in the world, and we don't recommend it. Travellers who decide to hitch should understand that they are taking a small but potentially serious risk.

Hitching is possible, but again, the distances involved make it difficult. Expect to be stuck for a day or so waiting for a ride. Katherine (where the Victoria Hwy branches off west to WA) and Three Ways (where the Barkly Hwy heads east for Queensland) are renowned spots for this.

For more information on hitching in the Territory, see the Getting Around chapter.

SEA
It is simply not possible to get to Darwin (or any other Australian port for that matter) on a scheduled shipping service. It may be possible to pick up a ride on a yacht in Indonesia or Singapore, but you'd have to be lucky – ask around during the Darwin-Ambon Yacht Race (see Special Events in the Darwin chapter for details).

ORGANISED TOURS
A number of tour operators offer transport into the Territory from other states. These

alternatives to the main bus companies usually get you off the beaten track on long interstate trips and the cost includes camping accommodation, meals and sightseeing en route. They're very informal and we've received some enthusiastic letters about this style of travel. YHA, VIP and student discounts are often available, and you should ask about stand-by rates.

One operator, Cool Croc (☎ toll-free 1800 688 458), does the popular Cairns-Darwin run and offers 4WD camping trips through the remote Gulf of Carpentaria; the six day trip costs $540 (YHA, VIP and students $489).

The Wayward Bus (☎ toll-free 1800 882 823) does an eight day trip between Adelaide and Alice Springs ($640) that takes in the Flinders Ranges, Coober Pedy, Oodnadatta Track, Uluru-Kata Tjuta and Watarrka (Kings Canyon) National Parks, and Alice Springs.

Wilderness Challenge (☎ 07 4055 6504) offers comfortable nine-day camping 4WD trips from Broome to Darwin, although at $1495 these are not cheap.

A similar trip with Northern Territory Adventure Tours (☎ toll-free 1800 063 838) travels from Broome to Darwin ($995; eight days) via the Gibb River Rd in the Kimberley.

An alternative route to/from Perth is via the Great Victoria Desert – some of the most remote and least-visited country on earth. Travelabout (☎ toll-free 1800 621 200) offers a six day bush camping 4WD trip from Perth to Alice Springs for $599. It also has an Overland Express ($250; 2½ days) that follows the same route and departs from Alice Springs every Monday.

Another way of tackling the Great Victoria Desert is on a bicycle, and Remote Outback Cycle Tours (☎ toll-free 1800 244 614) offers a tour including bikes and bike treks along the way; the five day trip costs $650.

OZ Experience (☎ 1300 301 359) offers Air-Bus Passes, many of which can include the Territory. The air travel component is with Qantas and various tour companies throughout Australia cover the bus tour section. See the Air-Bus Passes section earlier in this chapter for details.

Getting Around

AIR

Ansett (☎ 13 1300) and Qantas (☎ 13 1313) fly throughout the Territory (see the Getting There & Away chapter for further details).

Another airline operating within the Northern Territory is Airnorth (☎ toll-free 1800 627 474 or ☎ 8945 2866 in Darwin) connects Darwin and Alice Springs with most places in the Territory, including Bathurst Island, Arnhem Land, Borroloola, Gove, Kalkaringi, Katherine, Tennant Creek and Victoria River Downs. See the chart for fare details.

The regional airline in Western Australia, Ansett Sky West (☎ 13 1300), also connects Darwin with the Kimberley.

BUS

Greyhound Pioneer Australia (☎ toll-free 13 2030) and McCafferty's (☎ toll-free 13 1499) both have extensive services throughout the Northern Territory – see the Getting There & Away chapter for details of the fares and passes offered by the two companies.

Backpackers Bus

A good budget alternative for travel around the Top End – at least between Darwin, Kakadu, Katherine, Nitmiluk (Katherine) and Litchfield – is The Blue Banana (☎ 8945 6800, banana@taunet.net.au), named after a similar service called Go Blue Banana in Scotland. It does a regular round trip – clockwise – from Darwin via Kakadu to Katherine and back via Litchfield, stopping at several other attractions and points of interest en route. A ticket, valid for three months, allows you to jump on and off as you choose. Departures are on Thursday, Friday, Sunday and Monday from Darwin, and Saturday, Sunday, Tuesday and Wednesday from Katherine. When you're ready to move on just phone and book the next sector (24 hours notice is required – more in the peak tourist season).

The full round trip costs $170 and other

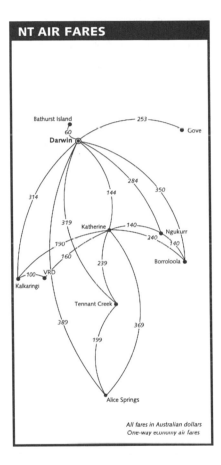

NT AIR FARES

All fares in Australian dollars
One-way economy air fares

options are Darwin to Katherine via Kakadu ($100), Katherine to Darwin via Litchfield ($90), a round trip from/to Darwin excluding Katherine ($140), and Jabiru to Katherine via Ubirr, Cooinda and Gunlom ($70). Prices do not include Kakadu National Park entrance fees.

The Blue Banana picks you up from your accommodation in Darwin or Katherine, and offers a 10% discount to YHA, VIP, ITC and Nomads card holders.

Blue Banana scheduled stops are listed in the relevant Getting There & Away sections of the Around Darwin, Kakadu & Arnhem Land and Katherine & Victoria River District chapters.

CAR

Distances in the Northern Territory are enormous. Access to many places by public transport is not possible, so the car is the accepted means of getting from A to B. More and more travellers are also finding it the best way to see the country. Between three or four people the costs are reasonable and the benefits many, provided of course you don't have a major mechanical problem.

Road Rules

Australians drive on the left-hand side of the road just like in the UK, Japan and most countries in south and east Asia and the Pacific. There are a few local variations from the rules of the road as applied elsewhere in the West. The main one is the 'give way to the right' rule – if an intersection is unmarked (unusual), you must give way to vehicles entering the intersection from your right.

The general speed limit in built-up areas is 60km/h. On the open highway in the Northern Territory, there is no speed limit outside built-up areas unless marked.

Almost all cars in Australia have seat belts front and back which you're required to wear – or face a fine if you don't. Small children must be belted into an approved safety seat.

On the Road

Road Conditions All major highways are bitumen roads engineered to a pretty high standard. A number of secondary roads are just a single-lane strip of bitumen known as 'beef roads'. By 1975 the Commonwealth government had spent $30 million on 2500km of roads in an effort to promote the beef cattle industry. One of these single-lane bitumen roads is the Delamere Rd, which runs from the Victoria Hwy to Wave Hill station, another is the Carpentaria Hwy from the Stuart Hwy to Borroloola.

However, you don't have to go far to find yourself on dirt roads, and anybody who sets out to see the country in reasonable detail will have to do some dirt-road travelling. If you seriously want to explore, then you'd better plan on having four-wheel drive (4WD) and a winch. A few useful spare parts are worth carrying if you're travelling on highways in the Northern Territory. A broken fan belt can be a damned nuisance if the next service station is 200km away.

Drink-Driving This is a big problem, especially in country areas. Serious attempts have been made in recent years to reduce the road toll – random breath tests are not uncommon in built-up areas. If you're caught with a blood-alcohol concentration of more than 0.08% then be prepared for a hefty fine and the loss of your licence.

Fuel Super, diesel, unleaded and LPG are available from stations sporting well-known international brand names. Prices vary from place to place, but generally it's in the 80-90c a litre range and closer to $1 in remote areas. In the outback the price can soar and some outback service stations are not above exploiting their monopoly. Distances between fill-ups can be long in the outback.

Hazards Cows and kangaroos are two common hazards on country roads throughout Australia, and camels and horses are two others in the Territory. A collision is likely to kill the animal and seriously damage your vehicle. Kangaroos are most active around dawn and dusk, and often travel in groups. If you see one hopping across the road in front of you, slow right down – its friends are probably just behind it. If one hops out right in front of you, hit the brakes and only swerve to avoid the animal if it is safe to do so. Many people have been killed in accidents caused by swerving to miss an animal. It's better to damage your car and probably kill the animal than kill yourself and others with you.

Many Australians try to avoid travelling altogether between 5 pm and 8 am, because of the hazards posed by animals.

Another thing to watch for are the road trains throughout the Territory. These consist of a prime mover and two, or usually three, trailers. On dual-lane highways they pose few problems, although you do need to allow a surprisingly long distance when overtaking. On single-lane bitumen roads you need to get right off the road if one approaches, because you can be sure it won't! On dirt roads you also need to pull over, and often stop altogether while you wait for the dust cloud to clear. Overtaking road trains on these roads is hazardous. Often it's best just to have a break for a while and let the road train get well ahead of you.

Outback Travel If you really want to see outback Australia there are still a lot of roads where the official recommendation is that you report to the police before you leave one end, and again when you arrive at the other. That way if you fail to turn up at the other end they can send a search party. Nevertheless many of these tracks are now much better kept than in years past and you don't need a 4WD or fancy expedition equipment to tackle them. However, you must be carefully prepared and carry important spare parts. Backtracking 300km to pick up some minor malfunctioning component or, much worse, to arrange a tow, is unlikely to be easy or cheap. When travelling to really remote areas it is advisable to travel with a high-frequency outpost radio transmitter that is equipped to pick up the Royal Flying Doctor Service bases in the area.

You will need to carry a fair amount of water in case of disaster – around 20 litres a person is sensible – stored in more than one container. Food is less important and the space might be better allocated to an extra spare tyre.

The Automobile Association of the Northern Territory (AANT) can advise on preparation and supply maps and track notes. Most tracks have an ideal time of year. In the Centre it's not wise to attempt the tough tracks during the heat of summer (November-March) when the dust can be severe; chances of mechanical trouble are much greater; and water will be scarce and hence a breakdown more dangerous. Similarly in the north travelling in the Wet may be hindered by flooding and mud.

If you do run into trouble in the back of beyond, stay with your car. It's easier to spot a car than a human from the air, and you wouldn't be able to carry your 20L of water very far anyway. For the full story on safe outback travel, get hold of Lonely Planet's *Outback Australia*.

Some of the favourite tracks in the Territory are:

Simpson Desert Crossing the Simpson Desert from Birdsville (Qld) to the Stuart Hwy is becoming increasingly popular but this route is still a real test. A 4WD vehicle is definitely required and you should be in a party of at least three or four vehicles equipped with long-range two-way radios.

Warburton Road/Gunbarrel Hwy This route runs west from Uluru by the Aboriginal settlements of Docker River and Warburton to Laverton in Western Australia. From there you can drive down to Kalgoorlie and on to Perth. The route passes through Aboriginal reserves and permission to enter must be obtained in advance if you want to leave the road. A well-prepared conventional vehicle can complete this route although ground clearance can be a problem and it is very remote. From the Yulara resort at Uluru to Warburton is 567km, and it's another 568km from there to Laverton. It's then 361km on sealed road to Kalgoorlie. For 300km near the Giles Meteorological Station the Warburton Road and the Gunbarrel Hwy run on the same route. Taking the old Gunbarrel (to the north of the Warburton) all the way to Wiluna in Western Australia is a much rougher trip requiring 4WD. The Warburton Road is now commonly referred to as the Gunbarrel – just to make life simple.

ARABELLA BAMBER

A welcome landmark up the Tanami Track

Tanami Track Turning off the Stuart Hwy just north of Alice Springs the Tanami Track (or Road) goes north-west across the Tanami Desert to Halls Creek in Western Australia. It's a popular short-cut for people travelling between the Centre and the Kimberley. See the North of Alice Springs chapter for more information.

Plenty Hwy & Sandover Hwy These two routes run east from the Stuart Hwy north of Alice Springs, to Mt Isa in Queensland. They're suitable for robust conventional vehicles. See the North of Alice Springs chapter for more information.

Travel Permits

If you wish to travel through the outback on your own, you may need special permits to pass through or visit Aboriginal land or to camp in national parks.

Aboriginal Land Permits A glance at any up-to-date land-tenure map of the Northern Territory shows that vast portions are Aboriginal land. Generally this has either government-administered reserve status or it may be held under freehold title vested in an Aboriginal land trust and managed by a council or corporation. With either format, the laws of trespass apply just as with any other form of private land, but the fines attached can be somewhat heftier.

In some cases permits won't be necessary if you stay on recognised public roads that cross Aboriginal territory. However, as soon as you leave the main road by more than 50m, even if you're 'only' going into an Aboriginal settlement for fuel, you may need a permit. If you're on an organised tour the operator should take care of any permits, but this is worth checking before you book.

Applications To make an application, you must write to the appropriate land council as outlined below, enclosing a stamped, self-addressed envelope and giving all details of your proposed visit or transit. In general, the following information is required: the names of all members of the party; the dates of travel; route details; purpose of the visit; the make, model and registration number of the vehicle; and contact address and telephone number.

Allow plenty of time: the application process may take one or two months as the administering body generally must obtain approval from the relevant community councils before issuing your permit. Keep in mind also that there is no guarantee that you'll get one. It may be knocked back for a number of reasons, including the risk of interference with sacred sites, or disruption of ceremonial business. As well, some communities simply may not want to be bothered by visitors.

The Central Land Council administers all Aboriginal land in the southern and central regions of the Territory. Write to the Permits Officer (☎ 8951 6211, fax 8953 4345) at PO Box 3321, Alice Springs, NT 0871.

A transit permit is required for the Yulara-Docker River road, but not for either the Tanami Track or the Sandover Hwy where these cross Aboriginal land. Travellers may camp overnight without a permit within 50m of the latter two routes. On the Tanami Track, you can call in to Yuendumu and fuel up without a permit.

Arnhem Land and other northern mainland areas are administered by the Northern Land Council. Write to the Permits Officer (☎ 8920 5100, fax 8945 2633) at PO Box 42921, Casuarina (Darwin), NT 0811.

Visitors to Bathurst and Melville islands (known as the Tiwi Islands) also need permits. Apply in advance to the Tiwi Land Council, Unit 5/3 Bishop St, Stuart Park NT 0820 (☎8981 4898).

National Park Permits You sometimes need a permit to camp in a national park or even to visit, such as for Gurig National Park, and such a permit must be obtained in advance. It often includes maps and other useful information. Details of required permits are provided in the relevant sections in this book.

Car Rental

There are plenty of car-rental companies ready and willing to put you behind the wheel. Competition in the car-rental business is pretty fierce so rates tend to be variable and lots of special deals pop up and disappear again. Whatever your mode of travel on the long stretches, it can be very useful to have a car for some local travel. Between a group it can even be reasonably economical. There are some places, like around Alice Springs, where if you haven't got your own transport you really have to choose between a tour and a rented vehicle because there is no public transport and the distances are too great for walking or even bicycles.

The four major companies are Budget, Hertz, Avis and Territory Thrifty Car Rentals, with offices or agents in most towns. Then there are a number of local firms or firms with just one outlet. People assume that the big operators generally have higher rates than the local firms but it ain't necessarily so – make inquiries.

However, the big firms have a number of big advantages. First of all they're the ones at the airports – Avis, Budget, Hertz and Territory Thrifty are represented at Darwin and Alice Springs airports. If you want to pick up a car or leave a car at the airport then they're the best ones to deal with.

The major companies offer a choice of deals, either unlimited kilometres or a flat charge plus so many cents per kilometre. On straightforward off-the-card city rentals they're all pretty much the same price. It's on special deals, odd rentals or longer periods that you find the differences. Weekend specials, usually three days for the price of two, are often good value. If you just need a car for three days make it the weekend rather than midweek. Budget offers 'stand-by' rates and you may see other special deals available.

Daily rates are typically about $50 a day for a small car (Holden Barina, Ford Festiva, Daihatsu Charade, Suzuki Swift), about $75 a day for a medium car (Mitsubishi Magna, Toyota Camry, Nissan Pulsar) or about $100 a day for a big car (Holden Commodore, Ford Falcon), all including insurance. You must be at least 21 to hire from most firms.

There is a whole collection of other factors to bear in mind about this rent-a-car business. For a start, if you're going to want it for a week, a month or longer then they all have lower rates. If you're in the really remote outback (places like Darwin and Alice Springs are only vaguely remote) then the choice of cars is likely to be limited to the larger, more expensive ones.

And if in Darwin, don't forget the 'rent-a-wreck' companies. They specialise in renting older cars and have a variety of rates, typically around $35 a day. If you just want to travel around the city, or not too far out, they can be worth considering.

One thing to be aware of when renting a car in the Northern Territory is that if you are travelling on *any* dirt road you are generally not covered by insurance. So if you have an accident, you'll be liable for *all* the costs involved. This applies to all companies, although they don't always point this out. This condition does not apply to 4WD vehicles. Always check the insurance coverage before planning to venture off the bitumen.

4WD Rental Having a 4WD vehicle enables you to get right off the beaten track and out to some of the great wilderness and outback places. A variation is the 4WD campervan, which is fitted with bedding, stove, sink and other essentials.

Renting a 4WD vehicle is within the budget range if a few people get together. Something small like a Suzuki or similar costs around $100 per day; for a Toyota Landcruiser you're looking at around $150, which should include insurance and some free kilometres (typically 100km per day). Check the insurance conditions, especially the excess, as they can be onerous – $4000 is typical, although this can often be reduced to around $1000 on payment of an additional daily charge (around $20). Even in a 4WD the insurance cover of most companies does not cover damage caused when travelling 'off-road', which basically means anything that is not a maintained bitumen or dirt road. Make sure you know exactly what you are covered for, and that it applies to the areas you intend visiting.

Hertz and Avis have 4WD rentals, and one-way rentals are possible between the eastern states and the Northern Territory. Budget also rents 4WD vehicles from Darwin and Alice Springs. Britz: Australia (☎ toll-free 1800 331 454) has the largest range of 4WD vehicles fitted out as campervans. These have proved extremely popular in recent years, although they are not cheap at $120 per day for unlimited kilometres,

plus Collision Damage Waiver ($15 per day). They have offices in Darwin, Alice Springs and all the mainland capitals, so one-way rentals are also possible.

Car Purchase

If you want to explore Australia by car and haven't got one or can't borrow one, then you've either got to buy one or rent one. Australian cars are not cheap, but if you're buying a second-hand vehicle reliability is all important. Mechanical breakdowns way out in the outback can be very inconvenient (not to mention dangerous).

Shopping around for a used car involves much the same rules as anywhere in the Western world but with a few local variations. First of all, used-car dealers in Australia are just like used-car dealers from Los Angeles to London – they'd sell their mother into slavery if it turned a dollar. You'll probably get any car cheaper by buying privately through newspaper small ads rather than through a car dealer. Buying through a dealer does give the advantage of some sort of guarantee, but a guarantee is not much use if you're buying a car in Darwin and intend setting off for Perth next week.

There's a popular travellers' used car market near the main backpackers' hang-out in Darwin – see the Darwin chapter for details.

The further you get from civilisation, the better it is to be in a locally-made car (unless you're in a new car of course), such as a Holden or Ford. If you're travelling in an older vehicle life is much simpler if you can get spare parts anywhere from Bourke to Bulamakanka.

Note that third-party personal injury insurance is always included in the vehicle registration cost. This ensures that every vehicle (as long as it's currently registered) carries at least minimum insurance. You're wise to extend that minimum to at least third-party property insurance as well – a minor collision with a Rolls-Royce can be amazingly expensive.

When you come to buy or sell a car there are usually some local regulations to be complied with. In the Northern Territory safety checks are compulsory every year when you come to renew the registration. Stamp duty has to be paid when you buy a car and, as this is based on the purchase price, it's not unknown for buyer and seller to agree privately to understate the price. It's much easier to sell a car in the same state or territory that it's registered in, otherwise it has to be reregistered in the new state. It may be possible to sell a car without re-registering it, but you're likely to get a lower price.

Finally, make use of the Automobile Association of Australia (AANT). It can advise you on any local regulations you should be aware of, give general guidelines about buying a car and, most importantly, for a fee (from $85 to $100 for members and affiliate members depending on the type of vehicle) will check over a used car and report on its condition before you agree to purchase it. It also offers car insurance to members.

MOTORCYCLE

Motorcycles are a very popular way of getting around. The climate is just about ideal for biking much of the year, and the many small trails from the road into the bush often lead to perfect spots to spend the night in the world's largest camping ground.

The long, open roads are really made for large-capacity machines above 750cc, but that doesn't stop enterprising individuals – many of them Japanese – from tackling the length and breadth of the continent on 250cc trail bikes. Doing it on a small bike is not impossible, just tedious at times.

If you want to bring your own motorcycle into Australia you'll need a *carnet de passages*, and when you try to sell it you'll get less than the market price because of restrictive registration requirements (though these aren't so severe in the Northern Territory). Shipping from just about anywhere is expensive.

However, with a little bit of time up your sleeve, buying a motorcycle is quite feasible, although you'll get a much better range of machines and more competitive prices in the other state capitals, particularly Sydney and Melbourne.

You'll need a rider's licence and a helmet. A fuel range of 350km will cover fuel stops up the Centre. Beware of dehydration in the dry, hot air – force yourself to drink plenty of water, even if you don't feel thirsty.

The 'roo bars' (outsize bumpers) on large trucks and many cars tell you one thing: never ride on the open road from early evening until after dawn. Kangaroos are nocturnal, sleeping in the shade during the day and feeding at night, and roadside ditches often provide lush grass for them to eat. Cows and sheep also stray onto the roads at night. It's wise to stop riding by around 5 pm.

It's worth carrying some spares and tools even if you don't know how to use them, because someone else often does. If you do know, you'll probably have a fair idea of what to take. The basics include: a spare tyre tube (front wheel size, which will fit on the rear but usually not vice versa); puncture repair kit with levers and a pump (or tubeless tyre repair kit with at least three carbon dioxide cartridges); a spare tyre valve, and a valve cap that can unscrew same; the bike's standard tool kit, for what it's worth (after-market items are better); spare throttle, clutch and brake cables; tie wire, cloth tape ('gaffer' tape) and nylon 'zipties'; a handful of bolts and nuts in the usual emergency sizes (M6 and M8), along with a few self-tapping screws; one or two fuses in your bike's ratings; a bar of soap for fixing tank leaks (knead to a putty with water and squeeze into the leak); and, most important of all, a workshop manual for your bike (even if you can't make sense of it, the local motorcycle mechanic can). You'll never have enough elastic straps (octopus or 'ocky' straps) to tie down your gear.

Make sure you carry water – at least 2 litres on major roads in central Australia, more off the beaten track. And finally, if something does go hopelessly wrong in the back of beyond, park your bike where it's clearly visible and observe the cardinal rule: don't leave your vehicle.

BICYCLE

Whether you're hiring a bike to ride around a city or wearing out your Bio-Ace chain-wheels on a Melbourne-Darwin marathon, you'll find that Australia is a great place for cycling. There are bike tracks in Darwin, Katherine and Alice Springs, and in the country you'll find thousands of kilometres of good roads which carry so little traffic that the biggest hassle is waving back to the drivers. Especially appealing is that in many areas you'll ride a very long way without encountering a hill.

Bicycle helmets are compulsory in all states and territories. It's rare to find a reasonably sized town that doesn't have a shop stocking at least basic bike parts.

If you're coming specifically to cycle, it makes sense to bring your own bike. Check your airline for costs and the degree of dismantling/packing required. Within Australia you can load your bike onto a bus or train to skip the boring bits. Note that bus companies require you to dismantle your bike, and some don't guarantee that it will travel on the same bus as you.

You can buy a good steel-framed touring bike in Australia for about $400 (plus panniers). It may be possible to rent touring bikes and equipment from a few of the commercial touring organisations.

You can get by with standard road maps, but as you'll probably want to avoid both the highways and the low-grade unsealed roads, the Government series is best. The 1:250,000 scale is the most suitable but you'll need a lot of maps if you're covering much territory. The next scale up, 1:1,000,000, is adequate. They are available in Darwin and Alice Springs.

Until you get fit you should be careful to eat enough to keep you going – remember that exercise is an appetite suppressant. It's surprisingly easy to be so depleted of energy that you end up camping under a gum tree just 10km short of a shower and a steak. No matter how fit you are, water is still vital. Dehydration is definitely no joke and can be life-threatening.

It can get very hot in summer, and you should take things slowly until you're used to the heat. Cycling in 35°C-plus temperatures isn't too bad if you wear a hat and plenty of sunscreen, and drink *lots* of water.

Of course, you don't have to follow the larger roads and visit towns. It's possible to fill your mountain bike's panniers with muesli, head out into the mulga and not see anyone for weeks. Or ever again – outback travel is very risky if not properly planned. Water is the main problem in the 'dead heart', and you can't rely on it where there aren't settlements. That tank marked on your map may be dry or the water from it unfit for humans, and those station buildings probably blew away years ago. That little creek marked with a dotted blue line? Forget it – the only time it has water is when the country's flooded for hundreds of kilometres.

Always check with locals if you're heading into remote areas, and notify the police if you're about to do something particularly adventurous. That said, you can't rely too much on local knowledge of road conditions – most people have no idea of what a heavily loaded touring bike needs. What they think of as a great road may be pedal-deep in sand or bulldust; on the other hand, cyclists have happily ridden along roads that were officially flooded out.

HITCHING

We don't recommend hitching. Travellers who decide to hitch should understand that they are taking a small but potentially serious risk. Before doing it, talk to local people about the dangers, and it is a good idea to let someone know your destination before you set off. If you do choose to hitch, the advice that follows should help to make your journey as fast and safe as possible.

- More than two people hitching together will make it difficult to get a lift, and solo hitching is unwise for both men and women. Two women hitching together may be vulnerable, and two men hitching together can expect long waits. The best option is for a woman and a man to hitch together.
- Stand at a place where vehicles will be going slowly and where they can stop easily. A junction or freeway slip road is a good place if there is stopping room. The ideal location is on the outskirts of a town – hitching from way out in

the country is as hopeless as from the centre of a city. Take a bus out to the edge of town.

- The ideal appearance for hitching is a sort of genteel poverty – threadbare but clean. Don't carry too much gear because if it looks like you're going to take half an hour to pack your bags aboard you'll be left on the roadside.

- Know when to say no. Saying no to a car-load of drunks is pretty obvious, but you should also be prepared to abandon a ride if you begin to feel uneasy for any reason. Don't sit there hoping for the best; make an excuse and get out at the first opportunity.

- Wait for the right, long ride to come along. It can be time-saving to say no to a short ride that might take you from a good hitching point to a lousy one. On a long haul, it's pointless to start walking as it's not likely to increase the likelihood of your getting a lift and it's an awfully long way to the next town.

- Trucks are often the best lifts but they will only stop if they are going slowly and can get started easily again. Thus the ideal place is at the top of a hill where they have a downhill run. Truckies often say they are going to the next town and if they don't like you, will drop you anywhere. As they often pick up hitchers for company, the quickest way to create a bad impression is to jump in and fall asleep.

- While you're in someone else's vehicle, you are their guest and should act accordingly. Many drivers no longer pick up people because they have suffered from thoughtless hikers in the past. It's the hitcher's duty to provide entertainment!

Of course people do get stuck in outlandish places but that is the name of the game. If you're visiting from abroad a prominent flag on your pack will help, and a sign showing your destination can also be useful. University and hostel notice boards are good places to look for hitching partners. The main law against hitching is 'thou shalt not stand in the road' so when you see the law coming, step back.

Just as hitchers should be wary when accepting lifts, drivers who pick up fellow travellers to share the costs should also be aware of the possible risks involved.

LOCAL TRANSPORT

Public transport is virtually unknown in the Northern Territory – the long distances and small population make such services generally unviable. There are limited public bus networks in Darwin and Alice Springs.

At the major tourist centres most backpackers hostels and some hotels have courtesy coaches which will pick you up from the airport or bus station. Most tour operators include transfers to and from your accommodation in the price. Larger towns have a taxi service.

ORGANISED TOURS

There are all sorts of tours around the Territory, including some interesting camping tours and 4WD safaris. Some of these go to places you probably couldn't get to on your own.

There are plenty of tour operators, a number of which are aimed at backpackers, and the emphasis is on active, fun tours. Particularly popular are the tours out of Darwin to Kakadu and Litchfield National Parks, and from Alice Springs to Watarrka (Kings Canyon) and Uluru-Kata Tjuta (Ayers Rock) National Parks. Other interesting options are extended bushwalking trips in Kakadu and elsewhere in the Top End, and camel trips through the beautiful central Australian bush.

Tours on Aboriginal Land

A number of tourist operations, some of them Aboriginal owned, run trips to visit Aboriginal land and communities in the Northern Territory. This is the best way to have any meaningful contact with Aboriginal people, even though you may feel that by being on a tour what you're getting is not the 'real thing'. The fact is that this is the way the Aboriginal owners of the land want tourism to work, so that they have some control over who visits what and when.

Arnhem Land offers the most options, mainly because of its proximity to Kakadu. The tours here generally only visit the very western edge of Arnhem Land, and take you to Oenpelli and other places which are normally off limits. Some of the tour operators include Umorrduk Safaris, Davidson's Arnhem Land Safaris, Northern Expeditions and AAT-Kings (see the Kakadu & Arnhem Land chapter for more details).

Other places in the Top End with similar tourist operations include the Tiwi Islands and the Litchfield and Katherine areas, while in the Centre they are at Kings Canyon and Uluru-Kata Tjuta. See those sections for details.

Darwin

• pop 86,576 ✉ 0800

The 'capital' of northern Australia comes as a surprise to many people. It's a lively, modern place with a young population, an easy-going lifestyle, a great climate and a cosmopolitan atmosphere.

In part this is thanks to Cyclone Tracy, which flattened Darwin on Christmas Eve in 1974. People who were there during the reconstruction say a new spirit grew up with the new buildings, as Darwinites took the opportunity to make their city one of which to be proud. Darwin became a brighter, smarter, sturdier place.

More recently it has been the city's proximity to Asia that has become the focus of interest as Australia looks increasingly to the region for trade and business opportunities. This should come as no surprise really: after all, Darwin is closer to Jakarta than it is to Canberra!

Despite its burgeoning sophistication, in many ways Darwin still retains a small-town atmosphere. It's a long way from any other major Australian city and even today the remoteness gives it a distinct 'far off' feel. A lot of people only live here for a year or two – it's surprising how many people you meet elsewhere in Australia who used to live in Darwin. It's reckoned you can consider yourself a 'Territorian' if you've stuck it for five years.

From the traveller's point of view Darwin is a major stop. There is a constant flow of travellers coming and going from Asia, or making their way around Australia. Darwin is an obvious base for trips to Kakadu and other natural attractions of the Top End, such as Litchfield National Park. It's a bit of an oasis too – whether you're travelling south to Alice Springs, west to Western Australia or east to Queensland, there are a lot of kilometres to be covered before you get anywhere, and having reached Darwin many people rest a bit before leaving.

HIGHLIGHTS

- Cruise Darwin Harbour at sunset on an old pearling lugger
- Sample an array of food at the Mindil Beach open-air market
- Meet other travellers in the Mitchell St backpackers' precinct
- Delve into the history of the Territory at the Museum & Art Gallery
- Fondle a crocodile at Crocodylus Park

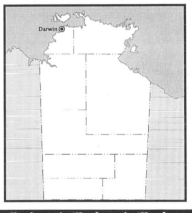

HISTORY

The Darwin peninsula had been the preserve of the Larrakiah Aboriginal clan for thousands of years before the arrival of whites in the 18th century. (The word 'larakia' is actually trade-Malay for 'lead-in', used in reference to vessels turning into the wind as they anchor.) With the arrival of whites they were forced to vacate their traditional lands and inevitably came into violent conflict with the new arrivals, despite attempts by the first administration under George Goyder to avoid conflict.

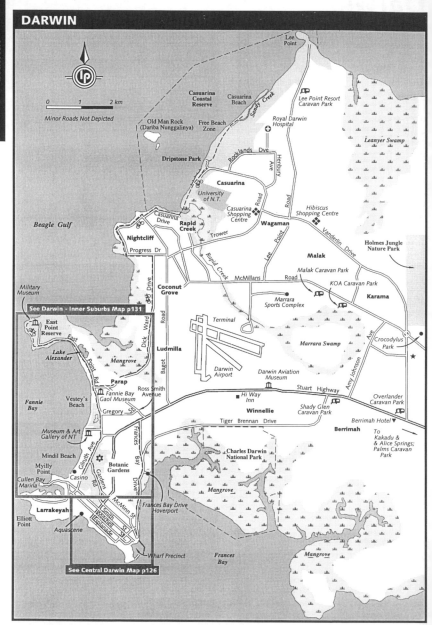

DARWIN

Minor Roads Not Depicted

0   1   2 km

Lee Point

Casuarina
Coastal
Reserve

Casuarina
Beach

Sandy Creek

Lee Point Resort
Caravan Park

Leanyer Swamp

Old Man Rock
(Dariba Nunggalinya)

Free Beach
Zone

Royal Darwin
Hospital

Rocklands Dve

Dripstone Park

Henbury Road

Rockland Ave

Casuarina

University
of N.T.

Casuarina
Shopping
Centre

Hibiscus
Shopping Centre

Holmes Jungle
Nature Park

Beagle Gulf

Casuarina
Drive

Rapid
Creek

Wagaman

Lee Point Road

Vanderlin Drive

Nightcliff

Progress Dr

Trower

Malak

Rapid Creek

McMillans   Road

Malak Caravan Park

KOA Caravan Park

Karama

Military
Museum

Coconut
Grove

Dick Ward Drive

Marrara
Sports Complex

Crocodylus
Park

See Darwin - Inner Suburbs Map p131

East
Point
Reserve

East Point Rd

Lake
Alexander

Mangrove

Bagot Road

Ludmilla

Terminal

Darwin
Airport

Marrara Swamp

Amy Johnson Ave

Parap

Fannie Bay
Gaol Museum

Ross Smith
Avenue

Darwin Aviation
Museum

Stuart   Highway

Overlander
Caravan Park

Fannie
Bay

Vestey's
Beach

Gregory St

Hi Way
Inn

Shady Glen
Caravan Park

Berrimah Hotel

Museum & Art
Gallery of NT

Winnellie

Tiger Brennan Drive

Berrimah

To
Kakadu &
& Alice Springs;
Palms Caravan
Park

Mindil Beach

Frances Bay Drive

Botanic
Gardens

Charles Darwin
National Park

Myilly
Point

Casino

Cullen Bay
Marina

Gardens Rd

Gilruth Ave

Mangrove

Larrakeyah

Smith St

Mitchell St

Esplanade

McMinn St

Frances Bay Drive
Hoverport

Elliott
Point

Aquascene

Wharf Precinct

Frances
Bay

Mangrove

See Central Darwin Map p126

From the early 19th century the British were keen to establish a major base in northern Australia (see the Facts about the Northern Territory chapter). However, it took a long time to decide on Darwin as the site for the region's main centre and, even after the city was established, growth was slow and troubled.

In 1864 Boyle Travers Finniss, an ex-British army officer, established a settlement at Escape Cliffs on the mouth of the Adelaide River, about 50km north-east of Darwin's present location. However, as it was surrounded by huge mangrove and melaleuca swamps, and reefs made shipping treacherous, it was a poor choice. In the words of explorer John McKinlay (who led the search for Burke and Wills in 1861): 'A greater sense of waste and desolation is unimaginable. As a seaport and a city this place is worthless'. It was finally abandoned in 1866.

Finally, South Australian Surveyor-General George Goyder was sent north in 1869 to have a go at settling and surveying the area. He headed straight for the city's current location, Port Darwin, having read the journals of John Lort Stokes who sailed into the harbour in 1839 aboard the *Beagle* and named it Port Darwin after a former shipmate, the great scientist and evolutionist Charles Darwin. The settlement was called Palmerston, but in 1911 the name was officially changed to Darwin.

Arrival of the Overland Telegraph
In 1871 Palmerston was chosen as the Australian landfall point for the overland telegraph link to Adelaide. At this time the settlement still had a population of less than 500 and a small collection of buildings, which included a Government House, a police barracks, some weatherboard shops and a few log huts.

Activity in the area increased with the discovery of gold at Pine Creek about 200km south. By 1874 the town had 1700 residents (of whom only about 50 were women), its own newspaper, the *Northern Territory Times & Government Gazette*, and plots of land which had been almost worthless only a few years before but were now fetching prices of up to £500.

But once the gold fever had run its course Palmerston slipped into a period of stagnation and by 1880 the population had dwindled to less than 500, of whom 300 were Chinese labourers who had been encouraged to immigrate in the hope that they would provide a source of cheap labour.

The discovery of pearl shell in Port Darwin in 1884 led to the development of a small industry which lasted for 70 years and became a vital part of the local economy. By the turn of the century there were more than 50 luggers operating out of Port Darwin, most of them employing Indonesian or Japanese divers.

Despite the hardships development continued and during the 1880s a number of important buildings were built, some of which still stand (see Things to See later in this chapter). The construction of a railway line south to Pine Creek to service the goldfields also boosted hopes but by the time it was finished in 1889 the gold was exhausted and the state government had incurred a massive debt. Any hope that pastoralists might use the railway to transport their stock was unfounded because the nearest cattle markets were in the Kimberley region of WA and in Queensland.

In 1897 Palmerston was hit by a devastating cyclone (probably the most destructive until Tracy in 1974). Hardly a building survived undamaged and many were destroyed completely. Again in 1937 the city of Darwin was badly damaged by a cyclone.

When the Federal Government assumed control of the Northern Territory in 1911 there was a brief flurry of building activity, but this was short-lived and for the next 20 years the city slipped back into inactivity.

WWII
WWII put Darwin permanently on the map when the town became an important base for Allied action against the Japanese in the Pacific.

When things started hotting up in Europe in the late 30s Darwin became the focus of military activity in Australia. The Darwin Mobile Defence Force was established in 1939, an anti-submarine boom net was constructed across the harbour in 1940, and an air force squadron was stationed at the civil airfield.

As the Japanese advanced rapidly through South-East Asia in late 1941 women and children were evacuated from Darwin, so that by the time the first raid hit on 18 February 1942 only 63 women and children remained in the city. The raid was launched from five aircraft carriers in the Timor Sea and a force of 188 fighters and bombers attacked the city virtually unopposed. Despite the preparations against exactly such a raid there was heavy loss of life and property. This first attack on Australia by a hostile power was followed almost immediately by another, which was delivered by 54 heavy bombers stationed in Ambon and Sulawesi.

These early raids led to a mass evacuation of the city as everyone headed south by whatever means possible. The road south at that stage only went as far as Adelaide River, 100km away, and the little town was soon swamped with evacuees. In all, Darwin was attacked 64 times during the war; 243 people lost their lives and more than 400 were injured; it was the only place in Australia to suffer prolonged attacks.

At the end of the war the city's administrators seized the chance to rebuild the city into something it had never been – attractive. The Chinatown area of Cavenagh St was seen as the major problem and so instead of handing the buildings back to their former owners the government bulldozed the lot.

Post-War Development

The late 1940s was another period of stagnation for Darwin, but during the 1950s and 60s it was rebuilt and expanded rapidly. New homes and buildings shot up everywhere, although carelessness crept in and the cyclone threat was disregarded. Consequently when the worst happened – and it did on 24 December 1974 – the devastation was far worse

than it should have been. Cyclone Tracy ripped through Darwin, seriously damaging 95% of its domestic dwellings and killing 66 people. For the second time in 50 years the city was virtually rebuilt.

Modern Darwin has an important role as the front door to Australia's northern region, and as a centre for administration and mining. Its modern port facilities mean it is well placed to become the main connection between Australia and Asia.

ORIENTATION

Darwin's centre is a fairly compact area at the end of a peninsula. The Stuart Hwy does a big loop entering the city and finally heads south to end as Daly St. The city-centre peninsula stretches south-east from here, and the main city centre shopping area, Smith St and its Mall, is about 500m from Daly St.

Long-distance buses arrive right in the city centre – Greyhound at the Transit Centre at 69 Mitchell St and McCafferty's nearby at 71 Smith St – and accommodation options start less than a minute's walk away. Most of what you'll want in central Darwin is within two or three blocks of the Transit Centre or Smith St Mall.

The suburbs spread a good 12 to 15km away to the north and east. Larrakeyah is immediately north of the centre and then the Botanic Gardens and the golf course form a buffer between the centre and the old suburbs of Parap and Fannie Bay, the latter with its old gaol and the East Point Reserve.

The Stuart Hwy to Alice Springs swings off to the east through the light-industrial suburbs of Winnellie and Berrimah, and eventually to Palmerston, a new satellite town 20km from the city centre.

The city is well endowed with open spaces and parks, and has an excellent series of bicycle tracks. The best beaches are to the north of the city.

INFORMATION
Tourist Office

The Darwin Regional Tourism Association Information Centre (☎ 8981 4300, fax 8981

7346) is on the corner of Knuckey and Mitchell Sts. It's open Monday to Friday from 8.30 am to 5.45 pm, Saturday from 9 am to 2.45 pm and Sunday from 10 am to 2.45 pm. It stocks hundreds of brochures and can book just about any tour or accommodation in the Territory. Information provided by DRTA is for places to stay and tour companies that belong to the association – they do not promote those that do not, and not all operators belong.

There's also a tourist information desk at the airport (☎ 8945 3386) which opens to meet all international and major domestic incoming flights.

The National Parks & Wildlife Service (☎ 8999 5511) has a counter in the Information Centre with an excellent range of free leaflets covering all the main national parks and reserves (with the exception of Kakadu) of the Top End, plus maps and a limited range of publications. Permits for Kakadu are available here.

Noticeboards in most of the backpacker hostels are useful for buying and selling vehicles or cheap tickets, or if you're looking for rides or long-term accommodation.

Weather information is posted outside the ANZ bank in the Smith St Mall.

Publications There are a couple of free publications which have some useful detail but are far from comprehensive. *Darwin & the Top End Today* is published twice yearly and has information on Darwin and the surrounding area. Possibly of more use is *This Week in Darwin*, which is updated weekly.

The *Daily Plan It* is a free monthly newspaper which is sometimes helpful. The Friday edition of the *Northern Territory News* newspaper has its *Your Weekend* liftout with details of theatres, live bands and cinemas.

The *Backpackers Information Guide – Northern Territory* (BIG-NT) is a free booklet produced locally every year, and it's also worth getting hold of.

Money
There are bureaux de change at the Transit Centre and in the Smith St Mall, open daily

from 8 am to 10 pm (at the Transit Centre until 9.30 pm). Another one at the airport opens to meet incoming flights.

There are ATMs all over the city centre, including Westpac on the corner of Peel and Smith Sts; a National Bank next to McDonald's in Cavenagh St; and an ANZ at the Knuckey St end of the Smith St Mall.

Post & Communications
The Darwin main post office is on the corner of Cavenagh and Edmunds Sts. Opening hours are Monday to Friday 8.30 am to 5 pm and on Saturday from 9 am to 12 pm. Outside there are phone booths taking both coins and cards. More phone booths are at the Transit Centre.

The poste restante is computerised and efficient; a computer-generated list of all mail held is printed each morning and is available by the poste restante counter. This saves you queuing for mail only to find there's nothing there. You'll need some form of identification to collect any mail.

There's a Hello International booth opposite the Transit Centre which accepts coins, credit cards and travellers cheques, and has EFTPOS. It sells Hello International cards ($10 minimum) and is open from 4 pm to midnight every day.

Email & Internet Access Several places around the city centre provide access. Rates are about $2/5/8 for 10/30/60 minutes.

Student UNI Travel
    50 Mitchell St (opposite the Transit Centre)
Internet Outpost
    At the Planet OZ bookshop in the Transit Centre; open every day from 10 am to 10 pm
Gondwana Tours
    In the Transit Centre; open every day from 9.30 am to 7.30 pm
Multigamer
    20 Knuckey St; large range of games, plus email and net surfing; open weekdays from 9 am to 9pm, weekends from 12 pm to 9 pm
Northern Territory Library
    Parliament House, Mitchell St; 30 minutes free access – book on the day but get there early

Useful Organisations

The Automobile Association of the Northern Territory (AANT; ☎ 8981 3837) has its office in the MLC Building at 81 Smith St. It can provide current information about the status of various Top End roads which may be closed in the Wet.

The National Trust (☎ 8981 2848) is at 52 Temira Crescent in Myilly Point – pick up a copy of its *Darwin Heritage Guide* leaflet (also available from the tourist office).

The Department of Mines & Energy (☎ 8999 5511) is in the Centrepoint Building in the Smith St Mall; fossicking permits are available on the 5th floor and geological maps and publications on the 3rd floor.

For reference material and other information on just about anything to do with the Territory, visit the State Library (☎ 8999 7177) in the new Parliament House. As well as the excellent Northern Australia Collection there's a fully catalogued collection of images available for viewing on CD-ROM, and international phone books and newspapers. It's open Monday to Saturday from 10 am to 6 pm.

Permits to visit Arnhem Land are issued by the Northern Land Council (☎ 8920 5100, fax 8945 2633) at 9 Rowling St, Casuarina, behind the Casuarina Shopping Centre. Tiwi Island permits are available from the Tiwi Land Council (☎ 8981 4898) at 5/3 Bishop St, Stuart Park.

If you want to get involved in fighting the Jabiluka uranium mine or some other hot issue, the Environment Centre (☎ 8981 1984) is at 24 Cavenagh St. A noticeboard advises what's happening in the environmental arena.

Foreign Consulates

For a list of consulates in Darwin, see Embassies & Consulates in the Facts for the Visitor chapter.

Travel Agencies

To book or confirm flights, bus travel or virtually anything but local travel, there's no shortage of agents in Darwin. The following are centrally located:

Flight Centre
   (☎ 8941 8002) 24 Cavenagh St
Jalan Jalan Tours & Travel
   (☎ toll-free 1800 802 250) Suite 35, 21 Cavenagh St (upstairs); specialises in tickets to Indonesia and other parts of South-East Asia
STA
   (☎ 8941 2955) Galleria Shopping Centre, Smith St Mall
Student UNI Travel
   (☎ 8981 3388) 50 Mitchell St (opposite the Transit Centre)

Freight Agents

If you need to get some gear freighted overseas, Perkins Shipping (☎ 8982 2000) on Frances Bay Drive is used to handling anything from a backpack up.

Within Australia, try TNT (☎ 13 1150) at 5 Lancaster Rd, Airport. McCafferty's bus line (☎ 8941 0911), 71 Smith St, has reasonable rates, but doesn't service Western Australia.

Bookshops

Planet OZ (☎ 8981 0690), 69 Mitchell St (next to the Transit Centre), is open every day from 10 am to 10 pm. It has an excellent range of travel guides, including Lonely Planet titles, and some foreign language books.

Bookworld (☎ 8981 5277), 30 Smith St on the Mall, has a large range of titles of local interest, as well as general books. There's a well-stocked branch of Angus & Robertson (☎ 8941 3489) in the Galleria Shopping Centre, also off the Smith St Mall.

For a large range of second-hand books as well as CDs and videos, Read Back Book Exchange (☎ 8981 8885) is in Darwin Plaza off the Smith St Mall.

Maps

The NT General Store (☎ 8981 8242), 42 Cavenagh St, has a good range, including maps of Indonesia and topographic maps for bushwalking.

For good maps of the Territory try Maps NT (☎ 8999 7032), in the Department of Lands, Planning & Environment, 1st floor, corner of Cavenagh and Bennett Sts. It's open only on weekdays from 8 am to 4 pm, unfortunately.

Most bookshops and many tour desks sell maps of Darwin, Kakadu and the Top End.

A $2 tourist map of the city, called *The Map*, is available at the Information Centre, but the maps in this book are just as useful.

Other Shops

Camping Gear For general camping equipment one of the best places is the NT General Store at 42 Cavenagh St. Adventure Equipment Darwin (☎ 8941 0019), down the road at 41 Cavenagh St, specialises more in rock-climbing and abseiling gear but has a good range of backpacks.

There's a branch of Snowgum (☎ 8941 7370), for lightweight tents and bushwalking gear, at 2/16 Bishop St, Stuart Park.

Barbecues Galore (☎ 8985 4544), 301 Bagot Rd, Coconut Grove, stocks larger tents, portable fridges and camping gear.

Bicycle Sales & Repairs There's a large bike section at the back of Rossetto's Sports Centre (☎ 8981 4436) at 30 Smith St Mall, and Wheelman Cycles (☎ 8981 6369) is centrally located at 64 McMinn St.

Fishing Gear Fishing & Outdoor World (☎ 8981 6398) at 27 Cavenagh St (the one with the artillery piece above the door) has an extensive range of tackle, lures, rods and anything else you might need to hook a big 'un.

Laundry

Most backpackers and other places to stay have laundry facilities. There's also a coin laundrette opposite the Transit Centre in Mitchell St, open from 6 am to midnight every day.

Medical & Emergency Services

There are various medical and emergency services in Darwin and they include:

Vaccinations
  The Federal Department of Health runs an International Vaccination Clinic (☎ 8981 7492) at 43 Cavenagh St. It is open on weekdays from 9 am to 5 pm. There's a $20 consultation fee, plus charges for whatever vaccinations you have
Medical Treatment
  For emergency medical treatment phone the Royal Darwin Hospital on ☎ 8922 8888. It is located in the northern suburb of Tiwi. There's also a Marine Stinger Emergency Line ☎ toll-free 1800 079 909
Counselling
  Lifeline Crisis Line (☎ 131114),
  AIDS Hotline (☎ toll-free 1800 011 144),
  Rape & Sexual Assault Referral Centre (☎ 8922 7156), Mensline (support for gay & bisexual men; ☎ toll-free 1800 181 888)
Dental
  For emergency dental treatment until 9 pm try the Night & Day Medical & Dental Surgery (☎ 8927 1899), Shop 31, Casuarina Shopping Centre
Chemist
  For prescription filling the Darwin Mall Pharmacy (☎ 8981 9202) is open from 9 am to 8 pm Monday to Saturday and 9 am to 5 pm Sunday
Ambulance
  For ambulance attendance phone ☎ 000 or ☎ 8927 9000
Police
  For emergency police assistance phone ☎ 8927 8888 or ☎ 000. There is a police station at the southern end of Mitchell St

THINGS TO SEE
City Centre

Despite its shaky beginnings and the destruction caused by WWII and Cyclone Tracy, Darwin has a number of historic buildings.

One of the most famous city landmarks is the **Victoria Hotel** on Smith St Mall. The 'Vic' was originally built in 1890 and badly damaged by Cyclone Tracy. The building on the corner of the Mall and Bennett St only dates from 1981 but it incorporates the colonnade of the 1884 stone **Commercial Bank building**, which at the time was one of the finest buildings in the city. It was known locally as the 'stone bank', to distinguish it from the 'tin bank', a termite-proof, prefabricated structure erected on Smith St around the same time.

The **old Palmerston town hall** on Smith St was also built during the gold boom in 1883 and during its life was a bank, occupied by the navy during WWII and later by

CENTRAL DARWIN

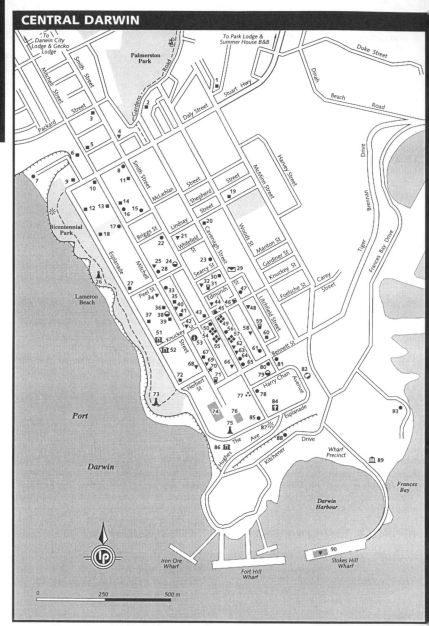

CENTRAL DARWIN

the Museums Board. Unfortunately it was virtually destroyed by Tracy, despite its solid Victorian construction. Today only remnants of its walls remain.

Across the road, **Brown's Mart**, a former mining exchange dating from 1885, was badly damaged in the fierce cyclone of 1897 and again by Tracy. It was restored on both occasions and now houses a theatre.

The 1884 **police station** and **old courthouse** at the corner of Smith St and the Esplanade were in use by the navy until 1974. They were badly damaged, but have been restored and are now used as government offices. A small plaque in the garden bed on the Smith St side of the building marks the spot where the first Telegraph Station stood.

Right across the road from here, perched on the edge of the escarpment, is the **Survivors' Lookout**, a reminder of the wartime bombing raids over Darwin. The lookout has a number of interesting interpretive signs and some old photos, and a staircase leads from here down to the harbour and Wharf Precinct.

A little further along the Esplanade, **Government House**, built in stages from 1870, was known as the Residency until 1911 when the Territory came under the control of the Commonwealth Government. Initially it was little more than a large room with hand-cut stone walls and canvas roof. George Scott, the Resident in 1873, added a second storey in 1874, but it was virtually rebuilt soon after because termites had made a mess of things and there was a real danger of collapse. The current building dates from 1877 and, although damaged by virtually every cyclone since, it is in fine condition today. It is opened to the public once a year in July or August.

Almost opposite Government House is a new memorial housing an old plaque which used to mark the spot where the original telegraph cable from Banyuwangi in Indonesia was brought up the cliffs to the Telegraph Station. This cable put Australia into instant communication with Britain for the first time. The original cairn was removed to make way for the new **Parliament House** building.

Further along is the **Old Admiralty House** at the corner of Knuckey St, one of the few 1930s Burnett buildings still standing in Darwin (see Myilly Point Historic Precinct for details of the work of BCG Burnett, the Northern Territory government architect in the 1930s). It was built in 1937 and originally stood on the corner of Peel St. It was moved to its present site in 1951 and until 1984 it was used by the navy; it's not open to the public.

On the opposite corner of Knuckey St is **Lyons Cottage** an attractive stone building with a blue roof and shutters. It was built in 1925 of locally-quarried stone as the executive residence for the British Australian Telegraph Company (and is sometimes known as BAT House), the company which laid the submarine cable between Java and Australia. Lyons Cottage is now a good little museum and the walls are lined with interesting photographs of early Darwin. Entry is free and it's open daily from 10 am to 5 pm.

The Esplanade is fronted by **Bicentennial Park**, a very pleasant expanse of grass and trees with some excellent views over the harbour, in which there are some memorials. Almost opposite the Hotel Darwin is the **Anzac Memorial**, with plaques to commemorate those who fought in WWI and other campaigns. Further along, what looks like a slab of suburban brick wall is actually a memorial to the scientist and explorer

Ludwig Leichhardt. Further again is a **lookout** over the harbour.

Parliament House & Supreme Court

The Territory's new Parliament House and adjoining Supreme Court buildings dominate the edge of town just south of the Smith St Mall.

The grand $117 million **parliament** building was opened in 1994 and drew much criticism for 'lacking outback ambience'. But, perhaps more appropriately, it owes something to South-East Asian architecture and evokes the grandeur of such buildings worldwide. Judge for yourself – tours are conducted at 10 am and noon; inquire at reception.

The building also houses the **Northern Territory Library**, which is open on weekdays between 10 am and 6 pm, and weekends from 1 to 5 pm.

The nearby **Supreme Court** building is chiefly of interest for the fine artwork on display inside. On the floor there's a mosaic by Aboriginal artist Nora Napaltjari Nelson. Called *Milky Way Dreaming*, some 700,000 pieces of Venetian glass were used in its construction. Also on display is *Kooralia and the Seven Sisters*, a rug woven by Tim Leura Tjapaltjarri that was the centre of a copyright dispute and marked a landmark decision in favour of an Aboriginal artist.

The Supreme Court building is open to the public on weekdays between 8 am and 5.30 pm. It's a short walk from the Smith St Mall.

Wharf Precinct

The Darwin Wharf Precinct centres around the old Stokes Hill Wharf, below the cliffs at the southern end of the city centre. It's worth spending a morning wandering around this area – it's a short stroll down from the Survivors' Lookout at the end of Smith St.

At the end of the jetty there is an old warehouse, now known as the Arcade, which houses a food centre that's great for an alfresco lunch or cool afternoon beer.

Government House, Darwin, rebuilt in 1883 after termites ate the original!

HUGH FINLAY

CHRIS MELLOR

The Smith Street Mall, Darwin

HUGH FINLAY

Evening at Mindil Beach Market

HUGH FINLAY

Northern Territory Parliament House, designed by Meldrum Burrows & Ptns, completed in 1994

Katherine River, Nitmiluk (Katherine Gorge) National Park

Cockatoo congregation and boab

Wangi Falls, Litchfield National Park

Indo-Pacific Marine Exhibition Probably the focal point of the precinct is this excellent marine aquarium. It's a successful attempt to display living coral and its associated life. Each small tank is a complete ecosystem, with only the occasional extra fish introduced as food for some of the carnivores such as stonefish or angler fish. They sometimes have box jellyfish, as well as more attractive creatures like sea horses, clownfish and butterfly fish. The living coral reef display is especially impressive.

The exhibition is open daily from 9 am to 6 pm, entry costs $10 (children $4). Night shows, including a seafood buffet, are held on Wednesday, Friday and Sunday at 7.30 pm; these cost $45 ($22.50) and must be booked ☎ 8981 1294.

The Tour Tub drops passengers here (see Getting Around at the end of this chapter).

Australian Pearling Exhibition Housed in the same building, the Pearling Exhibition describes the fascinating history of the pearling industry in the Top End. While pearling around Darwin doesn't have the importance it has in, say, Broome (WA), quite a bit still goes on in places such as the Cobourg Peninsula in Arnhem Land. The exhibition has excellent displays and informative videos.

The exhibition is open from 10 am to 5 pm weekdays (last entry 4.30 pm); entry costs $6/15 per adult/family.

WWII Oil-Storage Tunnels After Japanese air raids destroyed above-ground oil tanks near Stokes Hill Wharf, five oil-storage tunnels were dug into the cliff behind what is now the Wharf Precinct. It was an ambitious project that ultimately failed because of the high water-table and seepage, and the tunnels were never used.

It sounds pretty naff, but in fact is worth a look and quite impressive when you consider the tunnels were hacked into the solid rock by hand. Tunnels 5 (171m long) and 6 (78m) are open to the public, and on the walls there's a series of interesting wartime photos.

The tunnels are open daily from 9 am to 5 pm during the Dry, and Tuesday to Sunday from 10 am to 2 pm during the Wet. Entry costs $4 per person and family concession is available.

It's an easy walk from the city centre and the Tour Tub stops here.

Aquascene
At Doctor's Gully, near the corner of Daly St and the Esplanade, fish have been fed every day at high tide since the 1950s. Half the stale bread in Darwin gets dispensed to a horde of milkfish, mullet, scats, catfish and butterfish. It's a great sight and children love it – the fish will take bread out of your hand. Feeding times depend on the tides – phone ☎ 8981 7837 for feeding times or ask at the Information Centre.

Admission is $4 (children $2.50); the bread is free. As you can stand on a concrete ramp right in the water, it's not a bad idea to wear bathers, particularly for kids.

Doctor's Gully is an easy walk from the north end of the Esplanade.

Myilly Point Historic Precinct
Right at the far northern end of Smith St is this small but important historic precinct of four houses built in the 1930s. The houses were designed specifically for the tropical climate by the Northern Territory Principal

A 'climate-controlled' Burnett house

HUGH FINLAY

Architect, BCG Burnett, who came to Darwin in 1937 after spending many years working as an architect in China. The small elevated point was a prime residential spot as it had fine views and enjoyed any sea breezes, and so it was here that the top civil and military officials were housed.

At one stage in the early 1980s it looked as though the houses would be flattened to make way for the casino (it was eventually built on lower ground to the north). They are now on the Register of the National Estate; one, now called Burnett House, is the home of the National Trust (☎ 8981 2848), while another is a gallery and café. Burnett House is open from 10 am to 3 pm Monday to Friday; entry is free.

Botanic Gardens
The 42 hectare Botanic Gardens site was first used in the 1870s to establish a fruit and vegetable plantation so the settlement would be less dependent on unreliable shipments.

It's a pleasant, shady place for a walk. Many of the plants were traditionally used by local Aborigines, and self-guiding Aboriginal Plant Use trails have been set up – pick up a brochure at the gardens' information centre. Among the botanical highlights there's a rainforest gully and some 400 species of palms. Guided walks with Parks & Wildlife staff cover a number of topics – check at the Information Centre for times.

Over the road, between Gilruth Ave and Fannie Bay, there's a coastal habitat section which features sand dunes, a small wetland and a mangrove boardwalk that leads along the bay to the museum.

It's an easy 2km bicycle ride out to the gardens from the centre along Gilruth Ave and Gardens Rd, or there's another entrance off Geranium St, which runs off the Stuart Hwy in Stuart Park. The Gardens Rd gate is open from 7 am to 7 pm daily; the Geranium St access is 24 hour. Entry is free.

Museum & Art Gallery of the Northern Territory
This excellent museum and art gallery is on Conacher St at Fannie Bay, about 4km from the city centre. It's an eclectic collection, but well presented and not too big. A highlight is the Northern Territory Aboriginal art collection, with just the right mix of exhibits and information to introduce visitors to the different styles. It's particularly strong on carvings and bark paintings from the Tiwi Islands and Arnhem Land.

Don't miss the Cyclone Tracy display that graphically illustrates life before and after the disaster. You can stand in a little room and listen to a recording of Tracy at full throttle – a sound you won't forget in a hurry.

There's an interesting exhibition on the Chinese in Darwin upstairs, and outside there is an excellent maritime display that includes a pearling lugger and a boat used by Vietnamese refugees. Pride of place among the stuffed animals undoubtedly goes to 'Sweetheart', a 5m, 780kg saltwater crocodile, which became a Top End personality after attacking several fishing dinghies on the Finniss River south of Darwin.

Admission to the museum (☎ 8999 8211) is free and it's open Monday to Friday from 9 am to 5 pm, and weekends from 10 am to 5 pm.

Bus Nos 4 or 6 will drop you close by, or you can get there on the Tour Tub or along the bicycle path from the city centre. There's also a good licensed restaurant which makes a great spot for lunch (see Places to Eat).

Fannie Bay Gaol Museum
Another interesting museum is a little further out of town at the corner of East Point Rd and Ross Smith Ave. Built in 1883, this was Darwin's main jail for nearly 100 years. Among its locally famous inmates were Harold Nelson, who lobbied for political representation and eventually became the Territory's first member of parliament and Nemarluk, an Aboriginal bushranger who murdered three Japanese fishermen.

You can wander round the old cells, see a gallows constructed for a hanging in 1952, and a minimum security section used at various times for juvenile delinquents, lepers and Vietnamese refugees. The gaol

DARWIN - INNER SUBURBS

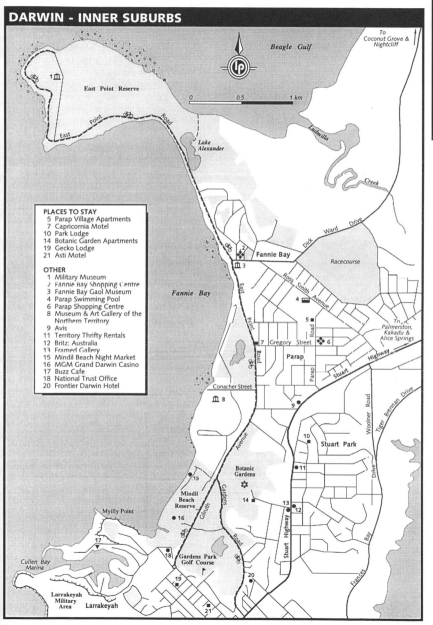

Beagle Gulf

To
Coconut Grove &
Nightcliff

East Point Reserve

Ludmilla

East Point Road

Lake
Alexander

Creek

0   0.5   1 km

PLACES TO STAY
5 Parap Village Apartments
7 Capricornia Motel
10 Park Lodge
14 Botanic Garden Apartments
19 Gecko Lodge
21 Asti Motel

OTHER
1 Military Museum
2 Fannie Bay Shopping Centre
3 Fannie Bay Gaol Museum
4 Parap Swimming Pool
6 Parap Shopping Centre
8 Museum & Art Gallery of the
   Northern Territory
9 Avis
11 Territory Thrifty Rentals
12 Britz: Australia
13 Framed Gallery
15 Mindil Beach Night Market
16 MGM Grand Darwin Casino
17 Buzz Cafe
18 National Trust Office
20 Frontier Darwin Hotel

Fannie Bay

Fannie Bay

Dick Ward Drive

Racecourse

Ross Smith Avenue

East Point Road

Gregory Street

Parap

Parap Road

Stuart Highway

To
Palmerston,
Kakadu &
Alice Springs

Conacher Street

Woolner Road

Tiger Brennan Drive

Stuart Park

Avenue

Botanic
Gardens

Mindil
Beach
Reserve

Myilly Point

Gilruth

Gardens

Stuart Highway

Bay

Frances

Road

Cullen Bay
Marina

Gardens Park
Golf Course

Larrakeyah
Military
Area

Larrakeyah

closed in 1979, when a new maximum security lock-up opened at Berrimah.

The museum is open weekdays from 9 am to 5 pm and on weekends from 10 am to 5 pm; admission is free.

Bus Nos 4 and 6 from the city centre go very close to the museum, and it's on the Tour Tub route.

Military Museum

Devoted to Darwin's WWII experiences, this well-presented little museum is in the East Point Reserve north of Fannie Bay (see next section). There's a 15 minute video on the bombing of Darwin, and cabinets showing various weapons and wartime photos. One curio is a captured bible in Japanese.

Outside there's an assortment of military hardware – check out the tail gunner's bubble, about the size of a large beach ball, from an American bomber. The centrepiece is a concrete emplacement housing a 9.2 inch gun. This massive gun could lob a shell weighing 172kg over a distance of 27km, although it was not installed and tested until 1945, by which time the war was all but over! Ironically, the gun was sold for scrap to a Japanese salvage company in 1960.

The museum (☎ 8981 9702) is self-funding and run by volunteers, and well worth a visit if you're into militaria. It's open daily from 9.30 am to 5 pm and entry costs $8. It's on the Tour Tub route and there's bicycle parking.

East Point Reserve

This spit of undeveloped land north of Fannie Bay is good to visit in the late afternoon when wallabies come out to feed, cool breezes spring up and you can watch the sunset across the bay. On the northern side there are some wartime gun emplacements and associated buildings; monsoon vine forest rings the peninsula and there are some walking and riding trails as well as a road to the tip of the point.

Also part of the East Point Reserve is Lake Alexander, a small, recreational saltwater lake that was made so people could enjoy a swim year-round without having to worry about box jellyfish.

A 1.5km mangrove boardwalk leads off from the car park. Signs explain the uses the Larrakiah people made of mangrove communities. The boardwalk is open daily from 8 am until 6 pm.

Vehicles are permitted in the reserve, and there's also a good bicycle track and footpath.

Parks & Reserves

Three reserves have been set aside in the Darwin vicinity for their natural, cultural and historic value. All have picnic areas, toilets, barbecues and walking trails.

Parks & Wildlife rangers lead informative walks through the parks – check with their desk at the Information Centre for details.

Casuarina Coastal Reserve
  Sites of Aboriginal and historical significance are preserved in this stretch of fine, sandy beaches between Rapid Creek and Lee Point. There's a nude bathing area and a rock offshore, known to the Larrakiah as *Dariba Nunggalinya*, is a registered sacred site. It is said that interference with the rock led to Cyclone Tracy.
Holmes Jungle Nature Park
  This 250 hectare park in Darwin's eastern suburbs features a small remnant of monsoon rainforest which is sustained by a permanent spring. This patch of forest is typical of the monsoon forest which once covered much of the Darwin area. Banyan trees and various palms, vines and ferns form the monsoon habitat, while the woodland area is dominated by eucalypts and grevilleas.
Charles Darwin National Park
  Declared in 1998, this little national park on the shore of Darwin Harbour preserves extensive stands of mangroves and some storage bunkers that date back to 1941. There's a pleasant grassed area with fine views over the harbour. Walking trails are being developed.

Australian Aviation Heritage Centre

Darwin's aviation museum (☎ 8947 2145) is a large hangar that's crammed with aircraft and aircraft bits. The centrepiece is a mammoth B52 bomber, one of only two displayed outside the USA, which has somehow been squeezed inside. It dwarfs the other aircraft, which include a Japanese Zero fighter shot down in 1942 and the remains of a RAAF Mirage jet that crashed in a nearby swamp. A short video on the mighty B52 runs daily. It's worth a look for the B52 alone, but there are many interesting displays.

The museum is on the Stuart Hwy in Winnellie, about 10km from the centre. It is open daily from 9 am to 5 pm; entry costs $8/20 per adult/family.

Bus Nos 5 and 8 run along the Stuart Hwy and it's on the Tour Tub route.

Crocodylus Park

Out on the eastern edge of town, this park was set up for crocodile research and features hundreds of the giant reptiles. There's an excellent display on the life cycle and behaviour of crocs, and graphic information on croc attacks. Allow about two hours to look around.

Crocodylus Park (☎ 8947 2510) is open from 9 am to 5 pm every day; feeding and a tour are held daily at 10 am, and 12 and 2 pm. Entry is a bit steep at $15 (children $7.50), but the price includes the chance to be photographed holding a crocodile.

To get there, take bus Nos 5 or 9 and ask to be dropped at the park entrance.

ACTIVITIES
Beaches

Darwin has plenty of beaches, but it's unwise to venture into the water between October and May because of the deadly box jellyfish (beach parties and concerts are held on May Day to celebrate the stingers' departure). Popular beaches include **Mindil** and **Vestey's** on Fannie Bay, and **Mandorah**, across the bay from the city (see the Around Darwin chapter).

In north Darwin, there's a stinger net protecting part of **Nightcliff** beach off Casuarina Drive, and a stretch of the 7km **Casuarina** beach further east is an official nude beach (despite the ample sunshine, topless bathing is illegal elsewhere). This is a good beach but at low tide it's a long walk to the water's edge.

Swimming Pools

The main public swimming pool is on Ross Smith Ave, Parap (☎ 8981 2662), and has a water slide; entry costs $2.50/1.20 for adults/children.

Scuba Diving

Although Darwin Harbour is not exactly crystal-clear, there are some easily accessible wrecks thanks to Cyclone Tracy. Cullen Bay DIVE! (☎ 8981 3049) at the Cullen Bay Marina conducts instruction courses and wreck dives throughout the year. Including equipment hire, basic open water instruction costs $374. Experienced divers can take a wreck dive for $29 per dive, plus $25 for equipment hire. Lycra suits to protect against box jellyfish stings are included.

The other main dive company is Coral Divers (☎ 8981 2686), 42 Stuart Hwy, Stuart Park.

Cycling

Darwin has a series of excellent bicycle tracks. The main one runs from the northern end of Cavenagh St to Fannie Bay, Coconut Grove, Nightcliff and Casuarina. At Fannie Bay a side track heads out to the East Point Reserve. See the Getting Around section for details of bicycle hire.

Golf

The nine-hole Gardens Park Golf Links (☎ 8981 6365) is centrally located on Gardens Rd near the Botanic Gardens. It is open to the public from 6.30 am to sunset daily and a round costs $11 ($12 on weekends and public holidays). There's also an 18-hole mini golf round costing $4 ($5).

Sailing

The Winter School of Sailing (☎ 8981 9368) has a 12m sloop which takes six passengers on a three hour cruise around the harbour. You can learn and participate or just sit and relax. Cruises operate throughout the year and cost $45 per person.

Longer cruises can also be arranged, for example, 24 hours for six people would come to $1000 including all meals.

Abseiling & Rock-Climbing

Adventure Bound NT (☎ 8988 2951) does beginners abseiling instruction for $30; longer courses and outings for experienced people are also available.

The Rock Climbing Gym (☎ 8941 0747), on Doctor's Gully Rd (near Aquascene), is open seven days and charges $8 with no time limit. Harness and shoe hire is available. It's open from 3.30 to 9.30 pm on weekdays (except Friday, when it closes at 8 pm) and from 10 am to 9.30 pm on weekends.

Skydiving & Parasailing

Pete's Parachuting (☎ 1800 811 646) offers tandem skydiving at $249 for the first jump.

Odyssey Adventures (☎ 0418 891 998) operates parasailing daily from Stokes Hill Wharf for $60 a go or $55 each for a tandem ride.

Fishing

See Activities in the Facts for the Visitor chapter for details of fishing charter operators.

ORGANISED TOURS

There are innumerable tours in and around Darwin offered by a host of companies. The Information Office in the Mall is the best place to start looking. Most tour prices should include transfers from your accommodation. See also the warning in the boxed text.

Many tours go less frequently (if at all) in the wet season. Some of the longer or more adventurous ones have only a few departures a year; inquire in advance if you're interested.

Aboriginal Cultural Tours

The four hour White Crane Dreaming tour operated by Northern Gateway (☎ 8941 1394) includes a 25 minute flight to the homelands of the Kuwuma Djudian people, and a chance to sample bush tucker.

Better are the full-day tours to Bathurst and Melville islands, operated by Tiwi

---

Which Tour?

There are a bewildering number of tours available for the visitor to the Top End. By the time you read this, more companies will have sprung up and others will have disappeared or changed hands. It's a competitive market and before parting with your money there are a few points to consider.

Find out the age group you'll be travelling with, the amount of walking you'll have to do (it can get extremely hot in the Top End's national parks) and the number of people you'll be travelling with. Large groups can mean an impersonal tour which may not suit you as much as one of the more adventurous trips available.

The reception desk at backpackers hostels can help organise and book tours, but beware that some hostels get a commission for recommending certain tours and may not be impartial in their advice. In fact, we have had complaints from readers who were abused and threatened for not taking a certain tour. Should this happen, do not hesitate to take your business elsewhere – there's plenty on offer.

Also, check what time your trip is due back – some tours return to Darwin late at night, so you should check with your accommodation that this is OK. If it's not, consider staying in accommodation where it won't cause a problem – at least on the night of your return.

Tours (☎ 8981 5115) – see the Around Darwin chapter for more on the Tiwi Islands.

Other day tours operate to Umorrduk in Arnhem Land (from $200 to $600 per person) – see the Kakadu & Arnhem Land chapter for details – and Peppimenarti at the Daly River ($314).

City Sights

Among the Darwin city tours, Darwin Day Tours (☎ 8981 8696) does a pretty comprehensive, four hour morning and afternoon trip departing at 8.15 am and 2 pm daily (adults $29, children $15). Keetleys Tours (☎ toll-free 1800 807 868) does similar tours.

The Tour Tub (☎ 8981 5233) is an open-sided minibus which tours around the various Darwin sights throughout the day (see Getting Around later in this chapter). For $18 (children $7) you can either stay on board and do a full circuit or get on and off at the various stops. The Darwin Road Runner Shuttle (☎ 8932 5577) is a similar service that allows 1½ hours at most of the sights and costs $18.

If you fancy a ride on a Harley-Davidson, Top End Classic Bike Tours (☎ 8945 5197) does tours around town ranging from five minutes ($5) to one hour ($60).

Harbour Cruises

Darwin Hovercraft Tours (☎ 8981 6855) operates 1¼ hour, 35km hovercraft flights around the harbour for $48 (children $30), and these can be a lot of fun.

For a sunset cruise there are plenty of options leaving from Cullen Bay Marina, including the Pearling Lugger *Kim* (☎ 8983 2892) and the schooner *City of Darwin* (☎ 8981 4300). Most cruises depart daily and last two to three hours. Prices range from $25 to $35 for adults and usually include cheap champagne and nibblies.

Darwin Duchess Cruises (☎ 8978 5094) leaves Stokes Hill Wharf at 2 pm Wednesday to Sunday for a two hour cruise around the harbour ($22 adults, $12 children), and again at 5.30 pm for a two hour sunset cruise.

Scenic Flights

For a view of Darwin from the air, Seawing Airways (☎ 8945 4337) has scenic flights over the Darwin area in an amphibious Beaver aircraft.

Heli North (☎ toll-free 1800 621 77) will whisk you over the city for $65 (children $50) for 15 minutes or $100 ($80) for a half-hour flight. The helipad is almost opposite the WWII Oil-Storage Tunnels near Stokes Hill Wharf.

Tours Around Darwin

A number of operators do trips to the jumping crocodiles at Adelaide River, the Crocodile Farm and to the Territory Wildlife Park. For Adelaide River try Adelaide River Queen Cruises (☎ 8988 8144), which does half-day trips at 7 am for $55 (children $40) that includes the two hour boat ride on the Adelaide River and a visit to Fogg Dam.

Darwin Day Tours (☎ 8981 8696) offers a variety of trips, including half/full-day trips to the Territory Wildlife Park ($34/38, children $21/24); a full-day Wildlife Spectacular Tour which takes in the Territory Wildlife Park, Darwin Crocodile Farm, the Jumping Croc cruise and nearby Fogg Dam costs $89/59. All prices include entry fees.

Keetleys Tours (☎ toll-free 1800 807 868) combines the Territory Wildlife Park and the jumping crocodiles in an eight hour trip which leaves Darwin at 7.30 am and costs $88 (children $78).

Lost Tours Wandering (☎ 8945 2962) has a full-day nature-oriented tour that includes Fogg Dam, Adelaide River, Berry and Howard Springs and sunset at Casuarina Beach costing $60 with lunch and morning tea.

SPECIAL EVENTS

Darwin has plenty of colour and flair when it comes to local festivals. Most of these take place in the Dry, especially during July and August.

Beer Can Regatta
    An utterly insane and typically Territorian festival which features races for boats made entirely out of beer cans. It takes places at Mindil Beach in July/August and is a good fun day (☎ 8927 5775).
Festival of Darwin
    This is mainly an outdoor arts and culture festival held each year in August which highlights Darwin's unique combination of high Asian and Aboriginal populations (☎ 8924 4411).
Royal Darwin Show
    Every July the showgrounds in Winnellie are the scene for the agricultural show. Activities include all the usual rides, as well as demonstrations and competitions.

Darwin Cup Carnival
The Darwin Cup racing carnival takes place in July and August of each year, and features eight days of horse races and associated social events. The highlight is the running of the Darwin Cup.

Darwin to Ambon Yacht Race
Darwin is the starting point for the fiercely-contested Darwin to Ambon Yacht Race, which takes place in July/August. It draws an international field of contestants and there is a real feeling of anticipation in Darwin in the few days leading up to the event.

Darwin Rodeo
Yee ha! August.

PLACES TO STAY

Darwin has accommodation to suit every budget and a thriving tourist industry seems to keep prices competitive and reasonable. There are backpacker hostels, guesthouses, motels, holiday flats and several upmarket hotels to choose from. There's also half a dozen or so caravan parks/camp grounds, but unfortunately none of these is close to the city centre.

Places to Stay – Budget

Darwin City Council actively patrols for people sleeping in parks or in their vehicles in public places (including Mindil Beach) and offenders are liable to a fine.

Camping & Caravan Parks There are no caravan parks close to the city centre and not all will allow you to pitch a tent anyway. If you have your own transport, you may be as well staying out of town at Howard Springs (see the Around Darwin chapter).

If you're going to be staying for a few days it's worth inquiring about weekly rates, as these are usually significantly cheaper, and can be better value even if you're not staying a full seven days.

Shady Glen Caravan Park (☎ 8984 3330), 10km east, is at the corner of Stuart Hwy and Farrell Crescent, Winnellie. This is the closest park to the city centre and is a good, shady place with a shop and pool. Campsites are $16 ($19 with power), or there are small on-site vans at $46.

Backpacker's Lament

As I wandered down Darwin's Mitchell St and the tourist precinct I saw myself as a breed of traveller I barely recognised. In 1983 when I bought my first Lonely Planet guide, people travelled to discover places, to see things, to experience what they hadn't previously experienced. They travelled light and did what the locals did, which meant eating at local places and travelling on local buses.

But the young people I saw in Darwin hardly seemed to go anywhere near the locals. The Mitchell St tourist precinct was like a cocoon with everything a 1990s backpacker could need – shops selling didgeridoos, the obligatory laundrette, an Irish pub, a multitude of small takeaway food shops, old station wagons bearing 'for sale' signs, 4WD vehicles belonging to tour operators and a travel agent advertising special airfares for European passport holders only.

Has the desire to discover the world been superseded by the desire to be part of a distinct backpackers culture, feeling comfortable because each backpacker enclave encountered contains all the necessary amenities (including nightclubs with cheap, abundant beer) that they feel is necessary?

Ian Loftus

Lee Point Resort (☎ 8945 0535) is 15km north of the city on Lee Point Rd. This is an attractive, spacious park, close to the beach at Lee Point, with excellent facilities. Unpowered/powered sites cost $15/18 daily ($90/95 weekly); powered sites with en suite cost $20. Air-con cabins with microwave and TV but no kitchen or bathroom are also available and cost $60 a single or double.

Malak Caravan Park (☎ 8927 3500) and the adjacent *KOA Caravan Park* (☎ 8927 2651) on McMillans Rd near the airport are actually one place. It's for caravans or campervans only but it's well maintained and not too far from the centre. Sites cost $20 per day and $95 per week.

Overlander Caravan Park (☎ 8984 3025) is 12km east of the centre on the corner of McMillans Rd and Stuart Hwy, Berrimah. Camp sites here are $10/60 a night/week ($15/90 powered) and are probably the cheapest you'll find. There are also basic cabins (no fan or air-con) costing from $86 a week.

Palms Caravan Park (☎ 8932 2891) is a good choice, with shade, a 24-hour mini-mart and pools, but it's 17km south-east of the city on the noisy Stuart Hwy at Palmerston. Campsites are $16 ($96 per week) and $18 with power ($108); on-site vans cost $39.90 and self-contained cabins $71.40.

Hostels – City Centre There's a host of choices in this bracket, most of which are on or near Mitchell St a stone's throw from the Transit Centre. Most have a courtesy phone at the airport.

Competition is keen and standards are pretty high, so it's always worth asking about discounts for the first night (currently $2 at some hostels), for a weekly rate (usually seventh night free) if you plan to stay that long, or during the Wet when things are likely to be slack. The usual YHA/VIP and other discounts apply.

Facilities normally include communal kitchen and pool, but most places turn on the air-con only at night. Free breakfasts are usually available.

Chilli's (☎ toll-free 1800 351 313, 69A Mitchell St) is part of the Nomads chain and is right next to the Transit Centre. There's no pool, but it has two outdoor spas, a breezy kitchen and meals area overlooking Mitchell St, a pool table and an air-con TV room. This is a well-run and clean place with very helpful staff. Dorms are $16 ($15 with discounts), doubles are $44 ($42) and doubles with en suite are $46. Prices drop slightly during the Wet.

The *Darwin City YHA* (☎ 8981 3995, 69 Mitchell St) is at another part of the Transit Centre. It offers a pool, 24-hour reception, a games room, TV rooms and lockers for valuables. The choice includes four-bed dorms for $16 per person, doubles or twins for $19 per person and doubles with en suite for $25 per person.

Fawlty Towers (☎ toll-free 1800 068 886, 88 Mitchell St) is a friendly place in one of the few surviving elevated tropical houses in the city centre. It has a shady backyard and swimming pool. A bed in a four-bed dorm costs $16, or there are doubles for $40.

Another popular place, right across the road, is *Globetrotters* (☎ toll-free 1800 800 798, 97 Mitchell St). All dorms have an attached bathroom, and there's a pool, free breakfast, two kitchens, frequent barbecues and a very popular bar with cheap meals. A dormitory bunk is $16 in a four to seven-bed room with fridge and attached bathroom. Double rooms are available for $44 with TV and attached bathroom. Bike hire is available.

Across the road from the Transit Centre is the *Melaleuca Lodge* (☎ toll-free 1800 623 543, 50 Mitchell St), which boasts two pools, good laundry and kitchen facilities, and free pancakes for breakfast. Dorm beds are $15 (in four to 10-bed rooms), or there are doubles with TV and fridge for $44 and triples for $50.

Frogshollow Backpackers (☎ toll-free 1800 068 686, 27 Lindsay St) is about 10 minutes walk from the Transit Centre. It's spacious and clean with a park across the road; there's a swimming pool and spa in the garden. The charge is $16 a night in a four, eight or 12-bed dorm (air-con at night), and there are good-sized double rooms with fridge and fan for $35 ($40 with air-con) and $44 with air-con and en suite. This place does pick-ups from the Transit Centre and organises free trips for guests out to East Point at sunset.

Hostels – Elsewhere Outside the hustle, but still within walking distance of the action, there are a couple of budget choices north of Daly St. *Elke's Inner City Backpackers* (☎ toll-free 1800 808 365, 112

Mitchell St) is actually in a couple of renovated adjacent houses. There's a pool and spa between the two buildings and it has much more of a garden feel to it than those right in the heart of the city. A bed in a four or six-share dorm costs $17, or twin/double rooms are $42/45.

Further out towards Mindil Beach is the *Gecko Lodge (☎ toll-free 1800 811 250, 146 Mitchell St)*. This is a smaller hostel in an elevated house, and there's a pool, bike hire and free pancakes for breakfast. Dorm beds cost $15, or there are singles/doubles for $35/45. The reception is upstairs.

The big YWCA *Banyan View Lodge (☎ toll-free 1800 249 124, 119 Mitchell St)* takes women and men and has no curfew. Rooms have fans and fridges, and are clean and well kept; there are two TV lounges, a kitchen and an outdoor spa. The charge is $15 per person in a four-bed dorm with fridge, and fan-cooled singles/doubles cost $30/40 or $32/45 for air-con. Weekly rates are also available.

If you're planning to stay a while the *YMCA (☎ 8981 8377)* at Doctors Gully charges $33 for a single per night but is good value at $110 per week. It's more for seasonal workers and long-stayers but is quite acceptable.

Places to Stay – Mid-Range
Guesthouses Darwin has a number of good small guesthouses, and these can make a pleasant change from the hostel scene, especially if you're planning a longer stay.

Right in the city centre there's the *Air Raid City Lodge (☎ 8981 9214, 35 Cavenagh St)*, opposite the main post office, which has air-con rooms with attached bathroom for $55/65/75 a single/double/ triple, including tax. There's also a communal kitchen and laundry. It's a roomy place and not bad value, although there's no garden or outdoor area.

Not too far from the centre there's the friendly, quiet and airy *Park Lodge (☎ 8981 5692, 42 Coronation Drive, Stuart Park)*, only a short cycle or bus ride from the city centre. All rooms have air-con, fridge, sink

and private balcony; bathrooms, kitchen, TV room and laundry are communal. Singles/doubles cost $35/40 including a light breakfast. Numerous city buses, including Nos 5 and 8, run along the highway nearby; ask the driver where to get off.

Hotels The charming old *Hotel Darwin (☎ 8981 9211)*, at the bottom end of the Esplanade, is good value in this range and makes a nice change from the rash of indistinguishable modern-style hotels. It's right in the heart of the city, facing the bay, and features lawns, a lush garden and a big pool. The rooms are big and comfortable, with air-con, en suite, TV, phone and fridge. The room rates are $72/83 a single/double, and this includes a light breakfast. Wet season rates are about 20% less.

Also good is the *Value Inn (☎ 8981 4733, 50 Mitchell St)*, opposite the Transit Centre. The rooms are comfortable though small, and have fridge, TV and en suite. Including tax, the price is $67.20 for up to three people during the Dry and a few dollars less during the Wet.

The *Don Hotel (☎ 8981 5311, 12 Cavenagh St)* is also in the centre, and air-con singles or doubles with en suite, TV and fridge cost $63 (including tax) including a light breakfast.

At the other end of the city centre is the *Top End Hotel (☎ toll-free 1800 626 151)* on the corner of Daly and Mitchell Sts. Singles/doubles in this modern two-storey hotel cost $110/120 including tax, although they can drop to $95 a double during the Wet.

Apartments & Holiday Flats There are plenty of modern places in Darwin, but prices in this range often vary immensely between the Dry and the cheaper Wet. Many of them give discounts if you stay a week or more – usually of the seventh-night-free variety. All these places have a swimming pool.

Good value here and well located is the *Peninsular Apartment Hotel (☎ toll-free 1800 808 564, 115 Smith St)*, just a short walk from the city centre. The studios have a double and a single bed, and cost $80 ($65 in the Wet), while the two-bedroom apartments accommodate four people and cost $130 ($95) including tax. All rooms have a microwave, hot plates, fridge, TV and en suite. Downstairs there's also a bar and shaded saltwater swimming pool.

The *Alatai Holiday Apartments* (☎ toll-free 1800 628 833), on the corner of McMinn and Finniss Sts, are modern, self-contained apartments at the northern edge of the city centre. The three-storey block is built around a swimming pool, and there's also a licensed café and a restaurant. Self-contained two-bed studio apartments cost $89 ($79 in the Wet), while two-bedroom apartments are $142 ($128) plus tax.

Further from the city centre and with a great location right by the Botanic Gardens in Stuart Park is the *Botanic Gardens Apartments* (☎ 8946 0300, 17 Geranium St). Spacious, two-bedroom, self-contained apartments cost from $169 ($129 in the Wet) for two people, three-bedroom apartments sleeping up to seven start at $209 ($169) and motel rooms are $129 ($99); all prices include tax. All apartments are air-conditioned, and have a balcony, full cooking facilities and a laundry.

In Parap, a little further again from the centre, there's another option, the *Parap Village Apartments* (☎ toll-free 1800 620 913, 39 Parap Rd). All apartments have their own balcony and laundry, and outside there are two pools and a children's play area. Including tax, the rates are $155/185 for a standard/deluxe two-bedroom apartment ($140/170 in the Wet) and $175 ($160) for a three-bedroom townhouse.

Motels In Darwin motels tend to be expensive, but a good option – and the first motel you'll pass if you're arriving by road from the south is the *Hi Way Inn* (☎ 8947 0979, 430 Stuart Hwy, Winnellie). A budget room with shared bathrooms and kitchen costs $42, although these fill up fast; large rooms with en suite start at $57.50.

Conveniently central is the *Asti Motel* (☎ toll-free 1800 063 335) on the corner of Smith St and Packard Place just a couple of blocks from the city centre. Excluding the 5% tax, rooms cost $90 ($68 in the Wet), and there are some four-bed family rooms for $105 ($89).

The *Metro Inn* (☎ toll-free 1800 022 523, 38 Gardens Rd) is a comfortable modern motel. Double rooms cost $115 ($90 in the Wet), or studio rooms with cooking facilities are $130 ($110) including tax. All rooms have private bathroom, fridge and TV. There's also a pool and restaurant. Gardens Rd is the continuation of Cavenagh St beyond Daly St.

For motel accommodation in Fannie Bay the *Capricornia Motel* (☎ 8981 4055, 44 East Point Rd) is good value, with big, tiled rooms with sink and fridge costing $63/78.75 for a single/double in the Dry ($47.25/63 in the Wet), including tax. There's a communal kitchen and a pool, and it's handy for the museum and Mindil Beach.

Places to Stay – Top End
Most of Darwin's upmarket hotels are on the Esplanade, making best use of the prime views across the bay. All offer the usual facilities, including pool, and most offer excellent off-season discounts and stand-by rates. Remember to add 5% tax to all prices.

Hotels The modern *Carlton Hotel* (☎ 1800 891 119) is on the Esplanade side of the Darwin Entertainment Centre and has double rooms for $290 and suites from $420; stand-by rates can drop to $180 a double.

Centra Darwin (☎ 8981 5388, 122 The Esplanade) has singles/doubles for $190, although discounts can bring the price down as low as $135.

Close by is the *Novotel Atrium* (☎ 8941 0755), which does indeed have an atrium, complete with lush tropical plants, and has rooms for $190 and up ($135 during the Wet).

The *Holiday Inn* (☎ toll-free 1800 681 686) is right behind the Transit Centre. It has a range of choices, from studios ($210), spacious hotel rooms ($195) and one/two/three-bedroom suites from $220/320/370.

DARWIN

Expect to pay about 10% more for a harbour view.

One block back from the Esplanade but still with the fine views is the city's only five-star hotel, the **Rydges Plaza Darwin** (*☎ 8982 0000, 32 Mitchell St*). It has all the facilities you'd expect, including some non-smoking floors. Rooms here start at $265 for a single or double, but weekend deals as low as $145 including breakfast are sometimes available.

The newest of the posh hotels is the **Darwin Central Hotel** (*☎ 8944 9000*), right in the centre at the corner of Smith and Knuckey Sts. Double rooms start at $215 ($166 in the Wet) and executive suites cost $239 ($189).

Serviced Apartments For self-contained accommodation at this end of the market there's the **Marrakai Serviced Apartments** (*☎ toll-free 1800 653 732, 93 Smith St*) in the city centre. The two-bedroom suites here all have cooking facilities, dishwasher, laundry and balcony, and cost $196 ($163 in the Wet) plus tax. The complex has underground parking and a great pool.

Also in the city centre is the **Mirrambeena Tourist Resort** (*☎ toll-free 1800 891 100, 64 Cavenagh St*). This large place has a variety of accommodation, all of it upmarket, ranging from $114/124 for a standard single/double and $144/155 for a deluxe unit to $199 for a split-level townhouse sleeping four – plus tax.

PLACES TO EAT

Dining out is not yet the obsession it has become in some other Australian cities, but Darwin's thriving tourist industry has spawned a rash of good – and reasonably priced – eateries. The standard is much better than virtually anywhere else in the Territory, so enjoy it while you're here.

A number of places in the vicinity of Mitchell St offer discount meals for backpackers. These can be extremely good value so keep an eye out for meal vouchers at the hostels. Of course, if you want to spend the dough there are plenty of upmarket choices,

but in general we found that in these you're paying for ambience and décor as much as food, and several mid-range restaurants were fine. The city's much-vaunted proximity to Asia has spawned few decent Asian eateries.

City Centre

Breakfast, Bakeries & Coffee All-night revellers and early starters can get a cooked breakfast at the 24-hour **Major's on Mitchell** opposite the Transit Centre on Mitchell St; it's the one with the condom dispenser outside.

The **Banyan Tree**, where the buses pull in at the rear of the Transit Centre, opens at 5.30 am and has cooked breakfasts as well as takeaways. **About Coffee**, also in the Transit Centre, opens at 10 am and has a good selection of breakfasts plus coffees. It sets up tables on the footpath in Mitchell St.

Salvatore's, on the corner of Knuckey and Smith Sts, opens early and has good Italian-style coffee. For fresh bread and pastries there's the **My Linn** Vietnamese bakery at the Transit Centre, which opens early, and in Anthony Plaza off the Smith St Mall, **Le Pierrot** French bakehouse has quiche and vol-au-vents.

Budget & Takeaway There are a number of cheap eateries at the Transit Centre in Mitchell St, in the thick of all the backpackers hostels. Most are hole-in-the-wall outlets but there are sheltered tables and stools out the back; the choice includes Mexican, Japanese, Chinese, vegetarian and Thai.

Coyote's Cantina (*☎ 8941 3676*) is an authentic Mexican place that's extremely popular with travellers and has a reputation that spans the country; there's both a hole in the wall and a sit-down restaurant upstairs (bookings essential on weekends).

The Mental Lentil is also popular and has very good vegetarian fare, including lentil burgers for $5.50, vegetable curry or dhal for $7, and lassis and fruit smoothies.

It would be hard to beat the meal deals at **Globetrotters Lodge** (*97 Mitchell St*) – $3.50 for nachos or lasagne, $3.95 for fish and chips, and $5 for a T-bone steak!

Rumpoles, in the Supreme Court building, is a good lunchtime café serving coffee, gourmet sandwiches and cakes.

Sizzler, on Mitchell St, is also popular, with queues out onto the footpath some nights. The reason is that it's very good value: for around $15 you can fill your plate from a wide range of dishes, and have a dessert too. At lunch time you can fill your plate several times over for as little as $5.90.

The city centre is also takeaway heaven, with outlets of *Red Rooster*, *KFC*, *McDonald's*, *Pizza Hut* and others.

Pubs Several watering holes along Mitchell St – two of them Irish – offer decent food at reasonable prices. *Shenannigans*, next to the YHA hostel, is Darwin's original Irish pub and offers traditional fare such as Irish stew. *Kitty O'Shea's Irish Bar & Café*, opposite the Darwin Plaza Hotel, is newer and roomier, and has similar dishes.

Rorke's Drift (46 Mitchell St) has good pub grub for breakfast, lunch and dinner. Good choices include huge serves of fish and chips for $10, and freshly baked pies, such as steak and stout or turkey and wild mushroom, for $7.50.

Restaurants The *Pancake Palace (☎ 8981 5307)* on Cavenagh St near Knuckey St, is open daily for lunch and in the evening until 1 am. Conveniently close to many of Darwin's night spots, it has sweet and savoury pancakes from $8, as well as meaty offerings such as buffalo and barra crepes for around $15.

For something different you could try the *Swiss Cafe & Restaurant (☎ 8981 5079)* tucked away in the Harry Chan Arcade off Smith St. It serves good, solid European food including popular favourites such as fondue, and is reasonably priced with main dishes for around $12 to $15.

Pente (☎ 8941 1444, 26 Mitchell St) is a relatively new place with a high standard; mains start at $15.50 for pasta and range up to $22.50 for barramundi; good pizzas from a wood-fired oven are from $11.50 to $13.50.

The very popular open-air *Lindsay St Cafe (☎ 8981 8631, 2 Lindsay St)* in the garden of a typical elevated tropical house. The menu is varied, with a tendency towards Asian cooking. Main courses are about $15 to $17 at lunchtime and up to $22 at dinner.

Meat eaters recommend the *Hog's Breath Cafe, (☎ 8941 3333)* right opposite the Vic in the Smith St Mall (see Entertainment). This popular American-style grill prides itself on its 18-hour tenderised rib steaks. There's also a wide range of burgers.

The licensed *Cafe Capri (☎ 8981 0010, 37 Knuckey St)* has a Mediterranean ambience and a good range of meat and pasta standards, plus burgers, bagels and kebabs. Pasta dishes are $10 to $13 and steaks around $18.

The *Sugar Club (☎ 8981 9887, 21 Cavenagh St)* is a café and bar with a pleasant, friendly ambience that stays open till late every night. It serves imaginative dishes, such as Mediterranean vegetables with curried lentil and mint couscous, as well as standard pasta and other mains ($14.50 to $19.50).

Guiseppe's (☎ 8941 3110, 64 Smith St) is a well-established place that serves seafood as well as pasta ($14 to $16), pizza ($8 to $16) and other Italian standards. Seafood entrees are in the $12 to $14 range and mains are $15 to $20.

Asian There are plenty of Asian eateries, although few stand out at the budget price end and others are decidedly expensive. One cheap exception is the excellent *Rendezvous Cafe* in the Star Village Arcade off the Smith St Mall, a no-frills place with Thai and Malaysian food – the laksa has a legendary reputation. Darwin's best range of cheap Asian fare is at the Mindil beach market, though it's open only during the Dry (see the following section).

The *Hanuman (☎ 8941 3500, 28 Mitchell St)* is an award-winning, mainly Thai restaurant, although the menu includes some Indian and Malay dishes. It ain't cheap – expect to pay around $17 for a main course.

DARWIN

Another good choice is *Nirvana (☎ 8981 2025)*, at the top end of Smith St over Daly St, which is open every day for dinner only. It offers a good range of Thai, Malaysian and Indian standards – main courses are $15 to $17 but half serves are available so you can sample more dishes. This place also has live music (see the Entertainment section).

For Chinese, *The Magic Wok (☎ 8981 3332)*, next to the main post office on Cavenagh St, offers a self-serve which you hand to the chef for cooking. It's $12.90 for one serve and $16.90 for all you can eat at lunchtime, and $26 per person at dinner. It's not cheap but it's good, fresh fare and a favourite among locals.

The more expensive hotels all have at least one major restaurant, and some of these can be fine places to eat – at fine dining prices.

Self-Catering There's a grotty Woolworth's *supermarket* on the corner of Smith and Knuckey Sts that's open seven days. If you're heading out to Kakadu or Litchfield and have your own transport there's a better Woolie's at Palmerston on the way.

If you're stocking up to go to Kakadu (not a bad idea) be aware that you must get a quarantine certificate for your fruit and vegetables at the checkout, and keep the produce sealed until you pass the checkpoint on either the Arnhem or Stuart Hwys.

Cullen Bay & Fannie Bay

Cullen Bay, the new marina/condo development north of the city centre, is providing Darwin's discerning diners and beautiful people with a new class of restaurant. There is certainly some good grub to be had here and the setting is very nice, but you'll pay well over the odds for the privilege and probably have to book well ahead for a seat.

Buzz Cafe (☎ 8941 1141) is setting the pace, with an enviable waterside decked area and a good menu that includes imaginative salads ($10.50 to $14.50), pastas (around the $15 mark, but up to $18.50 at dinner!) and main courses are $14.50 to $21.50. The men's bathrooms are a talking point.

Cheek by jowl around the marina are *Yots Café (☎ 8981 4433)*, *Sakura (☎ 8981 4949)* for Japanese and *Portofino (☎ 8981 4988)* for Italian. There are plenty of others, and upmarket Chinese dining is to be had at *Hoi King Chinese Seafood Restaurant (☎ 8981 0788)*.

At the other price extreme is the bustling *Mindil Beach Market* where food stalls are set up on Thursday night from May to October and, to a lesser extent, Sunday night from June to September. Big crowds begin arriving from 5.30 pm with tables, chairs, rugs, grog and kids to settle under the coconut palms for sunset and decide which of the tantalising food-stall aromas has the greatest allure. It's difficult to know whether to choose Thai, Sri Lankan, Indian, Chinese, Malaysian, Brazilian, Greek or Portuguese – or something else. All prices are reasonable at around $3 to $5 a serve. There are cake stalls, fruit-salad bars, arts and crafts stalls, and sometimes entertainment in the form of a band or street theatre.

Mindil Beach is about 2km from the city centre, off Gilruth Ave. Bus Nos 4 and 6 go past the market area.

Further along Fannie Bay the licensed *Cornucopia* at the Museum & Art Gallery has a good reputation. You can sit outside under the swishing fans on the verandah close to the sea, or inside with the air-conditioning. It's open from 9 am until late every day.

ENTERTAINMENT

Darwin is a lively city with bands at several venues and a number of clubs and discos. More sophisticated tastes are also catered for, with theatre, film and concerts.

Your Weekend is a liftout in the Friday edition of the *NT News* which lists live music and other attractions. It's probably the best source of information on what's on around town.

Bars & Live Music

You won't have to wander far down Mitchell St to find some form of distraction and it's as good a place as any to start.

Starting from the top, on the corner of Daly St there are two bars side by side, part of the Top End hotel complex. The *Sportsmen's Bar* is a 'blokey' kind of place, with poker machines, TAB and televised sport. *Blah Blah Bar* next door has pool tables, pizzas and good bar food, and also a DJ from Wednesday to Saturday; it stays open till 4 am.

Backpackers are catered for at *Globetrotters*, 97 Mitchell St, where the bar features happy hours and fun nights such as karaoke. Another popular choice is *Rattle'n'Hum* on Cavenagh St, which has barbecue evenings, theme nights and happy hours. Both places have a good earthy atmosphere and stay open late seven days.

Shenannigans and *Kitty O'Shea's* are two pleasant Irish-style pubs on Mitchell St that serve Guinness and other delights; on Monday night there's an acoustic music session at Shenannigans to which all comers are welcome.

The décor at *Rorke's Drift*, also on Mitchell St, features memorabilia of the Zulu War and even a scale model of the famous engagement. It's a good English-style pub with a beer garden that gets really jumping on Friday night.

Over Daly St on Smith St there's *Nirvana*, a good eatery (see Places to Eat) that hosts live jazz/blues every night. Entry is free and it's open until about 2 am, but you must eat as you drink; bar snacks are available at reasonable prices.

Live bands play upstairs at the *Victoria Hotel* (known simply as 'The Vic') from 9 pm Wednesday to Saturday, but it's also a good place for a drink in the early evening. Live music can also be heard on weekends at the *Billabong Bar* in the Novotel Atrium and at *Squires Tavern* in Edmunds St, which has a popular beer garden.

The *Jabiru Bar* in the Novotel Atrium is the venue on Friday evening for Crab Races. It's all very light hearted and there are prizes for the winners.

For a change of pace, the *Hotel Darwin* is a pleasant place for a quiet drink in the evening.

Nightclubs

Next to Squires Tavern on Edmunds St is the *Time Nightclub*. It's probably the most popular nightspot in the city and claims to be Darwin's only dance club. It's open from 10 pm until 4 am, but only on Monday and Thursday to Saturday.

Petty Sessions on the corner of Mitchell and Bennett Sts is a combination wine bar and nightclub. It's quite a popular place and stays open to 2 am. Another late night venue is *Caesars* nightclub at the Don Hotel on Cavenagh St.

Folk Music

For something a bit more laid back there's the *Top End Folk Club* which meets on the 2nd and 4th Friday of the month at the Rock, Doctors Gully. Visitors are welcome. Phone ☎ 8988 1301 for more details.

Also check what's on at the two Irish pubs in Mitchell St for a bit of Guinness and reeling.

Jazz & Classical Music

On Sunday afternoon during the dry season there's *Jazz on the Lawns* at the MGM Grand Darwin casino. Entry is free, and food and alcoholic drinks are available. It's a pleasant way to watch the sunset.

The Darwin Symphony Orchestra (DSO) holds concerts of popular favourites periodically at the Darwin Entertainment Centre and other venues; check with the Information Centre for what's coming up.

Cinema

The *Darwin Film Society* (☎ 8981 2215) has regular showings of offbeat/arthouse films at the Museum Theatrette, Conacher St, Bullocky Point. During the dry season the society runs the *Deckchair Cinema* (☎ 8981 0700) near Stokes Hill Wharf. Here you can watch a movie under the stars while reclining in a deckchair. Screenings are listed in the newspapers, or on flyers around town.

There's a commercial *cinema complex* on Mitchell St showing latest releases, and another at the Casuarina Shopping Square.

Theatre

The ***Darwin Entertainment Centre*** on Mitchell St houses the Playhouse and Studio Theatres, and hosts events from fashion-award nights to plays, rock operas, panto-mimes and concerts. Bookings and 24-hour information are available on ☎ 8981 1222.

The ***Darwin Theatre Company*** (☎ 8981 8424) often has play readings and other performances around the city.

The old ***Brown's Mart*** (☎ 8981 5522) on Harry Chan Ave is another venue for live theatre performances.

Casino

Finally, there's the tasteless ***MGM Grand Darwin*** casino on Mindil Beach, where you can spend as much money as you like as long as you're 'properly dressed' – that means no thongs and 'dress' shorts! Cheap meals are also available for losers.

SPECTATOR SPORTS

There's quite a bit happening on the local sports scene but very little in the way of interstate (let alone international) events.

The Northern Territory Football League is the local Australian Rules league, and there are matches most weekends in the dry season. Phone ☎ 8945 2224 for venues and match details.

Rugby Union matches are played at Rugby Park in Marrara (☎ 8981 1433), while Northline Speedway (☎ 8984 3469) is where the petrol heads cut loose.

SHOPPING

The city centre has a good range of outlets selling a range of art and crafts from the Top End – such as bark paintings from western Arnhem Land, and interesting carvings by the Tiwi people of Bathurst and Melville islands – and work from further afield in central Australia. Prices are generally very reasonable and if you have the bucks some very fine pieces are available. Taste and try – there's plenty to choose from.

Two long-established shops on Knuckey St are Raintree Aboriginal Fine Arts, at No

20 (☎ 8941 9933), and Wadeye Arts & Crafts Gallery, at No 31.

Aboriginal Fine Arts, above Red Rooster on the corner of Mitchell and Knuckey Sts, has some very fine pieces, as does the excellent Framed, a gallery at 55 Stuart Hwy in Stuart Park near the entrance to the Botanic Gardens. Both are worth a browse just for pleasure, even if you can't afford the price tags.

Indigenous Creations is a chain with several outlets in Darwin; the one at the Transit Centre is called Cultural Images and there are two shops in the Smith St Mall. Cultural Images offers didgeridoo lessons for $25 to $30 – inquire at the shop for details.

On Cavenagh St there's the Arnhemland Art Gallery (☎ 8981 9622), which has some fine bark paintings.

You can find Balinese and Indian clothing at Mindil Beach market (Thursday and Sunday evening – see Places to Eat). There's a Night Market on the corner of Mitchell St, open every night from 5 to 11 pm, where you can buy T-shirts, didgeridoos and sarongs for every occasion.

GETTING THERE & AWAY
Air

Darwin is becoming increasingly busy as an international and domestic gateway. The airport is only a short bus or taxi ride from the city centre.

On the international scene, there are flights to Brunei, Indonesia (Bali), Timor, Malaysia, Singapore and Thailand – see the Getting There & Away chapter for more information.

Domestically Darwin is not so well served. Ansett and Qantas fly direct to Adelaide, Alice Springs, Brisbane, Broome, Kununurra and Sydney, but the number of flights is limited and there is very little discounting as it's not a heavy traffic route.

On a more local level, Airnorth fly daily to Katherine ($144) and Monday to Saturday to Tennant Creek ($319) and Alice Springs ($389); see the relevant sections for details of flights to various other smaller settlements in the Top End.

See the Getting There & Away chapter for details of flights in and out of Darwin.

Airlines The main airline offices in Darwin include:

Airnorth
(☎ 8945 2866 or ☎ toll-free 1800 627 474 outside Darwin), Darwin Airport
Ansett
(☎ 13 1300), 19 Smith St Mall
Garuda
(☎ 1300 365 330), 9 Cavenagh St
Malaysia Airlines
(☎ 13 2627) 2nd floor, 38 Mitchell St
Merpati
(☎ toll-free 1800 060 188), 22 Knuckey St
Qantas
(☎ 13 1313), 16 Bennett St
Royal Brunei Airlines
(☎ 8941 0966), 22 Cavenagh St
Singapore Airlines
(☎ 131011),1st floor, Paspalis Centrepoint, Smith St Mall

Bus
Both major bus lines servicing the Top End stop in the centre of Darwin. Greyhound Pioneer (☎ 13 2030) pulls in at the rear of the Transit Centre on Mitchell St, and the McCafferty's (☎ 13 1499) terminus is a short walk away at 71 Smith St (on the corner of Peel St).

See the Getting There & Away and Getting Around chapters for route and fare details.

Blue Banana This backpackers bus service (☎ 8945 6800) does a regular circuit from Darwin to Katherine, via Kakadu and Litchfield and a few other stops. A three-month ticket allows you the flexibility to jump on and off as you like. It picks you up at your accommodation and discounts are available for YHA/VIP card holders.

Darwin to Katherine via Kakadu costs $100 or a round trip via Kakadu and Litchfield costs $170. A round trip to Darwin excluding Katherine is $140.

Car Rental
Darwin has numerous budget car-rental operators, as well as all the major national and international companies.

For driving around Darwin, conventional vehicles are cheap enough, but most companies offer only 100km free and any extra cost about 25c/km; around Darwin 100km won't get you very far. Some companies offer 150km free, but you may be restricted to a 70km radius of the city, so you can't go beyond Humpty Doo or Acacia Store (about 70km down the Stuart Hwy). The prices invariably drop for longer rentals for both conventional and 4WD vehicles.

Nifty Rent a Car is about the cheapest, starting at $25 per day; Delta is another budget option with cars from $39, but these cheap deals don't include any free kilometres.

Territory Thrifty Car Rentals is far and away the biggest local operator and is probably the best value. Discount deals include cheaper rates for four or more days hire, weekend specials (three days for roughly the price of two), and one-way hires (to Jabiru, Katherine or Alice Springs). Daily charges start at around $55 daily for a small car.

There are also plenty of 4WD vehicles available in Darwin, but you usually have to book ahead, and fees and deposits can be hefty. Larger companies offer one-way rentals plus better mileage deals for more expensive vehicles.

The best place to start looking is probably Territory Thrifty, which has several different models – the cheapest, a Suzuki four-seater, starts at around $99 a day, plus 28c per kilometre over 100km. Territory also has camping equipment packages costing $25 per vehicle per day.

Britz Australia has the largest range of 4WD campervans and motorhomes, starting from around $120 per day with unlimited kilometres. Backpacker Campervans has budget-priced campervans with cooking facilities from $60 per day including unlimited kilometres.

Rental companies, including the cut-price ones, generally operate a free towing or replacement service if the vehicle breaks down. But (especially with the cheaper operators) check the paperwork to see exactly what you're covered for in terms of damage to vehicles and injuries to passengers. The usual age and insurance requirements apply in Darwin and there may be restrictions on off-bitumen driving, or on the distance you're allowed to go from the city. Even with the big firms the insurance may not cover you when driving off the bitumen, so make sure you know exactly what your liability is in the event of an accident. It is certainly worth taking out comprehensive insurance: we get letters from travellers who didn't and paid out thousands of dollars for repairs.

Most rental companies are open every day and have agents in the city centre. Avis, Budget, Hertz and Territory Thrifty all have offices at the airport.

Avis
(☎ toll-free 1800 672 099), 145 Stuart Hwy, Stuart Park
Britz: Australia
(☎ 8981 2081), 44 Stuart Hwy, Stuart Park
Budget
(☎ 8981 9800), corner of Daly and Mitchell Sts
Delta
(☎ 131390), corner of Cavenagh and McLachlan Sts
Hertz
(☎ 8941 0944), corner of Smith and Daly Sts
Nifty Rent a Car
(☎ 8981 2999), 86 Mitchell St
Rent-a-Rocket
(☎ 8941 3733), 7 McLachlan St
Territory Thrifty Car Rentals
(☎ 8924 0000), 64 Stuart Hwy, Parap
Value Rent a Car
(☎ 8981 5599), 50 Mitchell St

Car Purchase
If you're trying to buy or sell a car for the next leg of your journey, the Travellers' Car Market (☎ mobile 0418 600 830) is behind the Mitchell St Night Market and is open daily from 8 am to 4 pm.

GETTING AROUND
To/From the Airport
Darwin's busy airport terminal is about 6km from the centre of town, and handles both international and domestic flights. The taxi fare into the centre is about $13 during the day and $15 at night.

There is an airport shuttle bus (☎ 1800 358 945) for $6/10 one way/return, which will pick up or drop off almost anywhere in the centre. When leaving Darwin book a day before departure.

Bus
City Bus Darwin has a fairly good city bus service that leaves from the small terminal (☎ 8924 7666) on Harry Chan Ave, near the corner of Smith St. Buses enter the city along Mitchell St and leave along Cavenagh St.

Fares are on a zone system – shorter trips are $1.20 to $1.60, and the longest costs $2.10.

Bus No 4 (to Fannie Bay, Nightcliff, Rapid Creek and Casuarina) and No 6 (Fannie Bay, Parap and Stuart Park) are useful for getting to Aquascene, the Botanic Gardens, Mindil Beach, the Museum & Art Gallery, Fannie Bay Gaol Museum and East Point.

Bus Nos 5 and 8 go along the Stuart Hwy past the airport (but not near the terminal building) to Berrimah, from where No 5 goes north to Casuarina and No 8 continues along the highway to Palmerston.

Tour Tub The Tour Tub (☎ 8981 5233) is a private bus which does a circuit of the city, calling at the major places of interest, and you can hop on or off anywhere. In the city centre it leaves from Knuckey St, near the end of the Smith St Mall (opposite Woolworth's). The set fare is $18 and the buses operate hourly from 9 am to 4 pm. Sites visited include Aquascene (only at fish-feeding times), Indo-Pacific Marine and Wharf Precinct, MGM Grand Darwin casino, the Museum & Art Gallery, East Point and the Military Museum, Fannie Bay Gaol Museum, Parap markets (Saturday only) and the Botanic Gardens. Users of this service are entitled to discounts at places along the route – see its brochure for details and for exact times.

A similar service operated by Galaxy Tours and Charters costs $18 per day, and also visits Crocodylus Park and Casuarina Shopping Square.

Darwin City Shuttle This 24-hour minibus service (☎ 8985 3666) will take you anywhere within 4km of the CBD for a flat fare of $2.

Taxi
Taxis congregate outside Woolworth's on Knuckey St and are generally easy to flag down.

Bicycle
Darwin has an extensive network of excellent bike tracks. It's a pleasant ride out from the city to the Botanic Gardens, Fannie Bay, East Point or even, if you're feeling fit, all the way to Nightcliff and Casuarina.

Many of the backpackers hostels have bicycles; the usual charge is $15 per day or $3 per hour.

Around Darwin

There are plenty of attractions within a few hours drive of Darwin. Litchfield, a major national park to the south, is very popular among locals, while the Territory Wildlife Park is an excellent place to get a look at, and photograph, a wide variety of animals.

Along the Arnhem Hwy (the main access route into Kakadu National Park from Darwin), there's the little town of Humpty Doo and the new Mary River National Park, which is set to become the next major attraction of the Top End.

Down the Stuart Hwy there's plenty of history to relive at the Grove Hill pub and the old gold-mining town of Pine Creek; thermal pools at Douglas Hot Springs and scenic gorges; and fishing enthusiasts will be in heaven on the Daly River.

All the places listed in this chapter are easily accessible by car and are only a few hours at the most from Darwin. Organised day tours run to most of these places, usually combining a number of attractions in one hit.

It's well worth spending a few days exploring this area as it offers a wealth of things to do.

MANDORAH

This popular beach resort on the tip of Cox Peninsula is about 110km by road from Darwin, the last 30km or so of which is unsealed, but only about 10km across the harbour by boat.

The ***Mandorah Beach Hotel*** (☎ 8978 5044) is right by the beach and has air-con motel units at $65 for a single or double with attached bathroom. There's a reasonable restaurant and beachfront beer garden.

Getting There & Away

The Mandorah Jet Shuttle (☎ 8981 7600) operates about eight times daily in each direction, with the first departure from the Cullen Bay Marina in Darwin at 6.30 am, the last at 6.05 pm; the latest return ferry is at 6.20 pm.

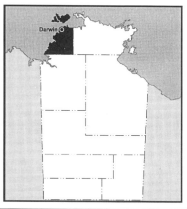

HIGHLIGHTS

- Sit under a waterfall in beautiful Litchfield National Park
- View the native fauna at the Territory Wildlife Park
- See the jumping crocs at Adelaide River Crossing
- Have a beer at the historic – and oddball – Grove Hill pub
- Dangle a line for barramundi at Daly River

The journey takes about 20 minutes, and the cost is $15 return (children $10).

HOWARD SPRINGS NATURE PARK

The 383 hectare Howard Springs Nature Park offers the nearest natural crocodile-free swimming hole to Darwin. Turn off 24km down the Stuart Hwy, beyond Palmerston.

The forest-surrounded swimming hole can get uncomfortably crowded because it's so convenient to the city. Nevertheless, on

AROUND DARWIN

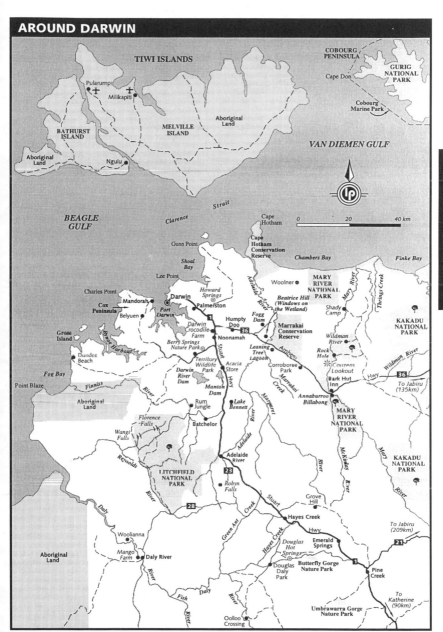

TIWI ISLANDS

COBOURG PENINSULA

GURIG NATIONAL PARK

Cape Don

Pularumpi

Milikapiti

Aboriginal Land

Cobourg Marine Park

BATHURST ISLAND

MELVILLE ISLAND

VAN DIEMEN GULF

Aboriginal Land

Ngulu

Strait

Clarence

Cape Hotham

BEAGLE GULF

Chambers Bay

Finke Bay

Gunn Point

Cape Hotham Conservation Reserve

Shoal Bay

MARY RIVER NATIONAL PARK

Woolner

Lee Point

Charles Point

Howard Springs

Beatrice Hill (Windows on the Wetland)

Shady Camp

KAKADU NATIONAL PARK

Mandorah

Darwin

Palmerston

Cox Peninsula

Port Darwin

Humpty Doo

Fogg Dam

Marrakai Conservation Reserve

Belyuen

Darwin Crocodile Farm

Noonamah

Wildman River

Grose Island

Berry Springs Nature Park

Leaning Tree Lagoon

Rock Hole

Dundee Beach

Territory Wildlife Park

Acacia Store

Corroboree Park

Couzens Lookout

Fog Bay

Darwin River Dam

Bark Hut Inn

To Jabiru (135km)

Point Blaze

Finniss

Manton Dam

Annaburroo Billabong

Aboriginal Land

Rum Jungle

Lake Bennett

MARY RIVER NATIONAL PARK

Florence Falls

Batchelor

KAKADU NATIONAL PARK

Wangi Falls

Reynolds

Adelaide River

LITCHFIELD NATIONAL PARK

Robyn Falls

Grove Hill

Woolianna

Hayes Creek

To Jabiru (209km)

Mango Farm

Daly River

Douglas Hot Springs

Emerald Springs

Butterfly Gorge Nature Park

Pine Creek

Aboriginal Land

Douglas Daly Park

Umbrawarra Gorge Nature Park

To Katherine (90km)

Oolloo Crossing

0   20   40 km

a quiet day – especially in the early morning – it's a pleasant spot for an excursion.

Fish and turtles can usually be spotted from the path across the weir, and agile wallabies graze quite unafraid of humans. Goannas also frequent the picnic area scrounging for hand-outs. There's a 1.8km walking track around the springs which is good for birdwatching before the crowds arrive, and at the southern end of the park you can see the springs themselves.

The park is open daily from 8 am to 8 pm.

Places to Stay

The small township of Howard Springs is about 4km short of the nature park. The *Howard Springs Caravan Park* (☎ *8983 1169)*, on Whitewood Rd, makes a nice alternative to the van parks in Darwin itself, with a saltwater pool, shop and good amenities. It has powered ($17) and unpowered ($12) sites, and comfortable cabins for $65; weekly rates are also available.

Getting There & Away

The Blue Banana bus stops at Howard Springs en route to Kakadu – see the Getting Around chapter for details.

DARWIN CROCODILE FARM

On the Stuart Hwy, 40km south of Darwin, the crocodile farm (☎ 8988 1450) has around 8000 saltwater & freshwater crocodiles. This is the residence of many of the crocodiles that have been taken out of Territory waters because they've become a hazard to people. But don't imagine they're here out of charity. This is a farm, not a rest home, and around 2000 of the beasts are killed each year for their skins and meat – you can find crocodile steaks or even crocodile burgers in a number of Darwin eateries.

There's a small exhibition area with photos and the skull of Charlie, a massive croc killed in 1973 that measured nearly 7m and was an estimated 80-90 years old. One of the live attractions is Burt, a 5m croc that appeared in the film *Crocodile Dundee*.

The farm is open from 10 am to 4 pm daily. There are guided tours on the hour

and feedings – the most spectacular times to visit – occur daily at 2 pm and most other days at noon. Entry is $9.50 (children $5) and you can sample a croc burger for $5.

Many of the day trips from Darwin include the croc farm on their itinerary.

TERRITORY WILDLIFE PARK & BERRY SPRINGS

The turn-off to Berry Springs is 48km down the Stuart Hwy from Darwin, then it's 10km along the Cox Peninsula road to the Territory Wildlife Park and the adjoining Berry Springs Nature Park – two worthwhile attractions that could be combined as a day trip from Darwin.

Territory Wildlife Park

Situated on 400 hectares of bushland, some 60km south of Darwin, the Territory Wildlife Park (☎ 8988 7200) is an excellent open-air type zoo that shouldn't be missed. The state of the art enclosures feature a wide variety of Australian wildlife, some of which is quite rare, and there's even one of feral animals.

Highlights of the park are the **nocturnal house**, where you can observe nocturnal fauna such as bilbies and bats; 12 small **aviaries**, each representing a different habitat from mangroves to monsoon forest, and a huge **walk-through aviary**; and the **arthropod and reptile exhibit**, where snakes, lizards, spiders and insects do their thing.

Pride of place must go to the **aquarium**, where a walk-through clear acrylic tunnel puts you right among giant barramundi, stingray, sawfish, saratoga and a score of others. Not to be missed.

To see everything you can either walk around the 4km perimeter road, or hop on and off the little shuttle trains which run every 15 minutes and stop at all the exhibits.

A number of free talks and activities are given by the staff each day at the various exhibits, and these are listed on noticeboards at the main entrance. There's a free-flying birds of prey demonstration at 10 am and 3 pm daily.

It's well worth the $12 entry fee ($6/30 for children/family) and you'll need at least half a day to see it all. The park is open daily from 8.30 am to 4 pm (gates close at 6 pm).

Day tours are run by various companies (see the Darwin chapter).

Berry Springs Nature Park

Close by is the Berry Springs Nature Park which is a great place for a swim and a picnic. There's a thermal waterfall, spring-fed pools ringed with paperbarks and pandanus palms, and abundant birdlife. If you have a snorkel and mask you could get a closer look at the aquatic life.

Under shady trees there's a pleasant grassed picnic ground with tables and fireplaces. Other facilities include toilets, changing sheds, showers and disabled toilet.

There's an information centre with displays about the park's ecology and history.

The park is open daily from 8 am to 6.30 pm, and there's no entry fee.

Places to Stay The *Tumbling Waters Caravan Park (☎ 8988 6255)* is past Berry Springs along the Tumbling Waters Road – and one of the nicest such places we found in the Top End. Camp sites are $14/17 without/with power and A-frame cabins with shared amenities are $50. There's a bar, pool, tame wildlife and nice shady gardens.

In Berry Springs itself there's the *Lakes Resort & Caravan Park (☎ 8988 6277)*, about 2.5km east of the Wildlife Park. It's well set up for watersports, with a pool with a water slide and a small lake for waterskiing and jet-skiing. Camp sites cost $15/18 and there's a variety of cabins from $60 to $75.

BATCHELOR
• pop 645   ✉ 0845

This small town lies 14km west of the Stuart Hwy. The establishment of the Rum Jungle uranium mine – Australia's first – nearby in the 1950s really put Batchelor on the map. During WWII it was a defence-force base.

Uranium mining ceased in the 1960s, and these days Batchelor owes its existence to the Aboriginal Teacher Training College

WWII Airstrips

One feature of the Stuart Hwy between Darwin and Batchelor is a number of old airstrips right by the side of the road. These date back to WWII when American and Australian fighter aircraft were stationed in the Top End. Owing to the threat of Japanese bombing raids these squadrons were based along the highway rather than in Darwin itself. Strips such as Strauss, Hughes and Livingstone are all signposted by the highway.

and the fact that it is the main access point for Litchfield National Park.

For some outback kitsch, there's a scale replica of **Karlstein Castle** in the town park.

The **Batchelor Butterfly Farm** *(☎ 8976 0199)* is a pleasant diversion, with large walk-through enclosures decked with tropical vegetation full of butterflies bred on the farm. Entry costs $5.50 and there's a good restaurant.

Places to Stay & Eat

Batchelor has a choice of accommodation presenting an alternative to camping at Litchfield.

The *Batchelor Caravillage (☎ 8976 0166, Rum Jungle Rd)* has camp sites at $16 ($20 powered), dorm beds for $13 and self-contained cabins for $75 a double.

The *Batchelor Motor Inn (☎ 8976 0123, Rum Jungle Rd)* has singles/doubles at $78/98. A new place, *Jungle Drums*, was being built next to the Butterfly Farm at the time of writing and is planned to have backpackers rooms; phone for an update ☎ 8976 0555.

There's good food at the *Butterfly Farm*, where you can sit in air-con or on the shady verandah; mains are about $12 to $14 and there are cakes and desserts.

Down the road towards Litchfield there's the *Banyan Tree Caravan Park (☎ 8976 0330, Lot 8a Windmill Rd)*, a pleasant place to stay with a magnificent spreading banyan tree. Camp sites cost $10 ($14 with power), there are budget four-bed fan rooms for $16.80 per person and air-con on-site vans for $21 per person. There's a pool and licensed bistro.

About 14km from Batchelor along the Litchfield road there's the friendly, informal *Mango Cafe at Maurie's*, (☎ *8976 0093)*, which has snacks, drinks, cakes and takeaways.

Getting There & Away
The Blue Banana bus stops here en route to Litchfield and Darwin.

LITCHFIELD NATIONAL PARK
This 146 sq km national park, 115km south of Darwin, encloses much of the spectacular Tabletop Range, a wide sandstone plateau mostly surrounded by cliffs. The park's main attractions are four waterfalls, which drop off the edge of this plateau, unusual termite mounds and curious sandstone formations. Beautiful country, excellent camp sites, and the 4WD, bushwalking and photography opportunities are also highlights. It's well worth a few days, although weekends can get crowded – the local saying in Darwin is 'Kaka-don't, Litchfield-do'.

There are two routes to Litchfield Park, both about two hour drive from Darwin. One, from the north, involves turning south off the Berry Springs to Cox Peninsula road onto a well-maintained dirt road, which is suitable for conventional vehicles except in the wet season. The second, and more popular, approach is along a bitumen road from Batchelor into the east of the park. The two access roads join up so it's possible to do a loop from the Stuart Hwy. The Finniss and Reynolds Rivers may cut off sections of the park during the Wet.

History
The Wagait Aboriginal people lived in this area, and the many pools and waterfalls and other prominent geographical features had great significance for them.

In 1864 the Finniss Expedition explored the Northern Territory of South Australia, as it was then called. Frederick Litchfield was a member of the party, and some of the features in the park still bear the names he gave them.

In the late 1860s copper and tin were discovered, and several mines opened in the area. The ruins of two of these are still visible at Bamboo Creek and Blyth Homestead.

The area was then opened up as pastoral leases, and these lasted until the proclamation of the national park in 1986.

Information
Permits are not required to enter the park unless you plan to walk and camp in remote areas.

There is no visitor centre, but an information bay 5km inside the park's eastern boundary has a map showing walks and lists road conditions. Informative signboards at most sites explain geology, flora and fauna, and Aboriginal activity. There's another information bay inside the northern boundary.

Parks & Wildlife publishes a very good map of the park, available at their desk in Darwin. If more detail is required, the topographic sheet maps that cover the park are the 1:100,000 Reynolds River (5071) and the 1:50,000 Sheets NO 5071 (I-IV). These are available from the Department of Land, Planning & Environment in Darwin.

A ranger is stationed near the northern entrance to the park, but should only be contacted in an emergency (☎ 8976 0282). There are emergency call devices (ECD) at Florence, Tolmer and Wangi Falls.

Litchfield is open all year and the main access road, which passes the main sights, is sealed. The southern access road is unsealed and normally closed during the Wet, even to 4WD vehicles. For an update on road conditions phone ☎ 8922 3394.

If you bring fresh fruit and vegetables from Darwin, remember to get a certificate (see the Darwin chapter for details) when you buy it because there's a quarantine checkpoint on the Stuart Hwy before the turn-off to Batchelor. The nearest fuel is at

Batchelor and there's a kiosk at Wangi Falls (no fuel or alcohol).

Dangers & Annoyances Scrub typhus is spread by a tiny mite which lives in long grass and several cases – including one recent death – have been associated with Litchfield National Park. The danger is small, but cover up your legs and feet should you need to walk in this habitat (most visitors won't encounter the problem). If you fall ill after a visit to the park, advise your doctor that you have been to Litchfield.

Magnetic Termite Mounds

About 17km from the eastern boundary of the park is the first major batch of curious grey termite mounds that are all aligned roughly north-south. A small boardwalk takes you out close to some of the mounds, and there's an excellent information display.

Nearby are some giant mounds of the aptly-named cathedral termites.

LITCHFIELD NATIONAL PARK

To Cox Peninsula Road (40 km)

Windmill Rd

Rum Jungle Road

Road

To Darwin (85km)

Banyan Tree Caravan Park

Batchelor

Batchelor

(4WD   Only)   Park   Rd

Bamboo Creek Tin Mine

Walker Creek

Litchfield

Florence Falls

Magnetic Termite Mounds

Petherick's Rainforest Reserve

Buley Rockhole

Aida Creek Jumpup

Miles Road

Highway

TABLETOP RANGE

Wangi Falls

Tabletop Swamp

Tjaetaba Falls

Tolmer Falls

(4WD)

The Lost City

Milton Road

Stuart

Adelaide River

Greenant Creek

(4WD Only)

Blyth Homestead (Ruins)

Tjaynera (Sandy Creek) Falls

Adelaide River

Dorat Road

Reynolds River

Reynolds River (east)

LITCHFIELD NATIONAL PARK

Minooke Creek

Surprise Creek Falls

Unsealed roads can vary from excellent to impassable, depending on many factors.

Reynolds River (4WD Only)

Table Land Creek

To Pine Creek

0   5   10 km

To Daly River

Daly   River   Road

Queens in Grassland Castles

The savanna woodlands of the Top End are dotted with innumerable, regularly-spaced mounds of earth. Some are football-sized domes, others towering monoliths or dirt cones that spread in every direction. From a distance they can look like herds of grazing antelope in the waving grass and, in a sense, that is what they represent, for they are built by the most abundant grazing animals in tropical Australia – termites.

Termite mounds – erroneously called anthills – are a wonder of natural engineering. Termites are blind, silent insects only a few millimetres in length, but somehow they cooperate to surround themselves with these vast, protective fortresses. Grains of earth, cemented with termite saliva, can grow to house a colony of millions. Collectively termites consume tonnes of grass and wood annually, and storage chambers in the mound may be filled with vegetation; other passages serve as brood chambers and ventilation ducts.

Cathedral termite mound

The hub of the colony is the queen, whose main task in life is to squeeze out millions of eggs. Most eggs hatch into workers, who tend the queen, forage for food and build the mound. Others become soldiers that defend the nest against raiders – termites are a favourite food of lizards, birds and echidnas. Every year a few develop into sexually mature, winged nymphs which leave to mate and raise a new colony. This is the moment other grassland inhabitants have been waiting for, and as the winged termites leave the nest they are snapped up by frilled lizards and birds. The toll is enormous and only one in a million termites survives to found a mature colony.

Several species of termites make recognisable and distinctive mounds. Magnetic termites (*Amitermes meridionalis*) make broad, flattened mounds about 2m high – rather like tombstones – that are aligned roughly north-south. The morning sun heats the flat surface and raises the mound's internal temperature; during the heat of the day, when the sun is overhead, the mound's narrow profile ensures an even temperature is maintained. But not all these mounds face exactly the same direction, as local climatic and physical conditions, such as wind and shade, dictate just how much sun each should receive. Scientists are mystified as to how the termites align their mounds.

Another species, *Coptotermes acinaciformis*, hollows out the trunk and branches of living trees, and in the process forms the tubes essential for that famous Aboriginal musical instrument, the didgeridoo.

The aptly named cathedral termites (*Nasutitermes triodiac*) make the most massive mounds of all, huge buttressed and fluted columns over 6m high. The same engineering feat in human terms would be a skyscraper nearly 2km high that covers eight city blocks, built by a million workers – blindfolded!

Magnetic termite mound

Florence Falls & Buley Rockhole

Almost immediately after the termite mounds the road climbs the escarpment up the Aida Creek Jumpup and after 6km you come to the Florence Falls turn-off on the eastern edge of the plateau. The falls lie in a pocket of monsoon forest 5km off the road along a good track.

Florence Falls has a walking track (with wheelchair access) that leads to a spectacular lookout over the sheer-sided pool, while a steeper path heads down to the excellent swimming hole. The track completes a loop back to the car park. There are picnic tables and fireplaces here.

Buley Rockhole is another popular swimming spot, with toilets and picnic tables, and there's a walking trail to the Tabletop Range escarpment. A track leads to Florence Falls (3.2km return) and the return trip can be done in 1½ hours including time for a swim.

There are two camp grounds here, one accessible only by 4WD. These are pleasant sites and are far less heavily used than Wangi Falls (see the following Facilities section for information about camping at Buley Rockhole).

From Florence falls a 4WD track takes you north across the Florence Creek and swings around to the east to join the main Litchfield Park Road near the park's eastern boundary.

Lost City

Back on the main road it's another 4.2km to the turn-off to the Lost City, 10.5km south of the road along a 4WD track. The feature here is the large sandstone block and pillar formations which, with a little imagination or a good joint, resemble ruined buildings. It's rather a fanciful proposition really but the area is undeniably atmospheric.

This track continues another 3.5km along a *very* rough section as it comes down off the range, to the **Blyth Homestead Ruins**. This section of track should not be attempted by inexperienced drivers.

Tabletop Swamp

About 5km past the Lost City turn-off a track to the left leads the few hundred metres to

Tabletop Swamp, a small, paperbark-ringed wetland that usually supports a few waterbirds. A short walking track goes around the swamp and there are shady picnic tables.

Tolmer Falls

It's a further 5.5km to the Tolmer Falls turn-off. Here the escarpment gives great views over the tropical woodland stretching away to the horizon, and the falls themselves screen a series of caves, the largest known breeding site for the endangered Orange Horseshoe Bat.

You'll probably not see any of these unless you get there at dusk, and access to the falls themselves has been restricted to protect the habitat. But a 450m walking track (with wheelchair access) leads to a lookout with views over the falls. You can continue along this track to complete a 1.5km loop back to the car park (45 minutes). This takes you past some excellent small rock pools above the falls. You are not permitted to swim in the rock pools directly behind the falls, but those further back up the creek are fine.

There are toilets, an information shelter and an emergency call device in the car park.

Blyth Homestead Ruins & Tjaynera Falls

Another 2km along the main road there's **Greenant Creek,** which has a picnic area and a 2.5km walking trail to **Tjaetaba Falls** (allow 1½ hours). It's a pretty spot but sacred to local Aboriginal people and swimming is not permitted.

Just beyond Greenant Creek is the turn-off to Tjaynera (Sandy Creek) Falls, which lie 9km off the road along a corrugated 4WD track. From the end of the track it's a 1.7km walk to the falls from the car park and camp ground along a track lined with lofty paperbark trees. The pool here is deep and cool, and is far less crowded than Wangi.

On the way to the falls from the main road, there's a turn-off to the north after 5.5km, and this is the southern end of the Lost City track. The Blyth Homestead is 1.5km along this track. This 'homestead' was built in 1929 by the Sargent family, and it's hard to believe now but it remained in use until the area was declared a national park in 1986.

After another 2km the main track forks, the left (eastern) fork heading to the falls (1.5km), the right (southern) fork continues right down through the isolated southern reaches of the park to a camp ground on the east branch of the **Reynolds River** (6km), and then another at **Surprise Creek Falls** (13km). Don't be tempted to swim here as saltwater crocodiles may be lurking. The track crosses the Reynolds River and eventually links up with the Daly River road, 17km beyond Surprise Creek. From this intersection you can head east to the Stuart Hwy or south-west to Daly River. This track through the south of the park is impassable during the Wet.

Wangi Falls

The main road through the park continues from the Tjaynera turn-off another 6.5km to the turn-off to the most popular attraction in Litchfield – Wangi Falls (pronounced 'wong-gye'), 1.5km along a side road.

The falls here flow year-round and fill a beautiful plunge pool which is great for swimming. Although the pool looks safe enough, the currents can be strong if the flow of water is large enough and the level high. Beside the pool a multi-language sign points out the dangers, and markers indicate when the water is considered to be too high to be safe. There's an emergency telephone at the car park here – every year a few people get into difficulty while swimming in the pool.

A colony of fruit bats lives near the waterhole, and goannas and kites are a little too friendly round the picnic area.

There are also picnic and camping areas by the pool, and a kiosk that's open from 9 am to 5 pm daily. This area can really become overrun on weekends. A marked 1.6km return, 1½ hour **walking trail** takes you up and over the falls for a great view, but it's quite a steep walk.

Reynolds River

About 4km north of the Wangi turn-off you can take a cruise on the Reynolds River or

a scenic chopper flight over the park. A three hour cruise costs $20/8 for adults/children and helicopter flights are $55/45 for 15 minutes.

Petherick's Rainforest Reserve

From the Wangi turn-off it's 5.5km to Petherick's Rainforest Reserve, also known as the Cascade Wilderness Park. It's a small freehold forest reserve which actually lies outside the park and has a few attractions of its own – Mt Ford Gorge, Curtain Falls, some thermal springs and a two hour walk to the wreck of a WWII Spitfire.

There's a picnic area and camp ground with toilets and showers, and an entry fee of $3 which is waived if you camp here ($5 per person).

Walker & Bamboo Creeks

From Petherick's the road loops back into the park, and after about 6km there's a turn-off to Walker Creek, not far off the road, where there are more rock pools and a camp ground.

At Bamboo Creek, a further 1.5km up the road, there's a track round the ruins of the tin mines that operated here in the 1940s. It's worth a look – there are informative signs and the loop takes about 30 minutes to complete.

It's only another 3km to the northern boundary of the park, and from there it's around 40km of dirt road to the Cox Peninsula road.

Activities

Nearly everyone who goes to Litchfield has a swim and in the Top End there are few better places to do just that. The park is riddled with idyllic waterholes and crystal clear cascades, and crocs are absent from all but a few. Our favourites are Florence and Buley, but it's also safe to swim at Sandy Creek and Wangi. Take a mask and snorkel and you might see some aquatic life. Saltwater crocs are alive and well in the nearby Finniss and Reynolds Rivers.

During the winter months the rangers conduct a number of activities aimed at increasing your enjoyment and knowledge of the park. The schedule varies, but should be posted at the information bays on the way into the park.

Organised Tours

There are plenty of companies offering trips to Litchfield from Darwin. Most day tours cost about $95, which normally includes a pick-up from your accommodation, guided tour of various sights, at least one swim, morning tea and lunch, and a billabong cruise. A one day trip is adequate if you are including Kakadu on your travels. Readers have recommended Coo-ee Tours (☎ 8981 6116) and Goanna Eco Tours (☎ 8927 3880).

If you have energy to burn, Track'n Trek Adventures (☎ toll-free 1800 355 766) does a two day trip that includes mountain biking through certain sectors for $169.

Campers can take a **cruise** on McKeddies Billabong, an extension of the Reynolds River, for $20 ($10 for children) – book at the Wangi kiosk.

Scenic flights can be organised through Batchelor Air Charter (☎ 8976 0023), which charges $95 per person for a 50 minute flight over the falls and other park highlights. See the preceding Reynolds River section for information about helicopter flights.

Facilities

Parks & Wildlife maintains a number of camp grounds within the park for which no permit is required, although a nightly fee must be paid into an honesty box at each site.

Those at Florence Falls (separate 2WD and 4WD areas), Buley Rockhole and Tjaynera Falls have toilets, showers and fireplaces, while the bush camps in the south of the park are very basic. The cost is $5/12 per adult/family at Florence Falls 2WD, and $1 at the others. The 2WD camp ground is closer to the falls and has disabled facilities.

At Wangi the camping area is relatively small and can get crowded. In the dry season it is very dusty underfoot and it is often full by late afternoon. There is an amenities block with showers, toilets and disabled facilities.

Fireplaces are provided, but collect wood before you get to the camp ground as there is very little in the vicinity. It costs $5/12 per person/family to camp here. There's a kiosk at Wangi that's open from 9 am to 5 pm daily.

Sandy Creek is another 4WD camp ground with showers and toilets.

Getting There & Away

En route from Katherine the Blue Banana bus stops at various points around Litchfield (Florence, Tolmer and Wangi Falls) before moving on to Darwin – see the Getting Around chapter for details.

Arnhem Hwy

The Arnhem Hwy branches off towards Kakadu National Park 34km south of Darwin. Most people belt along here intent on reaching Kakadu in the shortest possible time. The eastern boundary of Kakadu is 120km from the Stuart Hwy, and there are a number of interesting stop-offs and detours along the way.

HUMPTY DOO
• 4790   ✉ 0836

Only 10km along the highway you come to the small town with the incredible name – Humpty Doo.

The **Humpty Doo Hotel** is a colourful pub with some real character. It's worth stopping for a counter meal on your way along the highway – Sunday, when local bands sometimes play, is particularly popular.

Places to Stay

The *Humpty Doo Homestay (☎ 8988 1147)*, 2.5km north of the Arnhem Hwy (turn off just past the pub), is a weatherboard cottage with early Australian furniture that can sleep up to five for $90 a night. It's a lovely quiet place with a pool, and is an unofficial orphanage for injured animals.

Overnight cabins are available behind the *Humpty Doo Hotel* for $68.25 including tax and continental breakfast.

Getting There & Away
The Blue Banana bus stops here.

FOGG DAM CONSERVATION RESERVE
About 15km beyond Humpty Doo is the turn-off to Fogg Dam, which lies 6km north of the highway. This is a great place for watching waterbirds – there are some excellent stands of paperbark trees and a viewing platform out over the wetlands, which form part of the Adelaide River flood plain.

Although the dam's function these days is primarily as a waterbird habitat, it has an interesting history. In the 1950s investors pumped a load of money into a scheme to turn the Adelaide River flood plains into a major rice-growing enterprise, the Humpty Doo Rice Project. It lasted just a few short years, one of the causes of its demise being the flocks of magpie geese which feasted on the ripening crop.

The road into the reserve goes right across the old dam wall, although with the massive growth of water plants it's hard to tell on which side of the low wall was the actual dam. On the western side of the wall is an elaborate two-storey viewing platform with interpretive signs.

As you enter the reserve there are two walks: the **Rainforest Walk** takes you through the monsoon forest (3.6km; about two hours return) and on the opposite side of the road there's the **Woodlands to Waterlilies Walk** (2.2km; 45 minutes return), which skirts the southern edge of the dam through woodlands.

There's a picnic area with shelter and toilets and the Rainforest Walk is accessible to wheelchairs. Nocturnal walks are conducted by rangers during the Dry (check with Parks & Wildlife for times).

Fauna
In the late dry season as other water sources dry up, Fogg Dam hosts plenty of magpie geese and other birds such as brolgas, jabirus, white-bellied sea-eagles, kingfishers, ibis and egrets.

In the patch of monsoon rainforest you're likely to come across birds such as scrub-fowls and pittas, and other flying creatures such as butterflies and mosquitoes – be prepared. The reserve also holds large numbers of water pythons, which feed almost exclusively on the large population of dusky rats.

Agile wallabies can also be seen in large numbers grazing on the lush grass of the flood plain.

Saltwater crocs inhabit Fogg Dam.

Getting There & Away
The Blue Banana stops here en route to Kakadu.

ADELAIDE RIVER CROSSING
A further 8km along the Arnhem Hwy is the Adelaide River Crossing. In August 1998 a pile slipped in the bed of the Adelaide River, buckling the bridge and nearly tipping a road train, a motorbike and a ute into the drink. When you consider that the main attraction here is hand-fed crocodiles, you'll sympathise with the drivers' close call.

Popular river cruises leave from here, and from a few kilometres downstream, on which saltwater crocodiles jump for bits of meat held out on the end of poles. The whole thing is a bit of a circus really, but it is quite an amazing sight. The number of crocs waiting for handouts varies, but among the regulars are some giants measuring 6m.

The original cruises were run by Adelaide River Queen Cruises (☎ 8988 8144), and their jetty and office/shop is right by the bridge. The main vessel, the *Adelaide River Queen*, has a fully enclosed air-con lower deck from where you can get some spectacular pictures of crocs jumping right outside the window. The cost is $26 (children $15) for a 1½ hour cruise (daily at 9 and 11 am and 1 and 3 pm in the Dry; 9 and 11 am and 2.30 pm in the Wet).

There's another jumping croc cruise downstream, about 2km beyond Beatrice Hill, run by Adventure Cruises NT (☎ 8988 4547).

Adelaide River crocodile

MARY RIVER NATIONAL PARK

The latest major reserve in the Top End covers the Mary River wetlands, which extend north and south of the Arnhem Hwy. This area offers excellent fishing and wildlife-spotting opportunities, and because there is not much in the way of infrastructure it is far less visited than nearby Kakadu.

Information

The Window on the Wetlands Visitor Centre (☎ 8988 8188) acts as a de facto information centre for the park. It is an ultramodern creation atop Beatrice Hill, a small hill by the Arnhem Hwy a few kilometres east of the Fogg Dam turn-off.

The centre has some excellent 'touchy-feely' displays which give some great detail on the wetland ecosystem, as well as the history of the local Aboriginal people and the pastoral activity which has taken place in the area. There are also great views over the Adelaide River flood plain.

The centre is open from 7.30 am to 7.30 pm daily. Bush tucker sampling sessions are held twice a week during the Dry – check at Parks & Wildlife.

The Park

There are plans to increase the infrastructure once the park has been fully established, although there are already a number of places where you can camp and get out on the water. Currently access is via the Point Stuart Road, a good dirt road that heads north off the Arnhem Hwy about 22km west of Annaburroo.

Mary River Crossing This small reserve is right by the highway near the Bark Hut Inn. A boat ramp provides access to the river and there's also a picnic ground.

Couzens Lookout & North Rockhole Another dirt road 16km north of the Arnhem Hwy heads west to the Mary River 16km away. Couzens Lookout offers some great views (especially at sunset), and North Rockhole, also on the river but 6km away, has a boat ramp and a shady but basic camp ground.

Brian Creek Monsoon Forest About 9km beyond the North Rockhole turn-off another road heads west, this one leading to the Wildman River Wilderness Lodge (see the following Places to Stay section). About 800m along this road is the turn-off to a small pocket of rainforest.

Mistake Billabong About 3km past the Wildman turn-off, Mistake Billabong is an attractive wetland with a viewing platform and picnic ground.

Shady Camp This is an excellent and popular fishing spot right on the Mary River, about 40km north of the Arnhem Hwy. It's also an excellent place to view birdlife and crocodiles of both species – including the world's highest concentration of salties. Boat hire is available (see River Cruises, following).

Facilities include a picnic ground and toilet, but water must be drawn from the river. The dirt access road is in good condition and suitable for conventional vehicles, not just 4WDs.

Activities

Fishing The fishing fraternity is of course interested chiefly in the barramundi which is found in the Mary River waterways. Boat ramps are located at Mary River Crossing, Rockhole and Shady Camp.

Warning In case you had any ideas about swimming, the waterways that come within the park boundaries are home to the highest concentration of saltwater crocodiles in the world! There's also a significant population of freshies.

Organised Tours

From Darwin As the popularity of this area increases so does the number of tour operators visiting the park. A number of companies operating out of Darwin combine a trip to Kakadu with a detour to the Mary River wetlands. They include Gondwana (☎ toll-free 1800 242 177) and Holiday AKT (☎ toll-free 1800 891 121).

NT Adventure Tours (☎ toll-free 1800 063 838) have a basic two day backpackers tour for $55 which doesn't include any meals.

River Cruises There are a couple of private concessions within the park, and these offer both accommodation (see Places to Stay, following) and trips out on the river during the Dry. The Wildman River Wilderness Lodge runs two-hour river trips from North Rockhole daily at 9.30 am at a cost of $24. From the Point Stuart Wilderness Lodge, a wetland tour costs $25, and there are departures at 10.30 am and 2.30 and 4.30 pm daily.

Shady Camp Boat Hire (☎ 8978 8937) has self-drive 3.7m boats for $65/95 a half/full-day.

Places to Stay

Apart from the camp grounds at North Rockhole and Shady Camp, the only other accommodation options are two wilderness lodges.

The *Wildman River Wilderness Lodge* (☎ 8978 8912) charges $80 for a double room, or $150 including all meals. A powered site costs $15. The lodge has a beauti-ful position on the edge of the flood plains, and has good facilities including a swimming pool and a licensed dining room.

The other choice is the *Point Stuart Wilderness Lodge* (☎ 8978 8914) a little further north and a few kilometres off the main track. The lodge is actually part of an old cattle station, and the setting is quite nice and the facilities very good. There's a good grassy camping area and a swimming pool. It costs $8 per person to camp, there are dorm beds for $20, and four-bed self-contained units costing from $85 for singles or doubles plus $20 per extra person.

Mary River Houseboats (☎ 8978 8925) has a variety of vessels including dinghies ($65/95 per half/full-day), six-berth (from $380 for two days) and eight-berth ($470) house boats. Fishing tackle can also be hired. The turn-off to the houseboats berth is 12km east of Corroboree Park then it's 20km to the Mary River on a dirt road.

Getting There & Away

The Blue Banana stops at the Window on the Wetlands Visitor Centre.

Tiwi Islands

Two large, flat islands – Bathurst and Melville – about 80km north of Darwin are owned by the Tiwi Aboriginal people and thus commonly known as the Tiwi Islands. The Tiwis have a distinct culture and although the islands have little in the way of tourist facilities they can be visited on organised tours.

The Tiwi people's island homes kept them fairly isolated from mainland developments until this century, and their culture has retained several unique features. Perhaps the best known are the *pukumani* burial poles, carved and painted with symbolic and mythological figures, which are erected around graves. More recently the Tiwi have turned their hand to art for sale – bark painting, textile screen printing, batik and pottery, using traditional designs and motifs. The Bima Wear textile factory was set up in

Nourlangie from Nawurlandja Rock, Kakadu National Park

m Jim Falls & Creek, Kakadu National Park

Nourlangie & Anbangbang Billabong, Kakadu

Jbirr & East Alligator flood plain, Kakadu National Park

Rainbow Serpent rock art at Ubirr, Kakadu National Park

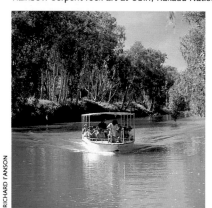
Cruising the East Alligator River, Kakadu

Yellow Water Wetlands, Kakadu National Park

Late afternoon at Berkley Bay, Gurig National Park, Cobourg Peninsula

1969 to employ Tiwi women, and today makes curtains, towels and other fabrics in distinctive designs (Bima designed and printed the vestments worn by Pope John Paul on his visit to the Territory in 1987).

The main settlement on the islands is **Nguiu** in the south-east of Bathurst Island, which was founded in 1911 as a Catholic mission. On Melville Island the settlements are **Pularumpi** and **Milikapiti**.

Most Tiwi live on Bathurst Island and follow a non-traditional lifestyle. Some go back to their traditional lands on Melville Island for a few weeks each year. Descendants of the Japanese pearl divers who regularly visited here early this century also live on Melville Island.

History
The Tiwi had generally poor relations with the Macassans who came from the island of Celebes (now Sulawesi) in search of the trepang, or sea cucumber, from the 17th century. This earned them a reputation for hostility which stayed with them right through the colonial era.

In their efforts to colonise the north of Australia, in 1824 the British established a settlement at Fort Dundas, near Pularumpi on Melville Island. Like the other British settlements in the north, initial hopes were high as the land seemed promising, but the climate, disease, absence of expected maritime trade and, to a degree, the hostility of the local people, took their toll and the settlement was abandoned within 18 months.

In the late 19th century two South Australian buffalo shooters spent a couple of years on Melville Island and, with the help of the Tiwi, reputedly shot 6000 buffaloes. The Tiwi speared one of the shooters; the other, Joe Cooper, fled to Cape Don on the Cobourg Peninsula, but returned in 1900 and spent the next 16 years with the Tiwi.

Efforts by the Catholic church to establish a mission on Melville in 1911 met with resistance from Joe Cooper, so the mission was set up on Bathurst Island. The Tiwi were initially extremely suspicious as the missionaries had no wives, but the situation

improved in 1916 when a number of French nuns joined the mission!

Information
You need a permit to visit the islands, for which you must apply in writing to the Chairman, Tiwi Land Council, Nguiu, Bathurst Island (☎ 8978 3755, fax 8978 3943).

The easier option is to take a tour; Tiwi Tours, a company which employs many Tiwi among its staff, is the main operator, and its tours have been recommended.

Organised Tours
Tiwi Tours (☎ toll-free 1800 183 630) and Aussie Adventure (☎ toll-free 1800 811 633) operate full-day trips to Bathurst Island. For about $250 these include the necessary permit, return flights, visits to the early Catholic mission buildings and craft workshops, a trip to a pukumani burial site and lunch. Two-day tours are also available, although one day is long enough to see the sights. Tours offer a good opportunity to converse with indigenous people.

Places to Stay
The *Munupi Wilderness Lodge* (☎ *8978 3783)* at Pirlangimpi on Melville Island, near the ruins of Fort Dundas, is a comfortable setup that offers outdoor recreation such as cycling, fishing, tennis and Australia's most northerly golf course. The tariff is from $55 per person in safari tents and from $90 per person in four-share bunk rooms, including all meals. The lodge also runs two-day fishing trips from Darwin costing from $370 per person. Air fares are extra.

Transport is through Air North (☎ toll-free 1800 627 474) which flies to Melville Island from Darwin every day except Sunday ($85).

Down the Track

The Stuart Hwy ('the Track') is the bitumen artery that connects Darwin on the coast with Alice Springs, 1500km to the south in the heart of the Red Centre. In the Top End it is a busy road with plenty to see.

AROUND DARWIN

ADELAIDE RIVER

• **pop 280**   ✉ **0846**

This sleepy settlement is 110km south of Darwin and little more than a refuelling and refreshment stop for travellers on the Track. It does, however, have a long history, with beginnings in the days of the Overland Telegraph Line and the North Australia Railway last century. The town was also an important rest camp and supply depot during WWII, and it's worth having a poke around.

The town comes alive during June when the Adelaide River Show, Rodeo, Campdraft & Gymkhana are held at the showgrounds.

Things to See

The town's most famous resident is Charlie, a water buffalo who shot to international fame for his appearance in *Crocodile Dundee*; you can see him in a pen outside the Adelaide River Inn.

Just over 1km east of the highway is the well-signposted **Adelaide River War Cemetery**. Set in an immaculate walled garden, this is the largest war cemetery in the country. It contains the graves of 434 people killed in WWII and a memorial to 287 others lost in the Timor Sea. Adjoining is the cemetery of 63 civilians killed in WWII.

There's a small **pioneer cemetery** on the southern side of the bridge with five graves dating back to 1884.

Places to Stay

The basic *Shady River View Caravan Park* (☎ 8976 7047) behind the BP station has grassy sites at $12, or $14 with power. There is also the *Adelaide River Inn* (☎ 8976 7047), which has single/double rooms with en suite for $55/65. Bistro meals are available and there's a shady beer garden.

The town's *showground*, 500m or so along the old Stuart Hwy (now the road to Daly River), has camp sites for $10 ($12 with power), backpackers beds for $5 and air-con singles/doubles for $30/40. Showers and barbecues, and evening meals are available.

Getting There & Away

The Blue Banana stops here en route to Darwin.

OLD STUART HWY

From Adelaide River the Stuart Hwy runs straight and boring south-east for 100km or so to the historic town of Pine Creek. The old highway is only slightly longer, but is infinitely more interesting and lacks the speeding traffic of the main highway. It's just a single lane of bitumen which winds lazily through open woodland.

The old highway also gives access to the Daly River road, which leads to Daly River, a popular fishing spot on the river of the same name about 80km from the main road (see later in this chapter for details).

Robyn Falls

The turn-off to these small waterfalls is about 15km along the highway from Adelaide River. From the car park it's a 15 minute scramble along a rocky path to the small plunge pool at the base of the falls.

Douglas Hot Springs

To reach Douglas Hot Springs Nature Park, turn south off the old highway just before it rejoins the Stuart Hwy and continue on for about 35km. The nature park here incorporates a section of the Douglas River, a pretty camping area with shady paperbarks, and several hot springs – a bit hot for bathing at 40-60°C, but there are cooler pools. The best swimming area is 200m upstream and there's a 1km return billabong walk.

There are a number of Aboriginal sacred sites in the area, and the reserve is actually owned by the Wagiman people, who know it as Tjuwaliyn, and managed on their behalf by Parks & Wildlife. Don't be tempted to swim in the river itself unless you want to tangle with a saltwater crocodile.

The camp ground here has pit toilets, barbecues, picnic tables and drinking water; camping costs $3.50/8 per adult/ family.

The Blue Banana stops here en route to Litchfield and Darwin.

Butterfly Gorge

About 17km beyond Douglas Hot Springs, **Butterfly Gorge Nature Park** is along a 4WD road which is closed in the Wet. True to its name, common crow butterflies sometimes swarm in the gorge, which is reached via a short walking track from the car park. The gorge itself is a 70m-deep gash cut through the sandstone escarpment by the Douglas River. There are numerous rock pools, the large one at the base of the gorge being a popular swimming hole. There are no saltwater crocs this far up the river, although you may well see freshies. The paperbark forest features some of the largest trees of this type in the Territory – some are close to 50m high. Camping is not permitted here and the gorge can get a bit dry at the end of the Dry season – check with a local before making the trip.

The gravel road continues south from Douglas Hot Springs for about 45km to the Daly River (the river, not the township), famed for its good fishing. The very pleasant *Douglas Daly Park (☎ 8978 2479)* is 7.5km beyond the Douglas Hot Springs turn-off. It's a clean, well-kept park with ample river frontage, swimming holes and fishing spots. A camp site costs $12 ($17 with power), there are dongas (demountable cabins) for $30 a double and air-con cabins with shared amenities from $50. Cooked meals and takeaways are available and there's a bar.

Grove Hill

Where the old highway rejoins the Stuart Hwy you can cross straight over and do a loop on the east side of the highway before rejoining it near Pine Creek. This well-maintained road is mostly gravel, and follows the line of the old railway. This is in fact the original 'north road', which was in use before the 'new road' (now the Old Stuart Hwy!) was built. It's a worthwhile detour to see the eccentric corrugated-iron pub at Grove Hill.

The *Grove Hill Heritage Hotel (☎ 8978 2489)* is part museum and part hotel which lies on the route of both the old railway

North Australian Railway

In the 1880s the South Australian government decided to build a railway line from Darwin (Palmerston) to Pine Creek. This was partly to improve the conditions on the Pine Creek goldfields, as the road south from Darwin was often washed out in the Wet, but was also partly spurred by the dream of a transcontinental railway line linking Adelaide and Darwin.

The line was built almost entirely by Chinese labourers, and was eventually pushed south as far as Larrimah. It continued to operate until 1976, but was forced to close because the damage inflicted by Cyclone Tracy drained the Territory's financial resources.

Completion of the transcontinental link continued to be a subject of much discussion in the Territory. Then in February 1999 the dream came a little closer to reality. An agreement was signed between the Northern Territory government and the Aboriginal land owners enabling the construction of the link between Darwin and Alice Springs to go ahead. It is envisaged it will take four years to construct and cost about $1 billion.

line and the Overland Telegraph Line. It was built by the Lucy family in the 1930s and is completely original, even down to the corrugated iron accommodation wing at the back. Inside is a fascinating and bizarre mix of bric-a-brac, old photos, farm and household implements and furniture. It's definitely worth the short detour for a look around and a cool ale. Entry is free.

Accommodation is in 30s-style rooms with ceiling fans ($23 per person), air-con demountable cabins ($26) or there are dorm beds for $13. You can also camp for $5 per person, although there is little shade.

The Blue Banana stops here en route to Darwin.

HUGH FINLAY

Grove Hill Hotel, built in the 1930s on the original 'north road'

DALY RIVER
• pop 350   ✉ 0822

The settlement of Daly River lies 81km west of the old Stuart Hwy along a bitumen and good gravel road. Daly River was devastated by floods in January 1998 – residents escaped with small overnight bags and essential papers as the waters rose an incredible 16.8m above the normal level virtually overnight. Fortunately there was no loss of life but much of the town was washed away or destroyed.

In happier times this is one of the most idyllic spots in the Territory. It's just far enough away from Darwin (240km) to remain pleasantly uncrowded. The big draw here is the chance of hooking a barra in the river, but even if you're not into fishing it can be a very pleasant spot to while away a few days.

History
The first white man to venture through this way was our old friend John MacDouall Stuart in 1862. He named the river after the then Governor of South Australia, Sir Dominick Daly, and a settlement of the same name was slowly established. In the 1880s there was a brief flurry of activity when a rich copper find was made by two prospectors. They were joined by three mates and together they mined and stock-

piled the ore. In September 1884 the men were attacked by local Aboriginal people who, up until that time, had been considered friendly – one of the attackers had even worked for the miners for some time. Four of the five died of the wounds they received, and the attack sparked a vicious response. A punitive party was dispatched and massacred men, women and children at will. When the incident became public there was a major outcry. The leader of the party, Corporal George Montagu, and other members were quizzed by a board of inquiry established by the South Australian government, but all were cleared of any wrongdoing.

The bulk of the copper-mining ceased in the 1890s, although there was still one mine operating in 1915. Pastoral ventures over the years have generally met with little success. In the 1880s sugar cane came and went quickly; in 1915 a dairy herd was brought in and taken out again just a year later; and in the 1920s peanut farming was favoured and survived into the 1950s. These days it is the surviving cattle runs and the increasing tourism industry that keeps the area alive.

Information
The bulk of the population are part of the Nauiya Nambiyu Aboriginal community, about 6km away from the rest of the town. There's a well-stocked general store, ser-

vice station and medical clinic (☎ 8978 2435), and visitors are welcome without a permit, although note that this is a dry community. Also here is Merrepen Arts, a resource centre which is also an outlet for locally made arts and crafts. Each year in June/July several Aboriginal communities from around the district, such as Wadeye, Nauiyi and Peppimenarti, display their arts and crafts at the **Merrepen Arts Festival**.

The rest of the town consists largely of the colourful Daly River Pub, and the police station (☎ 8978 2466).

Things to See & Do

The main activity is getting out on the river and dangling a line. If you don't have your own, boat hire is available at the Mango Farm and Woolianna tourist outfits (see Places to Stay). At the Mango Farm you can hire a dinghy with outboard motor and a full tank for $18 per hour (minimum of two hours), $65 for a half day and $100 for a full day.

Places to Stay

The best option is to camp. Just 500m from town on the road that takes you to the Mango Farm is the Daly River crossing, where a huge sandbar is a popular, although dusty, *camping spot*. There are only a couple of good spots with shade.

Further along this road, and well signposted 7km from the river crossing, is the *Mango Farm (☎ 8978 2464)*, right on the banks of the river. This was once the site of a Jesuit mission and it has a grove of magnificent mango trees that were planted more than 90 years ago. A camp site in the shade of these massive trees is $14 (it's not wise to set up under a tree during mango season!), $3 more with power, and there are cabins sleeping up to five for $55. Facilities include a pool, communal kitchen and barbecues. This place was hard hit by the floods and its future was uncertain at the time of writing – phone for an update.

About 5km before you actually get to Daly River a gravel road heads west for 15km to *Woolianna on the Daly Tourist Park (☎ 8978 2478)*, another low-key caravan park right on the banks of the Daly River. There's a beautiful shady green lawn for camping and an in-ground swimming pool. Camping here costs $18 for a site ($20 powered) and there's a self-contained two-bedroom flat costing $96 for two and $36 for each extra person (maximum of four). There's a kiosk selling snacks and fishing gear. It's a good spot.

Getting There & Away

The Nauiya Nambiyu community runs a thrice-weekly dry-season minibus service between Daly River and Darwin. It departs the community at 8 am and Darwin at 3 pm on Monday, Wednesday and Friday; the cost is $70 return (☎ 8978 2422 for details).

PINE CREEK
• pop 520   ✉ 0847

This small town, 245km from Darwin, is one of only a handful of towns in the Territory that have anything more than a baked, desperate atmosphere. Pine Creek was once the scene of a gold rush, from which some of the old timber and corrugated-iron buildings survive. As it lies 1km or so off the highway it also manages to retain a peaceful atmosphere, undisturbed by the road trains thundering up and down the highway.

Pine Creek is also where the Kakadu Hwy branches north-east off the Stuart Hwy to Kakadu National Park.

History

In the early 1870s labourers working on the Overland Telegraph Line found gold here, sparking a rush that was to last nearly 20 years. A telegraph station was opened in 1874 and around the same time there was a large influx of Chinese workers, who were brought in to do all the tough work on the goldfields. It wasn't long before more Chinese began arriving under their own steam to work the goldfields themselves. Such was the Chinese influx that by the mid-1880s Chinese outnumbered whites 15 to one in Pine Creek.

Not all the Chinese who arrived to work on the goldfields were labourers; many were merchants and businesspeople with money behind them. Pine Creek boasted a number of Chinese stores, although all but one of them were destroyed by a fire in 1892. Once the gold ran out the population of Pine Creek dwindled; many Chinese returned home in the 1890s.

Everyone going to Pine Creek in the hope of striking it rich faced a difficult journey from Palmerston (Darwin). There was no road to the diggings, and the government was unwilling to spend money on building one. Although a person on horseback could do the journey in a few days in the Dry, a fully laden wagon could take up to six weeks. Finally the decision was made to build a railway, and in 1889 Pine Creek became the terminus of the North Australian Railway.

The pastoral industry has been the mainstay of the town throughout this century, although recently an open-cut gold mine has been established right on the edge of town.

Information

The old railway station residence now houses the local information centre, although it keeps very irregular hours.

The ANZ on Railway Terrace is the only bank in town. There's a post office in Moule St, opposite the BP station, with public phones outside.

Things to See & Do

The railway station dates from 1888 and is worth a quick wander. There are a number of old buildings still standing, as well as an old steam loco and a couple of carriages. Next to the station is the Miners' Park which has a number of old bits of equipment scattered about, and some fairly dry information boards.

More interesting perhaps is the Pine Creek Museum, which is housed in the old mining warden's residence, a prefabricated steel building that was moved here from Burrundie, a town close by, in 1913. The building is on Railway Terrace and is now owned by the National Trust. There are displays on smithing, telecommunications, WWII and mining, and there's a preserved pioneer hut. Like all such rural museums, it's an eclectic collection with some little surprises. It is supposedly open from 11 am to 5 pm on weekdays and 11 am to 1 pm on weekends during the Dry, but don't be surprised if it's not. Entry costs $2 and the building also houses the town's library.

Gun Alley Gold Mining offers gold panning for $5 a pop; it also has fully operational steam equipment and is open from 8.30 am to 3 pm.

For an excellent view over the town and the open-cut mine, follow the signs on Main Terrace to a lookout. Also on Main St, across from the football oval, is the former Playford Club Hotel, a corrugated-iron relic of the gold rush days and mentioned in the famous novel We of the Never Never. For nearly 70 years it was the town's only pub; these days it's a private residence.

Places to Stay & Eat

There are three caravan parks in Pine Creek, but the best choice is *Kakadu Gateway Caravan Park* (☎ 8976 1166, Buchanan St), about 600m from Main Terrace, which has excellent facilities, meals and a range of accommodation. Camp sites are $16 ($18 with power), but have a carport and en suite; budget rooms start at $30/45 a single/double; and there are also 'swag rooms' – empty, air-con carpeted rooms where you can store a bicycle and roll out your swag for $15/20. The park's facilities include barbecues, free laundry, TV room, store and communal kitchen; meals are also available.

Alternatives in town include the *Pine Creek Hotel* (☎ 8976 1288, Moule St), opposite the BP station, which has motel rooms at $78.75 for singles or doubles and budget rooms for $30; and the *Pine Creek Diggers Rest Motel* (☎ 8976 1442, 32 Main Terrace), where self-contained units sleeping up to five people cost from $60 including tax.

In town there's *Famished*, a café next to the pub that does light sit-down meals and takeaways, and the *pub* itself, which offers counter lunches from $5.

In the old (1888) station master's house near the railway museum there's the *Swampy Croc*, which does mango smoothies, ice creams and drinks, plus free tea and coffee. At *Kakadu Gateway Caravan Park* you can get three meals a day for $22 or breakfast, lunch and dinner each for a reasonable price.

Getting There & Away
All buses along the Stuart Hwy pull into Pine Creek. Buses stop at the Ah Toy store in Main Terrace and will pick up from Kakadu Gateway, 600m away.

The Blue Banana stops at Pine Creek.

UMBRAWARRA GORGE NATURE PARK
About 3km along the Stuart Hwy south of Pine Creek is the turn-off to Umbrawarra Gorge Nature Park, 22km south-west along a dirt road (often impassable in the Wet). It's a quiet, little-visited spot with some Aboriginal rock art sites and safe swimming.

The gorge was first explored in 1872 and takes its name from the Umbrawarra tin mine, which in 1909 was the Territory's largest. However, little ore was ever removed because malaria swept through the area and left more than 40 miners dead. As the European miners left for better prospects, Chinese miners moved in and about 150 of them worked the area up until about 1925. The former mine site is now the car park area.

In Aboriginal legend, the gorge is the Dreaming site of *Kuna-ngarrk-ngarrk*, the white-bellied sea-eagle. Here he caught and ate a barramundi; the white flakes in the granite rock are said to be the scales of the barra, the quartz outcrops are the eagle's shit. Rock art can be seen along the gorge walls at its eastern end.

A marked walking track leads from the car park to swimming holes in the gorge and you can swim and scramble the rest of its 5km length. There's a camp ground with pit toilets and fireplaces.

Kakadu & Arnhem Land

East of Darwin lies Kakadu National Park, without a doubt the biggest attraction of a visit to the Top End and one of Australia's most-visited national parks. Kakadu is magnificent at any time of year and should definitely be part of your itinerary.

Further east again, across the East Alligator River, lies the vast expanse of Arnhem Land and at its tip is the Cobourg Peninsula, a wilderness protected by Gurig National Park and the Cobourg Marine Park. This entire area is Aboriginal owned and only accessible with a permit, and then only in limited areas and usually only with an organised group.

Kakadu National Park

Kakadu National Park is one of the natural marvels of the Northern Territory. The longer you stay, the more rewarding it is. It encompasses a variety of habitats, including some stunning wetlands, boasts a mass of wildlife and its Aboriginal people have left significant rock art sites. All these combine to make it one of the top tourist destinations in the country, and have gained it World Heritage Listing as an area of both cultural and ecological importance.

The name Kakadu comes from the language of the Gagadju people, the traditional owners of the area. Much of Kakadu is Aboriginal land, leased to the government for use as a national park. The entire park is jointly managed by Parks Australia and the traditional Aboriginal owners, 10 of whom sit on the 14-member board of management. There are around 300 Aboriginal people living in several Aboriginal settlements in the park and in the township of Jabiru, and about one-third of the park rangers are Aboriginal people. In addition, a number of the Aboriginal elders are em-

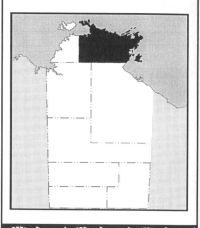

ployed to advise Parks Australia staff on management issues.

The traditional owners are represented through five associations, which own a number of the park's material assets – for example, the hotels at Jabiru and Cooinda, the Border Store and the Yellow Water cruise operation – and the Ranger Uranium Mine Lease.

HISTORY

At nearly 22,000 sq km Kakadu is the largest national park in Australia. It was proclaimed a national park in three stages. Stage One, the eastern and central part of the park including Ubirr, Nourlangie, Jim Jim and Twin Falls and Yellow Water Billabong, was declared in 1979. Stage Two, in the north, was declared in 1984 and gained World Heritage listing for its natural importance. Stage Three, in the south, was finally listed in 1991, bringing virtually the whole of the South Alligator River system within the park.

Aboriginal Heritage

It is known that Aboriginal people have lived in the Kakadu area for at least 23,000 years, and possibly even 50,000 years. Artefacts such as stone tools, ochre and grindstones found at a number of sites indicate that Aboriginal people were constantly in the area.

As elsewhere in Australia, they led a hunter-gatherer existence, with the men doing the hunting and the women gathering vegetable foods and seeds. They moved through the country as necessary, but never aimlessly, and along defined paths that had been used for generations in the search for food, water or other natural resources such as ochre or spears.

The rocky nature of the rugged countryside that typifies much of the park offered excellent shelter to the Aboriginal people, and many of these shelters bear art sites of world importance.

Today the park is occupied by a number of different groups (or clans), each with a different language and often different traditional practices. Although many of these traditional practices have been modified or lost altogether in the years since contact with whites, the traditional owners still

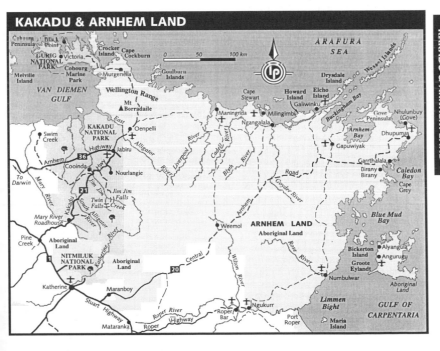

KAKADU & ARNHEM LAND

have strong personal and spiritual links with the land.

Recent Exploration

Although a number of vessels had sailed along the coast on exploratory voyages since the mid-17th century, it wasn't until Captain Phillip King made a number of voyages between 1818 and 1822 that any of the hinterland was investigated. King travelled up the East Alligator and South Alligator rivers, and it was in fact he who named them after mistaking the many saltwater crocs for alligators.

The first European to come through this area overland was the remarkable Prussian naturalist Ludwig Leichhardt, who set out from Queensland in October 1844 for Port Essington on the Cobourg Peninsula. He crossed the Arnhem Land plateau and the South Alligator River many months later and somewhat worse for wear, before finally staggering into Port Essington in December 1845.

Some 20 years later, a party led by experienced explorer John McKinlay was sent out by the South Australian government to find a better site than Escape Cliffs by the Adelaide River mouth for a northern settlement. McKinlay botched the expedition by not setting out until the middle of the wet season, which that year had been particularly severe. The party took months to travel just the relatively short distance to the East Alligator River, and ended up bailing out by shooting their horses, constructing a makeshift horse-hide raft and floating all the way back to Escape Cliffs!

In the 1870s the surge of prospectors to the goldfields at Pine Creek led to increased activity in the Kakadu area, and this was followed by the commencement of pastoral activity.

In the 1890s a few Europeans started to make a living from shooting buffalo for hides in the Alligator rivers region. Foremost among these men was Paddy Cahill, who dominated European settlement in this area until 1925. In that year the Church Missionary Society was given permission by the government to establish a mission at Oenpelli, one of a number throughout the Arnhem Land Aboriginal Reserve, which had been established in 1921. By this stage any attempts to set up pastoral properties had failed and parts of the area had become vacant crown land.

The buffalo industry continued throughout the first half of the 20th century, but with the introduction of synthetics demand fell away and hunting became unviable.

In 1969 and 1972 the precursors to Kakadu, the Woolwonga and Alligator rivers wildlife sanctuaries, were declared. These were followed in 1978 by the granting of some land titles to the traditional Aboriginal owners under the Aboriginal Land Rights (NT) Act of 1976, and the proclamation of the Kakadu National Park the following year.

In the late 1990s, Kakadu was receiving some 220,000 visitors per year, mostly in the Dry.

Mining

In 1953 uranium was discovered in the region. Twelve small deposits in the southern reaches of the park were worked in the 1960s but were abandoned following the declaration of Woolwonga.

In 1970 three huge deposits, Ranger, Nabarlek and Koongarra, were found, followed by Jabiluka in 1973. The Nabarlek deposit (in Arnhem Land) was mined in the late '70s, and the Ranger Uranium Mine started producing ore in 1981. Most of the Aboriginal people of the area were against the mining of uranium on traditional land, but were enticed with the double lure of land title and royalties.

The Jabiluka mine was the scene of widespread protest and sit-in demonstrations during the 1998 dry season. Things came to a head when a UN delegation inspected the mine site to assess whether the damage it was causing would endanger Kakadu's World Heritage Listing. The delegation found that Jabiluka could degrade Kakadu's pristine environment – a decision which shook the Federal government and which is currently the subject of an appeal.

GEOGRAPHY & FLORA

Kakadu's weather, landforms, vegetation, wildlife and culture are subtly and inextricably linked, and an understanding of one is virtually impossible without some appreciation of all the others.

Kakadu has six major landforms: the sandstone Arnhem Land plateau, the riverine flood plains, the coastal estuaries and tidal flats, monsoon rainforests, lowlands and the southern hills. Each has its own distinct type of vegetation, and this in turn dictates what fauna is found in each. Over 1600 plant species have been recorded in the park, and a number of them are still used by the local Aboriginal people for food, bush medicine and other practical purposes.

Arnhem Land Escarpment & Plateau

The meandering Arnhem Land escarpment cuts into the eastern boundary of the park and marks the start of the vast Arnhem plateau, a rugged expanse of sandstone that stretches 500km through east and south-east Kakadu. The eroded cliffs range from 30m to 300m high and provide a dramatic backdrop to many parts of the park. The plateau itself is surprisingly dry, mainly because the water drains away quickly into the deep gorges and tumbles off the escarpment as thundering waterfalls in the wet season.

The soil on the plateau is also relatively shallow and low in nutrients, and supports vegetation that can tolerate the generally poor conditions, such as spinifex grass and the endemic sandstone pandanus palm.

Flood Plains

Kakadu is drained by four major rivers – from west to east the Wildman, West Alligator, South Alligator and East Alligator – which during the Wet overflow to form vast shallow wetlands. These wet season floods are a chaotic yet vital part of the park's ecology. Areas on river flood plains which are perfectly dry underfoot in September will be under 3m of water a few months later. As the waters recede in the Dry, some loops of wet season watercourses become cut off, but don't dry up. These billabongs are a magnet for wildlife.

The wetlands offer some of the most spectacular sights of the park, and have been considered sufficiently important to be placed on the List of Wetlands of International Importance. Some of the more accessible wetland areas include Yellow Water, Mamukala, Ubirr and Bubba.

Many of the wetlands and permanent waterholes are fringed by stands of tall trees, predominantly paperbarks, and also freshwater mangroves and pandanus palms.

Coastal Estuaries & Tidal Flats

The coastal zone has long stretches of mangroves, important for halting erosion and as a breeding ground for marine and bird life. Mangroves line the South Alligator River for much of its length upstream, but most of this habitat is not generally accessible.

Monsoon Rainforest

Isolated pockets of monsoon rainforest appear throughout the park, and are of one of two types: coastal and sandstone. Coastal monsoon rainforest is dominated by banyan, kapok and milkwood trees, and generally appears along river banks or other places where there is permanent water – either above or below ground. Sandstone monsoon rainforest grows along the gorges of the escarpment, such as at Jim Jim Falls.

Lowlands

About half the park, predominantly the southern section, is dry lowlands with open grassland or woodland. The main tree of the woodland, and one which dominates much of the Top End, is a eucalypt, the Darwin woollybutt. Other important tree species include Cooktown ironwoods and Darwin stringybarks. Below their canopy pandanus palms and other small trees grow, while the ground is covered by annual grasses. Naturally enough these grasses are the dominant form of vegetation in the grasslands, and after the Wet can shoot up to 2m high, making the most of the moisture before the ground dries up during the Dry.

Much of the Arnhem Hwy from the Stuart Hwy into Jabiru passes through this habitat.

Southern Hills
Some rocky hills in the southern part of the park are of volcanic origin. Erosion of this material has led to different soil types, giving rise to distinctive flora and fauna. One of the most noticeable and widespread eucalypts found here, especially in the Gunlom vicinity, is the salmon gum, which has a smooth pink trunk.

FAUNA
Impressive though the totals are, to enumerate the park's many species of animals would be fairly meaningless since most are small or rarely seen by visitors. But if your enjoyment of nature includes number-crunching, cop this: Kakadu has about 60 types of mammals, 280 bird species, 120 or so types of reptile, 25 species of frog, 51 freshwater fish species and at least 10,000 different kinds of insect. There are frequent additions to the list and a few of the rarer species are unique to the park.

Most visitors see only a fraction of these creatures in a visit since many of them are shy, nocturnal or few in number. Take advantage of talks and walks led by park rangers, mainly in the Dry, to get to know and see more of the wildlife (see Activities later in this chapter).

Mammals
Eight types of kangaroos and wallabies inhabit the park, mostly in the open forest and woodland areas, or on the fringes of the flood plains. Most commonly seen are the agile wallaby and antilopine wallaroo. Those not so often sighted include the short-eared rock wallaby, which can sometimes be seen at Ubirr first thing in the morning and at sunset. It is well camouflaged and can easily be missed even when in full view at medium distance. Also keep your eyes open for the black wallaroo at Nourlangie Rock, they sometimes rest in the shade of the occupation shelter.

Nocturnal northern brushtail possums, sugar gliders and northern brown bandicoots are also common in the woodlands. Kakadu is home to 26 bat species and is a key refuge for four rare varieties. At dusk, look out for streams of huge fruit bats leaving their camps to feed on fruit.

Dingoes are sometimes encountered along roadsides.

Birds
Unlike most of the park's fauna, birdlife is both abundant and easy to see. Those with a general interest will find much to enjoy on the wetlands and walking tracks; keen birdwatchers should head straight for Nourlangie Rock or Gunlom to winkle out some of the rarer or unique species before enjoying the waterbird spectacle. The greatest variety is seen just before the Wet, when masses of birds congregate at the shrinking waterholes, the migrants arrive from Asia, and many species start their breeding cycle.

Kakadu is internationally famous for its abundant waterbirds, and the huge flocks that congregate in the dry season are a highlight. The park is one of the chief refuges in Australia for several species, among them the magpie goose, green pygmy-goose and Burdekin duck. The park supports some 85% of Australia's magpie geese during the Dry. Other fine waterbirds include pelicans, darters and the jabiru, with its distinctive red legs and iridescent plumage. Herons, egrets, ibis and cormorants are common. Waterbirds are most easily seen at Mamukala and other wetlands, and on the Yellow Water cruise.

The open woodlands are home to yet more birds. You're quite likely to see rainbow bee-eaters and kingfishers (of which there are six types in inland Kakadu), as well as parrots and cockatoos (especially red-tailed black cockatoos). Birds of prey include majestic white-bellied sea eagles, which are often seen near inland waterways, and whistling and black kites are common. At night you might hear barking owls calling – they sound just like dogs.

Reptiles

Kakadu is home to an extraordinary number of reptile species. Of the 120 species so far recorded, 11 are endemic, and the striking Oenpelli python was first seen by whites in 1976. The world's largest reptile – the estuarine or saltwater crocodile – is abundant in Kakadu. Several large specimens normally hang around Yellow Water, where one individual munched its way through a dog and a horse during our stay. Both Twin and Jim Jim Falls have resident freshwater crocodiles, which are considered harmless. While it's quite a thrill to be so close to nature 'red in tooth and claw', crocodiles are not to be meddled with on any account.

After the crocodiles, Kakadu's most famous reptilian inhabitant is probably the frilled lizard. These large members of the dragon family can grow to 1m in length and are common during the Wet. Look for them sitting upright by the roadside, or trundling through the bush on their hind legs like bizarre joggers.

Although Kakadu has many snakes, there is no need to panic because most are nocturnal and rarely encountered. Several beautiful species of python include the olive python (the scourge of chicken keepers) and the superbly marked children's python.

Fish

Among the 52 species of fish are saratoga, rainbow fish and catfish. The famous barramundi can grow to well over 1m long and changes its sex from male to female at the age of five or six years. The archer fish is so-named because it swims just below the surface and squirts drops of water at insects above to knock them down as prey.

Insects

Mosquitoes seem to be the most noticeable insect in the park, although they become less of a menace as you move south, and so they are worse at Ubirr than at Cooinda.

Termites are probably more abundant still, although their earth mounds are much more obvious than the actual insects. There are some giant examples along the highways.

One of the most famous of the park's insect inhabitants is Leichhardt's grasshopper, a beautiful blue and orange insect that was not seen by science until 130 years after its discovery in 1845. The Aborigines knew it though, and called the grasshoppers Aljurr, the children of Namarrgon (Lightning Man) because they are said to call their father to start the storms before the Wet.

CLIMATE

Kakadu's climate is typical of the Top End, but not exactly the same as Darwin – it is usually a bit hotter and doesn't have the cooling sea breezes. Broadly speaking, the Dry is from April/May to September/October and the Wet is from October/November to March/April; the average maximum temperature is 34°C year-round, but most of the average rainfall of 1600mm falls in the Wet.

The great change between the Dry and the Wet makes a big difference to visitors to Kakadu. Not only is the landscape transformed as the wetlands and waterfalls grow, but Kakadu's unsealed roads become impassable in the Wet, cutting off some highlights, such as Jim Jim Falls. The local Aboriginal people recognise six seasons in the annual cycle.

Gunmeleng This is the 'build-up' to the Wet, which starts in mid-October. Humidity and the temperatures rise (to 35°C or more) – and the number of mosquitoes, always high near water, rises to near plague proportions. By November the thunderstorms have started, billabongs are replenished and the waterbirds and fish disperse. Traditionally this is when the Aboriginal people made the seasonal move from the flood plains to the shelter of the escarpment.

Gudjuek The Wet proper continues through January, February and March, with violent thunderstorms and an abundance of plant and animal life thriving in the hot, moist conditions. Most of Kakadu's rain falls during this period.

Banggereng April is the season when storms (known as 'knock 'em down' storms) flatten the spear grass, which during the course of the Wet has shot up to 2m in height.

Yekke From May to mid-June is the season of mists, when the air starts to dry out. It is quite a good time to visit – there aren't too many other visitors, the wetlands and waterfalls still have a lot of water and most of the tracks are open.

Wurrgeng & Gurrung This is the late Dry, July and August, and the most comfortable time to visit Kakadu. It is when wildlife, especially birds, congregate in big numbers around the shrinking billabongs, but it's also when most tourists come to the park.

ABORIGINAL ART

Kakadu's rock art sites were critical to the park's World Heritage listing. More than 5000 sites are known, the oldest dating from more than 20,000 years ago; two of the finest collections are the galleries at Ubirr and Nourlangie.

The paintings have been classified into three roughly defined periods: Pre-estuarine, which is from the earliest paintings up to around 6000 years ago; Estuarine, which covers the period from 6000 to around 2000 years ago, when rising sea levels flooded valleys and brought the coast to its present level; and Freshwater from 2000 years ago until the present day. (See the section on Aboriginal art in the Facts About the Northern Territory chapter for a full discussion of the various styles.)

For the local Aboriginal people the rock art sites are a major source of traditional knowledge – their historical archives, if you like, because they have no written language. The most recent paintings, some executed as recently as the 1980s, connect the local community with the artists. Older paintings are believed by many Aboriginal people to have been painted by spirit people, and depict stories which connect the people with creation legends and the development of Aboriginal law.

The majority of rock art sites open to the public are relatively recent, and some visitors feel somewhat cheated when they learn that the paintings were only done in the 1960s. Many people are also surprised to learn that the old paintings they are seeing have actually been touched up by other Aboriginal people quite recently. In fact this was not uncommon, although the repainting could only be done by a specific person

Fire as a Management Tool

Many first-time visitors to the Top End in the Dry comment on the amount of smoke in the sky from large bushfires. In a country where bushfires are normally associated with enormous damage and loss of life, it sometimes seems as though huge tracts of the Top End are being reduced to ashes. In fact the truth is that the fires, although uncontrolled, are deliberately lit and are rejuvenating the country.

For thousands of years Aboriginal people have used fire as a tool for hunting and environmental management. In fact, they have been doing it for so long that many plant species have not only evolved to survive fires, they rely on them for seedling regeneration. The usual practice was to light fires in the early dry season to burn the lower shrubs and spear grass which grows so prolifically during the Wet. Fires late in the Dry were avoided as they could burn out of control over huge areas. The fires in the early dry season would burn over a fairly small area, and the result was a mosaic of burnt and unburnt areas. Populations of plants and animals that would have been destroyed in a wildfire could thus shelter in unburnt refuges and recolonise burnt areas.

Since European settlement of the Top End and the decline in Aboriginal people leading a traditional existence, the burning patterns have changed. This led to the accumulation of unburnt material on the ground and any fires late in the dry season would destroy huge areas.

The benefits of the traditional methods of environmental management have now been recognised by Parks Australia, which manages Kakadu with the assistance of the traditional owners and attempts are being made to recreate the mosaic burn pattern.

who knew the story that was being depicted. What also comes as a surprise is the way the paintings in a particular site are often layered, with newer paintings being placed right over the top of older ones.

The conservation of the Kakadu rock art sites is a major part of the park management task. As the paintings are all done with natural, water-soluble ochres, they are very susceptible to water damage from drip lines running across the rock. To prevent this sort of damage small ridges of clear silicon rubber have been made on the rocks above the paintings, so the water flowing down the rock is diverted to either side, or actually drips right off. Dust also affects the paintings; most of the accessible sites – which may receive up to 3000 visitors a *week* – have boardwalks which keep the dust down and keep people at a suitable distance from the paintings.

ORIENTATION

Kakadu National Park is huge. It's 170km from Darwin at its nearest boundary, and stretches another 130km from there across to the western edge of Arnhem Land. It is roughly rectangular and measures about 210km from north to south.

Only two main roads traverse the park, both sealed and accessible year-round, and most points of interest and places to stay are reached off these highways.

Access from the west (Darwin and the Stuart Hwy) is via the Arnhem Hwy, which stretches from the Stuart Hwy past the resort at South Alligator to the township of Jabiru (90km from the boundary).

Mamukala is a wetland 7km past the South Alligator bridge and from there it's 29km to the turn-off to one of the major sites in the park, Ubirr, 36km to the northeast near the East Alligator River. This road also gives access to Oenpelli, Arnhem Land and the Cobourg Peninsula, but note that a permit is needed to enter Arnhem Land (inquire at the Northern Land Council in Jabiru).

The Kakadu Hwy turns south off the Arnhem Hwy shortly before Jabiru. It runs past the Park Headquarters and Bowali Visitor Centre (2.5km), the Nourlangie turn-off (21km), Muirella turn-off (28km), Jim Jim Falls turn-off (41km), Cooinda turn-off (47km) and on to the Gunlom turn-off

(88.5km), the southern entrance to the park (137km) and Pine Creek on the Stuart Hwy (202km).

The road is bitumen all the way to the southern park gate and beyond to the Stuart Hwy.

Maps

The *Kakadu National Park Visitor Guide* booklet, which includes good maps, is included with your entrance fee. It's an excellent publication and will get you around the park safely.

The Hema *Kakadu National Park* 1:390,000 map is updated regularly and is widely available. Bowali Visitor Centre sells 1:100,000 topographic maps covering most parts of the park; they can also be studied at the Bowali resources centre. These are essential for bushwalking in some areas of Kakadu.

INFORMATION

Kakadu National Park is open year-round. Access roads to Jim Jim and Twin Falls, and to West Alligator Head are closed during the Wet, and attractions in the southern part of the park, such as Gunlom, are accessible only to 4WDs in the Wet.

Bowali Visitor Centre

The excellent Bowali Visitor Centre (☎ 8938 1121) is itself a highlight of the park. The centrepiece of this award-winning building is a walk-through, state-of-the-art display which explains Kakadu's ecology from both the Aboriginal and non-Aboriginal perspectives. It's informative and interesting, and a few features should keep the kids happy.

The building also houses an information desk with plenty of leaflets on various aspects of the park, toilets (including disabled), café and gift shop. A high-tech theatrette shows a 25 minute audio-visual presentation on the seasonal changes in the park (screened on the hour); and an excellent resource centre has a comprehensive selection of reference books and maps. Another air-con theatrette shows various

KAKADU & ARNHEM LAND

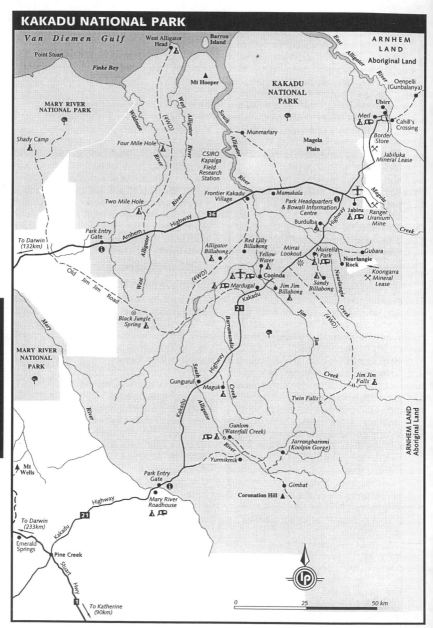

KAKADU NATIONAL PARK

documentaries made about Kakadu in the last few years, and these are also shown throughout the day between 8.30 am and 4.30 pm.

The Marrawuddi Gallery sells a good range of souvenirs, T-shirts and books on Kakadu.

Bowali is open daily from 8 am to 5 pm; allow at least two hours and preferably three to get the most out of a visit. It's on the Kakadu Hwy about 2.5km south of the Arnhem Hwy, and a walking track connects it to Jabiru, about 2km away (30 minutes).

Warradjan Aboriginal Cultural Centre

This centre near Cooinda gives an excellent insight into the culture of the park's traditional owners. The building itself is circular, which symbolises the way the Aboriginal people sit in a circle when having a meeting; the shape is also reminiscent of the *warradjan* (pig-nosed turtle), hence the name of the centre.

Inside, the displays depict creation stories when the Nayuhyunggi (first people) laid out the land and the laws, and the winding path you follow through the display symbolises the way the Rainbow Serpent moves through the country.

It's an excellent display, with crafts made by the local people and audio-visual displays. There's also a craft shop selling locally made items such as didgeridoos and T-shirts.

Warradjan is an easy walk (15 minutes) from the Cooinda resort.

Entry Fees

An entry fee of $15 (children under 16 free) is paid at the park gates as you enter. This entitles you to stay in the park for 14 days. You may be approached by someone trying to sell you their ticket once they've finished with it – after all, most people stay far less than 14 days. Avoid the temptation to buy a used park entrance ticket, no matter how many days 'credit' remaining – tickets are checked by park staff and recycled tickets are easily detected. If you're caught with an unofficial one you'll be obliged to fork out the $15 for a new ticket. Ticket sales account for a substantial portion of park revenue and you're not doing anyone a favour by trying to avoid the cost.

A 'Territorian Ticket' ($60) covers one vehicle and all its occupants, as well as camping fees at the Mardugal, Muirella Park, Merl and Gunlom camp grounds. It's a good option if you plan to visit the park several times – and will get you into Uluru-Kata Tjuta as well – but it is available only to Australian residents and can't be used for a rented vehicle.

Disabled Access

There is wheelchair access to the main gallery and Rainbow Serpent art sites at Ubirr, Anbangbang rock shelter (the main gallery at Nourlangie), the plunge pool at Gunlom, Bowali Visitor Centre and Warradjan Aboriginal Cultural Centre.

Wheelchairs can also be accommodated on the Yellow Water cruise – advise staff when booking.

ACTIVITIES
Bushwalking

Kakadu is excellent but tough bushwalking country. Many people will be satisfied with the marked tracks. For the more adventurous there are infinite possibilities, especially in the drier south and east of the park, but take great care and prepare well. Tell people where you're going and don't go alone. You need a permit from the Bowali Visitor Centre to camp outside established camp grounds.

Kakadu by Foot is a helpful guide to the marked walking tracks in Kakadu. It is published by Parks Australia ($3) and should be on sale at the Visitor Centre.

Marked Tracks in the Park There are some excellent marked tracks within the park. They range from 1km to 12km long and are all fairly easy. Many of the ranger-led activities involve a guided walk along various tracks, and there's usually a Park

KAKADU & ARNHEM LAND

Notes fact sheet for each so you can do a self-guided walk. These sheets are available from the visitor centre and usually from a box at the start of each track.

Walking Information A bushwalking permit is needed if your walk is for more than one day. These are available from the Bowali Visitor Centre. It's a good idea to allow a few days for the permit to be issued.

Topographic maps are necessary for extended walks; these are available in Darwin from the Department of Lands, Planning & Environment (see Maps under Information in the Darwin chapter) and in Kakadu at the Bowali Visitor Centre.

The Darwin Bushwalking Club (☎ 8985 1484) welcomes visitors and may be able to help with information too. It has walks most weekends, often in Kakadu.

Guided Walks & Talks

In the Dry there's a variety of free activities put on by the park staff. It's well worth going along to some of these activities as it's a great opportunity to learn some more about various aspects of the park.

The schedule of activities differs somewhat from one season to the next, but the following outline gives you a rough idea of what's on. Full details are given on a leaflet that you will be given on entering the park.

Art-Site Talks These are held at the various rock art sites at Ubirr (six daily) and Nourlangie (six daily).

Guided Walks These are held at Ubirr (three times weekly), Nourlangie (twice weekly), Yellow Water (three times weekly), Mardugal (once weekly), Maguk (twice weekly) and Gunlom (three times weekly). Kids' activities are held once a week at Gunlom.

Slide Shows These are held in the early evening once a week at various venues: the Hostel Kakadu at Ubirr, the Frontier Kakadu Lodge in Jabiru (three times weekly), Muirella Park camp ground, Frontier

Kakadu Village at South Alligator, Cooinda Caravan Park (twice weekly), Mardugal camping area and Gunlom camping area (three times weekly).

River Trips

Yellow Water The boat rides on the Yellow Water wetlands that operate throughout the dry season are probably the most popular activity within the park. They provide an opportunity to get right out into the waterways, and get surprisingly close to the waterbirds and crocs. The dawn trip is the best, but the other trips throughout the day can be equally good. Take mosquito repellent if you opt for the dawn trip.

Cruises last either 1½ or two hours, depending on time of year and day. During the Dry, 1½ hour trips depart daily at 11.15 am, and 1 and 2.45 pm, and cost $23.50 (children $12.50); the two-hour cruises leave at 6.45 and 9 am, and 4.30 pm, and cost $27 ($13.50). During the Wet only 1½ hour trips are available, leaving daily at 7, 9 and 11 am, and at 1, 3 and 5 pm.

All tours are operated by Yellow Water Cruises and can be booked through the travel desk at Cooinda (☎ 8979 0111) and at other resorts in the park. A shuttle bus connects Cooinda with Yellow Water 20 minutes before each cruise, or you can make your own way. It's a good idea to make reservations, especially during the Dry, and especially for the dawn trip.

East Alligator River Aboriginal-guided Guluyambi river trips are held on the East Alligator River near the Border Store in the north of the park. These are excellent trips with the emphasis on Aboriginal culture and their relationship with the land. The boats are a bit smaller than those used at Yellow Water which makes for a more personal experience.

Dry season trips leave from the upstream boat ramp at East Alligator and cost $25/11 per adult/child. Book at the Border Store or Jabiru airport. The cruise takes 1¾ hours and is marketed as an Aboriginal cultural tour. Aboriginal guides are often on board. It leaves at 9 and 11 am, and 1 and 3 pm.

KAKADU & ARNHEM LAND

During the Wet, Guluyambi operates a half-day tour leaving from Jabiru at 8 am and 12 pm daily. This tour includes a boat transfer across the picturesque Magela Creek and a bus drive on to Ubirr. This tour provides the only means by which visitors can get to Ubirr when it is at its best.

In general, both Guluyambi tours are highly recommended and do not duplicate Yellow Water. If you have the time and cash, both are worthwhile as they are different in almost every respect. A free shuttle bus runs between the boat ramp and the Border Store and Merl camp ground. For information and bookings phone ☎ toll-free 1800 089 113.

Scenic Flights

The view of Kakadu from the air is spectacular. Kakadu Air (☎ toll-free 1800 089 113) at Jabiru runs half-hour flights on the hour between 8 am and 5 pm for $65, or hour-long flights for $110.

Rotor Services (☎ 8945 0944) operates half-hour helicopter rides at $125 per person.

SOUTH ALLIGATOR

This area, 2.5km west of where the Arnhem Hwy crosses the South Alligator River, is not quite as heavily used as other areas, such as the rock art sites. There's a camp ground, bar, well-stocked shop (see Places to Stay & Eat later in this chapter) and some easy walks in the vicinity.

At the river itself there's a boat ramp and picnic area near the bridge.

Walking Tracks

There are two easy walks in this area.

Gu-ngarre Monsoon Rainforest (3.5km return; 90 minutes; easy) This is a flat walk that skirts the South Alligator resort through monsoon forest and woodlands then passes Anggardabal billabong. It's an excellent walk for learning about Aboriginal plant use.
Mamukala Wetlands (1km or 3km; up to two hours; easy) This large wetland area is an excellent place to watch waterbirds and experience the paperbark woodlands that fringe many waterholes. It is at its best during September-

October, when truly spectacular congregations can build up, including thousands of magpie geese. A short walk from the car park leads to a comfortable observation hide overlooking the wetlands, or you can take longer walks to see more of the wetlands. Visit early or late in the day for best photographic opportunities.

UBIRR

Ubirr is an outlying outcrop of the Arnhem escarpment, some 39km north of the Arnhem Hwy, famous for its spectacular Aboriginal rock art site.

An easily followed path from the Ubirr car park takes you through the main galleries and up to a lookout with superb views. There are paintings on numerous rocks along the path, but the highlight is the main gallery with a large array of well-executed and preserved x-ray-style wallabies, possums, goannas, tortoises and fish, plus a couple of *balanda* (white men) with hands on hips. Also of major interest here is the Rainbow Serpent painting, and the picture of the Namarkan Sisters, shown with string pulled taut between their hands.

The Ubirr paintings are in many different

The Rainbow Serpent

The story of the Rainbow Serpent is a common subject in Aboriginal traditions across Australia, although the story varies from place to place.

In Kakadu the serpent is a woman, Kuringali, who painted her image on the rock wall at Ubirr while on a journey through this area. This journey forms a creation path that links the places she visited: Ubirr, Manngarre, the East Alligator River and various places in Arnhem Land.

To the traditional owners of the park, Kuringali is the most powerful spirit. Although she spends most of her time resting in billabongs, if disturbed she can be very destructive, causing floods and earthquakes, and one local story has it that she even eats people.

KAKADU & ARNHEM LAND

styles. They were painted during the period from over 20,000 years ago right up to the 20th century. Allow plenty of time to seek out and study them.

The rock art site is open daily from 8.30 am to sunset from 1 May to 30 November and from 2 pm to sunset between 1 December and 30 April.

The view across the Nardab flood plain from the top is stunning, especially at sunset. Other activities in the area include walking tracks, fishing and cruises on the East Alligator River (see River Trips earlier in this chapter).

Shortly before Ubirr you pass the Border Store. There is a **backpackers hostel** and **camp ground** nearby (see Places to Stay & Eat later in this chapter), and boat ramps upstream and downstream of Cahill's Crossing. There are picnic tables on the river bank opposite the Border Store.

The Namarkan Sisters

The story of the Namarkan sisters is told to warn young children about the dangers of crocodiles. It seems the sisters were sitting together by a billabong one day when one dived into the water, changed into a crocodile, then paddled back and frightened the life out of her sister. She then changed herself back and returned to her sister, who related how she had been terrified by a crocodile.

The first sister got such a kick out of this, that she repeated it over and over. Finally the other sister realised what was going on, and retaliated in the same way. The sisters then realised that if they were to turn themselves into crocodiles permanently, they could scare and eat anyone they pleased.

Today the Namarkan sisters are present in all crocodiles, evident in the lumps behind the eyes and their great skill and cunning as hunters.

UBIRR AREA

KAKADU & ARNHEM LAND

All road access is sealed, although low-lying areas may be inundated during the Wet.

This part of the park is as far east as you can go, and the East Alligator River marks the boundary with Arnhem Land. If you have a permit, access to Arnhem Land and Oenpelli is via Cahill's Crossing – a tidal ford. Exercise caution when crossing here – vehicles are occasionally swept away – and on no account should you attempt to cross on foot because death by crocodile is a distinct possibility.

Walking Tracks

There are four tracks in the Ubirr area:

Ubirr Art Site Walk (1km return; one hour; easy) An informative track around the rock art galleries, and there's a short but steep side track to a lookout with great views over the East Alligator River flood plain – it's popular at sunset.

Manngarre Monsoon Rainforest Walk (1.2km return; 20 minutes; easy) This walk starts by the boat ramp near the Border Store, and for much of the way is along a raised boardwalk.

Bardedjilidji Sandstone Walk (2.5km; 90 minutes; easy) This is a slightly longer walk starting from the upstream picnic area car park. It takes in wetland areas of the East Alligator River and some interesting eroded sandstone outliers of the Arnhem Land escarpment.

Rock Holes Sandstone Walk (8km; three hours; moderate) This is an extension of the Bardedjilidji Walk, taking in more of the same country.

JABIRU
• **pop 1700**   ⊠ **0886**

The township of Jabiru was built to accommodate workers at the nearby uranium mines and was completed in 1982. It was intended to be a temporary settlement, but has developed into the major service centre for Kakadu.

Unless you're staying at one of the resorts here (see Places to Stay & Eat later in this chapter), the only reason to visit Jabiru is for a permit to visit Oenpelli, to take a tour of the mine or to buy supplies.

Information

The town's shopping centre has a good range of amenities. The post office is in the newsagency and there's a branch of the Westpac Bank with an ATM outside. EFTPOS is available at the supermarket and at the Mobil service station on Leichhardt St.

Email access is available at the public library (☎ 8979 2097) next to the shopping centre.

For permits to visit Oenpelli, across the East Alligator River, contact the Northern Land Council (☎ 8979 2410) on Flinders St near the shopping centre. The office is open weekdays from 8 am to 4.21 pm!

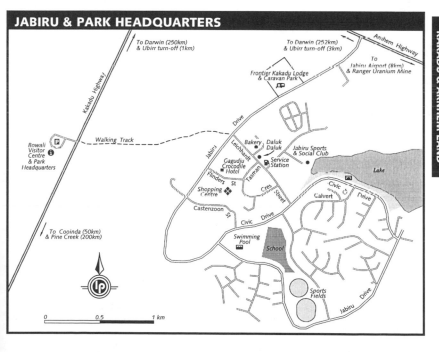

JABIRU & PARK HEADQUARTERS

KAKADU & ARNHEM LAND

The medical centre (☎ 8979 2018) is also in the main group of shops, and doctors are available for consultation from 8 am to 4 pm weekdays (except Wednesday when it closes at 2.30 pm). On weekends you can call the duty sister.

The police station (☎ 8979 2122) is in the centre on Tasman Crescent.

For fuel, mechanical repairs, camping gas and ice there's the Mobil service station (☎ 8979 2001) on Leichhardt St, which is open daily from 7 am to 8.30 pm.

The supermarket in the shopping centre is open weekdays from 9 am to 5.30 pm, Saturday from 9 am to 5 pm and Sunday from 10 am to 2 pm.

If you need a drink you should stock up in Darwin and bring it with you: takeaway liquor is not available to casual visitors to Jabiru. Alcoholic drinks can be bought and drunk on the premises at the hotels in Jabiru, Cooinda and South Alligator.

If you feel like a dip there's an Olympic sized public swimming pool just off Civic Drive. It's open daily from 9 am to 7 pm.

For car hire, Territory Thrifty Car Rentals has a desk at the Gagudju Crocodile Hotel (☎ 8979 2552).

Things to See

About the only option is a tour of the **Ranger Uranium Mine** east of the town. These are operated by Kakadu Parklink (☎ toll-free 1800 089 113) daily at 10.30 am and 1.30 pm during the dry season. The 90-minute bus tours leave from the Jabiru airport, and the cost is $15 (children $7).

Daluk Daluk is an Aboriginal arts and crafts shop specialising in screenprinting and textiles created on the premises. It's on Leichhardt St near the service station and most items are for sale.

NOURLANGIE

The sight of this looming, mysterious, isolated outlier of the Arnhem Land escarpment makes it easy to understand why it has been important to Aboriginal people for so long. Its long, red, sandstone bulk, striped in places with orange, white and black,

slopes up from surrounding woodland to fall away at one end in sheer, stepped cliffs, at the foot of which is Kakadu's best-known collection of rock art.

The name Nourlangie is a corruption of *nawulandja*, an Aboriginal word which refers to an area bigger than the rock itself. The Aboriginal name for part of the rock is Burrunggui. You reach it at the end of a 12km sealed road which turns east off the Kakadu Hwy, 21km south of the Arnhem Hwy. Other interesting spots nearby make it worth spending a whole day in this corner of Kakadu. The last few kilometres of the road are closed from around 5 pm daily.

From the main car park a walk takes you first to the **Anbangbang shelter**, which was used for 20,000 years as a refuge from heat, rain and the frequent wet-season thunderstorms. The shelter may have housed up to 30 people of the Warramal clan. Archaeological finds have revealed that the shelter was in almost constant use from about 6000 years ago to the time of contact.

Walking Tracks

Nourlangie is probably the most visited part of the park, and there are five other walking tracks at points along the access road.

Nourlangie Art Site (1.5km; one hour; easy to moderate) The best way to view the excellent rock art sites around the base of Nourlangie Rock. The Anbangbang rock shelter is the main gallery, and is accessible by wheelchair. Elsewhere the track is steep in parts; to have a good look at the paintings allow at least one hour.

The gallery here was repainted in the 1960s by Nayambolmi (also known as Barramundi Charlie), a respected artist, fisherman and hunter. From the gallery you can walk on to Gunwarrdehwarrde Lookout where you can see the distant Arnhem Land escarpment, which also includes Namarrgon Djadjam, the home of Namarrgon.

Nawurlandja Lookout (600m; one hour; moderate) This is just a short walk up a gradual slope, but it gives excellent views of the Nourlangie Rock area and is a good place to watch the sunset.

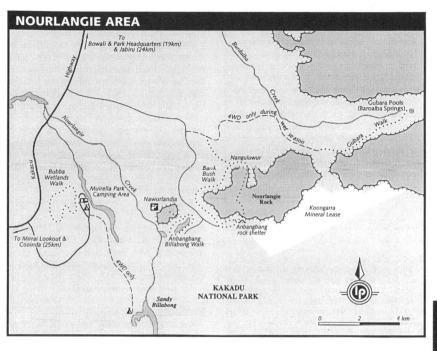

NOURLANGIE AREA

(map labels) To Bowali & Park Headquarters (19km) & Jabiru (24km); Highway; Nourlangie; Burdulba; Creek; 4WD only during wet season; Gubara Pools (Baroalba Springs); Gubara Walk; Nanguluwur; Bark Bush Walk; Kakadu; Bubba Wetlands Walk; Muirella Park Camping Area; Nawurlandja; Nourlangie Rock; Koongarra Mineral Lease; Creek; Anbangbang rock shelter; To Mirrai Lookout & Cooinda (25km); Anbangbang Billabong Walk; 4WD only; Sandy Billabong; KAKADU NATIONAL PARK; 0 2 4 km

Anbangbang Billabong Walk (2.5km; one hour; easy) This pretty billabong lies close to Nourlangie, and the picnic tables dotted around its edge make it a popular lunch spot. The track starts on the left about 1km from the main Nourlangie car park.

Nanguluwur Gallery (3.5km; two hours; easy) This outstanding, but little visited, rock art gallery sees far fewer visitors than Anbangbang simply because it's further to walk and has a gravel access road. Here the paintings cover most of the styles found in the park, including a good example of 'contact art', a painting of a two-masted sailing ship towing a dinghy.

Gubara Pools (6km; two hours; moderate) Further along the same road from Nanguluwur is the turn-off to this 3km walk, which skirts some clear pools in a patch of monsoon rainforest also known as Baroalba Springs. Remarkably, at least 14 species of freshwater fish are found in these small pools and it's a major breeding ground for saratoga.

Barrk Sandstone Bushwalk (12km; eight hours; strenuous) Barrk is the male black wallaroo

and you might see this elusive marsupial if you set out early. This difficult walk starts at the Nourlangie car park and involves some steep climbing to the top of Nourlangie Rock. Start as early as possible and carry plenty of water; it's also probably a good idea to tell staff at Bowali that you're going on this walk, and let them know when you get back.

MUIRELLA PARK AREA

Muirella Park is an excellent camping area in the central part of the park. It is convenient as a base for visiting Nourlangie, 25km away, and for Cooinda and Yellow Water which are about 30km south along the Kakadu Hwy.

A 6km 4WD track leads from Muirella Park to a free bush camping area at Sandy Billabong. There are no facilities there.

Walking Tracks

Three tracks can be enjoyed in the Muirella area.

Nourlangie Art

The major character in the main gallery at Nourlangie is **Namondjok** ('na-mon-jock'), who committed incest with one of his clan sisters. Next to Namondjok is **Namarrgon** ('na-mad-gon'), or the Lightning Man. He is responsible for all the spectacular electrical storms which occur during the Wet, and here is depicted surrounded by an arc of lightning. **Barrginj** ('bar-geen'), is the wife of Namarrgon, and is the small female figure just to the left and below Namondjok. Their children are called the Aljurr, beautiful orange and blue grasshoppers which are only seen just before the onset of the Wet.

Bubba Wetlands Walk (5km; two hours; easy) This walk skirts the edge of the Bubba Wetlands, and starts near the camp ground (signposted). There are wooden benches at intervals around the edge. This walk is closed in the Wet.

Mirrai Lookout (1.8km return; one hour; steep) This lookout is just off the Kakadu Hwy, 4km south of the Muirella Park turn-off. The track scales the dizzy heights of Mt Cahill (120m).

Iligadjarr Wetlands Walk (4km loop; 90 minutes; easy) The name refers to the ancestral file snakes that live in the billabong and on this interesting walk you can learn something of the uses the Aboriginal people had for the various wetland plants. Don't try it in the Wet.

JIM JIM & TWIN FALLS

These two spectacular waterfalls are along a 4WD dry season track that turns south off the Kakadu Hwy between the Nourlangie Rock and Cooinda turn-offs. It's about 60km – of which the last 10km can take up to 45 minutes, with the last 1km on foot – to Jim Jim Falls and 70km to Twin Falls, where the last few hundred metres are through the water up a snaking, forested gorge – great fun on an inflatable air bed. Jim Jim, a sheer 215m drop, is awesome after rain, but its waters shrink to nothing by about June. Even so, the gorge itself is impressive at any time, and the plunge pool makes a great swimming hole. There's even

a brilliant white sandy beach. There's a popular camp ground at Jim Jim.

Twin Falls is possibly more impressive for most visitors as it flows year-round. The track to Twin Falls is often blocked until well into the Dry by the Jim Jim Creek at the Jim Jim camping area. Markers indicate the depth in the middle of the creek but these should be used as a rough guide only as wheel tracks in the sandy creek bed can mean the water is deeper than you think. If you're unsure, wait for a tour vehicle or someone else with local knowledge to cross before attempting it. This crossing is only suitable for high clearance 4WDs with snorkel.

Several backpacker-style adventure tours visit Jim Jim and Twin regularly – they're worth the trip (see the Organised Tours section). Road access to Twin Falls closes off in the early Wet, much earlier than access to Jim Jim. Jim Jim alone is worth the visit in the early Wet as there is usually plenty of water dropping over the cliffs.

Walking Tracks

Some rough scrambling and a paddle are all that's required to get the most out of these two magnificent waterfalls.

Jim Jim Falls (1km; one hour; moderate) This is more of a scramble than a walk, as you climb over and around boulders of increasing size as you approach the falls. It is definitely not suitable for small children unless you can carry them. Allow at least an hour for a swim in the fantastic plunge pool at the foot of the falls.

Twin Falls Gorge (10km drive each way; two hours) Twin Falls flows year-round and is well worth the effort of getting there. After leaving the Jim Jim camp ground drive 10km then float upstream to the falls.

Budjmii Lookout (1km; 45 minutes; moderate) There are excellent escarpment views on this fairly rugged walk which starts from the Jim Jim camp ground.

YELLOW WATER & COOINDA

The turn-off to the Cooinda accommodation complex and the superb Yellow Water wetlands is 47km down the Kakadu Hwy from its junction with the Arnhem Hwy. It's then 4.5km to the Warradjan Cultural Centre (see the Information section earlier in this

Estuarine Crocodiles

A large crocodile lounging on a mud bank is an awesome sight. The entire length of its broad body and massive tail is armour-plated against the bite of anything but larger crocodiles. Its powerful jaws are held agape to help it stay cool, and in the process show an impressive array of teeth. It sits motionless, weighing perhaps a tonne, but if you approach it can launch itself into the water with a surprising burst of speed. There is no more formidable predator in the tropics, and its watchful, unblinking eyes remind you that here you are no longer at the top of the food chain.

The estuarine or saltwater crocodile is Australia's largest, heaviest – and most dangerous – reptile. It is common in both fresh and salt water in the Top End, including billabongs, estuaries and major river systems. It is often seen at sea, and sometimes far from land.

Most of its diet consists of crabs, fish and turtles, but for a large 'saltie' any animal is potential game, including wallabies, livestock, dogs and even humans. A hunting crocodile waits submerged, superbly camouflaged with only its eyes and nostrils above the surface. Should an animal get too close it lunges with incredible power and speed, propelled by its massive tail, and drags its victim under water. Although those powerful jaws can crush a pig's head in one bite, the croc first drowns its prey by rolling over and over. Crocs cannot swallow under water and after the 'death roll' must surface to eat.

But even an estuarine crocodile's life has its trials. The young are born only 30cm in length and to reach maturity must dodge birds, fish and larger crocodiles. To find a mate, a male must run the gauntlet of confronting older, territorial males which sometimes inflict fatal injuries. Travelling overland at night to reach a new waterhole, crocs sometimes perish in bushfires. Or, trapped in a drying swamp, they can suffer death by dehydration. Should it survive these hardships a croc can live 50 years and some very large specimens are estimated to be 80 years old.

The female lays 50-60 eggs in a nest of vegetation during the Wet. She defends the nest against intruders and, in a remarkable show of maternal care, carries the hatchlings to safety *in her jaws* and guards them for the first few weeks of life.

The saltie's ancestors can be traced back some 65 million years, but this unbroken lineage nearly ended during the 20th century, when its numbers were decimated by hunting. They are easy to spot at night because their eyes reflect the light of a strong torch. All crocs are now totally protected in the Territory, although Parks & Wildlife spend considerable time and money checking waterways and making them safe for people to enjoy.

KAKADU & ARNHEM LAND

chapter), a further 1km to the Yellow Water wetland turn-off, and about another 1km again to Cooinda.

A boat trip on the wetlands is one of the highlights of most people's visit to Kakadu (see the Activities section for details).

Yellow Water is also an excellent place to watch the sunset, particularly in the dry season when the smoke from the many bushfires which burn at this time of year turns bright red in the setting sun. Bring plenty of insect repellent with you as the mosquitoes can be voracious and rather detract from the experience.

Visitors should be particularly careful of crocodiles at Yellow Water – some impressive specimens hang around here. Keep well away from the water's edge and don't dangle legs over the edge of the floating pontoons.

Walking Tracks

Being the most accessible wetland and also having boat cruises, this is the busiest part of the park.

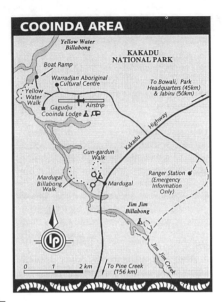

COOINDA AREA

KAKADU NATIONAL PARK

Yellow Water Billabong

Boat Ramp

Warradjan Aboriginal Cultural Centre

To Bowali, Park Headquarters (45km) & Jabiru (50km)

Yellow Water Walk

Gagudju Cooinda Lodge

Airstrip

Kakadu Highway

Gun-gardun Walk

Mardugal Billabong Walk

Mardugal

Ranger Station (Emergency Information Only)

Jim Jim Billabong

0 1 2 km

To Pine Creek (156 km)

Jim Jim Creek

Yellow Water (1.5km return; one hour; easy) The one walk here is little more than a stroll along a raised boardwalk out to a small viewing platform over the wetland. Nevertheless, it's a very pretty area with birds everywhere, and you can get some great photos at sunset (just be liberal with the mosquito repellent).

Mardugal Billabong (1km; 30 minutes; easy) Close by at Mardugal camping area a short walk takes you along the shore of Mardugal Billabong.

Gun-gardun (2km; one hour; easy) Also near the Mardugal camp ground, this circular walk showcases Kakadu's most widespread habitat, woodlands.

COOINDA TO PINE CREEK

Just south of the Yellow Water and Cooinda turn-off the Kakadu Hwy heads south-west out of the park to Pine Creek on the Stuart Hwy, about 160km away.

About 45km south of the Cooinda turn-off is the turn-off to **Maguk** (also known as Barramundi Gorge), a fine little camp ground on the Barramundie Creek 12km off the highway along a 4WD track.

After another 42km a road to the left (east) leads the 37km (mostly gravel but suitable for 2WD in the Dry) to **Gunlom (Waterfall Creek)**. This is another superb escarpment waterfall and plunge pool, and the only one accessible by conventional vehicle. There are also camping and picnic areas. This gravel road presents a challenge to foreign drivers who are unfamiliar with driving on rough corrugated roads. Rollovers are a common occurrence.

East of Gunlom, accessible by 4WD only and then with a permit, is Jarrangbarnmi (Koolpin Gorge), a beautiful and little-visited gorge with rock art sites. This area is best visited as part of a tour, since the rock art galleries are hard to find (see the Organised Tours section for operators).

Walking Tracks

The southern section of the park is less frequented than others, although the car park at Gunlom is sometimes full.

Maguk (2km; 90 minutes; moderate) This flat walk takes you to a plunge pool at the base of a small waterfall which flows year-round. Allow time for a swim.

Gunlom Waterfall (1km; one hour; strenuous) This is a short but steep walk which takes you to the top of the dramatic Gunlom Waterfall, above the plunge pool. It has great views and is worth the effort. This is a good place to look for some of the rare escarpment wildlife, such as black wallaroos. There's also a short walk to the large pool at the base of the waterfall (200m) with disabled access, and another to Murrill Billabong (1km) which carries on to the bank of the South Alligator River (2.5km).

Jarrangbarnmi (Koolpin Gorge) (2km; 90 minutes; moderate) This unmarked track follows Koolpin Creek to a series of pools and waterfalls. There's a rock art site and safe swimming in the creek.

Yurmikmik Walking Tracks

Five walks of varying difficulty penetrate the southern stone country of the park from Yurmikmik, 5km south of the South Alligator on the road to Gunlom. Some are day or half-day walks, others overnight and involve bush camping and navigational skills;

these should only be attempted by experienced bushwalkers.

Boulder Creek Walk (2km; 45 minutes; moderate) The easiest of the Yurmikmik walks, this short loop crosses Plum Tree Creek through woodlands and monsoon forest to return to the car park.

Yurmikmik Lookout Walk (5km; 90 minutes; moderate) The lookout gives fine views over Jawoyn country – the rugged ridges of the southern park area, the South Alligator River and the high, flat Marrawal Plateau.

Motor Car Falls Walk (7.5km; three hours; moderate) So named after the exploits of an old tin miner who drove his truck up here in 1946, this is actually a disused vehicle track. Markers lead to a plunge pool.

Motor Car Creek Walk 11km; seven hours; difficult) From Motor Car Falls, this is an unmarked section along the creek to the South Alligator River. It is essential to carry a topographic map (Topographic Map Sheet 5370/NatMap Series or Callaman 1:50,000) and compass, and a camping permit is required.

Motor Car and Kurrundie Creek Circular Walk (14km; 10 hours; strenuous) A topographic map, compass and camping permit are also essential for this overnight walk. The effort will be repaid by remote and seldom-visited country along Kurrundie Creek, returning by the South Alligator River and Motor Car Creek.

ORGANISED TOURS

There are a bewildering number of tour operators who can take you into Kakadu. Tours suit every taste from comfortable 'soft adventure' to 4WD trips that get right into the wrinkles of the escarpment. Ask about student/YHA discounts, stand-by rates and wet season specials. Don't forget that the park entry fee of $15 is generally not included in tour prices.

Most tours start from Darwin although a few start inside the park itself. There's lots of choice so shop around – and read the advice in the Darwin Organised Tours section.

Two-day tours typically take in Nourlangie, Ubirr and the Yellow Water cruise, and cost from around $170. A three day tour could include the art sites, Yellow Water cruise and access to 4WD areas such

---

Sickness Country

During the 1950s and 60s the southern part of what is now Kakadu National Park was the site of about a dozen small mines through the South Alligator River valley. The mines pulled high-grade uranium, gold, zinc, lead, silver and palladium, tin and copper from the ground.

The Jawoyn people call this area Buladjang – Sickness Country – and believe it was created by Bula, a powerful spirit who still lives underground, and that Bolung, the rainbow serpent, inhabits the billabongs in this country. They also believe that if disturbed both these creation ancestors can wreak havoc in the form of great storms, floods, disease and even earthquakes.

In geological terms, the Buladjang contains high levels of uranium and unusually high concentrations of arsenic, mercury and lead. In the 1980s preparations to mine Guratba (Coronation Hill) in the Buladjang created great fear among the Jawoyn people. In the words of one elder: 'My father know that gold was there longa Guratba. He said "Don't take any white man there. Bulardemo (Bula) will rock im, you and me, Shake the ground. We won't be alive. He will push and burn the trees ... no hope, nobody can stop him".'

But of course we all know that Australian uranium is used only for peaceful purposes ...

---

as Jim Jim Falls; expect to pay $330 and up. Four days should cover the above sights but give longer time at each for about $430; and longer trips – for $550 or so onwards, will give time to really appreciate the park and maybe get into somewhere remote.

Some companies also offer extented tours into Arnhem Land and packages that combine Litchfield and Katherine Gorge (Nitmiluk).

From Darwin

Two companies that aim at backpackers (and other sprightly travellers) and have been recommended are Gondwana (☎ toll-free 1800 242 177) and Wilderness 4WD Adventures (☎ toll-free 1800 808 288); you will certainly get a memorable trip and value for money with both outfits. Other operators that cater for younger travellers include Billy Can Tours (☎ toll-free 1800 813 484), Hunter Safaris (☎ toll-free 1800 670 640) and Backpacking Australia Tours (☎ 8945 2988).

A one day tour to Kakadu from Darwin is really too quick, but if you're short of time it's better than nothing. You could try Australian Kakadu Tours (☎ toll-free 1800 891 121), which will whiz you to Yellow Water for a two hour cruise (included) and Nourlangie Rock and back to Darwin for $75 ($85 including lunch), plus the $15 park entry fee.

Willis' Walkabouts (☎ 8985 2134) organises bushwalks guided by knowledgeable Top End walkers following your own or preset routes of two days or more.

If you have a tight schedule and the money, Outback NT Air Safaris (☎ toll-free 1800 089 113) runs Kakadu and combination Kakadu/Arnhem Land flights from Darwin.

From Jabiru & Cooinda

You can take 10-hour, 4WD tours to Jim Jim and Twin Falls from Jabiru or Cooinda ($120) with Kakadu Gorge & Waterfall Tours (☎ 8979 0111). Lord of Kakadu (☎ 8979 2567) and AAT-Kings (☎ 8947 1207) do similar trips.

Kakadu Park Connection (☎ 8979 0111) has half-day, 4WD trips from Cooinda for $55, but these only visit Maguk. Full-day trips cost $105 and head into Gunlom in the south of the park.

Northern Adventure Safaris (☎ 8981 3833) operates good two-day trips out of Jabiru, visiting Ubirr, Nourlangie and Yellow Water, for $203 ($160 for Greyhound Pioneer pass holders). Three-day trips also include Jim Jim and Twin falls, and cost $310 ($265).

For day trips to Ubirr, which include the Guluyambi river cruise and a visit to the Ranger mine, tours are run by Kakadu Parklink (☎ 8979 2411) for $100 (children $80) from Jabiru. It also does day trips down to Nourlangie and Yellow Water for the same price.

Guided full or half-day fishing trips are operated by Kakadu Fishing Tours (☎ 8979 2025). These depart from Jabiru and cost $180 for one person or $110 per person for groups of two or three; full-day trips including lunch cost $220 per person.

Into Arnhem Land

A couple of outfits offer trips into Arnhem Land from Kakadu, although they only nip across the East Alligator River to Oenpelli. Aboriginal-owned Magela Cultural & Heritage Tours (☎ 8979 2422) runs one-day tours from Jabiru costing $150 (children $100) and Lord of Kakadu Tours (☎ 8979 2567) does a four-hour fly/drive combo for $120.

PLACES TO STAY & EAT

With the exception of camp grounds, accommodation prices in Kakadu can vary tremendously depending on the season – dry-season prices (given here) are often as much as 50% above wet-season prices.

Cooinda

This is by far the most popular place to stay, mainly because of the proximity of the Yellow Water wetlands and the early-morning boat cruises. It gets mighty crowded at times, and bookings are advised well ahead of your intended dates of travel, especially if you want the cheaper rooms.

The *Gagudju Lodge Cooinda* (☎ toll-free 1800 500 401) has comfortable air-con units for $135 a single or double. Basic air-con 'budget rooms', which are just transportable huts of the type known as 'demountables' or 'dongas', cost $25 per person. They are quite adequate, if a little cramped (two beds per room), with shared cooking facilities.

The large camping area is OK with plenty of shade, although the facilities are stretched at times. It costs $9 per site, or $11 with power.

There's a *shop* at the resort selling fuel plus basic food needs, film and souvenirs; opening hours are 6 am until 9 pm (7.30 pm during the Wet). Barbecues and picnic tables are located throughout the camp ground.

Meals are available at the *Barra Bar & Bistro* from 6.30 am onwards. The food is unexciting and costs around $11 to $15. The choice at dinner includes a self-cook barbecue with a range of meats and salads. The bar can get quite lively at night and takeaway alcohol is available.

For good but expensive à la carte dining there's the *Mimi Restaurant* overlooking the resort's swimming pool. Main courses are around $20. It's open for lunch and dinner during the dry season only and bookings are essential.

Jabiru

The *Frontier Kakadu Lodge* (☎ 8979 2422) has the best range of accommodation in Jabiru and a great swimming pool. Shady and grassed powered sites in the well-equipped caravan park cost $20 and unpowered sites are $15. There are also four-bed air-con dorms for $25 ($20 during the Wet); linen is supplied and bathroom and cooking facilities are shared. Quad rooms with bunks cost $95 ($70) and self-contained cabins are also available for $165 ($120) plus tax.

The *Gagudju Crocodile Hotel* (☎ toll-free 1800 808 123) was built in the shape of a 250m crocodile. The shape is only really apparent from the air, but it's a comfortable enough hotel with bars, a good restaurant, souvenir shop and art gallery. Room prices start at $210 (plus tax) for a double during the Dry and drop to $150 during the Wet. Their swimming pool is surprisingly small.

The licensed poolside *bistro* at Frontier Kakadu Lodge serves reasonable pub-style meals for around $12 and there's a *shop* with basic groceries.

Gagudju Crocodile has upmarket *licensed restaurants*.

There's a *café* in the Jabiru shopping centre, and a *bakery* near the fire station which has a range of fresh pies and is the only place to get a cheap takeaway breakfast in the early morning (it's closed on Sunday).

South Alligator

Just a couple of kilometres west of the South Alligator River on the Arnhem Hwy is the *All Seasons Frontier Kakadu Village* (☎ 8979 0166). Sites in the grassed camp ground cost from $15, or $20 with power, and resort-style singles or doubles cost $132.

The resort has two restaurants, a general store and coffee shop, shaded swimming pool and bar. Fuel is available.

Ubirr

The popular *Kakadu Hostel* (☎ 8979 2232) behind the Border Store is the only place in Kakadu that offers what could be called budget accommodation with decent facilities. It's open year-round (as long as the road remains open) and offers a fully-equipped kitchen, pool and barbecues; cooked meals are available some nights. A bed costs $15 and accommodation is in dorms (one with air-con) or fan-cooled twins and doubles. Walking tracks connect the hostel with the East Alligator River and two pleasant walking tracks. Cheap meals are available, including evening barbecues for $6 and a full breakfast for $5.

The Border Store (☎ 8979 2474) stocks a good range of groceries, snacks and takeaway food (alcohol is not available), and fuel. By the time you read this it should be serving barbecue meals as well. It is open daily during the Dry from 8 am to 8 pm.

Camping

Facilities at camp grounds operated by National Parks range from basic sites with pit toilets to full amenities blocks with hot showers, although there's no electricity at any of them. There are also remote bush sites, usually accessible only by 4WD, with no facilities. As mentioned, commercial

KAKADU & ARNHEM LAND

sites with more facilities, such as restaurants and swimming pools, are attached to the various resorts at South Alligator, Jabiru and Cooinda.

National Park Camp Grounds There are four main National Parks camp grounds. All have hot showers, flushing toilets, and drinking water and the fee is $5 per person over 16 years. These are the only sites which are really suitable for caravans.

Merl This is close to Ubirr and the Border Store in the north of the park. There's plenty of shade, but the mosquitoes are thick and it's closed in the Wet.

Muirella Park Situated right on a paperbark-lined billabong, Muirella Park is 6km off the Kakadu Hwy and 7km south of the Nourlangie Rock turn-off. It's actually on a reclaimed airstrip which was part of a safari camp in the 1950s. There's not much shade and parts of the site can be flooded during the Wet.

Mardugal Just off the Kakadu Hwy, 1.5km south of the Cooinda turn-off, Mardugal is the only site not affected by the Wet. It's a nice, shady spot with big trees.

Gunlom This excellent and popular site in the south of the park has flush toilets, hot showers and drinking water. Salmon gums provide shade. Access is by a gravel road from the Kakadu Hwy, open to conventional vehicles during the Dry.

Other Sites National Parks provide 12 more basic camp grounds around the park at which there is no fee. They have fireplaces, some have pit toilets and at all of them you'll need to bring your own drinking water. To camp away from these grounds you will need a permit from the Bowali Visitor Centre.

GETTING THERE & AROUND
Ideally, take your own vehicle. It doesn't have to be a 4WD, since roads to most sites of interest are sealed, but a 4WD will give greater flexibility and is the only possible way to see Jim Jim or Twin Falls. Sealed roads lead from the Kakadu Hwy to Nourlangie, to the Muirella Park camping area and to Ubirr. Other roads are mostly dirt and blocked for varying periods during the Wet and early Dry. Hire cars (including 4WDs) are available from the Gagudju Crocodile Hotel in Jabiru (see Places to Stay & Eat earlier in this section).

Bus
Greyhound Pioneer runs daily buses from Darwin as far as Cooinda, and back. The buses stop at the Yellow Water wetland in time for the 1 pm cruise, and wait here for 1½ hours until the cruises finish. The bus leaves Darwin at 6.30 am, Jabiru at 9.55 am and arrives at Cooinda at 12.10 pm. It leaves from Cooinda at 2.30 pm, Jabiru at 4.20 pm, and arrives in Darwin at 7 pm. The cost is $65, Darwin to Cooinda, including two stopovers. To travel one way from Darwin to the park costs $25.

Blue Banana This company (☎ 8945 6800) runs out to Kakadu, stopping at South Alligator, Jabiru, the Border Store/Ubirr, Nourlangie Rock, Cooinda and Gunlom. You can alight at any or all of these stops.

The fare from Darwin to Kakadu and back via Litchfield is $140; Jabiru-Katherine via Ubirr, Cooinda and Gunlom is $70, and Darwin-Katherine via Kakadu is $100. A ticket is valid for three months.

Arnhem Land

The entire eastern half of the Top End comprises the Arnhem Land Aboriginal Reserve, a vast, virtually untouched area with spectacular scenery, few people and some superb rock art sites. The only settlements of any size are Gove, on the peninsula at the north-eastern corner, and Oenpelli (Gunbalanya), just across the East Alligator River from Ubirr in Kakadu National Park.

To the north is the remote Cobourg Peninsula, most of which is preserved as Gurig National Park and features the ruins of the ill-fated Victoria Settlement, some fine fishing and the world's only wild herd of banteng, or Indonesian cattle.

Access to Arnhem Land is by permit only and numbers are strictly controlled. It has long been known for its superb fishing, but the 'stone country' – the Arnhem escarpment and its outliers – also hosts literally thousands of Aboriginal rock art sites of incredible variety, age and interest.

Access to Oenpelli and Cobourg Peninsula is across the East Alligator River from Ubirr in Kakadu. Access to the northeastern section of Arnhem Land is from Katherine.

ORGANISED TOURS

There are a number of tours into Arnhem Land, but these usually only visit the western part.

The Aboriginal owned and operated Umorrduk Safaris (☎ 8948 1306) has a two day fly-in/fly-out tour from Darwin to the remote Mudjeegarrdart airstrip in north-western Arnhem Land. The highlight of the trip is a visit to the 20,000-year-old Umorrduk rock art sites. The cost is from $200 to $600 per person.

Davidson's Arnhemland Safaris (☎ 8927 5240) has been taking people into Arnhem Land for years to its concession at Mt Borradaile, north of Oenpelli, where there is a comfortable safari camp. The cost of staying at the camp is from $200 per person per day, which includes meals, guided tours and fishing; transfers from Darwin can be arranged.

Venture North Australia (☎ 8927 5500, fax 8927 7883) operates tours to remote areas and features expert guidance on rock art. It also has a safari camp near Smith Point in Gurig National Park.

AAT-Kings (☎ toll-free 1800 334 009) has two-day coach trips operating out of Darwin which take you through Kakadu and on to Davidson's Safari Camp. The cost of these trips is $499.

Gove Diving & Fishing Charters (☎ 8987 3445) runs fishing trips from Gove, costing $210 per person or $930 for a day's boat charter. They also run four day/three night camping safaris.

OENPELLI (GUNBALANYA)
• pop 740　　　　　　✉ 0822

Oenpelli is a small Aboriginal town 17km into Arnhem Land across the East Alligator River from the Border Store in Kakadu. The town is generally not accessible to visitors and the main reason to come here is to visit the Injalak Arts & Crafts Centre (☎ 8979 0190). Injalak is both a workplace and shopfront for artists and craftspeople who produce traditional paintings on bark and paper, plus didgeridoos, pandanus weavings and baskets, and screenprinted fabrics. Prices are very competitive with other outlets in the region and credit cards are accepted. All sales benefit the artists and therefore the community. Injalak offers discounts to YHA members.

It's best to visit Injalak in the morning, which is when most of the artists are at work. Tours can be arranged to the small hill north of Oenpelli known as Long Tom Dreaming. There are some fine rock art galleries here and a knowledgeable local guide explains their significance. The guide's services cost $60 per group for a two hour tour – it's a hot climb – and you must be at Oenpelli by 10 am. Injalak is closed on Sunday.

Before you can visit you must obtain a permit from the Northern Land Council in Jabiru (☎ 8979 2410), which collects a fee of $12 per person. Permits can usually be issued the same day, although 24 hours notice is appreciated; see the Jabiru section for NLC office hours.

Check the tides at the East Alligator crossing before setting out so you don't spend hours sitting around on the bank.

COBOURG PENINSULA

This remote wilderness, 200km north-east of Darwin, is protected by the Aboriginal-owned **Gurig National Park**, and its surrounding waters are included in the **Cobourg Marine Park**. The peninsula juts nearly 100km into the Timor Sea from the north-west tip of Arnhem Land and features some excellent beaches, although of course the water is full of nasties. Gurig is also home to a wide variety of introduced animals – Indonesian banteng cattle, sambar deer and pigs – all imported by the British when they attempted to settle the region in the 19th century.

It's not really possible to explore the inland parts of the park as there are virtually no tracks, so the focus here is on water-based activities. Apart from fishing and boating, you can wander along the deserted beaches gathering shells – of which there is an amazing variety and number – and it's a beautiful spot to kick back and relax.

One of the natural highlights of the peninsula is the Cobourg Marine Park, which protects 229,000 hectares of the peninsula's surrounding waters. The fishing is legendary, and sought-after species include blue water fish such as tuna and mackerel. Underwater life is rich and features coral reefs and seagrass meadows which attract dugong. Other large marine animals include six species of turtles and dolphins – Indo-Pacific humpbacks are seen regularly in Port Essington. And of course there's the usual rogue's gallery of estuarine crocs, sharks and sea stingers.

The park is jointly managed by Parks & Wildlife and the local Aboriginal inhabitants through the Cobourg Peninsula Sanctuary Board.

History

Various Aboriginal clans lived off the rich marine life of the area and fleets of Macassan traders, from what is now Sulawesi, fished for sea cucumbers (trepang) in the shallow coastal waters. Some of their words were absorbed into the Aboriginal languages, such as *balanda* (white man) and *mutiyara* (pearl shell), and artefacts such as pottery, fabrics, tobacco, gin, steel blades and food were traded.

In 1818 Captain Phillip Parker King explored and named the Cobourg Peninsula and Port Essington. British fears of French and Dutch expansion into the area led to unsuccessful attempts at settlement at Melville Island, then Raffles Bay on the Cobourg Peninsula, and a third attempt at Port Essington in 1838. This garrison town was named Victoria Settlement, and at its peak was home to over 300 people. Victoria was intended to become a major base for trade between Australia and Asia. Within a year the colony had been devastated by a cyclone and in ensuing years the colony's food supplies were raided by rats and insects. The poor soil meant a poor harvest and termites took a toll of the buildings. Disease also took its toll, and many settlers died of malaria before Victoria was abandoned in 1849.

Victoria Settlement

Victoria Settlement is tucked into the far reaches of Port Essington, the superb 30km-long natural harbour that virtually cleaves the peninsula in two. Only a few buildings remain and the site is now overgrown, but it's a peaceful spot that repays the effort of getting there. An information sheet, available from the visitor centre at Black Point, gives a brief history of the site and a self-guiding walk. It is remarkable to think that where there's now only woollybutts and vines, soldiers and civilians once strutted about in Victorian finery. Among the ruins are some peculiar beehive-shaped stone cottages and the cemetery where many of the original settlers were buried.

Victoria Settlement is accessible only by boat. A charter-boat service (☎ 8979 0263) is available from Black Point and costs $75 per person (children $40); departure times and days of operation are posted at the Gurig Store.

Permits, Fees & Information

Entry to Gurig is by permit. It's advisable to apply up to a year ahead because to get there by road you must pass through Arnhem Land and the Aboriginal owners restrict the number of vehicles going through to 15 at any one time. Permit application forms are available from the Cobourg Peninsula Sanctuary and Marine Park Board, PO Box 496, Palmerston NT 0831, or by phoning the Administration Office ☎ 8999 4555 or Ranger Station ☎ 8979 0244.

It is not necessary to obtain a permit for Kakadu National Park if you are just passing through en route to Gurig. If you are planning to stay in Kakadu on the way back, the most convenient place to get a permit is at the Bowali Visitor Centre.

Visitors arriving by road are charged a camping fee of $211 per vehicle carrying up to five adults for a maximum stay of seven nights. Extra passengers over the age of 16 must pay an extra $10. Visitors arriving by air or sea are charged $15 per person per night.

At Black Point there is a ranger station and a visitor centre (☎ 8979 0244) that has an interesting section about the Aboriginal people, as well as Europeans and Maccassans.

For information on conditions at Cahill's Crossing phone the East Alligator Ranger Station (☎ 8979 2291).

Places to Stay

Accommodation is available only at Smith Point, Cape Don and Seven Spirit Bay. *Northern Expeditions* (☎ 8927 5500) has a *safari camp* near Smith Point (see the Organised Tours section).

There's a good, shady Parks & Wildlife *camp ground* about 100m from the shore at Smith Point. Facilities include showers, toilets, barbecues and limited bore water.

For a bit more luxury, the *Cobourg Beach Huts* (☎ 8979 0263) at Smith Point overlooking Port Essington cost from $135 per night for up to four people, plus $10 per night for each additional person (maximum of six). The huts are equipped with solar electricity, gas stove, fridge and kitchen utensils and linen, but you need to bring your own supplies. Pit toilets and bush showers are separate.

At Cape Don the lighthouse keeper's *homestead* has been renovated to cater for packaged fishing tours that include all meals, accommodation, return air fares, and fishing guide and tackle. Prices start at $1495 for three nights on a twin share basis and range up to $2995 for seven nights. Daily rates range from $485 for a single to $360 for triple share.

The only other accommodation option is the *Seven Spirit Bay Resort* (☎ 8979 0277), a luxury wilderness resort turned fishing haven and accessible only by air or boat. It charges $350 per person for twin or double accommodation and $395 for singles; this includes three gourmet meals.

At Black Point there's the small *Gurig Store* (☎ 8979 0263), which is open Monday to Saturday from 4 to 6 pm only. It sells a good range of basic provisions, plus ice, camping gas and fishing tackle. Fuel is available at the nearby jetty between 6 and 6.30 pm only; because it must be shipped in by barge it is very expensive.

There's an airstrip at Smith Point which is serviced by charter flights from Darwin.

Getting There & Away

The quickest way to get to Gurig is by air, although it will leave you without transport when you arrive. The return fare from Darwin is about $300.

It's a long haul by road. The track to Cobourg starts at Oenpelli and is accessible by 4WD vehicle only – and access may be restricted during the Wet. The 288km drive to Black Point from the East Alligator River crossing takes about six hours and the track is in reasonable condition, the roughest part coming in the hour or so after the turn-off from Murgenella. The trip must be completed in one day as only emergency stops are permitted on Aboriginal land.

Straight after the Wet, the water level at Cahill's Crossing on the East Alligator River near the Border Store can be high, and you can drive across the ford only about an hour either side of low tide. A tide chart is included with your permit, or the Bowali Visitor Centre in Kakadu has a list of tide times.

EASTERN ARNHEM LAND

The eastern part of Arnhem Land that is of interest to visitors is the Gove Peninsula.

Groote Eylandt, a large island off the east Arnhem Land coast, is also Aboriginal land, with a big manganese-mining operation. The main settlement here is Alyangula (pop 670).

History

Dutch navigators in the 17th century were followed by an Englishman, Matthew Flinders, who named the area after one of the earlier Dutch ships. Early overland visitors to Arnhem Land were the explorer Ludwig Leichhardt in 1845 and the South Australian surveyor David Lindsay in 1883.

During the late 19th century cattle stations covered much of the area, although the land was largely unsuitable for stock, and there were also a number of Christian missions.

In 1931 the area was proclaimed an Aboriginal reserve on the recommendations of an investigation in the Northern Territory by the Federal government.

In 1963 the Aboriginal people of Yirrkala (pop 520) made an important step in the land rights movement when they protested against the plans for a manganese mine on their land. They failed to stop it, but forced a government inquiry and won compensation.

Permits

A permit is essential for travel through eastern Arnhem Land – not to travel the road, but to stop and camp overnight along the way (at designated camp grounds only). Obtaining permits to travel to Gove should be a straightforward matter, but it's best to plan ahead. Contact the East Arnhem Regional Tourist Association (☎ 8987 2255) who can get you on the right track. A minimum of 10 working days is normally required to process a permit. The NLC must contact the traditional owners in each case.

If you are flying in to Gove no permit is needed, but to venture outside the town – even to the beaches close by – you need to get a recreational permit ($11) from the traditional owners through the local Dhimurru

Land Management & Aboriginal Corporation (☎ 8987 3992) in Nhulunbuy (a formality).

Nhulunbuy

• pop 3719   ✉ 0880

At Nhulunbuy, on the Gove Peninsula, there is a bauxite-mining centre with a deep-water export port. The township itself was built in the 1970s to service the mine. On Friday morning there are tours of the **bauxite mine and plant**, which is 15km from the town.

It's worth visiting the **Yirrkala Arts & Crafts** (☎ 8987 1701) and you can buy locally made crafts at the **Nambara Arts & Crafts** Aboriginal gallery (☎ 8987 2811).

You can hire vehicles in Nhulunbuy to explore the coastline (there are some fine beaches but beware of crocodiles).

Places to Stay Nhulunbuy has two motels – the *Gove Peninsula Motel (☎ 8987 0700)*, where a single/double costs $99.75/110.25 including tax and the *Hideaway Safari Lodge (☎ 8987 3933)*.

The beachfront *Walkabout Arnhem Land Resort Hotel (☎ 8987 1777)* is a resort complex close to the town's facilities, and has a pool, restaurant and car hire. Standard singles or doubles cost $145 and a premier room, with a nicer aspect, costs $155, plus tax. It can process beach walking permits.

Getting There & Away

Air Ansett has almost daily flights between Darwin and Gove ($260), and from there to Cairns ($355). Airnorth flies between Darwin and Gove ($253), and also serves outstations in eastern Arnhem Land such as Maningrida ($170), Ngukurr ($284), Numbulwar ($314) and Ramingining ($200). All these prices are for one-way tickets.

Land Access to Gove (during the Dry only) is via the gravel road which leaves the Stuart Hwy 52km south of Katherine and cuts north-east across Arnhem Land the 700km or so to Gove. Locals do the trip in as little as nine hours, but it's better to take your time and do it in a couple of days.

Katherine & Victoria River District

The town of Katherine is the Territory's third largest settlement and a major crossroads for tourists. There's not much to see in Katherine itself, but nearby there's the majestic Katherine Gorge and 100km to the south the popular Mataranka Hot Springs.

The country west of Katherine contains some of the Territory's best scenery. The Victoria Hwy passes through the beautiful sandstone escarpments of the Gregory National Park to the little town of Timber Creek. Known as the Victoria River District, this is an area of vast cattle stations which gradually gives way to the spinifex-dotted expanses of the Tanami Desert to the south. In the far west of the Territory, there's little-visited Keep River National Park, from where it's a short trip to the border and beyond to Western Australia.

HIGHLIGHTS

- Paddle a canoe along the spectacular Katherine Gorge
- Delve into Aboriginal culture at Manyallaluk
- Soak tired limbs in the thermal pools at Mataranka
- Photograph giant boab trees and beautiful scenery at remote Keep River National Park

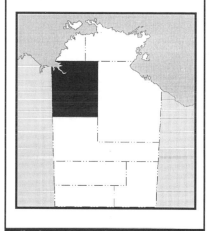

Katherine

· **pop 9856**   ✉ **0850**

This is the biggest town by far between Darwin and Alice Springs and a bustling little place where the Victoria Hwy branches off to the Kimberley and Western Australia.

Katherine has long been an important stopping point, since the river it's built on and named after is the first permanent running water on the road north from Alice Springs. It's a mixed blessing really, because Katherine suffered devastating floods in January 1998 – not for the first time – that inundated the surrounding countryside and left their mark up to 2m high on buildings all over town. Some good did come of the floods for Katherine however, as they forced a major clean up. Some buildings still stand empty, but many more have been given a new lease of life and with it the local tourist authority seems to have made a great effort to promote the town.

There are some historic buildings to see, but the main interest here is the beautiful Nitmiluk National Park – better known as Katherine Gorge – 30km to the east. The gorge is a great place to camp, walk, swim, canoe, take a cruise or simply float along on an air mattress.

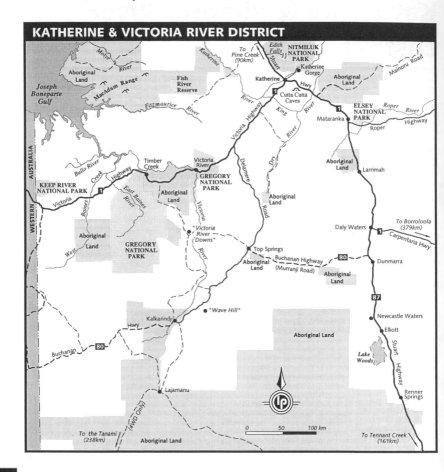

KATHERINE & VICTORIA RIVER DISTRICT

History

The Katherine area is the traditional home of the Jawoyn and Dagoman Aboriginal people, and following land claims in recent years they have received the title to large parcels of land, including Nitmiluk (Katherine Gorge) National Park.

The first Europeans through the area were those in the expedition of Ludwig Leichhardt in 1844. The river was named the Catherine by John McDouall Stuart in 1862, but for some reason the current

spelling was adopted. As was so often the case with Territory towns, it was the construction of the Overland Telegraph Line and the establishment of a telegraph station (at Knott's Crossing, a few kilometres along the gorge road from the current town) which really got the town going.

Pastoral ventures soon followed, one of the most notable being the establishment of Springvale Station by Alfred Giles in 1878. Although his attempts at sheep and cattle farming were not outrageously successful, he laid the foundations for the cattle industry which is important in the Katherine region today.

The town found its current site when the railway bridge over the Katherine River was opened in 1926. WWII saw Katherine become a major defence-force base, and it even received a bit of attention from the Japanese when nine bombers raided the town in March 1942.

The town now survives largely on the tourism generated by Katherine Gorge and the business from nearby Tindal air force base.

Orientation

The Stuart Hwy forms the backbone of Katherine. Approaching from Darwin, the bridge over the Katherine River marks the northern end of town; once south of the bridge, the highway becomes the main street, Katherine Terrace. On the right, about 300m south of the bridge, is the turn-off to the Victoria Hwy (for Victoria River, Timber Creek and Western Australia). Another 300m on the left is Giles St, the road to Katherine Gorge.

The transit centre, banks, main post office, most places to eat, a modern shopping centre and three roadhouses are along Katherine Terrace.

Information

At the south-eastern end of the town centre on the Stuart Hwy is the office of the Katherine Region Tourist Association (☎ 8972 2650), which is open Monday to Friday from 8 am to 5 pm, and Saturday and Sunday from 10 am to 3 pm. The staff are helpful and there's an excellent range of printed material on tours, sights and accommodation.

The local newspaper is the *Katherine Times* and tourism information is broadcast on 88 MHz FM.

Diagonally opposite the information centre at the 24-hour BP station, is Travel North (☎ 8972 1044), a major tour operator in the area. The BP station is also the transit centre where the long-distance buses pull in. Luggage can be left behind the counter at the bus check-in desk.

The main post office is on the corner of Katherine Terrace and Giles St. Telephones are located outside the main post office on Giles St and outside the information centre.

Email access is possible at Katherine Art Gallery, 12 Katherine Terrace (just up from the transit centre).

There are branches of the ANZ, Commonwealth and Westpac banks in Katherine Terrace, all with ATMs. There's a chemist in the main street and a shopping arcade at the southern end with a large supermarket. There are fast film processing labs opposite the transit centre and in the shopping arcade.

In case of emergency the hospital (☎ 8973 9294) is on Giles St, about 2.5km north of the town centre. Also on Giles St, but closer to the centre, there's a Parks & Wildlife office (☎ 8973 8770). The police station (☎ 8972 0111) is inconveniently located south of town along the Stuart Hwy.

Annual events in Katherine include the Katherine Show (July), the Katherine Rodeo (July) and the Fabulous Flying Fox Festival, which runs throughout October and features local artists and performers.

Things to See

The railway arrived in 1926 as an extension of the line which until then had terminated at Pine Creek. Katherine's old railway station has been restored and is now the **Railway Museum**, owned by the National Trust. It's on Railway Terrace, tucked away behind the Shell station on Katherine Terrace, and is open Monday to Friday from 10 am to noon and from 1 to 3 pm in the Dry season. Admission is $2.

The small **Katherine Museum** is on the site of the town's original airport and is housed in the old terminal building. It's on Gorge Rd (the continuation of Giles St), about 3km from the centre of town. Displays include a good selection of historical photos, agricultural equipment, old trucks and other bits and pieces. Pride of place goes to the original Gypsy Moth biplane flown by Dr Clyde Fenton, the first Flying Doctor. There's also a tiny helicopter used for cattle mustering. From March to October it is open weekdays from 10 am to 4 pm, November to February from 10 am to 1 pm and year-round on Sunday from 2 to 5 pm. Admission is $3.

Springvale Homestead is an attractive collection of stone buildings established in 1879 by Ernest Giles, who drove 2000 cattle and horses and 12,000 head of sheep from Adelaide to the site in 19 months. The stone homestead still stands by the river, about 8km from town, but it suffered terrible flood damage in 1998 and its future was uncertain at the time of writing.

A few kilometres beyond the museum and signposted off Gorge Rd is **Knott's Crossing**, the site of the original Katherine River crossing. The building here was formerly the Sportsman's Arms & Pioneer Cash Store and was used in the filming of *We of the Never Never*. A little further on again, and visible from the road, is one of the original pylons of the **Overland Telegraph**, which was built across the river in 1871.

On Riverbank Drive, near the Victoria Hwy, is **O'Keeffe House**, one of the oldest buildings in the town. It was originally built of simple bush poles, corrugated iron and flywire mesh by the Army in 1942 as a recreation hut. After WWII the building passed through a number of hands, until it was bought in 1963 by Olive O'Keeffe, a nursing sister who became well known for her work throughout the Territory over many years. The building was bought by the National Trust after 'Keeffie's' death in 1988. O'Keeffe House is open Monday to Friday from 1 to 5 pm during the Dry.

The **School of the Air**, 1.5km along on Giles St, offers an opportunity to see how kids in the remote outback are educated. Guided tours are held at 9, 10 and 11am, and 1 and 2 pm on weekdays from April to October; the cost is $4/2 for adults/children.

Activities
Swimming It comes as some relief to find Katherine has a choice of natural swimming places – Edith Falls and Nitmiluk (Katherine Gorge) are the most spectacular (see the relevant sections), but there are two others closer to town.

The pleasant **thermal pools** are beside the river, about 2km south of town along the Victoria Hwy, (accessible to wheelchairs from Croker St).

The 105 hectare **Katherine Low Level Nature Park** is 5km from town, just off the Victoria Hwy. It's a great spot on the Katherine River, taking in 4km of its shady banks, and the swimming hole by the weir is very popular in the Dry; in the Wet flash-flooding can make it dangerous. Facilities provided here include picnic tables, toilets and gas barbecues.

There's also a good public **swimming pool** beside the Stuart Hwy, about 750m past the information centre towards Mataranka.

Horse Riding Brumby Tracks Tours (☎ 8972 1425) runs a range of riding options on Granite Creek Station north-west of Katherine. Options range from 1½-hour trail rides for $35 to overnight wilderness campouts.

Campbell's Trail Rides out at Springvale Homestead runs short rides along the banks of the Katherine River. An hour's riding costs $20.

Cycling Katherine is pretty flat and cycling is a good way to get around town. Bikes may be hired at some backpackers hostels – prices are about $8/5 per full/half day.

Organised Tours
Katherine has a plethora of tour operators, offering everything from local history to Aboriginal art and culture, Nitmiluk and further afield to Kakadu and Arnhem Land. There's ample brochures available at the information centre, where you can also make bookings. Tour desks are also located at places to stay. Most tours will pick you up from where you're staying.

There are excellent **Aboriginal tours** at Manyallaluk (see the Around Katherine section later in this chapter) and Jankanginya Tours (☎ 8971 0318) take you out onto traditional Aboriginal land, sometimes referred to as Lightning Brothers country. Here you

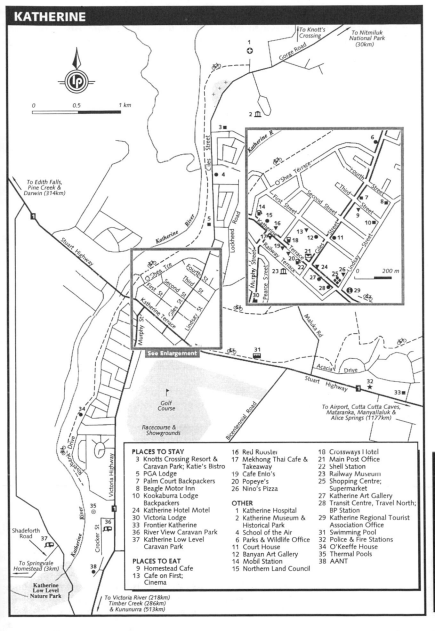

KATHERINE

PLACES TO STAY
3 Knotts Crossing Resort & Caravan Park; Katie's Bistro
5 PGA Lodge
7 Palm Court Backpackers
8 Beagle Motor Inn
10 Kookaburra Lodge Backpackers
24 Katherine Hotel Motel
30 Victoria Lodge
33 Frontier Katherine
36 River View Caravan Park
37 Katherine Low Level Caravan Park

PLACES TO EAT
9 Homestead Cafe
13 Cafe on First; Cinema

16 Red Rooster
17 Mekhong Thai Cafe & Takeaway
19 Cafe Enlo's
20 Popeye's
26 Nino's Pizza

OTHER
1 Katherine Hospital
2 Katherine Museum & Historical Park
4 School of the Air
6 Parks & Wildlife Office
11 Court House
12 Banyan Art Gallery
14 Mobil Station
15 Northern Land Council

18 Crossways Hotel
21 Main Post Office
22 Shell Station
23 Railway Museum
25 Shopping Centre; Supermarket
27 Katherine Art Gallery
28 Transit Centre, Travel North; BP Station
29 Katherine Regional Tourist Association Office
31 Swimming Pool
32 Police & Fire Stations
34 O'Keeffe House
35 Thermal Pools
38 AANT

KATHERINE

learn about bush tucker, crafts and medicine, and hear some of the stories associated with the rock art of the area.

For a trip along the Katherine River, Gecko Canoeing (☎ toll-free 1800 634 319) has three-day guided tours for $435 including meals and safety gear.

Trips out to a working Brahman cattle station are offered by Ironwood Station Adventure Tours (☎ 8972 3868), which include riding four-wheel motor bikes, inspecting the day to day running of the property and a visit to natural rock pools. Half-day trips cost $50 and a full day including a barbecue lunch is $90.

Scenic Flights One of the most unusual flights you'll ever do is to tag along with the Outback Mail Run. This is a regular service which leaves Katherine on Tuesday, Thursday and Friday to drop mail at various remote stations, and towns such as Borroloola, Roper Bar and Kununurra. Two seats are available on most flights, but you must take your own lunch and drinks. The cost is $240 per person and you're advised to book ahead (☎ 8972 3777).

Katherine Scenic Flights (☎ 8972 3777) operates tours over Nitmiluk ($65; 30 minutes), Nitmiluk and Kakadu ($175; 1¾ hours; this is also available with a 2¼ hour flight and two hour cruise of Yellow Water Wetlands for $260). A one hour helicopter flight over Nitmiluk costs $220.

To Kakadu Travel North (☎ toll-free 1800 089 103) has two-day camping trips, which for $249 include all meals, most of the sights, a Yellow Water cruise and the park-entry fee, and end in Darwin.

Places to Stay

Camping & Caravan Parks There are several possibilities here and most are very pleasant places. Don't forget you can camp out at the gorge as well – the facilities are good and it has the biggest natural swimming pool in the Top End. All of Katherine's caravan parks have pools, barbecues and oodles of tourist literature.

Close to the Low Level Nature Park, 5km from town, is the *Katherine Low Level Caravan Park* (☎ 8972 2238), a grassy place with shady sites and a great swimming pool. Campsites are $14 for two, or $18 with power. Self-contained cabins start at $65.

Closer to town, on the Victoria Hwy, is the *Riverview Caravan Park* (☎ 8972 1011), which has cabins with cooking facilities but shared bathroom for $50 or $70 with en suite; tent sites at $14 ($17 with power); and motel rooms for $65. The thermal pools are five minutes walk away from here.

The *Frontier Katherine* (☎ toll-free 1800 812 443), 4km south of town on the Stuart Hwy, is an upmarket motor inn (see Motels) with a pleasant, shady camp ground. Campsites cost $15 or $18 with power and en suite.

The *Knott's Crossing Resort* (☎ 8972 2511) on the corner of Cameron and Giles Sts on the way out of town is a rather swish park with a good range of facilities, including a restaurant (see Places to Eat). Camp sites are $19/14 with/without power. It also has a range of rooms (see Motels).

Closest to Nitmiluk and 6km from the town centre, *Shady Lane Caravan Park* (☎ 8971 0491) offers camp sites for $16/14 with/without power, air-conditioned budget cabins for $40 for 4 single beds or $45 for a double and two singles and self-contained cabins for $60. Canoe hire is available.

Hostels Katherine has four backpackers hostels. All are within a short walk of the transit centre, but you should book ahead because they fill up fast. Each has a pool and cooking facilities, and does pick-ups from the transit centre.

Closest to the transit centre is the *Kookaburra Lodge Backpackers* (☎ toll-free 1800 808 211), on the corner of Lindsay and Third Sts. A bed in a four or eight-bed dorm costs $15 or $13, or there are some twin rooms for $40. It can get overcrowded at times, but it's a clean and well-run place. Kookaburra also does bike and canoe hire.

Around the corner is the *Palm Court Backpackers* (☎ toll-free 1800 089 103), on the corner of Third and Giles Sts. The air-con rooms are uncrowded, and have their own lockers, TV, fridge and bathroom. Costs are $13/15 per person in an eight/four-bed dorm; twins or doubles are $45. The staff work hard to make this a pleasant place and discounts are available for various services around town.

The *Victoria Lodge (☎ toll-free 1800 808 875, 21 Victoria Hwy)* is not far from the main street. The tiled six-bunk rooms cost $14 per person and singles/doubles are $35/40.

Motels Inquire about low-season discounts and weekend specials at Katherine's motels. Prices here do not include tax.

The best value is at *PGA Lodge (☎ 8971 0266, 50 Giles St)*, where single/double motel rooms go for $35/45; budget singles are also available for $25. This place is popular with seasonal workers and it's often full.

The *Beagle Motor Inn (☎ 8972 3998)*, on the corner of Lindsay and Fourth Sts, is one of the cheapest motels in Katherine. Air-con budget singles/doubles with a fridge and shared bathroom cost $40/50; singles/doubles with attached bathroom cost $60/70. It's in a quiet location and meals are available.

Knotts Crossing Resort (☎ 8972 2511) on Giles St has a variety of accommodation, ranging from self-contained cabins with a double and 2 single beds and en suite for $65, standard motel rooms for $96 and those with limited cooking facilities for $108.

Even more upmarket is the *Frontier Katherine (☎ toll-free 1800 812 443)* on the Stuart Hwy south of the town centre, where rooms start at $109 and better rooms with cooking facilities cost $124.

Places to Eat

Eating out in Katherine comes a distant third to Darwin and Alice Springs, but since the flood purged the town several new places have sprung up and others got a much-needed facelift.

For budget eating there are plenty of greasy choices at the transit centre's 24-hour *café* and there's a branch of *Red Rooster* further up the main street towards Darwin. The *Homestead Café* opposite Palm Court Backpackers opens early for breakfast.

Self-caterers should visit the large Woolworth's *supermarket*, at the southern end of Katherine Terrace, which is open seven days. This is the cheapest place for hundreds of kilometres around to stock up for trips into the outback.

If you have transport, the *Kumbidgee Lodge Tea Room*, 10km out of town along the gorge road (Giles St), offers a hearty 'bush breakfast' in a pleasant outdoor setting for $8; cooked meals are available throughout the day for around $12.

Café Enio's (385 Katherine Terrace) next to the ANZ bank on the main street, is a popular lunch spot that does delicious focaccias, quiches and sandwiches, and has the best range of coffee in Katherine. Unfortunately, it's not open for dinner.

Café on First (17 First St), in the cinema complex, does reasonable snacks and light meals. It's one of the few places open for lunch on weekends.

Pizza outlets include *Nino's Pizza & Pasta Bar*, opposite the information centre, and **Popeye's** *(32 Katherine Terrace)*, which offers all-you-can-eat deals some nights for $7.

On the corner of Katherine Terrace and Murphy St (Victoria Hwy) is the *Mekhong Thai Cafe & Takeaway*. This is an unusual find in an outback town and it has an extensive menu with entrées at around $6 and main courses from $9.50 to $13.

The best grub we found in Katherine was at *Katie's Bistro* at the Knotts Crossing Resort. The food is good, fresh and well prepared, and the menu changes regularly. Mains are in the $16 to $19 range.

Shopping

Mimi Aboriginal Art & Craft in the shopping complex on Lindsay St is an Aboriginal-owned and run shop selling products made over a wide area, from the deserts in the west to the Gulf coast in the east.

KATHERINE

Banyan Art Gallery, in the arcade off First St, has a good range of bark paintings and other crafts. On the main street, there's Katherine Art Gallery, just up from the transit centre.

You are free to inspect the workshop at Coco's Katherine Didjeridoos at 21 First St, opposite the cinema, and works are on sale. A plain or decorated didj will set you back $100 to $300.

Getting There & Away

Air Katherine Airport is 8km south of town, just off the Stuart Hwy. Airnorth (☎ toll-free 1800 627 474) flies to Katherine daily from Darwin ($144), and daily except Sunday to Alice Springs ($369) and Tennant Creek ($239). It also has flights to Borroloola ($240; thrice weekly) and Kalkaringi ($170; twice weekly).

Bus All buses between Darwin and Alice Springs, Queensland or Western Australia stop at Katherine, which means two or three daily to and from Western Australia, and usually four to and from Darwin, Alice Springs and Queensland. Typical fares from Katherine are: Darwin ($39; four hours), Alice Springs ($133; 15 hours), Tennant Creek ($65; eight hours), Cairns ($253; 34 hours), Kununurra ($67; 4½ hours) and Broome ($180; 20 hours). Greyhound Pioneer offer up to 50% off on special fares and 15-day advance purchases.

The Blue Banana bus (☎ 8945 6800) has round trips from Katherine to Darwin via Litchfield National Park and Kakadu with many stops en route. A ticket is valid for three months and allows as many stops as you like. Katherine to Darwin via Litchfield is $90 and the round trip is $170. Discounts are available – see the Getting Around chapter for details.

Car Rental There are a few car rental agencies in town. Avis (☎ 8971 0520) on the corner of Bicentennial Rd and Victoria Hwy, Territory Thrifty Car Rentals (☎ 8972 3183) has a desk at the transit centre, and Hertz (☎ 8971 1111) is at Knott's Crossing Resort on Giles St.

Getting Around
The town centre is compact enough to walk around, although some sights, such as the thermal pools and museum, are a bit far – you can rent bicycles at some backpackers hostels.

Around Katherine

Katherine is the hub for a number of worthwhile attractions, chief among which is the spectacular series of gorges in Nitmiluk National Park.

NITMILUK (KATHERINE GORGE) NATIONAL PARK
This 2920 sq km park is one of the most visited sites in the Northern Territory. The best-known feature is the series of 13 sandstone gorges – known as Katherine Gorge – in the eastern part of the park, about 30km from Katherine. It is a beautiful place that's well worth a visit. The lesser-known Edith Falls, also part of Nitmiluk, is accessible from the Stuart Hwy 40km north of Katherine. It features a great swimming hole, waterfalls and walking trails. Access roads to both sections of the park are sealed but may be cut off for short periods during the Wet.

What was once Katherine Gorge National Park was proclaimed in 1962. In 1989 the Jawoyn Aboriginal people gained ownership following a land claim hearing; the name was changed to Nitmiluk and the land leased back to Parks & Wildlife (then known as the Conservation Commission). It is now managed by the Nitmiluk Board of Management, which has a Jawoyn majority, and traditional practices such as hunting, food gathering and ceremonies are still carried out in the park. Nitmiluk is the Jawoyn name for the Cicada Dreaming, which takes in the area from the park headquarters up to the end of the first gorge.

Flora & Fauna
The most obvious vegetation feature is the open woodland so typical of the Top End,

dominated by trees such as bloodwoods and ironwood. Pockets of monsoon rainforest grow in sheltered well-watered sites, such as at Butterfly Gorge; along the main waterways grow lofty paperbarks and stands of pandanus; and the higher sandstone ridges are typically covered in spinifex grass and hardy shrubs such as grevilleas and acacias. A number of endangered native plants are found within the park, such as the endemic *Acacia helicophylla*.

The park's animal life is also typical of the Top End. Large goannas are a common sight around the boat ramp area, and agile wallabies can be seen in the camp ground. Flying foxes can be seen flying along the waterways at dusk.

Birds are abundant and about 170 species have been recorded in the park. Around the camp ground and Visitor Centre look for parrots such as the gorgeous rainbow lorikeet and red-winged parrot, and flocks of white cockatoos called little corellas. Great bowerbirds, blue-faced honeyeaters and blue-winged kookaburras are also common around the park HQ, and in dry weather look for small birds, such as finches and honeyeaters, coming in to drink at sprinklers. One of the park's most valued inhabitants is the rare and endangered Gouldian finch.

Information

The Visitor Centre (☎ 8972 1886) has excellent displays and information on the park's geology, wildlife and Aboriginal lore, as well as the white history. The Visitor Centre is open daily from 7 am to 7 pm.

Information sheets detail the wide range of marked walking tracks that start here and traverse the picturesque country south of the gorge (see following sections). Some of the tracks pass Aboriginal rock paintings up to 7000 years old. The *Guide to Nitmiluk (Katherine Gorge) National Park* goes into more detail on these walks and is available from the Visitor Centre.

A free slide show and ranger talk is held in the Visitor Centre every night at 7.30 pm during the high season. Bookings can be made at the centre.

The Katherine Gorge Canoe Marathon, organised by the Red Cross, takes place in June.

In line with the desires of the traditional owners, there's no entry fee to the park, although this is to some degree built into the price you pay for cruises.

The Visitor Centre, camp ground and boat tours have disabled facilities.

Activities

Swimming The gorge is safe for swimming in the Dry season and there's a designated swimming area near the picnic area. However, it's probably best enjoyed by taking a canoe and finding your own space somewhere upstream.

In the Wet the gorge is closed to boats and canoes. The only crocodiles around are the harmless freshwater variety and they're more often seen in the cooler months.

Bushwalking The park has approximately 100km of walking tracks, ranging from short strolls of a few minutes length to the 66km one-way trek to Edith Falls; a map is available from the Visitor Centre.

Walkers setting out on any walk (apart from the short walk to the lookout at the gorge and to Leliyn Loop at Edith Falls) must register and deregister at the Visitor Centre. There's a $20 refundable deposit for any overnight walk ($50 for the Edith Falls walk) and a camping fee of $3 per person per night. The deposit is to ensure that people deregister when they've completed their walk (and get their money back) and don't instigate a time-wasting search by neglecting to let someone know they've returned.

The main walks, all of which are clearly marked, are listed here. Note that all distances and timings are one-way only. Inquire at the Visitor Centre for updated information.

Lookout Loop (2km; one hour; medium) A short, steep climb with good views over the Katherine River.
Windolf (4km; 1½ hours; medium) The nearest long walk to the Visitor Centre and the best for the not so ambitious. Windolf leads to the southern rockhole near the end of the first gorge and features Aboriginal rock art.

Butterfly Gorge (5.5km; two hours; hard) A shady walk through a pocket of monsoon rainforest leads to midway along the second gorge. There are often large numbers of crow butterflies here, hence the name.

Lily Ponds (9km; three hours; strenuous) This walk leads to Lily Pond Falls, at the far end of the third gorge, where there's a swimming hole that can usually be used throughout the Wet when swimming in the gorge itself is not possible.

Smitt's Rock (11km; five hours; strenuous) A rugged trek which takes you to Smitt's Rock near the start of the fifth gorge. There are excellent gorge views along the way, and you can swim and camp overnight at Dunlop Swamp.

Eighth Gorge (16km; overnight; strenuous) Most of the way this trail is actually well away from the edge of the gorge, only coming down to it at the end.

Jawoyn Valley (20km; overnight; strenuous) A wilderness loop trail leading off the Eighth Gorge walk into a valley with rock outcrops and rock art galleries.

Jatbula Trail (Edith Falls) (66km; five days; strenuous) This walk climbs the Arnhem Land escarpment, taking in features such as the swamp-fed Biddlecombe Cascade (11.5km from the Visitor Centre), the 30m Crystal Falls (20.5km), the Amphitheatre Rainforest (31km) and the Sweetwater Pool (61.5km). (Note that this walk can only be done one-way – you can't walk from Edith Falls to Katherine Gorge – and that a minimum of two people are required to do the walk.)

Canoeing Paddling a canoe is a great way to see the gorges, although it can be hot, back-breaking work for the inexperienced, and during the Dry canoes have to be carried over the rock bars that separate the gorges. An informative leaflet on canoeing the gorge, available from the

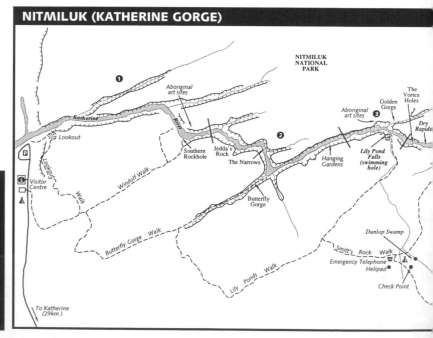

Visitor Centre, shows points of interest along the way, such as rock art, waterfalls and plant life.

Canoe hire is available at the boat ramp by the main car park, about 500m beyond the Visitor Centre. You can rent single and double canoes from Nitmiluk Tours (☎ 8972 1253) at the park. These cost $24/37 for a half-day, or $34/50 for a whole day. The price includes the use of a waterproof drum for cameras and other gear, a map, and life jackets if you feel the need.

You can also be adventurous and take the canoes out overnight, but you must book because a limited number of people are allowed to camp out in the gorges.

It's also possible to use your own canoe in the gorge for a registration fee of $5 per person per day, plus a refundable $10 deposit.

Organised Tours

Gorge Cruises The other, much less energetic way to get out onto the water is on a cruise. These depart daily and there's a variety to choose from. None is particularly cheap but bear in mind that part of the fee goes to the traditional owners in lieu of a park-entry fee. During the high season there's up to 1000 people coming through here each day, so it's no surprise that bookings on some cruises can be tight. It's a good idea to make a reservation the day before on ☎ toll-free 1800 089 103 or ☎ 8972 1253.

The two hour run goes to the second gorge and includes a visit to some gorge-side rock paintings. They leave daily at 9 and 11 am, and at 1 and 3 pm; the cost is $28/12 for adults/children. The four-hour trip goes to the third gorge for $41/19, leaving at 9 and 11 am, and 1 pm. Finally,

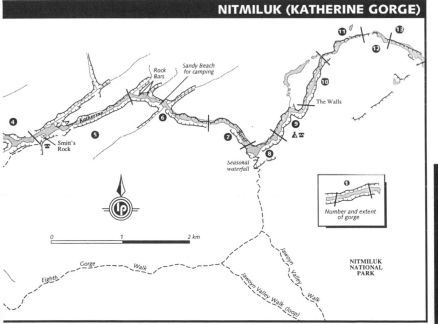

NITMILUK (KATHERINE GORGE)

Rock Bars

Sandy Beach for camping

The Walls

Katherine

Smitt's Rock

Seasonal waterfall

Number and extent of gorge

0   1   2 km

Gorge Walk

Eighth

Jawoyn Valley Walk

Jawoyn Valley Walk (loop)

NITMILUK NATIONAL PARK

KATHERINE

there's an eight-hour trip which takes you up to the fifth gorge, and also involves walking about 4km. The cost is $73 per person and it departs daily at 9 am.

The two and four-hour trips run all year, but the eight hour trip runs only from April to November.

Bushwalking Extended bushwalks with overnight camping are led by Willis' Walkabouts (☎ 8985 2134), which offers a five day walk through remote country from Manyallaluk to Nitmiluk with an Aboriginal guide for $825. Advance bookings are essential.

Scenic Flights Helicopter flights with Katherine Gorge Heli Tours (☎ 8972 1253) are $65/50 for adults/children for approximately 15 minutes and $100/80 for 25 minutes.

Edith Falls

The Edith Falls are in the western corner of the park and can be reached by car from the Stuart Hwy, 40km north of Katherine. The falls themselves cascade into the lowest of three large pools; it's a beautiful, safe place for swimming and a ranger is stationed here throughout the year. The pool is closed from 7 pm to 7 am daily.

Bushwalking opportunities include the Leliyn Trail, a 2.6km round trip that takes about two hours. The trail leads past scenic lookouts to the Upper Pool and a self-guiding leaflet available at the trailhead explains the history, plants and Aboriginal lore of the area.

Places to Stay & Eat

In the Park The only option out at the gorge itself is to camp. The *Gorge Caravan Park* (☎ 8972 1253) has plenty of grass and shade and is well-equipped, with showers, toilets, barbecues and laundry. A campsite costs $18/14 with/without power, and wallabies and goannas are frequent visitors.

Nitmiluk Café at the Visitor Centre is open from 7 am to 8 pm daily and serves snacks, drinks and hot meals. An all-you-can-eat deal costs about $15.

At Edith Falls there's a Parks & Wildlife *camp ground* (☎ 8975 4869) with shady unpowered sites, toilets, cold showers, laundry and disabled facilities. There's a *kiosk* selling snacks and basic supplies, open from 8 am to 5 pm (open only during the Dry). This is also where you pay the camping fee of $5/12 per person/family.

Getting There & Away

It's 30km by sealed road from Katherine to the Nitmiluk Visitor Centre and camp ground, and nearly 1km further to the car park where the gorge begins and the cruises start.

Travel North (☎ 8972 1044) runs a shuttle bus between Katherine and the gorge five times daily. It leaves at 15 minutes past the hour every two hours from 8.15 am til 4.15 pm from the transit centre in town, and on the hour every two hours from 9 am to 5 pm from the gorge. The fare is $9 each way, $15 return.

To Edith Falls it's 40km north of Katherine along the Stuart Hwy then 19km along a sealed road to the falls and camp ground. Access is possible to both parts of the park year round.

The Blue Banana stops at both Katherine Gorge and Edith Falls.

CUTTA CUTTA CAVES NATURE PARK

The 1499 hectare Cutta Cutta Caves Nature Park protects an extensive karst (limestone) landscape about 30km south of Katherine. The caves have a unique ecology and are home to the endangered ghost and orange horseshoe bats. During the Dry the bats move into the far recesses of the caves and visitors have little chance of seeing them. It is the only cave system open to the public in the Territory.

Cutta Cutta is a Jawoyn name meaning many stars; it was taboo for Aborigines to enter the cave, which they believed was where the stars were kept during the day. The first white person to see the cave was a local stockman in 1900, after whom it was known as Smith's Cave.

Only one cave is currently open to the public and it was badly damaged by Australian soldiers during WWII, who used the limestone curtains and stalactites for target practice.

In the Dry the caves are in fact quite dry, but in the Wet they can literally fill up with water.

The only way to see the caves is as part of a guided tour of the main cave, Cutta Cutta; these run at 9, 10 and 11 am and 1, 2 and 3 pm in the Dry. The tours last about 45 minutes and cost $6.75; bookings can be made by phoning ☎ 8972 1940. Nearby Tindal Cave is in better condition and may open this year. There are also some walking trails in the park.

MANYALLALUK

Manyallaluk is the former 3000 sq km Eva Valley cattle station which abuts the eastern edge of the Nitmiluk (Katherine Gorge) National Park, the southern edge of Kakadu and the western edge of Arnhem Land. It is owned by the Jawoyn Aboriginal people, and the community here is showing the way when it comes to Aboriginal tourism – people generally speak very highly of them.

The name Manyallaluk comes from a Frog Dreaming site found to the east of the community, and on it are members not only of the Jawoyn but also the Mayali, Ngalkbon and Rembarrnga language groups, with whom the Jawoyn share some traditions.

While it's possible to just turn up to the community and camp, the real reward comes in taking one of the tours offered by the community. Unlike many tourist operations in the Top End, these run throughout the year.

Organised Tours

There's a variety of tours to choose from, all operated by and from the community, although they also make pick-ups in Katherine.

The one-day trip includes transport to and from Katherine, lunch, billy tea and damper, and you learn about traditional bush tucker and medicine, spear throwing and how to play a didgeridoo. The day trip operates on Monday, Wednesday and Saturday, pick-up

from Katherine at 8.30 am, and costs $100/50 for adults/children, or with your own vehicle you can drive to Manyallaluk and take the day tour from there, which costs $65/40; this trip leaves at 9.45 am.

The two day trip ($205/100) includes visits to some excellent rock art sites and bush camping by a swimming hole. It is possible just to camp without taking the tour, but you are restricted to the camping area.

Bookings for the tours can be made through the community on ☎ toll-free 1800 644 727.

Places to Stay

It costs $10 to pitch a tent in the grassy camp ground, or $15 with power.

There is a reasonably well-stocked community store, which also sells some reasonably priced locally-made artefacts. Note that this is a dry community and alcohol is prohibited.

Getting There & Away

The community is equidistant – around 100km – from Katherine and Mataranka, and 35km off the main track in to Arnhem Land. This 35km stretch is along a well-maintained, all-season gravel road. The trip takes about 90 minutes.

MATARANKA

• pop 630   ✉ 0852

Mataranka is 103km south-east of Katherine on the Stuart Hwy. The town itself is just a stop on the highway and the real attractions are at the nearby hot springs and Elsey National Park.

The first European explorers through this region were Leichhardt (1845) and John McDouall Stuart (1862). When AC Gregory came through in 1856 on his exploratory journey from Victoria River Depot (Timber Creek), he named Elsey Creek after Joseph Elsey, a young surgeon and naturalist in his party. The name went on to became famous as Elsey Station (established in 1881) – the setting for the story *We of the Never Never*.

During WWII the town was one of a string of supply bases for the defence forces,

MATARANKA POOL & ELSEY NATIONAL PARK

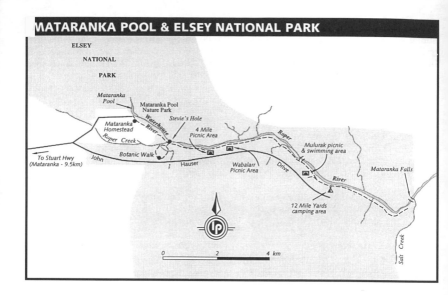

An All-Australian Game

The Alice and Darwin casinos offer plenty of opportunities to watch the Australian gambling mania in full flight. You can also observe a part of Australia's cultural heritage, the all-Australian game of two-up.

The essential idea of two-up is to toss two coins and obtain two heads. Players stand around a circular playing area and bet on the coins showing either two heads or two tails when they fall. The 'spinner' uses a 'kip' to toss the coins and the house pays out and takes in as the coins fall – except that nothing happens on 'odd' tosses (one head, one tail) unless they're thrown five times in a row. In this case you lose unless you have also bet on this possibility. The spinner continues tossing until either a pair of tails, five odds or three pairs of heads are thrown. When the spinner finally loses, the next player in the circle takes over.

and it had a camp hospital, although one member of the infantry battalion stationed here during the war remembers it as 'a disorganised convalescent camp, situated right in the middle of several extremely well-organised two-up schools.' (See boxed text.)

The **Museum of the Never Never** has displays on railway history, the Overland Telegraph Line and WWII. It's open weekdays from 8.30 am to 4.30 pm; entry costs $2.

Information

The town is little more than a gaggle of roadhouses, a police station (☎ 8975 4511) and a pub. All facilities are along the west side of the main street.

The Stockyard Gallery (☎ 8975 4530) is a gallery and souvenir shop that stocks a rather eclectic range of tourist information.

The Back to the Never Never Festival takes place in May.

Places to Stay & Eat

There are camping facilities in Mataranka itself, but you can camp in more natural surroundings at Mataranka Hot Springs and

Elsey National Park only a few kilometres from town.

In town itself, the **Shell Roadhouse Caravan Park** (☎ 8975 4571) has sites at $14/10 with/without power and cabins at $63/74 with fan/air-con.

The historic **Old Elsey Roadside Inn** (☎ 8975 4512) next to the Mobil service station, has motel rooms in an old tin shed built in 1942. They're better than they sound, with air-con and en suite, and cost $50/60 a single/double; backpackers beds are also available and cost $11.

Somewhat more sophisticated is the **Territory Manor** (☎ 8975 4516), 300m off the highway along Martin's Rd at the north end of town. It's a spacious, upmarket caravan park with a good restaurant, outdoor spa and a pool full of barramundi which are fed daily. A camp site costs $18/14 with/without power and attractive motel rooms made of rammed earth start at $68/81 a single/double, including tax.

A nice alternative is **Mataranka Cabins** (☎ 8975 4838), a few hundred metres past Territory Manor on Martin's Rd. Secluded, air-con cabins that can sleep up to six people and include fridge, TV, en suite and kitchen cost $60 (including tax) a double plus $10 per extra adult.

Like everything else in Mataranka, the **Café Barramundi** is on the main street. As you may have guessed, its speciality is barra and they put the famous fish to many good uses, including takeaways and à la carte dishes with an Asian flavour.

MATARANKA POOL NATURE PARK

The turn-off to the springs is 1.5km south of Mataranka, and then it's 8km along a bitumen road.

The crystal clear thermal pool here, in a pocket of pandanus palms, is a great place to wind down after a hot day on the road, though it can get crowded as it's very popular among the tour groups. There's no need to worry about the freshness of the water because it comes out of the ground at more than 16,000L per minute at a temperature of 34°C.

Jeannie Gunn

Probably the most famous woman in the history of the Territory is Jeannie Gunn. Originally from Melbourne, where she had run a school for young ladies, she arrived in the Territory in 1902 with her husband, Aeneas, who had already spent some years there and was returning to take up the manager's position at Elsey Station.

It was a brave move on the part of Jeannie, as at that time there were very few European women living in the Territory, especially on isolated cattle stations. The trip from Darwin to Elsey station was made during the Wet and took several weeks.

Station life was tough, but Jeannie adapted to it and eventually gained the respect of the men working there. She also gained a good understanding of the local Aboriginal people, a number of whom worked on the station.

Only a year after their arrival at Elsey, Aeneas contracted malarial dysentery and died. Jeannie returned to Melbourne and soon after recorded her experiences of the Top End in the novel *We of the Never Never*, published in 1908. While at the station she had been a keen observer of the minutiae of station life; recorded in her book, these observations captured the imagination of the people down south who led such a different existence. These days her depiction of Aboriginal people seems somewhat patronising.

Jeannie went on to become involved with the RSL, and in 1939 was awarded an OBE for her contribution to Australian literature. She died in Melbourne in 1961 at the age of 91.

Her book remains one of the classics of outback literature, recording in detail the lives of the early pioneers, and was made into a film in 1981.

The pool is just a short walk from the car park, which is at the very touristy Mataranka Homestead Tourist Resort. **Stevie's Hole** is another pool about 1km away that's usually uncrowded.

About 200m away is the **Waterhouse River**, where you can walk along the banks, or rent canoes and rowing boats for about $5 an hour.

Outside the homestead entrance is a replica of the **Elsey Station Homestead** which was made for the filming of *We of the Never Never*. There are interesting historical displays inside the replica and entry costs $2.50.

Places to Stay & Eat

Mataranka Homestead Tourist Resort (☎ *toll-free 1800 089 103*) is only 100m or so from the hot springs, and has accommodation to suit all budgets. It's a popular place and bookings are advised.

Backpackers can stay in dorms at the *hostel*. It's quite comfortable, although the kitchen is a bit small, and there are some double and twin rooms. A bed costs $16 per person ($14 with YHA card) including linen or it's $30 for a twin or double.

The large *camp ground* has plenty of grass and shade, and decent facilities including hot showers; camping is $18/14 for a site with/without power. Air-con motel rooms with fridge and private bathroom are $65/77 a single/double and cabins with en suite and kitchen start at $82 (plus tax).

There's a *store* where you can get basic groceries, a bar with snacks and meals (not cheap), or you can use the camp ground barbecues. There's often live entertainment here on weekend evenings during the Dry.

Getting There & Around

Long-distance buses travelling up and down the Stuart Hwy make the detour to the homestead.

ELSEY NATIONAL PARK

This 138 sq km national park abuts the Mataranka Pool Nature Park and is reached along John Hauser Drive, which leaves the Mataranka access road about 2km before the homestead.

The park takes in a long stretch of the Roper River, which has some excellent monsoon forest along its banks. If you're coming up from the south this is the first really good example of this type of habitat. Also within the park are colourful tufa limestone formations, which form the Mataranka Falls on the eastern edge of the park.

The area is the site of some Dreaming trails of the Yangman and Mangari people. Mataranka Station was selected as an experimental sheep station in 1912; the sheep didn't prosper and were removed in 1919; cattle did better and some of the yards are still standing at 12 Mile Yards.

While the park doesn't have the thermal pools of Mataranka Pools, neither does it have the masses of people who flock to them, and it's a much more peaceful and low-key place.

Activities

There are some tranquil and safe **swimming spots** along the river, two of the best being at 4 Mile and 12 Mile Yards camping area. Freshwater crocs inhabit the river but it is safe to swim above the falls.

A 4km **walking track** takes you along the bank of the Roper River between the Mulurak day-use area and the Mataranka Falls at the eastern edge of the park. There's an interesting 1.5km **botanical walk** near the park entrance with signs explaining the Aboriginal uses for various species. Mataranka Homestead runs a **guided nature walk**; the 45 minute walk around the area starts daily at 11.00 am and is free.

Canoe hire is available from the 12 Mile Yards camp ground. Costs are $7/5 per hour for two/one persons; all-day hire costs $35/25.

Fishing is permitted and prized catches include barramundi, black bream and saratoga. Barramundi controls apply in the park.

A four hour **cruise** of the Roper River is run by Brolga Tours (☎ 8975 4538) on Saturday, Sunday and Wednesday. The cost is $55/35 for adults/children.

Facilities

The 12 Mile Yards *camp ground* has lots of grass and shade. The good facilities, include a kiosk and solar hot showers, although there is no electricity. Camping here costs $5 per person.

There is access to the river, with picnic grounds and toilets, at 4 Mile Yard and Mulurak.

ELSEY CEMETERY

A few kilometres off the Stuart Hwy, 5km south of the Roper Hwy turn-off, is Elsey Cemetery, where a number of the real-life characters portrayed in the novel *We of the Never Never* are buried. Among them are Aeneas Gunn, the manager of the station and husband of Jeannie Gunn, the book's author.

During WWII the army located the bodies of a number of them, including Henry Ventlia Peckham ('The Fizzer'), and moved their remains here.

The site of the original homestead, as near as can be determined, is 500m or so beyond the cemetery, by the bridge over the Elsey Creek. A plaque and cairn mark the spot.

Victoria River District

The Victoria River itself, one of the largest in northern Australia, starts in rugged country on the northern fringes of the Tanami Desert and winds its way north through some of the Territory's best pastoral land before entering the sea in the Joseph Bonaparte Gulf.

Travellers to the area today tend to just pass along the Victoria Hwy, which bisects the region, from Katherine to Kununurra over the border in Western Australia. The main attractions of the region are found along the highway. These are two of the territory's least-visited national parks – the Gregory and Keep River – and the historic town of Timber Creek.

It's 513km on the Victoria Hwy from Katherine to Kununurra. The road is bitumen for its entire length and in very good condition except for a few narrow strips.

As you approach the border you'll start to see the boab trees found in much of the

north-west. There's a 1½ hour time change when you cross the border and a quarantine inspection post, where all fruit and vegetables must be left. When entering the Territory from WA a variety of fruits and vegetables must also be deposited here. For more details, contact the NT Department of Primary Industries & Fisheries in Darwin (☎ 8981 8733).

History

Exploration started when the British naval vessel, HMS *Beagle* surveyed the north coast in 1839, having recently completed a five year worldwide journey with a young naturalist on board by the name of Charles Darwin. The *Beagle* negotiated the difficult mouth of the Victoria River (named by the *Beagle*'s captain, John Wickham, in honour of Queen Victoria) and sailed 200km up-river to its navigable limit, which today is the site of Timber Creek.

In the 1850s the Colonial Office in London, with the prompting of the Royal Geographic Society, funded an expedition which was to travel from the Victoria River east to the Gulf of Carpentaria. The expedition was led by a young surveyor, Augustus Gregory, and the party landed at, and named, Timber Creek, when their ship, the *Tom Tough*, ran aground in shallows and was repaired with local timber.

For the next six months Gregory and his party surveyed the area extensively, and it was largely thanks to his glowing reports of the region that pastoral activity and European settlement followed. His reports also prompted the South Australian government's demand that the northern part of Australia should come within its borders.

The 1880s saw a pastoral boom, and it was during this time that the major stations of the Victoria River district were established – Victoria River Downs (the so-called 'Big Run' or VRD), Wave Hill, Bradshaw, Auvergne and Willeroo.

The cattle industry became the backbone of the Territory economy, and in the post-war recovery period of the 1950s there was strong worldwide demand for meat, particularly from Britain. This led to the development of an infrastructure across the Territory and Queensland, but particularly in the Victoria River district where cattle were so important. Vesteys, a huge British company which owned more than 100,000 sq km of stations in the Territory, developed the 'road train' for cattle haulage, and the Commonwealth government started pouring money into 'beef roads'. By 1975, $30 million had been spent on 2500km of roads. One of these single-lane bitumen roads is the Delamere Rd, which runs from the Victoria Hwy to Wave Hill Station (a Vesteys property).

The Wave Hill Stockmen's Strike

Aboriginal stockmen played a large role in the early days of the pastoral industry in the Northern Territory. Because they were paid such paltry wages (which often never even materialised) a pastoralist could afford to employ many of them, and run his station at a much lower cost. White stockmen received regular and relatively high wages, were given decent food and accommodation, and were able to return to the station homestead every week. By contrast Aboriginal stockmen received poor food and accommodation and would often spend months in the bush with the cattle.

In the 1960s Vincent Lingiari was a stockman on the huge Wave Hill Station, owned by Vesteys, a British company. His concern with the way Aboriginal workers were treated led to an appeal to the North Australian Workers' Union (NAWU), which had already applied to the federal court for equal wages for Aboriginal workers. The federal court approved the granting of equal wages in March 1966, but it was not to take effect until December 1968. Lingiari asked the Wave Hill management direct for equal wages but the request was refused and, on 23 August 1966, the Aboriginal stockmen walked off the station and camped in nearby Wattie Creek. They were soon joined by others, and before long only stations which gave their Aboriginal workers not only good conditions but also respect were provided with workers by Lingiari and the other Gurindji elders.

The Wattie Creek camp gained a lot of local support, from both white and Aboriginal people, and it soon developed into a sizeable community with housing and a degree of organisation. Having gained the right to be paid equally, Lingiari and the Gurindji people felt, perhaps for the first time since the arrival of the pastoralists, that they had some say in the way they were able to live. This victory led to the hope that perhaps they could achieve something even more important – title to their own land. To this end Lingiari travelled widely in the eastern states campaigning for land rights, and finally made some progress with the Whitlam government in Canberra. On 16 August 1975, Prime Minister Gough Whitlam attended a ceremony at Wattie Creek which saw the handing over of 3200 sq km of land, now known as Daguragu.

Lingiari was awarded the Order of Australia Medal for service to the Aboriginal people, and died at Daguragu in 1988.

The story has a short postscript: late in December 1998 secret government documents on the Wave Hill Strike were made public for the first time and revealed that the government feared the strikers were being infiltrated by Communists.

In 1966 Wave Hill Station became the focus for the Aboriginal land rights issue when 200 Gurindji Aboriginal workers and their families, led by Vincent Lingiari, walked off the job in protest against poor living and working conditions (see the boxed text). It wasn't until 1975 that the Gurindji received title to 3200 sq km of claimed land at Wave Hill, and it was 1986 before full ownership was granted.

VICTORIA RIVER CROSSING

The spot where the Victoria Hwy crosses the Victoria River, 192km south-west of Katherine, is known, not surprisingly, as Victoria River Crossing (on some maps it's simply marked Victoria River).

The setting here is superb. The crossing is snug among sandstone gorges, and the high cliffs and flat-top range are quite a sight. Much of the area around the crossing, either side of the road, forms the eastern section of the **Gregory National Park** (see that section later in this chapter), and there are picnic facilities at **Sullivan Creek**, about 10km east of the crossing.

The settlement basically consists of a roadhouse, the *Victoria River Wayside Inn* (☎ 8975 0744), which has a very pleasant camp ground ($10/6 for a site with/without power), air-con budget rooms for $26 and motel units from $42. It also has a well-stocked store, a bar, and a dining room with decent meals from $11 to $14. It's open daily from 7 am to 11 pm.

Access to the river itself is via a track 500m west of the crossing. Bush camping is permitted 10km upstream from the crossing – accessible by boat only.

TIMBER CREEK
• pop 560   ✉ 0852

Almost exactly 100km west of Victoria River Crossing is Timber Creek, the only town between Katherine and Kununurra. It is close to the Victoria River at the foot of the rugged Newcastle Range.

It's a tiny place – more a glorified lay-by than a town – where everything is crowded around a little park. The town relies almost entirely on passing trade as people stop to rest and refuel, and it can get surprisingly busy if a few buses and cars pull in at the same time.

Timber Creek is a good place to stock up with supplies and fuel before heading off into the Gregory National Park.

History
In 1839 the *Beagle* negotiated the river to a spot about 8km from town which came to be known as the Victoria River Depot. The depot was established to service the new pastoral leases that had opened up the country to the south.

Race relations were an early problem, and a police station was set up here at the turn of the century to establish order and help control the 'hostile' Aboriginal people. These days the police station is a museum.

Information
The town has a supermarket and a store (both with fuel), medical clinic (☎ 8975 0727), police station (☎ 8975 0733), pub, caravan park and motel. There's no bank, but the roadhouses have EFTPOS facilities. Fuel is available 24 hours at the Mobil station. The next available fuel is at Kununurra, 232km to the west, where there's a 24-hour roadhouse.

There's also a Parks & Wildlife office (☎ 8975 0888) about 1km west of town on the highway, which has informative displays on the region and good wall maps of Gregory National Park.

Boat hire is available from Fogarty's store and there's a boat ramp nearby. Timber Creek Boat Hire (☎ 8975 0722) has punts with 15hp outboards for $60/90 a half/full day hire.

The colourful Timber Creek Races are held over three days on the first weekend of September, the highlight being the Saturday night Ball.

Things to See
The **Police Station** was built in 1908 to replace the 1898 original, and displays old police and mining equipment. It's open from 3 to 5 pm Monday to Saturday during the Dry

and entry costs $2. About 200m past the museum is an old **cemetery**. The museum turn-off is about 2km west of town.

The **Timber Creek Heritage Trail** is a 3.5km return walk that starts next to the BP station at the west end of town. It takes a leisurely two hours, including time to look at the police station and graves.

There's a scenic **lookout** about 5km west of town, and after another 12km a cairn marks the turn-off to the **Gregory's Tree Historical Reserve**, a great boab on which Augustus Gregory carved the date July 2nd 1856. It's 3.5km down a corrugated dirt road.

Organised Tours

Max's Victoria River Boat Tours runs a four hour trip on the Victoria River, where you'll be shown crocodiles, fish and turtles being fed, and you can try billy tea and crack a stock whip. The tours leave daily at 8 am during the Dry, and cost $40/25 for adults/children; if there's sufficient demand, a shorter tour sometimes leaves in the afternoon. Bookings can be made at Pike's Booking Centre in Timber Creek (☎/fax 8975 0850).

Barra Fishing Safaris (☎ 8975 0688) does a full day trip for $160 per person, including all fishing gear, lunch and refreshments.

Places to Stay & Eat

The *Circle F Caravan Park (☎ 8975 0722)*, by the Timber Creek Hotel/Fogarty's Store, has sites for power for $16 or without power for $7.50 per person. There are also single/double budget rooms at $35/55 and four-bed, self-contained cabins for $70. The caravan park is also the site of the motel, and there are five units at $70 for up to three people.

Much the same is offered next door at the *Timber Creek Wayside Inn (☎ 8975 0732)*, with camp sites for $12/8 with/without power, rooms with common facilities costing $30/48 for a single/double, and motel rooms at $79.

The *Wayside Inn* and the pub both do meals.

There's a Parks & Wildlife *camp ground* at Big Horse Creek, on the river 10km west of town – see the Gregory National Park section.

Getting There & Away

The long-distance buses call through on the route between Darwin and Perth.

GREGORY NATIONAL PARK

At 12,860 sq km Gregory is the second largest national park in the Territory. Apart from the beautiful sandstone scarps that the Victoria Hwy passes through, most visitors see little of Gregory. But some parts are accessible to 2WDs and for those properly equipped the park's rugged 4WD tracks will provide a challenge rewarded with superb gorge country and solitude.

The park was gazetted in 1990 and apart from its scenic values protects reminders of the early pioneers and links to the region's Aboriginal people – the Wardaman, Ngariman, Ngaliwurri, Nungali, Jaminjung and Karrangpurra groups. The park's core is the former Bullita Station, but it also includes parts excised from neighbouring stations, such as Victoria River Downs, Humbert River, Delamere, Auvergne and Innesvale.

The park actually consists of two separate sectors: the eastern sector, known as the Victoria River section, which surrounds the Victoria River Crossing (see that section earlier in this chapter), and the much larger Bullita sector in the west. The two areas are separated by the Stokes Range Aboriginal land. Bullita was originally an outstation of the Durack family properties.

The park offers a chance to get off the beaten track. There's excellent fishing, bush camping and a 4WD track which tests both vehicle and driver.

Flora & Fauna

The northern part of the park consists of grassy woodland, with pockets of monsoon forest, while the southern hills are dominated by spinifex; less common plants include the Victoria palm, a Livistona palm

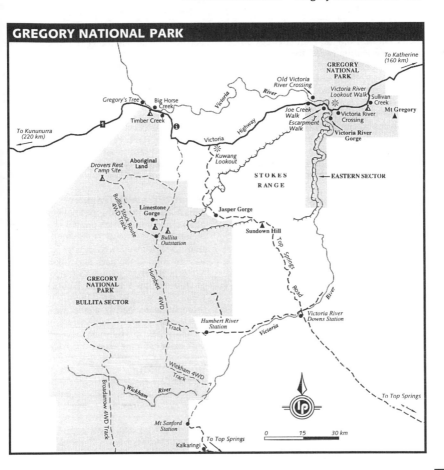

GREGORY NATIONAL PARK

that grows on the sandstone escarpments, and the northern grey box, a eucalypt endemic to the park. Despite the arid conditions, some 900 plant species grow in the park, including 70 acacias and 30 eucalypts.

There is not a great deal of animal life to be seen, although wallabies are reasonably common. Among the 140 bird species recorded are the white-quilled rock-pigeon of rocky escarpments, the white-browed robin and the rare Gouldian finch.

Information

Information on the park can be obtained from the Parks & Wildlife office in Timber Creek (☎ 8975 0888) and at Bullita (☎ 8975 0833) or Wickham River (☎ 8975 0600) ranger stations. Road condition reports are available from the Parks & Wildlife offices at Katherine (☎ 8973 8888) or Timber Creek.

There's an information bay just inside the park's eastern boundary, about 165km west of Katherine and 31km east of Victoria River.

To travel on either of the 4WD tracks you need a permit from the Timber Creek office, and on the Bullita Stock Route track there is a book at each end of the track which you have to sign. Parts of the 4WD tracks are pretty rugged and it is not recommended for 'light' 4WDs; high ground clearance is essential and it is recommended that two spare tyres be carried.

No provisions are available in the park and all visitors must be self-sufficient. The nearest stores are at Timber Creek and Victoria River – see the relevant sections for details.

Water should be carried at all times and any taken from rivers or billabongs should be boiled before drinking. Both saltwater and freshwater crocodiles live in the park.

The Bullita sector of the park is sometimes closed during the Wet and both the 4WD tracks are closed from October to May.

Bullita Outstation

The old homestead here still has the original timber stockyards, and the name of one of the Duracks is carved in a boab tree nearby. The homestead is 52km from the Victoria Hwy along a well-maintained gravel road suitable for conventional vehicles. There's a shady camp ground with river views.

Limestone Gorge

Limestone Gorge is 9km off the main Bullita access track and accessible by 2WD vehicle during the Dry. There's excellent swimming in Limestone Creek, not least because saltwater crocs are absent, and a walk to Limestone Ridge takes about 1½ hours.

Bullita Stock Route 4WD Track

This 90km track follows part of an old stock route into the western part of the park through some beautiful limestone-gorge country to the Drovers Rest camp site (50km from Bullita Outstation), then loops back to join the main Bullita access track, 27km from the Victoria Hwy. Average driving time to complete the track is eight hours.

Cattle were taken from Bullita and Humbert River Stations along this track to the Auvergne Stock Route further north, and from there on to the meatworks in Wyndham (WA). The Spring Creek Yards (13km from Bullita Outstation) were typical of yards used during cattle drives, when up to 500 head were moved.

At the junction of the Spring Creek and East Baines River (21km), a huge boab was obviously the site of a regular drovers' camp – 'Oriental Hotel' is carved into it and still clearly visible.

Humbert 4WD Track

This track along an old packhorse trail is an alternative entry or exit point to the park. It connects Bullita with Humbert River Station 62.5km away, just outside the southeastern edge of the park and 30km west of Victoria River Downs. The track was originally a supply trail for Humbert River from Victoria River Depot. It passes through some superbly scenic and quite isolated country, and it takes about six hours from Bullita to Humbert River. There is only bush camping along this route.

Bushwalking

The smaller eastern section of the park has a few short walks up and along the Victoria River escarpment.

Victoria River Lookout Walk (2km return; one hour) Starting a few kilometres before the crossing, this walk is steep, but you'll be rewarded with views of the river and the start of the Victoria River Gorge.

Escarpment Walk (3km return; 90 minutes) This walk starts 1.5km past Victoria River. Interpretive signs along the way help you get more out of the landscape and the great views. Watch out for the loose surface in places.

Joe Creek Walk (1.7km return; 1½ hours) The turn-off to this walk is 5km west of the Crossing. This is a beautiful, tranquil spot where you can scramble up the escarpment for more stunning views. It's best in the early morning. After wet season storms small cascades water the Livistona palms lining the foot of the cliffs. There's a picnic ground and toilets but no camping.

Kuwang Lookout Between Victoria River Crossing and Timber Creek, this lookout gives a fine, sweeping view over the peaks of the Gregory National Park 12km away. An interpretive sign explains the Aboriginal significance of what you see.

Facilities

There are good *camp grounds* at Bullita Homestead, Limestone Gorge and Big Horse Creek in the western part of the park, which have picnic tables, fireplaces and pit toilets. A nightly fee of $2.50/6 per person/family is payable into an honesty box at each site. There's a boat ramp at Big Horse Creek.

Basic camping is also available at Sullivan Creek in the eastern section.

KEEP RIVER NATIONAL PARK

From Timber Creek the Victoria Hwy continues west for 188km to the WA border. The 570 sq km Keep River National Park abuts the border, on the northern side of the highway, and the entrance is 3km east of the border.

This is a beautiful and little-used national park, with some stunning sandstone formations and a number of significant Aboriginal rock art sites. This region of the Territory is the tribal area of the Mirriwung and Gadjerong people.

Information

There's an information bay 400m along the entrance road with facts about the park's landscape, culture and wildlife. A noticeboard advises if any trails are closed. There's a rangers' station (☎ 9167 8827) 3km into the park from the main road, although this is only a residence, not a visitor centre, and should be used only in an emergency.

Bushwalkers intending to camp overnight in the park away from the designated camp grounds must notify the rangers before setting off. It's probably a good idea to carry a topographic map (1:100,000 Keep 4766) and compass, and definitely carry water. Reliable water is available only from a tank near the park entrance and at Jarrnarm camp ground. Summer temperatures of 37°C can make it very unpleasant for walking.

Access to the park's sights and camp grounds is along gravel roads suitable for 2WDs, but they may be cut by floods during the Wet.

Things to See

Apart from beautiful scenery, Keep River has interesting **wildlife**, plenty of **boab trees** and a couple of Aboriginal rock art sites.

Some 170 bird species and 50 mammals have been recorded in the park, although many are nocturnal or active only at dawn and dusk. The sandstone outcrops are home to some creatures specialised to this environment – look out for short-eared rock wallabies, and listen for the melodious call of the sandstone shrike thrush echoing among the rocks.

The **rock art site** at Nganalam has an estimated 2500 petroglyphs (rock carvings), although they are off limits to the public. Rather, there is a neat little gallery with numerous painted images, including *gurri-*

Distinctive rock formations, Keep River

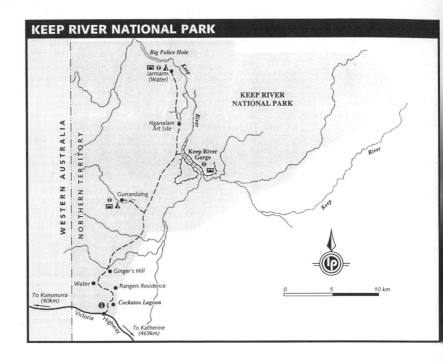

KEEP RIVER NATIONAL PARK

malam the rainbow snake, echidnas, kangaroos, tortoises and crocodiles.

Bushwalking

Pamphlets about self-guiding walks are available at the start of the trails. Remember to carry sufficient water and wear a hat – even in the Dry the heat can be punishing. Check the information bay for updates on trail conditions.

Keep River Gorge (4km; 1½ hours) An easy walk along the floor of the gorge. Look for Aboriginal paintings along the steep red walls and enjoy the frenetic birdlife near the permanent waterholes. There are picnic tables and fireplaces at the car park.

Gurrandalng Walk (1km; one hour) This pleasant walk heads off from the Gurrandalng (Brolga Dreaming) camping area and scrambles up an escarpment for some fine views. Excellent interpretive signs explain the wildlife and flora.

Cockatoo Lagoon Walk (2km return; one hour) Just 3km from the highway near the ranger station, this is an easy stroll to a bird-hide overlooking a lagoon. Its at its best during the Dry, although it sometimes dries up completely.

Nganalang (500m; 10 minutes) This short walk leads to a rock art site on a beautiful sandstone outcrop.

Ginger's Hill (500m; 10 minutes) An easy walk off the main entrance road to an interesting rock shelter used by Aboriginal hunters to catch unwary birds.

Jarrnarm walks Two interesting walks start at the camp ground in the north of the park. The Nigli Gap walk (5.5km return; 2½ hours) leads to a photogenic eroded sandstone formation; the Dilirba Gap walk (6km return; 2½ hours) leads to Big Police Hole. There are no trails – follow the markers.

Facilities

There are two *camp grounds*, Gurrandalng and Jarrnarm, with pit toilets, picnic tables and fireplaces. Gurrandalng is 15km into the park and Jarrnarm sits in a stand of fine boab trees 28km from the entrance. A camp site costs $2.50/6 per person/family, payable in honesty boxes.

There is drinking water at Jarrnarm and at a tank 4km in from the main entrance.

OVER THE BORDER INTO WA

A few kilometres past the Keep River turnoff there's a 24-hour agricultural checkpoint where you must leave all fruit, vegetables, nuts and honey before proceeding. If you're only heading into WA for a day ask the staff to keep it safe for 24 hours.

BUCHANAN HWY

The Buchanan Hwy, named after legendary stockman Nat Buchanan, is one of the Territory's loneliest stretches of road, but it's not without interest. It offers an alternative route into Western Australia, running roughly parallel to (and between 100 and 150km south of) the Victoria Hwy, connecting Dunmarra, 36km south of Daly Waters on the Stuart Hwy, with Halls Creek in Western Australia. Although you'll see very few vehicles on it, the road is in good condition and is mostly gravel; only the section from Kalkaringi to Top Springs is bitumen, as this forms part of the beef road that connects Wave Hill Station with the Victoria Hwy and Katherine.

From the Stuart Hwy it's 180km to Top Springs, a stretch of fairly monotonous road which can seem never ending. Only in the last 10 or 20km before Top Springs does it go through some scenic undulating hills studded with termite mounds.

Top Springs

Top Springs is not a pretty place; it consists solely of a roadhouse and a road junction. The Top Springs themselves are nearby and good for a swim. The **Murranji Stock Route**, which connected Newcastle Waters with Wave Hill and was pioneered by Nat Buchanan (see the boxed text), passed through Top Springs.

From Top Springs the bitumen **Delamere Road** heads north to join the Victoria Hwy

Nat Buchanan

Although Nathaniel Buchanan was not a great land-holder in the mould of Kidman or the Duracks, he was a great cattleman and drover, and was responsible for the settlement of huge areas of the outback.

Known as Old Bluey because of his shock of red hair, Buchanan led many drives through Queensland and the Northern Territory, including what was probably the largest cattle drive ever to be undertaken in Australia: the movement of 20,000 head from Aramac in Queensland to Glenco Station, near Adelaide River, in the Northern Territory.

In 1896, at the age of 70, Buchanan set off from Tennant Creek, trying to find a direct route across the Tanami Desert to Sturt Creek in the north of Western Australia. He hoped to find a route suitable for droving cattle, rather than having to take them much further north. The hoped-for route didn't eventuate, but this was probably the first European crossing of the Tanami Desert.

Buchanan was accompanied on some of his drives by his son Gordon, who wrote about his experiences in the book *Packhorse & Waterhole*.

(164km), or you can head south-west to Kalkaringi and WA, or travel north-west to Victoria River Downs and Timber Creek.

Places to Stay & Eat At the roadhouse, the *Wanda Inn* (☎ 8975 0767), there's a very lively bar, patronised largely by the local Aboriginal people. There's a grassy camping area ($12/8 with/without power), swimming pool, three air-con single/double motel units at $57/67, and pub rooms with common facilities for $40.

Victoria River Downs

The dirt road heading north-west from Top Springs takes you to the famous Victoria River Downs Station (100km). The road is generally in good condition and can easily be travelled by conventional vehicles in the Dry.

Victoria River Downs, known throughout the Top End as VRD, or the Big Run, is one of the largest stations in the area (over 12,000 sq km), and is the focal point of the area. It was one of the many large pastoral leases established in the 1880s and stocked with cattle brought in on the hoof from Queensland. There's even been a book written about the place (*The Big Run* by Jock Makin).

The road passes right by the homestead area, which looks more like a small town than a station. There are no tourist facilities, although the station has a general store (☎ 8975 0853) which the public are welcome to use. Opening hours are 7 am to 5.30 pm.

From VRD the road continues north to the Victoria Hwy (140km), passing through the spectacular **Jasper Gorge** (57km; good camping) on the edge of the Gregory National Park. If you are heading for the Gre-

gory National Park and are travelling by 4WD vehicle, it's possible to enter the park via a rough track from Humbert River Station, 30km west of VRD. Before doing so, however, phone the Parks & Wildlife office in Timber Creek (☎ 8975 0888) and advise them of your plans.

Kalkaringi
• pop 260   ✉ 0852

From Top Springs the Buchanan Hwy becomes bitumen and swings south-west on the 170km stretch to Kalkaringi on the Victoria River. This small town exists basically to service the Aboriginal community of **Daguragu**, 8km north. Daguragu was formerly known as Wattie Creek and grew out of the Aboriginal stockmen's strike of 1966, which ultimately led to the granting of land to Aboriginal people (see the boxed text 'The Wave Hill Stockmen's Strike' earlier in this chapter).

For visitors, the town offers a chance to refuel and refresh, and there are limited fishing and swimming opportunities in the

Yard work on a cattle station, Victoria River District

river. The town is basically a dry area, the only place with a liquor licence being a club that changes hands regularly.

The gravel road west to Halls Creek in WA is generally good, although it can be made treacherous and even cut (usually only for short periods) by creeks during the Wet.

Information Facilities in the town include a police station (☎ 8975 0790), a medical centre and a service station (which is also the store, takeaway and caravan park, open 8 am to 5 pm weekdays, 10 am to 2 pm Saturday and 1 to 5 pm Sunday).

Place to Stay The only accommodation is camping at the *Kalkaringi Service Station Caravan Park* (*☎ 8975 0788)*, where there's plenty of grass and shade for $10 a site. Air-con dongas cost $20 per person.

Getting There & Away Airnorth (☎ toll-free 1800 627 474) has twice-weekly flights to Darwin ($314), Lajamanu ($100) and Katherine ($190).

Lajamanu & the Tanami Track

The other possibility from Kalkaringi is to head south to Lajamanu (104km) in the Tanami Desert, from where it's a further 232km to the Tanami Track. Again, this track is generally in pretty good condition and a 4WD vehicle is probably not necessary, but check with the police in Kalkaringi before heading off. The road passes through some beautiful country, and about 10km south of the Buchanan Hwy the country changes from good cattle country (Mitchell grass plains with sparse trees) to much less hospitable spinifex country – the change is so sudden that it's almost as though a dividing line has been drawn between the two.

Lajamanu is an Aboriginal community, and while you don't need a permit to enter the town for fuel and supplies from the Lajamanu Store (10 am to noon and 3 to 5 pm weekdays, Saturday to noon only; ☎ 8975 0896), there's nowhere to stay and no other facilities. There's also a police station (☎ 8975 0622) here.

The Barkly Region

The Barkly region occupies a huge area of the Territory and marks the transition zone from the green of the Top End to the distinctive reds and ochres of the centre. The Stuart Hwy splits the Territory neatly down the middle – with the Barkly Tableland plateau and Gulf region to the east, and the rich Victoria River pastoral district to the west (see the Katherine & Victoria River District chapter). This is predominantly cattle country.

Down the Track

From Mataranka the Stuart Hwy runs south to Alice Springs. There are long stretches on this road where there's not a great deal to see, but there are enough distractions in between to break up the journey.

LARRIMAH
• pop 20   ✉ 0852

The tiny settlement of Larrimah would be just another fuel stop on the Stuart Hwy were it not for its historical importance as the southern terminus of the North Australian Railway. The town is one of many along the highway which were important during WWII, and there are still reminders of that era around town. There's also a great outback pub.

History
Late last century settlers established themselves at Birdum Creek, about 5km from the town, and it was to here that the railway line ran. During WWII the Army established a base on the highway – largely because Birdum was subject to flooding – which they named Larrimah ('meeting place').

In 1942 the Royal Australian Air Force (RAAF) started work on Gorrie Airfield, 10km north of Larrimah. It became one of the largest in the Pacific and at its peak, Gorrie was the base for 6500 military personnel.

HIGHLIGHTS

• Enjoy a beer at the quaint old Daly Waters Pub

• Camp at the bizarre Devil's Marbles

• Explore the eerie ghost town of Newcastle Waters

• See a gold stamp battery in action at Tennant Creek

• Take a helicopter ride over the 'Lost City' formations near Cape Crawford

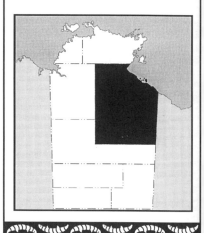

After WWII Larrimah's population fell to less than 50. The Birdum Hotel was dismantled and moved to its current location in Larrimah; the rest of the settlement was abandoned.

In 1976 the railway line closed as it had long since become uneconomical to run.

Things to See
There's a small **museum** in town which has displays mainly about the railway and

THE BARKLY REGION

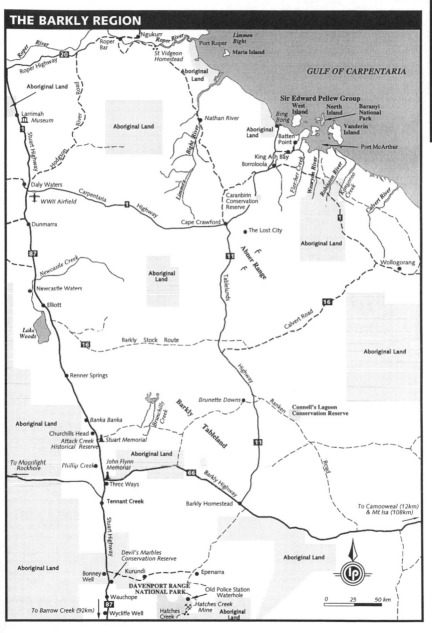

GULF OF CARPENTARIA

Roper River
Ngukurr
Roper Bar
Roper River
Port Roper
Limmen Bight
Maria Island
St Vidgeon Homestead
Aboriginal Land
Roper Highway
Aboriginal Land
River Road
Larrimah
Museum
Stuart Highway
Hodgson
Aboriginal Land
Nathan River
Bight River
Aboriginal Land
Sir Edward Pellew Group
West Island
North Island
Baranyi National Park
Bing Bong
Batten Point
Vanderin Island
Port McArthur
King Ash Bay
Daly Waters
WWII Airfield
Carpentaria Highway
Borroloola
Fletcher Creek
Dunmarra
Cape Crawford
Limmen
Caranbirin Conservation Reserve
Wearyan River
Robinson River
Kingoroo Creek
Calvert River
The Lost City
Aboriginal Land
Newcastle Creek
Aboriginal Land
Abner Range
Wollogorang
Newcastle Waters
Elliott
Tablelands
Lake Woods
Calvert Road
Barkly Stock Route
Aboriginal Land
Renner Springs
Highway
Brunette Downs
Connell's Lagoon Conservation Reserve
Ranken
Aboriginal Land
Brunchilly Creek
Barkly Tableland
Banka Banka
Churchills Head
Attack Creek Historical Reserve
Stuart Memorial
Road
To Moonlight Rockhole
Phillip Creek
John Flynn Memorial
Aboriginal Land
Barkly Highway
Three Ways
Tennant Creek
Barkly Homestead
To Camooweal (12km) & Mt Isa (108km)
Stuart Highway
Devil's Marbles Conservation Reserve
Aboriginal Land
Aboriginal Land
Bonney Well
Kurundi
Epenarra
DAVENPORT RANGE NATIONAL PARK
Old Police Station Waterhole
To Barrow Creek (92km)
Wauchope
Hatches Creek Mine
Wycliffe Well
Hatches Creek
Aboriginal Land

0   25   50 km

WWII. It's open from 9 am to 5 pm and admission is by donation.

It's worth having a look at the remaining military buildings, the airstrip at **Gorrie Airfield**, though it'slargely overgrown, and the remains of the abandoned settlement of **Birdum**. A mud map is available at the museum.

Places to Stay & Eat

The **Wayside Inn** (*☎ 8975 9931*) has powered/unpowered camp sites for $10/8. It also has backpacker rooms at $10 per bed and simple hotel rooms for $20/25 a single/double.

The **Green Park Tourist Complex** (*☎ 8975 9937*) is slightly more sophisticated and has a swimming pool. Camp sites cost $8, ($14 with power), backpacker beds are $15 and a donga for two is $40. Adjacent is the **Top of the Town Roadhouse** (*☎ 8975 9932*), where air-con budget rooms cost $15/25 a single/double, or $40/50 with attached bathroom. Camp sites are $8 ($12 with power). This is a good place, with pool, barbecues and a licensed café.

Fran's Devonshire Tea House is an eccentric eatery opposite the Top of the Town where you can indulge in fresh-baked pasties and home-made ginger beer while flipping through interesting photo albums on local history. Counter meals are available at the **Wayside Inn**.

DALY WATERS

The historic little settlement of Daly Waters lies 4km west of the Stuart Hwy. With just a handful of houses it would be easy to pass over, but the pub here is an eccentric little place and the nearby airfield was Australia's first international airport. This is one of the detours off the Stuart Hwy that shouldn't be missed.

On the highway itself, 4km south of the Daly Waters turn-off, is the Daly Waters Junction, where the Carpentaria Hwy heads east the 234km to Borroloola and the Gulf.

The Daly Waters Rodeo, held over two days in September, is the social event of the year, with a dance held at the pub on the Saturday evening.

History

It was on John McDouall Stuart's third attempt to cross the continent from south to north that he came upon the small creek here, which he named in honour of the then governor of South Australia.

In 1872 the Overland Telegraph Line came through and a repeater station was built. An exploration party in the Kimberley led by Alexander Forrest was rescued by a party sent out from Daly Waters, after Forrest rode to the line and followed it to Daly Waters. A memorial cairn alongside the Stuart Hwy about 50km north of Daly Waters marks the approximate spot where Forrest found the line.

In the 1890s a pub sprang up, catering for drovers who had started using Daly Waters as a camp on the overland stock route between Queensland and the Kimberley. The current building dates from the late 1920s, and from the outside at least looks now much like it probably looked then.

The next wave of activity to hit Daly Waters came from the air. In the early 1930s Qantas, then a fledgling airline, used Daly Waters as a refuelling stop on the Singapore leg of its Sydney-London run. The airstrip became one of the major stops in northern Australia.

The RAAF also used Daly Waters as a refuelling stop for its bombers en route to Singapore, and in 1942 established a base here. It was in constant use throughout the war, and the recently restored hangar now belongs to the National Trust.

Things to See

The **Daly Waters Pub** is an attraction in itself. It has changed little since the 1920s, and inside has the most unusual array of mementos left by passing travellers – everything from bras to banknotes adorn the walls! The actual liquor licence has been used continuously since 1893, and so the pub claims to be the oldest in the Territory.

About 1km from the pub there's the remains of a tree where John McDouall Stuart carved a large letter 'S' (signposted) and at the **Daly Waters Aerodrome** there's

HUGH FINLAY

The Daly Waters Pub, licensed since 1893

a historical display in the old hangar (they should have a key at the pub).

Places to Stay & Eat

The *pub* (☎ 8975 9927) has a camp ground with shade and grass. A site costs $6, $10 with power. There are also some basic motel-type rooms at $28/38 a single/double. There's a pool here.

Meals at the pub are good, and the beef 'n' barra barbecue ($14) in the evening is very popular; there's often live music in the dry season. The menu on the wall inside is the product of a local wit – our favourite is the Dingo's Breakfast (A piss and a look around – no charge!).

Out on the highway, at the junction of the Stuart and Carpentaria Hwys, there's the *Hiway Inn Roadhouse* (☎ 8975 9925), with camping $8 (powered $14), and motel rooms at $47.25/57.75 for a single/double. It's open from 7 am to 11 pm.

DUNMARRA

Like so many other spots on the Stuart Hwy, Dunmarra is these days little more than a roadhouse providing fuel and other services to travellers.

The **Buchanan Hwy**, a beef road which runs right through to Halls Creek in Western Australia, starts 8km north of town (see the Katherine & Victoria River District chapter).

About 35km south of town is a **historic marker** to Sir Charles Todd, builder of the Overland Telegraph Line, and it commemorates the joining of the two ends of the line in August 1872.

Places to Stay

The *Dunmarra Wayside Inn* (☎ 8975 9922) has camping ($2.50 per person or $10 for a powered site), as well as air-con motel rooms with attached bath and fridge, at $30/40 a single/double. There's also a bar and restaurant, and takeaway food is available.

NEWCASTLE WATERS

Newcastle Waters is a former droving town which was right at the intersection of northern Australia's two most important stock routes – the Murranji and the Barkly. Today it is virtually a ghost town, the only permanent inhabitants being the families of employees from Newcastle Waters Station. It is wildly atmospheric and, being 3km off the Stuart Hwy, sees relatively few visitors. It's worth making the detour as the town is probably the best place in the Territory to get a feel for the hard life led by the early drovers.

History

The original inhabitants of this area are the Jingili Aboriginal people, and their name for it is Tjika. The English name comes once again from John McDouall Stuart, who in 1861 named the stretches of water after the Duke of Newcastle, Secretary for the Colonies.

The first pastoral activity was in the 1880s when the lease was taken up by AJ Browne of Adelaide, who employed Alfred Giles to stock it. Cattle were brought overland from Queensland but the station did poorly and it was sold 20 years later for a pittance.

The Murranji stock route was pioneered by Nat Buchanan in 1886 to connect Newcastle Waters with the Victoria River. This way was 'only' 250km or so, compared with the alternative route via Katherine, which was something like 600km further. The only trouble was that there were long stretches without reliable water on the Murranji route (the name comes from a desert frog which is capable of living underground for extended periods without water).

The government recognised the need for permanent water along the stock routes, and to this end Newcastle Waters was made the depot for a bore-sinking team in 1917. Once the 13 bores along the Murranji were operational in 1924, use of the route increased steadily.

The town site for Newcastle Waters was leased from the station by the government in 1930 and a store and pub were built; a telegraph repeater station followed in 1942.

The town's death knell was the demise of the drovers in the early 1960s, with the advent of road transport for moving stock, and the fact that the Stuart Hwy bypassed the town.

Things to See

The first place you see on arrival in the town is the **Drovers' Memorial Park**, which commemorates the part played by the drovers in the opening up of the Territory. Its construction was part of Australia's Bicentennial Project and it was from here that the Last Great Cattle Drive headed off in 1988 as another Bicentennial activity. For the drive, 1200 head of cattle, donated by pastoralists in the Territory, set off for Longreach in Queensland, 2000km away to the south-east. They reached there almost four months later and the cattle were auctioned off in a televised sale.

Today the town's remaining buildings stand in its one and only street. The **Junction Hotel** was built in 1932 out of scraps collected from abandoned windmills along the stock routes, and it became the town's focus. After weeks on the track thirsty drovers would get into Newcastle Waters and cut loose. The beer was kept cool in wet straw, and it seems the barman would keep the limited supplies of cool beer for those who were sober; those who couldn't tell the difference were served it warm.

The other notable building in town is **Jones Store**, also known as George Man Fong's house. It was built in the 1930s by Arnold Jones, who ran it until 1949, after which time it changed hands a couple of times until 1959 when it was acquired by George Man Fong, a saddler who worked on the premises until 1985. The building was restored by the National Trust in 1988 and houses a small museum.

There are no facilities of any kind in the town, the nearest being at Dunmarra and Elliott.

ELLIOTT

• **pop 430**   ✉ **0862**

The one-street town of Elliott is a cattle service town, and is one of the cattle 'bath' centres where cattle coming from the north are given a chemical bath to kill any ticks so they don't infect herds to the south. The actual 'Tick Line' is the boundary of Banka Banka and Phillip Creek Stations, about 250km south of Elliott.

The town includes a roadhouse with a supermarket, a general store and post office, and a police station (☎ 8969 2010).

If it's any help, Elliott is the half-way point between Alice Springs and Darwin.

Places to Stay & Eat

There's the usual range of accommodation, although nothing stands out. The *Halfway Caravan Park* (☎ 8969 2025) is part of the Mobil roadhouse, and has camp sites for $8.50 ($14.50 with power) or cabins from $50. There's a *supermarket* here serving takeaways.

Much nicer is the *Midland Caravan Park* (☎ 8969 2037), despite the rather unfriendly proprietors. A camp site costs $10 ($15 with power); on-site vans cost from $35 and cabins are $50 ($60 with en suite).

RENNER SPRINGS

Renner Springs, an hour or so down the track from Elliott, is another roadhouse by the highway. It's more interesting than it sounds because it is actually an old army hut which was removed after WWII from the staging camp at Banka Banka Station to the south. It's built entirely of corrugated iron – even the bar is tin. It's worth stopping for a look around or a bite to eat.

Renner Springs is generally accepted as being on the dividing line between the seasonally wet Top End and the dry Centre.

The often monotonous country which the highway passes through is relieved around here by the Ashburton Range, which parallels the road for some distance either side of Renner Springs.

Place to Stay

The only choice here is the *Renner Springs Desert Inn* (☎ 8964 4505), which has camping ($8, $10 with power), 'budget' cabins for $50 and motel units for $55. The meals at the bar are quite acceptable.

Fuel and supplies are available from 7 am to 11 pm.

ATTACK CREEK HISTORICAL RESERVE

About 90km south of Renner Springs the highway crosses Attack Creek, and on the southern side is a memorial to John McDouall

Stuart. There's a picnic area with shade and water.

On Stuart's first attempt at a south-north crossing of the continent in 1860 he got as far as this creek before he was forced to return to Adelaide, partly because he was low on supplies. Stuart's version was that his party was attacked by hostile Warumungu Aboriginal men and that this forced the turn around. The attack certainly occurred, but it seems it was exaggerated by Stuart and that this was simply the last straw.

About 1km north of Attack Creek an old section of the highway loops west off the new for a few kilometres. Some 9km along it passes a rock by the roadside in a cutting, which soldiers working on the road during WWII thought looked liked Britain's wartime prime minister, Winston Churchill. It's still there, complete with cigar in mouth (a large stick). It's pretty dumb, really, but I guess there wasn't much else to do out there. You can keep going and end up back on the new highway, just for something to do.

A grid about 10km south of Attack Creek is the boundary fence between Banka Banka and Phillip Creek Stations, and this is also the Tick Line, as a large sign points out (see the earlier Elliott section).

THREE WAYS

Being the point where the Stuart Hwy meets the road east to Queensland, the Barkly Hwy, it didn't take much wit to come up with the name Three Ways. Basically it's a bloody long way from anywhere apart from Tennant Creek, which is 26km down the Track: it's 537km north of the Alice, 988km south of Darwin and 643km west of Mt Isa. Three Ways is a classic 'get stuck' point for hitchhikers and a 'must stop' point for road trains.

On the north side of the junction next to the highway there's a construction that looks like a brick water tower. This is in fact the Flynn Memorial, commemorating the founder of the Royal Flying Doctor Service, the Reverend John Flynn. It's one of the least aesthetically pleasing monuments you're ever likely to see.

Place to Stay

It's probably a good idea to time your trip so you don't have to stay at the **Threeways Roadhouse** (☎ 8962 2744). We found the food execrable and the service surly – and we're not the only ones (see *Sean And David's Long Drive*, by Sean Condon, in Lonely Planet's Journeys series).

If you're stuck you can camp ($10, $15 with power), or there are air-con dongas for $31.50/50 a single/double and motel rooms for $49.50/59.50. There's a pool, bar, shop and a restaurant. Showers are available if you're just passing through.

Fuel and supplies are available from 5.30 am to midnight.

TENNANT CREEK

- pop 3862   ✉ 0860

Apart from Katherine, Tennant Creek is the only town of any size between Darwin and Alice Springs. It's 26km south of Three Ways and 511km north of Alice Springs. The local tourist authority works hard to promote the town's few attractions, but it's a scruffy place and not worth more than an overnight stop.

History

To the Warumungu people, Tennant Creek is Jurnkurakurr, the intersection of a number of Dreaming tracks.

The recent history of the town, as with so many places on the Track, starts with the expeditions of John McDouall Stuart. He passed through here in 1860 before turning back at Attack Creek some distance north. He named the creek, which is about 10km north of town, after John Tennant, a prominent pastoralist from Port Lincoln in South Australia.

When the Overland Telegraph Line was put through in the 1870s a repeater station was set up at Tennant Creek. The story goes that the town itself was established 10km south of the repeater station because that was where a wagonload of beer broke down here in the early 1930s; rather than take the beer to the people, the people went to the beer and that's where the town has stayed.

Although it spoils a good story, the truth is far more prosaic: the present site is close to the gold fields, the telegraph station area isn't.

The discovery of gold here in the 1930s led to a minor gold rush and by WWII there were some 100 small mines in operation.

Once the mining was under way the local Aboriginal people were moved to the Phillip Creek settlement on the Stuart Hwy north of Tennant, where the mud brick ruins are still visible.

However, the gold rush was short-lived and the town might well have gone the way of a number of 'boom and bust' towns in the Territory, except that viable quantities of copper were found in the 1950s. Even today there are commercial gold mines in the area, the main one being Poseidon Gold's White Devil mine 42km north-west of town.

Orientation & Information

Tennant Creek sprawls north-south along the Stuart Hwy, which is called Paterson St where it passes through town. Along the main drag you'll find the transit centre, most places to stay and a few places to eat, banks and a supermarket. There's also the police station (☎ 8962 2606), two roadhouses, a pub and post office. Fuel is available 24 hours at the BP roadhouse.

The helpful Visitor Centre (☎ 8962 3388) is inconveniently located 2km east of town on Peko Rd at the historic gold stamp battery (see Things to See following). The office is open Monday to Friday from 9 am to 5 pm, and Saturday (and Sunday during the tourist season) from 9 am to 12 noon.

A couple of blocks west on Schmidt St is the Tennant Creek Hospital (☎ 8962 4399) and there's a chemist on the main street opposite the transit centre.

The Central Land Council (☎ 8962 2343) has an office on Paterson St, and the Department of Mines & Energy (☎ 8962 1288), also on Paterson St, is where you need to go if you want a fossicking permit.

Anyinginyi Arts is an Aboriginal shop on Davidson St specialising in arts and crafts from the Barkly Tablelands. Most of the

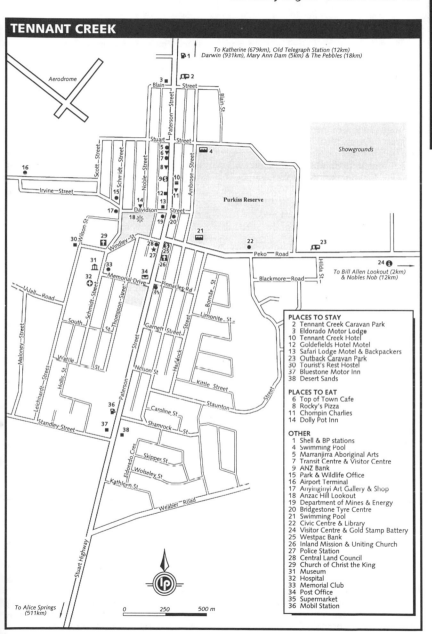

TENNANT CREEK

To Katherine (679km), Old Telegraph Station (12km)
Darwin (931km), Mary Ann Dam (5km) & The Pebbles (18km)

Aerodrome

Showgrounds

Purkiss Reserve

Blain Street

Paterson Street

Stuart Street

Noble Street

Schmidt Street

Scott Street

Ambrose Street

Irvine Street

Davidson Street

Windley St

Wilson St

Peko Road

Hilda St

Blackmore Road

To Bill Allen Lookout (2km)
& Nobles Nob (12km)

Memorial Drive

Pinnacles Rd

U Wall Road

Schmidt Street

Thompson Street

Garnett Street

Haddock Street

Bornite St

Limonite St

Maloney Street

Leichhardt Street

Hollis St

Wattle St

South St

Nelson St

Kittle Street

Staunton St

Caroline St

Shamrock St

Paterson Street

Standley Street

Eldorado Cres

Skipper St

Wolseley St

Kathleen St

Weaber Road

Stuart Highway

To Alice Springs
(511km)

0   250   500 m

PLACES TO STAY
2 Tennant Creek Caravan Park
3 Eldorado Motor Lodge
10 Tennant Creek Hotel
12 Goldfields Hotel Motel
13 Safari Lodge Motel & Backpackers
23 Outback Caravan Park
30 Tourist's Rest Hostel
37 Bluestone Motor Inn
38 Desert Sands

PLACES TO EAT
6 Top of Town Cafe
8 Rocky's Pizza
11 Chompin Charlies
14 Dolly Pot Inn

OTHER
1 Shell & BP stations
4 Swimming Pool
5 Marranjirra Aboriginal Arts
7 Transit Centre & Visitor Centre
9 ANZ Bank
15 Park & Wildlife Office
16 Airport Terminal
17 Anyinginyi Art Gallery & Shop
18 Anzac Hill Lookout
19 Department of Mines & Energy
20 Bridgestone Tyre Centre
21 Swimming Pool
22 Civic Centre & Library
24 Visitor Centre & Gold Stamp Battery
25 Westpac Bank
26 Inland Mission & Uniting Church
27 Police Station
28 Central Land Council
29 Church of Christ the King
31 Museum
32 Hospital
33 Memorial Club
34 Post Office
35 Supermarket
36 Mobil Station

pieces on sale – including boomerangs, coolamons, spears and shields – are made locally and prices are lower than in Alice Springs. Murranjirra Aboriginal Arts is another gallery on Paterson St, near the transit centre.

Things to See

For a good view of the town there's a small **lookout** on Anzac Hill, right next to the Safari backpackers on Davidson St. It takes only a minute to climb but you won't want to linger long among the broken bottles.

About 2km east of the Visitor Centre along Peko Rd there's the **Bill Allen Lookout** with views over the town and the McDouall Ranges to the north, and signboards explaining the sights.

In Town The small National Trust **museum**, on Schmidt St opposite the Memorial Club, dates from 1942 when it was built as an army hospital. Until 1978 it was used as an outpatients clinic for the hospital next door. It has some interesting displays, including a re-creation of a miner's camp and is open daily during winter from 3 to 5 pm ($2).

The corrugated-iron **Church of Christ the King** on Windley St was originally built in Pine Creek early this century, but was trucked to Tennant Creek in 1935.

On the main street just south of Peko St is another church building, this one the old **Australian Inland Mission** (Uniting Church). This corrugated-iron building was built in the 1930s by the Sidney Williams Co. (Many corrugated-iron buildings along the track are of Sidney Williams construction, see the boxed text.)

On the walls of the Central Land Council building in Paterson St is the **Jurnkurakurr Mural**, painted by the local Aboriginal people and depicting the Dreamings from this area – among them the snake, crow, white cockatoo, budgerigar, fire and lightning.

Around Town East of town, about 2km along Peko Rd, is the **Gold Stamp Battery**, which also houses the Visitor Centre (see Orientation & Information). It was erected in 1939 so local miners could process their ore locally instead of shipping it to South Australia. The site is now a museum and the 10-head battery gets cranked up for visitors daily at 9.30 am and 5 pm ($12 adults, $24 family), but you are free to wander around at other times. A 1½ hour tour of the mine itself leaves at 11 am daily (and at 3.30 pm during winter) and costs the same as the battery tour.

A further 12km along Peko Rd brings you to **Nobles Nob Open Cut Mine**. The gold here was discovered in 1933 by one-eyed Jack Noble and his blind mate William Weaber. By the time it closed in 1985 it had yielded $65 million worth of gold, making it the richest mine in the country at the time. It was originally an underground mine but was converted to open-cut following a huge cave-in.

About 3km north of town is the **Mary Ann Recreational Dam**, a good spot for a swim or a picnic. A bicycle track runs next to the highway to the turn-off and then it's a further 1.5km.

You'll see the green-roofed stone buildings of the old **Telegraph Station** near the highway about 12km north of town. Built in 1872, it is one of only four of the original 11 stations remaining in the Territory (the others are at Barrow Creek, Alice Springs and Powell Creek). This station was the most northerly station to be provisioned from Adelaide, and the supplies were brought by camel from the railhead at Oodnadatta. The station's telegraph functions ceased in 1935, when a new office opened in the town itself, but it was in use until 1950 as a linesman's residence and until 1985 as a station homestead. Today it is being restored by Parks & Wildlife. It's an interesting and pleasant spot and well worth a look.

Just north of the Telegraph Station is a turn-off to the west to **The Pebbles**, a formation of granite boulders like a miniaturised version of the better-known Devil's Marbles 100km or so south of Tennant Creek. To the Aboriginal people the Pebbles are known as Kundjarra, and is a Women's Dreaming sacred site. It's about 6km along a good dirt road to the Pebbles, but only worth the trip at sunset or sunrise.

The Sidney Williams Hut

Time and again visitors to the Territory who have an interest in history and architecture come across corrugated-iron buildings known as Sidney Williams Huts. These prefabricated buildings were supplied by Sidney Williams & Co, a Sydney-based company that was established in the 1920s by Sidney Williams, an architect and engineer.

Initially the company specialised in windmills, but from experience gained on his travels throughout remote parts of the country, Williams realised that there was the need for a building system that was cheap, easy to transport and simple to erect. The company developed the Comet Building, a system of interchangeable steel sections which bolted together so that any configuration of walls, doors and windows could be achieved. The beauty of the steel frame was that it was not only stronger than local wood, but was also termite proof.

Sidney Williams huts went up in all corners of the Territory from the 1920s onwards and became very much a part of it – in 1935 the civic buildings in the new township of Tennant Creek were almost exclusively of Sidney Williams construction. The defence forces bought and built large numbers of Sidney Williams huts all the way from Alice Springs to Darwin during WWII, as they were cheap and quick to assemble, and had none of the limitations of canvas tents.

The company was wound up in 1988 and all records destroyed, so it is not known just how many were shipped to the Northern Territory. Many of the original buildings have been moved, often to remote locations, but many still survive – the old Inland Mission building in Tennant Creek and the Totem Theatre buildings in Alice Springs were all supplied by Sidney Williams & Co.

Activities

If you're into fossicking, head for **Moonlight Rockhole** fossicking area, about 60km west of town along the Warrego road. Note that a permit must be obtained from the Department of Mines & Energy (on the main street).

You can take part in a cattle drive or go horse riding at **Juno Horse Centre** (☎ 8962 2783). A four hour horseback cattle muster, including cooked breakfast and tea, costs $55 and trail rides of various length start at $30 per rider.

There's a good outdoor **swimming pool** on Peko Rd; entry costs $2. Most places to stay have a pool, but check that it's heated before leaping in after a cold desert night.

Organised Tours

Kraut Downs Station (☎ 8962 2820) runs informative half-day tours where you can learn about bush tucker and medicine, try whip-cracking and boomerang-throwing and wash down a witchetty grub with billy tea and damper for $25.

Norm's Gold & Scenic Tours (☎ mobile 0418 891 711) offers a 'Gold Fever Tour' ($25), where you can pan for gold and keep the proceeds, and afternoon trips to the Devil's Marbles ($45 including dinner).

Tours of the Dot Mine, an old gold mine dating from the 1930s, start each evening during winter at 7 pm ($14). For details phone ☎ 8962 2168.

The Tourist's Rest Tennant Creek Hostel (see Places to Stay) runs 'Devil's Deals' – trips out to the Devil's Marbles for $50 including a night's accommodation.

Special Events

Tennant Creek hosts a number of interesting annual events. As well as the usual Tennant Creek Show (July), there's the Renner Springs Races (not held in Renner Springs at all!; Easter weekend), the Goldrush Folk Festival (August) and the Desert Harmony Arts Festival (September). If you happen to be in town for the show, you can witness the handbogging competition! A Go-kart Race is held in May.

Places to Stay

Camping & Caravan Parks The *Outback Caravan Park* (☎ 8962 2459) is a shady, quiet park 1½km east of town along Peko Rd. Tent sites cost $13 ($17 with power), there's one on-site van for $25 and cabins (some with air-con) cost from $38 with shared facilities to $50 for self-contained ones.

The other choice – also good – is the *Tennant Creek Caravan Park* (☎ 8962 2325) on Paterson St on the northern edge of town. It has grassed camp sites for $6 per person ($8 with power), on-site vans for $35, 'bunkhouse' rooms at $20 a double, and air-con cabins for $55.

Hostels There are only two options here. The *Safari Lodge Motel* (☎ 8962 2207, 12 Davidson St) has a block of backpacker rooms across the road from its main building on Davidson St. A bed costs $12, and there are shared cooking and bathroom facilities.

The budget alternative is the *Tourist's Rest Tennant Creek Hostel* (☎ 8962 2719), in a shady location on the corner of Leichhardt and Windley Sts. Beds in air-con triple dorms cost $14 and twins/doubles are $30/32; YHA/VIP/Nomads discounts are available. Its combination accommodation/ Devil's Marbles trips are good value – see Organised Tours, earlier.

Hotels & Motels The *Safari Lodge Motel* (☎ 8962 2207, 12 Davidson St) has singles/doubles for $69/79 and budget rooms with shared bathroom facilities for $34. It's centrally located, and there's a spa and laundry.

The *Goldfields Hotel Motel* (☎ 8962 2030), just around the corner on Paterson St, is good value, with singles/doubles with bathroom for $45/65.

On the northern edge of town on the highway is the upmarket *Eldorado Motor Lodge Motel* (☎ 8962 2402), where units start at $53/56 for a budget single/double with bathroom and range up to $72/78 for a deluxe room.

At the southern end of town and also on the highway, the *Bluestone Motor Inn* (☎ 8962 2617) has comfortable self-contained units ranging from $55 to $85.

The best value in this category is offered by the *Desert Sands* (☎ 8962 1346), opposite the Bluestone, where self-contained units with kitchen, en suite and washing machine start at $50/55.

Places to Eat

After passing through the string of roadhouses along the Stuart Hwy, it is disappointing to find that Tennant Creek actually has very few places to eat.

Believe it or not, one of the most highly regarded is in the local squash centre. The *Dolly Pot Inn* (☎ 8962 2824), on the corner of Davidson and Noble Sts, is open daily from 11 am to midnight. You can eat good-value meals while watching sporting types thrash a ball around.

A popular place with locals for night time takeaways is *Chompin' Charlies (114 Paterson St)*, near the Tennant Creek Hotel, which has good barramundi and chips for $3.50.

At the front of the transit centre building, *Priester's Café* opens for light meals and snacks whenever a bus pulls in; it's a nice enough place to kill time if you're just passing through. Next door to the transit centre is the recently opened *Top of Town Cafe* which is open every day from 8.00 am to 3.30 am.

Rocky's Pizza & Pasta (☎ 8962 2522), next to the ANZ bank on Paterson St, has, yep, pizzas and pasta.

For takeaway snacks and ice cream there's *Mr Perry's Ice Creamery* near the supermarket on Paterson St, and opposite the Goldfields Hotel Motel the *Barkly Bakehouse* sells fresh bread and pastries.

There's a *Chinese restaurant* in the Goldfields Hotel Motel that offers a $7.50 lunch special, and a good range of Chinese favourites and Aussie food; the pub itself offers $5 counter meals in the evening.

Margo Miles Steakhouse (☎ 8962 2227) in the bluestone Tennant Creek Hotel on the main street has Italian and steak dishes.

The Memorial Club on Memorial Drive welcomes visitors and has good, straightforward counter meals at its *Memories Bistro*, including a $5 lunch special.

The *Bluestone Motor Inn* and the *Eldorado Motor Lodge* both have licensed restaurants and are open for breakfast.

Getting There & Around

Air Airnorth (☎ toll-free 1800 627 474) has flights to Alice Springs (daily except Sunday; $199 one way), Darwin and Katherine (both daily except Saturday; $319 and $239 one way respectively).

Bus The long-distance buses all stop at the transit centre in Paterson St.

Car Rental The Outback Caravan Park is an agent for Hertz (☎ toll-free 1800 891 112), while Ten Ant Tours at the BP station acts for Territory Thrifty Car Rentals (☎ toll-free 1800 891 125).

Bicycle If you're feeling energetic and want to pedal around, bike rental is available from the Bridgestone tyre centre (☎ 8962 2361) on Paterson St.

DEVIL'S MARBLES CONSERVATION RESERVE

The huge boulders known as the Devil's Marbles are one of the most famous geological sights in the Territory. The reddish rocks make a spectacular sight at sunrise or sunset, and a challenge to photographers by moonlight.

The 1827 hectare reserve straddles the Stuart Hwy about 105km south of Tennant Creek and 393km north of Alice Springs.

Over an estimated 1640 million years a huge granite block crisscrossed with fault lines eroded into slabs roughly 3m to 7m square; the extreme desert temperatures forced the expansion and contraction of the blocks, and slabs flaked off like the peel of an onion (a process known as exfoliation). Their corners are now rounded and many have eroded into symmetrical geometric shapes, such as eggs and spheres. Some are stacked in precarious piles, with some balanced at unlikely angles – they look as if a good shove could send them tumbling.

The area is a registered sacred site of the local Warumungu tribe, who know it as Karlukarlu. Several Dreaming trails cross the area and the rocks are believed to be the eggs of the Rainbow Serpent.

Interpretive signs and diagrams can be read along a **self-guided walk** which does a 20 minute loop from the car park. This walk is well worth doing, and at one point you pass an amazing 4m high boulder that has been neatly split in half – it is so neat it's as if a giant tomato has been sliced with a sharp knife.

Facilities

There are pit toilets at the car park, and during the peak months (July-August) an ice-cream van from nearby Wauchope often sets up during the day.

There's a *camp ground* with remarkably hard ground around the eastern side of the boulders. Pit toilets, a shade shelter and fireplace are provided (BYO firewood). Camping costs $2.50/6 per adult/family.

Tours to the marbles are run from Tennant Creek. If you don't want to camp, there's accommodation about 10km south of the reserve at Wauchope.

WAUCHOPE

Pronounced '*war*-kup', this settlement is nothing more than a fuel stop by the highway. At least this one has some character, as the pub itself dates back to the 1930s, and the 'town' itself to the discovery of wolfram in the area in 1914. At its height around 50 miners worked the small but rich field 12km east of here. Many more worked larger fields at Hatches Creek, about 140km to the east in the Davenport Ranges. After WWI the price of wolfram halved almost overnight as the British no longer needed it in their war effort, and the Wauchope field became unviable.

The price of wolfram revived in the late 1930s in the build-up to WWII, and it was at this time that the pub was established. During the war the wolfram fields were taken over by the Commonwealth government and the few miners remaining (most had joined the army) were paid wages to dig the ore, along with 500-odd Chinese quarrymen whom the government had evacuated from islands in the Pacific. For a second time a war finished and the demand for wolfram fell dramatically. Before long the fields were deserted (the Chinese were transferred to Brisbane to work for the US Army) and Wauchope became the stop on the highway that it is today.

With a 4WD vehicle it's possible to visit the old wolframite field today. Ask at the pub for directions.

Places to Stay

The *Wauchope Hotel (☎ 8964 1963)* has grassed camp sites at $8 ($12 powered), backpacker beds for $12 and rooms from $60 a double. There's also a bar full of the paraphernalia that outback pubs seem to accumulate, and decent meals are available in the restaurant. Fuel is available from 6 am to 11 pm.

Bicycle hire is available ($10 a day) if you feel like pedalling the 10km to the Devil's Marbles.

This is a quiet, pleasant place to stay if you don't want to camp at the Devil's Marbles, and it's closer and more attractive than Tennant Creek.

WYCLIFFE WELL

The next service stop along the track is Wycliffe Well, just 18km south of Wauchope, a large accommodation complex where in recent years a spate of UFO sightings has been claimed.

The well referred to in the name dates from 1872 and the Overland Telegraph Line, although the water quality was not all that flash. In the 1930s a bore was sunk to provide good water on the North-South Stock Route. During WWII a two hectare army vegetable farm was established to supply the troops further up the Stuart Hwy.

Wycliffe Well's most (and probably only) famous resident was one Doreen Crook (later Doreen Braitling). While still a young girl her family set up here around 1920, hauling water for cattle on the stock route, having had no luck at the wolfram field at Wauchope. She married pastoralist Bill Braitling, and they went on to establish Mount Doreen Station on the Tanami Track north-west of Alice Springs. Doreen spent a great deal of time looking after the welfare of Aboriginal people on the station, and after her husband died she moved to Alice Springs and became involved with the preservation of historic buildings (it's largely thanks to her that the Stuart Town Gaol was not demolished in 1972). She eventually went on to form the National Trust of the Northern Territory, and was elected its first president.

Places to Stay

The *Wycliffe Well Holiday Park (☎ 8964 1966)* has a variety of accommodation and lots of facilities, including barbecues, laundry and an indoor pool. Camp sites cost $13 ($17 with power), and there are on-site vans costing $32; budget cabins range from $40/50 for singles/doubles with shared facilities up to $78 for a chalet with cooking facilities and en suite; motel rooms are also available for $75.

As the sign at the front says, 'earthlings are welcome at Wycliffe Wells', and facilities at the roadhouse include a pool, licensed restaurant and bar. You can read all about the UFO sightings while sampling the good variety of international beer brands available at the bar. The roadhouse is open from 6 am to 9 pm every day.

Barkly Tableland & The Gulf

To the east of the Stuart Hwy lies the huge expanse of the Barkly Tableland and, beyond it, the Gulf region. It is primarily cattle country, characterised by arid grasslands of the tableland and open woodland country of the Gulf.

Out here the distances are vast and the population sparse. Most visitors pass through on the Barkly Hwy, which connects the Stuart Hwy with Mt Isa in Queensland and virtually the only attraction is some fine fishing – the Roper River, on the southern edge of Arnhem Land, and the waterways around Borroloola close to the Gulf of Carpentaria are renowned among fisherfolk.

If fishing is not your bag then the pickings are pretty slim, but there is some fine scenery and camping by the Gulf at Wollogorang Station near the Queensland border and on the sometimes rough gravel road that links Roper Bar with Borroloola. If you're not in a hurry it's worth the diversion to visit this little-touristed corner of the Territory.

The Barkly Tableland, named after the Governor of Victoria in 1861, comprises a relatively featureless plain, dominated by tussock grasses. Only in the few creek lines do many trees occur.

ROPER BAR

From just south of Mataranka on the Stuart Hwy, the Roper Hwy strikes out east for 175km to Roper Bar, a popular fishing spot on the Roper River. It's also an access point into south-eastern Arnhem Land, or you can fuel up and continue south to Borroloola.

The 'bar' itself is a ford across the Roper River, the 'town' is a store/motel/caravan park with a population of less than a dozen. The road crosses the river here, then continues on for a further 30km to the Aboriginal community at **Ngukurr**, which is off limits to visitors. In the early days, steam ships and large sailing vessels tied up at the bar to discharge cargo. The wreck of one of them, the *Young Australian*, lies about 25km downstream.

From the Stuart Hwy, all but the last 40km are sealed, and even the gravel section is generally well maintained and poses few problems if you're sensible.

Although it's on Aboriginal land, permits are not required for visits to the area.

Places to Stay

The one and only choice here is at the *Roper Bar Store* (☎ 8975 4636), which caters mainly to tourist traffic and nearby Aboriginal communities. It dispenses fuel (9 am to 6 pm daily), groceries and fishing tackle and has accommodation and a caravan park. Overnight rates in air-con dongas are $35 a single plus $15 for each additional person (up to four). Sites in the grassed camping area, which is only about 100m from the river, cost $10.

ROPER BAR TO BORROLOOLA

The road from Roper through to Borroloola is usually pretty good. It certainly does not require 4WD, but it's prudent to carry two spares because the shale can be sharp in places if the grader has been over it recently.

About 70km from Roper Bar you arrive at the old **St Vidgeon Homestead** – a lonely ruin on a stony rise conjuring up stark images of battlers eking a scant living from the hostile bush. The station is owned by the Northern Territory government, and is set to become part of a 10,000 sq km national park in the not-too-distant future. Close by is the superb **Lomarieum Lagoon**, a stone's throw from the homestead and only about 1km from the Roper River. Fringed by paperbarks and covered by large water lilies, the lagoon has many birds and a peaceful atmosphere.

After crossing the Limmen Bight River, 178km from Roper Bar, the countryside changes. For about 50km southwards from here, the road runs up narrow valleys between rugged ridges, with some dramatic scenery along the way.

You pass the turn-off to **Nathan River Homestead** 13km from the Limmen Bight crossing. Nathan River is set to be included in the same national park as St Vidgeons. It contains some superb rock formations (known as the Lost City) which are said to rival the Bungle Bungles in Western Australia. For the moment, it is off-limits because it is the subject of an Aboriginal land claim.

Finally the track joins the bitumen Carpentaria Hwy 30km from Borroloola.

BORROLOOLA
- pop 550   ✉ 0854

Borroloola is a small service town close to the Gulf of Carpentaria. It is connected to the outside world by bitumen roads leading to the Stuart and Barkly Hwys, and by air services to Darwin and Katherine. Among fisherfolk it's something of a mecca, but it's a dirty, unpleasant place – part town, part rubbish dump – with expensive accommodation and no redeeming features; unless you're here to catch fish it's probably best avoided.

History
Until 1885 there were no facilities at all between Burketown (then a busy little port in Queensland's Gulf country) and the store at Roper Bar. Then a racketeer by the name of John 'Black Jack' Reid brought his boat, the *Good Intent*, loaded with 'duty free' alcohol and supplies up the McArthur River to the Burketown Crossing. There he built a rough store, which became the Royal Hotel, and from this the settlement grew.

A year later, by which time traffic on the Gulf Track had greatly increased thanks to the Kimberley gold rush, the embryonic township had a population of up to 150 whites – 'the scum of northern Australia', according to the government resident. It boasted four corrugated-iron stores (three of which doubled as pubs), a bakery, a Chinese market garden, police station and a dairy farm. A decade later, the gold rush and the great cattle drives were over and the white population had shrunk to six.

Borroloola probably would have died altogether were it not for its location on one of the Gulf's largest rivers; it survives today as a minor administrative centre and supply point for the region's cattle stations. After a century of obscurity, however, the town is set to boom again, with the on-going development of a giant silver, lead and zinc mine

and the creation of a deep-water port on the Gulf at the fabulously-named Bing Bong.

Sprawled along 2km of wide main street, Borroloola was blown away by Cyclone Kathy in 1984 and much of its old character was lost in the rebuilding.

Information
Facilities and services include a medical centre (☎ 8975 8757), post office, police station (☎ 8975 8770), Parks & Wildlife office (☎ 8975 8792), aerodrome, mechanical repairs, car hire, tourist accommodation, supermarkets, butchery and marine suppliers. A number of businesses sell fishing tackle and bait.

Gulf Mini Mart and Borroloola Bulk Discounts are general stores that act as the Westpac and ANZ agencies, respectively; both are open seven days a week and have EFTPOS and credit card facilities. The post office acts as the Commonwealth Bank agency.

There are public phones at Gulf Mini Mart and near the police station.

Things to See
Unprepossessing though it is today, Borroloola has an undeniably colourful past. Much of the town's history is recorded and displayed in the old police station, which dates from 1886 and is now a National Trust museum. The museum contains photos and artefacts on pastoralism, the police, Macassan contact, aboriginal lore and exploration.

The museum is open from 10 am to 5 pm Monday to Friday (at other times the key is available from the motor mechanic nearby) and admission costs $2.

Fishing
The McArthur River is tidal as far as the Burketown Crossing near town and there are boat ramps at Borroloola and King Ash Bay, about 40km downstream. Fishers with large enough craft can venture out into the Gulf around the Sir Edward Pellew Group. Don't despair if you don't have a boat: you can catch a wide variety of fish, including barramundi and threadfin salmon, from

various spots along the river's tidal section, between Batten Point (near King Ash Bay) and the Burketown Crossing.

Special Events
Most of Borroloola's 10,000 annual visitors come for the fishing and the Borroloola Fishing Classic, held in June each year, draws a large number of enthusiasts. Other annual events include the inevitable rodeo (August) and the Borroloola Show (July).

Places to Stay & Eat
There are three choices for accommodation in town, all in the main street and all securely fenced in. They often get booked out so it's advisable to ring ahead.

The *Borroloola Inn* (☎ 8975 8766) has air-con dongas starting at $45 for a twin. The pub's Sunday night carvery is excellent value at $8 and the swimming pool, which is surrounded by large mango trees, is arguably the nicest place in Borroloola.

Just down from the pub, the *McArthur River Caravan Park* (☎ 8975 8734) has unpowered camp sites costing $12 ($15 for power). There are dongas at $30/40 for singles/doubles, but the park's on site vans and cabins are rarely available because of the shortage of long-term accommodation in town. If you strike it lucky, the self-contained cabins cost $65/75, vans are $40 for a double.

The *Borroloola Holiday Village* (☎ 8975 8742) has air-con units with attached bath, cooking facilities, TV and telephone ($79/92 a single/double). There are four economy rooms sleeping just one person ($50), while budget beds in the bunkhouse cost $30.

Any option that doesn't involve staying in Borroloola itself is an attractive one There's good fishing from the river bank at King Ash Bay, where the *Borroloola Boat & Fishing Club* (☎ 8975 9861) has its headquarters, and if you join the club (a life membership costs $500 and annual membership $30) you can make use of its toilet, shower and bar facilities. Otherwise there are powered ($14) and unpowered sites ($10). The

bar is open from 5 to 8 pm daily and grills are available from 6 to 8 pm.

A good option if there is a group of you is to hire a houseboat on the McArthur River. *Borroloola Houseboats* (☎ toll-free 1800 658 529) berth at the fishing club at King Ash Bay; the costs for four or eight-berth boats in the high/low season are $1050/750 and $2050/1350 per week.

Borroloola has little to choose from in the way of eateries. The unimaginatively-named *Aussie Barra Van* at the north end of town does fish and chips; and takeaways are available at both *general stores*.

Getting There & Away
Airnorth (☎ toll-free 1800 627 474) has three flights a week to Darwin ($409) and Katherine ($265), and less frequently to Ngukurr ($155) and Numbulwar ($135) in Arnhem Land (all one-way fares).

AROUND BORROLOOLA
Barranyi National Park
The islands of the Sir Edward Pellew Group lie in the Gulf of Carpentaria about 30km north of the McArthur River mouth. One of the islands, North Island, is owned by the Yanyuwa people and part of it is managed by Parks & Wildlife as the Barranyi National Park.

The park features sandy beaches and sandstone cliffs, and four species of marine turtle nest there. The waters of the park provide excellent fishing, including Spanish mackerel, northern bluefin tuna and several of the trevally family.

While there are no facilities in the park, it is possible to camp if you have your own gear.

Contact Parks & Wildlife in Borroloola (☎ 8975 8792) before heading out to the park. Access is only by boat via the McArthur River and Carrington Channel (35km); the closest boat ramp is at King Ash Bay, 40km north of Borroloola. Even in the Dry the waters of the Gulf can be quite rough and the 30km crossing to North Island should be attempted only by experienced sailors.

Caranbirini Conservation Reserve

This small reserve 46km south of Borroloola lies at the western extremity of the Bukalara Range, and protects a rugged sandstone escarpment, some attractive outlying sandstone spires, known as 'Lost City' formations and a semi-permanent waterhole.

The local Aboriginal people, the Gadanji, used the reserve's waterhole as a source of food such as turtles, mussels and waterlilies, and two Dreaming trails, the Emu and the White Cockatoo, have associations with the site.

There are no facilities and camping is not permitted, but there's a 1.5km **walking trail** that takes in the 25m high Lost City formations. It's a pleasant spot in the early morning or evening, and lots of birds congregate around the waterhole in the drier months. The escarpment country to the east is home to the rare Carpentarian grasswren; if you go looking for this bird take plenty of water and a compass – it's tough work walking through this rocky spinifex country.

CAPE CRAWFORD

Despite its name, Cape Crawford is nowhere near the coast – it's at the junction of the Carpentaria and Tablelands Hwys 113km south-west of Borroloola and 234km east of the Stuart Hwy. There's nothing there except a roadhouse, the Heartbreak Hotel, that offers a nice alternative to staying in Borroloola.

Organised Tours

Helicopter tours are operated from the Heartbreak Hotel and take in the Lost City rock formations in the Abner Range, some of which tower 50m high, cool ferneries and tumbling waterfalls, none of which is otherwise accessible to the general public. Scenic flights cost $70 per person and Lost City tours cost $125.

Places to Stay

The *Heartbreak Hotel* (☎ 8975 9928) is a pleasant enough place to park, with a grassy, shaded camp ground ($10, $16 powered), and clean, air-con dongas for $50/60 a single/twin with shared facilities.

There's also a pool, fuel, shop with basic supplies, air-con restaurant and a bar. From here it's a desolate 374km across the Barkly Tablelands to the Barkly Hwy and the Barkly Homestead.

WOLLOGORANG

From Borroloola a good gravel road heads south-east to Wollogorang Station, on the NT-Queensland border, 268km away. This road is best traversed with a 4WD vehicle, but conventional vehicles with high ground clearance should have no difficulty. Highlights of this stretch include some fine river crossings (the Wearyan, Robinson and Calvert Rivers), and 60km beyond the Calvert River there's some dramatic scenery.

Wollogorang Station itself covers over 7000 sq km, and it boasts a fully licensed roadhouse and an 80km frontage of pristine sandy beaches on the Gulf of Carpentaria. The coast can only be reached by 4WD vehicle; a small fee is charged for access.

Organised Tours

Fishing, exploring and pig-shooting safaris operate from the roadhouse, with costs for fishing and exploring tours starting at $80 per person per day for six people. Hunting expeditions are more expensive.

Places to Stay & Eat

The *Wollogorang Roadhouse/Gulf Wilderness Lodge* (☎ 8975 9944), open seven days a week, has a licensed restaurant offering good, wholesome country cooking at reasonable prices. There is also a snack menu.

The roadhouse has six air-conditioned units, each sleeping three, at $55/70/80 a single/double/triple. Camp sites cost $14 ($19 with power). Fuel and takeaway beer are also available.

BRUNETTE DOWNS

Brunette Downs Station, covering a shade over 12,000 sq km, is on the Tablelands Hwy 140km north of the Barkly Homestead. It is accessible by conventional vehicles with care.

This station would be no different from any other in the region if it wasn't for the **Brunette Downs Bush Races**, held in June each year. A cast of hundreds flocks in from miles around and it's a lively four days that includes a rodeo and ball. There is no charge for camping or to use the showers and toilets, and a professional caterer supplies meals (around $10) and keeps the beer flowing. The race track is around 20km from the homestead.

It's a great outback event and one well worth the detour if you happen to be in the area. You can find out exact dates from the station itself (☎ 8964 4522), but they offer nothing in the way of facilities for travellers.

CONNELL'S LAGOON CONSERVATION RESERVE

This lonely reserve is on the Barkly Stock Route east of Brunette Downs Station. Here 259 sq km of pancake-flat land was set aside to preserve undisturbed Mitchell grass habitat. It may look pretty uninspiring, but there's a surprising range of botanical diversity – 189 plant species are known to exist in the area.

The namesake lagoon doesn't amount to much and in fact only fills after good rains. When it does, it attracts migratory wading birds, as well as grassland species such as flock bronzewings and Pictorella mannikins. Another inhabitant, the long-haired rat, forms plagues after big rains when grass seeds are abundant. It in turn becomes food for predators such as owls, kites and dingoes.

There's no drinking water and there are no visitor facilities within the reserve, with the exception of an information bay on the southern side of the track. Access is via a gravel track between Brunette Downs and Alexandria Stations.

DAVENPORT RANGE NATIONAL PARK

This proposed national park will protect 1120 sq km of the ancient Davenport and Murchison Ranges east of Wauchope. The ranges were the site of wolfram mines at **Hatches Creek** early this century, but the remains of these lie on the Anurrete Aboriginal land, which is surrounded on three sides by the park. The Davenport Ranges are not the most spectacular on earth, but they are probably the oldest as their eroded peaks are all that remains of a geological formation that's more than 1800 million years old.

For visitors the only real attraction is the **Old Police Station Waterhole**, which can be reached by 4WD vehicle from the Stuart Hwy from the north (170km via the track to Kurundi and Epenarra Stations, which leaves the Stuart Hwy at Bonney Well, 90km south of Tennant Creek) or from the south (also 170km via the Murray Downs Station track, which heads east off the Stuart Hwy close to where it crosses Taylors Creek, about 40km north of Barrow Creek). Access is by 4WD only and a vehicle with high ground clearance is advised.

The park's only facilities are at the Old Police Station Waterhole, where there's a *camp ground* with pit toilets. All visitors must be completely self-sufficient. Fuel is available at Kurundi, Epenarra and Murray Downs (☎ 8964 1958) Stations. Roads can be flooded between December and March; for information about conditions phone the police station at Ali Curung ☎ 8964 1959.

BARKLY HOMESTEAD

Last stop before the Queensland border and probably your first contact with people in some time if you've just come down off the Barkly Tablelands, the *Barkly Homestead* (☎ 8964 4549) is a roadhouse that has the most expensive fuel between the Queensland coast and Tennant Creek. It's 210km east of Tennant Creek and 265km west of Camooweal in Queensland, so if your vehicle has the range you can save money by giving it a miss.

As a place to stay, however, it's not such a bad choice – there's a licensed restaurant, clean accommodation, watered lawns and decent food. Camp sites are $16 ($18 with power) and motel units, $62/72 a single/double. The roadhouse is open from 7 am until midnight every day.

From the roadhouse it's 252km east to the border and another 13km to Camooweal in Queensland. Across the border the road instantly deteriorates into a potholed, decaying beef road with blind rises and few places to overtake. Exercise extreme caution along this stretch, particularly in the early morning and evening, when you'll have the sun in your eyes as well as kangaroos, wandering stock and road trains to look out for.

North of Alice Springs

While there's not a great deal to see directly north of Alice Springs itself, there are a couple of interesting stops you can make on the Stuart Hwy on the way to Barrow Creek and beyond. There are also outback tracks that branch off the highway north-west across the Tanami Desert to Halls Creek in the Kimberley, and east to Camooweal and Mt Isa in Queensland. All these roads are traversable by conventional (2WD) vehicles with care, but it's not for inexperienced drivers and you should check locally for an update on road conditions before setting off. If there has been any rain recently you may need a 4WD vehicle.

Up the Track

The Stuart Hwy heads north from Alice Springs, snaking through the low outliers of the MacDonnell Ranges before flattening out after about 20km for the long haul north to Darwin. You may get a sinking feeling when you see the sign saying Tennant Creek 504km and Darwin 1491km!

Twenty kilometres north of Alice Springs is the turn-off for the Tanami Track, a gravel road connecting Alice with the Kimberley.

A further 11km brings you to the marker for the Tropic of Capricorn, and another 19km further on is the turn-off for the Arltunga Tourist Drive, an alternative route to the historic town of Arltunga in the East MacDonnell Ranges. This gravel road is generally in good condition to Claraville Station, 110km east of the highway, but the 13km stretch from there to Arltunga can be rough. Between The Garden and Claraville Stations lie the Harts Range Gem Fields, but these are 5km off the track and accessible by a 4WD vehicle only.

Leaving the Stuart Hwy a further 20km north is the Plenty Hwy, which spears 742km east across the northern fringes of

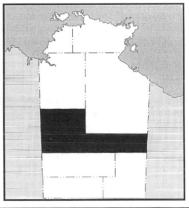

the Simpson Desert to Boulia in Western Queensland. The Sandover Hwy leaves the Plenty Hwy after 27km and heads north-east for 552km to the Queensland border and then on to Camooweal.

NATIVE GAP CONSERVATION RESERVE

This is a rest stop on the Stuart Hwy 110km north of Alice Springs. It marks a gap in the Hann Range, and the first European reference to it is by William Wills, a surveyor on the central section of the Overland Telegraph Line in 1872.

The Gap is a registered sacred site and is known to the local Aboriginal people as Arulte Artwatye.

There is a shady picnic ground with pit toilet but camping is prohibited.

RYAN WELL HISTORIC RESERVE

After another 19km the road crosses this small historic reserve, which preserves the ruins of a well and the remains of an early homestead.

The well was one of a number sunk in the late 1880s by a party led by Ned Ryan to provide water along the Overland Telegraph Line. The water was initially raised to the surface by bucket and windlass, but as the number of stock using the route increased and more water was needed, holding tanks were installed and these were filled by a larger bucket raised by a draught animal. While the head works of the well are all that remain today, it's still possible to make out the tank and trough foundations.

On the other side of the highway are the remains of **Glen Maggie Homestead**. This pastoral lease was taken up by Sam Nicker in 1914 and was named after his daughter, Margaret.

AILERON

About 1km west of the Stuart Hwy, 138km north of Alice Springs, Aileron roadhouse sits next to the homestead of Aileron Station. Photos in the roadhouse show the region's history and local characters.

Aileron Hotel Roadhouse (☎ 8956 9703) offers grassed camp sites ($10, $15 with power), backpacker accommodation for $12 and motel-style single/double units at $55/65. There's a pleasant licensed restaurant, pool table and swimming pool.

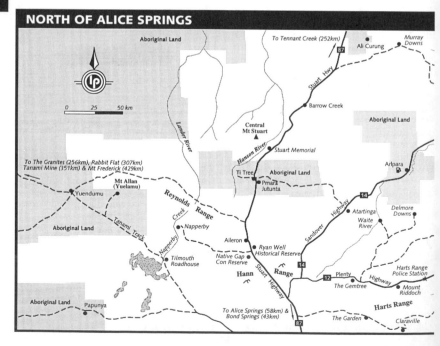

NORTH OF ALICE SPRINGS

TI TREE
• pop 105 ✉ 0872

The small town of Ti Tree is 193km north of Alice Springs. It is a service centre for the surrounding Aboriginal communities, such as Pmara Jutunta and Utopia, as well as for travellers on the Stuart Hwy.

The town, originally called Tea Tree Wells after the ti-tree lined waterhole about 300m west of the roadhouse, started life as a settlement on the Overland Telegraph Line. In 1971 the Anmatjera Aboriginal people won the lease of the Ti Tree Station, and this is now the settlement of Pmara Jutunta.

Facilities in the town include a medical centre (☎ 8956 9736) and police station (☎ 8956 9733).

Along from the roadhouse is the AAKI Gallery, which is an outlet for locally-made art and crafts. The prices for the unmounted dot paintings here are generally very com-petitive. Over the road, Gallereaterie (see Places to Stay & Eat following) also sells some good quality dot paintings, didgeri-doos and other creations, made at Utopia and Ti Tree, at reasonable prices.

Places to Stay & Eat
The *Ti Tree Roadhouse* (☎ 8956 9741) offers camping ($10, $15 with power), backpacker dorms for $12 and single/dou-ble motel rooms at $55/65. There's also a restaurant and bar, and a *Golden Fried Chicken* outlet.

The *Gallereaterie* is a little café/gallery a few hundred metres west of the highway, serving bistro meals and takeaway.

CENTRAL MOUNT STUART HISTORICAL RESERVE
This cairn beside the Stuart Hwt 20km north of Ti Tree commemorates Stuart's naming of

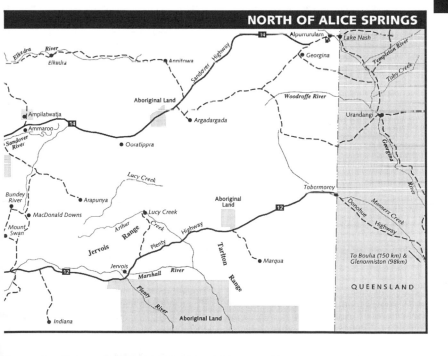

NORTH OF ALICE SPRINGS

Selling Camels to Arabia

OK, which country has the only wild dromedary camels in the world? The answer is Australia, where an estimated 200,000 roam the outback – some 60,000 of them in the Northern Territory alone. The other 13 million camels in the world are domesticated and live mainly in north Africa. Superbly adapted to life in arid conditions, it is not surprising that camels were imported as beasts of burden before the advent of railways and motor vehicles. Their descendants run wild today.

The first camel was brought to Australia from the Canary Islands in 1840, but it was in 1860 that the first major group arrived, and these were imported especially for the ill-fated Bourke and Wills expedition. By the late 1860s camels were arriving in large numbers, many of them going to the stud set up by Thomas Elder (founder of the Beltana Pastoral Co which evolved to today's multinational Elders Ltd) at Beltana in South Australia, which was established to meet the growing demand for these 'entirely new animals', as explorer Ernest Giles described them.

Other studs were set up in Western Australia, and for more than 50 years these provided high-class stock for domestic use. Imports from then British India continued until 1907, and between 1860 and 1907 an estimated 12,000 camels were imported.

By far the most commonly imported was the Arabian camel or dromedary (that's the one-humped variety). Being from hot desert areas it was at home in the Australian climate. Different breeds were imported according to requirements – some were larger and more suited to heavy loads, others suitable for riding and light baggage and still others for riding and speed. Fewer than 20 Bactrian (two-humped) camels were ever imported and none survives in the wild today.

So-called 'Afghans' were also brought to Australia to handle the animals. Although these men came from various parts of west Asia (mainly from Peshawar in present-day Pakistan) they were all Afghans to the locals. They played a vital role in the development of central Australia, and the *Ghan* train was named after them. While the Afghans were generally treated well, they tended to live apart from the local population, often in so-called 'Ghan towns' on the edge of fledgling outback towns.

The camel strings were used both in exploration and to haul goods from the railheads in central Australia as the line gradually crawled further north. The poles on the Overland Telegraph Line were carted by camel, as were supplies and mail for Alice Springs, sheep and cattle stations and remote missions, and for Aboriginal communities.

The biggest camel teams in use consisted of up to 70 camels with four Afghans, although strings of 40 camels were more common. In the desert they could travel up to 40km a day, with each beast carrying 300-600kg. When Giles first used camels he travelled 354km in eight days without watering his animals, while one 1891 expedition travelled over 800km in a month.

By the 1920s motor vehicles had largely rendered the camel obsolete, although they continued to be used for exploration – the last major expedition to make use of them was Dr CT Madigan's 1939 crossing of the Simpson Desert. Gradually all the domesticated beasts were released and they formed the free-ranging herds which are found today.

Central Mt Stuart, a hill about 12km to the north-west. Stuart thought he had reached the centre of Australia, and named the 'mountain' Central Mt Sturt, after his former expedition leader and friend, Charles Sturt. The name was later changed to honour Stuart himself. A cairn by the highway commemorates Stuart's visit.

Selling Camels to Arabia

In the last decade or so there has been a great resurgence of interest in the camel, the main emphasis being on recreational use. In central Australia there are three camel farms in the Alice Springs area.

Alice Springs is also home of the Camel Cup, an annual camel race. What started out as a race between two camels more than 20 years ago is now one of the major events on the Alice Springs calendar. As well as racing there is the unique sport of 'pocamelo' – camel polo.

Australian camels are exported live to countries as wide ranging as the USA, Taiwan and Saudi Arabia. Camel meat and other products are also becoming increasingly popular and there's an abattoir in Alice Springs. Camel milk keeps for six months without refrigeration or preservatives, and, unlike dairy herds, camels do not require supplementary feeding to maintain milk supply and quality. Camel hides are also tanned in Alice Springs and a small amount of camel wool is shorn, which makes an excellent insulating, warm fabric.

The camel has evolved to become an efficient desert dweller and no animal of similar size can survive in the arid places where camels range. Camels have a number of adaptations which help them to survive. The metabolic rate is extremely low, mainly because its 60m of intestines (humans have about 7m) allow it to extract nourishment out of little more than dry twigs. Digestion is aided by rumination, the process of regurgitating food for further chewing once indigestible substances, such as cellulose, have been destroyed by bacteria in the gut.

Camels also pass very little urine, with virtually all the moisture being reabsorbed into the body. Urine is also recycled by the kidneys and used to digest salty food and synthesise proteins. Other water-saving measures are the membrane in the nasal cavity which prevents moisture loss during exhalation, and the thick coat of hair which insulates the body and prevents sweating. When a human starts to dehydrate, the blood thickens rapidly and loses volume, reducing its ability to cool the body and stressing the heart. A 12% loss of body weight through dehydration is enough to kill a human. A camel can lose up to 40% of its body weight before it suffers unduly, mainly because it can use moisture from stores such as muscle tissue and digestive juices before taking it from the bloodstream.

But the most famous of the camel's attributes is the hump – a fat store which can be drawn on in times of scarcity. It also helps in cooling the body as it shields the vital organs from the sun's heat and, because all the fat is concentrated in one place, heat is able to dissipate through the skin in other parts of the body.

Yet another feature of these remarkable animals is the ability to absorb heat during the day and dissipate it at night. Daytime body temperatures can rise as high as 41°C, while at night they can drop to 34°C – fluctuations which would kill a human.

Camels reach maturity at around seven years, although they can start to reproduce a couple of years before that. In good conditions females calve every two to three years until the age of about 20. The mating season lasts from about August to November. Gestation ranges from 12½ to 14 months, depending on conditions.

BARROW CREEK

Historic Barrow Creek sits next to the Stuart Hwy where it passes through a dramatic gap in the Watt Range about 70km north of Central Mount Stuart. It's the site of one of the few surviving Overland Telegraph Stations and has one of the quirkier outback pub-roadhouses along the Track.

About 30km to the north are the signposted ruins of an army staging camp from WWII.

History

The area around what was to become Barrow Creek was the home of the Kaytetye Aboriginal people, and two trees near the blacksmith's shop at the telegraph station are registered sacred sites.

John McDouall Stuart led the first white expedition through the area and named the creek after a South Australian journalist and politician, John Henry Barrow. The opening of the Overland Telegraph Line saw the establishment of a fort-like telegraph station in 1872.

In February 1874 the telegraph station, under stationmaster James Stapleton, was attacked by a group of Kaytetye men. Stapleton and a linesman were killed, and their graves are close to the station. The attack came as something of a surprise as Stapleton had adopted a fairly enlightened (for the time) approach with the local Aboriginal population, and had provided food for those who were ill. The South Australian government authorised a punitive expedition which led to a two month killing spree and the deaths of at least 50 Aborigines.

Telegraphic operations at the station ceased in 1910, but it was used as a depot until 1980.

The **pub** dates from 1932 and has been providing travellers with refreshments ever since. The walls are adorned with all manner of drawings, cartoons and bank notes – the idea being that you leave a bill and retrieve it next time you pass through.

The WWII **staging camp** of New Barrow, the largest in the Territory, lies signposted 1km east of the highway, about 30km north of Barrow Creek. Although it lies on Neutral Junction Station, the owners don't mind if you wander in for a look at the site, which consists only of concrete foundations and various bits of scrap metal lying around. From 1942 to 1945 the station accommodated up to 1000 troops and equipment travelling up and down the Stuart Hwy. (As it is private property, please leave no trace of your visit and leave gates how you found them.)

Places to Stay

The *Barrow Creek Hotel* (☎ 8956 9753) has twin rooms in dongas for $25 and hotel rooms at $25/35 single/double. A good, filling meal in the dining room will set you back about $8 to $10.

Fuel is available from 7 am to 11.30 pm daily.

Tanami Track

The Tanami Track cuts right through the heart of the Tanami Desert and some of Australia's least populated country. It connects Alice Springs in the Centre with the Kimberley's Halls Creek in the far northwest. Despite the remoteness – or perhaps because of it – the Tanami Track is becoming an increasingly popular route that can save hundreds of kilometres backtracking if you want to visit both the Top End and the Kimberley from Alice Springs. It's also possible to leave the Tanami Track at the Tanami Mine and head north for **Lajamanu** and **Kalkaringi** on the Buchanan Hwy (see the Katherine & Victoria River District chapter for details).

The 1097km track has been much improved in recent years; it's possible to cover it in a well-prepared 2WD vehicle. The Northern Territory section is wide and usually well graded, but between the border and Halls Creek there are some sandy patches which require care – a high-clearance vehicle is advisable. After rain (rare), sections of the track can become impassable.

In the cooler months there is quite a bit of traffic – up to 40 vehicles a day pass through Rabbit Flat – so a breakdown need not cause alarm if you are well prepared with food and water. In summer the heat can be extreme – days where the temperature hits 50°C are not uncommon – so think carefully before setting off at this time.

The Tanami Desert is the traditional homeland of the Walpiri Aboriginal people, and for much of its length the Track passes through Aboriginal land.

Permits are not required for travel on the Tanami Track, although if you want to venture more than 50m either side of the road a permit is required. This does not apply to the settlement of Yuendumu, which lies 2km off the road.

Although it is not compulsory to register with the police at either end of the Tanami Track, remember that travel in this area is no Sunday-school picnic and you should at least notify someone reliable of your travel plans.

The somewhat daunting sign at the junction of the Tanami Track and the Stuart Hwy informs you that it's 703km to the Western Australian border; the first 118km is sealed.

History

The first exploration of the Tanami Desert was undertaken by the surveyor and explorer AC Gregory in 1855. His party headed south from the Victoria River to what is now Lajamanu, then headed west until they came to a dry watercourse near the present WA/NT border, which Gregory named Sturt Creek, after the explorer. He followed the creek south-west to a lake south-west of Balgo, which he humbly named after himself, before returning to his Victoria River base.

The first white man to cross the desert was probably the pioneering cattle driver Nat Buchanan who crossed from Tennant Creek to Sturt Creek in 1896. See the boxed text in the Katherine and Victoria River District chapter.

Allan Davidson was the first white to explore the Tanami Desert in any detail. In 1900 he set out looking for gold and mapped likely looking areas. Gold was discovered at a couple of sites and for a few years there was a flurry of activity as hopefuls came in search of a fortune. The extremely harsh conditions and small finds deterred all but the most determined, and there were never more than a couple of hundred miners in the Tanami. The biggest finds were at Tanami and The Granites;

after many years of inactivity the latter was reopened in 1986 and is still being mined today. The Tanami Mine closed in 1994.

Pastoral activity has always been precarious, although some areas can support grazing. Suplejack ('soo-pull-jack') Downs and Tanami Downs, respectively 60km north and south-west of Rabbit Flat, are two that have survived. Suplejack is one of the few pieces of non-Aboriginal land in the Tanami Desert, while Tanami Downs is owned by the Mangkururrta Aboriginal Land Trust.

During the 1920s Michael Terry, a geologist, led a number of expeditions across the northern half of Australia in search of minerals. In 1928 he travelled from Broome, via Halls Creek (Old Halls Creek today) down to Tanami and then south-east to Alice Springs. His book *Hidden Wealth and Hiding People* recounts his adventures and describes life for the prospectors and Aboriginal people at the time.

TILMOUTH WELL

Napperby Station straddles the Tanami Track and its roadhouse, Tilmouth Well, sits on the banks of the (usually) dry Napperby Creek. This is the first watering hole along the track, 167km after leaving the Stuart Hwy. Visitors can take various tours on the property, including a six hour 'bore run' for $30, or you can follow a mud map to watch the sunset from Stuart Bluff for $20 per person.

Places to Stay

The modern *Tilmouth Well Roadhouse* (☎ 8956 8777) has camp sites for $10 and cabins at $50 for singles or doubles. There's also a restaurant, bar and takeaway food. The roadhouse is open daily from 7 am to 9 pm.

YUENDUMU

• pop 740   ✉ 0872

The turn-off to the Aboriginal community of Yuendumu, which lies 2km north of the track, is 289km from the Stuart Hwy. Visitors are welcome to buy fuel or provisions from the store, but permits are required to visit elsewhere and alcohol is prohibited.

The community also has a medical centre (☎ 8956 4030) and a police station (☎ 8956 4004).

Yuendumu has a thriving art community, and the work put out by the Warlukurlangi artists is highly regarded. However, it's not possible to visit the artists without a permit.

Every year on the long weekend in August the town becomes the centre of a major sporting and cultural festival for Aboriginal people from all over this region called the Yuendumu Festival. Visitors are welcome and no permits are required to visit the town over this weekend, although you will need your own camping gear.

Facilities

The *Yuendumu Store* (☎ 8956 4006) has fuel and a fairly well stocked supermarket. It's open on weekdays from 8.30 am to 5 pm, and on Saturday from 9 am to 12 pm.

The other option here is the *Yuendumu Mining Company* store (☎ 8956 4040). It is also well stocked and has fuel. Opening hours are Monday to Saturday from 9 am to 2 pm and 3 to 5 pm, and on Sunday from 1 to 5 pm.

THE GRANITES GOLD MINE

Just before the new gold mine of The Granites, 256km north-west of Yuendumu, a low rocky outcrop on the left of the road and a couple of old ruins can be seen. These are worth exploring as they are the original buildings dating back to the workings during the 1930s.

A rough vehicle track winds up to the top of the hill, about 500m from the road. It's best to leave the vehicle here and from this vantage point the new mine can be seen away to the west.

If you wander down the southern flank of the hill, you can see older relics, the most important of which is an excellent old ore stamper, or battery. The site has long been picked over for small relics, but it is still worth stopping and soaking up the atmosphere of this place. What the old miners went through is vastly different to what the present workers experience, flying in and out from Alice Springs on their weekly shift.

The Granites mine site was first pegged in 1927. The returns were small, with a yield of only about 1000 ounces per year, and the mine operated only until 1947. In 1986 it reopened and production is currently running at around 170,000 ounces of gold per year.

RABBIT FLAT

It's just 48km from The Granites to the most famous place in the Tanami, the Rabbit Flat Roadhouse, 1km or so north of the track. It's certainly not an attractive place – just a couple of breeze-block buildings and a few fuel tanks – but it's the social centre of the Tanami, not least because it's the only place for hundreds of kilometres where Aboriginal people can buy a drink. On Friday and Saturday nights it can get pretty lively with all the workers in from the mines.

Places to Stay

The quirky *Rabbit Flat Roadhouse* (☎ 8956 8744) stocks fuel, basic provisions and beer, and there's a bar. It's opening hours are 7 am to 10 pm, but be warned – the roadhouse is closed on Tuesday, Wednesday and Thursday, and business is conducted on a cash-only basis.

It's also possible to camp here, and there's no charge for this. You'd be advised to ring ahead to make sure it's open anyway. Fuel prices at Rabbit Flat are infamous – up to $1.25 a litre when this book was researched!

For road information on the rest of the Track to Halls Creek, phone the Halls Creek police (☎ 9168 6000).

RABBIT FLAT TO HALLS CREEK (WA)

From Rabbit Flat the track continues northwest for 44km to the now-defunct **Tanami Mine**. There is no public access to the mine site and there are no tourist services.

Just 1km or so past the Tanami Mine is the **Lajamanu Rd** turn-off which heads north (see the following section). After the turn-off, the Tanami Track swings west to the Western Australia border and beyond. The route between the Tanami Mine and **Billiluna Aboriginal Community** was established in the

The Rabbit Flat roadhouse, social centre of the Tanami

1960s by Father McGuire from what was then the Balgo Aboriginal Mission.

It is 78km from the Rabbit Flat roadhouse to the border, and another 86km will see you at the junction of the road to **Balgo Aboriginal Community**, nearly 40km to the south.

From the Balgo turn-off it's 73km to Billiluna along a stretch which is sandy in places and where low clearance vehicles could get stuck. You can usually get fuel here, and further up this stretch you'll pass the turn-off to **Wolfe Creek Meteorite Crater**, the second largest of its type in the world.

The major T-intersection with Hwy 1 is just 16km south-west of Halls Creek and all its facilities.

LAJAMANU RD

The Lajamanu Rd heads north off the Tanami Track at the Tanami Mine, although it's not even marked on many maps. It's generally kept in good condition, although it gets sandy towards Lajamanu, and there are numerous creek-bed crossings and the occasional washout. Even so, it is negotiable in dry conditions by a 2WD vehicle with care.

The road offers an interesting alternative to the Tanami Track and takes you through country that has very little tourist traffic. It passes through the Central Desert Aboriginal Land and the Lajamanu Aboriginal Land. A permit is not required to traverse the road, or to get fuel and supplies at Lajamanu.

From the Tanami Mine it's 231km to **Lajamanu**, and the trip takes around four hours. The road goes through some very pretty countryside, especially around Suplejack Downs Station, and is generally more interesting than the Tanami Track itself. See the Katherine & Victoria River District chapter for details of Lajamanu and further north.

Plenty Hwy

Leaving the Stuart Hwy 70km north of Alice Springs, the 742km long Plenty Hwy spears across a semi-arid plain and terminates at Boulia in western Queensland. This is very remote country and even in winter you can drive the entire route and see fewer than a dozen vehicles. Facilities are almost non-existent, there are none whatsoever in the final 456km to Boulia, so you must be self-sufficient in everything and have a fuel range of at least 500km.

The first 103km from the Stuart Hwy are sealed, but after that the road can be extremely rough and corrugated; large bull-dust holes usually pose a hazard on the Queensland side, which is not so well maintained and is often more like a track than a road. Once past the bitumen, the highway is suitable for use only in dry weather and is definitely not recommended for caravans. Fuel is available at the Gemtree (140km from Alice Springs), Atitjere Aboriginal Community (215km), Jervois Homestead (356km) and Boulia (812km).

Before setting out on the road, check conditions with the Boulia Shire Office (☎ 07-4746 3188) or the Alice Springs police (☎ 8951 8888).

History

The disappearance of the German explorer Ludwig Leichhardt and his large, well-equipped party is one of Australia's great unsolved mysteries. Leichhardt vanished somewhere in the interior on his final expedition, in 1846, and it's possible that he crossed the area of the Plenty Hwy while attempting to return to civilisation. The evidence that this actually happened is largely based on the discovery of marked trees in central Australia and far west Queensland.

In 1886 the surveyor David Lindsay, of Ruby Gap fame, found trees in the Harts Range that had been carved with Leichhardt's distinctive mark. Many years later, more trees bearing similar marks were discovered along the Georgina River on Glenormiston Station. Also of interest is the fact that the bones of several unknown whites had been found by a waterhole near Birdsville in the early 1870s, before the area was settled.

Henry Barclay was one of the next white men on the scene. In 1878, while carrying out a trigonometric survey from Alice Springs to the Queensland border, he was north-east of the Harts Range when he was faced with a critical water shortage. He dug into a sandy riverbed – this being the usual method of finding water in dry outback rivers – and found ample supplies of the precious fluid flowing beneath the surface. That is how the Plenty River got its name, and it's why the present beef road, which was first upgraded from a two-wheel track during the 1960s, is called the Plenty Hwy.

THE GEMTREE

70km from the Stuart Hwy you come to The Gemtree Caravan Park, on the gum-lined banks of Gillen Creek. This is the only tourist facility of note on the Plenty Hwy. Guests can take a fossicking tour and search for zircons 10km away at the **Mud Tank zircon field**. There are also garnet deposits about 3km from the roadhouse.

For a reasonable $40 you can take a tag-along trip to the park's zircon deposit (equipment provided) and get some practical experience with an expert. The top 80cm of soil conceals zircons of various colours (including yellow, light brown, pink and purple), ranging in size from small chips to large crystals. Provided they put their backs into it, even novices have an excellent chance of finding gem material with nothing more complicated than a shovel, a couple of small sieves and some water in a drum. If you find anything worth faceting, the caravan park's gem-cutter can turn your find into a beautiful stone ready to be set in gold or silver.

The zircon field and one or two of the garnet deposits can be reached by conventional vehicles (driven with care), provided it hasn't been raining. Don't forget that fossicking is illegal unless you hold a permit – it can be obtained at the Department of Mines & Energy office in Hartley Street, Alice Springs.

Places to Stay

The *Gemtree Caravan Park* (☎ *8956 9855*) offers good shade, a kiosk, fuel and a range of accommodation options. On-site caravans cost $37 for two people, while powered/unpowered sites cost $17/14. Bush camping (with access to shower and toilet facilities) costs $6 per person. Air-con budget cabins with fridge and stove cost $46 for singles or doubles plus $9 for each extra adult.

The store is open seven days a week from 8 am to 6 pm and serves takeaways. There are no facilities at the gem fields.

Games of paddymelon bowls, with tea and damper to follow, provide some light entertainment on Saturday night in the cooler months.

HARTS RANGE

The Harts Range starts at Ongeva Creek and is one of Australia's premier fossicking areas. It yields a host of interesting gems and minerals, including mica, smoky and rose quartz, aquamarine, black and green tourmaline, sphene, garnet, sunstone, ruby, iolite and kyanite. Among the many magnificent stones found here is the world's largest known specimen of sphene. However, the area is extremely rugged and the best fossicking spots are quite hard to get to – high-clearance 4WD vehicles are required for most tracks. It's essential to carry plenty of water at all times.

High ridges and mountains keep you company for the next 40km to the **Harts Range police station** (☎ 8956 9772). The two police officers based here have the awesome task of preserving law and order over a sparsely populated area of 120,000 sq km. Apart from constant travel, they do everything from investigating murders to issuing driving licences. By all accounts they're kept busy controlling revellers during the annual Harts Range Races, which take place over the first weekend in August. This is a good weekend's entertainment, with a barbecue and bush dance on the Saturday night, but you need to get there early to find a camp site handy to the action.

Facilities

There's no accommodation in Harts Range, but the *Atitjere Community Store* (☎ 8956 9773) sells fuel, basic food requirements and cold drinks. Aboriginal art and interesting gemstones from the nearby Harts Range are usually on sale. The store is open between 9 am and noon and 3 to 5 pm Monday to Friday and from 9 am to noon on Saturday.

In a medical emergency contact the Atitjere clinic (☎ 8956 9778).

JERVOIS

The road is wide and formed all the way from Harts Range to the border, but it can still be quite rough, depending on when it was last graded. The first 50km is extremely scenic, with attractive tall woodlands of

Bitter and poisonous paddymelons are used as a purge – and for the occasional game of bowls.

whitewood and weeping ironwood fronting the rugged Harts Range to the south. Later only flat-topped hills, scattered low ranges and occasional, beautiful gum-lined creeks break the monotony of the endless plain.

About 130km east of Harts Range you reach Jervois Station (☎ 8956 6307), where you can buy snacks and fuel during daylight hours. Just inside the homestead access road between the highway and the first gate (about 1km in) there's a camping area with barbecues and water. Shower and toilet facilities are available at the homestead. The many magnificent ghost gums growing along the nearby Marshall River make a beautiful setting for a bush camp.

For something different, you can inspect the huge rocket-proof shelter that was built at the homestead during the 1960s, when Blue Streak rockets were fired in this direction from Woomera in South Australia. Instead of huddling inside as they were supposed to, the stationfolk preferred to stand on top to watch the fireworks.

JERVOIS TO BOULIA (QLD)

The highlight of this section is right beside the road, 50km past the turn-off to Jervois Homestead. Here a conical **termite mound** nearly 5m high and 3m thick towers above the surrounding sea of stunted mallees and spinifex – it's an extraordinary sight. The mound is the highest point around, and the white splashes on top tell you that it's a favourite perch for hawks. You pass similar termite mounds in the next 10km but few of these surpass 2m.

At the Queensland border, the road changes its name and becomes known as the Donohue Hwy. Crossing the border grid, you'll also usually notice a dramatic change in road conditions – the Boulia Shire does its best, but it only takes a few road trains to break the surface and form deep bulldust holes.

At 118km from the border you come to the **Georgina River**, and other than the vast expanses of empty space, this waterway is the highlight on the Queensland section of the highway. The main channel features

shady coolabahs, good camp sites and abundant birdlife. The crossing is normally dry, but any flooding causes it to be closed until conditions improve – which can take many days.

Just 8km from **Boulia** you meet the bitumen and joyous relief from the bulldust and corrugations. This isolated township has a good range of facilities, including a hospital, police station, post office, hotel, caravan park, two garages and a café.

Sandover Hwy

Leaving the Plenty Hwy 27km east of the Stuart Hwy, the Sandover Hwy heads northeast across flat semi-desert for 552km to terminate at Lake Nash Homestead, near the Queensland border. Getting its name from the Sandover River, whose course it follows for about 250km, this long, wide ribbon of red dirt is an excellent short cut for adventurous travellers wishing to drive between central Australia and north-west Queensland. The highway offers a memorable experience in remote touring.

Road conditions depend to a great extent on the weather: prolonged rain creates bogs that can keep the highway closed for days. In the late 1980s the road was closed to all traffic for several months after exceptionally heavy rains caused long sections to be washed away. Although often rough, the road is normally suitable for conventional vehicles with high ground clearance and heavy-duty suspension.

There are no tourist facilities along the road but you can buy fuel and supplies at the Arlpara Store (180km from the Stuart Hwy) and the Alpurrurulam Aboriginal Community (573km from the Stuart Hwy).

The best sources of current information on road conditions are the Arlpara Store at Utopia and the Alpurrurulam Community Government Council Office (☎ 07-4748 4800) at Lake Nash. In the event of a medical emergency, you can obtain assistance at the Utopia Clinic (☎ 8956 9875) and at clinics at the Ampilatwatja (☎ 8956 9942) and

Alpurrululam (☎ 07-4748 3111) Aboriginal communities.

History

For most of its distance the Sandover Hwy crosses the traditional lands of the Alyawarra Aboriginal people, whose lives until recent times focused on the relatively rich environment of the Sandover River. Whites arrived in Alyawarra country in the 1880s, when Lake Nash and Argadargada Stations were established for sheep and cattle grazing.

The country to the south-west wasn't permanently settled until 40 years later; Ooratippra was the last station to be taken up, being leased in the late 1940s. The loss of food resources and the fouling of precious water by cattle caused bloody conflict between pastoralists and Aboriginal people. The Sandover Massacre of the 1920s resulted in the deaths of about 100 Alyawarra, who were either shot or poisoned after committing the grievous crime of cattle-spearing.

Atartinga Station, about 140km north-east of Alice Springs, was taken up by RH (Bob) Purvis in 1920. Known as the Sandover Alligator because of his extraordinary appetite, Purvis was contracted by the government in the late 1920s to sink wells along the newly gazetted Sandover Stock Route, which was intended to link the stations of far western Queensland with the Alice Springs railhead. The stock route was continued through to Lake Nash after the 1940s, when heavy drilling equipment became readily available in central Australia. Nevertheless, the Sandover Hwy was, for the most part, little more than a bush track until the 1970s, when it was upgraded to a standard where it was just suitable for road trains.

UTOPIA

Turning off the Plenty Hwy 27km from the Stuart Hwy, the Sandover crosses a vast, semi-arid plain virtually all the way to the Ammaroo turn-off. This is marginal cattle country – the average station en route has only about 25% useful grazing land. For example, Atartinga covers 2240 sq km but its 1200-head herd is concentrated on about 600 sq km. The spinifex areas along the highway carry billions of termites but only one cow to every 10 sq km.

At 127km from the Plenty Hwy you cross the western boundary of Utopia Station. Purchased by the federal government in 1976 for local Aboriginal people, the station is home to about 700 Alyawarra people, who live in 20 small outstations scattered over an area of 2500 sq km. These communities are governed by a council based at Arlparra, which you pass 27km further on. The fence 23km past Arlparra marks the boundary between Utopia and Ammaroo Stations. Almost all the minor roads that turn off the highway between the two fences lead in to Aboriginal communities and are off-limits to the travelling public.

Facilities

The *Arlparra store* (☎ 8956 9910) mainly serves the Aboriginal communities of that area. It sells fuel, and has a mini-supermarket and takeaways. The store is open from 9 am to 5 pm Monday to Friday and from 9 am to noon on Saturday.

LAKE NASH

It's 317km past Ammaroo that you see the glittering iron roofs of the **Alpurrurulam Aboriginal Community** come into view on the left. The end of the highway is just five minutes away, at Lake Nash Homestead. The largest of the Sandover's stations, Lake Nash covers 13,000 sq km and carries, on average, a herd of 41,000 high-quality Santa Gertrudis beef cattle.

Everything about Lake Nash is big: it has the world's largest commercial herd of Santa Gertrudis, the property's bore runs are so long that the vehicles assigned to them travel a total of 96,000km per year, and the average paddock covers several hundred sq km. The station's workforce of 80 is also huge by local standards.

The Sandover Hwy ends at Lake Nash Homestead, where you have a choice of three routes: north to Camooweal (183km), east to Mount Isa (205km) or south to Uran-dangi (172km). All are minor dirt roads, and as they include black clay soil sections, they become impassable after rain. When dry, they are normally suitable for conventional vehicles in the hands of experienced out-back motorists.

Caution must be exercised, as signpost-ing is poor throughout and available maps seldom show the roads' true positions. If in doubt, the best approach is to fill up with fuel at Alpurrurulam and ask for directions and an update on road conditions – if the people at the store can't help, ask at the council office across the road.

Facilities

The *community store* sells fuel and basic food requirements, and there's a garage for vehicle repairs (including tyres). The store is open from 8 to 11 am and 3 to 5 pm Mon-day to Friday and from 8 to 11 am on Sat-urday. Although visitors are welcome to use the commercial facilities, which are right at the entrance to Alpurrurulam, you should not proceed further into the community.

Alice Springs

• pop 25,520   ✉ **0870**

In its brief 125 year history, the Alice, as it's usually known, has gone from a simple telegraph station on the Overland Telegraph Line (OTL) to a modern town. While it is the country's biggest and most isolated outback town, outwardly it has little of the frontier atmosphere which many people expect to find. With the tourist boom of the last decade, most of the old buildings have made way for modern shopping plazas, hotels and offices, and the new sprawling suburbs are as unappealing as those in any Australian city.

But the outback is still only a stone's throw away, as are some of the country's most spectacular natural wonders, and the town has a unique atmosphere which is a major draw for travellers.

For many visitors the Alice is a place to relax and replenish supplies after a number of days on the road. It's tempting to rush off to the many surrounding attractions, but it's worth spending a few days to seek out the reminders of the Centre's pioneering days. A visit to places such as the Royal Flying Doctor Base can help you grasp what the Alice means to the people of central Australia.

HISTORY

The Alice Springs area is the traditional home of the Arrernte Aboriginal people, and to them it is Mparntwe. For them the heart of the area is the junction of the Charles (Anthelke Ulpeye) and Todd (Lhere Mparntwe) rivers, just north of Anzac Hill. All the topographical features of the town were formed by the creative ancestral beings – known as the Yeperenye, Ntyarlke and Utnerrengatye caterpillars – as they crawled across the landscape from Emily Gap (Anthwerrke), in the MacDonnell Ranges south-east of town. Alice Springs today still has a sizeable Aboriginal community with strong links to the area.

The European history of Alice Springs begins with the Overland Telegraph Line in

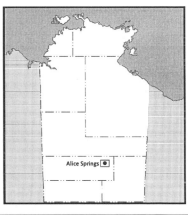

ALICE SPRINGS

1871. It was originally a staging point on the line, and a telegraph repeater station was built near a permanent waterhole in the otherwise dry Todd River. The river was named after Charles Todd, Superintendent of Telegraphs in Adelaide, and a spring near the waterhole was named after Alice, his wife.

The taking up of pastoral leases in the Centre, combined with the rush of miners who flocked to the gold and 'ruby' fields to the east, led to the establishment of Stuart in

255

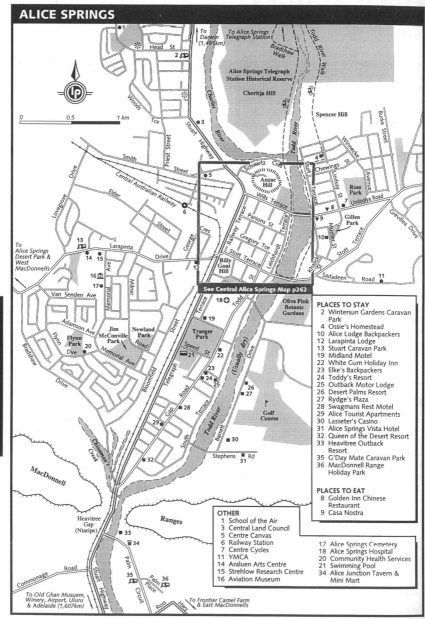

ALICE SPRINGS

0   0.5   1 km

To Darwin (1,491km)

To Alice Springs Telegraph Station

Bradshaw Walk

Head St

Woods Tce

Stuart Highway

Charles River

Alice Springs Telegraph Station Historical Reserve

Choritja Hill

Spencer Hill

Burke Street

Winnecke St

Todd River Walk

Smith Street

Priest Street

Central Australian Railway

Elder Street

Lovegrove Drive

Drive

Schwartz Cres

Anzac Hill

Wills Terrace

Chewings St

Lindsay St

Avenue

Ross Park

Undoolya Road

Gillen Park

Grevillea Drive

Stuart Terrace

To Alice Springs Desert Park & West MacDonnells

Larapinta Drive

George Street

Cres

Railway Terrace

Parsons St

Gregory Tce

Stott Terrace

Leichhardt Terrace

Terrace

Mueller St

Stott Terrace

Khalick St

Sadadeen Road

Milner Ave

Van Senden Ave

Adamson Ave

Flynn Park

Jim McConville Park

Newland Park

Bloomfield Street

Telegraph Road

Memorial Ave

Bradshaw Drive

Flynn Dve

Billy Goat Hill

See Central Alice Springs Map p262

Olive Pink Botanic Gardens

Terrace

Traeger Park

Speed St

Gap Road

South Terrace

Todd River (Usually dry)

Golf Course

Barrett Drive

Stephens Rd

MacDonnell

Chinaman's Creek

Heavitree Gap (Ntaripe)

Ranges

Palm Circuit

Commonage Road

Stuart Highway

Ross Hwy

Palm Place

To Old Ghan Museum, Winery, Airport, Uluru & Adelaide (1,607km)

To Frontier Camel Farm & East MacDonnells

ALICE SPRINGS

PLACES TO STAY
2 Wintersun Gardens Caravan Park
4 Ossie's Homestead
10 Alice Lodge Backpackers
12 Larapinta Lodge
13 Stuart Caravan Park
19 Midland Motel
22 White Gum Holiday Inn
23 Elke's Backpackers
24 Toddy's Resort
25 Outback Motor Lodge
26 Desert Palms Resort
27 Rydge's Plaza
28 Swagmans Rest Motel
29 Alice Tourist Apartments
30 Lasseter's Casino
31 Alice Springs Vista Hotel
32 Queen of the Desert Resort
33 Heavitree Outback Resort
35 G'Day Mate Caravan Park
36 MacDonnell Range Holiday Park

PLACES TO EAT
8 Golden Inn Chinese Restaurant
9 Casa Nostra

OTHER
1 School of the Air
3 Central Land Council
5 Centre Canvas
6 Railway Station
7 Centre Cycles
11 YMCA
14 Araluen Arts Centre
15 Strehlow Research Centre
16 Aviation Museum
17 Alice Springs Cemetery
18 Alice Springs Hospital
20 Community Health Services
21 Swimming Pool
34 Alice Junction Tavern & Mini Mart

1888, a few kilometres south of the telegraph station. The expectation was that the town would grow quickly, especially as it was announced in 1890 that the railway line from the south was to extend all the way to Stuart.

Unfortunately the gold finds didn't amount to much, the rubies turned out to be worthless garnets and the railway took another 40 years to reach the town. The first pub, the Stuart Arms, was built in 1889, and within five years there were just three stores, a butcher and a handful of houses. Ten years later, the adventurous JJ Murif, who was cycling across Australia from north to south, described the town as: 'Sleepy Hollow ... all shade, silence and tranquillity'.

When the railway finally reached Stuart in 1929 the white population stood at about 30, but by the time the name was officially changed to Alice Springs in 1933, this had grown to around 400. By the late 1930s the town had a hospital and a gaol, and a population of around 1000.

In WWII Alice Springs became a major military base and the administrative centre of the Northern Territory. It was the Army's northern railhead, arsenal and troop reserve. The Darwin Overland Maintenance Force (DOMF) was based in Alice Springs and numbered around 8000 troops, and something like 200,000 troops passed through on their way to or from the Top End. Many of the town's residents were actually classified as 'unessential' or 'undesirable' by the Army area commander and were shipped south. It was during WWII that Alice Springs was first connected to anywhere by a sealed road – the Stuart Hwy north to Darwin was tarred to hasten troop movements.

After the war Alice Springs settled back into a period of slow but steady growth. The 1950s saw the beginnings of the Centre's vital tourism industry, which has played a lead role in the prosperity of the town ever since. The final boost to the Alice came with the sealing of the Stuart Hwy from Port Augusta in 1987, and the Centre is now visited by almost half a million tourists each year.

CLIMATE

Summer days in Alice Springs can get very hot (up to 45°C) and even winter days are pretty warm. However, winter nights can freeze and a lot of people get caught off guard. In winter (June and July), you can feel the heat disappear five minutes after the sun goes down and the average minimum nightly temperature is 4°C. Despite the Alice's dry climate and low annual rainfall, the occasional rains, which usually fall in summer, can be heavy and the Todd River may flood – this happened in 1993 and 1995, forcing the cancellation of the Henley-on-Todd Regatta (see the Special Events section).

ORIENTATION

Alice Springs has one of the most dramatic locations of any inland town in the country. The MacDonnell Ranges form the southern boundary of the town, and the only access from the south is through the narrow Heavitree Gap (Ntaripe in Arrernte), named by OTL surveyor and discoverer of Alice Springs, William Mills, after his former school in Devon. The (usually dry) Todd River and the Stuart Hwy both run roughly north-south through the town.

The centre of town is a conveniently compact area just five streets wide, bounded by the river on one side and the highway on the other. Anzac Hill forms the northern boundary to the central area while Stuart Terrace is the southern end. Many of the places to stay and virtually all of the places to eat are in this central rectangle.

Todd St is the main shopping street of the town; from Wills Terrace to Gregory Terrace it is a pedestrian mall.

Greyhound Pioneer buses pull in at the corner of Gregory and Railway Terraces; McCafferty's is opposite the CATIA office on Gregory Terrace. The railway station is close to the centre, on the western side of the Stuart Hwy in the town's light industrial area. The airport is 15km south of town through the Gap and close to the Stuart Hwy.

Larapinta Drive is the main road heading west, and west of the city centre there are a number of places worth visiting – the Alice Springs Desert Park, Araluen Arts Centre, Strehlow Research Centre, Aviation Museum and cemetery. To the east of the Todd River are some of the town's newer suburbs, and the more upmarket accommodation and casino.

INFORMATION
Tourist Offices

The Central Australian Tourism Industry Association (CATIA) office (☎ 8952 5800) is on Gregory Terrace, across from McCafferty's in the centre of town. The staff here are helpful and have a large range of brochures and maps. The office is open weekdays from 8.30 am to 5.30 pm, and on weekends from 9 am to 4 pm. This office issues permits to travel on the Mereenie Loop Rd in the West MacDonnell Ranges.

Parks & Wildlife (☎ 8951 8211) has a desk at the CATIA office, with a comprehensive range of brochures on all the parks and reserves in the Centre.

There's an information desk at the airport that's open during normal business hours and at weekends.

The *Centralian Advocate* is the Alice Springs twice-weekly newspaper, and it's often a good source of info. The *Aboriginal Independent* is a fortnightly paper that covers Aboriginal issues Territory-wide.

Alice has an established gay and lesbian community; for information on social activities and support phone ☎ 8953 2844.

Money

There's a bureau de change near the corner of Todd St and Gregory Terrace. It's open daily from 8 am to 10 pm and charges commission on a percentage basis (and therefore is better for changing small amounts).

Major banks and ATMs can be found in the Todd St Mall.

Post & Communications

The main post office is on Hartley St and there's a post restante counter down the passage at the left hand side. There's a row of public phones outside and more telephones are lined up outside Melanka's on Todd St (see Places to Stay).

Internet and email access is available at some of the backpackers hostels (Melanka's Internet Café charges $2 for 15 minutes and is open from 9 am to 9 pm) and at the Alice Springs Library, where the cost is $2 for 30 minutes.

Useful Organisations

The Department of Lands, Planning & Environment office (☎ 8951 5344) on Gregory Terrace is a good source for maps.

The Automobile Association of the Northern Territory (AANT; ☎ 8953 1322), at 58 Sargent St (heading north out of town) should be able to advise on road conditions if you're travelling to remote areas.

For fossicking permits and information, the Department of Mines & Energy (☎ 8951 5658) has its office in Minerals House on Hartley St, across from the Diplomat Hotel.

The Alice Springs Library (☎ 8952 2303) is centrally located at the council offices on Todd St south of the Mall.

Permits to visit Aboriginal land are issued by the Central Land Council (☎ 8951 6211, fax 8953 4345) at 31-33 Stuart Hwy, north of the town centre.

The Arid Lands Environment Centre (☎ 8952 2497), 1st floor, Fan Lane (off Todd Mall) is a non-profit organisation which can advise on both local and national environmental issues.

Bookshops

Alice has a couple of good bookshops. The Aranta Gallery on Todd St just south of the Mall is one, and there's a branch of the Dymocks chain in the Alice Plaza.

Other Shops

Photographic There are several 'instant' film processing labs in the Todd St Mall. Major brands of slide and print film are readily available.

Camping Gear Alice Springs Disposals (☎ 8952 5701) is a small shop packed with a wide range of gear. It is in the small Reg

Harris Lane, which runs off the southern end of the Todd St Mall.

For locally made good quality swags, try Centre Canvas (☎ 8952 2453) on Smith St, west of the centre.

Bicycle Sales & Repairs Centre Cycles (☎ 8953 2966) at 14 Lindsay St, across the river east of the centre, has a good range and also does short and long-term hire (see the Getting Around section for details).

Medical & Emergency Services

For medical problems and emergencies these are the agencies to contact:

Police
    For emergency police assistance ☎ 8951 8888 or ☎ 000
Ambulance
    For ambulance service the number is ☎ 8951 6633, or simply ☎ 000.
Medical Treatment
    For emergency medical treatment phone the Alice Springs Hospital on ☎ 8951 7777. The hospital is on Gap Rd a short distance south of the town centre.
Chemist
    For prescription services the Alice Springs Amcal Chemist (☎ 8953 0089), in the Alice Plaza, is open from 7.30 am to 10.30 pm every day.
Counselling
    Lifeline Crisis Line (☎ toll-free 1800 019 116); AIDS Council of Central Australia (☎ 8953 1118); Sexual Assault Referral Counsellor (☎ 8951 5880).
Disabled Organisations
    For information on services for the disabled, contact the Disabled Services Bureau (☎ 8951 6722) at the Community Health Centre on Flynn Drive, south of the Araluen Arts Centre.

ANZAC HILL

The best place to get an overview of the town is from Anzac Hill, at the northern end of Todd St. You can make the short, sharp ascent to the top on foot, or there's vehicle access from the western side. Aboriginal people call the hill Untyeyetweleye (pronounced Onjeea-toolia), the site of the Corkwood Dreaming, the story of a woman who lived alone on the hill. The Two Sisters ancestral beings (Arrweketye therre) are also associated with the hill.

From the top of the hill you have a fine view over modern Alice Springs and down to the MacDonnell Ranges. At the western edge of the ranges is **Mt Gillen**, named after an explorer and naturalist. In Arrernte lore it is Alhekulyele, the nose of the wild dog creator where it lay down after an extended battle with an intruding dog from another area.

On the southern edge of the town centre you can see the small rise of **Billy Goat Hill** (Akeyulerra). Here the Two Sisters Dreaming passed on their way north through the area and the hill is now a registered sacred site.

At the foot of Anzac Hill is the RSL Club and **War Museum**, which features a collection of firearms, medals and photos of Alice during WWII. The museum is open daily from 10 am.

HISTORIC BUILDINGS

Although much of the town centre consists of modern buildings, there are still a surprising number of survivors from the old days.

Adelaide House

Right in the centre of the Todd St Mall is Adelaide House, the first hospital in Central Australia. Built in the 1920s as the Australian Inland Mission hospital, it was designed by the Reverend John Flynn and built of local stone and timber carted from Oodnadatta in South Australia. Flynn incorporated into its design an ingenious cooling system which pushed cool air from the cellar up into the building. When a government hospital was opened in 1939, the building became a convalescent home for women.

Today it houses the **John Flynn Memorial Museum**, which displays photographs and implements of the pioneering medical work undertaken in remote areas. At the rear of the building stands a small hut which once housed the radio where electrical engineer and inventor of the famous 'pedal radio', Alfred Traeger, and Flynn ran transmission tests of Traeger's new invention. (See the boxed text for more information.)

Alfred Traeger & the Pedal Radio

In the 1920s communication with isolated outback stations was a major problem. The Reverend John Flynn of the Inland Mission invited Alfred Traeger, an electrical engineer and inventor from Adelaide who for some years had been playing around with radio transmitters, to come to the Centre and test out some radio equipment.

Outpost transmitters were set up at Hermannsburg and Arltunga, putting both places in instant contact with the radio at the Inland Mission in the Alice. But the equipment was cumbersome and relied on heavy copper-oxide batteries that were impractical for use in the bush. Flynn employed Traeger to solve the problem, and he eventually came up with a radio set which used bicycle pedals to drive the generator.

Flynn commissioned Traeger to manufacture 10 similar sets, and these were installed in Queensland with a base at Cloncurry. Within a few years sets had been installed in numerous locations throughout the Territory, still using the Cloncurry base. The Alice Springs station officially started operation in April 1939.

Traeger's pedal sets revolutionised communications in the outback and by the late 1930s (before which Morse code only was used) voice communication had become the norm. Long after the pedal radios became obsolete, the two-way radios were often still referred to as 'the pedal'.

Traeger was awarded an OBE in 1944 and died in Adelaide in 1980.

It's open from 10 am to 4 pm Monday to Friday, and from 10 am to 12 noon on Saturday. Admission is $3 (students $2) and includes a cup of tea or coffee.

Flynn, who was the founding flying doctor, is also commemorated by the **John Flynn Memorial Church** next door.

Stuart Town Gaol

Hidden on Parsons St in the shadow of a modern building is the old gaol, the oldest surviving building in Alice Springs. It was built from 1907 to 1908 with locally quarried stone and had its first guests in 1909. Most of the early inmates were Aboriginal men whose usual crime was killing cattle, but plenty of white offenders were committed as well, for crimes ranging from horse theft to passing dud cheques. The last two prisoners were interned in 1938 for the heinous crime of travelling on the *Ghan* without a ticket!

The building was used as a gaol until a new one (now the Alice Springs Gaol) was built south of Billy Goat Hill in 1939. Redevelopment of the town centre in the 1970s threatened the building, but it was spared, largely

thanks to the efforts of Doreen Braitling (see Wycliffe Well in the Barkly Region chapter). She managed to arouse enough public interest to save the building, and these days it is owned by the National Trust.

It's open Monday to Friday from 10 am to 12.30 pm and Saturday from 9.30 am to 12 noon; admission costs $2.

Old Courthouse

On the corner of Parsons and Hartley Sts, this building was constructed in 1928 as the office of the administrator of Central Australia (as the area was known from 1927 to 1931). During the 1930s it was used as the local court, and it served this function until 1980. These days it houses the fledgling **National Pioneer Women's Hall of Fame**, which aims to document the exploits and achievements of pioneer women all over Australia. Currently there's an interesting photographic display.

It is open daily from 10 am to 2 pm, although it may be closed in summer on hot, quiet days; admission is by donation and for $5 you can 'buy a brick' in the proposed permanent exhibition space for the Hall of Fame.

The Residency

The low, wide-roofed building across the road from the courthouse was built as the home of the Government Resident of Central Australia between 1926 and 1931. In 1963 it served as digs for a Royal Visit and the twin bathrooms refitted for HM The Queen and the Duke of Edinburgh have been preserved for posterity.

There are a few historic photos on display inside, but the building mainly speaks for itself and is beautifully preserved. It is open from 9 am to 4 pm weekdays and 10 am to 4 pm on weekends, although it is often closed during lunchtime.

Hartley St School

Down Hartley St, on the other side of the post office from the Residency, is the old Hartley St School. The core of the building was built in the late 1920s, but additions were made in the 1940s. By the 1950s there were more than 400 students at the school, and it was also the School of the Air studio. The Hartley St School building was used until 1965 and since 1988 has been the National Trust office (☎ 8952 4516). Inside is a small classroom as it once was.

The school is open from Monday to Friday from 10.30 am to 2.30 pm; admission is free.

Tuncks Store

On the corner of Hartley St and Stott Terrace is the verandahed Tuncks Store. It was built in 1939 and managed by Ralph Tuncks until it closed in 1979. The verandah overhanging the footpath was a common feature of early Alice Springs shops; this is the last to survive.

Pioneer Theatre

Near the corner of Parsons St and Leichhardt Terrace, the old Pioneer Theatre is a former open-air, walk-in cinema dating from 1942. The cinema's owner, 'Snow' Kenna, opened a drive-in cinema in 1965 and this was the beginning of the end for the Pioneer Cinema; the coming of TV in 1972 was the real end. These days the cinema is a very comfortable YHA hostel.

Totem Theatre

During WWII up to 8000 troops of the DOMF camped by what is now Anzac Oval, between Anzac Hill and the Todd River. All that remains of this once substantial camp are two Sidney Williams huts which were part of the camp's first-aid post. They now serve as the Totem Theatre, the base for the Alice Springs Theatre Group for the last 30-odd years.

ROYAL FLYING DOCTOR SERVICE BASE

The RFDS base is close to the town centre in Stuart Terrace. It was established in 1939, largely with funds raised by the Women's Centenary Council of South Australia. A small museum here offers some interesting insights into the problems faced by many people isolated in central Australia.

Now that most stations have telephones, the RFDS radio-telephone service is not the vital link it once was. However, it still operates over-the-air routine medical clinics to isolated communities, with radio diagnosis by a doctor. It is also still the best way for vehicles travelling in remote areas to keep in touch.

The base (☎ 8952 1129) is open Monday to Saturday from 9 am to 4 pm, and on Sunday from 1 to 4 pm. Tours begin every half hour and last 30 minutes, including a 10 minute video. The cost is $3 (children $1).

SCHOOL OF THE AIR

The School of the Air (☎ 8951 6834), which broadcasts school lessons by HF radio to children living in the outback, is on Head St, about 1km north of the centre. This was the first school of its type in Australia; it serves an area of 1.3 million sq km and reaches about 140 children on remote stations, roadhouses, Aboriginal communities and national parks. During school terms you can hear a live broadcast (depending on class schedules).

The school is open from 8.30 am to 4.30 pm Monday to Saturday and 1.30 to 4.30 pm Sunday. Admission is $3 (children $2).

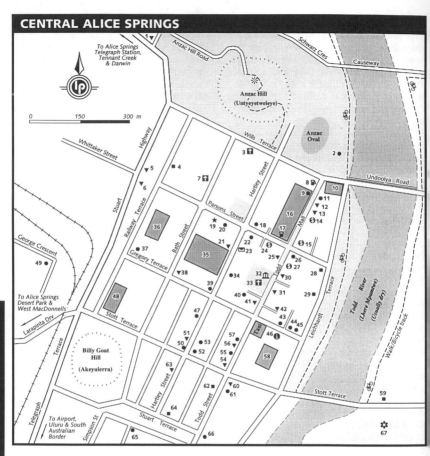

CENTRAL ALICE SPRINGS

AVIATION MUSEUM OF CENTRAL AUSTRALIA

This interesting little museum is housed in the former Connellan hangar on Memorial Ave, where the town's airport used to be. A small adjoining building houses the wreck of the *Kookaburra*, a two-man plane that went down in the desert in 1929. It's not all tragedy, however. There are exhibits on pioneer aviation in the Territory and, of course, the famous Royal Flying Doctor Service – that's Flynn's old plane out the front.

The museum is open Monday to Friday from 9 am to 5 pm and weekends from 10 am to 5 pm; admission is free.

STREHLOW RESEARCH CENTRE

This building on Larapinta Drive, close to the Araluen Arts Centre, is partly constructed of a massive rammed-earth wall. The centre (☎ 8951 8000), commemorates the work of Professor Strehlow among the Arrernte people of the district (see the Hermannsburg Mission section in the MacDonnell & James

CENTRAL ALICE SPRINGS

PLACES TO STAY
4   Desert Rose Inn
10   Todd Tavern
28   Pioneer YHA Hostel
29   Territory Inn
59   Alice Springs Pacific Resort
62   Melanka's Backpackers
64   Stuart Lodge

PLACES TO EAT
1   Hungry Jacks
5   Red Rooster
6   McDonalds
12   Al Fresco's
13   Oscar's
17   Stuart Arms Hotel
21   Hong Kong Chinese
      Restaurant
25   Puccini's Restaurant
30   Red Ochre Grill
31   Scotty's Tavern
38   Pizza Hut
41   Red Dog, La Cafetiere
      & Red Rock Cafe
42   Cafe Mediterranean Bar
      Doppio & Camel's Crossing
      Mexican Restaurant

51   The Overlander Steakhouse
54   KFC
56   Bojangles Restaurant
60   Dingo's Café
63   Oriental Gourmet
      Restaurant

OTHER
2   Totem Theatre
3   Catholic Church
7   Anglican Church
8   Shell Service Station
9   Bi-Lo Supermarket
11   Cinema
14   Westpac
15   ANZ Bank
16   Alice Plaza
18   Old Courthouse
19   Police Station
20   Stuart Gaol
22   The Residency
23   Main Post Office
24   Commonwealth Bank
26   Qantas
27   National Bank
32   Adelaide House
33   Flynn Church

34   Hartley St School
35   Yeperenye Shopping
      Centre
36   Coles supermarket
37   Greyhound Pioneer
39   Avis
40   Alice Springs Disposals
43   McCafferty's
44   Airport Shuttle Bus
45   Maps NT
46   CATIA (Tourist Office)
47   Minerals House
48   K-Mart
49   Pioneer Cemetery
50   Hertz & Tuncks Store
52   Territory Thrifty Car
      Rental
53   Panorama Guth
55   Aboriginal Art & Culture
      Centre
57   Papunya Tula Artists
58   Library & Council Offices
61   CAAMA Shop
65   Royal Flying Doctor
      Services
66   Budget Rent a Car
67   Olive Pink Botanic Gardens

ALICE SPRINGS

Ranges chapter) and houses the most comprehensive collection of Aboriginal spirit items in the country. These were entrusted to Strehlow for safekeeping by the Arrernte people years ago when they realised their traditional life was under threat. Unfortunately, these items cannot be viewed by an uninitiated male or *any* female, and are kept in a vault in the centre. However, there is a very good multimedia display to see on the works of Strehlow and on the Arrernte people.

The centre is open daily from 10 am to 5 pm; entry is $4.

MUSEUM OF CENTRAL AUSTRALIA

Housed in the Strehlow Research Centre building, the Museum of Central Australia (☎ 8951 5532) has a fascinating collection, including some superb natural history exhibits, an interesting exhibition on meteorites (including the Henbury meteorites)

and exhibits on Aboriginal culture. The museum is open Monday to Friday from 9 am to 5 pm and admission is $5.

ARALUEN CENTRE FOR ARTS & ENTERTAINMENT

The Araluen Arts Centre (☎ 8952 5022), on Larapinta Drive next to the Strehlow Centre, is the town's performing arts centre and there's often something on (see the Entertainment section).

The stained-glass windows in the foyer are the centrepiece of the centre. The largest window features the Honey-Ant Dreaming (a popular central Australian theme) and was designed by local artist Wenten Rubuntja. Other windows were designed by Aboriginal students at a local college. A large painting by Clifford Possum Tjapaltjarri was commissioned for the centre and is reproduced on the outside eastern wall.

The main interest to visitors is a small gallery which includes paintings by Albert

Namatjira, members of the Arrernte community and Rex Batterbee, the European man who first introduced the young Namatjira to watercolour painting.

The centre is open daily from 10 to 5pm. Entry to the Namatjira gallery is $2.

ALICE SPRINGS CEMETERY

Adjacent to the aviation museum is the town cemetery, which contains the graves of a number of prominent locals.

The most famous grave is that of Albert Namatjira – it's the sandstone one on the far side. This interesting headstone was erected in 1994, and features a terracotta tile mural of three of Namatjira's Dreaming sites in the MacDonnell Ranges. The glazes forming the mural design were painted on by Namatjira's granddaughter, Elaine, and the other work was done by other members of the Hermannsburg Potters.

Other graves in the cemetery include that of Harold Lasseter, who perished in 1931 while trying to rediscover the rich gold reef, 'Lasseter's Reef', he found west of Ayers Rock 20 years earlier, and the anthropologist Olive Pink, who spent many years working with the Aboriginal people of the central deserts. A number of Afghan cameleers are also buried here, facing Mecca.

The cemetery is open from sunrise to sunset daily.

PIONEER CEMETERY

This is the original cemetery, and today it lies almost forgotten and rarely visited in the light-industrial area on the western side of the railway line on George Crescent. The gravestones here tell some of the stories of the original settlers – including that of the young man who died of 'foul air'.

ALICE SPRINGS DESERT PARK

About 3km out of town along Larapinta Drive, the Desert Park (☎ 8951 8788) is a superb wildlife park built at the foot of the MacDonnell Ranges. The 1300 hectare park features the ecosystems of central Australia and their traditional relationship with Abo-

riginal people through walk-through enclosures, state-of-the-art interpretive displays and superb graphics.

It's best to kick off your tour with the 20 minute film (shown on the hour between 8 am and 5 pm) then take the 1.6km walking track through the major exhibits. The unique and endangered plants and animals of Central Australia are a highlight of the park and gems such as bilbies, mala, kowari and carnivorous ghost bats can be seen. There are **walk-through aviaries** housing desert parrots such as the magnificent princess parrot, and a brilliant **nocturnal house** with a great assortment of creatures you wouldn't have a hope of seeing otherwise. Free-flying birds of prey are exhibited daily and ranger talks are held at various exhibits throughout the day.

There's a cafeteria and a la carte restaurant (see Places to Eat).

Alice Springs Desert Park is open every day from 7.30 am to 6 pm. Admission is $12/30 per adult/family. Allow at least three hours to get the most out of the park.

Getting to and from the park is a problem if you don't have your own transport. The cheapest way to get there is by bike, but Desert Park Transfers (☎ 8952 4667) operates during park hours and does the return trip for $20 (students and children $14) including park entrance fee.

PANORAMA GUTH

Panorama Guth (☎ 8952 2013), at 65 Hartley St in the town centre, is a large, indoor, circular painted panorama which depicts most of the points of interest around the Centre. It's an exercise in high kitsch, really, although it has a saccharine charm. The artist responsible, Henk Guth, also paints doe-eyed women with large breasts, if you like that sort of thing, but the real reason to come here is to see his extensive collection of Aboriginal artefacts and other relics of outback life.

Panorama Guth is open Monday to Saturday from 9 am to 5 pm and Sunday from 2 to 5 pm; admission is $3.

TELEGRAPH STATION HISTORICAL RESERVE

This 450 hectare reserve lies 2km north of town by the Todd River, and it encloses the best-preserved telegraph station of any of the original 12 which were built along the line in the 1870s.

Laying the telegraph line across the dry, harsh centre of Australia was no easy task, as the small museum at the old telegraph station shows. The station was constructed of local stone and continued in operation until 1932.

The station was also the original site of the settlement of Alice Springs until the town of Stuart was established to the south. As the post office (opened in 1878) was at Alice Springs there was much confusion over the names, and so when the post office moved to Stuart in 1932 the town's name was officially changed to Alice Springs.

The buildings have been faithfully restored, and you get a good idea what life was like for the small community here, which consisted of the stationmaster and his family, four linesmen/telegraph operators, a cook, a blacksmith and a governess.

The original **Alice Springs** (which is in fact only a waterhole), is nearby and a nice spot for a cooling dip. There's also a grassy picnic area by the station with barbecues, tables and some gum trees – a popular spot on weekends. A number of walking tracks radiate from the reserve.

Guided tours operate hourly between 8.30 am and 4.30 pm (phone ☎ 8952 3993 to confirm times); there's also an informative self-guiding map. A free slide show is held three times weekly at 7.30 pm – check with Parks & Wildlife for details.

The station is open 8 am to 7 pm daily in winter and until 9 pm in summer; entry costs $4.

It's easy to walk or ride to the station from the Alice – just follow the path north along the riverbank; it takes about half an hour to ride. It's signposted to the right off the Stuart Hwy about 1km north of Anzac Hill.

The station also marks the start of the **Larapinta Trail**, a trail for bushwalkers which heads out west through the MacDonnell Ranges (see the MacDonnell & James Ranges chapter for details).

OLIVE PINK BOTANIC GARDEN

Just across the Todd River from the centre, the 16 hectare Olive Pink Botanic Garden has a fine collection of the native shrubs and trees found within a 500km radius of Alice Springs. There's a rammed earth visitors centre which explains the evolution and ecology of arid-zone plants, their traditional use by Aboriginal people, and the life of the garden's founder, prominent central Australian anthropologist and botanical artist Olive Pink.

The garden is open from 10 am to 6 pm and entry is free. The entrance is on Tuncks Rd at the southern end of the garden.

FRONTIER CAMEL FARM

About 5km along Palm Circuit, south of Heavitree Gap, is the Frontier Camel Farm (☎ 8953 0444), where you can ride one of the beasts. These strange 'ships of the

TELEGRAPH STATION

Walking track to Trig Hill & Cemetery

Walking track to Simpson's Gap (Larapinta Trail Stage 1)

Buggy Shed & Store

Battery Room

Historic Precinct

Barracks

Entrance

Exit Station Master's Kitchen

Post & Telegraph Office

Blacksmith

Evaporation Tank

Alice Springs Waterhole

Station Master's Residence

To Car Park

Todd River (usually dry)

Walking track to Alice Springs

ALICE SPRINGS

desert', guided by their Afghani masters, were the main form of transport before the railways were built. There's a museum with displays about camels, and a guided tour and camel ride is held daily at 10.30 am (and 2 pm April to October).

Also here is the **Arid Australian Reptile House**, which has an excellent collection of snakes and lizards. The farm is open daily from 9 am to 5 pm. The cost of the camel tour is $10 (children $5) including a visit to the reptile house.

OLD *GHAN* TRAIN & MUSEUM

At the MacDonnell siding, about 10km south of Alice Springs along the Stuart Hwy, a group of local railway enthusiasts have restored a collection of *Ghan* locomotives and carriages on a stretch of disused siding from the old narrow-gauge *Ghan* railway track. You can wander round the equipment and learn more about this extraordinary railway line. A 1930s style railway station, reconstructed from plans originally intended for the Alice, houses railway memorabilia and historical photos, and serves as an information centre.

The museum (☎ 8955 5047) is open from 9 am to 5 pm daily during the cooler months (phone for opening hours during summer). Admission is $4 (children $2.50).

There are also trips on the old *Ghan* on Wednesday, Friday and Sunday in winter to Mt Ertiva siding, 9km south of town. The trip starts at 10 am, takes 1½ hours and costs $13 (children $7.50), including entry to both the museums. On select Sundays during the cooler months it also runs to Ewaninga (adults $23/children $13).

MacDonnell siding is on the Alice Wanderer bus route (see Getting Around later in this chapter) and can be reached by bicycle.

ROAD TRANSPORT HALL OF FAME

The Road Transport Hall of Fame (☎ 8952 7161) is housed in two gigantic sheds a short walk past the Old *Ghan* Museum. It has a fine collection of old vehicles, including some very early road trains, vintage and veteran cars, and other transport memorabilia. Many are superbly restored and this is a motor vehicle buff's delight. The Hall of Fame is open daily from 9 am to 5 pm; admission is $4/9 per adult/family. Access is via a gate next to the Old *Ghan* Museum.

CHATEAU HORNSBY

The Territory's only winery, Chateau Hornsby (☎ 8955 5133) was established in 1972 and is a few kilometres south of Alice Springs along the Stuart Hwy. Most of the wine is sold to people intrigued by the novelty of a central Australian wine. It's a nice setting and free tastings, light meals and morning and afternoon teas are available. Sunday afternoon jazz sessions are a popular excursion from town.

Chateau Hornsby is open daily from 9 am to 5 pm. The jazz concerts are ususally held between 1 and 4 pm (6 and 9 pm in summer) and entry costs $3.

The turn off to the Chateau is 8km south of Heavitree Gap then 5km along Colonel Rose Drive. You could pedal there, but the easier option is to take the Alice Wanderer.

ACTIVITIES
Swimming

Almost without exception, all places to stay have a swimming pool, although these vary greatly in size. The council swimming centre on Speed St, just south of the town centre, is open from September to April.

Cycling

Alice is a flat town which lends itself to getting around by bicycle, and there are a number of marked bike tracks. An excellent track leads up from town along the Todd River to the Old Telegraph Station and you can ride to Simpsons Gap along a designated track. Be sure to carry plenty of water whenever you go cycling. See the Getting Around section for information on bike hire.

Steve's Mountain Bike Tours (☎ 8952 1542) offers short trips through the MacDonnell Ranges near town costing from $30 for an easy hour to $85 for four to five hours for experienced riders.

Golf

The Alice Springs Golf Club (☎ 8952 5440) is on Cromwell Drive east of the river.

Indoor Abseiling & Rockclimbing

At the YMCA (☎ 8952 5666), east of the river on Sadadeen Rd, there's an indoor climbing gym. Climbing costs $6, or $4 if you have your own equipment. The rock wall is open from 6 to 8 pm Monday to Thursday and 3 to 4.30 pm Sunday.

Abseiling is available by appointment.

Horse Riding

Ossie's Outback Horse Treks (☎ toll-free 1800 628 211) operates a variety of trail rides to suit all levels of experience. Three-hour morning, afternoon or sunset nature trail rides cost $65 per person including snacks and water; an all-day ride including barbecue lunch and billy tea costs $125; and an overnight ride, sleeping in a swag under the stars, costs $175. Longer tours are also available.

Camel Rides

Camel treks are another central Australian attraction. You can have a short ride for a few dollars at the Frontier Camel Farm (☎ 8953 0444), or take the longer Todd River Ramble, which is a one hour ride along the bed of the Todd River ($45, children $25).

Camel Outback Safaris (☎ 8956 0925), based at Stuart's Well 90km south of Alice Springs, also operates camel tours (see The South-East chapter).

Hot-Air Ballooning

Sunrise balloon trips are also popular and cost from $110 (children $55) for a 30 minute flight or $120 including breakfast. One-hour flights cost around $170 ($80) with breakfast, or you can just tag along as part of the chase crew for $35 ($25) or so.

Operators include Outback Ballooning (☎ toll-free 1800 809 790), Ballooning Downunder (☎ toll-free 1800 801 601) and Spinifex Ballooning (☎ toll-free 1800 677 893), which operates from Chateau Hornsby.

ORGANISED TOURS

The CATIA office can tell you about all sorts of organised tours from Alice Springs and every place to stay has a tour desk. Among the usual big-name operators and a host of small local operators you can choose from bus tours, 4WD tours, camel tours and even balloon tours. There's plenty of choice so shop around.

Note that although many of the tours don't operate daily, there is at least one trip a day to one or more of the major attractions: Uluru-Kata Tjuta National Park (Ayers Rock & the Olgas), Kings Canyon, Palm Valley, both the West and East MacDonnell Ranges, Simpsons Gap and Standley Chasm. Tours to less popular places, such as Rainbow Valley and Chambers Pillar, operate less frequently.

Most of the tours follow similar routes and you see much the same on them all; things like level of service and degree of luxury will determine the cost. All the hostels can book tours and should know exactly which company is offering the best deals.

Town Tours

Alice Wanderer Mini Town Tours (☎ toll-free 1800 669 111) can whizz you around some of the town's major sights in three hours for $60 including admission fees. The tours depart daily at 9 am and 2 pm, and you are collected from your accommodation. Check their brochure for details, but some options are not good value because they offer a ride to places within a few minutes walk of town with free entry anyway!

Aboriginal Culture Tours

Rod Steinert (☎ toll-free 679 418) operates the popular $69 (children $34.50) Dreamtime & Bushtucker Tour. It's a three hour trip in which you meet some Warlpiri Aboriginal people and learn a little about their traditional life. There are demonstrations of weapons and foods and samples of barbecued witchetty grubs. While this is basically a good tour, it caters for large bus groups and so can be impersonal. You can do the same tour with your own vehicle for $59 ($29.50).

ALICE SPRINGS

Oak Valley Day Tours (☎ 8956 0959) is an Aboriginal-owned and run organisation that makes day trips to Mpwellare and Oak Valley, both of cultural significance to Aboriginal people. The cost is $110 and this includes a barbecue lunch. Trips to Ewaninga and Rainbow Valley are also possible.

Visual Arts & Specialist Tours (VAST; ☎ 8952 8233) is a small company that specialises in taking small groups to remote Aboriginal communities and rock art sites that are otherwise inaccessible. The cost is $1200 per group per day (one to nine people), including permits, camping equipment and meals. Check out its Website at www.VAST.com.au.

Tours Farther Afield

MacDonnell Ranges Jim's Bush Tours (☎ 8952 5305) offers good-value day tours to the East and West MacDonnells. Itineraries vary, but the emphasis is on less driving and more time walking. A day tour costs $55 ($49 for YHA/VIP holders), although you must bring your own lunch.

Full day 4WD tours to Finke Gorge are run daily in winter by AAT King's (☎ 8952 1700) for $89 including lunch.

Uluru/Kings Canyon Several operators run two and three-day and longer tours that take in the Rock, Olgas with or without Kings Canyon and other sights such as the West MacDonnells. A two day trip is squeezing things a bit, but you'll certainly *see* most sights, even if that's the extent of your experience.

If your time is limited, Day Tours (☎ 8953 4664) will get you to the Rock and back for $140, including lunch and viewing the sunset.

Sahara Outback Tours (☎ 8953 0881) offers very good daily camping trips to the Rock and elsewhere and these are popular with backpackers. It charges $220 for a two day trip to Uluru-Kata Tjuta, or you can pay an extra $100 and spend an extra day taking in Kings Canyon – well worthwhile if you have the time. Its five day camping safari ($520) does the above three day trip plus

two days taking in many of the features of the West MacDonnells. Northern Territory Adventure Tours (☎ toll-free 1800 063 838) offers similar trips and fares.

There are plenty of other operators.

4WD Tours

The Outback Experience (☎ 8953 2666) has day trips from Alice Springs to Chambers Pillar and Rainbow Valley for $135 per person including lunch.

Austour (☎ toll-free 1800 335 009) offers a variety of tours that take in Uluru-Kata Tjuta, Kings Canyon and the MacDonnells, with 'soft options' such as hotel accommodation en route. One possibility is to tag along in your own vehicle on a five day camping safari; the cost for this is $475 per person if you have your own camping gear, or $1150 if you want budget accommodation and $1295 for slightly more expensive rooms.

Motorcycle Tours

High on the Hog (☎ toll-free 1800 240 230) is an outfit that offers tours on the back of a Harley-Davidson. A 20 minute tootle around town will set you back $28, and there are 1½ hour, three hour and full day tours to the East or West MacDonnells for $85/175/295.

Air Tours

If your time is really limited you can take a one day air safari to Uluru and back, flying over the West MacDonnells, Kings Canyon and the Olgas en route. The cost of $445 includes a tour around the Rock and Olgas, and park entry fee. Contact Alice Springs Air Charter (☎ 1800 811 240).

Personalised Scenic Flights (☎ 8952 4625) does a similar trip, plus a 90 minute flight over the West MacDonnells ($180) and all day at Kings Canyon for $350. Trips further afield include a flypast of Chambers Pillar and lunch at Old Andado Station for $350, or Old Andado for morning tea then lunch at the Birdsville Pub for $380.

An interesting option is an Outback Mail Flight to remote Aboriginal communities west of Alice with Ngurratjuta Air (☎ 8953

5000). Half day flights depart Tuesday and Thursday and full day flights leave on Wednesday and Friday. The cost is $220 for either option.

SPECIAL EVENTS

No Territory town would be complete without its list of eccentric festivals, and Alice Springs is no exception. Darwin has a race of boats made from beer cans; in Alice the boats have no bottom and the river has no water!

Heritage Week
Held in April, this is the week when the emphasis is on the town's European past. Re-enactments, displays and demonstrations of old skills are all held.

Alice Springs Cup Carnival
The autumn racing carnival takes place throughout April and May, the highlight being the Alice Springs Cup held on the holiday Monday in early May.

Camel Cup
This is one of the biggest events of the year and it's worth being around in early May just for the hell of it, as it's a great day out. It's held in Blatherskite Park, south of the Gap, and in addition to the camel races, there are sideshows, novelty events and lots of drinking.

Bangtail Muster
A parade of floats, also held on the Monday holiday in early May.

Alice Craft Acquisition
Held in May each year at the Araluen Arts Centre, this started out 20 years ago as the craft section of the local Alice Prize. Today it's a highly regarded national exhibition, where pieces are selected from entries to become additions to the Alice Crafts Acquisition Collection. Part of it is displayed at the airport, the rest at the Araluen Centre.

Country Music Festival
While this isn't Tamworth, Territorians give this June festival a bash, and there's plenty of live music and foot-tappin' goin' on, buddy.

Finke Desert Race
This is a motorbike race held on the Queen's Birthday weekend in June. The race takes riders from Alice Springs south the 240km to Finke along unmade roads, and the following day they race back again!

Alice Springs Show
The annual agricultural show, which is held in June, has the usual rides and attractions, as well as displays and events organised by local businesses.

Alice Springs Rodeo
Yep, Alice has one of these too and its held in August. All the usual events are featured including bareback riding, steer wrestling, calf roping and ladies' barrel races.

Henley-on-Todd Regatta
Arguably the Territory's most famous sports event, this boat race without water has been held since 1962. Barefoot crews race bottomless boats down the dry sandy bed of the Todd

Alice Springs' annual Henley-on-Todd Regatta

ALICE SPRINGS

ARABELLA BAMBER

River! It's a very colourful spectacle and worth catching if you're in town.

It is held annually on the 1st Saturday of October. (It was recently moved from January to October as it was washed out twice in the space of five years!)

Verdi Club Beerfest

This is held in early October, at the end of the regatta. It's held at the Verdi Club on Undoolya Rd and there are many frivolous activities including spit the dummy, tug of war, and stein-lifting competitions. Sample a wide range of Australian and imported beers, then fall over.

Corkwood Festival

This annual festival is held on the last Sunday in November. It's basically an arts and crafts festival, but there's also a good deal of music, other live entertainment and food. Craft stalls are the focus during the afternoon, while the evening is capped with a bush dance.

PLACES TO STAY

The Alice has an excellent range of accommodation options, from camping and caravan parks to luxury hotels; the thriving backpackers business is very well catered for. Competition is stiff during the main tourism season and many places combine several styles of accommodation to cater for different budgets.

Places to Stay – Budget

Camping & Caravan Parks None of the Alice Springs caravan parks is really close to the centre, the closest probably being the Stuart, on Larapinta Drive about 3km to the west. All have barbecues, laundry, swimming pool, shop with basic provisions and a swag of tour information; some offer discounts for longer stays and/or reduced rates during the hotter months. Prices quoted here are for two people and include the 5% bed tax.

G'Day Mate Caravan Park (☎ 8952 9589), on Palm Circuit, 600m from the Stuart Hwy has camp sites for $14, powered sites for $16, on-site vans from $38 and en suite cabins from $44.

Heavitree Gap Resort (☎ toll-free 1800 896 119), Palm Circuit, 3km south of town, also charges $14 for camp sites and $16 for powered sites. Economy rooms with bath-room are $45 and self-contained motel units are from $65. This is a huge resort with a bistro, tavern and supermarket.

MacDonnell Range Holiday Park (☎ toll-free 1800 808 373), Palm Place, 4km from town has camp sites for $15, powered sites for $18, basic/en suite cabins for $50/62 and two-bedroom villas from $70.

Stuart Caravan Park (☎ 8952 2547), 3km down Larapinta Drive has camp sites for $14, powered sites for $16.50, on-site vans for $39, budget cabins for $42, en suite cabins for $50 and four-bed deluxe cabins from $60.

Wintersun Gardens Caravan Park (☎ 8952 4080), 3.5km north on the Stuart Hwy; has grassed, shady camp sites for $14, powered sites for $17, on-site vans for $38, budget cabins for $42 and en suite cabins for $58 a single or double.

Hostels All the places catering to backpackers have the usual facilities and services – air-con (and heating!), kitchen and laundry, pool, courtesy bus and travel desk. Some also have bicycle hire and Internet access. VIP/YHA discounts apply and watch out for special offer coupons.

Right in the centre of town, on the corner of Leichhardt Terrace and Parsons St in the old Pioneer outdoor cinema, is the YHA *Pioneer* (☎ 8952 8855). It has 62 beds in air-con dorms, and charges $14 in a four or six-share room and $18 per person for a twin or double; linen hire is $2 extra. It's a spacious, clean and well-kept place offering disabled facilities, a well-appointed kitchen, Internet access, pool table, bike hire and security lockers.

Melanka's Backpackers (☎ toll-free 1800 815 066, 94 Todd St) is a huge place that really packs 'em in. Facilities are a bit cramped, but there's a choice of six or eight-bed dorms at $13, or three and four-bed dorms for $14 per person; twin-shares are $16 per person and singles cost $30. An adjoining block has single/double/triple motel rooms for $71.40/78.75/89.25 (tax included). There's a cafeteria with budget meals, an Internet café, bike hire and Rattle 'n'Hum nightclub, one of the most popular travellers drinking spots in the Alice (see Entertainment).

Further down Todd St, but an easy walk from the centre, *Elke's Backpackers Resort* (☎ toll-free 1800 633 354, 39 Gap Rd) is a comparatively new place. Dorms and all facilities are clean and well-maintained; each dorm has its own bathroom, kitchen and TV; a bed costs $16 ($13 for YHA/VIP members). Budget twin or double rooms with shared kitchen, TV and bathroom cost $45 ($35). Also available are well-appointed self-contained motel rooms costing $90 (plus 5% tax). Elke's also has free breakfast, and bike and tent hire – worth considering if you're heading out to Uluru.

Next door there's *Toddy's Resort* (☎ toll-free 1800 806 240, 41 Gap Rd) which has beds in eight/six/four-bed dorms with shared facilities for $10/12/14. There's also a six-bed dorm with TV and bathroom ($14) and the motel rooms cost from $36 for a budget twin/double to $48 for a twin/double room with all mod cons. Toddy's has email access, a bar and cheap meals.

Over the river, but still close to town, there's the relaxed *Alice Lodge Backpackers* (☎ toll-free 1800 351 925, 4 Mueller St). This is a small, quiet and friendly hostel with a courtyard garden, barbecue, free breakfast and fridges in each room. Nightly rates are $13 in the dorm, $15 in a four-share room and $32 for a double or twin. There's a small kitchen and laundry facilities.

Also on this side of the river is *Ossie's Homestead* (☎ toll-free 1800 628 211, 18 Warburton St), a quiet, friendly place with a small pool, free breakfast and linen, and pet kangaroos. A bed in the 12-bed dorm is $12, or $14 in a four-bed room; private rooms cost $30/32 a single/double. Ossie's organises horse riding treks (see the Organised Tours section).

Places to Stay – Mid-Range

There's no shortage of hotels and motels in Alice; all the caravan parks (see the preceding Camping & Caravan Parks section) also have cabins and/or motel rooms. Tax is included in these prices.

Hotels Right by the river is the *Todd Tavern* (☎ 8952 1255, 1 Todd Mall). This pub gets noisy when there are bands playing on weekends, but it's otherwise quite a reasonable place to stay. Room rates, including a light breakfast, are $39.40 for singles or doubles (with shared bathroom) or $51.70 with en suite.

At the southern end of Gap Rd, just before Heavitree Gap, is the *Queen of the Desert Resort* (☎ toll-free 1800 896 124), a large, more upmarket place about 1km from the centre. A deluxe single/double with bathroom, fridge and TV costs $90/100; a budget room sleeping up to four costs $80. Backpackers are also catered for, although there are no kitchen facilities – a bed in a six-bed dorm costs $13 (no linen) or there's one four-bed dorm for $15 (linen supplied). Facilities include a nightclub and good pool.

Stuart Lodge (☎ toll-free 1800 249 124) on Stuart Terrace is a nicely-placed cheap option run by the YWCA. Singles, twins/doubles and triples with shared bathrooms cost $35, $45 and $50 respectively. It's clean, quiet and well-run; shared facilities include kitchen, laundry, pool and TV rooms, and cheap breakfasts are available.

Apartments & Holiday Flats This is probably the category with the least choice. There are very few apartments and flats for rent; in most cases the best you can do is a motel-type room with limited cooking facilities, which usually consist of an electric fryingpan and a microwave oven.

The *Alice Tourist Apartments* (☎ toll-free 1800 806 142) is on Gap Rd. There's a choice of one or two-room apartments with kitchenette, bathroom and TV. One-room apartments cost $72 a single or double or $78 for three (including tax); the two-room apartments sleep up to six and go for $104 for up to four and $110/115 for five/six people. These places consist of a main room with sleeping, cooking and dining facilities, and the larger flats have a second room with two or four beds. There's a communal guest laundry and the obligatory

ALICE SPRINGS

swimming pool. This is a good option for families.

The *White Gum Holiday Inn (☎ toll-free 1800 896 131, 17 Gap Rd)* , has 20 rooms with kitchen, en suite and phone at $73 a double (tax included).

Another motel-type place with cooking facilities in the rooms is the *Outback Motor Lodge (☎ 8952 3888, 13 South Terrace)*. Rooms can sleep up to four people (one double and two single beds) and cost $75 for two and $95 for four people, plus 5% tax.

On Barrett Drive, next to the Rydge's Plaza hotel, the *Desert Palms Resort (☎ toll-free 1800 678 037)* has spacious bungalow-style rooms, each with kitchenette and en suite, at $79 a single or double and $89 for a triple (including tax). This is a quiet place with a large swimming pool and nicely land-scaped gardens.

Conveniently central is the *Larapinta Lodge (☎ 8952 7255, 3 Larapinta Drive)*, just over the railway line from the town centre. It has singles/doubles for $67/77, with communal kitchen and laundry, and the obligatory swimming pool.

Also close to the centre is the *Desert Rose Inn (☎ toll-free 1800 896 116, 15 Railway Terrace)*. There's a choice of single or twin budget rooms with shared bathroom for $49; comfortable standard singles/doubles with TV, shower and fridge for $80/88; and deluxe rooms with en suite, microwave, fridge and balcony for $105/115. Add 5% tax to all prices.

Motels Alice Springs has a rash of motels, and prices range from around $50 to $100 for a double room, although there are often lower prices and special deals during the hot summer months. Facilities normally in-clude pool, TV, phone, en suite and guest laundry.

There's *The Swagman's Rest Motel (☎ toll-free 1800 089 612, 67 Gap Rd)*, with sin-gles/doubles for $63/73, and close by, the *Midland Motel (☎ toll-free 1800 241 588, 4 Traeger Ave)* is a small but comfortable place with a licensed restaurant and saltwa-ter pool. Singles/doubles cost $65/75 and

economy rooms sleeping up to four people cost $65.

Places to Stay – Top End

Most of Alice's best hotels are on the east-ern side of the river and feature restaurants, bars, pools and shuttle buses to town. Week-end deals and special rates are often avail-able, but add the 5% bed tax to prices.

At the top of the range there's *Rydge's Plaza (☎ toll-free 1800 675 212)*, on Barrett Drive, with rooms from $190 up to $420. The hotel is very well equipped, with facil-ities including heated pool, spa/sauna and tennis courts.

Almost next door is *Lasseter's Casino (☎ toll-free 008 808 975)*, where standard single or double rooms go for $180 and suites cost $230. Facilities include bars, restaurant, complimentary bicycles, cour-tesy bus and of course gaming rooms.

Another top-end option is the *Alice Springs Pacific Resort (☎ toll-free 1800 805 055, 34 Stott Terrace)*, right by the Todd River, not far from the centre of town. Standard rooms here cost $178 and deluxe singles or doubles are $250.

Alice Springs Vista Hotel (☎ toll-free 1800 810 664) is out on Stephens Rd, at the foot of the MacDonnell Ranges. Singles or doubles here go for $110 each.

The only centrally-located posh hotel is the *Territory Inn (☎ 1800 089 644)* on Leich-hardt Terrace facing the Todd River. It offers standard singles or doubles with all mod cons from $120, or $130 for deluxe rooms.

Places to Stay – Around Alice Springs

There are a couple of places to stay in the Alice area which offer an interesting alter-native to staying in Alice Springs itself.

The *Ooraminna Bush Camp (☎ 8953 0170)* is half-an-hour's drive south of town along the road to Maryvale Station and Chambers Pillar. This is a tourism venture run by the owners of Deepwell Station and accommodation is in the 'Pioneer's Suite' – a swag under the stars with shared facilities – for $90 including dinner and breakfast.

There's also the Ooraminna Hut, a traditional wooden hut with open fireplace which can be booked by groups or families. Ooraminna also offers horse trail rides ($65 per day) bushwalking and a half-day 4WD Cattle Station Tour ($60 per person including refreshments). All prices include transfers from Alice Springs.

About 25km north of Alice Springs, **Bond Springs Outback Retreat** (☎ 8952 9888) offers accommodation in a comfortable, traditional homestead; bed and breakfast is $250 a twin or double and a self-contained suite or cottage sleeping up to four costs $200.

PLACES TO EAT
Alice has a reasonable range of eateries, but generally doesn't cater well for early risers or late-night diners.

Budget Dining & Self-Catering
The thriving backpackers market in Alice ensures a cheap meal is usually easy to come by.

Rattle'n'Hum at Melanka's and **Toddy's Backpackers Resort** both have cheap breakfasts and dinners – watch out for backpackers specials and special offer coupons around town.

If you're stocking up for a trip into the wilds, you can experience the joys of several large **supermarkets** around the city centre. All are open seven days; Coles is open 24 hours and the Bi-Lo at the north end of Todd St Mall is generally the cheapest.

Cafes, Snacks & Takeaway
There are numerous places for a sandwich or light snack along the Todd St Mall and in the arcades running off it. Many of them put tables and chairs outside – ideal for breakfast on a cool, sunny morning.

La Cafetiere is at the southern end of the Mall and is open for breakfast, burgers, sandwiches etc. Right next door are the **Red Dog** and **Red Rock Café**, very similar places with tables and umbrellas out on the footpath.

The **Alice Plaza** has a number of lunchtime cafeteria-style eating places serving snacks, light meals, sandwiches and salads. There's another **food court** in the Yeperenye shopping centre on Hartley St.

Territory Tucker (80 Todd St) is a good takeaway joint. There are pies baked on the premises, including roo, camel and emu ($3.50), and novelty takeaways such as roo on a stick ($4.50) or kangaroo tail soup and damper ($4).

And of course Alice Springs has its share of popular takeaway outlets such as **KFC**, **Hungry Jack's**, **Red Rooster**, **McDonald's** and **Pizza Hut**.

Pub & Counter Meals
Far and away the most popular place is the **Pub Caf** at the Todd Tavern. The counter meals are tasty and there are special nights when you can get a meal for $5 to $8.

Scotty's Tavern is a small bar in the Mall that has substantial meals for $12 to $16. Watch out for cheap meal deal coupons around town, where for $6 you can get a burger with fries and a drink.

The **Stuart Arms Hotel**, upstairs at the Alice Plaza, has a bar brunch menu and **Bojangle's** (☎ 8952 2873, 80 Todd St) is a bistro in a colonial-style bar with a good range of hot meals.

Restaurants
Swingers on Gregory Terrace (near the corner of Todd St) is something of an institution in Alice, but although it opens early it's not open for dinner. The food is good and includes filled pita bread, focaccia and treats like curry laksa. There's a big noticeboard here where you can check out what's happening around town.

Café Mediterranean Bar Doppio, in the small Fan Lane off the Mall, opposite the Red Dog café, has an excellent range of health-food dishes. You can BYO and the front window is covered with notices that may be of interest. It's open every day and most dishes cost between $5 and $10.

Next door is the **Camel's Crossing Mexican Restaurant** (☎ 8952 5522), which has a varied menu of both vegetarian and meat dishes. It's open nightly except Sunday, and a two course meal will set you back about $30.

There are a few good Italian options. *Puccini's Restaurant* is on the Mall and claims to be the Territory's most-awarded restaurant. It serves excellent home-made pasta and char-grilled fish but expect to pay around $18 to $20 for a main course.

Across the river from the centre, on the corner of Undoolya Rd and Sturt Terrace, is the *Casa Nostra* (☎ 8953 0930), a long-standing, family run pizza and pasta specialist. It is BYO, open every evening except Sunday and good value.

Good pasta with a choice from 26 sauces, plus a great range of pastries, cakes and gelati can be enjoyed at the licensed *Al Fresco's Café* (☎ 8953 4944), in the cinema complex at the northern end of the Mall. It's open from 10 am daily. Also recommended is *Oscar's* (☎ 8953 0930), next to the cinema complex.

Of course the Alice has to have a steakhouse, and you can try the *Overlander Steakhouse* (☎ 8952 2159, 72 Hartley St). It features 'Territory food' such as emu, crocodile, kangaroo and camel – and the 'Drover's Blowout' ($35) is a carnivore's delight! It's quite popular, although it's not that cheap and main courses are about $17.50 to $25.

Both the Chinese restaurants on Hartley St are said to be good. *Oriental Gourmet*, (☎ 8953 0888) at No 80 is only open in the evening, while the *Hong Kong Chinese Restaurant* (☎ 8952 3873) next to the Yeperenye shopping centre is open in the evening and also for lunch on week days except Tuesday. Also recommended is the bright-yellow *Golden Inn* (☎ 8952 6910, 9 Undoolya Rd), just over the bridge from the centre, where apart from the usual fare you can sample some Malaysian and Szechuan dishes.

Malathi's Restaurant (☎ 8952 1858, 51 Bath St) serves good Asian and Australian dishes – it's open in the evening. *Keller's Swiss & Indian Restaurant* (☎ 8952 3188, Shop 1 & 2, Diplomat Hotel, Gregory Terrace) is a long-standing Alice Springs restaurant with an unusual menu – half Indian, half Swiss! It is licensed and non-smoking until 9.00 pm.

The food is so-so at *Dingo's*, in the historic CWA (Country Wormen's Association) building on the corner of Stott Terrace and Todd St, but you can dine inside or out in a nice garden setting.

For very good upmarket dining in the town centre, the *Red Ochre Grill* (☎ 8952 2066, Todd Mall) features 'creative native cuisine' for breakfast, lunch and dinner. Quality native plants and animals are imaginatively combined in dishes such as wallaby mignons and yam gnocchi; more conventional dishes are also available. Lunch char-grills cost around $19.50 and most main courses at dinner are $17 to $22.

Madigan's (☎ 8955 1122), out at the Alice Springs Desert Park, is another very good restaurant serving native foods. It's open from Tuesday to Sunday for lunch and dinner.

Dining Tours

A few interesting possibilities involve taking a ride out of town, although none could be considered good value and are best experienced for their novelty value.

The Camp Oven Kitchen (☎ 8953 1411) offers substantial bush meals at sunset, consisting of kebabs, then soup, damper, roast beef and vegetables, all cooked in 'camp ovens' – cast-iron pots which are buried in hot coals – followed by golden syrup dumplings. A bush balladeer provides the entertainment. The cost per person is $69, including transfers from your accommodation, but doesn't include alcoholic drinks.

Tuits Old Ghan Bush Kitchen Dinner Tour departs MacDonnell Siding on Friday and Saturday at 7 pm and includes, for $75 per head, a 60 minute ride on the Old Ghan while sipping cheap champagne, a four course bush dinner and star gazing. It's also possible to have the meal without the train ride for $60. Bookings can be made on ☎ 8952 5443.

Take a Camel out to Breakfast/Dinner is another popular dining option. This combines a one hour camel ride with a meal at the Frontier Camel Farm (☎ 8953 0444). The cost is $55 (children $35) for breakfast and $80 ($60) for dinner.

Tailormade Tours (☎ 8952 1731) and Alice Limousine Tours (☎ 8955 5595) both operate evening *bush barbecues* where you head out of town and tuck into a barbecue with all the trimmings, while a minstrel sings Australian folk tunes. If you've never eaten food cooked on an open fire it may be worth the rather hefty price of $75.

ENTERTAINMENT
Pubs, Live Music & Nightclubs
Most backpackers drop into *Rattle'n'Hum* at Melanka's on Todd St – it's a good place for a beer and to meet other travellers, and there are occasionally live bands as well.

The *Todd Tavern*, by the river on the corner of Wills and Leichhardt Terraces, has a jam session from 9 pm on Monday night, which sometimes features better-known bands. Friday night is another popular night (munchies are provided on the bar) and a local band plays most Sunday afternoons.

Other pubs with live music are the *Stuart Arms*, which has something on most nights in its 'authentic' pioneer bar, and *Scotty's Tavern* in the Mall. *Sean's Irish Bar*, in the same building as Malathi's Restaurant (see Places to Eat), is a popular drinking spot with locals and visitors.

For some dance music you could try *Legends* at the Stuart Arms (Thursday, Friday and Saturday) or the *Alice Junction Tavern* on Palm Circuit, which has a disco on Friday and Saturday nights.

Bojangles on Todd St has live music every night and a didgeridoo session on Sunday and Monday nights.

Live Performance
Alice has two long-running and popular shows with an outback flavour.

Local 'character' Ted Egan puts on a performance of tall tales and outback songs four nights a week at *The Settlers* on Palm Circuit. The show costs $15 (students $10). It's popular with tour groups and bookings are advised (☎ 8952 9952).

At 40 Todd St Mall the *Sounds of Starlight Theatre* presents a musical performance evoking the spirit of the outback with a didgeridoo and various Latin American instruments. Performances are held at 7 pm from Tuesday to Saturday between April and November. Bookings can be made through the theatre (☎ 8953 0826), CATIA or the Original Dreamtime Gallery (☎ 8952 8861). It costs $15.

Performers on national tour often appear at the *Araluen Arts Centre* on Larapinta Drive. Bookings can be made at the Araluen booking office (☎ 8953 3111).

Cinema
There's a *cinema complex* at the top end of Todd St showing latest releases. Some nights, usually early in the week, dinner and a film is available at various restaurants around town – inquire at the cinema.

'Art house' films are shown on Sunday at the *Araluen Arts Centre* (☎ 8953 3111).

SHOPPING
There are plenty of shops along Todd St Mall selling souvenirs and Aboriginal arts and crafts including a forest of didgeridoos (an instrument not traditionally played in this part of the Territory). They haven't made into the supermarkets yet, but if you're desperately short of time you can even buy a didgeridoo at the chemist!

Plenty of art galleries and craft centres specialise in Aboriginal creations – if you've got an interest in central Australian art or you're looking for a piece to buy, there are a couple of places where you can buy direct from the artists, such as the Papunya Tula Artists shop, on Todd St just south of the Mall, or Jukurrpa Artists at 35 Gap Rd. Both of these places are owned and run by the art centres which produce the work.

Two of the better commercial outlets for Aboriginal art are Gallery Gondwana and the Original Aboriginal Dreamtime Gallery, both on the Todd St Mall.

The award-winning Aboriginal Art & Culture Centre, 86 Todd St, runs didgeridoo lessons, and has cultural displays and a gallery upstairs with some fine works.

The Central Australian Aboriginal Media Association (CAAMA) has a shop at 101 Todd St, just down from Dingo's, and is another very good outlet with reasonable prices.

GETTING THERE & AWAY
Air
You can fly to Alice Springs with Qantas (☎ 13 1313) or Ansett (☎ 13 1300). Qantas have an office on the Todd St Mall and Parson St intersection. Ansett's office is at the airport.

Both companies connect Alice Springs with Yulara ($187 one way), Cairns ($493), Darwin ($392), Adelaide ($414), Perth ($555), Sydney ($577) and Melbourne ($575). Both also fly to Broome ($498) in WA.

You can also fly direct to Yulara from Adelaide, Sydney, Perth and Cairns. So if you're planning to fly to the Centre and visit Uluru it would be more economical to fly straight to Yulara, then continue to Alice Springs, or vice versa. See the Getting There & Away chapter for more details.

Bus
Greyhound Pioneer (☎ 13 2030), on the corner of Gregory and Railway Terraces, has daily services from Alice Springs to Yulara ($59 one way; 5½ hours), Darwin ($145) and Adelaide ($135). It takes about 20 hours from Alice Springs to Darwin (1481km) or Alice Springs to Adelaide (1543km). You can connect to other places at various points up and down the Track – such as Tennant Creek for Mt Isa and the Queensland coast, Katherine for Western Australia, Erldunda for Uluru and Port Augusta for Perth.

McCafferty's (☎ toll-free 13 1499), at 91 Gregory Terrace, also has daily departures to Adelaide ($135) and Darwin ($145), and connections to Uluru ($55) and Queensland.

Both companies offer passes for visiting Uluru from Alice Springs – see the Uluru-Kata Tjuta chapter for details.

Train
The *Ghan* between Melbourne, Adelaide and Alice Springs is a great way to enter or leave the Territory. There are two services weekly in each direction throughout the year, but it's a popular service, especially during winter.

Bookings are essential (☎ 13 2232) and there's a booking office next to the Ansett office on the Todd St Mall. See the Getting There & Away chapter for fares and times.

Car
The basic thing to remember about getting to Alice Springs is that it's a long way from anywhere, although most main roads are sealed and in good condition. Coming in from Queensland it's 1180km from Mt Isa to Alice Springs or 529km from Three Ways, where the Mt Isa road meets the Darwin to Alice Springs road. Darwin to Alice Springs is 1476km. Even Uluru is over 400km away.

Car Rental All the major hire companies have offices in Alice Springs, and Avis, Budget, Hertz and Territory Thrifty also have counters at the airport where cars can be picked up and dropped off. Prices may drop in the low season and some companies offer stand-by rates.

A conventional (2WD) vehicle will be adequate to get to most sights around Alice, such as Simpsons Gap and Standley Chasm; major firms and local companies offer competitive rates. Local companies are usually cheaper but can't do one-ways.

If you want to go further afield, say to Chambers Pillar and Finke Gorge, a 4WD is essential. Prices depend on size of vehicle and length of hire, and not all companies offer unlimited kilometres. Shop around and ask about stand-by rates.

Avis, Budget, Hertz and Territory Thrifty all have 4WDs for hire. You're looking at around $99 per day for a Suzuki, including insurance and 100km free per day. For a Toyota Landcruiser or similar vehicle the price jumps to around $150 per day, excluding insurance. Discounts apply for longer rentals (more than four to seven days, depending on the company).

Britz: Australia has the biggest range of campervans and motorhomes, and with branches in all major cities one-way rentals are an option. The cost is around $125 per day for unlimited kilometres (excluding insurance).

Comprehensive insurance is a good idea and check the small print for your liabilities – not all vehicles are covered for tyres or windscreen damage. The main care hire places are:

Avis
   (☎ 8953 5533) 52 Hartley St
Britz: Australia
   (☎ 8952 8814) North Stuart Hwy (corner of Power St)
Budget
   (☎ 8952 8899) 10 Gap Rd
Centre Rentals
   (☎ 8952 1405) Shell Service Station, corner of Todd Mall and Willis Terrace
Hertz
   (☎ 8952 2644) 76 Hartley St
Koala Campervan Rentals
   (☎ toll-free 1800 998 029) North Stuart Hwy (corner of Power St)
Outback Auto Rentals
   (☎ 8953 5333) 78 Todd St
Territory Thrifty Car Rentals
   (☎ toll-free 1800 891 125) corner Stott Terrace & Hartley St

GETTING AROUND

Although there is a limited public bus system, Alice Springs is compact enough to get around on foot, and you can reach quite a few of the closer attractions by bicycle. The main exceptions are sights further afield such as the Desert Park and Transport Hall of Fame, for which your cheapest option is to take a taxi. If you want to go further afield you'll have to take a tour or rent a car.

To/From the Airport

The Alice Springs airport is 15km south of the town, about $20 by taxi. There is an airport shuttle bus service (☎ 8953 0310) that meets all flights and takes passengers to all Alice accommodation and to the railway station. It costs $9 one way or $15 return. Most backpacker joints will get you to your flight on time for a similar fee.

Bus

Asbus A local public bus service – Asbus – leaves from outside the Yeperenye shopping centre on Hartley St. There are only four routes and not all places of interest are served, but useful routes are as follows:

West Route (No 1)
   Goes along Larapinta Drive, with a daily detour (Route 1C) for the Strehlow Centre, Araluen Arts Centre and the Aviation Museum. Route 1C leaves at 9.45 am and returns at 3.35 pm.
North Route (No 3)
   Heads north along the Stuart Hwy and passes the School of the Air.
South Route (No 4)
   Runs along Gap Rd – past many of the hotels and hostels – through Heavitree Gap and along Palm Circuit (useful for the southern caravan parks).

Buses run approximately every 1½ hours from 7.45 am to 6 pm on weekdays and Saturday morning only. The fare for a short trip is $2.

Alice Wanderer Starting at Todd St Mall, the Alice Wanderer is a minibus that does a loop around the major sights – Olive Pink Botanic Garden, Frontier Camel Farm, Old *Ghan* Museum and Transport Hall of Fame, Strehlow Research Centre (alight here for the Aviation Museum, Araluen Centre and Cemetery), Old Telegraph Station, School of the Air, Anzac Hill, Panorama Guth and the Royal Flying Doctor Base. You can get on and off wherever you like, and it runs every 70 minutes from 9 am to 4 pm. The cost is $20 for a full day, and if you phone ahead (☎ toll-free 1800 669 111) you can be picked up from your accommodation in time for the 9 am departure.

Alice Mini Bus Another privately-run bus service (☎ 8955 1222) runs short trips between 8 am and midnight which cost $6 for up to five people.

Taxi

A taxi (☎ 131 008 or 8952 1877) to most places near the town centre should cost around $4.

Bicycle

Alice Springs has a few bicycle tracks and a bike is a great way of getting around town and to the closer attractions, particularly in winter.

Several backpackers hostels offer bike hire; typical rates are $8/13 per half/full day.

Centre Cycles (☎ 8953 2966), 14 Lindsay Ave, east of the town centre, has 15-speed mountain bikes for $9/15 per half/full day (including lock, helmet and pump), or longer term it's $50 per week and $130 a month.

Penny Farthing Bike Shop (☎ 8952 4551) on the North Stuart Hwy also do repairs.

MacDonnell & James Ranges

The rugged MacDonnell Ranges form an imposing red barrier from east to west for 400km across the vast central Australian plain, with Alice Springs situated conveniently in the middle. West of the Alice there is some rugged and spectacular scenery, and it is here that many of the features associated with the Centre can be enjoyed – Simpsons Gap, Standley Chasm, Finke Gorge and the awesome Kings Canyon (Watarrka). There is also a rich Aboriginal heritage and some Aboriginal communities worth visiting, such as historic Hermannsburg. Much of the area is preserved in the West Mac-Donnell National Park.

The ranges consist of a series of long, steep-sided, parallel ridges that rise between 100m and 600m above the intervening valley floors. Scattered along the entire length are deep gorges carved by ancient rivers that flowed south into the Simpson Desert. Here also you find the four highest peaks west of the Great Dividing Range: Mt Zeil, the highest, is 1531m above sea level and 900m above the surrounding plain.

Many of the most spectacular landscapes and most important biological areas are now included in national parks and reserves, most of which are readily accessible by conventional vehicle. The largest of these, the 2100 sq km West MacDonnell National Park, stretches 160km from the outskirts of Alice Springs. To the east, a string of generally small parks and reserves lies scattered through the ranges for nearly the same distance. The ranges were explored a number of times by John Mc-Douall Stuart on his various attempts to cross the continent from south to north, and he named the range after the South Australian governor, Sir Richard Mac-Donnell.

A vehicle is virtually essential to get the best out of the MacDonnells. The entire region is accessible by 2WD along good

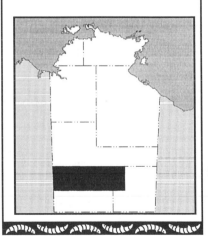

sealed roads or maintained gravel roads, and one could easily spend a week or two walking, relaxing and enjoying the different moods the change of light on the landscape creates at different times of day.

MACDONNELL & JAMES RANGES

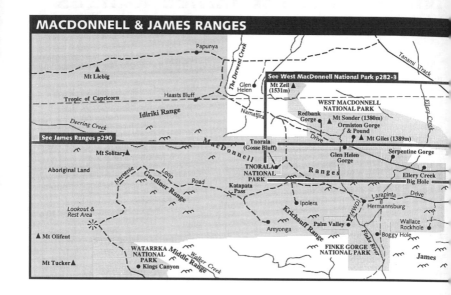

Map labels:
Papunya; Mt Liebig; The Darwent Creek; Glen Helen; Mt Zeil (1531m); Tanami Track; See West MacDonnell National Park p282-3; Haasts Bluff; Tropic of Capricorn; WEST MACDONNELL NATIONAL PARK; Idiriki Range; Namatjira; Redbank Gorge; Mt Sonder (1380m); Ormiston Gorge & Pound; Ellery Creek; Deering Creek; Drive; Mt Giles (1389m); See James Ranges p290; MacDonnell; Tnorala (Gosse Bluff); Glen Helen Gorge; Serpentine Gorge; Mt Solitary; Ranges; Aboriginal Land; Meereenie; Gardiner Range; Loop; Road; TNORALA NATIONAL PARK; Ellery Creek Big Hole; Ellery Creek Drive; Katapata Pass; Ipolera; Larapinta; Drive; Lookout & Rest Area; Krichauff Range; Palm Valley; Hermannsburg; Wallace Rockhole; Areyonga; Boggy Hole; Mt Olifent; Finke River; Mt Tucker; WATARRKA NATIONAL PARK; Middle Range; Walker Creek; FINKE GORGE NATIONAL PARK; James; Kings Canyon

West MacDonnell National Park

The West MacDonnell National Park was proclaimed in the early 1990s and stretches unbroken along the range from the Stuart Hwy just north of Alice Springs to Mt Zeil, 170km to the west. There are a number of spectacular red gorges and several deep waterholes along the way, with all but Standley Chasm located within the park. In dry conditions, all the main attractions along this route are accessible to conventional vehicles. Spearing between high ridges, Larapinta Drive (the road west from Alice Springs) is sealed for the first 135km, to the Finke River crossing near Glen Helen. From here the final 37km past Redbank Gorge to the road between Haasts Bluff and Hermannsburg is rough dirt.

FLORA & FAUNA

Wildlife enthusiasts will be delighted by the chance to observe some of the 167 species of birds, 85 species of reptiles, 23 species of native mammals, five frog species and various fish; a number of the mammals are rare or endangered elsewhere in the arid zone. To the casual observer the wildlife is not immediately apparent. Although it is diverse and at times abundant, its visibility depends on factors such as time of day, proximity to water and time of year.

Although arid, the ranges are covered with a huge variety of plants, including many tall trees, with the majestic ghost gums an outstanding feature. In hidden, moist places are relics of the rainforest flora that covered this region millions of years ago.

Most mammals are nocturnal and shy, although black-footed rock wallabies have become used to visitors at several spots, such as Standley Chasm and Ormiston Gorge. Birds are easier to find, and several colourful species of parrots will probably cross your trail at some point. Look for the plump spinifex pigeons on rocky hillsides and in picnic grounds.

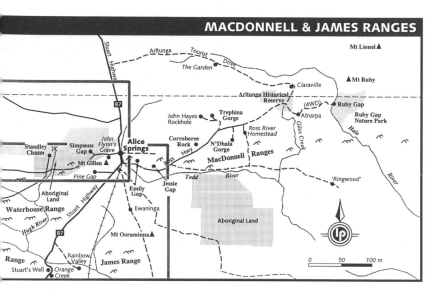

MACDONNELL & JAMES RANGES

INFORMATION

The best place for park information is the Visitor Centre (☎ 8955 0310) at Simpsons Gap, 16km west of Alice Springs, where there are a number of interpretive displays. Advice on road conditions can be obtained here and at Glen Helen. There's another Visitor Centre (☎ 8956 7799) at Ormiston Gorge.

At the main sites of interest throughout the park there are generally excellent information signs and displays.

If you're camping, stock up in Alice Springs, where commodities are a whole lot cheaper, and try to avoid buying fuel at remote places, where it is very expensive.

ACTIVITIES
Bushwalking

The ranges provide ample opportunity for walking and many excellent trails have been laid in the various parks and reserves – see the relevant sections for details.

Anyone attempting an overnight walk is urged to register with the Voluntary Walker Registration Scheme (☎ 1300 650 730). A refundable deposit of $50 is requested (payable by credit card over the phone or cash at CATIA in Alice) to offset the cost of a search should anything go wrong. More information can be obtained from Parks & Wildlife (☎ 8951 8211).

Larapinta Trail The Larapinta Trail is an extended walking track along the backbone of the West MacDonnell Ranges. When finally completed in the next few years, it will offer walkers a 13 stage, 220km trail of varying degrees of difficulty stretching from the telegraph station in Alice Springs to Mt Razorback, beyond Glen Helen. It will then be possible to choose anything from a two day to a two week trek, taking in a selection of the attractions in the West MacDonnells. At the time of writing, the following sections (with length, recommended walking time, and degree of difficulty) were open:

Section 1
Alice Springs Telegraph Station to Simpsons Gap
24km; two days; Class B.

Section 2
  Simpsons Gap to Jay Creek
  23km; two days; Class B.
Section 3
  Jay Creek to Standley Chasm
  14km; eight hours; Class C.
Section 8
  Serpentine Gorge to Inarlanga Pass (Ochre Pits)
  18km; eight hours; Class B.
Section 9
  Inarlanga Pass (Ochre Pits) to Ormiston Gorge
  27km; two days; Class C.
Section 10
  Ormiston Gorge to Glen Helen Gorge
  12.5km; seven hours; Class B.
Section 11
  Glen Helen to Redbank Gorge
  29km; two days; Class C.
Section 12
  Redbank Gorge to Mt Sonder
  16km return; eight hours return; Class C.

Class B trail is defined as being wide, well constructed and suitable for inexperienced walkers. Class C trail is narrow, steep and rough in places, suitable for experienced walkers.

Detailed trail notes and maps ($1 per section) are available from the Parks & Wildlife desk at the CATIA office in Alice Springs, or contact the Parks & Wildlife office (☎ 8951 8211) for further details.

The problem lies in getting to the various trailheads, as there is no public transport out to this area. Jim's Bush Tours (☎ 8953 1975) can pick you up or drop you off for a fee, depending on distance; and Trek Larapinta (☎ toll-free 1800 803 174) offers transport and catering for one-day walks ($95), overnight walks ($160 for one night, $250 for two days/one night) or a three day/two night Mt Sonder special for $350.

Cycling

Simpsons Gap Bicycle Track The 17km sealed cycling path between Flynn's Grave on Larapinta Drive and Simpsons Gap wanders along timbered creek flats and over low rocky hills, with occasional kangaroos to keep you company. There are many bush picnic spots en route, and excellent views of **Mt Gillen**, **Rungutjirba Ridge** and the rugged **Alice Valley**. Flynn's

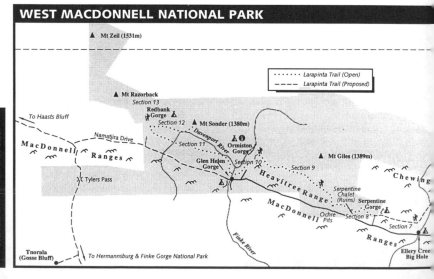

WEST MACDONNELL NATIONAL PARK

Grave is 7km from the town centre, and you do this part along Larapinta Drive. For the best views (not to mention comfort), cycle out in the early morning and return in the afternoon. Carry plenty of drinking water in warm weather as there is none along the way. The one-way trip takes one or two hours, depending on fitness, and is generally easy.

A useful map is available from the Parks & Wildlife counter at CATIA in Alice.

Guided Walks & Talks

During the main tourist season (May to September), Parks & Wildlife rangers conduct a number of excellent activities in the park, and it's well worth making the effort to get along to any which may be on.

The program varies, but may include walks, talks or a slide show – check with Parks & Wildlife for times and locations.

Nature walks are held at the Ochre Pits (Sunday) and Kathleen Springs in Watarrka (Wednesday).

Ranger **talks** are held at Simpsons Gap (four times weekly), Ormiston Gorge (daily), Palm Valley (four times weekly) and Watarrka (weekly); Watarrka also hosts **slide shows** three times weekly.

ORGANISED TOURS

One and two-day tours of the MacDonnell Ranges are very popular and there are numerous operators and styles to choose from – contact CATIA in Alice Springs for details. Costs vary, but as a rule of thumb expect to pay anything up to $100 for a day tour that includes lunch, and about $100 a day for overnight camping trips. Camping safaris often include places such as Palm Valley and Kings Canyon on the itinerary. Discounts often apply during the low season and it's also worth asking about stand-by rates.

Centreman Tours (☎ 8953 2623) has a half-day tour taking in Standley Chasm, Simpsons Gap and Flynn's Grave for $35 and a full-day West MacDonnells trip for $80 including lunch.

Alice Springs Holidays (☎ toll-free 1800 801 401) offers a full-day tour that covers most sights between Simpsons Gap and Ormiston Gorge for $98 including a picnic lunch.

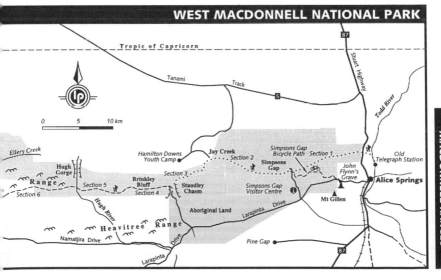

If you have the money, you could do a more leisurely five day tour which also takes in Kings Canyon and Uluru for $525 with NT Adventure Tours (☎ toll-free 1800 063 838) or $545 with Sahara Outback Tours (☎ toll-free 1800 806 240).

FLYNN'S GRAVE

Just outside the eastern boundary of the West MacDonnell National Park, 7km west of Alice Springs along Larapinta Drive, is the grave of Dr John Flynn, founder of the RFDS and the Australian Inland Mission. It's sited on a low rise with ghost gums and a Devil's Marble brought down from Tennant Creek. From here there is a magnificent view of nearby Mt Gillen.

SIMPSONS GAP

The nearest of the West MacDonnells' features to the Alice is Simpsons Gap, 22km to the west along Larapinta Drive. Roe Creek has exploited a fault in the quartzite Rungutjirpa Ridge and gouged a red gorge with towering cliffs. The actual Gap is 7km north of Larapinta Drive.

The area is popular with picnickers and also has some good walks. Early morning and late afternoon are the best times to see the rock wallabies that live among a jumble of huge boulders right in the gap. You might also see dusky grass wrens here – they hop about among the boulders at the Gap like chubby brown fairy-wrens.

There's a good Visitor Centre 1km from the park entrance, with displays on local wildlife; information on road conditions and the Mereenie Loop Rd is also available here. Simpsons Gap is open between 5 am and 8 pm daily.

Ranger talks are given four times a week – inquire at the Parks & Wildlife office for times.

History

To the Arrernte people, Simpsons Gap is known as Rungutjirpa, the home of giant goanna ancestral beings.

During explorations which would eventually lead to the construction of the Overland Telegraph Line, Stuart advised that the line should cross the ranges at a place about 60km west of here, but it was later deemed too rugged and an alternative route was sought. Consequently OTL surveyor, Gilbert McMinn, found the gap in the ranges in 1871, and described it as 'one of the finest pieces of scenery I have met with for a long time ...'.

It's not known who the gap was named after, although it appears on early survey maps as Simpsons Gap.

Bushwalking

There are some pleasant and not too strenuous walks around Simpsons Gap. Starting at the Visitor Centre there's the **Ghost Gum Walk**, a 20 minute loop with information boards describing some of the vegetation of the area, including a beautiful 200 year old ghost gum.

A short track (500m) to the top of **Cassia Hill** gives fine views over the range and Larapinta Valley.

You can also do day walks on the Larapinta Trail – peaceful **Bond Gap** (to the west) and **Wallaby Gap** (to the east) are both worthwhile – or take the Woodland Trail to **Rocky Gap**. This track continues on to Bond Gap via the Larapinta Trail, but it's hard walking through rough hills and won't appeal to many. The flatter wooded country south-east of Simpsons Gap, between **Rungutjirpa Ridge** and Larapinta Drive has plenty of potential for off-track walks.

STANDLEY CHASM

From the Simpsons Gap turn-off, you cross Aboriginal land for 29km to the Standley Chasm turn-off. This part of the MacDonnells is owned and managed by the nearby community of **Iwupataka**, who know it as Angkerle. Its English name honours Ida Standley, who became the first school teacher in Alice Springs in 1914. The school for Aboriginal children was moved to Jay Creek (Iwupataka today) in 1925 and Mrs Standley was the first white woman to visit the chasm.

The chasm was formed where a tributary of the Finke River has worn a narrow cleft through the surrounding sandstone. In places the smooth vertical walls rise to 80m and at its widest the chasm is only 9m across. It's cool and dark on the chasm floor, but for about an hour either side of midday the stone walls are lit up by reflected sunlight that causes the rocks to glow red and triggers the shutter of every camera for miles around.

The 15 minute **walk** up the rocky gully from the kiosk to the chasm is crammed with moisture-loving plants such as river red gums, cycad palms and ferns, creating an unexpected lushness in this arid world of craggy bluffs. It's one of the best walks in the area but most visitors are in too much of a hurry to notice. Once the crowds depart the birds, dingoes and rock wallabies come out to play and you'll have the place more or less to yourself. For a real walking challenge with many rewards, you can return to Alice Springs along the Larapinta Trail (see that section earlier in this chapter).

Standley Chasm is open daily between 7.30 am and 6 pm and there's an entry fee of $4. There's a kiosk at the site selling snacks and drinks.

The chasm itself is 9km north of Larapinta Drive along a sealed road.

ELLERY CREEK BIGHOLE

Ellery Creek Bighole, 87km from Alice Springs on Namatjira Drive, is a popular swimming hole in summer but, being shaded by the high cliffs of Ellery Gorge, is generally too cold for comfort a lot of the year.

The Ellery Creek was named by explorer Ernest Giles in 1872 after a Victorian astronomer. The 'bighole' is a local name used to distinguish the hole at the foot of the gorge from other smaller waterholes along the creek. The Aboriginal name for the waterhole is Udepata, and it was an important gathering point along a couple of Dreaming trails which pass through the area.

The 20 minute **Dolomite Walk** is worth doing. An information shelter at the car park explains the area's fascinating geological history, which is exposed in the creek banks downstream from the waterhole.

Facilities

There's a small, usually crowded *camp ground* with wood-burning barbecues (no wood provided), tables, pit toilet and very limited shade within easy reach of the waterhole. Fees (honesty box) are $2.50/6 per person/family.

SERPENTINE GORGE

About 11km further along Namatjira Drive is the (often rough) gravel track which leads to the Serpentine Gorge car park. From here it's a 1.3km walk (30 minutes each way) along the sandy creek bed to the main attraction, and this makes a pleasant introduction to the area. It's no accident that the car park is so far from the gorge – it limits the number of people who visit the gorge to those prepared to walk though the sand. The gorge and its waterholes contain some rare (for this area) plant species, such as the Centralian flannel flower.

A waterhole blocks access to the entrance of the narrow gorge, which snakes for over 2km through the Heavitree Range. You can swim through the first (bloody cold!) section, and then walk up the rocky creek past large cycads to a second waterfilled cleft. There is some stunning scenery here, which can also be enjoyed from a lookout located a short scramble above the gorge entrance.

Section 8 of the Larapinta Trail (see earlier in this chapter) starts at the car park and takes you via Counts Point Lookout to Serpentine Chalet dams and Inarlanga Pass, then on to the Ochre Pits.

There is no camping at the gorge.

SERPENTINE CHALET RUINS

Continuing on from Serpentine Gorge you soon arrive at the Serpentine Chalet turnoff. A rough track leads to the ruins of the old Serpentine Chalet. It seems an unlikely spot, but this was the site for an early 1960s tourism venture. Visitors would travel all day from Alice Springs to reach the chalet which was a haven of relative – though still basic – comfort in the harsh bush. Lack of water caused the chalet to close after only a couple of years and all that remains are the concrete foundations and floor slabs.

Facilities

Eleven bush camp sites scattered along the track to and beyond the old Serpentine Chalet site have wood-burning fireplaces (collect your own wood) and a sense of isolation. These are ideal for winter camping but are too exposed in hot weather. The first five sites are accessible to conventional vehicles, the last six to 4WD vehicles only. No fees are charged.

OCHRE PITS

The nearby Ochre Pits, with extensive parking and picnicking areas (free gas barbecues), has some interesting information signs relating to ochre and its importance to Aboriginal people. Except for a small deposit of yellow ochre, which is still used today, the material at this minor quarry site is of poor quality. Nevertheless, the swirls of red and yellow ochre in the walls of this little ravine make an attractive picture in the afternoon sun.

Bushwalking

A three hour return walk takes you to scenic **Inarlanga Pass** at the foot of the Heavitree

The Magic of Ochre

Ochre was an important commodity in local Aboriginal culture. It was used medicinally and was also a valuable trade item. Red ochre was mixed with grease and eucalyptus leaves to form a decongestant balm; and it was believed that white ochre had magical powers – it was mixed with water and then blown from the mouth, a practice which was said to cool the sun and calm the wind. Ochre was also used extensively for body decoration and in painting.

Layers of deposited silt containing varying amounts of iron were compressed, folded and buckled over millions of years – creating the different coloured vertical layers of the Ochre Pits.

Range. Although the track passes through uninspiring country, the gorge is most interesting, as is the old Serpentine Chalet dam, an hour's walk to the east along the Larapinta Trail. For details, see the brochure on Section 8 of the Larapinta Trail.

ORMISTON GORGE

From the Ochre Pits it's a further 26km to Ormiston Gorge, where soaring cliffs, stark ghost gums, rich colours and a deep waterhole combine in some of the grandest scenery in the central ranges. Most visitors congregate at the gorge entrance, but for those who want to explore further afield several walks that start and finish at the Visitor Centre are recommended.

The gorge itself features towering crags that glow red and purple in the sunlight, hemming in jumbles of fallen rocks and a series of waterholes. Ormiston Gorge is a good spot for wildlife enthusiasts, thanks to the variety of habitats (mulga woodland, spinifex slopes, rock faces, large river gums and permanent water) that you find in close proximity to each other. Even in the dry of summer the waterholes can support a few waterbirds such as ducks.

The waterhole itself is part of the Aboriginal Emu Dreaming and is a registered sacred site. Although the water is pretty cold year round, it is still a popular summer swimming spot.

It's also an ideal base for exploring the western half of the West MacDonnells.

Bushwalking

This park has some of the best short walks in the MacDonnell Ranges. The *Walks of Ormiston Gorge & Pound* brochure gives more detail on each.

The short (10 minute) walk to the **Waterhole** has signs explaining the Aboriginal lore and wildlife of the waterholes.

The **Ghost Gum Walk** (1½ hour loop) climbs the western cliffs via many steps, past **Ghost Gum Lookout** (30 minutes return), which has superb views down the gorge itself, and returns along the floor of the gorge.

The **Pound Walk** (7km; two-three hour loop) is a superb walk that climbs to an elevated spinifex-clad gap in the range, passes into remote Ormiston Pound then follows the floor of the gorge back to the camp ground. Start early and take plenty of water. Do it first thing in the morning in an anticlockwise direction so you can enjoy a sunlit view of the big cliffs.

Longer walks to **Bowman's Gap** (9km; one-two days return) and **Mt Giles** (21km; two-three days return – includes a 600m ascent of Mt Giles) can be attempted by experienced bushwalkers. The view at dawn across Ormiston Pound from Mt Giles to Mt Sonder is sensational. Section 10 of the **Larapinta Trail** winds over rocky hills and along gum-lined creeks from Ormiston Gorge to Glen Helen, with fine views to Mt Sonder en route. Anyone attempting these walks must obtain a camping permit from the rangers at Ormiston Gorge before setting out. Water is not always available.

Facilities

This relatively upmarket *camp ground* almost in the shade of Ormiston Gorge features hot showers, toilets, disabled facilities, picnic furniture and free gas barbecues, but there is no room for caravans. Fees are $4/10 per person/family. Water supplies become severely limited during times of drought, when restrictions may apply.

GLEN HELEN GORGE & HOMESTEAD

There is another large waterhole at Glen Helen Gorge, 135km from Alice Springs. The has been carved through the Pacoota Range by the Finke River as its floodwaters rush

Back from the Dead

Inland Australia has lost many species of small mammals since white settlement, a tragedy blamed on feral predators and changing land use.

For example, the rare long-tailed dunnart is a small marsupial that was last recorded in the West MacDonnell Ranges in 1895. Nearly 100 years passed with no further sign of it and scientists wrote it off as extinct – an all too familiar story.

But in 1993 a prisoner from Alice Springs gaol, working on the construction of the Larapinta Trail, noticed a small mouse-like animal inside a discarded bottle. Thinking it was dead he placed it under a clump of spinifex. Another prisoner noticed the animal's curiously long tail and put it in his pocket. At this point the 'mouse' made a bid for freedom, hotly pursued by the prisoners, who managed to retrap it and hand it over to the ranger at Ormiston Gorge.

Upon examination, the 'mouse' turned out to be a female of the long-lost long-tailed dunnart! There was an immediate flurry of public and media interest and within the month a male had been trapped alive in the same area. But despite intensive searching the dunnart has never been seen since.

Perhaps more perplexing is the fate of the closely related sandhill dunnart, which was discovered in 1894 near Lake Amadeus, lost then rediscovered in 1969 at a site 1000km away; it too hasn't been seen since.

Scientists and conservationists keep their fingers crossed that these and other lost species are clinging on in remote areas of the outback.

MACDONNELL RANGES

south to the Simpson Desert; a major flood in 1988 backed up so high that it flooded the nearby tourist accommodation.

A 10 minute stroll takes you from the car park to the gorge entrance, where you can admire the 65m high cliffs, but if you want to go further you'll have to either swim through the waterhole or climb around it.

History
To the Arrernte people the gorge is a sacred site known as Yapulpa, and is part of the Carpet Snake Dreaming.

In 1872 Ernest Giles was the first white to explore the area. The pastoral lease was first taken up by prominent pastoralists, Frederick Grant and Stokes, and the station (and gorge) was named after Grant's eldest daughter by their surveyor, Richard Warburton, in 1876.

In 1901 the station was bought by Fred Raggatt, and remnants from that time, such as the timber meathouse, still survive.

Facilities
A high red cliff provides a dramatic backdrop to the *Glen Helen Homestead* (☎ 8956 7489), which is built on the site of the early homestead of Glen Helen station. The resort was in the throes of refurbishment at the time of writing, but the redevelopment plans look very grand. The only accommodation was camping for $10 a site ($15 with power), and basic groceries and takeaways are available at the store.

If you're travelling further west, check here for information on road conditions beyond the bitumen; permits for the Mereenie Loop Rd can also be bought at Glen Helen.

REDBANK GORGE
The bitumen ends at Glen Helen, and for the next 20km to the Redbank Gorge turn-off you're on occasionally rough dirt with numerous sharp dips. As is the case anywhere, as soon as dirt roads are encountered, the number of vehicles drops dramatically. This is great for the few who

don't mind the dirt roads as they have the places pretty much to themselves, and this is certainly the case with the beautiful Redbank Gorge.

From the Redbank turn-off on Namatjira Drive it's 5km to the Redbank car park, from which the final stage is a 20 minute walk up a rocky creek bed to the gorge. Redbank Gorge is extremely narrow, with polished, multi-hued walls that close over your head to block out the sky. To traverse the gorge you must clamber and float along the freezing deep pools with an air mattress, but it's worth doing – the colours and cathedral atmosphere inside are terrific. Allow two hours to get to the end.

Bushwalking
Redbank Gorge is the starting point for Section 12 of the Larapinta Trail to nearby Mt Sonder. The full day return walk along the ridge from Redbank Gorge to the summit of Mt Sonder will appeal to the well-equipped enthusiast. While the trek itself is rather monotonous, the view from Mt Sonder and the sense of achievement are ample reward. As on Mt Giles (see the Ormiston Gorge section), the atmosphere and panorama of timeless hills at sunrise makes it worth camping out on top.

Facilities
There are two *camp grounds* at Redbank. The Woodland camping area is on a creek flat with shady coolabahs and is very well set up. The sites are well spaced so there is some degree of privacy. Each site has a sand patch for a tent, fireplace (no wood provided), free gas barbecues and picnic tables, and there's a block with pit toilets. Fees are $2.50/6 per person/family, payable at the honesty box. An early morning stroll down the Davenport River, with the sun softly lighting the river gums, is a great way to start the day.

From there it's 3.5km down a rough track to the more basic Ridgetop camp ground, which has a pit toilet, fireplaces for each site and excellent views of the ranges. It is, however, quite exposed and the ground is stony.

Hospital kitchen, Victoria Settlement, Gurig National Park, Cobourg Peninsula

Camel riding, West MacDonnell Ranges

Waterhouse River, Elsey National Park

Huge, precariously balanced boulders of the Devil's Marbles at sunset

HUGH FINLAY

The church at Hermannsburg Mission

RICHARD I'ANSON

The Old Telegraph Station, Alice Springs

RICHARD I'ANSON

Kings Canyon, Watarrka National Park

RICHARD I'ANSON

Alice Springs and the MacDonnell Ranges from Anzac Hill

TNORALA (GOSSE BLUFF) CONSERVATION RESERVE

An alternative return route to Alice Springs once you reach Redbank Gorge is to continue west on Namatjira Drive for 17km, then turn south over Tylers Pass on the sometimes rough dirt road to Hermannsburg and Larapinta Drive. En route you pass Gosse Bluff, the spectacular remnant of a huge crater that was blasted out when a comet plunged into the ground 140 million years ago. The power of such an impact is almost impossible to comprehend – the 5km diameter crater you see today was originally 2km below the impact surface, and is just the core of the original 20km diameter crater. The best overall view is from the signposted lookout at Tylers Pass, a short distance to the north; in the early morning the light is stunning.

The crater was named by Ernest Giles in 1872 after Harry Gosse, a telegraphist at the Alice Springs telegraph station. In 1991 title was handed back to the traditional Aboriginal owners.

The Aboriginal name for the crater is Tnorala, and in the local mythology it's a wooden dish belonging to some star ancestors that crashed down from the sky during the Dreamtime. The area is a registered sacred site and is protected by a 4700 hectare conservation reserve. Although no permit is required to travel along this road, you do need a permit to enter the Tnorala Conservation Reserve, which lies about 8km off the main track. These permits are available from the tourist office in Alice Springs, and Glen Helen Homestead and the resort at Kings Canyon.

Access to Gosse Bluff is along a rough track, best tackled in a 4WD, which goes right into the crater. There's a picnic ground with pit toilet and information boards. Camping is not permitted.

Gosse Bluff is about 50km from the Redbank Gorge turn-off, and it's about 42km from the bluff to the junction rejoining Larapinta Drive. From here you can travel west and south along the **Mereenie Loop Rd** to Kings Canyon, and from there on to

Uluru without returning to the Stuart Hwy (see later in this chapter).

Alternatively, it's 21 km to the historic mission settlement of **Hermannsburg**.

JAMES RANGES

The spectacular James Ranges form an east-west band south of the West MacDonnell Ranges. While they are relatively unknown in comparison to the MacDonnells, the ranges are still well visited as they contain a few of the Centre's best attractions: Hermannsburg, Palm Valley and Kings Canyon.

Most people visit Hermannsburg and Palm Valley on a day-trip from Alice Springs, and Kings Canyon on a separate trip which includes Uluru. However, you can save a lot of back-tracking if you continue from Hermannsburg around the western end of the James Ranges on the gravel Mereenie Loop Rd, which brings you out at Kings Canyon.

LARAPINTA DRIVE

Taking the alternative road to the south from Standley Chasm in the West MacDonnells, Larapinta Drive crosses the Hugh River before reaching the turn-off for Wallace Rockhole, 18km off the main road and 117km from Alice Springs.

Wallace Rockhole

The Arrernte community of Wallace Rockhole was established in 1974 as an outpost of Hermannsburg Mission. You can take a **rock art tour** (9.30 am and 1.30 pm; $7) and sample bush tucker in season ($40 including rock art tour) – kangaroo tail and damper cooked in the ground is a speciality.

The **Wallace Rockhole Tourist Park** (☎ 8956 7993) has a pleasant camping area ($14, $16 with power), plus on-site vans ($40) and en suite cabins (from $95). The general store sells ice and locally produced Aboriginal crafts.

Namatjira Monument

Back on Larapinta Drive, just east of Hermannsburg, is the Namatjira Monument.

JAMES RANGES

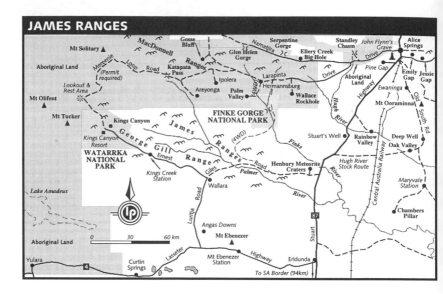

Today the artistic skills of the central Australian Aboriginal people are widely known and appreciated. This certainly wasn't the case when the artist Albert Namatjira started to paint his central Australian landscapes in 1934 (see the boxed text).

HERMANNSBURG
• **pop 460**   ✉ **0872**

Only 8km beyond the Namatjira monument you reach the Aboriginal settlement, Hermannsburg, 125km from Alice Springs.

Although the town is restricted Aboriginal land, permits are not required to visit the mission or store, or to travel through. Supermarket shopping is available at the mission store near the historic precinct, and at the Ntaria Supermarket at the main entrance to town. There's a service station next door.

Hermannsburg Mission
This fascinating monument to the skill and dedication of the Territory's early Lutheran missionaries is a fine example of traditional German farmhouse architecture. Shaded by tall river gums and date palms, the white-washed walls of this old mission stand in stark contrast to the colours of the surrounding countryside that were captured so eloquently by the settlement's most famous inhabitants, the painters of the Namatjira family.

Among the low, stone buildings there's a church, a school and various houses and outbuildings, restored with a federal government grant in 1988. One building houses an art gallery which provides an insight into the life and times of Albert Namatjira and contains examples of the work of 39 Hermannsburg artists.

The best place to start a visit to the historic precinct is the ***Kata-Anga Tea Room*** (☎ 8956 7402) in the old missionary house. Open seven days a week from 9 am to 4 pm (10 am to 4 pm from December to February), the tea room has a marvellous atmosphere and the walls are adorned with interesting photos by eminent anthropologist Baldwin Spencer.

For a reasonable price, you can relax with a light lunch, or a bottomless cup of tea or coffee and a large slice of home-baked cake. If you're making a special trip out from Alice Springs in the summer months, call first to check that they'll be open.

The tea room sells a good range of traditional and watercolour paintings, artefacts and pottery, all items being the work of local Aboriginal people. The quality is generally very good and the prices reasonable. The staff here also issue permits for travel on the Mereenie Loop Rd (see that section later in this chapter).

Admission to Hermannsburg costs $4 per adult, $2.50 per child; a leaflet explains the various buildings and their history which you can wander through. For $3 extra per person you can take a guided tour that includes the Namatjira private collection, which you can't see for the basic entrance price. Tours leave at 10 minutes past the hour between 10.10 am and 3.10 pm from April to November.

History In 1876, fresh from the Hermannsburg Mission Institute in Germany, pastors AH Kempe and WF Schwarz left Adelaide bound for central Australia with a herd of cattle and several thousand sheep. Eighteen months later they finally arrived at the new mission site, having been held up by drought at Dalhousie Springs for nearly a year. It was a nightmarish introduction to the harsh central Australian environment, but the pastors were committed to the task of bringing Christianity and 'civilisation' to the Aboriginal people. They weren't to make any converts for 11 years but, despite treating sickness in the interim, regarded this feat as their most significant achievement.

The missionaries faced incredible hardships, including strong opposition from white settlers to their attempts to protect Aboriginal people from genocide, but they

Albert Namatjira (1902-59)

Probably Australia's best-known Aboriginal artist, Albert Namatjira lived at the Hermannsburg Lutheran Mission west of Alice Springs. He was introduced to the art of European-style watercolour painting by a non-Aboriginal artist, Rex Batterbee, in the 1930s.

Namatjira successfully captured the essence of the Centre with paintings which were heavily influenced by European art. At the time his pictures were seen purely for what they appeared to be – renderings of picturesque landscapes.

These days, however, it is thought he chose his subjects carefully, as they were Dreaming landscapes to which he had a great bond.

Namatjira supported many of his people with the income from his work, as he was obliged to do under tribal law. Because of his fame, he was allowed to buy alcohol at a time when this was otherwise illegal for Aboriginal people. In 1957 he was the first Aboriginal person to be granted Australian citizenship, but in 1958 he was jailed for six months for supplying alcohol to Aborigines. He died the following year, aged 57.

Although Namatjira died disenchanted with white society, he did much to change the extremely negative views of Aboriginal people which prevailed at the time. At the same time he paved the way for the Papunya painting movement which emerged a decade after his death.

Albert Namatjira's headstone

HUGH FINLAY

JAMES RANGES

established what became the first township in central Australia. It eventually became run down and neglected; many of the Aboriginal residents drifted away and the mission was abandoned in 1891.

This was all turned around with the arrival of Pastor Carl Strehlow in 1894. Strehlow was a tireless worker who learnt the Arrernte language, translated the New Testament into Arrernte and wrote a number of important works on the Arrernte people. On the downside, however, he also had the touch of arrogance which typified missions at the time (dubbed 'muscular Christianity'), believing that the Aboriginal beliefs and customs were wrong.

At one time Hermannsburg had a population of 700 Western Arrernte people, a herd of 5000 cattle and various cottage industries, including a tannery. In 1982 the title was handed back to the Arrernte people under the Aboriginal Land Rights (NT) Act of 1976. Since that time most of its residents have left and established small outstation communities on traditional clan territories. There are now 35 such outstations on the old mission lease. Although about 200 Aborigines still live at Hermannsburg, its main function is to provide support and resources for the outlying population.

One of Hermannsburg's most famous residents was Professor TGH (Ted) Strehlow, youngest child of Carl Strehlow. He was born on the mission and spent more than 40 years studying the Arrernte people. His books about them, like *Aranda Traditions* (1947), *Australian Aboriginal Anthropology* (1970) and *Songs of Central Australia* (1971), are still widely read. The Arrernte people entrusted him with many items of huge spiritual and symbolic importance when they realised their traditional lifestyle was under threat. These items are now held in a vault in the Strehlow Research Centre in Alice Springs.

FINKE GORGE NATIONAL PARK

From Hermannsburg the trail follows the Finke River south to the Finke Gorge National Park. It's only 12km away, but a 4WD is essential to tackle the sandy and rocky access road.

Famous for its rare palms, Finke Gorge National Park is one of central Australia's premier wilderness areas. Its most popular attraction is Palm Valley, but the main gorge features high red cliffs, stately river gums, cool waterholes and plenty of clean white sand.

For thousands of years, the Finke River formed part of an Aboriginal trade route that crossed Australia, bringing goods such as sacred red ochre from the south and pearl shell from the north to the central Australian tribes. The area around Hermannsburg had an abundance of animals and food plants. It was a major refuge for the Western Arrernte people in times of drought, thanks to its permanent water, which came from soaks dug in the Finke River bed. An upside-down river (like all others in central Australia), the Finke flows beneath its dry bed most of the time. As it becomes saline during drought, the Western Arrernte call it Lhere Pirnte (pronounced 'lara pinta' hence Larapinta), which means salty river. It was their knowledge of its freshwater soaks that enabled them to survive in the harshest droughts.

Access into the park is restricted to 4WD vehicles, but there are plenty of tour operators who do day-trips here from Alice Springs.

History

The explorer Ernest Giles arrived on the scene in 1872, when he travelled up the Finke on his first attempt to cross from the Overland Telegraph Line to the west coast. To his amazement he found tall palms growing in the river, which had been named 12 years earlier by John McDouall Stuart, and he went into raptures over the beauty of the scenery.

Palm Valley

Leaving the Finke at its junction with Palm Creek, you head west past an old ranger station and 1km further on arrive at the Kalarranga car park. En route there's a small information bay that gives you an introduction to the area and to some of the walks you can do (see the following Bushwalking section). Kalarranga, more usually known as the **Amphitheatre**, is a semi-circle of striking sandstone formations sculpted by a now-extinct meander of Palm Creek. Be there in early morning or late afternoon for the best views.

Continuing on from the Amphitheatre, the track becomes extremely rough and rocky for the final 3km to Palm Valley. Along the way you pass the camp ground and picnic area before arriving at **Cycad Gorge**, where a chocolate-coloured cliff towers over a clump of tall, slender palms. The gorge is named for the large number of shaggy cycads growing on and below the cliff face. Lending a tropical atmosphere to their barren setting, the palms and cycads are leftovers from much wetter times in central Australia. They only survive here because of a reliable supply of moisture within the surrounding sandstone.

Just past Cycad Gorge you come to Palm Valley itself, with the first oasis of palms just a stone's throw away. The valley is actually a narrow gorge that in places is literally choked with lush stands of waving **Red Cabbage Palms** up to 25m high. Found nowhere else in the world, the species (*Livistona mariae*) grows within an area of 60 sq km and is over 800km from its nearest relatives. To the Arrernte people the palms are associated with the Fire Dreaming. There are only 3000 mature palms in the wild, so the rangers ask that you resist the temptation to enter the palm groves – the tiny seedlings are hard to see and are easily trampled underfoot.

The gorge is a botanist's paradise, as it is home to over 400 plant species, which is almost one fifth of all those found in the Centre, and about 10% of them are either rare or have a restricted distribution.

Finke Gorge

If you have your own 4WD vehicle there's a track which traverses the full length of the picturesque Finke Gorge, much of the time along the bed of the (usually) dry Finke River. It's a rough but worthwhile trip and the camp sites at Bogey Hole, about 2½

hours from Hermannsburg, make an excellent overnight stop (if you are in a hurry you can get from Palm Valley all the way to Kings Canyon in less than eight hours via this route). This is a great trip, but it's also serious 4WD territory and you need to be suitably prepared. See Lonely Planet's *Outback Australia* for full details.

The 4WD track is closed over the hot summer months. Be sure to inform a ranger at Finke Gorge (☎ 8956 7401) or Watarrka (☎ 8956 7460) of your plans and safe arrival.

Bushwalking

There are four walking tracks in the Palm Valley area, all of them suitable for families.

The **Arankaia** walk is a short walk (2km) along the valley, returning via the sandstone plateau where there are great views over the park. Allow one hour to complete the loop.

The most popular walk is the 5km **Mpulungkinya Track**, a two hour loop through Palm Valley that joins the Arankaia walk on the return. It passes dense stands of palms and offers excellent views down the gorge and signboards show how the availability of water determines plant life in the area.

A second 5km track, the **Mpaara Track**, starts and finishes at the Kalarranga car park and takes in the Finke River, Palm Bend and the rugged Amphitheatre. It leads you in the footsteps of two heroes from the Aboriginal Dreamtime, Mpaara (Tawny Frogmouth Man) and Pangkalanya (Devil Man), whose adventures are explained by signs along the way. There are superb views of the Finke River.

A relatively short track takes you up to **Kalarranga Lookout** (45 mins; 1.5km) on a sandstone knob; the view over the Amphitheatre is striking.

Facilities

A small *camp ground* beside Palm Creek has shady trees, hot showers, gas barbecues and flush toilets as well as numerous friendly birds on the lookout for a free feed. It's a very pleasant place in a scenic setting of red sandstone ridges and the spectacular Amphitheatre is just a few minutes walk away.

Overnight charges are $5 per adult or $12 per family, paid into the honesty box; dead wood cannot be collected past the park entry sign in the Finke River, so if you want a fire, be sure to collect firewood in advance.

Day-trippers on the way to Palm Valley have free use of the nearby *picnic area* and its shade shelters, flush toilets and gas barbecues. There are also disabled facilities.

Ranger talks are held at the camp ground four nights a week from May to October.

MEREENIE LOOP RD

Larapinta Drive continues west past the turn-off to Palm Valley. After the Areyonga turn-off (no visitors) it becomes the unsealed Mereenie Loop Rd, which loops around the western edge of the James Ranges to Kings Canyon. This dirt road offers an excellent alternative to the Ernest Giles Rd as a way of reaching Kings Canyon.

You need a permit from the Central Land Council to travel along the Mereenie Loop Rd, because it passes through Aboriginal land. The permit includes the informative *Mereenie Tour Pass* booklet, which provides details about the local Aboriginal culture and has a route map. Permits are issued on the spot by CATIA in Alice Springs, Glen Helen Homestead, the Kata-Anga Tea Rooms at Hermannsburg, and the Kings Canyon Resort. A permit costs $2.

The countryside is interesting and varied, although hardly breathtaking, the highlight perhaps being the classic outback road sign which you pass on the southern part of the track – a rusty old 44-gallon drum sits by the side of the road on the approach to a sharp bend, and it carries a warning to slow down: 'lift um foot'. If you are travelling towards Kings Canyon, you reach the sign after the danger, and so the message reads: 'puttum back down'!

The road is generally in reasonable condition, and it takes around four hours to travel the 204km from Hermannsburg to Kings Canyon. It is quite OK for conventional vehicles, although it can become corrugated if the grader hasn't been through for a while. Caravans should probably give it a miss.

HENBURY METEORITE CRATERS CONSERVATION RESERVE

About 40km south of Stuart's Well along the Stuart Hwy, the **Ernest Giles Rd** heads west for 200km to Kings Canyon. The first 97km is a notoriously rough stretch with many narrow, winding sections through the dunes and sudden washouts; a 4WD is the preferred mode of transport. After this the track joins the Luritja Rd from the Lasseter Hwy (and Uluru) and is bitumen the rest of the way to Kings Canyon.

Eleven kilometres west of the Stuart Hwy a corrugated side road on the right leads 5km to the Henbury Meteorite Craters, where a cluster of small craters dots an exposed, stony plain. About 4500 years ago a meteorite clocking an estimated 40,000km/h broke up as it entered the earth's atmosphere. The craters were formed when the fragments hit the ground – the largest is 180m wide and 15m deep, and was formed by a piece of rock about the size of a 44-gallon drum.

The facts are interesting, but it's only worth a quick stop to stretch the legs or if you have a deep interest in this sort of thing. The road is rough but OK for 2WD if it's dry. Beyond the craters turn-off, the Ernest Giles Rd is not recommended for 2WDs.

Facilities

There's a *camp ground* here, but it is extremely exposed and the ground is very hard and stony – on a cold, windy day it's pretty grim; on a hot, windy day it's worse. There are also fireplaces (although wood may be hard to find) and a pit toilet.

WATARRKA NATIONAL PARK (KINGS CANYON)

The western half of the George Gill Range, an outlier of the James Ranges, is protected by Watarrka National Park, which includes one of the most spectacular sights in central Australia – the sheer, 100m high walls of **Kings Canyon**. If you have the time, a visit here is a must.

The name Watarrka comes from the Luritja Aboriginal word for the umbrella bush

(*Acacia ligulata*) and it also refers to the Kings Canyon district. The park offers spectacular walking and photographic opportunities, and there's a range of accommodation options nearby.

More than 600 plant species – including 17 relict species – have been recorded in the park, giving it the highest plant diversity of any place in Australia's arid zone. At the head of the 1km gorge is the spring-fed **Garden of Eden**, where a moist microclimate supports a variety of plants. The narrow, rocky bed of Kings Creek along the floor of the canyon is covered with tall ghost gums and an unusual bonsai variety. Also seen along the valley walls is the MacDonnell Ranges cycad, a bushy palm which appears only in the range country of central Australia.

The gorge is surrounded by a sandstone plateau which is covered in many places by bizarre, weathered sandstone domes.

History

The Luritja Aboriginal people have lived in this area for at least 20,000 years and there are a number of registered sacred sites within the park. There are also three communities of Aboriginal people living within the park boundaries.

In 1872 Ernest Giles named the George Gill Range after his brother-in-law, who also helped fund the expedition. Giles also named Kings Creek after his friend Fielder King, and a number of other natural features in the area.

William Gosse camped at Kings Creek a year later on an exploratory trip and went on to become the first white man to see Uluru, which Giles had missed. The Horn Scientific Exploring Expedition of 1894, led by Charles Winnecke, also camped at Kings Creek, and it was thanks to its finds that the botanical importance of the area was identified.

Being the first European to explore the area, Giles had first option on applying for a pastoral lease, and this he did in 1874. It covered almost 1000 sq miles and included the area of Watarrka. By 1885 Giles' land had become part of the Tempe Downs lease to the east, and it was run from there until the formation of the national park in the 1980s.

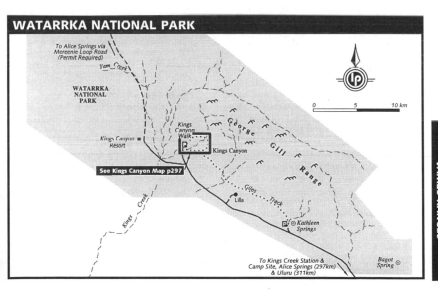

WATARRKA NATIONAL PARK

To Alice Springs via Mereenie Loop Road (Permit Required)

Yam Creek

WATARRKA NATIONAL PARK

Kings Canyon Walk

Kings Canyon Resort

Kings Canyon

See Kings Canyon Map p297

George Gill Range

Kings Creek

Giles Track

Lilla

Kathleen Springs

To Kings Creek Station & Camp Site, Alice Springs (297km) & Uluru (311km)

Bagot Spring

0   5   10 km

JAMES RANGES

The first tourism venture in the area was set up by Jack Cotterill in 1960 on Angus Downs Station. It was operated by Jack's son, Jim (see Stuart's Well in The South-East chapter) until 1990. Jack Cotterill built the road from Wallara to Kings Canyon, and a small cairn and plaque at Kings Canyon commemorates the huge effort he put into developing the tourist trade in this area.

Information

There are information boards, shelter, water and toilets at the car park. In case of medical emergencies, there is a solar radiophone at the canyon car park and at the eastern edge of the Garden of Eden, and a comprehensive first-aid kit up on the plateau on the northern side of the canyon.

There's a sunset-viewing area 1km short of the car park.

Ranger Talks

Talks, guided walks and slide shows are held between May and October – check with the Parks & Wildlife office in Alice or at Kings Canyon Resort for the latest schedule. Slide shows are held weekly at the resort and twice-weekly at Kings Creek Station (see Places to Stay & Eat) at 7.30 pm; guided walks generally leave from the canyon car park.

Bushwalking

The best way to appreciate Kings Canyon is to walk – either through the gorge or, if you're feeling energetic, up onto the plateau and around the canyon edge. There's another walking trail at Kathleen Springs, about 12km to the east.

In addition there's the excellent two-day Giles Track – if you're attempting this one, contact the rangers beforehand (☎ 8956 7488) for a map and further information.

Kings Canyon Walk (6km; four hour loop)
After a short, steep climb, this walk skirts the rim of the canyon and passes through a maze of giant eroded domes. It's an excellent walk which offers some stunning views – as far as Uluru on a good day – and this gives you enough time to make the short detour to the

Garden of Eden on the northern edge of the canyon. The trail is clearly marked with flashes on metal posts along the way. Start before sunrise to get the jump on the crowds and enjoy the canyon in its best light. A certain level of fitness is necessary, and the wind can be strong at the top – take care near the edge.

Kings Creek Walk (2.6km; one hour return)
This is a much shorter walk (more of a scramble really) along the rocky bed of Kings Creek. While you do get some good views of the canyon walls through the ghost gums, it's not a patch on those from the canyon rim. After rains the waterfall at the canyon's end should be flowing. There is wheelchair access for the first 700m.

Kathleen Springs (2.5km; one hour return)
This wheelchair accessible path leads to a beautiful spring-fed rock pool at the base of the range. There is a picnic ground with barbecues, shade, water and toilets.

Giles Track (22km one way; overnight)
This is an easy marked trail which follows the ridge from Kings Canyon to Kathleen Springs. If you don't want to do the whole two days, it's possible to do a day walk as there is also access from Lilla (Reedy Creek), which is about half-way along the trail. Although there are waterholes in the area, these cannot be relied upon so you need to be fully self-sufficient in both food and water. There's a designated camp site along the ridge above Lilla, and small campfires are permitted here. Get a map from the ranger before setting out and remember to register with the Volunteer Walker Registration Scheme (☎ 1300 650 730) – see the Activities section at the start of this chapter.

Organised Tours

Aboriginal Tours (☎ 8956 7442) Lilla is an Aboriginal-owned and run tour company which runs a couple of trips from the Kings Canyon Resort. Depending on demand, the four hour **Guided Canyon Walk** departs at 7 am and an Aboriginal guide takes you on the canyon-rim walk. Inquire at reception.

The **Willy-Wagtail Tour** is a two hour tour which takes in cave paintings and an introduction to Luritja traditions. It departs daily at 9 and 11 am and 4 pm, and the cost is $25 ($20).

Scenic Flights Helicopter flights are available from Kings Creek Station (see Places to Stay & Eat) and at Kings Canyon Resort; a 15 minute flight costs $80, and 33 minutes costs about $150 per person.

Places to Stay & Eat

The only accommodation in the park is at the **Kings Canyon Resort** (☎ *toll-free 1800 089 622*), which has a range of choices from expensive camping to very expensive motel rooms.

A camp site for two people costs $20 ($25 with power); the camp ground is grassy and shady with a pool, laundry and barbecues, and facilities are clean and well kept.

There's a choice of rooms, including four-share dorms where a bed costs $35 or the whole room costs $138; lodge rooms with shared kitchen and bathrooms are $83 a single or double and $152 for a family room sleeping up to five people. Motel rooms with private facilities cost $270 with

a view and $328 for a deluxe room. Prices include tax.

For meals you have the choice of **Carmichael's**, an à la carte restaurant where the buffets are reasonable value, or the **Desert Oaks Café & George Grill Bar**, which opens at 5.30 am for breakfast and serves light meals through till 9 pm. The latter has a 'stockman's supper' which is good value at $12.50; the 'stockman's lunch' costs $9.50. The complex includes a shop with limited, and expensive, food supplies. Fuel is available from 7 am to 7 pm seven days a week. Kings Canyon had the most expensive fuel this side of Alice, at 99.8c/litre, when we visited.

For something friendlier, cheaper and more akin to a bush experience, try **Kings Creek Station** (☎ 8956 7474), on Ernest Giles Rd just outside the national park's eastern boundary and 33km from the canyon

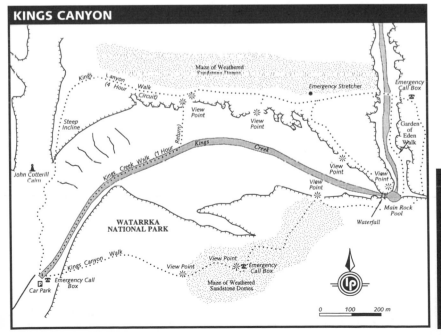

turn-off. The very pleasant camp ground has individual fire pits among shady desert oaks and costs $8 per person (power is $1 extra per site). There are also very comfortable tent cabins which cost $38.85 per person including a cooked breakfast. Amenities are shared and there's a kitchen/barbecue area where you can cook your evening meal. Fuel, ice, snacks, barbecue packs and limited stores are available seven days a week at the shop (open from 8 am to 7 pm).

Getting There & Away

There are no commercial flights or buses to Kings Canyon – unless you're part of an organised tour, it's self-drive only.

The most interesting route from Alice Springs is via the West MacDonnells, Hermannsburg and the Mereenie Loop Rd (see that section earlier in this chapter). You can then continue on to Uluru and back to the Stuart Hwy at Erldunda, from where you can head north to Alice Springs (200km), or south to the South Australian border (94km) and beyond. This round trip circuit from the Alice is about 1200km, only 300km of which is gravel.

Getting Around

The Kings Canyon Resort operates a shuttle bus between the resort and the canyon for $9.50 return (children $4.50). Inquire at reception.

East MacDonnell Ranges

The East MacDonnells stretch in a line for about 100km east of Alice Springs, the ridges cut by more gaps and gorges that culminate in beautiful Ruby Gap. (See the map at the beginning of this chapter.)

The road from Alice Springs east to Arltunga is extremely scenic for the most part, taking you through a jumble of high ridges and hills drained by gum-lined creeks. Along the way you pass several small parks and reserves where you can explore a variety of attractions such as rugged gorges, Aboriginal culture and abandoned mining areas. Despite the attractions it is a poor cousin to the much more popular West MacDonnells and thus attracts fewer visitors. But this fact makes it altogether more enjoyable.

The Ross Hwy from Alice Springs is sealed for the 80km to Ross River Homestead. The turn-off to Arltunga is 9km before Ross River. Arltunga is 32km from the Ross Hwy, and the unsealed road can be quite rough, as can the alternative return route via Claraville, Ambalindum and The Garden homesteads to the Stuart Hwy.

Access to John Hayes Rockhole (in Trephina Gorge Nature Park), N'Dhala Gorge and Ruby Gap is by 4WD vehicle only, but other main attractions east of Alice Springs are normally accessible to conventional vehicles.

EMILY & JESSIE GAPS NATURE PARK

Following the Ross Hwy east of the Stuart Hwy for 10km you arrive at **Emily Gap**, the first of two scenic gaps in the range. Nobody knows for sure how they got their English names, but both gaps are associated with an Arrernte Caterpillar Dreaming trail.

It's a nice spot with **rock paintings** and a deep waterhole in the narrow gorge. Known to the Arrernte as Anthwerrke, this is one of the most important Aboriginal sites in the Alice Springs area as it was from here that the caterpillar ancestral beings of Mparntwe (Alice Springs) originated.

Jessie Gap, 8km further on, is an equally scenic and normally a much quieter place.

Both sites are popular swimming holes and have picnic tables and fireplaces. Camping is not permitted.

Bushwalking

For a minor challenge, the 8km walk along the high, narrow ridge between these two gaps has much to recommend it. You get sweeping panoramas all the way and there's usually wildlife, such as euros, black-footed rock wallabies and wedge-tailed eagles, to see. The idea is to get someone to drop you off at Emily Gap, then have them continue on to Jessie Gap to get the picnic ready. Allow at least 2½ hours for the walk, which isn't marked.

CORROBOREE ROCK CONSERVATION RESERVE

Past Jessie Gap you drive over eroded flats, the steep-sided MacDonnell Range looming large on your left, before entering a valley between red ridges. Corroboree Rock, 43km from Alice Springs, is one of a number of unusual tan-coloured dolomite hills scattered over the valley floor. A small cave in this large dog-toothed outcrop was once used by local Aboriginal people as a storehouse for sacred objects. It is a registered sacred site and is listed on the National Estate. Despite the name, it is doubtful if the rock was ever used as a corroboree area, owing to the lack of water in the vicinity.

A short walking track leads from the car park around the base of the rock.

TREPHINA GORGE NATURE PARK

About 60km from Alice Springs you cross the sandy bed of **Benstead Creek**, with its lovely big gums. The thousands of young river gums that line the road germinated in the mid-1970s, when the Alice Springs region received unusually high rainfall. This delightful scenery, which is totally at odds with the common perception of central Australia, continues for the 6km from the creek crossing to the Trephina Gorge turn-off.

Trephina Gorge Nature Park, 3km north of the Ross Hwy, offers some magnificent gorge, ridge and creek scenery, excellent walks, deep swimming holes, wildlife and low-key camping areas. The main attractions are the Gorge itself, **Trephina Bluff** and **John Hayes Rockhole**. The rockhole, a permanent waterhole, is reached by a rough track that wanders for several kilometres up the so-called **Valley of the Eagles** and is often closed to conventional vehicles.

The first explorers to pass through the gorge were an advance survey party of the Overland Telegraph Line, led by John Ross, which came through here in 1870. The gorge contains a stand of huge river red gums, and many of these were logged in the 1950s to provide sleepers for the *Ghan* railway line. The area was excised from The Garden Station in 1966 and gazetted as a park to protect both the gums and the gorge.

Trephina Gorge has a restful atmosphere and some grand scenery, making it a great spot to camp for a few days. It also boasts a colony of black-footed rock wallabies on the cliff above the waterhole – wander down first thing in the morning and you'll usually spot them leaping nimbly about on the rock face. The gorge area is also home to a number of rare plants, including the Glory of the Centre Wedding Bush.

Bushwalking

There are several good walks here, ranging from a short wander to a five hour hike. The less energetic can simply wander along the banks of Trephina Creek back towards the park entrance and admire the superb red gums, or there's a short walk along the entrance road that leads to a magnificent ghost gum, estimated to be 300 years old. The marked walking trails are as follows:

Trephina Gorge Walk
An easy walk along the edge of the gorge, from where the trail drops to the sandy creek bed and loops back to the starting point. Allow about 45 minutes return.

Panorama Walk
Slightly longer (one hour) but still easy, this one gives great views over Trephina Gorge and examples of bizarre, twisted rock strata.

Ridgetop Walk
This is the most difficult of the park's marked trails, and traverses the ridges from Trephina Gorge to the delightful John Hayes Rockhole, a few kilometres to the west. Here a section of deep gorge holds a series of waterholes long after the more exposed places have dried up. The one-way trip takes about five hours, but affords splendid views and isolation.

Chain of Ponds Walk
From the John Hayes Rockhole camp ground

TREPHINA GORGE NATURE PARK

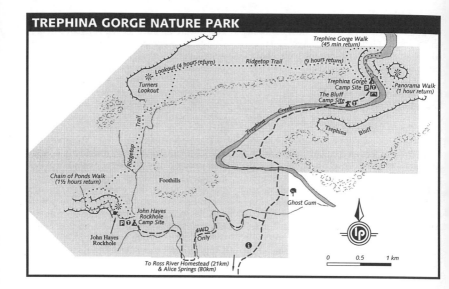

this 90 minute loop walk leads through the gorge past rock pools up to a lookout above the gorge.

The walks are outlined in the *Walks of Trephina Gorge Nature Park* published by Parks & Wildlife ($1).

Facilities

Small camp grounds at Trephina Gorge, The Bluff and John Hayes Rockhole offer a variety of camping experiences, and all are cheap: $2.50/6 per person/family (payable into honesty boxes). You can collect firewood from a heap just before the first Trephina Creek crossing on the Trephina Gorge access road.

The *Trephina Gorge camp ground* is in a timbered gully a short stroll from the main attraction, and has running water, pit toilets, fireplaces and picnic tables. It is suitable for caravans, unlike *The Bluff camp ground*, which is about five minutes walk away. The Bluff has similar facilities, in addition to free gas barbecues, but a more spectacular creek bank setting under tall gums in front

of a towering red ridge. There are disabled toilets between the two camp grounds.

John Hayes Rockhole has basic sites beside a rocky creek down from the waterhole.

If you need any emergency assistance, there is a ranger stationed in the park (☎ 8956 9765). Rangers give talks around the campfire on Tuesday and Thursday evenings during the winter.

N'DHALA GORGE NATURE PARK

Shortly before reaching Ross River homestead you come to the 4WD track to N'Dhala Gorge Nature Park, where some 6000 ancient **rock carvings** (petroglyphs) decorate a deep, narrow gorge.

The 11km access track winds down the picturesque **Ross River valley**, where a number of sandy crossings make the going tough for conventional vehicles. As the sign says, towing is costly. You can continue on downstream past N'Dhala Gorge to the Ringwood Rd, then head west to rejoin the Ross Hwy about 30km east of Alice Springs.

The petroglyphs at N'Dhala (known to the Arrernte people as Irlwentye) are of two major types: finely pecked, where a stone hammer has been used to strike a sharp chisel such as a bone or rock; and pounded, where a stone has been hit directly on the rock face. The carvings, which are generally not that easy to spot, are thought to have been made in the last 2000 years. Common designs featured in the carvings are circular and feather-like patterns, and these are thought to relate to the Caterpillar Dreaming.

The walking trail is 2km return and an easy 45 minute walk. The main petroglyphs are about 300m and 900m from the car park.

Facilities

There is a *camp ground* at the gorge entrance. Facilities are limited to fireplaces (collect your own wood), tables and a pit toilet; shade is limited. Camping fees are $2.50/6 per person/family, payable into an honesty box.

ROSS RIVER HOMESTEAD

Originally the headquarters for Loves Creek Station, the Ross River homestead (☎ 8956 9711) has a pretty setting under rocky hills beside the Ross River. It's a friendly sort of place that offers walks in the spectacular surrounding countryside, short camel and wagon rides and horse riding, or simply lazing around with a cold one.

A large grassy *camp ground* across the (usually dry) river has unpowered sites ($12), powered sites ($16) and bunkhouse accommodation for $13 per person ($18 with linen supplied). There are picnic shelters and a small, rustic-style bar where you can enjoy a cold drink.

The old homestead on the other side of the river has cosy timber cabins with en suite that sleep up to five people for $75 (single or double) plus $15 per extra person.

The *bar* is open for breakfast, lunch and dinner and has generous meals at reasonable prices. A three-course 'campoven cookout' under the stars, chauffeured on a horse-drawn wagon, costs $35/20 for adults/children.

For something out of the ordinary, the resort puts on an overnighter with either horses or camels. This involves a three hour ride to a bush camp in the hills, where you enjoy a three course campoven meal before unrolling the swag under the stars. In the morning you eat breakfast before returning to the resort. It's an expensive excursion, however, at $165 per adult and $115 for children.

ARLTUNGA HISTORICAL RESERVE

Leaving the Ross Hwy, the first 12km of the Arltunga Rd passes through scenic **Bitter Springs Gorge**, where red quartzite ridges tower high above dolomite hills. This was the route taken by the early diggers as they walked from Alice Springs to the goldfields at the turn of the century. The road can be quite rough at times and is impassable after heavy rain.

Arltunga Historical Reserve is all that's left of what was officially central Australia's first town – a gold rush settlement that once housed nearly 3000 people. This superb historic reserve preserves significant evidence of gold-mining activity, including a partly-restored ghost town. There are walking tracks and old mines to explore, now complete with bat colonies, so make sure to bring a torch (flashlight).

The richest part of the goldfield was **White Range**, but showing remarkable short-sightedness, authorities allowed almost all the ruins and small mines that once dotted this high ridge to be destroyed during a recent open-cut mining operation. The White Range Mine operated for a few years in the late 1980s and was reopened in early 1996 as new technology made the area viable once more. Fortunately the mine is out of sight on the far side of the range and the new operations are all underground.

Fossicking is not permitted at Arltunga, but there is a **fossicking reserve** in a gully just to the south where you may (with luck) find some gold. A permit is required, and can be obtained from the Department of Mines & Energy in Alice Springs.

EAST MACDONNELL RANGES

From Arltunga it is possible to do a loop back to Alice Springs along Arltunga Tourist Drive.

History

The rush to the so-called ruby fields east of here (see Ruby Gap Nature Park following) led to the chance discovery of alluvial gold at Paddy's Rockhole in 1887, and further exploration uncovered the reefs at White Range in 1897.

The field was not particularly rich, and the miners faced huge problems, especially against the extremes of weather and the lack of water. In 1898 the South Australian government constructed a 10-head gold-stamping battery and cyanide processing works at Arltunga, in itself a major logistical feat as all the equipment had to be brought by camel train from the railhead at Oodnadatta, 600km to the south.

However, the improved facilities did little for the prosperity of the field, and even at its peak in the early 1900s there were never more than a few hundred miners working here; most of the time there were less than 100. By the time it closed, battery had treated 11,500 tons of rock, yielding around 15,000 ounces of gold.

Information

There's a Visitor Centre (☎ 8956 9770) which has interesting displays of old mining machinery and historic photographs. A free, self operated 20 minute slide show describes the reserve and its history. The Visitor Centre is open every day from 8 am to 5 pm. Drinking water is available and there are toilets, including disabled facilities.

Self-guiding walks are scattered through the reserve (see next section). On Sunday at 11 am the rangers crank up the old Jenkins

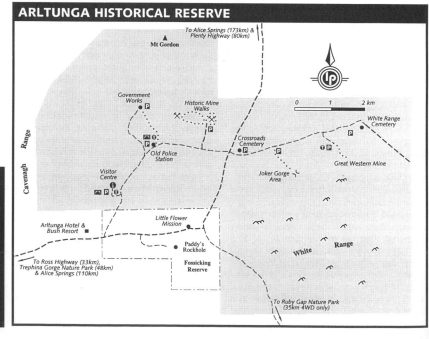

ARLTUNGA HISTORICAL RESERVE

To Alice Springs (173km) & Plenty Highway (80km)

Mt Gordon

Government Works

Historic Mine Walks

0   1   2 km

White Range Cemetery

Range

Crossroads Cemetery

Old Police Station

Great Western Mine

Cavenagh

Visitor Centre

Joker Gorge Area

Arltunga Hotel & Bush Resort

Little Flower Mission

Paddy's Rockhole

White   Range

To Ross Highway (33km), Trephina Gorge Nature Park (48km) & Alice Springs (110km)

Fossicking Reserve

To Ruby Gap Nature Park (35km 4WD only)

EAST MACDONNELL RANGES

Battery behind the centre and crush some gold-bearing ore. Guided tours are conducted three times a week between May and October.

Things to See

Arltunga is a fascinating place for anyone interested in history and gives an idea of what life was like for the early diggers. The main sites are scattered over a wide area and you'll need a vehicle to get around, but you could easily spend a day here.

Allow 40 minutes to walk around the **Government Works** area, where the best collection of drystone buildings survives. Among the ruins are the site of the Government Battery and Cyanide Works, and the partly restored Manager's and Assayer's Residences. A short walk (1.5km; 30 minutes) leads to the **Old Police Station**, or you can drive there.

Two mines are open in this area, but a torch (flashlight) is essential to get the most out of them. At the **MacDonnell Range Reef Mine** you can climb down steel ladders and explore about 50m of tunnels between two shafts. The **Golden Chance Mine** nearby offers the chance to see old drystone miners' huts.

At the **Crossroads** there's an old cemetery plus the ruins of the old bakehouse; this was the site surveyed for the township that never eventuated. **Joker Gorge** features more old stone buildings and a good view reached by a 200m path up a hill.

The **Great Western Mine** is another short self-guided walk. After climbing some steep ridges with great views to the east, the road ends at **White Range Cemetery**, where lie the remains of Joseph Hele, the man who first found gold here, and numerous other miners.

The remains of **Little Flower Mission** can be seen outside the Reserve. About 200 people lived here from 1942 until 1953, when the Mission moved to Santa Theresa.

Facilities

Camping is not permitted within the historical reserve, but the nearby *Arltunga Hotel &* *Bush Resort* (☎ 8956 9797) is a friendly little pub with excellent home cooking and real coffee, where you can camp for $10 a site.

RUBY GAP NATURE PARK

This little-visited and remote park, accessible only by 4WD, is well worth the effort of getting there. Its gorge and river scenery is some of the wildest and most attractive in central Australia, and being remote and hard to get to, it doesn't have the crowds that often destroy the atmosphere at more accessible places. The waterholes at **Glen Annie Gorge** are usually deep enough for a cooling dip.

It is essential to get a map from Parks & Wildlife, and to register at the Arltunga Visitor Centre before setting out – and when you return. Do not attempt the trip if you are inexperienced, especially in summer. All visitors must carry sufficient water and, as the last 5km is through boggy sand, a shovel and jack may come in useful.

Leaving Arltunga, head east towards Atnarpa homestead. Turn left immediately before the gate 11km from the Claraville turn-off. The road then deteriorates and is restricted to 4WD vehicles thanks to sandy creek crossings and sharp jump-ups. After

Arltunga Jail

another 25km you arrive at the **Hale River**; follow the wheel ruts upstream (left) along the sandy bed for about 6km to the turn-around point, which is through **Ruby Gap** and just short of rugged Glen Annie Gorge. If you're first on the scene after a flood, always check that the riverbed is firm before driving onto it, otherwise you may sink deep in sand.

Allow two hours each way for the trip.

History

Ruby Gap was named after a frantic ruby rush in the late 1880s that crashed overnight when it was found that the rubies were worthless garnets. The man responsible for the rush was David Lindsay, an explorer and surveyor who came through this way while leading an expedition from Adelaide to Port Darwin. The word spread and before long more than 200 hopefuls had made the arduous trek from the railhead at Oodnadatta. It's easy to see how the prospectors got carried away because the surface of the river bed shimmers a deep-claret colour as the sun reflects off the millions of garnet specks. They faced incredible hardships here, not least of which were the lack of water and the fierce climate.

Bushwalking

There are no marked walks here, but for the enthusiast a climb around the craggy rim of **Glen Annie Gorge** features superb views of this beautiful spot. You can climb up on the southern side and return from the north along the sandy floor, or vice versa.

The lonely **grave** of a ruby miner is located at the gorge's northern end.

Facilities

There are no facilities of any kind. *Camping* is allowed anywhere along the river, but you'll need to bring your own firewood and drinking water.

The park is managed by the rangers at Arltunga (☎ 8956 9770), so check road conditions with them before heading out here.

The South-East

To the south of Alice lies a sparsely inhabited region where rolling sand dunes are broken by incredible rock formations, Aboriginal settlements host cultural programs and there's fine bush camping under the desert sky. Many sights can be reached by conventional vehicle, and with a 4WD the visitor will have virtually unlimited access to some little-visited sights of central Australia. The remote Simpson Desert in the far south-eastern corner of the Territory is an almost trackless region of spinifex and shifting sands that is one of the last great 4WD adventures.

North Simpson Desert

Even without a 4WD vehicle excursions are possible into the Simpson Desert, east of the Stuart Hwy, and with a little effort you can travel to the geographical centre of Australia. It was along here that the Overland Telegraph Line and the old *Ghan* railway line ran, and it's still possible to follow the latter along its route from Alice to the small town of Finke, about 150km east of the highway.

The 'Old South Road' turns off the road to Alice Springs airport and runs close to the old *Ghan* railway line. It's beautiful country, the road cutting through red sand dunes in places, and worth a look just to imagine a road train battling through.

Most of the places listed here are accessible by 2WD in dry conditions. However, Chambers Pillar is definitely 4WD only.

EWANINGA ROCK CARVINGS

This small conservation reserve 39km out of Alice on the Old South Road protects an outcrop of sandstone next to a claypan sacred to Arrernte people. The carvings found here and at N'Dhala Gorge are thought to have been made by Aboriginal people who lived

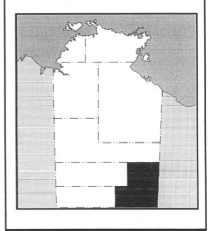

here before those currently in the Centre. The carvings (petroglyphs) are chiselled in the soft rock, but their meaning is regarded as too dangerous for the uninitiated.

There's a 30 minute loop walk with informative signboards, and it's well worth the short stop for a look around.

RAINBOW VALLEY CONSERVATION RESERVE

This is one of the more extraordinary sights in central Australia yet sees relatively few visitors. Out of the low dunes and mulga on the eastern edge of the James Ranges rises

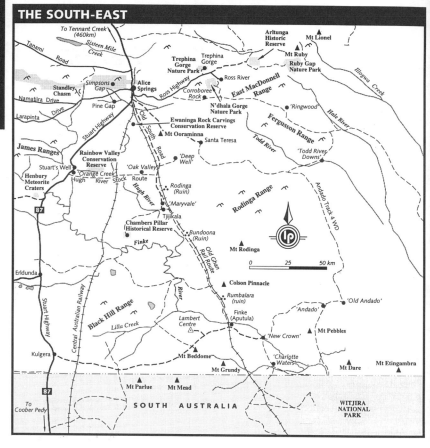

THE SOUTH-EAST

a series of sandstone bluffs and cliffs which seem to glow at sunset. Although colourfully named, the crumbling cliffs are various shades of cream and red. If you're lucky enough to visit after rain, when the whole show is reflected in the claypans, you could get some stunning photos. It's only at sunset that this park attains its real beauty, but it's a nice place to soak up the timeless atmosphere of the Centre.

The rocks here were laid down about 300 million years ago, and weathering and

leaching has led to a concentration of red iron oxides in the upper layers; lower down the stone is bleached almost white. The reserve is important to the southern Arrernte people, and the large rock massif known as Ewerre in the south of the reserve is a registered sacred site.

There's a sunset viewing platform near the car park and a 30 minute boardwalk leads around the claypan to the foot of the bluff. The sandstone here is extremely soft and brittle, and is very easily damaged, so visitors are asked to tread lightly. It is also forbidden to drive on the claypans.

The reserve lies 22km east of the Stuart Hwy along a well-used but unsignposted track 14km north of Stuart's Well by a cattle grid. A sign at the start of the track warns that access is by 4WD vehicle only; a conventional vehicle could make the trip in dry conditions, although there are a couple of deep sandy patches where you could get bogged.

Organised Tours
A number of companies do 4WD trips to Rainbow Valley, usually combined with visits to Chambers Pillar. Companies to contact include the Aboriginal-owned and run Oak Valley Tours (☎ 8956 0959), which does a day trip for $110, and The Outback Experience (☎ 8953 2666) which covers Chambers Pillar as well for $135.

Extended camel safaris from Camel Outback Safaris (☎ 8956 0925) at Stuart's Well also visit Rainbow Valley (see the Stuart's Well section).

Facilities
The small car park about 500m from the foot of the bluff doubles as the *camp ground*. It's a bit exposed, with little shade and no water, but the location is superb and perfectly positioned for sunset viewing – sitting here with a cooling ale watching the show (especially if a full moon is rising) is something not to be missed. There are fireplaces, picnic tables and a pit toilet. The fee is $2.50/6 per person/family, paid into the honesty box. Firewood must be collected on the way in from the highway.

There's a shelter with information about the reserve and a ranger talk is held here on Friday evening during winter.

OAK VALLEY
It's worth calling in at this small Aboriginal community if you happen to be passing. It's on the Hugh River Stock Route, a good track which connects the Stuart Hwy with the old *Ghan* line and Maryvale Station.

The community (☎ 8956 0959) operates day tours out of Alice Springs, but there's

also a 2½ hour guided tour which operates from Oak Valley. The tour takes in local rock art and fossil sites and delves into bush tucker, and costs $15 (children $7).

If you want to stop there for the night there's a *camp ground* with hot showers, toilets, shade shelters and barbecues (firewood supplied). The cost is $7 per person.

CHAMBERS PILLAR HISTORICAL RESERVE
This extraordinary sandstone pillar towers 50m above the surrounding plain and is all that's left of a layer of sandstone laid down 350 million years ago. It's carved with the names of early explorers and the dates of their visit – and, unfortunately, the work of some possibly less worthy modern-day graffiti artists. To the Aboriginal people of the area Chambers Pillar is the remains of Itirkawara, a gecko ancestor of great strength.

There's a basic *camp ground* with toilet and fireplaces, but you need to bring water and firewood. The camping fee is $2.50/6 per person/family. Ranger talks are held weekly between May and October – check with Parks & Wildlife in Alice.

Although Chambers Pillar is only 160km from Alice Springs the trip takes a good four hours. A 4WD is required for the last 44km from the turn-off at Maryvale Station; there's a great view along the way from a high ridge 12km to the west of the pillar.

See the Rainbow Valley section for details of 4WD tour operators who go to Chambers Pillar.

FINKE
Back on the Old South Road, you eventually arrive at Finke, a small Apatula Aboriginal settlement 230km south of Alice Springs. This is another town that owes its existence to the railway line. It started life as a railway siding and gradually grew to have a white population of about 60. With the opening of the new *Ghan* line further west in 1982, administration of the town was taken over by the Apatula Aboriginal community. The community store here is also an outlet for the local artists, who make crafts such as

carved wooden animals, bowls, traditional weapons and seed necklaces. Be aware that this is Aboriginal land – alcohol and the taking of pictures are prohibited.

Finke is linked to the Stuart Hwy, 147km to the west, by the well-maintained dirt road sometimes known as the Goyder Stock Route. It's a fairly uninteresting stretch of road, although the Lambert Centre (see the following section), just off the road, makes an interesting diversion.

From Finke there are some exciting possibilities – east to New Crown Station, and then south to Oodnadatta (passable with a robust conventional vehicle), or further east to Old Andado Station then south to Dalhousie Springs in the Witjira National Park, South Australia. This is definitely 4WD territory; for full details of travel in this area, see the Lonely Planet *Outback Australia* book.

Facilities

There's a basic *community store* (☎ 8956 0968) and a petrol station. Opening hours for both are Monday to Friday 8.30 to 11.30 am and 1.30 to 4 pm, and Saturday from 9 am to 11 am (there's a $10 surcharge for opening up after hours).

LAMBERT CENTRE

A point 21km west of Finke along the Kulgera road, and 13km north of the road along a sandy, signposted track, has been determined as Australia's geographical centre. And to mark the spot there's a 5m high replica of the flagpole, complete with Australian flag, that sits on top of Parliament House in Canberra! For those of you who like precision, the continent's centre is at latitude 25°36'36.4"S and longitude 134°21'17.3"E, and was named after Bruce Lambert, a surveyor and first head of the National Mapping Council. In addition to the flagpole there's a visitors' book which makes interesting reading. Some people get all emotional on reaching this point and blabber on with some of the most parochial and rabidly nationalistic crap you're ever likely to come across!

The track is sandy in patches, but you could probably make it in a 2WD vehicle with care.

South Down the Track

South from Alice along the Stuart Hwy there are a couple of roadhouses but not much else till you reach the South Australian border. Erldunda marks the turn-off to Uluru-Kata Tjuta National Park (Ayers Rock) and the road is sealed and in good condition all the way.

STUART'S WELL

Stuart's Well is a stop on the Stuart Hwy 90km south of Alice Springs, where the highway passes through a gap in the James Ranges. The main attraction here is the **Camel Outback Safaris** operation (☎ 8956 0925), founded by central Australia's 'camel king', Noel Fullerton. It's a good opportunity to take a short camel ride ($4 around the yard, $15/25 for 30/60 minutes and $55/75 for a half/full day). Extended safaris of seven to 14 days into places like nearby Rainbow Valley or Palm Valley also operate on a regular basis. The rate for these is around $110 per person per day.

Places to Stay

Next door to the camel farm is *Jim's Place* (☎ 8956 0808), run by another central Australian identity, Jim Cotterill. The Cotterills opened up Kings Canyon to tourism and Jim is a font of knowledge on the area.

There's camping ($12, $15 powered) with grass and shade, four-bed dorms at $15 per person and self-contained cabins at $60/75. There's a pool and spa, a store that stocks basic provisions, and a licensed restaurant and bar. On the wall is an interesting collection of photos, particularly of the old Wallara Ranch on the Ernest Giles Rd.

Fuel is available from 6 am to 10 pm.

ERLDUNDA

Erldunda is a modern roadhouse and motel complex on the Stuart Hwy 200km south of Alice Springs, at the point where the Lasseter Hwy branches off 244km west to Uluru. It's a very popular rest and refuelling stop, but the fuel prices are among the highest along the 2700km length of the Stuart Hwy.

In addition to accommodation there's a licensed restaurant/bistro, and the roadhouse sells takeaway food, souvenirs, groceries and vehicle parts. Fuel is available from 7.30 am to 10 pm.

Places to Stay

The *Desert Oaks Motel – Caravan Park* (☎ *8956 0984*) has shaded and grassy camp sites for $14 ($18 with power), and there's a shaded swimming pool and tennis court. The air-con bunkhouse section consists of interconnected dongas with four-bed rooms and communal facilities, where accommodation costs $26/36/47/52 for one to four people, respectively. Comfortable motel rooms with en suite, fridge and TV cost $66/78.

KULGERA

Depending on which way you're heading, the scruffy settlement of Kulgera will be your first or last taste of the Territory. It is on the Stuart Hwy 20km north of the South Australian border, and from here the gravel road known as the Goyder Stock Route heads off east for the 147km trip to Finke.

The pub/roadhouse and police station (☎ *8956 0974*) here service the outlying Pitjantjatjara Aboriginal community and pastoral leases.

Places to Stay

At the *Kulgera Roadhouse* (☎ *8956 0973*) there are air-con units with fridge and en suite for $48, air-con backpackers' rooms at $10 a bed, and camping is $10 a site ($15 with power). The roadhouse also has a shop, bar and dining room, and does takeaways.

SOUTH TO PORT AUGUSTA

From the border, 20km south of Kulgera, there's lots of very little to see as you head south the 900km or so to Port Augusta. The main exception is the town of Coober Pedy, which is one of the more interesting outback towns and definitely worth a stop.

Port Augusta isn't terribly attractive or interesting, but it's a convenient place to rest overnight. Coober Pedy is 391km south of the border and a long day's drive from Ayers Rock or Alice; Port Augusta is another 695km down the track and an important junction of traffic east, west and north.

There are several roadhouses at intervals along the route. All sell fuel (the longest distance between fill-ups is 254km, between Coober Pedy and Glendambo) and meals during regular business hours, and decent accommodation is available.

For details, see Lonely Planet's *South Australia* guide.

Uluru-Kata Tjuta National Park

The south-west section of the Territory consists largely of sweeping spinifex grass sand plains that stretch west into the formidable Gibson Desert in Western Australia. It's cold and windy in winter and unimaginably hot in summer, but this inhospitable land supports large stands of desert oaks and mulga trees, and is a blaze of colour after spring rains when dozens of varieties of wildflowers bloom.

You probably wouldn't spare it a passing thought except for one thing, it is in this area that you find one of Australia's most readily identifiable icons – Uluru (Ayers Rock). 'The Rock' lies some 250km west of the highway along a fine bitumen road.

LASSETER HWY

The bitumen Lasseter Hwy connects the Stuart Hwy with Uluru-Kata Tjuta National Park, 244km to the west. It is a wide, well-engineered road which takes only a couple of hours to travel – a far cry from the old days when a journey to Uluru was a major expedition.

Mt Ebenezer

Mt Ebenezer is an Aboriginal-owned station 56km west of the Stuart Hwy in the shadow of the Basedow Range and Mt Ebenezer to the north. There's a roadhouse which dates back to the 1950s and the original part is built from hand-sawn desert oak logs.

The roadhouse is the art-and-craft outlet for the local Imanpa Aboriginal community and prices here are very competitive. At the time of writing the *Mt Ebenezer Roadhouse (☎ 8956 2904)* was upgrading its accommodation and had no facilities other than fuel, snacks and souvenirs.

Opening hours are 7 am to 8 pm.

Luritja Rd

Just over 50km beyond Mt Ebenezer is the Luritja Rd turn-off. This sealed 68km road links Uluru with the Ernest Giles Rd and

- Spend a few days exploring Uluru and vicinity
- Take your time on the walk around the base of the Rock
- Walk the Valley of the Winds at sunrise in magnificent Kata Tjuta
- Learn about Anangu traditions at the Aboriginal Culture Centre
- Gaze at a million stars in the desert sky

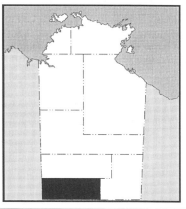

Kings Canyon (see the MacDonnell & James Ranges chapter).

Mt Conner

From the Luritja Rd the Lasseter Hwy swings towards the south, and it's along this stretch that you get the first glimpses of Mt Conner, the large mesa (table-top mountain) which looms 350m high out of the desert about 20km south of the road. On first sighting many people mistake this for Uluru, but on closer inspection it bears no resemblance. There's a rest area on the highway 26km beyond the Luritja Rd turn-off which is a good vantage point to take in the scene.

Mt Conner was discovered by explorer William Gosse in 1873, who named it after ML Conner, a South Australian politician. It has great significance for the local Aboriginal people, who know it as Artula, the home of the ice-men.

Organised Tours Mt Conner lies on Curtin Springs Station and there is no public access. Half/full-day tours ($75/155) of Mt Conner and the station are run by Day Tours (☎ 8953 4664) from Curtin Springs roadhouse. If you're staying at Yulara, Uluru Experience (☎ toll-free 1800 803 174) runs an afternoon/sunset tour, including dinner, from the resort for $125 (children $104).

Curtin Springs

The Curtin Springs homestead roadhouse is a further 26km from the rest area and can be a very lively little spot, not least because the bar is popular among the local Aboriginal community. The station was named after the nearby springs, which were in turn named after the prime minister at the time, John Curtin.

Facilities In addition to the bar, the *roadhouse* (☎ 8956 2906) has fuel, a store with limited supplies and takeaway food and a swimming pool (guests only). Camping is free, unless you want power ($10), and there's accommodation in demountables for $42 with common facilities or $65 with attached bathroom. A good three-course dinner is available for $18.

Fuel is available from 7 am until about 11 pm.

Uluru-Kata Tjuta National Park

For most visitors to Australia a visit to Uluru is a must, and it undoubtedly ranks among the world's greatest natural attractions. The national park is one of eleven places in Australia included on the UN World Heritage list.

The entire area is of deep cultural significance to the local Pitjantjatjara and Yankuntjatjara Aboriginal people (who refer to themselves as Anangu). To them the Rock area is known as Uluru and the Olgas as Kata Tjuta.

There are plenty of walks and other activities at Uluru, Kata Tjuta and the township of Yulara, and it is not at all difficult to spend several days here. Unfortunately most group tours are very rushed and squeeze in a quick afternoon Rock climb, photos at sunset, a morning at the Olgas next day and then off – 24 hours in total if you're lucky.

HISTORY
Aboriginal Heritage

Archaeological evidence suggests that Aboriginal people have inhabited this part of Australia for at least 10,000 years. According to Aboriginal law laid down during the creation period (*Tjukurpa* 'chook-oor-pa'), all landscape features were made by ancestral beings; the Anangu today are the descendants of the ancestral beings and are the custodians of the ancestral lands. Tjukurpa is a philosophy providing answers to fundamental questions about existence.

The most important ancestors in the Uluru area are the Mala (rufous hare wallaby), the Kuniya (woma python) and the Liru (brown snake), and evidence of their activities is seen in features of the Rock.

According to Anangu legend, Uluru was built by two boys who played in the mud after rain in the Tjukurpa; it is at the centre of a number of Dreaming tracks which criss-cross central Australia.

The Anangu officially own the national park, although it is leased to Parks Australia, the Commonwealth government's national parks body, on a 99 year lease. The traditional owners receive an annual rental of $150,000 plus 25% of the park entrance fees. Decisions related to the park are made by the 10 members of the Board

ULURU-KATA TJUTA

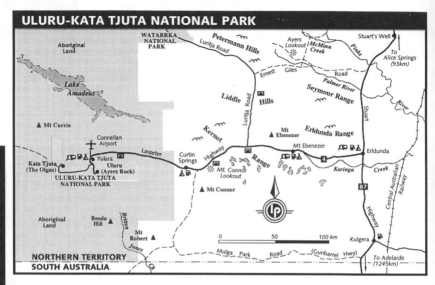

ULURU-KATA TJUTA NATIONAL PARK

of Management, six of whom are nominated by the traditional owners.

Mala Tjukurpa The Mala wallabies travelled from the Yuendumu area to Uluru for ceremonies (*inma*). The men climbed to the top of Uluru to plant a ceremonial pole, while the women collected and prepared food at Taputji, a small isolated rock on the north-eastern side.

During the ceremonies, the Mala were invited by the Wintalka (mulga-seed) men to attend dance ceremonies away to the west. Being already committed to their own celebrations, the Mala refused and the angered Wintalka created a nasty, dingo-like creature (Kurpany) which sneaked up on the women's dancing ceremonies at Tjukatjapi on the northern side of the Rock. The frightened women fled right into the middle of the men's secret ceremony, ruining it, and in the confusion a Mala man was killed and eaten by the Kurpany. The remaining Mala fled south towards the Musgrave Ranges.

Kuniya & Liru Tjukurpa The Tjukurpa tells of how the Kuniya (woma python)

came from the east to hatch her young at Uluru. While she was camped at Taputji, she was attacked by a group of Liru (brown snakes), who had been angered by Kuniya's nephew. At Mutitjulu she came across a Liru warrior and performed a ritual dance, mustering great forces. In an effort to dispel this terrifying force she picked up a handful of sand and let it fall to the ground. The vegetation where the sand fell was poisoned and today remains unusable to Anangu.

The force within her remained strong and a great battle with the Liru was fought. She hit him on the head, attempting to inflict a 'sorry cut', but overcome with anger she hit him a second time and killed him. The two wounds received by the Liru can be seen as the vertical cracks on the Rock near Mutitjulu.

Lungkata Tjukurpa The Lungkata Tjukurpa is the story of how Lungkata (blue-tongue lizard man) found an emu, which had been wounded by other hunters, at the base of the Rock. He finished it off and started to cook it. The original hunters, two bellbird brothers, found Lungkata and asked him if he had seen their emu. He lied, saying he hadn't seen it, but the hunters did not believe him and chased him around the base of the Rock. While being pursued Lungkata dropped pieces of emu meat, and these are seen as the fractured slabs of sandstone just west of Mutitjulu, and at Kalaya Tjunta (emu thigh) on the south-eastern side of Uluru, where a spur of Rock is seen as the emu's thigh.

White History

The first white man to venture into the area was Ernest Giles on his attempted crossing from the Overland Telegraph Line to the west of the continent in 1872. His party had travelled west from Kings Canyon, and sighted Kata Tjuta, which he named Mt Ferdinand after his financier, the noted botanist Baron von Mueller. However, von Mueller later changed the name to Mt Olga, after Queen Olga of Wurttemburg. Giles tried to reach Kata Tjuta in the hope of finding water around its base, but was repeatedly thwarted by the large salt lake which lay in front of him. He named it Lake Mueller, again after von Mueller, and described it as 'an infernal lake of mud and brine'. Baron von Mueller also renamed this one, calling it instead Lake Amadeus, after the King of Spain.

The following year a party led by William Gosse set out to cross to the west. Hot on his heels was a disappointed Giles, who was keen to have another go. Gosse reached the area first, and after sighting and naming Mt Conner, sighted a hill to the west. His account states:

The hill, as I approached, presented a most peculiar appearance, the upper portion being covered with holes or caves. When I got clear of the sandhills, and was only two miles distant, and the hill, for the first time, coming fairly into view, what was my astonishment to find it was one immense rock rising abruptly from the plain ... I have named this Ayers Rock, after Sir Henry Ayers the premier of South Australia.

The early explorers were followed by pastoralists, missionaries, doggers (dingo hunters) and various miscellaneous adventurers who travelled through the area. Among these was Harold Lasseter, who insisted he had found a fabulously rich gold reef in the Petermann Ranges to the west in 1901. He died a lonely death in the same ranges in 1931 trying to rediscover it.

As white activity in the area increased, so did the contact and conflict between the two cultures. With the combined effects of stock grazing and drought, the Anangu found their hunting and gathering options becoming increasingly scarce, which in turn led to a dependence on the white economy.

In the 1920s the three governments of Western Australia, South Australia and the Northern Territory set aside a reserve (the Great Central Aboriginal Reserve) for Aboriginal people. In the era of assimilation, reserves were seen, according to the *NT Annual Report* of 1938, as '... refuges or sanctuaries of a temporary nature. The Aboriginal may here continue his normal existence until the time is ripe for his further development'. 'Development' here refers to the assimilation aim of providing Aboriginal people with skills and knowledge which would enable them to fit into white society. The policy failed across the country; the Anangu shunned this and other reserves, preferring instead to maintain traditional practices.

By 1950 a road had been pushed through from the east and tourism started to develop in the area. As early as 1951 the fledgling Connellan Airways applied for permission to build an airstrip near Uluru. In order to facilitate this, the area of Uluru and Kata Tjuta was excised from the reserve in 1958 for use as a national park. Soon after motel leases were granted and the airstrip constructed.

The first official ranger and Keeper of Ayers Rock at the Ayers Rock & Mt Olga National Park was Bill Harney, a famous Territorian who spent many years working with Aboriginal people and contributed greatly towards white understanding of them.

With the revoking of pastoral subsidies in 1964, which until that time had compensated pastoralists for food and supplies distributed to passing Aboriginal people, many Anangu were forced off the stations and

ULURU-KATA TJUTA

gravitated to Uluru. As they could no longer sustain themselves completely by traditional ways, and needed money to participate in the white economy, they were able to earn some cash by selling artefacts to tourists.

By the 1970s it was clear that planning was required for the development of the area. Between 1931 and 1946 only 22 people were known to have climbed Uluru. In 1969 about 23,000 people visited the area. Ten years later the figure was 65,000 and now the annual visitor figures are approaching the 500,000 mark!

The 1970s saw the construction of the new Yulara Resort some distance from the Rock, as the original facilities were too close and were having a negative impact on the environment. Many of the old facilities, close to the northern side of the Rock, were bulldozed, while some are still used by the Mutitjulu Aboriginal community.

Increased tourism activity over the years led to Aboriginal anxiety about the desecration of important sites by tourists. The Federal government was approached for assistance and by 1973 Aboriginal people had become involved with the management of the park. Although title to many parcels of land in the Territory had been handed back to Aboriginal people under the Aboriginal Land Rights (NT) Act of 1976, the act did not apply here as national parks were excluded from the legislation.

It was not until 1979 that traditional ownership of Uluru-Kata Tjuta was recognised by the government. In 1983, following renewed calls from traditional owners for title to the land, the Federal government announced that freehold title to the national park would be granted and the park leased back to what is now Parks Australia for a period of 99 years. The transfer of ownership took place on 26 October 1985.

Since then the park has become one of the most popular in Australia.

GEOLOGY

The Rock itself is 3.6km long by 2.4km wide, stands 348m above the surrounding dunes and measures 9.4km around the base.

It is made up of a type of coarse-grained sandstone known as arkose, which was formed from sediment from eroded granite mountains. Kata Tjuta, on the other hand, is a conglomerate of granite and basalt gravel glued together by mud and sand.

The sedimentary beds which make up the two formations were laid down over a period of about 600 million years, in a shallow sea in what geologists know as the Amadeus Basin. Various periods of uplift caused the beds to be buckled, folded and lifted above sea level, and those which form Uluru were turned so that they are almost vertical, while at Kata Tjuta they were tilted about 20°. For the last 300 million years or so erosion has worn away the surface rocks, leaving what we see today. Yet it's believed that two-thirds of the Rock still lies beneath the sand.

The sculptured shapes seen on the surface of Uluru today are the effects of wind, water and sand erosion. At Kata Tjuta the massive upheavals fractured the Rock, and erosion along the fracture lines has formed the distinctive valleys and gorges.

CLIMATE

The park is in the centre of the arid zone, which covers 70% of the Australian continent. Here the average yearly rainfall is around 220mm. Although rainfall varies greatly from year to year, the most likely time for rain and thunderstorms is during the Top End's wet season, from November to March, when the tails of tropical depressions moving over the centre of Australia bring widespread rainfall. Droughts are not uncommon and a year or two may go by without rain; the longest drought on record ended in 1965 after lasting for more than six years. Not surprisingly, humidity is low throughout the year.

Many people are surprised at how cold it gets at Uluru in winter. Daytime temperatures in winter can be pleasant, but if there's cloud and a cold wind around it can be bitter. Clear nights often see the temperature plunge to well below freezing – campers beware!

In summer the temperatures soar, peaking during February and March when it gets as hot as 45°C. Normally it's a mere 30 to 35°C. Climbing the Rock is prohibited between 10 am and 4 pm on days when the temperature is forecast to reach 38°C or above.

FLORA & FAUNA
Flora
The plants of the red sand plains of central Australia have adapted to the harsh, dry climate – mainly spinifex grasses, mulga bushes and desert oak trees. These plants remain virtually dormant during times of drought and shoot into action after good rains.

The mulga has heavy, hard wood and so was used by Anangu for firewood, and for making implements such as boomerangs and digging sticks. Stands of desert oaks are usually found in areas of deep sand. The rough, corky bark protects and insulates the trunk, giving it a level of fire protection.

Common eucalypts found in the area include the Centralian bloodwood, the river red gum and the blue mallee.

Except in the times of severe drought, numerous grevilleas and fuchsias thrive in the sand dunes.

Late winter/early spring (August-September) usually turns on a display of wildflowers with some surprisingly showy blooms.

As is the case in the Top End, Aboriginal people in central Australia used fire to manage the land. Controlled burns encourage regrowth and limit the amount of accumulated vegetation. Large fires burn too hot over a large area and can be very destructive. These days the park managers are trying to recreate the 'mosaic' pattern of small burns which occurred before white settlement.

Fauna
Although this arid country around Uluru doesn't look very fertile, it is home to a wide variety of animals – the fact that most of the Tjukurpa sites within the park are animal related is evidence of that. Anangu knowledge of ecosystems and animal behaviour is essential to wildlife surveys and provides background for conservation programs.

Nearly 20 species of native – and another six introduced – mammals are found within the park. The most common native mammals include red kangaroos, euros, dingoes and small marsupials such as dunnarts and marsupial moles. The moles have become specialised desert dwellers – they are blind and use their short, strong limbs to burrow through the loose sand, feeding on insect larvae and small reptiles.

Most of the park's mammals are active only at night, but you're bound to see some birds. Crested pigeons are common around Yulara and while walking round the Rock you'll probably see colourful galahs, budgerigars and zebra finches. After rains nomadic flocks of chats and honeyeaters can arrive virtually overnight. A checklist of birds found within the park is available from the Visitor Centre.

ORIENTATION
The 1326 sq km Uluru-Kata Tjuta National Park takes in the area of Uluru (Ayers Rock) and Kata Tjuta (the Olgas). Yulara is the modern town which has been built to service the almost half a million tourists who visit the area each year. The township lies outside the northern boundary of the national park, and is 20km from the Rock; the Olgas lie 53km to the west. All roads within the park are bitumen and are open year-round.

INFORMATION
The Uluru-Kata Tjuta National Park Cultural Centre (☎ 8956 3138) is inside the national park, just 1km before the Rock on the road from Yulara. This excellent facility is open from 7 am to 5.30 pm in winter (to 6 pm in summer). It's worth putting aside at least one hour, preferably more, to have a good look around the Cultural Centre before visiting Uluru itself.

There are two main display areas, both with multilingual information: the Tjukurpa display features Anangu art and Tjukurpa; while the Nintiringkupai display focuses on the history and management of the national park.

The centre also houses the Aboriginal-owned Maruku Art & Crafts shop (8 am to 5.30 pm), and there's the opportunity to see artists at work and dancers performing. Everything is created in the surrounding desert regions, and certificates of authenticity are issued with most paintings and major pieces. It's about the cheapest place in the Centre to buy souvenirs (carvings etc) and you're buying direct from the artists.

There's also the Aboriginal-run Ininti Store, which sells a tasteful range of T-shirts and other souvenirs, plus snacks, books and videos (open 7 am to 5.30 pm).

The centre has a picnic area with free gas barbecues and the Anangu Tours desk (☎ 8956 2123), where you can book Aboriginal-led tours around Uluru.

There's also a Visitor Centre at Yulara. This one is open daily from 8 am to 9 pm and is also a good source of information (see the Yulara section later in this chapter).

The park is open daily from half an hour before sunrise to sunset.

Entry Fees

Entry to the national park costs $15 (free for children under 16), and this is good for a five day visit. Entry permits should be bought at the park entry gate on the road between Yulara and Uluru.

A $60 'Territorian Pass' is available for Australian residents and valid for a year. It includes access to Kakadu.

ULURU (AYERS ROCK)

The world-famous Uluru towers above the pancake-flat surrounding plain. Its colour changes as the setting sun turns it a series of deeper and darker reds before it fades into grey and blends into the night sky. A similar performance in reverse, with fewer spectators, is performed at dawn each day.

Uluru Walks

There are a number of walking trails around Uluru and park rangers lead informative tours which delve into a particular aspect of the area. On some of the walks there are tours operated by Anangu Tours.

Note that there are several Aboriginal sacred sites around the base of Uluru. They're clearly fenced off and signposted

and to enter or photograph these areas is a grave offence, not just for non-Aboriginal people but for 'ineligible' Aboriginal people as well.

Carry water at all times and drink at least one litre per hour when walking during hot weather.

Full details of the Mala and Mutitjulu walks are given in a self-guided walks brochure available from the Visitor Centre for $1.

Circuit Walk It takes around three or four hours to walk around the base of Uluru, looking at the caves and paintings on the way. This is a good way to explore Uluru because most people are in too much of a rush to do this walk and you'll often have the path pretty much to yourself.

Pick up a brochure for the self-guided walk around the base.

Mala Walk This walk starts from the base of the climbing point and takes about 1½ hours at a very leisurely pace. The Tjukurpa of the Mala is of great importance to the Anangu. You can do this walk on your own, or there are ranger-guided walks daily at 10 am (8 am in summer) from the car park (no booking necessary). This walk is suitable for disabled visitors.

Mutitjulu Walk Mutitjulu is a permanent waterhole on the southern side of Uluru. The Tjukurpa tells of the clash between two ancestral snakes, Kuniya and Liru. The waterhole is just a short walk from the car park on the southern side, and you can either do the walk yourself, or go with Anangu Tours (see Organised Tours later in this chapter), where you'll learn more about the Kuniya Tjukurpa, and also about food and medicinal plants found here. Swimming is not permitted in the waterhole.

Climbing the Rock

The consensus is Uluru shouldn't be climbed (see the following boxed text). Those of you who decide to do so should

ULURU (AYERS ROCK)

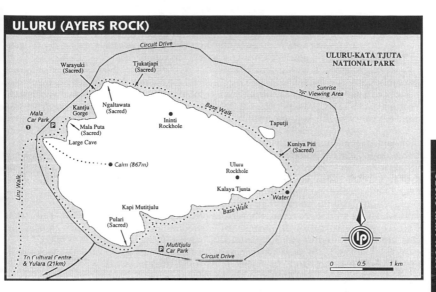

Warayuki (Sacred)
Tjukatjapi (Sacred)
Circuit Drive
ULURU-KATA TJUTA NATIONAL PARK
Sunrise Viewing Area
Kantju Gorge
Ngaltawata (Sacred)
Base Walk
Mala Car Park
Mala Puta (Sacred)
Ininti Rockhole
Taputji
Large Cave
Kuniya Piti (Sacred)
Cairn (867m)
Uluru Rockhole
Kalaya Tjunta
Water
Liru Walk
Kapi Mutitjulu
Base Walk
Pulari (Sacred)
Mutitjulu Car Park
Circuit Drive
To Cultural Centre & Yulara (21km)
0   0.5   1 km

ULURU-KATA TJUTA

take care – in the last 30 years 28 people have met their maker in the attempt, usually by having a heart attack, but some by taking a tumble. Avoid climbing in the heat of the day during the hot season – start climbing at 6 or 7 am. The climb is actually closed between 10 am and 4 pm on days when the forecast temperature is more than 38°C. There is an emergency phone at the car park at the base of the climb, and another at the top of the chain, about halfway up the climbing route.

And don't underestimate the cold in winter – wear clothing which can be peeled off or put back on according to conditions. Gloves and a woollen hat may come in useful.

The climb itself is 1.6km and takes about two hours up and back with a good rest at the top. The first part of the walk is by far the steepest and most arduous, and there's a chain to hold on to. It's often extremely windy at the top, even when it isn't at the base, so make sure your hat is well tied on.

There's no food or water at the top or bottom – carry all your requirements.

Climbing Uluru

For years climbing the rock was considered a highlight of a trip to the Centre. It's important to note, however, that climbing Uluru goes against Aboriginal spiritual beliefs, and the Anangu would prefer that you didn't. The route taken by visitors is associated closely with the Mala Tjukurpa (see the History section earlier in this chapter). The Anangu also feel responsible for all people on the rock, and are greatly saddened when a visitor to their land is injured or dies there.

Besides, they call the people climbing the 'Minga Mob'. You just have to look at them from a distance to get the joke – minga means ant.

Although the number of visitors to Uluru has risen steadily over the years, the number actually climbing the rock is declining, while sales of the ideologically sound 'I Didn't Climb Ayers Rock' T-shirts are on the rise.

Facilities

About half-way between Yulara and Uluru there's a **sunset viewing area** with plenty of car parking space. This place is amazingly busy at sunset and it's hardly a quiet and peaceful experience.

There is little in the way of facilities at the Rock itself. There is a toilet block at the climb car park, but this is just a small facility using composting methods and there are often long queues. It's better to use those at the Cultural Centre if possible.

KATA TJUTA (THE OLGAS)

Kata Tjuta, a collection of smaller, more rounded rocks, stands about 30 km to the west of Uluru (53km by road from Yulara). Though less well known, the monoliths are equally impressive and, indeed, many people find them more captivating. The tallest rock, Mt Olga, at 546m, is nearly 200m higher than Uluru.

Meaning 'many heads', Kata Tjuta is of great significance to Anangu and is associated with a number of Tjukurpa stories. However, as these relate to secret ceremonies involving the education and initiation of men, they are only revealed to men involved in these rituals and are not for general consumption.

A lonely sign at the western end of the access road points out that there is a hell of a lot of nothing if you travel west – although, suitably equipped, you can travel all the way to Kalgoorlie and on to Perth in Western Australia (see the Getting Around chapter).

Kata Tjuta Walks

There are two marked walking trails at Kata Tjuta, neither of them highly used compared with those at Uluru.

Valley of the Winds This walk takes around three hours and winds through the gorges giving excellent views of the domes. Although well constructed, the track can be rough in places and you'll need sturdy footwear, plus drinking water and a hat.

Olga Gorge (Tatintjawiya) There is a short signposted track into the extraordinary Olga Gorge from the car park. The return

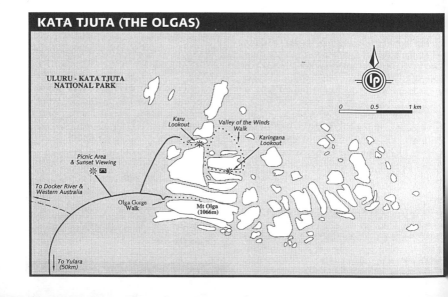

KATA TJUTA (THE OLGAS)

ULURU - KATA TJUTA
NATIONAL PARK

Karu Lookout

Valley of the Winds Walk

Karingana Lookout

Picnic Area & Sunset Viewing

To Docker River & Western Australia

Olga Gorge Walk

Mt Olga (1066m)

0   0.5   1 km

To Yulara (50km)

trip takes around an hour to complete and again offers good views.

Facilities

The car park, complete with toilet block, shade shelters and picnic tables, is close to the western edge of the Olgas. There's also a solar-powered radio here for use in an emergency.

A short distance to the west, on the main access road, is a **sunset viewing area** with picnic tables and toilets. It's worth organising your activities so you can be out here at sunset as the views are often stunning.

Along the road between Yulara and Kata Tjuta there's a marked **dune viewing area**. From the car park here it's a five minute walk along a boardwalk through the dunes to a viewing platform which gives sweeping views over the surrounding dune country, with Kata Tjuta in the background. Interpretive signs here outline the features of the complex dune environment.

ORGANISED TOURS
From Yulara

There's a Tour & Information Centre at Yulara (☎ 8956 2240) where operators each have a desk. It's open from 8.30 am to 9 pm. If you arrive here from anywhere other than Alice Springs without a tour booked (see the tours from Alice Springs section following) then you're limited to what's here.

Uluru Experience This company (☎ toll-free 1800 803 174) offers a number of possibilities. The five hour Uluru Walk includes the base walk and breakfast for $69/54 for adults/children; Spirit of Uluru is a four hour vehicle-based tour around the base of the Rock for the same price. The Olgas & Dunes Tour includes the walk into Olga Gorge and the sunset at the Olgas for $51/41. The Uluru Experience Pass lets you choose any two of the three tours above and also gives you a discount on the Night Sky Show (see the following Yulara section for details).

Uluru Experience also runs tours to Mt Conner (see that section earlier in this chapter for details).

AAT-King's To allow some flexibility with your itinerary AAT-King's (☎ toll-free 1800 334 009) has a range of options which depart daily. Check with the desk at the centre at Yulara for departure times.

A 'Rock Pass' which includes a guided base tour, sunset, climb, sunrise, Cultural Centre and Kata Tjuta (Olga Gorge only) tours costs $154/77 for adults/children. The pass is valid for three days and includes the $15 national park entry fee.

If you don't want to climb the Rock the 24-hour Super Pass costs $114 and includes the Valley of the Winds (Olgas). Other combinations are available.

All these activities are also available in various combinations on a one-off basis: base tour ($37/19), sunrise tour ($34/17), climb ($34/17), sunset ($24/12), base and sunset ($52/26), sunrise and climb ($57/29), climb and base ($62/31), sunrise and base ($57/29), sunrise, climb and base ($76/38), Olgas and Uluru sunset ($54/41). These prices do not include the park entry fee.

Another option is the Uluru Breakfast Tour, which includes breakfast at the Cultural Centre then hooks into the Anangu Tours' Aboriginal cultural walk for $81/41.

For Olgas viewing, there's the Morning Valley of the Winds Tour ($65/33) or you can do the three hour Valley of the Winds walk, then enjoy a relaxing barbecue with the sunset over the domes for $96/48. A combined Olgas and Uluru sunset costs $64/32.

Anangu Tours Owned and operated by Anangu from the Mutitjulu community, Anangu Tours (☎ 8956 2123) also has a tour desk at the Cultural Centre inside the park.

The Anangu tours are led by an Anangu guide and an interpreter, and they offer a wonderful chance to meet and talk with Anangu. The **Aboriginal Uluru Tour** departs daily, costs $78/63 for adults/children and lasts approximately 4½ hours. Starting with sunrise over Uluru, it takes in a base tour, Aboriginal culture and law, and demonstrations of bush skills and spear-throwing.

ULURU-KATA TJUTA

The **Kuniya Sunset Tour** ($65/49) leaves at 2.30 pm (3.30 pm between October and March) and includes a visit to Mutitjulu Waterhole and the Cultural Centre, finishing with viewing the sunset.

Both trips can be combined over two days with an **Anangu Culture Pass**, which costs $120/95.

Self-drive options are also available for $39/20. You can join an Aboriginal guide at 8.30 am (7.30 in summer) for the morning walk or at 3 pm (4 pm) for the Kuniya Tour.

Bookings are essential for all tours.

Camel Tours Frontier Camel Tours (☎ 8956 2444) has a depot at Yulara with a small museum and camel rides. Two popular rides are the Camel to Sunrise, a two hour tour which includes a saunter through the dunes before sunrise, billy tea and a chat about camels for $65 (breakfast box an additional $9.50); and the sunset equivalent, which costs the same. The sunrise trip can be combined with an Ayers Rock base tour ($100/83 for adults/children) and the sunset trip with a barbecue and Night Sky Show for $100/95.

Motorcycle Tours Sunrise and sunset tours can also be done on the back of a Harley-Davidson motorcycle, though for $105 a pop you'd have to be a motorcycle fanatic. Self-drive tours are also available. For bookings phone ☎ 8956 2019.

From Alice Springs

All-inclusive tours to Uluru by private operators start at about $285 for a three day camping trip which includes Kings Canyon. Companies such as Sahara Tours (☎ 8953 0881) and Northern Territory Adventure Tours (☎ toll-free 1800 063 838) are popular with the budget conscious.

You have to shop around a bit because the tours run on different days and you may not want to wait for a particular one. Other things to check for include the time it gets to the Rock and Kata Tjuta, and whether the return is done early or late in the day. Prices can vary with the season and demand, and sometimes there may be cheaper 'stand-by'

fares available. Bus-pass travellers should note that the bus services to the Rock are often heavily booked so if your schedule is tight it's best to plan ahead.

Tours which include accommodation other than camping are generally much more expensive.

Another option is the passes offered by Greyhound Pioneer and McCafferty's. These are good value as they give you return transport to Yulara, plus various activities options at the Rock (but don't include the park entry fee). See the Getting There & Away section for details.

YULARA
• **pop 2080 (including Mutitjulu)** ✉ 0872
Yulara is the service village for the national park and has effectively turned one of the world's least hospitable regions into an easy and comfortable place to visit. Lying just outside the national park, 20km from Uluru and 53km from Kata Tjuta, the complex is administered by the Ayers Rock Corporation and makes an excellent – though expensive – base for exploring the area's renowned attractions. Opened in 1984, the village was designed to blend in with the local environment and is a low-rise affair nestled between the dunes. Yulara supplies the only accommodation, food outlets and other services available in the region; demand certainly keeps pace with supply and you'll have little choice but to part with lots of money to stay in anything other than a tent here.

Orientation
Yulara is built around a vaguely circular drive through the low dunes and native shrubbery. Heading clockwise everything is on your left, starting with the Desert Gardens Hotel.

The central reserve is criss-crossed by walking trails and everything is within a 15 minute walk or a short drive. If you don't feel like joining the crowds at sunrise or sunset, there are lookouts on top of strategic dunes.

Information & Facilities
The Resort Guide is a useful sheet available at the Visitor Centre and hotel desks. It lists

The sleeping woman of Mount Sonder at sunrise, West MacDonnell Ranges

Trephina Gorge, East MacDonnell Ranges

Glen Helen Gorge, West MacDonnell Ranges

Spectacular Ormiston Gorge, West MacDonnell National Park

RICHARD I'ANSON

Kata Tjuta (the Olgas)

CHRIS MELLOR

The Anangu call them the 'Minga Mob'

PAUL SINCLAIR

Chambers Pillar Historic Reserve

CHRIS MELLOR

Uluru - Ayers Rock

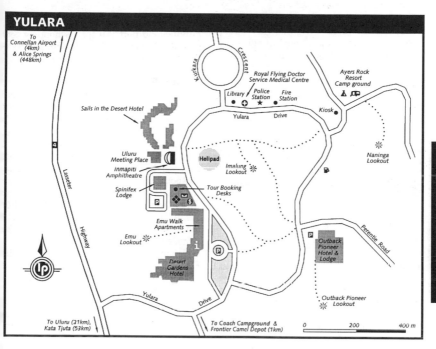

YULARA

To Connellan Airport (4km) & Alice Springs (448km)

Kurkara Crescent

Royal Flying Doctor Service Medical Centre

Library
Police Station
Fire Station

Ayers Rock Resort Camp ground

Kiosk

Sails in the Desert Hotel

Yulara Drive

Lasseter Highway

Uluru Meeting Place

Inmapiti Amphitheatre

Helipad

Imaliung Lookout

Naninga Lookout

Spinifex Lodge

Tour Booking Desks

Emu Walk Apartments

Emu Lookout

Desert Gardens Hotel

Perentie Road

Outback Pioneer Hotel & Lodge

Outback Pioneer Lookout

Yulara Drive

To Uluru (21km), Kata Tjuta (53km)

To Coach Campground & Frontier Camel Depot (1km)

0   200   400 m

ULURU-KATA TJUTA

facilities and opening times, and has a good map of Yulara on one side.

The Visitor Centre (☎ 8957 7377) is open from 8.30 am to 7.30 pm daily and contains good displays on the geology, flora and fauna, history and Aboriginal lore of the region.

Information is also available at the Cultural Centre inside the park, near the Rock itself.

Tours can be booked at the Tour & Information Centre (☎ 8956 2240), which is open from 8.30 am to 9 pm (see the Organised Tours section).

The shopping centre is built around an outdoor eating area, and includes a well-stocked supermarket, bank, post office (open every day), newsagency, various eateries and a same-day photo lab.

The only bank at Yulara is ANZ and it has an ATM. The supermarket and Mobil service station both have EFTPOS facilities.

There's a child care centre in the village for children aged between three months and eight years, which operates from 8 am to 5.30 pm daily (except public holidays). The cost is $18.50/39.50 for a half/full day. Bookings can be made by phoning ☎ 8956 2097.

Also within the village is a Royal Flying Doctor Service medical centre (☎ 8956 2286), which is open from 9 am to noon and 2 to 5 pm weekdays, and from 10 to 11 am on weekends, and a police station (☎ 8956 2166).

The service station sells all types of fuel, maps and ice, and a mechanic is on duty every day. It also has bikes for hire (see Getting Around). It is open daily from 7 am to 9 pm.

Wheelchair access is possible throughout the Yulara resort and the Cultural Centre at the Rock.

Alcohol Warning

Please be aware that alcohol (grog) is a problem among the local Mutitjulu Aboriginal people living near Uluru. It is a 'dry' community and, at the request of the Mutitjulu leaders, the liquor outlets have agreed not to sell it to Aboriginal people. For this reason you may be approached in the car park at the shopping centre by Aboriginal people who want you to buy alcohol on their behalf. The community leaders appeal to you not to do so.

Guided Walks & Talks

There are a number of activities in the village.

Garden Walk This is a guided tour through the native garden of the Sails in the Desert Hotel. It takes place on weekdays at 7.30 am and is led by the hotel's resident gardener. This tour is free and there's no need to book; it starts from the hotel lobby.

Night Sky Show Each evening there's the Night Sky Show, an informative look into Anangu and Greek astrological legends, with views of the startlingly clear outback night sky through telescopes and binoculars. Trips in English are at 8.30 and 10.15 pm, and bookings are required (☎ toll-free 1800 803 174). The cost is $25 (children $18) and you are picked up from your accommodation.

Cocktails at Sunset From the vantage point of a high dune within the village you can watch the sunset, sip cheap champagne and munch 'outback canapés'. It's all very civilised and very expensive too, at $28 (children $14).

Sounds of Silence Another popular excursion is the three hour Sounds of Silence tour, which includes watching the sunset from a vantage point 7km outside Yulara while listening to the sounds of a didgeridoo, sipping cheap champagne and munching canapés, followed by dinner, stargazing, billy tea and port. All for a whopping $90 (children $45) including transfers. Reservations are advised (☎ 8956 2200).

Scenic Flights

While the enjoyment of those on the ground may be diminished by the constant buzz of light aircraft and helicopters overhead, it's very popular and, for those actually up there, it's an unforgettable trip. Operators collect you from your accommodation. Bookings are essential, preferably a day in advance.

Rockayer (☎ 8956 2345) charges $67/55 for adults/children for a 30 minute plane flight over the Rock and Kata Tjuta. For $180/150 you can take a 110 minute flight that also takes in Kings Canyon and Lake Amadeus, and there's a six hour trip ($275) which includes breakfast and time to do the Kings Canyon walk before heading back.

Helicopter flights are operated by Professional Helicopter Services (PHS) (☎ 8956 2003) and Ayers Rock Helicopters (☎ 8956 2077). A 12-15 minute flight over the Rock costs about $70 and 25-30 minutes that includes the Olgas is $150.

There are no child concessions on any of the helicopter flights.

Places to Stay

If there's anything to put a damper on your visit to Uluru, it's the high cost of accommodation and dining at Yulara – you're over a barrel so you'll just have to fork out the dough and grit your teeth. Nonetheless, seemingly insatiable demand makes it advisable to book all accommodation, including dorm beds at the Outback Pioneer Lodge and tent or van sites at the camp ground, especially during school holidays.

All buildings are air-conditioned in summer and heated in winter, and most have a swimming pool.

Remember to add 5% tax to prices (except budget rooms and camping). Bookings can be made on a central reservations number (☎ toll-free 1800 089 622) outside the Sydney metropolitan area or on (☎ 9360 9099) in Sydney.

Budget 'Cheap' is a relative term at Yulara and both the camp sites and dormitories are the most expensive in the Territory. The camp ground is fine but backpackers facilities are looking pretty tired.

The *Ayers Rock Resort Camp Ground* (☎ 8956 2055) charges $22 for two people on an unpowered site, or $26 with power. Most of the camp sites have manicured patches of green grass; the camp ground is set among native gardens and there's quite a bit of shade. If you don't have your own tent, Elke's Backpackers in Alice has them for hire ($6/9 a day for two/three-person tents) and if you're not going back to Alice the Greyhound bus driver can drop it back at Elke's for $5.

Facilities at the camp ground include a swimming pool, phones, laundry, free barbecues and disabled amenities.

The next cheapest option is the dormitories at the *Outback Pioneer Lodge* (☎ 8956 2170), across the dunes from the shopping centre. A bed in a segregated 20-bed dorm costs $24 (YHA members pay $21, dropping to $20 for the 2nd and $18 the 3rd and subsequent nights). The communal cooking facilities are in desperate need of upgrading and noticeably light on utensils. Baggage storage lockers are available for $1 and linen is available for a $10 refundable deposit.

Also available are four-bed lodge cabin ('YBR') rooms, costing $30 per person ($27 for YHA members and $26/24 on 2nd/3rd nights).

Cabins & Units The *camp ground* has cabins sleeping up to six people for $115 per night. The price includes linen and cooking facilities, although bathrooms are shared. They get booked out pretty quickly during the cool winter months.

The *Outback Pioneer Lodge* also has budget rooms, sleeping up to four in combinations of twin or double beds plus bunks. Each has TV, linen, fridge and tea/coffee-making facilities, but bathrooms are communal. The cost is $124. Out the back of this place there's a good lookout point for sunset views of the Rock.

Next up is the *Spinifex Lodge* (☎ 8956 2131) near the shopping square. It has 68 one-bedroom units which accommodate from two to four people at a cost of $124 for a double. These are quite good value, with fridge, TV and microwave oven, although bathrooms are shared. There are guest laundry facilities.

Apartments Probably the best deal at Yulara is offered by the *Emu Walk Apartments* (☎ 8956 2100). There are one and two-bedroom flats which accommodate four and eight people, respectively. They have a lounge room with TV, a fully equipped kitchen and there's a communal laundry. They are also very central, being right between the Visitor Centre and the shopping square. The cost is $284 for the small apartments and $352 for the larger ones.

Hotels The most expensive part of the Outback Pioneer complex is known as the *Outback Pioneer Hotel*, where a single or double room with attached bathroom costs $280.

At the opposite side of Yulara, the *Desert Gardens Hotel* has 100 rooms with TV, phone, minibar and room service costing $312 for a standard single or double and $366 for deluxe rooms with a Rock view. The hotel has a pool and a restaurant.

At the top of the range is the *Sails in the Desert Hotel* (☎ 8956 2200, which has all the facilities you'd expect in a five-star hotel, including in-house movies, 24-hour room service, spa, tennis court and art gallery. High-season rates start at $382 for a double, soaring to $425 with a Rock view and $675 for a deluxe suite.

Places to Eat
The range of eating options is pretty good though self-catering is the only cheap option. The well-stocked *supermarket* at the shopping centre is open daily from 8.30 am to 9 pm and sells meats, fresh fruit and vegetables, and camping supplies; there's also a salad bar and delicatessen.

Yulara Take-Away, also in the shopping centre, does reasonable fast food which you can take back to eat wherever you are staying, or you can eat at the tables in the shopping area. It's open daily from 8.30 am to 7.30 pm. The *Pioneer Kitchen* at the Outback Pioneer Lodge is a kiosk offering light meals and snacks from 8.00 am until 9.00 pm.

The *bakery* has a good selection of pastries and breads, plus good pies and sausage rolls baked on the premises.

Nearby there's an *ice-cream parlour* which serves thick shakes and milkshakes.

For sit-down dining there are licensed restaurants in the hotels and at the shopping centre. Prices are astronomical, yet you'll probably have to book for dinner.

Geckos Café at the shopping centre offers a range of pasta ($15 to $20) and meat dishes ($20 to $25), and wood-fired pizzas ($14 to $19). The prices are way above the quality. Reservations (☎ 8956 2562) are advised.

One of the most popular deals at Yulara is the *Pioneer Barbecue* which takes place every night at the Outback Pioneer Lodge. For around $15 you can barbecue your choice of meat or fish and help yourself to a range of salads. There's also a cheaper vegetarian dish offered, or you can just have the salads for $8.50.

For more conventional dining the hotel also has the *Bough House (☎ 8956 2170)* which is open daily for breakfast, lunch and dinner. Its all you can eat dinner buffet is good and costs $35.

Upmarket à la carte dining can be enjoyed at the Desert Gardens Hotel, where the more formal *White Gums (☎ 8956 2100)* is open for breakfast and dinner only. Main courses here are in the $20 to $25 range, but you can choose any two courses à la carte for $40 and there's an excellent dinner buffet for $37.

The last word in upmarket dining is the Sails in the Desert Hotel, which has the *Rockpool* poolside restaurant; the *Winkiku*, which features buffet meals; and the more sophisticated *Kuniya* which is open for din-

ner only. Reservations for all three can be made by phoning ☎ 8956 2200.

Entertainment

The posh hotels have *bars* which are open daily until late, but remember to dress up a bit.

There are no dress standards at the Outback Pioneer's *BBQ Bar* and live music plays nightly. It's a good place to meet fellow travellers and takeaway alcohol can be bought here.

GETTING THERE & AWAY
Air

Connellan Airport is about 5km from Yulara. You can fly direct to Yulara from various major centres as well as from Alice Springs, which remains the popular starting point for Uluru. Ansett has two flights daily for the 45 minute, $205 hop from Alice to the Rock; Qantas has one for the same price.

The numerous flights direct to Yulara can be money-savers. If, for example, you were intending to fly to the Centre from Adelaide, it makes a lot more sense to go Adelaide-Yulara-Alice Springs rather than go to Adelaide-Alice Springs-Yulara-Alice Springs. You can fly direct between Yulara and Perth ($547), Adelaide ($587), Cairns ($537), Melbourne ($577), Sydney ($576) and Darwin ($549) with Qantas or Ansett.

Bus

Apart from hitching, the cheapest way to get to the Rock is to take a bus or tour. Greyhound Pioneer (☎ 132030) and McCafferty's (☎ 131499) have services between Alice Springs and Yulara – Greyhound Pioneer direct daily, and McCafferty's on Sunday, Tuesday, Thursday and Friday, connecting at Erldunda. The 441km trip takes about 5½ hours.

The fare for one-way travel with McCafferty's is $55 from Alice Springs to Yulara; with Greyhound Pioneer it's $59.

There are also services between Adelaide and Yulara (both companies four times weekly), although this actually means connecting with another bus (and a two hour wait) at Erldunda, the turn-off from the Stuart Hwy. Adelaide to Yulara takes about 22 hours for the 1720km trip and costs $135.

Passes If you don't already have a pass, McCafferty's has its Rock Pass. This is valid for three days and includes return transport from Alice Springs, and then at the Rock itself you can join all the AAT-King's tours: Kata Tjuta & sunset tour, Uluru climb, Uluru sunrise, Uluru sunset and Uluru base tour. The pass doesn't include the park entry fee or accommodation, and costs $148 (children $74). The only condition is that you must stay for two nights, and this is at your own expense.

A variant costing $219 allows you three of the AAT-King's trips plus Kings Canyon and on to Alice, with no time limit.

Greyhound Pioneer has similar deals. If you already have a Greyhound Pioneer pass which gets you to Yulara, you can opt to do the two half-day tours at no extra cost.

Car Rental
If you haven't got your own vehicle, renting a car in Alice Springs to go down to Uluru and back can be expensive. You're looking at $70 to $100 a day for a car from the big operators, and this only includes 100km a day, each extra kilometre costing 25c.

Some companies offer one-way deals from Yulara to Alice Springs. For example, Hertz offers two-day rental with 700km free for $195 and three days with 1000km free for $295. Beware of extras such as insurance, but between four people that's cheaper than taking a bus there and back.

Territory Thrifty Car Rentals in Alice Springs has a deal where a small car costs $70 per day which includes 300km free per day; this is a more realistic option. On one of these deals if you spent three days and covered 1000km (the bare minimum) you'd be up for around $400, including insurance and petrol costs.

The road from Alice to Yulara is sealed and there are regular food and petrol stops along the way. Yulara is 441km from Alice, 241km west of Erldunda on the Stuart Hwy, and the whole journey takes about six to seven hours.

Hertz (☎ 8956 2244), Avis (☎ 8956 2266) and Territory Thrifty Car Rentals (☎ 8956 2030) are all represented at Yulara.

GETTING AROUND
To/From the Airport
A free shuttle bus operated by AAT-King's meets all flights and drops at all accommodation points around the resort.

Around Yulara
A free shuttle bus runs between all accommodation points every 15 minutes from 10.30 am to 2.30 pm and from 6.30 pm to 12.30 am daily.

Bike hire is available at the petrol station for $8 per hour and $15/20 per half/full day.

Around the National Park
Several options are available if you want to go from Yulara to Uluru or Kata Tjuta in the national park. The ticket price includes a stop at the Cultural Centre, and you can then take a later bus to Uluru at no extra charge. The fare does not include the park entry fee.

Sunworth (☎ 8956 2152) runs shuttles to Uluru and return for $20 per person (sunset $15, sunrise $25). Morning/afternoon return services to Kata Tjuta cost $35/40.

Glossary

Basically, Australian (that's 'Strine') is a variant of English/American, owing much of its old slang to British and Irish roots, and often picking up the worst of newspeak from American TV. However, there are a few surprises and other influences, including Aboriginal terms.

Some words have completely different meanings in Australia than they have in English-speaking countries north of the equator; some commonly used words have been shortened almost beyond recognition.

Lonely Planet publishes the *Australian* phrasebook – an introduction to both Australian English and Aboriginal languages. The following Glossary may also help.

arvo – afternoon
avagoyermug – traditional rallying call, especially at cricket matches
award wage – minimum pay rate

back o' Bourke – back of beyond, middle of nowhere
bail out – leave
banana bender – resident of Queensland
barbie – barbecue (BBQ)
barra – the famous fighting barramundi (a fish)
barrack for – support sports team
bastard – general form of address which can mean many things, from high praise or respect ('He's the bravest bastard I know') to dire insult ('You rotten bastard!'). Avoid if unsure!
battler – hard trier, struggler
beaut, beauty, bewdie – great, fantastic
big mobs – a large amount, heaps
bikies – motorcyclists
billabong – water hole in dried up riverbed, more correctly an ox-bow bend cut off in the dry season by receding waters
billy – tin container used to boil tea in the bush

black stump – where the 'back o' Bourke' begins
block (ie 'do your block') – to lose your temper
bloke – man
blow-in – stranger
blowies – blow flies
bludger – lazy person, one who won't work
blue (ie 'have a blue') – to have an argument or fight
bluey – a can of Foster's beer (because it's blue)
bonzer – great, ripper
boomer – very big; a particularly large male kangaroo
boomerang – a curved flat wooden instrument used by Aboriginal people for hunting
booze bus – police van used for random breath testing for alcohol
bottle shop – liquor shop
brekky – breakfast
Buckley's – no chance at all
bulldust – fine and sometimes deep dust on outback roads; also bullshit
burl – have a try (as in 'give it a burl')
bush – country, anywhere away from the city
bushbash – to force your way through pathless bush
bushranger – Australia's equivalent of the outlaws of the American Wild West (some goodies, some baddies)
bush tucker – native foods, usually in the outback

camp oven – large, cast-iron pot with lid, used for cooking on an open fire
cark it – to die
cask – wine box (a great Australian invention)
cheers – drinking salutation
Chiko Roll – vile Australian fast food
chocka – completely full, from 'chock-a-block'
chook – chicken

chuck a U-ey – do a U-turn
clobber – to hit
coldie – a cold beer
compo – compensation, such as workers' compensation
come good – turn out all right
coolamon – Aboriginal wooden carrying dish
counter meal, countery – pub meal
cow cocky – small-scale cattle farmer
crook – ill, badly made, substandard
cut lunch – sandwiches

dag, daggy – dirty lump of wool at back end of a sheep, also an affectionate or mildly abusive term for a socially inept person
daks – trousers
damper – bush bread made from flour and water and cooked in a camp oven
dead horse – tomato sauce
dead set – fair dinkum, true
didgeridoo – cylindrical wooden musical instrument traditionally played by Aboriginal men
dill – idiot
dinkum, fair dinkum – honest, genuine
dinky-di – the real thing
dip out – to miss out or fail
dob in – to tell on someone
donga – demountable cabin
don't come the raw prawn – don't try and fool me
down south – the rest of Australia
drongo – worthless person, idiot
Dry, the – dry season in northern Australia (April to October)
dunny – outdoor lavatory

earbash – talk nonstop
esky – large insulated box for keeping beer etc cold

fair crack of the whip! – fair go!
fair go! – give us a break
flat out – very busy or fast
flog – sell, steal
fossick – hunt for gems or semiprecious stones
furphy – a rumour or false story

galah – noisy parrot, thus noisy idiot
game – brave (as in 'game as Ned Kelly')
gander – look (as in 'have a gander')
garbo – person who collects your garbage
g'day – good day, traditional Australian greeting
gibber – Aboriginal word for a stone or rock, hence gibber plain or desert
give it away – give up
good on ya – well done
greenie – Territory term for a can of VB beer (because it's green)
grog – general term for alcoholic drinks
grouse – very good

haitch – aitch, the 8th letter of the alphabet
hit pay dirt – strike it rich
homestead – residence of a station owner or manager
hoon – idiot, hooligan, yahoo
how are ya? – standard greeting, expected answer 'good, thanks, how are *you*?'

icy-pole – frozen lolly water on a stick
iffy – dodgy, questionable

jackaroo – young male trainee on a station (farm)
jillaroo – young female trainee on a station
jocks – men's underpants
journo – journalist
jumped-up – arrogant, full of self importance

knock – criticise, deride
knocker – one who knocks

lair – layabout, ruffian
lairising – acting like a lair
lamington – square of sponge cake covered in chocolate icing and coconut
larrikin – a bit like a lair
lollies – sweets, candy
lurk – a scheme

mate – general term of familiarity, whether you know the person or not
mozzies – mosquitoes
mud map – literally a map drawn in the ground, or any roughly drawn map

mulga – outback tree or shrub, usually covering a large area

nature strip – grass border beside road; verge
never never – remote country in the outback
no hoper – hopeless case
no worries – she'll be right, that's OK

ocker – an uncultivated or boorish Australian
off-sider – assistant or partner
OS – overseas, as in 'he's gone OS'
outback – remote part of the bush, back o' Bourke

paddock – a fenced area of land, usually intended for livestock
pastoralist – large-scale grazier
pavlova – traditional Australian meringue and cream dessert, named after the Russian ballerina Anna Pavlova
perve – to gaze with lust
pinch – steal
piss – beer
pissed – drunk
pissed off – annoyed
piss weak – no good, gutless
pokies – poker machines
Pom – English person
postie – mailman

ratbag – friendly term of abuse
ratshit (R-S) – lousy
rapt – delighted, enraptured
reckon! – you bet!, absolutely!
rego – registration, as in 'car rego'
rellie – relative
ridgy-didge – original, genuine
ripper – good (also 'little ripper')
road train – semitrailer-trailer-trailer
root – sexual intercourse
rooted – tired
ropable – very bad-tempered or angry

scrub – bush
sea wasp – deadly box jellyfish
sealed road – surfaced road
septic – American person (rhyming slang ie Septic tank/Yank)

session – lengthy period of heavy drinking
sheila – woman
shellacking – comprehensive defeat
she'll be right – no worries
shonky – unreliable
shoot through – leave in a hurry
shout – buy a round of drinks (as in 'it's your shout')
sickie – day off work ill (or malingering)
slab – carton of 24 beer bottles or cans
smoko – tea break
snag – sausage
sparrow's fart – dawn
spunk – good-looking person
station – large farm
sticky beak – nosy person
stinger – box jellyfish
stubby – 375mL bottle of beer
Stubbies – popular brand of men's work shorts
sunbake – sunbathe (well, the sun's hot in Australia)
swag – canvas-covered bed roll used in the outback, also a large amount

tall poppies – achievers (knockers like to cut them down)
tea – evening meal
thongs – flip-flops, an ocker's idea of formal footwear
tinny – 375mL can of beer; also a small, aluminium fishing dinghy
too right! – absolutely!
Top End – northern part of the Northern Territory
troopie – troop carrier ie 4WD Landcruiser
trucky – truck driver
true blue – dinkum
tucker – food
two-pot screamer – person unable to hold their drink
two-up – traditional heads/tails gambling game

uni – university
ute – utility, pick-up truck

vegie – vegetable

wag – to skip school or work

wagon – station wagon, estate car
walkabout – lengthy walk away from it all
weatherboard – wooden house
Wet, the – rainy season in the north
wharfie – dockworker
whinge – complain, moan
wobbly – disturbing, unpredictable behaviour (as in 'throw a wobbly')
woomera – stick used by Aboriginal people for throwing spears

woop-woop – outback, miles from anywhere
wowser – a fanatically puritanical person, a teetotaller

yahoo – noisy and unruly person
yakka – work (from an Aboriginal language)
yobbo – uncouth, aggressive person
yonks – ages, a long time
youse – plural of you, pronounced 'yooze'

LONELY PLANET

Guides by Region

Lonely Planet is known worldwide for publishing practical, reliable and no-nonsense travel information in our guides and on our Web site. The Lonely Planet list covers just about every accessible part of the world. Currently there are nine series: travel guides, shoestring guides, walking guides, city guides, phrasebooks, audio packs, travel atlases, diving and snorkeling guides and travel literature.

AFRICA Africa – the South ● Africa on a shoestring ● Arabic (Egyptian) phrasebook ● Arabic (Moroccan) phrasebook ● Cairo ● Cape Town ● Central Africa ● East Africa ● Egypt ● Egypt travel atlas ● Ethiopian (Amharic) phrasebook ● The Gambia & Senegal ● Kenya ● Kenya travel atlas ● Malawi, Mozambique & Zambia ● Morocco ● North Africa ● South Africa, Lesotho & Swaziland ● South Africa, Lesotho & Swaziland travel atlas ● Swahili phrasebook ● Tanzania, Zanzibar & Pemba ● Trekking in East Africa ● Tunisia ● West Africa ● Zimbabwe, Botswana & Namibia ● Zimbabwe, Botswana & Namibia travel atlas
Travel Literature: The Rainbird: A Central African Journey ● Songs to an African Sunset: A Zimbabwean Story ● Mali Blues: Traveling to an African Beat

AUSTRALIA & THE PACIFIC Australia ● Australian phrasebook ● Bushwalking in Australia ● Bushwalking in Papua New Guinea ● Fiji ● Fijian phrasebook ● Islands of Australia's Great Barrier Reef ● Melbourne ● Micronesia ● New Caledonia ● New South Wales & the ACT ● New Zealand ● Northern Territory ● Outback Australia ● Papua New Guinea ● Papua New Guinea (Pidgin) phrasebook ● Queensland ● Rarotonga & the Cook Islands ● Samoa ● Solomon Islands ● South Australia ● Sydney ● Tahiti & French Polynesia ● Tasmania ● Tonga ● Tramping in New Zealand ● Vanuatu ● Victoria ● Western Australia
Travel Literature: Islands in the Clouds ● Sean & David's Long Drive

CENTRAL AMERICA & THE CARIBBEAN Bahamas and Turks & Caicos ● Barcelona ● Bermuda ● Central America on a shoestring ● Costa Rica ● Cuba ● Dominican Republic & Haiti ● Eastern Caribbean ● Guatemala, Belize & Yucatán: La Ruta Maya ● Jamaica ● Mexico ● Mexico City ● Panama
Travel Literature: Green Dreams: Travels in Central America

EUROPE Amsterdam ● Andalucía ● Austria ● Baltic States phrasebook ● Barcelona ● Berlin ● Britain ● British phrasebook ● Canary Islands ● Central Europe ● Central Europe phrasebook ● Corsica ● Croatia ● Czech & Slovak Republics ● Denmark ● Dublin ● Eastern Europe ● Eastern Europe phrasebook ● Edinburgh ● Estonia, Latvia & Lithuania ● Europe ● Finland ● France ● French phrasebook ● Germany ● German phrasebook ● Greece ● Greek phrasebook ● Hungary ● Iceland, Greenland & the Faroe Islands ● Ireland ● Italian phrasebook ● Italy ● Lisbon ● London ● Mediterranean Europe ● Mediterranean Europe phrasebook ● Norway ● Paris ● Poland ● Portugal ● Portugal travel atlas ● Prague ● Provence & the Côte d'Azur ● Romania & Moldova ● Rome ● Russia, Ukraine & Belarus ● Russian phrasebook ● Scandinavian & Baltic Europe ● Scandinavian Europe phrasebook ● Scotland ● Slovenia ● Spain ● Spanish phrasebook ● St Petersburg ● Switzerland ● Trekking in Spain ● Ukrainian phrasebook ● Vienna ● Walking in Britain ● Walking in Italy ● Walking in Ireland ● Walking in Switzerland ● Western Europe ● Western Europe phrasebook
Travel Literature: The Olive Grove: Travels in Greece

INDIAN SUBCONTINENT Bangladesh ● Bengali phrasebook ● Bhutan ● Delhi ● Goa ● Hindi/Urdu phrasebook ● India ● India & Bangladesh travel atlas ● Indian Himalaya ● Karakoram Highway ● Nepal ● Nepali phrasebook ● Pakistan ● Rajasthan ● South India ● Sri Lanka ● Sri Lanka phrasebook ● Trekking in the Indian Himalaya ● Trekking in the Karakoram & Hindukush ● Trekking in the Nepal Himalaya
Travel Literature: In Rajasthan ● Shopping for Buddhas

LONELY PLANET

Mail Order

Lonely Planet products are distributed worldwide. They are also available by mail order from Lonely Planet, so if you have difficulty finding a title please write to us. North and South American residents should write to 150 Linden St, Oakland, CA 94607, USA; European and African residents should write to 10a Spring Place, London NW5 3BH, UK; and residents of other countries to PO Box 617, Hawthorn, Victoria 3122, Australia.

ISLANDS OF THE INDIAN OCEAN Madagascar & Comoros • Maldives • Mauritius, Réunion & Seychelles

MIDDLE EAST & CENTRAL ASIA Arab Gulf States • Central Asia • Central Asia phrasebook • Iran • Israel & the Palestinian Territories • Israel & the Palestinian Territories travel atlas • Istanbul • Jerusalem • Jordan & Syria • Jordan, Syria & Lebanon travel atlas • Lebanon • Middle East on a shoestring • Turkey • Turkish phrasebook • Turkey travel atlas • Yemen
Travel Literature: The Gates of Damascus • Kingdom of the Film Stars: Journey into Jordan

NORTH AMERICA Alaska • Backpacking in Alaska • Baja California • California & Nevada • Canada • Chicago • Florida • Hawaii • Honolulu • Los Angeles • Louisiana • Miami • New England USA • New Orleans • New York City • New York, New Jersey & Pennsylvania • Pacific Northwest USA • Rocky Mountain States • San Francisco • Seattle • Southwest USA • USA • USA phrasebook • Vancouver • Washington, DC & the Capital Region
Travel Literature: Drive Thru America

NORTH-EAST ASIA Beijing • Cantonese phrasebook • China • Hong Kong • Hong Kong, Macau & Guangzhou • Japan • Japanese phrasebook • Japanese audio pack • Korea • Korean phrasebook • Kyoto • Mandarin phrasebook • Mongolia • Mongolian phrasebook • North-East Asia on a shoestring • Seoul • South-West China • Taiwan • Tibet • Tibetan phrasebook • Tokyo
Travel Literature: Lost Japan

SOUTH AMERICA Argentina, Uruguay & Paraguay • Bolivia • Brazil • Brazilian phrasebook • Buenos Aires • Chile & Easter Island • Chile & Easter Island travel atlas • Colombia • Ecuador & the Galapagos Islands • Latin American Spanish phrasebook • Peru • Quechua phrasebook • Rio de Janeiro • South America on a shoestring • Trekking in the Patagonian Andes • Venezuela
Travel Literature: Full Circle: A South American Journey

SOUTH-EAST ASIA Bali & Lombok • Bangkok • Burmese phrasebook • Cambodia • Hill Tribes phrasebook • Ho Chi Minh City • Indonesia • Indonesia's Eastern Islands • Indonesian phrasebook • Indonesian audio pack • Jakarta • Java • Laos • Lao phrasebook • Laos travel atlas • Malay phrasebook • Malaysia, Singapore & Brunei • Myanmar (Burma) • Philippines • Pilipino (Tagalog) phrasebook • Singapore • South-East Asia on a shoestring • South-East Asia phrasebook • Thailand • Thailand's Islands & Beaches • Thailand travel atlas • Thai phrasebook • Thai audio pack • Vietnam • Vietnamese phrasebook • Vietnam travel atlas

ALSO AVAILABLE: Antarctica • Brief Encounters: Stories of Love, Sex & Travel • Chasing Rickshaws • Not the Only Planet: Travel Stories from Science Fiction • Travel with Children • Traveller's Tales

Index

Text

Bold indicates maps.

Boxed Text

MAP LEGEND

BOUNDARIES

▬▪▬▪▬▪▬	International
▪▬ ▪▬ ▪▬	State

HYDROGRAPHY

	Coastline
	River, Creek
	River Flow
	Lake
	Intermittent Lake
	Salt Lake
◎ ⟶	Spring, Rapids
	Swamp
	Waterfalls

ROUTES & TRANSPORT

	Freeway
	Highway
	Major Road
	Minor Road
	Unsealed Road
	City Highway
	City Road
	City Street, Lane
	Pedestrian Mall
⊢─○─	Train Route & Station
⊢─■─	Light Rail Route & Stop
═──Ⓜ──	Underground & Station
	Tramway
....	Walking Track
──⊗──	Bicycle Track
──────	Ferry Route

AREA FEATURES

	Beach
	Building
+₊+₊ +₊+₊	Cemetery
	Market
✿	Park, Gardens
	Urban Area

MAP SYMBOLS

✈	Airport, Airfield	ℙ	Parking
⊖	Bank	�	Petrol Station
⌓	Cave	★	Police Station
⊞ ✝	Church	✉	Post Office
⌢⌢⌢	Cliff or Escarpment	∴	Ruins
⌐	Golf Course	❖	Shopping Centre
)(	Gorge, Chasm	🏛	Stately Home
⊕	Hospital	▭	Swimming Pool
⌲	Lighthouse	☎	Telephone
※	Lookout	⊙	Toilet
✕	Mine	❶	Tourist Information
⚊	Monument	⋔	Trailhead
▲	Mountain	⊜	Transport
🏛	Museum, Art Gallery	△	Trig Station
⚑	National, State Park	⚲	Zoo

◎ **CAPITAL**	National Capital
◉ **CAPITAL**	State Capital
● **CITY**	City
● **Town**	Town
● **Town**	Small Town
○	Point of Interest
■	Place to Stay
⚑	Camping Ground
🚐	Caravan Park
▼	Place to Eat
🍺	Pub, Entertainment
▣	Picnic Area

Note: not all symbols displayed above appear in this book

LONELY PLANET OFFICES

Australia
PO Box 617, Hawthorn 3122, Victoria
tel: (03) 9819 1877 fax: (03) 9819 6459
e-mail: talk2us@lonelyplanet.com.au

USA
150 Linden St, Oakland, CA 94607
tel: (510) 893 8555 TOLL FREE: 800 275-8555
fax: (510) 893 8572
e-mail: info@lonelyplanet.com

UK
10a Spring Place, London, NW5 3BH
tel: (0171) 428 4800 fax: (0170) 428 4828
e-mail: go@lonelyplanet.co.uk

France
1 rue du Dahomey, 75011 Paris
tel: 01 55 25 33 00 fax: 01 55 25 33 01
e-mail: bip@lonelyplanet.fr

World Wide Web: www.lonelyplanet.com *or* AOL keyword: lp
Lonely Planet Images: lpi@lonelyplanet.com.au